Methodology in Private Law Theory

OXFORD PRIVATE LAW THEORY

Oxford Private Law Theory publishes leading work in private law theory. It commissions and solicits monographs and edited collections in general private law theory as well as specific fields, including the theoretical analysis of tort law, property law, contract law, fiduciary law, trust law, remedies and restitution, and the law of equity. The series is open to diverse theoretical approaches, including those informed by philosophy, economics, history, and political theory. Oxford Private Law Theory sets the standard for rigorous and original work in private law theory.

ALSO PUBLISHED IN THIS SERIES

Wrongs, Harms, and Compensation
Paying for our Mistakes
Adam Slavny

Standing in Private Law
Powers of Enforcement in the Law of Obligations and Trusts
Edited by Timothy Liau

Private Law and Practical Reason
Essays on John Gardner's Private Law Theory
Edited by Haris Psarras and Sandy Steel

Rights, Wrongs, and Injustices
The Structure of Remedial Law
Stephen A. Smith

Civil Wrongs and Justice in Private Law
Edited by Paul B. Miller and John Oberdiek

Methodology in Private Law Theory

Between New Private Law and Rechtsdogmatik

Edited by

THILO KUNTZ

Juristische Fakultät, Heinrich Heine Universität Düsseldorf

PAUL B. MILLER

Notre Dame Law School

OXFORD
UNIVERSITY PRESS

OXFORD
UNIVERSITY PRESS

Great Clarendon Street, Oxford, OX2 6DP,
United Kingdom

Oxford University Press is a department of the University of Oxford.
It furthers the University's objective of excellence in research, scholarship,
and education by publishing worldwide. Oxford is a registered trade mark of
Oxford University Press in the UK and in certain other countries

First Edition published in 2024

Published in the United States of America by Oxford University Press
198 Madison Avenue, New York, NY 10016, United States of America

British Library Cataloguing in Publication Data

Data available

Library of Congress Control Number: 2023919412

ISBN 978–0–19–888530–6

DOI: 10.1093/oso/9780198885306.001.0001

Printed and bound by
CPI Group (UK) Ltd, Croydon, CR0 4YY

To Marie, Theodor, and Moritz
TK

Dedicated to the memory of Stephen A Smith, whose ideas and character continue to inspire.
PBM

Acknowledgements

This book is the result of a workshop on methodology in private law theory convened at Bucerius Law School in Hamburg in the spring of 2022. We received generous financial support for the workshop from Bucerius Law School and from the Notre Dame Program on Private Law, and we are grateful for this support. We thank our contributors for rich and engaging conversation at the workshop and for their thought-provoking chapters. We are also grateful to Iris Kessler and Alicia Sachau for their logistical support. The late Stephen A Smith, formerly James McGill Professor of Law at McGill University, was to have contributed to the volume. Sadly, his grave illness prevented that. Smith's ideas are, nevertheless, reflected in the work of several contributors, and it is comforting to know that he contributed indirectly yet palpably to the volume. We know that his work will inspire and inform private law theory for generations to come. This book is dedicated to his memory. Thilo thanks Marie for her unwavering support and endurance of living with a spouse who has his head in the clouds too often, and Theodor and Moritz for bringing him back to planet earth. And Paul thanks Stella, Serena, and Kieran for their ongoing love and support.

Contents

List of Contributors

Marietta Auer, Director, Max Planck Institute for Legal History and Legal Theory

Ino Augsberg, Chair in Legal Philosophy and Public Law, Christian Albrechts Universität, Kiel

Christian Bumke, Commerzbank Foundation Chair in the Fundamentals of Law, Bucerius Law School

Johanna Croon-Gestefeld, Professor of Law, Leuphana Law School, Lüneburg University

Andrew S. Gold, Professor of Law, Brooklyn Law School

John C.P. Goldberg, Carter Professor of General Jurisprudence, Harvard Law School

Nils Jansen, Chair in Roman Law, Legal History, German and European Private Law, Universität Münster

Felipe Jiménez, Associate Professor of Law and Philosophy, University of Southern California Gould School of Law, and Profesor Adjunto Extraordinario, Universidad Adolfo Ibáñez

Lorenz Kaehler, Professor for Private Law, Civil Procedure and Philosophy of Law, Universität Bremen

Larissa Katz, Canada Research Chair in Private Law Theory, University of Toronto Faculty of Law

Paul Krell, Chair in Criminal Law, Bucerius Law School

Thilo Kuntz, Chair in Private Law, Commercial and Corporate Law, Juristische Fakultät, Heinrich Heine Universität Düsseldorf

Paul B. Miller, Professor of Law and Associate Dean for International and Graduate Programmes, Notre Dame Law School

Jeffrey A. Pojanowski, Professor of Law, Notre Dame Law School

Fritz Schäfer, Research Assistant at the Commerzbank Foundation Chair in the Fundamentals of Law, Bucerius Law School

Kevin Tobia, Associate Professor of Law, Georgetown Law Center

W. Bradley Wendel, Edwin H Woodruff Professor of Law, Cornell Law School

Benjamin C. Zipursky, Professor and James H Quinn Chair in Legal Ethics, Fordham University School of Law

Introduction

Thilo Kuntz and Paul B. Miller

I. Background

Private law scholarship is undergoing an exciting revival in the United States, much of it driven by developments in private law theory. The most recent and auspicious of these is the rise of the New Private Law movement, inaugurated at Harvard Law School and since fostering a well-spring of scholarly interest in private law in the United States. While the New Private Law is a scholarly movement that operates on a mostly theoretical plane, it is notable for the emphasis it places on legal concepts (including doctrine), practices, and institutions.

Private law scholarship and interest in legal doctrine in Germany have not needed revival, however they are experiencing something of a reorientation. Private law has long been viewed as distinctive professional and academic enterprise in Germany, with scholarly interest in exposition and interpretation reflecting aspirations to order, systematicity, and comprehensiveness in the German civil code. In Germany, unlike the United States, private law was never overtaken by public law, nor were its concerns discounted by nominalism about legal concepts. Rather, German private law has been characterized between close ties between practice, adjudication, and scholarship rooted in common methodological commitments to doctrinal analysis: *Rechtsdogmatik*. Nevertheless, in recent years, German private lawyers—especially scholars—have advocated for openness to theory in a broad sense, for greater independence of legal scholarship and practice, and for use of theoretical methods the deployment of which entails detachment from doctrine and the functioning of legal institutions. Thus, though it remains a minority position, German scholars have increasingly looked to unconventional methods via domestic intellectual movements and those of foreign legal cultures (eg American neo-classical law and economics).

We are describing tendencies associated with emergent movements, not tenets of entrenched schools of thought. Accordingly, in bringing together in this volume representatives of different legal systems and cultures, we have not aimed for a direct and crosswise comparison of scholarly monocultures. Refreshingly, the methods and aims associated with the movements described

Thilo Kuntz and Paul B. Miller, *Introduction* In: *Methodology in Private Law Theory*. Edited by: Thilo Kuntz and Paul B. Miller, Oxford University Press. © Thilo Kuntz and Paul B. Miller 2024. DOI: 10.1093/oso/9780198885306.001.0001

here break with orthodoxy but do not aim to replace defeated orthodoxies with new ones. Rather, they are movements that contain multitudes and are, in that sense, heterodox, all while presenting certain sharp edges and points of distinction that demarcate old from new. This volume provides observers and participants in still-evolving intellectual movements with the opportunity to teach and to learn from one another, with the comparative element enabling the surfacing of presuppositions that might not otherwise be apparent.

Legal concepts travel—through transplantation, translation, and otherwise—and legal theories are incubated within but not hemmed in by culture. The historical development of private law in the United States, Germany, and other civil and common law jurisdictions provides ample evidence of this. However, the new scholarly movements shaping US and German private law have yet to take direct notice of one another.

The New Private Law has emerged partly in response to older movements that generated and have sustained lasting scholarly scepticism of, and disinterest in, private law in the United States (eg American legal realist and law and economics movements). The latter movements profoundly altered American private law scholarship and set it on a course that would diverge markedly from those taken elsewhere.

German private law scholarship is trending in an opposite direction, in part. Critics of *Rechtsdogmatik* are dissatisfied with the methodological and substantive limitations wrought by the traditionally close affinity between modes of analyses deployed in legal scholarship and legal practice. German private law scholars value rigorous intellectual exchange and argument between scholars, lawyers, and judges of the sort made possible by common acculturation within, and commitments to, *Rechtsdogmatik*. However, they also wish to establish the methods and aims of legal scholarship as a bona fide and distinctively scholarly endeavour, creating space for argument unshackled from the analytical and practical exigencies of legal practice and of adjudication. Some take inspiration from nineteenth- and early twentieth-century scholarship, which was not yet bound up with court practice and the development of statutory law, and is thought to have been more open to legal philosophy, comparative law, and continental antecedents of legal realism and law and economics. Others are influenced by research visits and/or graduate legal education undertaken in the United States.

As should be evident, current movements in German and American private law, while not culture-bound, reflect distinctive, domestic points of inspiration and reference. The New Private Law movement is meant, in part, to foster change in scholarly engagement with private law in the United States in particular, reviving private law as an academic subject while pointing it in a new and more productive direction. The latter holds true for contemporary German private law scholarship as well. Even though new critics of *Rechtsdogmatik* mostly work 'in house' (having no intention of dispensing with *Rechtsdogmatik* altogether or of unbundling scholarship from practice), they plead for plurality in methodology and emphasize the value of legal scholarship as a distinctive enterprise.

Until now, the proponents of new movements in private law theory in Germany and the United States had not taken notice of one another, but we approached this project in the belief (one that we think amply vindicated) that the vanguards of German and American private law theory had something to say to one another. We will note three factors that led us to think the exchange would be productive, as these may prove to be useful lodestars for readers.

First, the scholarly movements from which the volume emerges are movements in legal theory. Each involves generalizations about legal doctrine, practices, and institutions, and this proves auspicious as a focus on general precepts in theory-construction lends itself more readily to comparative analysis than might be possible in respect of movements that are domestic in foci and milieu.

Second, the new German and American scholarly movements in private law are shaped as much by the emergence of new theoretical *methodologies* as they are influenced by distinctive objects, substantive commitments, or metaphysical priors. The New Private Law, for instance, does not proclaim new objects of inquiry: it promises renewed attention to private law doctrines, practices, and institutions. What is 'new' is the set of methodologies that it embraces and how it combines and makes use of them: what it promises is a fresh way of *thinking* about something familiar (private law). Likewise, recent trends in German private law reflect a rethinking of methodology, or rather an opening up of a culture dominated by *Rechtsdogmatik* to perspectives afforded by different methodologies. Just like proponents of the New Private Law, German scholars hope to reinvigorate debates they regard as somewhat stale, providing fresh perspectives on inherited problems and questions.

The above two factors justify the thematic focus of our volume, with its billing as a work on *methodology* in private law *theory*. But we had be remiss if we did not mention a third: the fact that the emergent methodologies and milieus compared here enjoy certain resemblances and resonances. Amongst these are: shared rejection of nominalism about legal concepts and categories; common belief in the possibility, and value, of understanding private law from participants' vantage points; shared awareness that the law claims superordinate practical authority and trades in normative constructs; shared recognition that private law, where it functions well as a guide to conduct, does so in virtue of its functioning soundly as a *system*; and common recognition that private law is a construct of reason and thus exhibits excellences and deficiencies of human intelligence, integrity, and craft. As the chapters collected here illustrate, these resonances and resemblances shape methodological choices made by contemporary German and American private law theorists, just as they shape resulting analyses. When the movements are examined severally, each within their own milieu, the characteristic views about law just noted serve to distinguish the emergent movements from domestic movements that preceded them. But where, as here, they are examined jointly, they enable fruitful comparison and exchange.

II. General Perspectives on Private Law Theory

The chapters gathered in Part I examine methodologies of choice in contemporary German and American private law theory, while also commenting on alternative methodologies, past and present. Amongst other topics, our authors in Part I aim to clarify the nature of private law as an object of theoretical analysis, to identify and distinguish between specific methodologies apt to interpretive and normative theorizing, to present criteria according to which one might assess the successful deployment of different methodologies in interpretive and normative theory, and to comment critically upon the historical arc of private law theory by examining the strengths and weaknesses of methods latent within now- or once-dominant paradigms, movements, and schools of thought.

In 'A Genealogy of Private Law Epistemologies', Marietta Auer argues that approaches to legal theory depend on the prevailing scientific *zeitgeist*. Choosing Germany as her frame of reference, she presents a historical narrative in three phases. Her point of departure is early nineteenth-century philosophical-historical holism. Auer then discusses 'legal scientism', which emerged in the second half of the nineteenth century. She concludes with the 'jurisprudence of values', spanning roughly from 1950 to the present. Auer uncovers three recurring patterns of epistemic pathways: normative, descriptive, and analytical theories, approaches, and methods, reflected in idealistic, empirical, and analytical epistemologies of 'legal science'.

Philosophical-historical holism was ushered by the Historical School. Treating Roman law as a source of the '*Volksgeist*' (spirit of the people), it envisioned private law as a normative concept of society, autonomy-based, and tied to enlightenment philosophy, especially Kant's work on the transcendental foundations of private rights. Roman dualistic thinking about private law in terms of the law of persons and of things, and an associated tripartite division of private into property law, the law of obligations, and family law, continues to shape German private law. Legal scientism emerged partly in reaction to the perceived inability of the Historical School's methodology to adapt private law to the exigencies of an industrializing society. The legislator moved to the fore as the most important fount of private law. Echoing the new natural sciences' emphasis on empirical methods and objectivity, legal methodology was reconceived as an analytical and positivistic endeavour, not of doctrinal construction, but of legal interpretation. In the aftermath of the Second World War, scholars in German private law spurned positivism and turned to the 'jurisprudence of values', replacing empiricism with a balancing method focused on eliciting values in law, increasingly from the constitution, and culminating in the doctrine of the horizontal effect of constitutional rights. This generated a third paradigm: balancing constitutional primacy and constitutional rights with the distinctive normative aims of private law.

Auer concludes that private law was only successful when it struck a viable balance between the analytical and doctrinal standards of the legal system and the empirical and normative foundations of private law in society. Setting empiricist and analytical-doctrinal epistemologies against one another is a recipe for futility.

In 'Exploring the Paradigms of Private Law', Johanna Croon-Gestefeld observes that much private law scholarship suffers from a lack of clarity and transparency on methodology. After examining different ways of understanding what 'legal methodology' consists in, and noting an increasing openness towards interdisciplinary approaches in German scholarship, Croon-Gestefeld emphasizes the importance of legal paradigms in shaping the development of, and choices made between, legal methodologies.

Croon-Gestefeld first describes different understandings of legal methodology in German scholarship, noting how these differences depend on whether scholars concern themselves with matters of academic interest only or, as is more typical, also concern themselves with matters of practical application. Croon-Gestefeld explains that debates on methodology persist because of advances in methodological sophistication and changes in socio-legal context. She emphasizes the importance of *Rechtsdogmatik* as a method for making the structure of law understandable (ie its ordering and systematization) and as a method for reasoning about and with the law from an internal and specifically legal point of view. Croon-Gestefeld notes that with increasing openness to theories and methodologies drawn from other disciplines, scholars are now more willing to make their methodological choices explicit. What Croon-Gestefeld is interested in, however, is not the methodologies that scholars employ, but rather the perceptions and hidden assumptions ('paradigms') about law that covertly shape choice of methodology. Her attention to paradigms is meant to uncover preconceptions, narratives, and discursive mechanisms at play wherever scholars analyse law. By way of example, Croon-Gestefeld shows that scholarly attention to the phenomenon of 'sharenting' surfaces different preconceptions held by data protection scholars and family lawyers, with different paradigms and methodologies resulting in significant differences in legal analysis of 'sharenting'.

In 'When Private Law Theory is Close Enough', Andrew S. Gold examines and reframes methodological criteria according to which one might assess the adequacy of interpretive private law theories. The criteria are derived from the work of the late Stephen A Smith in his landmark book *Contract Theory*. Smith articulated several criteria, primarily in order to explain and to defend the methodology adopted in the interpretive theory of contract law presented in his book. As Gold notes, Smith's criteria subsequently gained wide recognition and influence, including amongst members of the New Private Law movement.

Gold focuses on two criteria in particular: transparency and morality. As Gold explains, the transparency criterion requires that a theory be faithful to the law's self-understanding, taking legal reasons given by lawmakers for law-making and law-enforcement actions as their genuine reasons, and aiming to understand them. The morality criterion requires that a theory recognize the law's claim to moral authority by articulating moral reasons for the law that allow one to appreciate how the law's claim to authority might be justified. As Gold explains, the object of justification picked out by this criterion is usually understood as the content of a given law or framework of laws (and not, for instance, the existence and operation of legal institutions, or the actions taken by legal officials).

Many New Private Law theorists accept the premises upon which Smith's criteria are based: that, as a theorist, one ought to presume that legal officials act in good faith when providing public justification for their actions, and that one ought also to examine posited legal reasons as being given impliedly on the basis of the law's claim to moral authority, to meet burdens of public justification. Gold does not question the reception of the criteria, or their importance. Instead, he argues that private law theorists ought to distinguish between interpretive and prescriptive theory in specifying them. He also argues that each of the criteria ought to be reformulated, with his proposed reformulation being focused on the demandingness of the criteria and their relative priority (for instance, Gold argues that in respect of work of interpretive theory, where the transparency and morality criteria conflict, the former ought to be given priority, consistent with the theorist's aim for interpretive fidelity).

In 'Understanding Private Law', Felipe Jiménez examines the methodological choices made by American private law theorists relative to their ambition to explain, and thus to improve public understanding of, private law. As Jiménez suggests, some of these choices are implicit and unargued for. Others reflect a presumption that theorists are operating on the basis of a common, and sound, understanding of what private law consists in; a presumption that, once prodded, proves dubitable. Jiménez rigorously examines methodologies used by private law theorists. He also explains how private law theory could be enriched through accommodation of comparative jurisprudential methods, noting that the New Private Law, in particular, is especially well suited to support and effectively channel insights that might be gleaned from application of these methods.

Jiménez begins by commenting on what counts as 'private law'. His aim is not the conventional one of tallying subfields that fall within private law, lie beyond it, or are situated across whatever boundaries might demarcate private from public law. Rather, his aim is to clarify what law generally (including private law) consists in, and, along the way, to question certain narrow conceptions of private law. More specifically, Jiménez rejects the notion that (private) law consists merely in posited law: authoritative legal text and the rules and other doctrines expressed in same. He suggests that posited law is intelligible only in the context of associated social practices.

According to Jiménez, interpretive private law theory ought to aim at elucidation of the intelligibility of law as a set of social practices. That, in turn, requires that one access and adequately represent the law as it is understood from participants' perspectives. To undertake this work is to begin—even if not, necessarily, to end—with examination of law from an internal point of view. And to complete this work properly, one needs to focus not merely on inputs and outputs of social practices crystallized in the form of posited law, but also on the attitudes, beliefs, values, and commitments that underlie and support law's social functions within political communities.

Jiménez capitalizes on this enriched conception of private law in offering a fresh critical perspective on methodological choices made by American private law theorists. Scholars associated with antecedent movements—adopting formalist and instrumentalist methodologies of different types—tended to miss their mark (ie private law) by construing it narrowly or reductively, missing the sense in which private law is a set of social practices, or else they ignored or overlooked implications of the socio-cultural contingency of aspects of private law (eg by treating doctrinal 'misfits' as marginal ephemera). The New Private Law fares better, Jiménez says, partly because its proponents take private law seriously as a set of social practices of rendering and relying on normative guidance; practices that encompass but are not exhausted by posited law. But, Jiménez says, the New Private Law would do better still to break loose of parochial concerns with outmoded American scholarly methodologies, adopting methods of comparative jurisprudence in examining points of divergence and convergence that emerge through comparative, practice-grounded analyses of law as culture-inflected practices that vary across legal systems.

In 'Against Essentialism in Private Law Theory: Private Law as an Artifact Kind', Thilo Kuntz questions internalist and externalist interpretive methodologies in private law theory. He argues that they reflect an untenable essentialism about private law. Drawing on artifact theory, Kuntz maintains that there is no essential or true nature of private law. Private law accommodates and rests on a mixed set of norms and values that change over time, rendering partisan accounts inapt. Kuntz argues that interpretive private law theory must acknowledge the ambivalent and multipolar nature of private law if it is to be methodologically sound.

Kuntz brings artifact theory to bear upon contemporary private law theory. Abstracting from substantive theories about the nature of private law, the artifactual interpretive model that he favours helps to shed new light on the ontological interdependency of posited law, understood positivistically, and insights generated by externalists (eg economic and other instrumentalist analyses that prescind from doctrine). Kuntz explains why externalist methodologies fail. They underestimate the significance of moral norms and values that underlie private law. Any judge creating private law must place the new artifact within an existing normative framework if they are to be successful. However, Kuntz maintains that internalist methodologies suffer from a parallel flaw insofar as they discount the consequentialist justifications given by lawmakers for much current private law.

Kuntz then makes his case against essentialist renderings of private law. Private law, he says, rests on a multiplicity of foundational norms and its doctrinal and institutional form is historically contingent. Legal officials take on a double role in judging and law-making. They evaluate the law 'as it is' and apply it to the facts of cases, governed by the criteria of fit and consilience. This implies they have to pay attention to what the law 'does'. Moreover, the law requires efficient and effective application with respect to the aims it serves, implying that private law's normative orientation is broadly consequentialist. Thus, private law's characteristics are diffuse and dynamic.

III. New Private Law and *Rechtsdogmatik*: Formalism and Conceptualism in Private Law Theory

The New Private Law has engendered methodologies that aim at interpretation of private law doctrine, practices, and institutions, as well as critique.

These methodologies include novel varieties of formalism, conceptualistic (ie non-reductive) functionalism, and pragmatism, supplemented by general jurisprudential analysis of the relationship between law and practical reason. The interest in formalism and conceptualism is, again, pitched at the level of self-conscious examination of theoretical methodology, and not traditional doctrinal analysis of the sort that has attracted pejorative accusations of 'empty formalism' or 'arid conceptualism'. Furthermore, the modes of interpretation favoured in the New Private Law are not pressed in service of apologia for posited law and or rejection of social scientific and other 'external' vantage points on private law. Along each of these dimensions, methodologies characteristic of the New Private Law allow for instructive comparison with developments in German private law. The durability of *Rechtsdogmatik* in German private law provides common ground for conversation about the varieties, techniques, and limitations of formalism and conceptualism, while the emergence of alternative methodologies—social scientific and otherwise—raises questions of common interest about the extent to which legal (ie juridical or lawyerly) knowledge may be enriched by methods that aim not to supplant legal epistemologies but rather to enrich, inform, direct, and to challenge legal thought.

The chapters in Part II treat formalism and conceptualism in German and American private law theory in different ways. Some present compelling original accounts of varieties of formalism, conceptualism, and allied methodologies that characterize contemporary American and German private law theory. Others provide critical historical perspective on methods of conceptual analysis favoured in the United States before the rise of the New Private Law, or in Germany before the incremental accommodation of methods other than *Rechtsdogmatik*.

Ino Augsberg advocates for the ambiguity of legal concepts in his 'In Defence of Ambiguity: Towards a Shandean Way for Legal Methodology'. Contrary to a popular view according to which legal methodologies (including formalist methodologies) should aid lawmakers in the reduction of conceptual ambiguity in the name of promoting rule of law values, Augsberg maintains that ambiguity can play a valuable role in legal systems, with the law reflecting strategies meant to discourage the disambiguation of legal concepts.

Augsberg begins by noting that most interpretive theorists believe that interpretation is meant to elicit the reason or logic of legal decision-making, reducing uncertainty about what the law permits or requires, thereby enabling wider conformity with the law and more accurate prediction of litigation outcomes. Augsberg argues that this way of thinking is flawed insofar as it treats uncertainties generated by legal ambiguity—and ambiguity itself—as aberrant and dysfunctional. Much legal ambiguity is intentional and is meant to be functionally adaptive. Augsberg cites the German Federal Constitutional Court which, in several decisions, has explicitly stated that legal issues raised in cases often do not admit of a single legally correct disposition. Against the view that ambiguity, legal indeterminacy, and associated uncertainty are markers of structural deficits in law, Augsberg points to several examples of lawmakers' deliberately introducing ambiguity (eg allowance for the issuance of dissenting opinions, or opinions that concur in a result but not legal reasoning meant to justify it).

Ambiguity is as often a feature as it is a bug of legal systems. Augsberg contends that well-conceived ambiguity can enable the legal system to more readily adapt to materially different circumstances without sacrificing the virtues of legality that depend on systematicity. Formalist methodologies, according to Augsberg, have a decisive role to play in supporting this function. He provides two examples: the balancing of principles as a tool for resolving interpretive conflicts and reliance on empirical facts. He regards both as difficult to reconcile with the idea of an autonomous legal system, because the first tends to consider almost any aspect of life as a legal problem, while the second sharply narrows the field. Augsberg claims that formalist methodologies help to preserve functionally adaptive ambiguity in law by protecting it against externalist-instrumentalists' efforts at colonizing the law through the adoption of ends foreign to law as such, thereby protecting the law from imported false certainties.

Christian Bumke and Fritz Schäfer reflect on 'The Nature and Value of Conceptual Legal Scholarship' by comparing *Rechtsdogmatik* and the New Private Law. In framing the comparison, they introduce a distinction between methodologies that aim to explain law positivistically and those that aim to explicate law's normative content and justification.

Bumke and Schäfer first identify three points of commonality. First, both *Rechtsdogmatik* and the New Private Law are oriented towards posited law. Second, both employ an 'internal' or participants' perspective. Finally, both reflect a shared belief in the law's aspiration to systematicity (ie to be a well-ordered system of norms).

Bumke and Schäfer next introduce three important differences between *Rechtsdogmatik* and the New Private Law. First, they note that whereas *Rechtsdogmatik* is dominant in Germany and is buttressed by widespread belief in the autonomy of law and distinctly legal epistemologies, the New Private Law is but one of many approaches to law in the United States, with the implication being that its methods face a higher burden of justification. Second,

Bumke and Schäfer emphasize differences in the legal traditions within which *Rechtsdogmatik* and the New Private Law are situated. Reflecting the divergent tendencies of civilian and common law thought, German scholars tend to start out from a rule, while New Private Law scholars typically begin with cases. As the latter is less well suited to serve as a basis for theoretical abstraction, New Private Law scholars might be less inclined to examine private law holistically, as an ordered system of norms. Finally, unlike the New Private Law, *Rechtsdogmatik* is closely connected to legal practice.

In the last section of their chapter, Bumke and Schäfer explore varieties of conceptual legal scholarship in greater detail. They focus particularly on distinguishing the aims and methods apt to normative and explanatory forms of conceptual analysis. Illustrating the point through a discussion of two property cases, they demonstrate that this distinction is important both for *Rechtsdogmatik* and New Private Law scholarship.

Nils Jansen's chapter, 'The Point of View of Doctrinal Legal Science', seeks an appropriate perspective from which to engage in doctrinal legal science. He argues against detached observers' vantage points, including those exemplified in 'law and ... ' approaches (eg in law and economics). Jansen pleads for a genuinely legal *and* scholarly perspective: one not of practising lawyers, but of scholars intimately knowledgeable about law but operating at a remove from concerns peculiar to legal practice. Jansen argues that the current sense of crisis amongst legal scholars in Germany results from the loss of scholarly distance from practice during the twentieth century.

Jansen begins by describing fundamental changes in the German legal system and their consequences for private law scholarship. He emphasizes a shift in the centre of gravity from the law faculties to the courts. As a result, innovations in legal dogmatics increasingly originated in leading decisions of the highest courts and not in work of legal scholarship. In tandem, Jansen argues, the nature of scholarly work changed. Instead of thinking about abstract questions, scholars began to focus on more specific questions relating to particular legal provisions, and they began writing for a practitioner audience. In criticism of these developments, Jansen offers three normative claims: first, merely contributing to law-making is not a legitimate function of doctrinal legal science; second, scholars should no longer regard contributions to commentaries or other practice-oriented publications as a legitimate way of engaging in doctrinal legal science; and third, the task of doctrinal science is to generate new legal knowledge that goes beyond mere description of norms of a legal system.

In the end, Jansen promotes comparative methodologies. He argues that where a broad majority of legal systems reach a convergent response to a specific issue, one might presume that it reflects convergence on basic moral principles rather than the *Sonderweg* of a single legal system. Moreover, Jansen finds that comparative surveys help scholars to describe law through transparent, normatively thin concepts. Combining comparative with doctrinal or philosophical perspectives will enable scholars to formulate alternative models that may be used by judges or legislators.

In 'Formalism, Legality, and the Rule of Law', Paul B. Miller builds on and extends his prior work on formalist methodology in the New Private Law. In that work, Miller argued that the New Private Law is characterized by implicit commitment to a novel kind of formalism attending, as it does, to the structural formality of private law rules and enabling doctrines, and to the deliberative formality of legal reasoning. There, and here, Miller cautions that the new formalism in the New Private Law ought not to be confused with other varieties of formalism, and emphasizes that its comparative advantages lie in a rejection of both excesses of older formalisms as well as a corrosive cynicism about private law doctrine, institutions, and practices found in movements that espouse nominalism about law and legal semantics.

Miller's chapter focuses on connections between scholarly and professional formalism, on the one hand, and aspirations to legality and the rule of law, on the other. He explains the sense in which legality depends on the relative structural formality of law and deliberative formalism in legal reasoning. Miller also explains the sense in which structural and deliberative formalism are requisite to realization of the rule of law. In turn, Miller locates contingent moral reasons for a preference for scholarly and professional formalism in aspirations to legality and the rule of law, noting that the reasons and preference they generate are contingent upon the moral soundness of a legal system and of the guidance its laws provide. According to Miller, the contingency arises because the practical point of law is the provision of practically reasonable normative guidance. The formality of law, and of deliberative engagement with law, loses its imperative quality where applicable law is practically unreasonable.

In 'Private Law Formalism and Jurisprudential Method', Jeffrey A. Pojanowski examines the relationship between methodological precepts in the New Private Law, Kantian formalism, and anglophone positivist general jurisprudence. Discussions of methodology in the New Private Law, Pojanowski observes, have been explicitly informed by debates over methodology in general jurisprudence, with particular attention to debates over vantage points on law. These engagements imply methodological continuity across private and public law theory, marking a significant break from American private law theory's immediate past. The New Private Law was preceded by

Kantian formalism, which asserted the normative distinctiveness of private law as a site for the realization of corrective justice and equal freedom, and claimed that private law's distinctive normative concerns are reflected in distinctive modes of legal reasoning. The most influential work of Kantian formalist thought is Ernest Weinrib's *The Idea of Private Law*. Given the assertions made by the Kantians, it might be supposed, Pojanowski allows, that their methods diverged sharply from those characteristic of positivist general jurisprudence.

Pojanowski acknowledges divergences but argues that there are nonetheless significant methodological similarities between Kantian formalism and positivist general jurisprudence. These include, notably: a focus on analysing law from an internal point of view; an emphasis on evaluating law indirectly in terms of the moral ends latent within it; and a belief that private law, like other social practices, can have essential properties, the elucidation of these being an abiding task of legal theory. According to Pojanowski, these points of similarity expose Kantian formalism to important, and as-yet unrefuted, objections to positivist methodology.

In 'How Can You Have Law Without Lawyers? Legal Formalism, Legality, and the Law Governing Lawyers', W. Bradley Wendel comments on the role morality of lawyers and on the relationship between legal ethics, private law theory, and general jurisprudence. Drawing on recent work on methodology in the New Private Law—Paul Miller's work on formalism, and John Goldberg and Benjamin Zipursky's work on pragmatic conceptualism—Wendel sees a gap and opportunity for enrichment in the literature on these topics.

The gap lies in inattention to the role of lawyers in enabling the law to function as New Private Law scholars say it does (ie as a practically authoritative source of normative guidance). Private law cannot function adequately as a source of guidance absent intermediation by lawyers, Wendel argues. The law is not self-executing: knowledge of law and acts of intermediation performed by lawyers are necessary for law to be effective. Accordingly, Wendel argues, the development of new scholarly methodologies in private law theory ought to account for the role of lawyers and modes of legal analyses apt for the advising, advocacy, and facilitative functions (lawyerly deliberative tasks) undertaken by lawyers.

The opportunity for enrichment lies in filling out the implications of this account for private law theory and legal ethics. For instance, attention to the deliberative tasks undertaken by lawyers for clients might help a formalist like Miller explain how the law invites and structures deliberatively formalistic reasoning by clients. In turn, insights gleaned from recent work on methodology in the New Private Law might profitably reorient debates over the role morality of lawyers in legal ethics. These debates have featured contrasting positions taken by legal ethicists with little comment on the nature of law, or on the private law bases of role-related obligations governing lawyers. At one extreme are proponents of client-centric models that belittle the moral seriousness of law's guidance function, treating lawyers as implements of client preferences. At the other are proponents of community-centric models that position lawyers as wise scolds with an obligation to mould client preferences. Wendel sees wisdom in a middle way: one according to which lawyers channel and help to constitute the guidance function of law, bringing the guidance supplied by law more completely into contact with the behaviour law is meant to shape by articulating (and, as necessary, questioning) practical reasons given by and for the law.

IV. Empirical, Philosophical, and Normative Approaches to Private Law Theory

In the United States and in Germany, it is increasingly common to supplement lawyerly methods with those drawn from other disciplines. In the United States, the New Private Law has ushered a new interdisciplinarity, announcing a detente between legal scholars and other social scientists through work that exemplifies the potential complementarity of internal and external vantage points on law. In Germany, legal academia witnesses interdisciplinary and comparative approaches gain prominence, promoted by a younger generation of scholars whose contributions are valued and well-regarded even by academics working in the tradition of *Rechtsdogmatik*.

The chapters gathered in Part III illustrate and examine the combination of legal and non-legal methods of scholarly analysis of law; they explain the sense in which scholarly methods prevalent in contemporary private law theory are philosophical, empirical, and normative; they examine the relationship between scholarly and professional methods of legal analysis; and they query relationships between description, explanation, interpretation, and evaluation of private law. Each chapter in its own way shows how private law theory is enriched by the careful deployment of non-legal scholarly methods by scholars who are also respectfully attuned to lawyerly methods of analysis and argument.

In 'The Place of Philosophy in Private Law Scholarship', John C.P. Goldberg and Benjamin C. Zipursky set out to explain the prominence of philosophical methods in the New Private Law and in American private law theory more widely. Goldberg and Zipursky recognize that, examined in comparative context, the interest in philosophical methods might seem peculiar. It is a departure from the formalism of *Rechtsdogmatik*, for example, which views conceptual analysis of law as a matter for lawyers, not philosophers. And it conflicts with longstanding, if now dated, views of American private law as having succumbed to the imperialistic ambitions of economic analysis or as having been eclipsed by public law.

Goldberg and Zipursky provide an explanation of Americans' predilection for philosophical theory. First, they attribute the rise of private law *theory* to several factors rooted in American federalism, including the need for synoptic representations of common law doctrine, owing to the fact that the United States is without a 'single apex court' with jurisdiction to resolve doctrinal questions about private law nationwide. They also note the desire of American law schools to establish scholarly bona fides in a university milieu long sceptical of law as an academic discipline. Second, Goldberg and Zipursky attribute a preference for *philosophical* theory to the proven value of philosophical analysis in surfacing unstated assumptions and in delineating the limitations of other scholarly methodologies. Finally, they emphasize that those who provide philosophical theories about private law differ in their aims. Some work is exclusively or predominantly normative, or blends normative with interpretive (Dworkinian) rational reconstruction of private law doctrine, institutions, and practices. Other work is exclusively or predominantly interpretive in an explanatory sense, deploying philosophical methods of conceptual analysis in examination of legal concepts.

In 'The Minimal Morality of Private Law', Lorenz Kaehler argues that normative private law theory ought to consider that private law rests on minimalistic (and, hence, easier to defend) moral foundations. He claims that more extreme positions asserting the separation of law and morality (hard legal positivism) or their pervasive and close connection (natural law theory) lose sight of a central feature of private law: that basic institutions of private law such as contract, property, and torts are less difficult to justify than are other frameworks of legal rules.

In order to illustrate this point first in respect of contract law, Kaehler conjectures that unduly complex theories aimed at justifying contractual obligation miss the moral simplicity of the core idea that voluntary obligations are a necessary condition of taking others and oneself seriously. Supplementary moral considerations come into play only once an agreement has been made. Similarly, Kaehler argues that property law does little more than elaborate on the thin moral insight that in order to facilitate social cooperation, it is necessary to distinguish between the 'external Mine and Yours'. Finally, Kaehler locates the morality of tort law in simple idea that one must not harm others and must compensate them if one has.

Kaehler extends his core thesis to gap-filling, arguing that the burden of giving reasons for gap filling in private law is different from, say, that faced in constitutional law. He thinks that arguments rooted in notions of good faith and equity draw on a minimal morality: they are easier to ascertain and are basic (ie not reducible to more primitive reasons). Kaehler notes that in drawing on notions like good faith and equity in gap-filling, judges do not aim to elicit thick moral reasons. Rather, they restrict attention to standards evincing minimal morality, such as the 'reasonable person' standard, eschewing standards keyed to contentious views about what is morally optimal.

After explaining how private law contents itself with a minimal morality, Kaehler argues that this is as it should be. He gives three reasons. First, a minimal morality is better able to justify the exercise of coercive power by the state. Second, a minimal morality enjoys virtues associated with simplicity, including that of making the justification of private law's rules more accessible to people of different backgrounds. And third, it supports the generality of private law's rules.

In 'Rights Without Standing: On the Nature of Equitable Rights', Larissa Katz examines the nature of private rights in law and equity, drawing together substantive, remedial, and procedural dimensions of private ordering. According to Katz, in common law systems, equity and law are both sources of private rights. However, the role of right-holder and judge differ significantly between equity and law, for reasons owing to wider differences in the contributions that equity and law make, respectively, to the public administration of justice. Private rights originating at law encompass—in a constitutive sense—standing (rights of enforcement), which may be exercised at the instance of the right-holder. By contrast, rights originating in equity do not encompass standing; in equity, unlike in law, the decision whether to recognize and remedy a right is a matter within the discretion of the judge.

Katz recognizes that this difference, and the two-step modality for the administration of justice that it involves (one is presumptively left to one's rights at law, unless one can motivate a court to intervene in equity), is foreign to civilian legal systems. Katz thus offers a novel account of the justification for the two-step approach to the public administration of justice, bearing in mind that civilians adopt different means to achieve cognate ends. According to Katz, equity's policy of denying standing to complainants, leaving the enforcement of equitable rights to judges, is rooted in the recognition that judges perform two key functions, neither of which can be ceded to private actors: the familiar adjudicative function where (at law) they provide for impartial enforcement of private rights, and a less familiar but important guardianship function where (in equity) they protect the integrity of public authority by responding to opportunistic misuse or abuse of law. Performance of the latter function requires that the decision whether to enforce an equitable right be left to judges.

In 'The Critical Potential of Doctrinal Analysis', Paul Krell investigates how doctrinal analysis may serve as an instrument of critique of existing law. To that end, he begins by painstakingly examining the nature of doctrinal analysis. Introducing a metaphor of doctrinal analysis as an intermediate layer between law and its application, Krell explains that it can also be understood as a discipline that produces rules, a method of producing rules, a rule-producing activity, and a product of that activity. The variation is a consequence of different ways in which doctrinal analysis makes reference to law. Krell distinguishes between constituent doctrinal analysis and constituted doctrinal analysis. In the former case, doctrinal analysis serves as the basis of law, whereas in the latter it is based on law and is a means by which to make sense of it.

Krell then examines the critical potential of doctrinal analysis. He considers two possible restrictions. The first is formal, being a function of doctrinal analysis's rootedness in law. The second is substantive, being a function of the prejudice that doctrinal analysis must remain neutral on the morality of law. In recognition that doctrinal analysis connotes different modes of engagement with law, Krell comes 'to the somewhat unsatisfactory conclusion that it is not always possible to say conclusively when a criticism can be classified as doctrinal'. These concerns have ramifications for the authority of doctrinal analysis. Contrary to what a dominant element in the German tradition claims, Krell assigns a limited critical role to doctrinal analysis, namely, highlighting points of contradiction in law, conflict, uncertainty, and other deficiencies. Krell concludes that the critical potential of doctrinal analysis lies in promoting critical discourse about, and reasoned improvement of, statutes and judge-made law.

In our concluding chapter, 'Private Law Theory from an Empirical Perspective', Kevin Tobia introduces a new school of legal philosophy—empirical jurisprudence—and explains how its methods and aims are congenial to those of the New Private Law.

Empirical jurisprudence, Tobia reports, combines empirical methods with those of philosophy, testing hypotheses or claims advanced in moral, political, and legal philosophy that are amenable of empirical confirmation or disconfirmation. Conventional jurisprudence (legal philosophy), Tobia notes, often makes use of devices like thought experiments and appeals to intuition in efforts to tether (usually normative) arguments to everyday life, and more specifically to the beliefs, opinions, and behaviour of people. Empirical jurisprudence dispenses with these devices as inadequate, supplanting them with empirical studies designed to generate more comprehensive, robust, and useful information about how law is understood by, and how it impacts, those meant to be guided by it.

Tobia suggests that empirical jurisprudence might make important contributions to the New Private Law. The New Private Law, he notes, favours conceptual analysis on the basis of its proponents' views on the significance of legal concepts to the nature of law, its administration, and its social functions. New Private Law scholars often investigate legal concepts in relation to ordinary concepts, and premise arguments and conclusions on empirical assumptions about how law influences human deliberation and behaviour. These assumptions, Tobia emphasizes, can and should be tested, and this sort of testing is central to empirical jurisprudence. To the extent that New Private Law scholars are interested in connections between legal concepts and cognate non-legal concepts, and to the extent they wish to know about social facts that indicate or predict the effectiveness of law, the aims and methods of the New Private Law point to those of empirical jurisprudence.

V. Concluding Reflections

The chapters collected here cover varied terrain and provide rich and suggestive views on choice of methodology in private law theory, while also providing insiders' views on emergent methods in private law theory in Germany and the United States. What have we learned? Perhaps the most important takeaway is that, notwithstanding differences in legal systems and traditions, transatlantic dialogue about private law theory is fruitful. Furthermore, and more specifically, our authors uniformly recognize the value of doctrinal, formalistic, and conceptual analysis of law, seeing in them a rich set of methodologies that bear little resemblance to the fictive formalist who practises 'mechanical jurisprudence'. Our authors value formalism, doctrinal analysis, and conceptualism precisely insofar as these methods enable one to understand and to critically analyse existing law in the context of social practices upstream and downstream of the work of legal institutions; practices through which we participate constitutively in systems of normative guidance meant to reliably indicate what we owe to each other and how we may effectively and justly coordinate and collaborate. These, the traditional aims and concerns of private law are also the concerns of the vanguard of new movements in private law in Germany and the United States.

I

METHODOLOGY IN PRIVATE LAW THEORY: GENERAL PERSPECTIVES

1

A Genealogy of Private Law Epistemologies

Marietta Auer

I. Introduction

Just a few years ago, the question of whether there can be anything like a concept of private law worthy of scholarly research might have sounded odd—if not incomprehensible—to all but a handful of legal scholars who still believed in the time-honoured German tradition of legal academia. In this tradition, formed in the early years of the nineteenth century by the works of the German 'Historical School', law is a 'science', and its study, if it is to be considered truly scientific, must be subject to scientific methodology.[1] This categorical imperative of legal science, however, leaves one crucial question open: just which methodology should legal science aspire to if it is to find its own, distinctive character as a science of the law? Is there any genuine legal methodology to cope with the doctrinal riddles of contracts, torts, and property? Does the social embeddedness of garden-variety private law institutions—everything from the market and the corporation to the family and the private person—push private law scholarship in the direction of more empirical, especially economic, sociological, and historical, research? Or is it, quite to the contrary, more philosophical reasoning on the value foundations of private contracts and property that engenders the essence of private law methodology?

In recent times, these and related questions have attracted a surprising amount of new attention on both sides of the Atlantic. While German academia, struggling with its ancient methodological paradigm of doctrinal scholarship under new interdisciplinary and international scrutiny, has embarked on a zealous journey of self-reflection under the influence of novel methodological paradigms,[2] the challenge in the common law world has been

[1] On the German tradition of 'law as a science', see extensively Jan Schröder, *Recht als Wissenschaft* (3rd edn, CH Beck 2020). On the relationship between the Historical School and present-day private law scholarship, see Gerhard Wagner, 'Zivilrechtswissenschaft heute: Zwischen Orakeldeutung und Maschinenraum' in Horst Dreier (ed), *Rechtswissenschaft als Beruf* (Mohr Siebeck 2018) 67–182, 71ff.

[2] The recent German debate on 'law as a science' is vast. See, eg, Matthias Jestaedt and Oliver Lepsius (eds), *Rechtswissenschaftstheorie* (Mohr Siebeck 2008); Gregor Kirchhof, Stefan Magen

Marietta Auer, *A Genealogy of Private Law Epistemologies* In: *Methodology in Private Law Theory.* Edited by: Thilo Kuntz and Paul B. Miller, Oxford University Press. © Marietta Auer 2024. DOI: 10.1093/oso/9780198885306.003.0001

to get private law onto the map of legal reasoning at all. This goal, however, has been surpassed by more than one recent development in Anglo-American legal theory. Perhaps the most striking example is the 'New Private Law' movement.[3] The explicit goal of this movement is the pursuit and formulation of a new paradigm of private law scholarship beyond, on the one hand, the ancient common law agnosticism of a conceptualized abstractum of private law and, on the other, the novel methodological orthodoxy of academic law and economics—both equally blind to the common principled core of private law in the fields of contracts, torts, property, corporations, trusts, succession, and family law.

This chapter seeks to contribute to these novel methodological debates in private law on a related, though not directly similar, path. The path taken here is that of the history of ideas of legal scholarship since the nineteenth century. The aim of this chapter is to present the scientific epistemologies of private law as a genealogical development within the general framework of the theory and history of science. Its goal is to show that there is no such thing as one 'right' methodology of private law, indeed of legal reasoning in general. Legal methodology always mirrors the scientific zeitgeist of its time. But there is more to understanding the genealogy of private law epistemologies: they show a recurring pattern of three epistemic pathways to legal knowledge, namely, normative, descriptive, and analytical approaches, theories and methods.[4] These

and Karsten Schneider (eds), *Was weiß Dogmatik? Was leistet und wie steuert die Dogmatik des Öffentlichen Rechts?* (Mohr Siebeck 2012); Matthias Jestaedt, 'Wissenschaft im Recht. Rechtsdogmatik im Wissenschaftsvergleich' (2014) JZ (Juristenzeitung) 1–12; Thilo Kuntz, 'Recht als Gegenstand der Rechtswissenschaft und performative Rechtserzeugung' (2016) 216 AcP (Archiv für die civilistische Praxis) 866–910; Christian Bumke, *Rechtsdogmatik: eine Disziplin und ihre Arbeitsweise* (Mohr Siebeck 2017); Jannis Lennartz, *Dogmatik als Methode* (Mohr Siebeck 2017); Marietta Auer, 'Privatrechtsdogmatik und Bereicherungsrecht. Möglichkeiten und Grenzen rationaler Theoriewahl in der Privatrechtswissenschaft' in Marietta Auer and others (eds), *Privatrechtsdogmatik im 21. Jahrhundert. Festschrift für Claus-Wilhelm Canaris* (Walter de Gruyter 2017) 509–46; Marietta Auer, *Zum Erkenntnisziel der Rechtstheorie* (Nomos 2018); Horst Dreier (ed), *Rechtswissenschaft als Beruf* (Mohr Siebeck 2018); Nils Jansen, *Rechtswissenschaft und Rechtssystem* (Nomos 2018); Nils Jansen, *Recht und gesellschaftliche Differenzierung* (Mohr Siebeck 2019); Eric Hilgendorf and Helmuth Schulze-Fielitz (eds), *Selbstreflexion der Rechtswissenschaft* (2nd edn, Mohr Siebeck 2021).

[3] For the scholarship assembled under the heading of 'New Private Law', see in particular the symposium issue in 125 Harvard LR 1640ff (2012) with contributions by John CP Goldberg, Shyamkrishna Balganesh, Henry E Smith, Stephen A Smith, and Benjamin C Zipursky, with comments in the Forum section of the same issue. For older works in Anglo-American private law theory, see, eg, Ernest J Weinrib, *The Idea of Private Law* (OUP 1995); James Gordley, *Foundations of Private Law* (OUP 2006); William Lucy, *Philosophy of Private Law* (OUP 2007).

[4] For a more detailed treatment and further references, see Marietta Auer, 'Selbstreflexion der Privatrechtswissenschaft: Formation, Herausforderungen, Perspektiven' in Erik Hilgendorf and Helmuth Schulze-Fielitz (eds), *Selbstreflexion der Rechtswissenschaft* (n 2) 301–25; Marietta Auer, 'Politische Theologie als Rechtswissenschaftstheorie. Kommentar zu Jean-François Kervégan' (2021) RphZ (Rechtsphilosophie) 131–40.

three epistemic pathways—the normative, the descriptive, and the analytical—have repeatedly emerged over time in various combinations. They amount to three complementary epistemologies of legal science: the idealistic, the empirical, and the analytical. Finally, they also mirror parallel methodological viewpoints and tensions between viewpoints in other fields of inquiry, notably in the economic sciences.[5]

This text consists of five sections. I start with an introduction to the recent debate on methodological self-reflection in German legal thought. I then attempt a historical sketch of three methodologically pivotal phases of private law scholarship since 1800. These three phases will be the focus of sections two, three, and four of my text. Section two will deal with the paradigm of the German Historical School prevalent in the first half of the nineteenth century. This is followed in section three by the analytical scientism of the late nineteenth and early twentieth centuries. The fourth section then addresses the turn to the 'conflicting considerations' mode of legal argument and the 'jurisprudence of values' since the second half of the twentieth century. On this basis, the fifth and final section changes the direction of analysis: from the inductive work of the history of ideas, I turn to the analytical, systematic and, ultimately, the philosophical task of interpreting the methodological findings from the historical parts. This final part ends with an outline of the three epistemic pathways—the normative, the descriptive, and the analytical—as concurring and recurring models of private law methodology.

II. Why and How to Theorize Private Law?

Why is there a dispute on the methodology of private law, or indeed law, at all? Why is the status of 'law as a science' disputed? What else can legal scholarship be if not an academic endeavour? Ever since Julius von Kirchmann's famous saying that three corrective words of the legislator are sufficient to turn entire law libraries into waste paper,[6] one recurring theme of the German debate on the academic merits of legal inquiry has been the contingency of legal doctrine, or more generally, the ephemerality of positive law, as an argument against its suitability as an object for serious scholarly inquiry. Serious scholarship seems

[5] For a similar tripartite methodological exposition of welfare economics, see Henner Kleinewefers, *Einführung in die Wohlfahrtsökonomie* (Kohlhammer 2008) 24–31.

[6] Julius Hermann von Kirchmann, *Die Werthlosigkeit der Jurisprudenz als Wissenschaft* (3rd edn, Julius Springer 1848) 17: 'drei berichtigende Worte des Gesetzgebers und ganze Bibliotheken werden zu Makulatur'.

to be an enterprise in need of an independent, unchanging object of study, while jurisprudence necessarily falls short of this demand because its object is in a constant state of flux. Worse still, doctrinal change occurs in part precisely because of the deliberate normative impact exercised by legal scholarship on its own object of study.[7] There is, in other words, no way of separating legal scholarship from legal practice. This holds true, particularly in German legal culture, where the mutual ties between legal academia and legal practice, expressed in common publishing formats, citation cultures, and discourse strategies, are particularly strong.[8]

This insight gives rise to yet another problem for the scientific character of legal study. Legal scholarship, particularly with legal doctrine at its core and understood as a hybrid of legal science and legal practice, seems to suffer from an incurable epistemological contradiction in terms: theory cannot be practiced and vice versa. At first glance, this practice-bound understanding of legal scholarship also conceptually excludes or at least burdens the possibility of a truly scientific legal methodology. If there is something like a relevant objective of legal theory, it seems to describe a conceptual lacuna, a topical absence where a theoretical methodology of jurisprudence should be situated. American law schools, in particular, are where the 'law and ...' fields come into play. Among them are research subjects such as law and economics, law and literature, philosophy of law, sociology of law, legal history, legal anthropology or comparative law. All of these classic pathways of interdisciplinary legal study share the aim of achieving scientificity in legal study by linking it to a field *outside* the law. In the same vein, the German Council of Science and Humanities issued a report on the perspectives of German legal scholarship. In this oft-cited 2012 report, the council maintained that in order to fully exhaust the depth of its matter of inquiry, academic legal research needs to incorporate the entire breadth of 'historical, linguistic, philosophical, social, political, economical, psychological, criminological, and other perspectives', as well as the respective repertories of methods. The Council concludes that there is no such thing as legal scholarship without interdisciplinary references.[9] Taken literally, however, this poses

[7] For a pointed critique of the epistemic dependency of legal scholarship on legal practice and vice versa, see Oliver Lepsius, 'Kritik der Dogmatik' in Kirchhof, Magen, and Schneider (eds), *Was weiß Dogmatik?* (n 2) 39–62.

[8] See, eg, Matthias Jestaedt, 'Wissenschaftliches Recht' in Kirchhof, Magen, and Schneider (eds), *Was weiß Dogmatik?* (n 2) 117–37; Matthias Jestaedt, 'Wissenschaft im Recht. Rechtsdogmatik im Wissenschaftsvergleich' (n 2) 5–6.

[9] German Council of Science and Humanities (Wissenschaftsrat), *Prospects of legal scholarship in Germany. Current situation, analyses, recommendations*, printed matter no 2558-12, https://www.wissenschaftsrat.de/download/archiv/2558-12_engl.pdf (2012) 33: 'When legal scholarship integrates historical, linguistic, philosophical, social, political, economical, psychological, criminological, and other

a serious challenge for law as an independent field of academic inquiry. While the Council of Science and Humanities is certainly right in urging for more interdisciplinary research in law, this ill-formulated demand appears to deliberately widen the antagonism between the 'merely practical' core of law, on the one hand, and 'truly scientific' interdisciplinary legal scholarship, on the other. This antagonism, mirrored in many statements within the recent debate, unnecessarily burdens the methodological self-reflection of legal study. It obscures or even cancels out the merits and scientific import of the established canon of legal methodology.

But, again, this raises the question: what exactly is the established canon of legal methodology, and of private law in particular? Has it always been the same? Or have shifts occurred, with various ramifications, not only between different legal fields, such as private and public law,[10] or even between different issues of private law,[11] but also in the development of private law over time? The present chapter supposes that the latter has indeed been the case. It is precisely here that self-reflection of legal scholarship seems most needed. I argue that over time, the methodology of private law has expressed different, historically contingent combinations of the three epistemic pathways to the study of law. What combination prevailed at a given time reflects not only historical shifts such as the 'social question' of the late nineteenth century or the post-World War II Western consensus of a new constitutionalized international law and value-based public policy but also, and more specifically, the general scientific paradigm of the time. Since the academization of legal scholarship in the European Middle Ages, legal culture has been a part of the general academic culture of its time and therefore can be read through the lens of the history of science. To demonstrate this, I will look at three pivotal phases for the development of the methodology of modern private law scholarship in the German discourse: the first is the philosophical-historical holism brought to perfection

perspectives, it simultaneously adopts their methodologies. It appropriates different epistemological methods to understand its object of inquiry, thereby unfolding the rich variety of meaning naturally entailed in the law (the conditions of its creation and validity, the legal permeation of various areas of life and of different social spheres, the durability and resilience of norms, questions of justice, etc). Legal scholarship cannot, therefore, afford to dispense with these interdisciplinary relations.'

[10] This question might be fruitful aside from the much-disputed 'collapse' of the divide between public and private law, as advocated, eg, by Duncan Kennedy, 'The Stages of the Decline of the Public/Private Distinction' (1982) 130 U Pennsylvania L Rev 1349–57. For the previous question, see, eg, Martin Bullinger, *Öffentliches Recht und Privatrecht. Studien über Sinn und Funktionen der Unterscheidung* (Kohlhammer 1968) 8–12; Wolfgang Hoffmann-Riem and Eberhard Schmidt-Aßmann (eds), *Öffentliches Recht und Privatrecht als wechselseitige Auffangordnungen* (Nomos 1996).

[11] One classic question is whether and how family and patrimony can be united into a single system of private law. See Duncan Kennedy, 'Savigny's Family/Patrimony Distinction and its Place in the Global Genealogy of Classical Legal Thought' (2010) 58 Am J Comp L 811–42.

by the Historical School during the first half of the nineteenth century. The second is the subsequent turn to legal scientism, the leading research paradigm around 1900. The final paradigm, which may be seen as governing private law scholarship and practice up to the current time, is the 'conflicting considerations' mode of the post-World War II normative consensus of the moderate-liberal 'value jurisprudence'.

III. 1800–50: Philosophical-Historical Holism

In Germany, the first and arguably most important formative period of modern private law was the first half of the nineteenth century. It was in this era that the concept of private law as a scientific and methodological enterprise was formed. The leading movement in this development was the Historical School, mostly associated with Friedrich Carl von Savigny.[12] To this day, Savigny is frequently, though not entirely correctly, identified as the founder of the modern canon of statutory interpretation.[13] The Historical School's impact, however, goes far beyond the formulation of rules of interpretation. Its truly lasting achievement lay in the forging of the separate subject matters of private law, that is, the different fields of patrimony and family law, into one coherent system of international rank.[14] What made Savigny's system coherent was on the one hand, its doctrinal elaboration, which reshaped the traditional Roman private law sources into the law of a modern nation. On the other hand, it would be a mistake to assume that the Historical School only carried out research in legal history. The hallmark of Savigny's and some of his contemporaries' writings was that they argued not only on historical but also on normative, philosophical, (conservative-)idealistic grounds.[15] They genuinely believed in the study of Roman law as the source of the '*Volksgeist*' as the basis of a nation's law, and more importantly, they derived from this study a unifying vision of private law as a normative concept of society. One of the key features of this early concept of a civil society based on private law was the 'will theory' as the governing principle of private

[12] See Friedrich Carl von Savigny, *System des heutigen Römischen Rechts* (Veit & Co 1840–48). For an English-language analysis of Savigny's method and influence, see Kennedy, 'Savigny's Family/Patrimony Distinction' (n 11); cf the comprehensive monographs by Hans-Peter Haferkamp, *Die Historische Rechtsschule* (Vittorio Klostermann 2018) and Joachim Rückert, *Idealismus, Jurisprudenz und Politik bei Friedrich Carl von Savigny* (2nd edn, Klostermann 2022).

[13] See, eg, Schröder, *Recht als Wissenschaft* vol 2 (n 1) 196 [§ 147].

[14] Kennedy, 'Savigny's Family/Patrimony Distinction' (n 11).

[15] ibid 813–30. On Savigny's historical-philosophical method, see generally Rückert, *Idealismus, Jurisprudenz und Politik bei Friedrich Carl von Savigny* (n 12).

transactions.[16] This normative, autonomy-based root of private law—still fundamental in private law scholarship today—is clearly derived from natural law and Enlightenment philosophy. And while the Historical School always denied this heritage and acted as though its scholarship was only concerned with the exegesis of historical sources, there is, in fact, a strong idealistic core contained in the idea that there is something like an autonomous, coherent system of private law even today.[17] According to this idea, private law relationships are not only separate from but also normatively prior to state and public law. Again, the root of this thinking lies in Enlightenment philosophy, which was transformed into modern law through the philosophical-historical holism of the Historical School. This is particularly evident in the work of Immanuel Kant, whose concept of private law, closely mirrored by Savigny's system, is identical to the entirety of transcendentally founded individual private rights.[18] A right, according to Kant, can appear in one of three forms: as a right against a person, a right to a thing, or a right to a person akin to a right to a thing. In Savigny's system, this triad reappears in the triad of obligations, property and family law. The main point of the Kantian philosophy of rights, however, is that private rights are innate rights; they precede the state and are carried over into the state by means of public law, the content of which is left unchanged by this transition.[19] In Savigny's system, this premise is elegantly left untouched.

Perhaps the Historical School's most innovative scholarly achievement consisted in blending this idealistic view of private rights with classic Roman law into a functioning system of modern private law. By a 'functioning' system, I mean a system that is 'systematic' enough to allow for general reasoning but not too abstract to solve specific cases. One can speak of an optimal level of abstraction where workable legal concepts and jurisprudential methods are typically situated.[20] It is precisely on this level that Savigny's 'System of Contemporary Roman Law' operates and creates a new mixed form out of

[16] Kennedy, 'Savigny's Family/Patrimony Distinction' (n 11) 831; cf also Duncan Kennedy, 'From the Will Theory to the Principle of Private Autonomy: Lon Fuller's "Consideration and Form"' (2000) 100 Col L Rev 94–175.

[17] This is not a statement of the philosophical merits but of the history of ideas of modern private law. For an extensive treatment and further references, see Marietta Auer, *Der privatrechtliche Diskurs der Moderne* (Mohr Siebeck 2014).

[18] Immanuel Kant, *The Metaphysics of Morals* (Mary Gregor tr & ed, CUP 1996) 85, 90 [§§ 41, 44]; cf Savigny, *System* vol 1 (n 12) 338ff, 367 [§§ 53–54, 56]. For the relationship between both systems, see Kennedy, 'Savigny's Family/Patrimony Distinction' (n 11) 833f; Auer, *Diskurs* (n 17) 26ff at n 71, 74, 76 and 83ff; Marietta Auer, 'Privatrecht ist doch wie Liebe' in M Grünberger and N Jansen (eds), *Privatrechtstheorie heute* (Mohr Siebeck 2017) 98–117, 100ff.

[19] Kant, *The Metaphysics of Morals* (n 18) 85, 90 [§§ 41, 44].

[20] This is not a new insight. For a modern law and economics rendering, see Isaac Ehrlich and Richard A Posner, 'An Economic Analysis of Legal Rulemaking' (1974) 3 J Legal Studies 257–86.

the Roman dualism of persons and things on the one hand and the threefold division of Kantian private rights on the other. The resulting system—that is, the threefold division between property law, the law of obligations, and family law—continues to shape the system of German private law to this day. Decisive for this integrative achievement was the so-called 'pandect system'.[21] This five-pronged system consists, in its three middle parts, of the three system categories developed by Kant and Savigny (ie property law, the law of obligations, and family law). Moreover, it recognizes the law of succession as a fifth, independent part of the system and summarizes the general doctrines on rights, persons, and so forth in a preceding first general part. Over the course of the nineteenth century, the pandect system, initially only conceived as a teaching aid, developed into the leading idea of what a principled system of scholarly private law should look like. Ironically, this system finally derived its normative power from the state by a 'wilful' legislative act, namely the enactment of the German Civil Code in 1900, which replicates the pandectist structure in its five books. Yet, the decisive factor for the success of the pandect system seems to lie in its productive mixture of historical private law sources, a normative concept of private right, and just the right amount of academic leeway to cater to the needs of private practice. Even today, this methodical mixture still represents a productive model for future private law scholarship.

IV. 1850–1930: Legal Scientism

By the mid-nineteenth century, however, it became increasingly clear that the pandect system, together with the historical-philosophical method developed by the Historical School, were not enough to cope with new challenges facing private law. Among those was the rise of the industrial society with an increasing need for economic and social regulation, which led to a new role of the legislator as the most important creator of binding sources of private law. Around 1850, the general sentiment had become apparent: the historical method was no longer adequate to the task of dealing with this shift in the

[21] The 'pandect system' has its origins in a textbook on Roman law: Georg Arnold Heise, *Grundriss eines Systems des gemeinen Civilrechts zum Behuf von Pandecten-Vorlesungen* (1st edn, Mohr und Zimmer 1807). For the development of private law systems during the nineteenth century, see Andreas B Schwarz, 'Zur Entstehung des modernen Pandektensystems' (1921) 42 ZRG Rom Abt 578–610; Lars Björne, *Deutsche Rechtssysteme im 18. und 19. Jahrhundert* (Rolf Gremer 1984), 131ff, 274ff; Hans-Peter Haferkamp, *Die Historische Rechtsschule* (n 12) 81ff. To this day the pandect system underlies not only the German Civil Code but also internationally related private law codifications, such as the Swiss Civil Code and the Swiss Code of Obligations.

canon of legal sources away from legal history. In its place grew the demand for a new, genuinely juridical method of legal interpretation.[22] One consequence of this new vision of a truly juridical method was the rising prestige of legal doctrine as a skilled endeavour that could only be mastered by the best legal minds.[23] In epistemological terms, this development can to some extent be described as aiming at a new analytical understanding of legal sources. But it was also inspired by the exact paradigm of the contemporary empirical and theoretical natural sciences. And while the most appropriate label is open to debate, one promise of this new vision of legal scholarship was clear: the contemporary paradigm of legal science was no longer found in the premises of the Historical School, which were at this point considered outdated.

For the present purposes, it is important to note that this novel paradigm did not develop in a theoretical vacuum. Behind this shift lies the simultaneous intensification of the norm of scientific objectivity in the contemporary natural sciences.[24] For a long time, the natural sciences had proceeded in the style of interpretive natural history, an approach not altogether different from the interpretive style employed by the historical sciences. But in the late nineteenth century, the formulation of scientific laws that left room for subjective interpretation was suddenly frowned upon in the natural sciences. Scientific exactitude became incompatible with the interpretation of facts by scientists. The facts had to speak for themselves or be reproducible through mechanistic devices or methods. The more mechanistic the process and the less room for interpretation, the better. Thus, legal scholarship, relying on interpretive methods even more than other social sciences or humanities, faced a major problem if it was to remain a science on par with the contemporary natural sciences. The response of private law scholarship to this challenge was complex. On the one hand, it developed the said analytic-positivist, genuinely doctrinal approach to legal scholarship. On the other, it embarked on the search for an objective reality of law purged of as many interpretive artifacts as possible, and it looked for this objective reality analogous to the contemporary natural sciences. This second characteristic is probably best described as 'legal scientism'.[25]

[22] Representative authors from this time include Burkard Wilhelm Leist, *Ueber die dogmatische Analyse römischer Rechtsinstitute* (Friedrich Frommann 1854); Johannes Emil Kuntze, *Der Wendepunkt der Rechtswissenschaft* (JC Hinrich 1856); Rudolf von Jhering, 'Unsere Aufgabe' (1857) 1 JherJB (Jhering's Jahrbücher) 1–52; cf Haferkamp, *Die Historische Rechtsschule* (n 12) 315ff.

[23] This aspiration is particularly present in Jhering, 'Unsere Aufgabe' (n 22).

[24] This development has been described extensively by Lorraine Daston and Peter Galison, 'The Image of Objectivity' (1992) 40 Representations 81–128; Lorraine Daston and Peter Galison, *Objectivity* (Princeton UP 2007).

[25] For this concept, although in a different context, see, eg, Andrew Lang, 'New Legal Realism, Empiricism, and Scientism: The Relative Objectivity of Law and Social Science' (2015) 28 Leiden J Intl Law 231–54.

The paradigmatic formulation of this scientistic research paradigm came from Rudolf von Jhering. In a programmatic essay published in 1857 at the launch of his new journal, the 'Jherings Jahrbücher', he formulated a new methodological ideal for private law scholarship that combined scientific objectivity with doctrinal and practical productivity. The key concept was 'higher jurisprudence', which, in Jhering's florid language, abounds with chemical metaphors.[26] In particular, higher jurisprudence was supposed to emerge from lower jurisprudence just as one aggregate state of a chemical element emerges from another. According to Jhering, all law consists of legal substance, which changes its character via the alchemistic processes of legal science. Through legal science, the legal raw substances are transformed into a coherent intellectual body, which, for Jhering, presents itself to experimental exploration. According to Jhering, a science of private law living up to this ideal of scientific objectivity would, at the same time, be the highest philosophy of law.[27]

Ultimately, this maximally holistic paradigm of legal scientism never succeeded. Legal scholarship is, after all, not an exact natural science. Legal scholarship was incapable of keeping pace with the rapid rise and mathematical formalization of physics and chemistry at the turn of the twentieth century. Nevertheless, the desideratum formulated by Jhering of a legal scholarship that was both analytically honed in its doctrine *and* empirically precise in terms of its scientific methods was by no means abandoned. This lofty epistemic goal lived on when the paradigm of physics and chemistry—of which the early Jhering had dreamt—was replaced by the methods of the new empirical social sciences, which formed their paradigms in the late nineteenth century. The later Jhering, who emphatically proclaimed law to be a means to an end, was again leading the charge of this development. His now commitment to 'purpose' as the 'creator of all law'[28] in no way meant that he had abandoned his earlier claim that legal science must make use of the most advanced methodologies sourced from all branches of science. In his later writings, he replaced the natural-historical method with purpose as the touchstone of legal epistemology. Even more tellingly, just a few years before Freud's 'Interpretation of Dreams',[29] Jhering defined the purposiveness in law as a 'psychological law

[26] Jhering, 'Unsere Aufgabe' (n 22) 8ff. For Jhering's method, see Ralf Seinecke, 'Rudolf von Jhering anno 1858' (2013) 130 ZRG GA (Zeitschrift für Rechtsgeschichte, germanistische Abteilung) 238–80; Joachim Rückert, 'Das Methodenorakel Rudolf von Jhering (1818–1892)' (2019) 219 AcP (Archiv für die civilistische Praxis) 457–87; cf also Auer, 'Privatrechtsdogmatik und Bereicherungsrecht' (n 2) 514–22; Lennartz, *Dogmatik als Methode* (n 2) 28ff; Haferkamp, *Die Historische Rechtsschule* (n 12) 317ff.

[27] Jhering, 'Unsere Aufgabe' (n 22) 19ff.

[28] Rudolf von Jhering, *Der Zweck im Recht* vol 1 (Breitkopf & Härtel 1877), front page motto.

[29] Sigmund Freud, *Die Traumdeutung* (1st edn, Franz Deuticke, 1900).

of causality' and thereby again tried to establish a connection to the exact sciences, in this case, neurology.[30] This combination of legal doctrine and methodological scientism is once again characteristic of private law scholarship in the second half of the nineteenth century.

The dawn of a new century placed the source basis of German private law on a new footing. On 1 January 1900, the German Civil Code came into force. What changed as a result? Ultimately, not that much—at least, much less than one might think. First, as argued before, the German civil code follows the structure of the pandect system. All older, especially historical-philosophical, readings of the existing private law system were therefore still plausible. It would be a fallacy to regard the codification of private law or, more generally, private law legislation since 1900 as an abrogation or delegitimization of nineteenth-century private law scholarship, even though the contemporary reader might be tempted to create an intellectual opposition between democratic legislation, on the one hand, and what Savigny and Puchta called 'scientific law', on the other.[31] More precisely, the primary fault lines between the state of private law scholarship before 1900 and that of today lies neither in the structure of legal sources nor in the abrogation of private law scholarship. After 1900, there was not less but rather more freedom for doctrinal construction. However, it changed its form: doctrinal construction became legal interpretation.[32] In other words, a reorientation of focus in private law scholarship had taken place that put the new codification at the centre of attention, but it did not curtail the interpretive freedom associated with it.

The decisive question in private law scholarship therefore became the following: how should this interpretative leeway be used? At first glance, it might seem surprising to see a continuation of the same scientistic paradigm established before the turn of the century again after 1900, when the battle cry of the 'free law' and 'social law' movements became an international affair.[33] But it is important to understand that free law became a theoretical problem around

[30] Jhering, *Zweck* (n 28) 4.

[31] This is the view taken by Lennartz, *Dogmatik als Methode* (n 2) 15ff; cf Ralf Seinecke, 'Die deutschsprachige Rechtswissenschaft seit 1800 und der Rechtspluralismus' (2020) 137 ZRG GA (Zeitschrift für Rechtsgeschichte, germanistische Abteilung) 272–363, 281f. For a critique, see Nils Jansen, 'Rechtsdogmatik, Rechtswissenschaft und juristische Praxis' (2018) 143 AöR (Archiv für öffentliches Recht) 623, 636ff.

[32] Lennartz, *Dogmatik als Methode* (n 2) 24ff, 40ff.

[33] For an overview of the contemporary German writings on free law, see Gnaeus Flavius (Hermann Kantorowicz), *Der Kampf um die Rechtswissenschaft* (Carl Winter 1906) 50. For the French social law movement, cf Duncan Kennedy and Marie-Claire Belleau, 'La place de René Demogue dans la généalogie de la pensée juridique contemporaine' (2006) 56 RIEJ (Revue interdisciplinaire d'études juridiques) 163–211.

1900 not because private law was now codified and thus its free interpretation amounted to a scandal in Germany. Instead, creative interpretation had already become objectionable as a scientific method long before, especially against the background of the renewed demand for scientific objectivity in the late nineteenth century.[34] Philipp Heck's 'jurisprudence of interests', developed in the first two decades of the twentieth century, is paradigmatic of these developments in German private law.[35] Sharply rejecting the free law euphoria present at the turn of the century, Heck's theory again strove to achieve the most comprehensive level of objectivity in the interpretation of law. For Heck, just as for Jhering, the scientific basis of legal knowledge had to be empirically rooted. The source of Heck's empiricism, however, differed fundamentally from that of Jhering, mirroring the shift in legal sources away from historic Roman law to private law legislation. Thus, Heck sharply rejected Jhering's 'higher jurisprudence' and instead proposed a strictly 'subjective' theory of statutory interpretation, which amounted to an early version of originalism strictly bound to the legislator's will.[36] At its root, however, Heck's attack on Jhering does not turn on legal sources but, again, on legal epistemologies. For Heck, the fallacy of Jhering's 'higher jurisprudence' was not to commit conceptual realism but, much more fundamentally, to condone scientific arbitrariness resulting from unfettered interpretation of legal materials. For Heck, only strict adherence to the 'subjective theory' of interpretation could deliver scientifically valid legal results.

Heck's writings, however, already reveal the methodological paradox that was to reappear in the development of private law throughout the twentieth century. On the one hand, there was the claim of scientific objectivity in the interpretation of the law, which, under a codified legal system, seems to repress scientific construction and limit legal scholarship to the strict interpretation of the law. On the other, experience soon began to show that limiting scientific construction to statutory interpretation by no means narrowed the scope

[34] It was only because of this shift that legal positivism was able to emerge as one of the leading jurisprudential theories since the late nineteenth century; cf at n 72.

[35] The three key texts are found in Philipp Heck, *Das Problem der Rechtsgewinnung—Gesetzesauslegung und Interessenjurisprudenz—Begriffsbildung und Interessenjurisprudenz* (Roland Dubischar ed, Gehlen 1968). For Heck's empirical method, see Heinrich Schoppmeyer, *Juristische Methode als Lebensaufgabe* (Mohr Siebeck 2001) 57ff; Marietta Auer, 'Methodenkritik und Interessenjurisprudenz' (2008) 16 ZEuP (Zeitschrift für Europäisches Privatrecht) 517–33, 521ff.

[36] Heck, *Das Problem der Rechtsgewinnung* (n 35) 56ff; cf Schoppmeyer, *Juristische Methode als Lebensaufgabe* (n 35) 102ff; Auer, 'Methodenkritik und Interessenjurisprudenz' (n 35) 528ff. For a critique, see Marietta Auer, 'Der Kampf um die Wissenschaftlichkeit der Rechtswissenschaft. Zum 75. Todestag von Hermann Kantorowicz' (2015) 23 ZEuP 773, 787ff; Auer, *Zum Erkenntnisziel der Rechtstheorie* (n 2) 68.

of doctrinal creativity but instead extended its possibilities far into the realm of judicial law-making.[37] During the Weimar Republic, this paradox was the starting point for a new style of boundless legal methodology, employed by both academics and judges. Among the lasting innovations of private law in the first half of the twentieth century were doctrinal developments that, on the one hand, appeared to be closely bound to the wording of the Civil Code, while they, on the other, opened it up for policy-based decision styles on a large scale. One milestone was the development of the general clauses of 'good faith' and 'good morals' into safety valves for substantive value corrections as well as judicial law-making in all areas of private law.[38] Both Justus Wilhelm Hedemann's warning against the 'flight into the general clauses' (expressed on the eve of the dictatorship) and Franz Wieacker's thesis of the transformation of the 'social model' underlying German private from a 'formal ethics of freedom' to a 'material ethics of social responsibility' are oft-cited testimonies that exemplify this critical self-reflection of the path of private law and underline its fundamental importance.[39] As a result, the methodological boundaries of private law inherited from the nineteenth century began to slip. And while the institutional division of labour between legislation, adjudication, and legal scholarship remained untouched for the time being, this too was soon to change under the rule of the Nazi dictatorship.[40] It shall suffice here to point out the radicalized use of the general clauses as supra-legal 'control norms' under Nazism, thus opening up space for free judicial law-making, which was now no longer interpreted as an arrogation of power but instead cherished—in a perverse reversal of contemporary scientific values—as 'personalised objectivity' of the politicized judges.[41]

[37] Lennartz, *Dogmatik als Methode* (n 2) 24.

[38] See, eg, Ludwig Raiser, *Das Recht der Allgemeinen Geschäftsbedingungen* (Hanseatische Verlags-Anstalt 1935). For the rise of the general clauses, see, eg, Hans-Peter Haferkamp, in *Historisch-kritischer Kommentar zum BGB* vol II/1 (Mohr Siebeck 2007) §242 n 56ff; cf Hans-Peter Haferkamp, 'Zur Methodengeschichte unter dem BGB in fünf Systemen' (2014) 214 AcP (Archiv für die civilistische Praxis) 60–92, 78ff; Bernd Rüthers, *Die unbegrenzte Auslegung* (9th edn, Mohr Siebeck 2022) 13ff; Marietta Auer, *Materialisierung, Flexibilisierung, Richterfreiheit: Generalklauseln im Spiegel der Antinomien des Privatrechtsdenkens* (Mohr Siebeck 2005) 103ff.

[39] Justus Wilhelm Hedemann, *Die Flucht in die Generalklauseln. Eine Gefahr für Recht und Staat* (JCB Mohr 1933); Franz Wieacker, *Das Sozialmodell der klassischen Privatrechtsgesetzbücher und die Entwicklung der modernen Gesellschaft* (CF Müller 1953) 18; cf Franz Wieacker, *Privatrechtsgeschichte der Neuzeit* (2nd edn, Vandenhoeck & Ruprecht 1967) 543ff.

[40] For comprehensive analyses of the law under the Nazi dictatorship, see Schröder, *Recht als Wissenschaft* vol 2 (n 1) 5–57 [§§ 95–113]; Bernd Rüthers, *Die unbegrenzte Auslegung* (n 38).

[41] See, eg, Heinrich Lange, 'Mittel und Ziel der Rechtsfindung im Zivilrecht' (1936) 3 ZAkDR (Zeitschrift der Akademie für deutsches Recht) 922, 924. For a comment, see Haferkamp, 'Methodengeschichte' (n 38) 73ff.

V. 1950–2020: Jurisprudence of Values

After 1945, the most obvious ideological content was quickly erased from the German private law system. What could not be erased, however, was the lasting shift in the institutional distribution of powers between private law legislation, adjudication, and legal scholarship. The most notable new feature, stemming from the Weimar era and the Nazi dictatorship, was a greatly expanded scope for judicial law-making by balancing conflicting considerations, understood as fundamental values of the legal system.[42] Accordingly, one of the most significant developments in private law methodology in the post-war period was the replacement of Heck's 'jurisprudence of interest' with the so-called 'jurisprudence of values'.[43] The 'jurisprudence of values' was carried over from the 1930s into the post-war period by former leading private law scholars of the Nazi era, such as Karl Larenz. Its main goal was to replace the epistemic empiricism of the jurisprudence of interests with a balancing method based on values. The critique targeted at Heck by Larenz and others since the 1930s was that the balancing of empirical interests, taken as a method of jurisprudence, amounted to a naturalistic fallacy in view of the necessarily normative character of the law.[44] The 'jurisprudence of values' thus suggested replacing the allegedly arbitrary balancing of interests by the balancing of values, as taken from the law itself. While this critique of the 'jurisprudence of interests' has to be read against the ideological background of the Nazi regime in the 1930s and 1940s, in which it clearly aimed to discredit Heck's politically neutral balancing method and replace it with Nazi ideology, this strong ideological content of the 'jurisprudence of values' was quickly abandoned in the post-war era.[45] After 1950, the widely uncritical spread of the 'jurisprudence of values' served to fill the ideological vacuum following the collapse of the Nazi regime with new substantive content, which now mostly stemmed from the German constitution, but also from an eclectic mix of other normative, idealistic, and philosophical beliefs about the law. The brief post-World War II renaissance of religious and secular

[42] Haferkamp, 'Methodengeschichte' (n 38) 81ff.

[43] 'Wertungsjurisprudenz'; see Karl Larenz, *Methodenlehre der Rechtswissenschaft* (6th edn, Springer 1991); cf Haferkamp, 'Methodengeschichte' (n 38) 84; Schröder, *Recht als Wissenschaft* vol 2 (n 1) 180f [§143].

[44] See, eg, Julius Binder, 'Bemerkungen zum Methodenstreit in der Privatrechtswissenschaft' (1934) 100 ZHR (Zeitschrift für das gesamte Handels- und Wirtschaftsrecht) 4–83. On the ideological nature of the controversy, see Bernd Hüpers, *Karl Larenz—Methodenlehre und Philosophie des Rechts in Geschichte und Gegenwart* (Berliner Wissenschaftsverlag 2010) 273ff, 375ff, 421ff; cf Auer, 'Der Kampf um die Wissenschaftlichkeit der Rechtswissenschaft' (n 36) 790 at n 62.

[45] Haferkamp, 'Methodengeschichte' (n 38) 73f.

natural law in German jurisprudence is the most conspicuous example of this renewed shift to normative epistemologies in legal scholarship.[46]

After 1950, the Civil Code, which had survived the dictatorship, once again provided the necessary authoritative basis for private law scholarship to create sophisticated doctrinal structures and to mould them into a new normative or 'teleological' system of private law.[47] In the resulting system, there was now a 'principle of reliance' that stood alongside contract law,[48] while 'social' regulation moderated the rigidity of the market economy in landlord-tenant law, labour law, and consumer protection. It is a signature of this epoch of the German 'social market economy' that social modifications of private autonomy were always moderate enough so as to not fundamentally call into question the principled unity of private law. The same held true of market regulations in new research fields like national and European capital market regulation, competition law, and antitrust law. One could say that the particular style of private law scholarship in Germany under the 'Bonn Republic' up to 1990 was characterized by an attempt to always strike a balance or find a middle ground between 'the market' and 'the social', both politically and epistemologically.[49] The political balance was achieved between the ordo-liberal, free-yet-regulated understanding of the 'private law society', which mostly succeeded at bracketing the heterogeneous forces of public law within the complementary paradigm of the welfare state.[50] The epistemic balance achieved was a surprisingly stable mélange of doctrinal and analytical jurisprudence with strong realistic and normative elements, partly grounded in empirical fields like sociology and economics, partly drawing on the 'jurisprudence of values' and the Enlightenment roots of classic private law. All of this was methodologically reinforced by a constitutionally renewed explanation of the binding power of statutory law and legal methodology.[51] Perhaps the single most significant German post-war innovation of private law scholarship was the doctrine of

[46] For this development, see Lena Foljanty, *Recht oder Gesetz. Juristische Identität und Autorität in den Naturrechtsdebatten der Nachkriegszeit* (Mohr Siebeck, 2013).

[47] Claus-Wilhelm Canaris, *Systemdenken und Systembegriff in der Jurisprudenz* (2nd edn, Duncker & Humblot 1983).

[48] Claus-Wilhelm Canaris, *Die Vertrauenshaftung im Deutschen Privatrecht* (CH Beck 1971).

[49] On the rise of the balancing paradigm, see Joachim Rückert, 'Abwägung—die juristische Karriere eines unjuristischen Begriffs oder: Normenstrenge und Abwägung im Funktionswandel' (2011) JZ (Juristenzeitung) 913–23; cf on the parallel international development Duncan Kennedy, 'A Transnational Genealogy of Proportionality in Private Law' in R Brownsword, H-W Micklitz, L Niglia, and S Weatherill (eds), *The Foundations of European Private Law* (Hart 2011) 185–220.

[50] On the paradigm of the 'private law society', see Franz Böhm, 'Privatrechtsgesellschaft und Marktwirtschaft' (1966) 17 ORDO 75; cf Karl Riesenhuber (ed), *Privatrechtsgesellschaft: Entwicklung, Stand und Verfassung des Privatrechts* (Mohr Siebeck 2007).

[51] For a summary, see Jörg Neuner, '60 Jahre Grundgesetz aus der Sicht des Privatrechts' (2011) 59 Jahrbuch des öffentlichen Rechts der Gegenwart 29–58.

the horizontal effect of constitutional rights. Its breakthrough moment came with the Federal Constitutional Court's famous 1958 'Lüth' decision.[52] In 'Lüth', the court held that a call for a boycott by Erich Lüth, chairman of the Hamburg press club, of a movie by Nazi director Veit Harlan was covered by the constitutional free speech clause and could not be banned by a threat of injunction. Initially, it seemed as if the 'Lüth' decision could be seamlessly embedded into the doctrinal structure of German post-war private law. The general clauses, which had served as access points for value-based innovations of private law doctrine since the 1920s, were now functioning as a ready-made doctrinal tool for introducing constitutional values into private law.[53] Expressed through the doctrine of 'indirect horizontal effect' and a convenient re-reading of constitutional rights as duties of protection, an initially stable balance was achieved between constitutional primacy on the one hand and the normative autonomy of private law on the other.[54]

This balance could be called the third defining methodological paradigm of German private law, after the philosophical-historical holism of the Historical School and the empirical-analytical paradigm of legal scientism in the late nineteenth and early twentieth centuries. Characteristic of this third paradigm was a combination of all three epistemic paths encountered in private law scholarship up to this point, with a combination of analytical-doctrinal, normative-teleological, and empirical-social thinking at its core.[55] The normative aim was always directed towards value compromise between 'the market' and 'the social', and from today's perspective is inseparable from history since Weimar and National Socialism. A pronounced increase in regulatory interventions by national and European Union legislation only occurred in the last third of the century, and initially, these could be dealt with using proven dogmatic constructions. Finally, there was a widely accepted consensus on the judicial power to interpret the Civil Code and advance doctrinal reasoning, a power usually exercised in constructive dialogue with private law scholarship. Could this harmonious balance hold forever? The possible tipping points are already visible in the present dynamics of the system:[56] on the one hand,

[52] 7 BVerfGE (Entscheidungen des Bundesverfassungsgerichts) 198 (15 January 1958).

[53] Haferkamp, 'Methodengeschichte' (n 38) 78ff.

[54] Claus-Wilhelm Canaris, 'Grundrechte und Privatrecht' (1984) 184 AcP 201; cf Matthias Ruffert, *Vorrang der Verfassung und Eigenständigkeit des Privatrechts* (Mohr Siebeck 2001).

[55] For a summary along these lines, see also Schröder, *Recht als Wissenschaft* vol 2 (n 1) 117f [§ 132].

[56] For a critique of this point, see Gerhard Wagner, 'Materialisierung des Schuldrechts unter dem Einfluss von Verfassungsrecht und Europarecht—Was bleibt von der Privatautonomie?' in U Blaurock and G Hager (eds), *Obligationenrecht im 21. Jahrhundert* (Nomos 2010) 13–84; Wagner, 'Zivilrechtswissenschaft heute' (n 1) 96ff.

they lie in the ever-increasing mass of private law regulation.[57] The other major threat lies in the dynamics of the ongoing constitutionalization of private law.[58] Both developments reinforce each other since they stem from the same pattern of emphasizing the primacy of legislative sources over the normative core of private law: the primacy of the constitution, on the one hand, and the primacy of European Union law, on the other.

VI. Three Paths of Legal Epistemology

Are there any general lessons to be learned from the three formative periods of private law methodology distinguished in the preceding sections? One lesson is this: private law was only able to achieve a classic, enduring gestalt when it succeeded in striking a viable balance between the analytical and doctrinal standards of the legal system, on the one hand, and the empirical and normative foundations of private law in society, on the other. Epistemologically, all three formative phases of private law scholarship followed similar paths in that they sought *and found* a connection to the most advanced methods of the contemporary natural and social sciences. For the Historical School, this connection lay in its common origin with the historical sciences, scientifically at their zenith in the early nineteenth century. For the legal scientism of the late nineteenth and early twentieth centuries, this connection shifted to the most advanced contemporary natural and social sciences. Perhaps the least pronounced of the three in terms of a specific scientific role model was the mixed paradigm of late twentieth-century private law, represented by the universal policy-based middle ground of the 'jurisprudence of values'.

More specifically, a methodologically defined relation between private law and the underlying empirical reality has always been a necessary, but never a sufficient, condition of its fully developed scientific paradigm. The same also holds true for the analytical and normative components of private law scholarship. An advanced methodology of private law has always demanded, but never been restricted to, a sophisticated analytical component that did justice

[57] On the regulatory paradigm in private law, see Gerhard Wagner, 'Prävention und Verhaltenssteuerung durch Private – Anmaßung oder legitime Aufgabe?' (2006) 206 AcP (Archiv für die civilistische Praxis) 352–476; cf Alexander Hellgardt, *Regulierung und Privatrecht* (Mohr Siebeck 2016).

[58] Among the most recent developments is the 'stadium ban' decision on the horizontal effect of the equal treatment clause, 148 BVerfGE (Entscheidungen des Bundesverfassungsgerichts) 267 (11 April 2018); cf Alexander Hellgardt, 'Wer hat Angst vor der unmittelbaren Drittwirkung?' (2018) JZ (Juristenzeitung) 901–10.

to its doctrinal complexity and the demands of legal practice. It is a futile endeavour to play empiricist and analytic-doctrinal epistemologies against one another, and the same applies to legal academia versus legal practice.[59] Both in its internal fruitfulness and external influence, the science of private law has reached its highest points of relevance when it was capable of establishing a connection to the contemporary natural and social sciences, while at the same time offering useful guidelines to legal practitioners.[60] Likewise, there is also an inevitably normative component involved, which rests on the Enlightenment foundations of private law and, beyond that, reflects the entire *nomos* or normative universe of the contemporary society.[61] A topical methodology of private law will ultimately lead to the question of what valuation society at large grants to relationships governed by private initiative. Measured against these standards, a fruitful methodology of private law should seek to combine both extra-legal, empirical, and normative insights and a core of analytical reasoning within a normatively thin and thus timeless system of doctrinal concepts.[62] Just to be clear, there is no such thing as a comprehensive 'system' of private law if understood as the result of a scholarly endeavour to collect and map all private law decisions, norms, and doctrines into one coherent scheme. Making such a system the aim or goal would indeed be an unrealistic task for private law scholarship.[63] Systematic thinking, however, can do more than this. In fact, private law scholarship cannot avoid updating both its system of fundamental values and its system of conceptual organization in such a way that both allow for an adequate representation of the meaning of private law in contemporary society. As a brief reminder, private law enables the autonomous formation of legal relationships as a residual power of social self-organization, and this vital social task is by no means obsolete. On the contrary, the heavier the regulatory load of national and European Union legislation becomes, the more urgent it

[59] But see Nils Jansen, *Rechtswissenschaft und Rechtssystem* (Nomos 2018) 47ff; Nils Jansen, 'Rechtsdogmatik, Rechtswissenschaft und juristische Praxis' (n 31) 638ff; Nils Jansen, *Recht und gesellschaftliche Differenzierung* (Mohr Siebeck 2019) 279ff, for a defence of the difference between legal scholarship and legal practice based on Niklas Luhmann's systems theory.

[60] One example for an attempt to bridge the gap between law and society is the recent exchange on 'responsive legal doctrine'; see Michael Grünberger, 'Verträge über digitale Güter?' (2018) 218 AcP (Archiv für die civilistische Praxis) 213–96, 238ff; Karl Riesenhuber, 'Neue Methode und Dogmatik eines Rechts der Digitalisierung?' (2019) 219 AcP (Archiv für die civilistische Praxis) 892–923; Michael Grünberger, 'Responsive Rechtsdogmatik – eine Skizze' (2019) 219 AcP (Archiv für die civilistische Praxis) 924–42.

[61] For the concept of *nomos*, see, fundamentally, Robert M Cover, 'The Supreme Court, 1982 Term, Foreword: Nomos and Narrative' (1983) 97 Harvard LR 4–68.

[62] For this demand, see Jansen, 'Rechtsdogmatik, Rechtswissenschaft und juristische Praxis' (n 31) 642ff, 651ff; cf also Thomas Lobinger, 'Perspektiven der Privatrechtsdogmatik am Beispiel des allgemeinen Gleichbehandlungsrechts' (2016) 216 AcP (Archiv für die civilistische Praxis) 28–106, 47f.

[63] For this critique, see Wagner, 'Zivilrechtswissenschaft heute' (n 1) 182.

seems at the same time to restate and reinforce the legal preconditions for social self-organization through private law.

What, then, has been the core of private law methodology since the nineteenth century? What I have attempted to show is that there is indeed no single core but rather a triad of recurring paths of legal epistemology that have time and again re-emerged since the nineteenth century. No single path was capable of exhausting the depth of legal scholarship. Any scholarly approach that was treated as an absolute to the exclusion of other paths quickly found itself, epistemically speaking, at a dead end—something that has happened several times since the early nineteenth century. In other words, there is what one could almost describe as a cyclical reoccurrence of all three paths since the nineteenth century, none of them able to definitively prevail over the others. In the remainder of this chapter, I will attempt a brief analytical sketch of the 'pure' form of each of the three paths, distilled from the history of legal thought.[64]

The first of these paths can be described as *normative*, *philosophical*, or *idealistic*. Idealistic epistemology was present in the holistic paradigm of the Historical School as well as in every later stage of German private law scholarship up to the late twentieth-century 'jurisprudence of values'. Its ancient legacy, however, goes back even further. The roots of modern private law can be traced back to the ancient and medieval systems of natural law, which were, in essence, all founded on idealistic epistemic premises.[65] But why should such premises still be relevant for present-day legal scholarship? Ever since the anti-metaphysical turn of post-Kantian philosophy, metaphysical normative foundations are no longer defensible as a guiding model for legal scholarship or, indeed, for science at large. And yet, this in no way implies that idealistic premises or normative patterns of reason have become meaningless for legal scholarship. The history of modern private law shows that the opposite is true. Modern private law abounds with norms and values that are derived not only from the Enlightenment philosophies of, among others, Hugo Grotius, Samuel Pufendorf, John Locke, and, most visibly in the case of German private law, Immanuel Kant, but also with a number of other, both older and more recent, philosophical influences on its *nomos*.[66] Just to mention a few more, Aristotelians, medieval scholastics, late scholastics, and even German idealists like Hegel have all, consciously or unconsciously, left their normative and

[64] For the following, see Auer, 'Politische Theologie als Rechtswissenschaftstheorie' (n 4) 133–36. References are kept to a minimum.

[65] See only Hans Welzel, *Naturecht und materiale Gerechtigkeit* (4th edn, Vandenhoeck & Ruprecht 1962).

[66] See, eg, Auer, *Diskurs* (n 17) 14ff.

ethical imprint on the shape of modern private law, despite the professed anti-metaphysics of modern legal positivism. Carl Schmitt, the conservative agent provocateur of the Weimar legal intelligentsia, expressed it thusly: the key concepts of modern state theory are ultimately secularized theological concepts.[67] Try as one might, there is no true anti-metaphysical way out of the 'political theology' of modern legal culture.

To disprove the metaphysical path has, however, precisely been the aim of the second type of legal epistemologies we encountered—legal *scientism*, *realism*, or *empiricism*. Recall Julius von Kirchmann's critique of legal scholarship:[68] this famous complaint about the worthlessness of jurisprudence as a science was essentially gauged against the methodological standards of the contemporary natural sciences.[69] Following Kirchmann's lead, late nineteenth-century legal scholarship attempted to bridge the epistemological divide between the natural sciences and the humanities in such a way that legal science would find itself, so to speak, on the modern, natural-scientific side of the divide. Being on the 'right' side of this debate meant framing legal science in terms of an empirical social science on par with contemporary exact methodology. Which methodology this specifically entails, however, has shifted several times since the end of the nineteenth century. Modelled on subsequent paradigms of sociology and psychology, one initial attempt was Rudolf von Jhering's 'jurisprudence of purpose'.[70] More recently, economics has superseded sociology as the guiding discipline in the social sciences, so that the emergence of law and economics as a new scientistic paradigm (with a temporal lag) was a foreseeable development in legal scholarship. From the standpoint of the history of sciences, if law and economics did not already exist, one would literally need to invent it in view of the ascent of economics to the leading epistemic paradigm of contemporary social sciences. One may even argue that the more mathematical and empirical the economic paradigm becomes, the more mathematical and empirical law and economics also need to become—a development that we already see, especially in American legal scholarship.[71] Yet, as the history of empirical methods in legal scholarship has shown, the promised exactitude is

[67] Carl Schmitt, *Politische Theologie* (11th edn, Duncker & Humblot 2021) 43; cf Auer, 'Politische Theologie als Rechtswissenschaftstheorie' (n 4) 134.

[68] See at n 6.

[69] Kirchmann compares jurisprudence to, for example, botany, zoology, physiology, psychology, mathematics and astrophysics; see Kirchmann, *Die Werthlosigkeit der Jurisprudenz als Wissenschaft* (n 6) 6ff.

[70] See at nn 28–30.

[71] See William M Landes and Richard A Posner, 'The Influence of Economics on Law: A Quantitative Study' (1993) 36 J Law & Economics 385–424.

in the end unobtainable. Legal scholarship evades empirical modelling whenever its own normative logic is at stake. The scientistic paradigm thus predictably proves to be a self-referential hall of mirrors of empiricist artifacts that move at an invariable equidistance to the intrinsic rationality of law. Taken as an absolute, this just means that the scientistic path, just like the idealist path, cannot conclusively solve the question of legal epistemology either.

The third *analytical* research paradigm we encountered as continually re-emerging can, in some ways, be seen as a reaction to the failures of the two paths just mentioned, but it also has a strong intrinsic connection to the structure of the modern legal system. If we leave aside its partially contradictory individual styles, the epistemic core of analytical legal thought lies in bracketing the contingency of the social, empirical, as well as normative surroundings of the legal system by focusing on its internal logic, normativity, or doctrinal structure. Positivist theories of law that have in regular cycles called for the 'purification' of legal science by eliminating idealistic and realistic premises belong to this path. Both Kelsen's 'Pure Theory of Law' and H.L.A. Hart's legal positivism are prime examples.[72] Another key example of an analytical 'high theory' of the law is Niklas Luhmann's concept of modern law as an autopoietic system.[73] Modern law understood in this sense presupposes a typical institutional backdrop, including a tiered structure of the legal order, a distinction between primary and secondary rules, as well as the adjudicability and alterability of legal acts in legal procedures. All of these features have been present since the early nineteenth century and constitute the background against which all discussions of methodology in private law take place. It is thus not surprising that doctrinal methods, including canons of interpretation, have played a major role in all paradigms of private law scholarship encountered since the nineteenth century. Although legal sources have changed over time, the avowed goal of doctrinal methodology has essentially stayed the same. Its focus continues to be on the most authentic application of the contemporary canon of authoritative legal sources possible. Yet the analytical paradigm, too, ultimately ends in a self-referential dead end when it loses touch with the empirical and normative reality underlying the law. This has been the source of numerous critiques of legal formalism and conceptual jurisprudence since the nineteenth century.[74]

[72] The classic texts are Hans Kelsen, *Reine Rechtslehre* (2nd edn, Franz Deuticke 1960) and HLA Hart, *The Concept of Law* (3rd edn, OUP 2012).

[73] Niklas Luhmann, *Das Recht der Gesellschaft* (8th edn, Suhrkamp 2020); cf Gunther Teubner, *Recht als autopoietisches System* (Suhrkamp 1989).

[74] See, paradigmatically, Kantorowicz, *Der Kampf um die Rechtswissenschaft* (n 33).

How does one, then, arrive at a productive methodology of private law? The solution involves striking the right balance between different epistemic pathways—a process that depends on the specific problem at hand. It should be clear that there is no universal principle of selection or combination of pathways that is equally productive for all times and all research questions. Private law research might focus on the rational reconstruction of legal doctrine, the observable social impact of private law institutions in society, or the fundamental values underlying private law. The choice between these objects of interest, which usually also entails respective epistemological choices, is obviously not neutral. There is also no guarantee that the combination of different epistemic pathways will always succeed at avoiding genuine antinomies of thought that limit their convergent use. The goal of this chapter, however, has been much more modest. I tried to show that however the balance between different epistemologies of private law is struck, it always bears the unmistakable features of the dominant scientific paradigm of its time, including the older layers that still define its *nomos*. In other words, the pre-modern metaphysical concept of law is still, albeit mostly unconsciously, present in modern private law scholarship, as is the dominant paradigm of the empirical sciences, while the positivist and analytical turns of the nineteenth and twentieth centuries appeared as a constant reaction to the post-metaphysical epistemic unsettledness of modernity. Whichever of the three epistemologies is the most fruitful or should prevail normatively is not a question to be discussed here. Indeed, this chapter suggests the opposite: there is no such thing as one single methodology of private law. If there is one lesson to be gleaned from the genealogy of private law epistemologies, it is this: the methodology of private law never failed because of conceptual contradictions or epistemological eclecticism. It failed whenever it was unable to account for the entirety of the normative, empirical, and analytical *nomos* of the private law of its time.

2

Exploring the Paradigms of Private Law

*Johanna Croon-Gestefeld**

I. Speaking of Method

The legal scholar Ernst Rabel is said to have commented on the topic of legal methodology: 'Every good jurist has a method; he just doesn't talk about it.'[1] The statement is referred to as an attestation of the viewpoint that legal scholarship can generate meaningful insights without an explicit discussion about the underlying methods. It draws its allure from the fact that Rabel was not just any jurist doubting the merits of methodological debates; he was one of the most influential scholars of private international law at the beginning of the twentieth century and contributed substantially to devising the functional method of comparative law.[2]

The quote is faintly reminiscent of artists refusing to comment on their works as they are supposed to speak for themselves. From a scientific point of view, however, it seems startling that a scientist has little interest in disclosing his methods. In the natural sciences, the common standard is to clearly describe the approach taken in an experiment. The main motive for this explicitness is that experiments ought to be reproducible to test the validity of their results. Another reason lies in other scientists' capacity to use the applied method to influence their work and thereby further the knowledge in a field. Within legal scholarship, few examples of experiments can be found,[3] and reproducibility is seldom a matter of concern. Yet, testing claims, assessing whether an argument is persuasive, and drawing inspiration from other people's publications is

* I would like to thank Ruben Dillmann and the participants of the workshop 'Methodology in Private Law Theory' for their helpful comments on the chapter.

[1] Reported by Wolfgang Fikentscher, *Methoden des Rechts in der vergleichenden Darstellung* (vol 1, Mohr Siebeck 1975) 10; mentioned by Holger Fleischer, 'Comparative Approaches to the Use of Legislative History in Statutory Interpretation' (2012) 60 Am J Comp L 401; Jan Smits, 'What is Legal Doctrine? On the Aims and Methods of Legal-Dogmatic Research' (2015) *M*-EPLI Working Paper 2015/06, 13 <https://papers.ssrn.com/sol3/papers.cfm?abstract_id=2644088> accessed 16 January 2023.

[2] Ernst Rabel, *Conflict of Laws: A Comparative Study* (2nd edn, UofM 1964).

[3] Though there are examples, such as in the field of criminology, see Dorothee Peters, *Richter im Dienst der Macht. Zur gesellschaftlichen Verteilung der Kriminalität* (Ferdinand Enke-Verlag 1973).

Johanna Croon-Gestefeld, *Exploring the Paradigms of Private Law* In: *Methodology in Private Law Theory.*
Edited by: Thilo Kuntz and Paul B. Miller, Oxford University Press. © Johanna Croon-Gestefeld 2024.
DOI: 10.1093/oso/9780198885306.003.0002

equally important for the jurists' work. Consequently, there are good reasons for lifting those parts of legal methodology that are not discussed out of the unarticulated.

In the conviction that methodology merits discussion, the contribution sketches an approach I will refer to as 'exploring legal paradigms'. The approach examines legal reasoning by focusing its attention not on the explicitly given arguments as in doctrinal analysis, but rather on the paradigms underlying legal argumentation. As will be explained in greater detail in Section IV.1., the term paradigm stands here for methods, techniques, principles, commonly shared attitudes, basic beliefs, and value judgments within an academic community. In order to situate the approach in the broader discussion on legal methodology, the contribution first sets out to explain its understanding of legal methodology (Section II). It continues with the current state of legal methods within German private law scholarship (Section III). This lays the groundwork for the presentation of the methodological approach that explores legal paradigms within German private law (Section IV).

II. Methodology—the Way to Go

The term 'legal methodology' has already come up at the beginning of the introduction. What has been missing so far is a more detailed description. The etymological origins of the word methodology offer substantial insights into what the notion is meant to convey. The Greek term 'meta-hodos' translates into 'following the road'[4] and the suffix '-ology' denotes that a discipline is being described. In conjunction, the word stands for the study of the approaches employed to generate insights and increase knowledge. Furthermore, the methodology can be referred to as 'legal' when it concerns the study of approaches within the realm of law.

At this point, the first terminological imprecisions regarding the object of the study appear: Is legal methodology only concerned with academic approaches to law, or does it also comprise the study of approaches that deal with the practical application of the law? At least as far as the German legal community is concerned, there are works that point towards a narrow, exclusively academic understanding of legal methodology centring on the practices of

[4] Rob van Gestel/Hans-Wolfgang Micklitz/Miguel Poiares Maduro, 'Methodology in the New Legal World' (2012) EUI Working Paper 2012/13, 1 <https://cadmus.eui.eu/handle/1814/22016> accessed 23 January 2023.

legal research[5] as well as contributions that encompass approaches to judicial decision-making in their study.[6] Yet, no increased need is felt to resolve the issue. Given the prevalence of doctrinal approaches in legal academia[7] and the strong interdependency between the faculties of law and legal practitioners in Germany, it seems superfluous to strictly draw the line between the different understandings of legal methodology. Offering arguments for why legal methodology should be engaged seems more relevant. From an academic's perspective, intrinsic and extrinsic motivations speak in favour of an analysis. Starting with the intrinsic side, if one is interested in furthering insights, it is beneficial—to say the least—to contemplate how to reach this goal. The work others have done before can be relied on in this exercise. Moreover, it is an act of self-reflection that can help a person to better understand her own modes of apprehension and analysis.

As far as the extrinsic side is concerned, additional reasons explain why the debate on legal methodology is long-standing, ongoing, and with no end in sight.[8] Owing to the research performed in the different disciplines, the amount of knowledge is constantly growing. As described with the applicable phrase of 'standing on the shoulders of giants', our present-day research sets out from a different starting point than that of our predecessors; we can build upon their work. Just as our knowledge of specific legal outcomes or appraisals of the law evolves over time, previously unknown tools or methods may offer new ways of analysis. Case in point, the idea of using computer programs to look for structural patterns in legal texts was floating around in the empirical study of law in the 1970s.[9] Fifty years later and with much more efficient computers available, the suggestion of that time has been developed into large scale research projects.[10] Given that researchers of today start at a higher level of methodological knowledge than the researchers that came before them, the

[5] Rolf Stürner, 'Die Zivilrechtswissenschaft und ihre Methodik – zu rechtsanwendungsbezogen und zu wenig grundlagenorientiert?' (2014) 214 AcP 8; Gerhard Wagner/Reinhard Zimmermann, 'Vorwort: Methoden des Privatrechts' (2014) 214 AcP 1, 2; Reinhard Zimmermann, 'Juristische Methodenlehre in Deutschland' (2019) 83 RabelsZ 242.

[6] Franz Bydlinski, *Juristische Methodenlehre und Rechtsbegriff* (2nd edn, Springer 2011); Thomas Möllers, *Juristische Methodenlehre* (4th edn, CH Beck 2021); Franz Reimer, *Juristische Methodenlehre* (2nd edn, Nomos 2020); Karl Riesenhuber (ed), *Europäische Methodenlehre* (4th edn, De Gruyter 2021).

[7] See Matthias Jestaedt, 'Wissenschaft im Recht' (2014) JZ 1; Zimmermann (n 5) 250.

[8] For historical depictions, see Hans-Peter Haferkamp, 'Zur Methodengeschichte unter dem BGB in fünf Systemen' (2014) 214 AcP 60; Jan Schröder, *Recht als Wissenschaft* (3rd edn, CH Beck 2021).

[9] eg Jürgen Rödig, 'Axiomatisierbarkeit juristischer Systeme' (1972) 1 Datenverarbeitung im Recht 170; Wilhelm Steinmüller, 'Gegenstand, Grundbegriffe und Systematik der Rechtsinformatik' (1972) 1 Datenverarbeitung im Recht 113.

[10] See eg Corinna Coupette, *Juristische Netzwerkforschung* (Mohr Siebeck 2019); Friedemann Vogel, Hanjo Hamann and Isabelle Gauer, 'Computer-Assisted Legal Linguistics: Corpus Analysis as a New Tool for Legal Studies' (2018) 43 Law & Social Inquiry 1340.

increased knowledge should prompt researchers to reconsider what methods are best suited to approach their research questions.

Another reason for renewed reflections on methodology are changes in the environment. When the circumstances of jurisprudence alter, these changes must be considered at the methodological level. The method must suit the research object in order to produce meaningful insights. For instance, the fact that potent, globally active private players can create their own legal rules and thereby create transnational law poses a challenge to predominant approaches to the law. This is due to the fact that established approaches, with the doctrinal approach leading the way, are primarily concerned with systematizing positive law[11] and thus mainly deal with state-made law. However, transnational law can stem from sources other than statutes or judicial decisions emanating from the state.[12] Consequently, approaches commonly used to analyse state-made law can only explain the workings of transnational law up to a certain point. Alternative approaches, such as institutional theory or systems theory, offer promising methods to make sense of this area of law.[13]

III. Fancy Theory or Method Syncretism?

Once the conviction has come about that legal methodology matters, the subsequent question results: What methods are actually employed in the analysis of law? In my response, I will limit myself to sketching a map of the methodological approaches of the academia of German private law. In doing so, I would like to point out that the perspective of the internal observer[14] is the only perspective from which I can set out to sketch the map. Accordingly, there is the risk of misperceptions that are owed to such a subjective reading. Where I see

[11] On the nature of doctrinal analysis, see Christian Bumke, *Rechtsdogmatik* (Mohr Siebeck 2017) 1; Winfried Hassemer, 'Dogmatik zwischen Wissenschaft und richterlicher Pragmatik: Einführende Bemerkungen' in G Kirchhof, S Magen, and K Schneider (eds), *Was weiß Dogmatik?* (Mohr Siebeck 2012) 3, 7, 8, 14; Nils Jansen, 'Theoriebildung in der europäischen Privatrechtsdogmatik' in R Alexy (ed), *Juristische Grundlagenforschung* (Franz Steiner Verlag 2005) 29 (32); Jan Smits, 'What is Legal Doctrine? On the Aims and Methods of Legal-Dogmatic Research' (2015) M-EPLI Working Paper 2015/06, 5 <https://papers.ssrn.com/sol3/papers.cfm?abstract_id=2644088> accessed 13 January 2023.

[12] Philip C Jessup, *Transnational Law* (YUP 1956) 2–3; see also Gralf-Peter Calliess and Peer Zumbansen, *Rough Consensus and Running Code* (Hart 2010) 11–12; Peer Zumbansen, 'Introduction, Transnational Law, with and beyond Jessup' in P Zumbansen (ed), *The Many Lives of Transnational Law. Critical Engagements with Jessup's Bold Proposal* (CUP 2020) 1, 18–22.

[13] Hans-Wolfgang Micklitz, 'Guest Editorial on the Politics of Legal Methodology' (2014) 21 MJ 589, 594; Jan Smits, 'European Legal Education or: How to Prepare Students for Global Citizenship' (2011) 45 The Law Teacher 163, 166, 175–176.

[14] cf Bumke (n 11) 8; Johanna Croon-Gestefeld, *Gemeininteressen im Privatrecht* (Mohr Siebeck 2022) 23.

a mountain, there may just be a hill; where I detect a small stream, there may flow a river. The only way to cope with this risk is to clearly articulate the subjectivity in the approach and scrutinize the findings.

On the map depicting German private law academia, the doctrinal method, with its emphasis on systematizing the law, takes up the largest space.[15] In fact, the doctrinal method is so ingrained in the study of German law that it sometimes comes as a surprise to law students when they are exposed to different ways of thinking about the law in classes on legal theory. A variety of reasons explain the pre-eminence of the doctrinal method. German legal scholarship can look back to a long history of making law understandable through rigorous ordering and systemization. The origins of the approach date back to a time when the nationwide codification of private law had not yet materialized.[16] Furthermore, the doctrinal method offers a way of reasoning about the law that is firmly rooted in the law, allowing for an examination from an internal perspective and enabling its applicants to gain insights into the law by means of interpretation. Different from other approaches to legal analysis, doctrinal work can produce meaningful insights into the law without reliance on the methods of other disciplines. In addition, doctrinal legal research has strong connections to legal practice since the same argumentative style is employed.[17] On account of this similarity, legal practice can readily make use of insights gained through doctrinal research and apply these when deciding individual cases.

On the map of German private law academia, areas of philosophical, theoretical, sociological, economic, historical, comparative, and historical-comparative approaches can be found next to the wide territory of doctrinal analysis. However, these areas take up significantly less room than the doctrinal works. Scholars working with these approaches analyse the law from a greater observatory distance than those using the doctrinal method alone. As far as non-doctrinal legal research is concerned, it can be subdivided into two types of works: One strand of work focuses exclusively on a theoretical, sociological,

[15] See n 7.

[16] Hans-Peter Haferkamp, *Georg Friedrich Puchta und die „Begriffsjurisprudenz"* (Vittorio Klostermann 2004) 221–47, 274; Joachim Rückert, 'Savignys Dogmatik im „System"' in A Heldrich and others (eds), *Festschrift für Claus-Wilhelm Canaris zum 70. Geburtstag* (CH Beck 2007) vol 2, 1263, 1282; Schröder (n 8) vol 1, 251–52.

[17] See Croon-Gestefeld (n 14) 99, 117–18; Thomas Gutmann, 'Intra- und Interdisziplinarität: Chance oder Störfaktor?' in E Hilgendorf and H Schulze-Fielitz (eds), *Selbstreflektion der Rechtswissensschaft* (2nd edn, Mohr Siebeck 2021) 93, 97; Matthias Jestaedt, 'Vom Beruf der Rechtswissenschaft – zwischen Rechtspraxis und Rechtstheorie' in H Dreier (ed), *Rechtswissenschaft als Beruf* (Mohr Siebeck 2018) 227, 241. Albeit they have a common engagement with doctrinal analysis, the access of legal academia and legal practice to doctrinal texts differs. Whereas academics are more concerned with developing and upgrading systematic accounts of the law, legal practitioners resort to doctrinal texts to understand the law and offer better advice to their clients.

etc. investigation of the law. The unfolding discussions take place in communities that are much smaller in size than that of doctrinal analysis. As a result, terminology and conceptualizations prevalent in those smaller communities can be highly specialized, making it difficult for outsiders to comprehend the analysis. Analyses that employ systems theory to explain the workings of the law are a case in point. Texts that reason from concepts such as *autopoiesis* or *re-entry* often come with great explanatory potential.[18] Yet, they are less often cited than could be expected because doctrinal analysis has difficulty in drawing on them. Another type of work complements doctrinal analysis with other approaches.[19] Such a combination is chosen when authors consider that their research would benefit from a diversity of perspectives. The blending of methods can be observed most notably in monographs, as their format offers room for the extensive examination of a topic. These works frequently dedicate chapters to an analysis of the historical and philosophical origins of the provision or legal institution examined, as well as its economic effects. Moreover, authors of comprehensive studies often enrich their analyses with comparative side glances, explaining how the legal topic under investigation is handled in other jurisdictions. Even though a combination of approaches is not uncommon, the quality achieved varies. Particularly insightful are works that connect the results obtained through different methodological approaches. By contrast, works that fail to integrate the insights gained by approaches more external to the law in their doctrinal analyses are less compelling and also less perceptive from a methodological point of view.[20]

Combining different approaches in the analysis of law is not unique to German private law academia. With regard to legal scholarship in the United States, Duncan Kennedy described his mixing and matching of different approaches without reservations as 'fancy theory'.[21] His description applies to approaches towards German private law that aim to integrate different research methods. The openness of fancy theory towards different approaches makes it attractive for authors no matter where they have received their education. They experience more freedom in approaching legal questions than they would if they had to strictly follow one method; the approach leaves ample room for

[18] On these concepts, see Niklas Luhmann, *Soziale Systeme* (Suhrkamp 1987) 60–61; ibid, *Das Recht der Gesellschaft* (Suhrkamp 1995) 30, 45; Gunther Teubner, *Recht als autopoietisches System* (Suhrkamp 1989).

[19] Zimmermann (n 5) 12; for a similar assessment of the methodology in German legal theory, see Marietta Auer, *Zum Erkenntnisziel der Rechtstheorie* (Nomos 2018) 33–35.

[20] A positive example of an analysis offering insights by the means of different methodological approaches is Alexander Hellgardt, *Regulierung und Privatrecht* (Mohr Siebeck 2016).

[21] Duncan Kennedy, *Sexy Dressing etc. Essays on the Power and Politics of Cultural Identity* (HUP 1993) XI.

creativity. Moreover, fancy theory is appealing due to its interdisciplinary nature and its ability to help 'break the culture of insularity'[22] that is often attributed to the doctrinal study of law.[23]

Nevertheless, there is also a more sceptical reading of fancy theory as a means of expanding the understanding of the law. A first question that may arise is to what extent research can be considered truly interdisciplinary if it is inherently content to borrow methods and insights from other disciplines[24] and does not demand a more long-standing, thorough exchange of ideas with the neighbouring sciences.[25] Fancy theorists may, however, object to this critique by stating that the label of interdisciplinarity has been assigned to them by others and that it is not their intent to present the theory as more elaborate than it is.

A second critique takes issue with the fact that the theory is less concerned with methodological rigour. 'Method syncretism'[26] may be contended to be at play. The mixing and matching of different methods to investigate the law is said not to advance the knowledge of the law but to obscure the foundations and workings of the law instead. The critique of method syncretism is far from being new. Among others, Hans Kelsen already considered legal academia to engage in method syncretism at the beginning of the twentieth century.[27] He argued with respect to contract theories of the state that scholars engaged in an improper mixing of normative and objective considerations.[28] The critique of method syncretism asks for nothing less than a clear division between strictly scientific endeavours in the exploration of the law and academic contributions that contain elements of valuation. But fancy theory need not be at odds with demands for such a demarcation: Nothing about fancy theory prohibits its applicants from combining different objective research methods to investigate

[22] Matyas Bodig, 'Legal Doctrinal Scholarship and Interdisciplinary Engagement' (2015) ELR 43, 45.

[23] For a critique of this aspect, see German Science and Humanities Council, *Perspektiven der Rechtswissenschaft in Deutschland* (Drs. 2558–12, 2012) 35–36 <https://www.wissenschaftsrat.de/download/archiv/2558-12.html> accessed 16 January 2023.

[24] For this self-depiction, see Kennedy (n 21) XI; ibid, *A Critique of Adjudication {Fin de Siècle}* (HUP 1997) 15–16.

[25] For this understanding of interdisciplinarity see Ino Augsberg, 'Multi-, inter-, transdisziplinär? Zum Erfordernis binnenjuristischer Metaregeln für den Umgang mit extrajuridischem Wissen im Verwaltungsrecht' in I Augsberg (ed), *Extrajuridisches Wissen im Verwaltungsrecht. Analysen und Perspektiven* (Mohr Siebeck 2013) 3, 16; Heinz Heckhausen, '»Interdisziplinäre Forschung« zwischen Intra-, Multi- und Chimären-Disziplinarität' in J Kocka (ed), *Interdisziplinarität* (Suhrkamp 1987) 129, 132; Anne Röthel, 'Interdisziplinarität in der Rechtswissenschaft: Besichtigung eines Ideals' in K Vieweg (ed), *Festgabe für Institut und Technik* (Carl Heymanns 2017) 213, 217–18.

[26] In lieu of many, Alexander Stark, *Interdisziplinarität der Rechtsdogmatik* (Mohr Siebeck 2020) 323–24.

[27] Hans Kelsen, *Über die Grenzen zwischen juristischer und soziologischer Methode* (Mohr 1911) 16–18.

[28] ibid.

the law. Moreover, if authors employing fancy theory make normative claims, they can (and should) highlight them as such.

Further insights into legal methodology can be gained through comparison of the map of German private law academia with its counterpart in the United States. It appears that the pendulum has swung towards emphasizing the benefit of doctrinal studies in the United States. The New Private Law movement[29] is a testament to this development. By contrast, German private law academia seems concerned with reconciling different methods of exploring the law at this time. This is part of the bigger enterprise of self-reflection inside German legal academia.[30] Although it remains to be seen how the debate will develop in the future, two results can already be observed. First, 'methodological honesty'[31] has gained momentum, with researchers being open to making their methods known and putting them up for debate. Second, the trend towards more intensive reflection on research methods has led to changes in the education of up-and-coming researchers. Whereas seminars on methodology and legal writing used to be a rarity at German law faculties, most universities now offer some form of methodological education for doctoral researchers. Graduate schools have sprung up to support young scholars in thinking about their research questions and the approaches that might help to answer them.

Overall, the methods employed in German private law academia can be summarized as follows: Doctrinal research is the dominant method for analysing the law, while there is an openness towards enriching doctrinal analysis with insights gained from perspectives more external to the law.

IV. Paradigms at the Centre of Attention

The greater openness towards methodological diversity has resulted in a greater willingness on the part of researchers to make methodological choices explicit. This is accompanied by an increased recognition of the fact that

[29] Andrew S Gold, 'Internal and External Perspectives: On the New Private Law Methodology' in AS Gold and others (eds), *The Oxford Handbook of the New Private Law* (OUP 2020); Paul B Miller, 'The New Formalism in Private Law' (2021) 66 Am J Jurisprud 175.

[30] On this self-reflection, see Horst Dreier (ed), *Rechtswissenschaft als Beruf* (Mohr Siebeck 2018); Thomas Duve and Stefan Ruppert (eds), *Rechtswissenschaft in der Berliner Republik* (Suhrkamp 2018); Christoph Engel und Wolfgang Schön (eds), *Das Proprium der Rechtswissenschaft* (Mohr Siebeck 2007); Eric Hilgendorf and Helmuth Schulze-Fielitz (eds), *Selbstreflexion der Rechtswissenschaft* (2nd edn, Mohr Siebeck 2021); Matthias Jestaedt and Oliver Lepsius (eds), *Rechtswissenschaftstheorie* (Mohr Siebeck 2008).

[31] Augsberg (n 25) 16; Andreas Voßkuhle in W Hoffmann-Riem, E Schmidt-Assmann, and A Voßkuhle (eds), *Grundlagen des Verwaltungsrechts* (2nd edn, CH Beck 2012) vol 1, § 1 para 39.

hidden assumptions about the law, as well as about proper legal scholarship, shape legal research. From acknowledging that subversive influences impact research, it is a small step towards using this insight for further analysis. Making these assumptions explicit and tracing their influences is in itself an approach for conceptualizing the law. For the purposes of this chapter, the approach shall be referred to as exploring legal paradigms.

First, an explanation is offered of what is meant by the notion of paradigms (section 1). As a second step, the foundations of the approach of exploring legal paradigms are elucidated (section 2), and its intellectual influences are disclosed (section 3). The examination continues by highlighting the potential of the approach (section 4) while also exposing the risks associated with it (section 5). Last, the approach is put into practice (section 6). The current debate in German private law academia on the conditions under which parents can consent to posting pictures of their children on social media is conceptualized by means of the approach.

1. The Many Forms of Paradigms

An approach described as exploring legal paradigms warrants some introductory remarks. Most notably, the term 'paradigm' merits explication, as it can take on different meanings, has undergone great changes over time and 'can be too nearly all things to all people'.[32] Just like methodology, the term paradigm can be traced back to its Greek roots. In Ancient Greek, 'parádeigma' stands for a model,[33] a clear example of something. The concept began to regain wider attention when Ludwig Wittgenstein characterized paradigms in his philosophical deliberations. According to Wittgenstein, paradigms have three different traits. First and in line with the Ancient Greek origins, a paradigm is 'something with which comparison is made'.[34] In other words, paradigms are 'means of representation'.[35] Second, participants in a language game must agree on paradigms to be able to 'come to any understanding'.[36] Without such shared agreement, speakers talk past each other. Third, since paradigms

[32] Thomas Kuhn, 'Second Thoughts on Paradigms' in T Kuhn (ed), *The Essential Tension. Selected Studies in Scientific Tradition and Change* (CUP 1977), 293.

[33] Entry for Παράδειγμα, Henry George Liddell and Robert Scott (eds), *A Greek-English Lexicon*, <https://www.perseus.tufts.edu/hopper/text?doc=Perseus%3Atext%3A1999.04.0057%3Aentry%3Dpara%2Fdeigma> accessed 10 January 2023.

[34] Ludwig Wittgenstein, *Philosophical Investigations* (Gertrude Anscombe tr, 3rd edn, Basil Blackwell 1967, reprint 1986) I-50.

[35] ibid.

[36] ibid I-242.

are designated means of representation, they are '*antecedent* to the correctness or incorrectness of a statement'[37] made with reference to such representation.[38] Thus, Wittgenstein argued that a paradigm cannot be appraised as true or false, right or wrong, by looking at particular cases that refer to a paradigmatic means of representation.[39]

The conception of a paradigm also prominently features in the work of Thomas Kuhn on scientific theory.[40] Kuhn is most known for his claim that the evolution of science is not to be understood as a linear, continuous progress. He argued instead that paradigm shifts at times force scientists to depart from long-held and commonly shared views and methods. These shifts are said to be necessary when new scientific knowledge cannot otherwise be incorporated into the existing body of knowledge.[41] Given the importance of the paradigm shift for his analysis of scientific revolutions, it is puzzling that Kuhn has not provided one fixed explanation of what he considered a paradigm. In fact, Margaret Masterman has counted twenty-one different senses in which Kuhn used the term paradigm in his work.[42] According to a noted version of the descriptions, a paradigm is a scientific 'achievement ... sufficiently unprecedented to attract an enduring group of adherents away from competing modes of scientific activity'.[43] Furthermore, a paradigm must be 'sufficiently open-ended to leave all sorts of problems for the redefined group of practitioners to resolve'.[44] Contrasting Wittgenstein's characterization of a paradigm with this description, differences between the two can easily be spotted. Kuhn has dropped the depiction of a paradigm as a means of representation on the one hand and moved the notion of paradigms exclusively to the sphere of science on the other hand. His portrayal centres on the idea of shared research premises, scientific methods or basic principles widely accepted within a scientific community.

Although both Wittgenstein and Kuhn have formulated what they mean by a paradigm, the concept has obtained a meaning beyond the authors'

[37] Ludwig Wittgenstein, *Remarks on the Foundations of Mathematics* (Gertrude Anscombe tr, MIT Press 1967, emphasis in the original) I-155.
[38] This depiction has been adopted from C Grant Luckhardt, 'Beyond Knowledge: Paradigms in Wittgenstein's Later Philosophy' (1978) 39 PPR 240, 244.
[39] See ibid 244–45.
[40] Thomas Kuhn, *The Structure of Scientific Revolutions* (3rd edn, UCP 1996).
[41] ibid 10–22.
[42] Margaret Masterman, 'The Nature of a Paradigm' in I Lakatos and A Musgrave (eds), *Criticism and the Growth of Knowledge* (CUP 1970) 59, 61–65; further elaborating on Kuhn's vague usage of the term, Daniel Goldman Cedarbaum, 'Paradigms' (1983) Studies in History and Philosophy of Science 173, 174.
[43] Kuhn, *Scientific Revolutions* (n 40) 10.
[44] ibid.

characterizations in everyday parlance. Nowadays, paradigms are considered to encompass not only methods, techniques, or scientific principles within an academic community but also commonly shared attitudes, basic beliefs, and value judgments. As a result, the term 'paradigm' has even less conceptual clarity. On a positive note, 'paradigm' now gives expression to the fact that scientific and academic progress is not solely due to the continuous acquisition of hard, objective truths but also owed to valuations and conventions that operate within a community and cannot be explained through a true/false or right/wrong dichotomy. Within the field of legal theory, Rudolf Wiethölter took up the conception of paradigm in its encompassing sense and stated: 'The consciousness, the orientation behavior and the methodological instruments characterize a scientific field of work. For a number of years, a word has made a career in this context: *paradigm*.'[45] When I use the term in this chapter, I refer to this latter conception.

2. Looking at Paradigms

Now that it has been clarified what paradigm means for this analysis, the approach of exploring legal paradigms can be explained in detail. As its name implies, the approach is concerned with looking at the paradigms encountered in legal communities. Even though my remarks almost exclusively relate to legal academia, it is possible to apply the approach to analysing the paradigms in communities of legal practice as well. With respect to legal research, the approach of looking at paradigms seeks to closely examine the methods and foundations of jurisprudence as well as the beliefs and valuations of the law commonly held in legal academia.

The description already indicates that the approach has connections to established practices. Just like other endeavours in legal theory, it shows an interest in the methods of legal scholarship. In this respect, it gives expression to the greater objective of explicating legal methodology. Moreover, it shares its emphasis on the fundamental principles and structures of the law with doctrinal analysis and other theoretically oriented approaches to law. Yet, in contrast to related approaches, the approach of exploring legal paradigms focuses

[45] Rudolf Wiethölter, 'Begriffs- oder Interessenjurisprudenz – falsche Fronten im IPR und Wirtschaftsverfassungsrecht' in Alexander Lüderitz and Jochen Schröder (eds), *Festschrift für Gerhard Kegel* (Alfred Metzner 1977) 213, 219. Habermas uses the term in an even broader sense. For him, paradigm stands for an 'implicit image' (Jürgen Habermas, 'Paradigms of Law' in M Rosenfeld and A Arato (eds), *Habermas on Law and Democracy* (UCP 1998) 13).

on the fundamental principles and structures *as perceived* in legal scholarship. For instance, the interplay of national private law and EU private law would not be the direct object of analysis in the approach, as the analytical focus would lie on the scholarly perception of the interplay.

In view of the clarification, the question may occur: Do these deviances from existing approaches justify the appraisal of the approach as discriminable? After all, nearly all statements issued in legal academia engage in the assessment of other people's positions on the discussed topic. In my opinion, one element makes the approach distinct: The emphasis on the appraisal of commonly shared beliefs and valuations is unique to it. Specifically, looking at the perceptions covertly shaping the legal discourse sets the approach of exploring legal paradigms apart from adjoining approaches.

In order to explain this facet of the approach in more detail, it makes sense to take a close look at what happens when a contribution to a legal discourse is made. Generally, an argument is put forward, and a discourse with other speakers ensues. In this discourse, participants try to convince the others that their legal assessments are to be preferred over alternatives.[46] The argument may support the claim that certain behaviour is legal or illegal; it may substantiate that a particular measure is proportionate or disproportionate; if it is an argument phrased in the terminology of an economic analysis of law, it might support or dismiss the assertion that legal regulation is efficient. In all these instances, speakers primarily articulate arguments for the purpose of convincing others of the soundness of their reasoning. Yet, giving reasons and defending one's viewpoint are not the only functions of argumentation in legal discourse. Articulating an argument positions the statement as well as the person who issues it within the discourse.[47]

Legal arguments can, therefore, be analysed in different ways: The substance of the argument can be examined at face value, or the subtext of the argument can be looked at, and its underlying assumptions explored. The approach of exploring legal paradigms is particularly involved with the latter aspects of legal reasoning. It seeks to investigate the unarticulated elements of the argument, as well as the position of the argument in the legal discourse. Therefore, the approach has content- and discourse-oriented elements. As far as the former is concerned, the questions may arise: Which assumptions about the law underlie the argument? Does the argument indicate if the speaker adheres

[46] Seminally Jürgen Habermas, *Faktizität und Geltung* (Suhrkamp 1994) 276 ff.

[47] Comp. Pierre Bourdieu, 'Zur Genese der Begriffe Habitus und Feld' in P Bourdieu (ed), *Der Tote packt den Lebenden* (Jürgen Bolder tr, VSA 1997, reprint 2011) 55, 57–60.

to a formalist or a functionalist conception of private law?[48] These questions would not be asked in a doctrinal analysis. Such analysis would examine the explicit content of the argument and seek to detect overarching patterns of substantial arguments. Exploring the underlying assumptions would be its subordinate concern. However, under the approach of exploring legal paradigms, the prioritization is reversed. The focus lies in the subtext, with the explicit text 'merely' as a point of reference for determining the subtext.

As far as the discourse-oriented side is concerned, the approach of exploring legal paradigms looks at the discursive mechanisms that are at play when a statement is issued. The speech act[49] becomes the centre of attention; its position in the legal discourse is investigated. The aim of the analysis is to deepen the understanding of the argument by examining its discursive context. In this exercise, these questions can be of relevance: Does the speaker mention keywords[50] to allude to discussions in neighbouring disciplines? Do the cited materials offer hints as to which thought collective[51] or academic school[52] the speaker feels connected to? And can conclusions be drawn from the presentation of the argument as to where the speaker positions the contribution in the legal discourse?

At first glance, it might seem as if the content- and discourse-oriented elements have little in common. Yet, the connections between the two components are strong. They share an interest in the less obvious, more subversive ways of legal reasoning. Besides, their common aim is to deepen our understanding of the law by looking underneath the surface of legal argumentation.

Someone bothered about the vagueness of the term paradigm might also ask a further question: Wouldn't *exploring schools of thought* instead of *exploring paradigms* more adequately describe the project? After all, the change in denomination would come with the benefit of not having to laboriously

[48] On the two-question theory, see Felipe Jiménez, 'Two Questions for Private Law Theory' (2021) Jurisprudence 1, 16–17; Miller (n 29); Ernest Weinrib, *The Idea of Private Law* (OUP 1995); ibid, 'Legal Formalism: On the Immanent Rationality of Law' (1988) 97 Yale LJ 949; Benjamin C Zipursky, 'Pragmatic Conceptualism' (2000) 6 Legal Theory 457, 463–74 (2000).

[49] On this concept, see John Austin, *How to Do Things with Words* (2nd edn, HUP 1975); Jaques Derrida, 'Die différance' in J Derrida (ed), *Randgänge der Philosophie* (Passagen 1972) 6; ibid, 'Signatur, Ereignis, Kontext' in J Derrida (ed), *Randgänge der Philosophie* (Passagen 1972) 124; John Searle, *Speech Acts* (CUP 1969); ibid, 'Reiterating the Differences. A Reply to Derrida' (1997) 1 Glyph 172.

[50] Susanne Baer, 'Schlüsselbegriffe, Typen und Leitbilder als Erkenntnismittel und ihr Verhältnis zur Rechtsdogmatik' in E Schmidt-Assmann and W Hoffmann-Riem (eds), *Methoden der Verwaltungsrechtswissenschaft* (Nomos 2004) 223, 225–28.

[51] Ludwik Fleck, *Entstehung und Entwicklung einer wissenschaftlichen Tatsache* (13th edn, Suhrkamp 2021) 53–70.

[52] See eg Helmuth Schulze-Fielitz, 'Leicht spekulative Notizen zur Reputationshierarchie in der deutschen Staatsrechtslehre' in H Schulze-Fielitz (ed), *Staatsrechtslehre als Mikrokosmos* (Mohr Siebeck 2013) 187, 193.

set out what is meant by a paradigm. However, there is one important argument speaking against the change in label: a small but critical nuance would get lost. According to Harold Koh, a school of thought 'comprises a group of likeminded individuals who share common opinion, outlook, philosophy, or membership in the same intellectual, artistic, social or cultural movement'.[53] The presented approach is not limited to researching the operations of schools of thought and the attribution of individuals to one school or another. It also examines the more subversive, less articulated forces that shape a discourse – a fact that is better captured via the reference to paradigms.

3. Intellectual Influences

As can be inferred from the description of the approach, exploring legal paradigms emphasizes the point that legal reasoning involves communication and understanding. Therefore, theories and movements concerned with the transmission and processing of information influence the approach. Its intellectual influences are hermeneutics, narrative jurisprudence, and discourse analysis.

To begin with, hermeneutics can be argued to be at the core of any approach trying to make sense of legal statements by means of interpretation. However, the influence of hermeneutics on the approach presented here goes beyond a mere reference to its interpretational character. Hermeneutics has produced profound insights into the understanding of texts. In 'Wahrheit und Methode',[54] Hans-Georg Gadamer explained why a person is never completely free in interpreting a text but is always bound by past experiences and previous schooling. According to Gadamer, an interpreter approaches a text with a conception in mind. The interpreting person's understanding of the text will rely upon her developed preconception of the text, even though the assessment of the text may adjust throughout the reading.[55] Josef Esser built on these insights and applied them to the legal sphere. He argued that pre-established expectations of how a given legal conflict can be solved predetermine the possible outcomes of interpretation.[56] In essence, both scholars pursued the objective

[53] Harold Hongju Koh, 'Is There a "New" New Haven School of International Law?' (2007) 32 Yale J Int'l L 559.

[54] Hans-Georg Gadamer, *Wahrheit und Methode* (1st edn, Mohr 1960).

[55] Hans-Georg Gadamer, 'Wahrheit und Methode' in H-G Gadamer, *Gesammelte Werke. Hermeneutik* (Mohr Siebeck 1999) vol 1, 271.

[56] Josef Esser, *Vorverständnis und Methodenwahl in der Rechtsfindung* (Athenäum 1970) 136. For an English translation consult <https://newprivatelawtheory.files.wordpress.com/2021/03/chapter-01-esser-p.-116-141.pdf> accessed 13 January 2023.

of presenting the idea that understanding depends on preunderstanding. They further shared the belief that said preunderstanding is not fixed but in flux, since the person is influenced by a constantly changing and evolving environment of understanding. In contrast to the hermeneutic studies of Gadamer and Esser, the approach of exploring legal paradigms does not focus on the perspective of the recipient of a text. Rather, it looks at that of the author to examine the communication process in the legal realm. This being said, the approach presented here borrows extensively from the insights produced by Gadamer and Esser because it is based on the idea that an author's preunderstandings and preconceptions heavily influence the creation of legal content.

The approach is furthermore loosely influenced by narrative jurisprudence. Relevant in this context is that engagement with narrative jurisprudence is less common in Germany[57] than in the United States.[58] There is no close interconnected movement of narrative jurisprudence in German legal academia. Instead, one can find individual works united by their shared attitude towards the law that acknowledges the existence of narratives in law and seeks to analyse their influence on the evolution of law. Studies of narratology explain that an important function of narratives is to make sense of the world.[59] Moreover, they further show that narratives are not confined to the realm of fiction but operate in the natural sciences and the humanities as well.[60] In Albrecht Koschorke's words:

> Narrative has refused to be locked up in the repository of beaux arts. The need to narratively model the world does not stop at the boundaries between different social systems. This affects all levels – from everyday narratives to scientific theories to master narratives in which a society as a whole recognizes

[57] Nonetheless, see Ino Augsberg, *Die Lesbarkeit des Rechts* (Velbrück 2020); Ruth Blufarb, *Geschichten im Recht. Übertragbarkeit von „Law as Narrative" auf die deutsche Rechtsordnung* (Nomos 2017); Christian Bumke, 'Rezeption und Rezeptionsabbrüche' in N Marsch, L Münkler, and T Wischmeyer (eds), *Apokryphe Schriften* (Mohr Siebeck 2018) 47, 55–56; Bertram Lomfeld, 'Narrative Jurisprudenz' (2019) JZ 369; Andreas von Arnauld, 'Was war, was ist – und was sein soll. Erzählen im juristischen Diskurs' in C Klein and M Martínez (eds), *Wirklichkeitserzählungen. Felder, Formen und Funktionen nicht-literarischen Erzählens* (Springer 2009) 14; Andreas von Arnauld (ed), *Völkerrechtsgeschichten. Historische Narrative und Konzepte im Wandel* (Duncker und Humblot 2017).

[58] For the US, see eg Peter Brooks and Paul Gerwitz (eds), *Law's Stories: Narrative and Rhetoric in the Law* (YUP 1996); Martha Nussbaum, *Poetic Justice: The Literary Imagination and Public Life* (Beacon Press 1995); Ian Ward, *Law and Literature: Possibilities and Perspectives* (CUP 1995); Richard Weisberg, *Poethics, and Other Strategies of Law and Literature* (Columbia UP 1992); Kenji Yoshino, 'The City and the Poet' (2005) 114 Yale LJ 1835.

[59] Albrecht Koschorke, *Wahrheit und Erfindung. Grundzüge einer Allgemeinen Erzähltheorie* (4th edn, S. Fischer 2017).

[60] Christian Klein and Matías Martínez (eds), *Wirklichkeitserzählungen. Felder, Formen und Funktionen nicht-literarischen Erzählens* (Springer 2009).

itself – and all forms ... Wherever matters of social relevance are negotiated, narratives are at play.[61]

Given that law has a system with substantial influence over the regulation of socially relevant topics, it comes as no surprise that legal narratives can be detected to be in operation. In conformity with Koschorke's observation, the sizes of legal narratives range from small to big. Two cases in point: The legal persona is an example of a small narrative. By denominating the association of people as persona, it is given a human-like constitution that can be of relevance when it comes to the attribution of fault or the appraisal of knowledge within the legal persona.[62] In addition, a more extensive (bigger) narrative is presented when the development of German private law from the end of the eighteenth century is depicted as the rise and fall of a liberal conception of private law.[63] As these cursory remarks reveal, narrative jurisprudence and the approach of exploring legal paradigms share the notion that legal texts are not just accessible to logically rigid study, but can also be read as works that have an element of storytelling to them. They both assume that legal texts work with linguistic imagery and allusions and, at times, are written in a style that excites certain emotions in the reader.[64] In this sense, they have the common goal of illustrating that texts are often accompanied by a meaningful subtext influencing its understanding.

Lastly, the approach of exploring legal paradigms can be described as a variant of discourse analysis, putting discourses that are held in private law at the centre of its examination and studying the discursive mechanisms at play.[65] The discourses under review can be limited in scope and, for example, only concern the requirements for the contraction of marriage or the conditions of product liability. However, the discourses can also be more wide-ranging and touch upon the foundations of private law, such as the freedom of contract or private autonomy. In order to investigate the operation of discursive mechanisms in legal discourse, the approach avails itself of methods and insights that were advanced

[61] Koschorke (n 59) 18–19, trans. by the author.

[62] See Jan-Erik Schirmer and Philipp Pauschinger, 'Im Griff der Metapher – eine (andere) Geschichte von juristischer Person und Dieselskandal' (2020) 220 AcP 211, 217–33.

[63] This powerful narrative has been put forward by Franz Wieacker, *Privatrechtsgeschichte der Neuzeit* (2nd edn, Vandenhoeck und Ruprecht 1967) 514–57; ibid, 'Das Sozialmodell der klassischen Privatrechtsgesetzbücher und die Entwicklung der modernen Gesellschaft' in Franz Wieacker, *Industriegesellschaft und Privatrechtsordnung* (Fischer-Athenäum 1952) 24; on this Marietta Auer, *Der privatrechtliche Diskurs der Moderne* (Mohr Siebeck 2014) 1; Croon-Gestefeld (n 14) 29.

[64] cf Weisberg (n 58) 10–11.

[65] Borrowing in particular from Foucault's mode of exploration in Michel Foucault, *Die Ordnung der Dinge* (26th edn, Suhrkamp 2020); ibid, *Archäologie des Wissens* (20th edn, Suhrkamp 2022); ibid, *Die Ordnung des Diskurses* (14th edn, Fischer 2017).

by linguists and post-structural theorists.[66] It aligns with the notion put forward in discourse analysis that the manner in which we talk about a topic influences our very perception of the topic. It further accepts the idea that contributions to a discourse can take on different meanings depending on the context in which they are uttered. That is to say, the approach subscribes to the view that the content of an argument can shift on account of repeatedly being brought forward in different circumstances. In other words, the iteration of an argument in different contexts can have an impact on the content of the argument.[67]

The mentioned references to discourse analysis have remained rather abstract so far. An example may illustrate to what extent an exploration of discursive mechanisms can provide insights.[68] Werner Flume, one of the most influential German private law scholars of the twentieth century, wrote an essay in which he elaborated on the concept of private autonomy. He stressed that private autonomy, first and foremost, guaranteed an individual's right to self-determination, even if such self-determination seemed unreasonable or even detrimental to an outside observer. Flume gave expression to this conception by referring to the Latin proverb *stat pro ratione voluntas*,[69] which can be translated as meaning that free will applies regardless of its reasonableness. He further argued that the exercise of private autonomy is premised on a person's capacity to form a free will without undue influence.[70] In the wake of Flume's work, the Latin saying has been alluded to numerous times with reference to the author in the discourse on the significance of private autonomy as a foundational principle of private law.[71] Yet, these contributions mention Flume's views on the inbuilt limitations to the exercise of private autonomy less often. From the point of view of discourse analysis, at least three discursive mechanisms are at play in the discourse on private autonomy that augment the status given to the principle in private law. First of all, the reference to the influential author's quote lends authority to the text mentioning it. The referring text can position itself in line with other texts emphasizing the importance of autonomy.

[66] esp Austin (n 49); Jaques Derrida, 'Die différance' in Jaques Derrida, *Randgänge der Philosophie* (Passagen 1972) 6; Searle (n 49).

[67] Jaques Derrida, 'Die différance' in Jaques Derrida, *Randgänge der Philosophie* (Passagen 1972) 6; ibid, 'Signatur, Ereignis, Kontext' in Jaques Derrida, *Randgänge der Philosophie* (Passagen 1972) 133–51.

[68] This paragraph is an abbreviated version of the examination in Croon-Gestefeld (n 14) 92–98.

[69] Werner Flume, *Allgemeiner Teil des Bürgerlichen Rechts* (4th edn, Springer 1992) vol 2, 6.

[70] ibid 10.

[71] See eg Claus-Wilhelm Canaris, 'Verfassungs- und europarechtliche Aspekte der Vertragsfreiheit in der Privatrechtsgesellschaft' in P Badura and R Scholz (eds), *Festschrift für Peter Lerche* (C.H. Beck 1993) 873, 881; Peter Derleder, 'Privatautonomie, Wirtschaftstheorie und Ethik des rechtsgeschäftlichen Handelns' in C Broda (ed), *Festschrift für Rudolf Wassermann* (Luchterhand 1985) 643; Franz Gamillscheg, 'Die Grundrechte im Arbeitsrecht' (1964) 164 AcP 385, 413; Eduard Picker, 'Antidiskriminierungsgesetz – Der Anfang vom Ende der Privatautonomie?' (2002) JZ 880.

In doing so, it draws on the authority of the previous texts. Moreover, texts that only refer to the Latin proverb but omit the limitations to private autonomy mentioned by Flume (free will-formation as a precondition) work with abbreviations. These abbreviations can alter the understanding of the source text over time because participants in the discourse will start to perceive the secondary mentions as accurate depictions of the original statement. In the end, danger is present that limitations, qualifications, and/or nuances in meaning get lost. Finally, the repetitive reference to a certain statement can contribute to setting a standard. Regarding *stat pro ratione voluntas*, the reference to the quote underlines the standard in private law discourse that private autonomy is of particular importance. Consequently, contributions to the discourse that deviate from this standard appear as objections to it, finding themselves in a defensive position from which to argue.

Having laid out the intellectual influences of the approach, one point, in particular, should be stressed: The approach of exploring legal paradigms, as presented here, does not aim to evaluate the operation of preconceptions, narratives or discursive mechanisms in terms of good or bad. Its sole purpose is to offer the means and terminology to make the functioning of underlying paradigms more explicit in analyses of the law.

4. Potential

The explanatory remarks have already offered an indication as to the potential benefits of the approach. The approach can make hidden assumptions about the law more visible, reveal the extent to which path dependencies impact the evolution of jurisprudence, and heighten awareness of the fact that stylistic choices influence the perception of the topic at hand.

The approach of exploring legal paradigms relies on the idea that each text can be the object of a second reading. The latter reading looks more closely at the subtext of a text, that is, the connotations and references in a text that are not always explicitly articulated. In doing so, the approach goes beyond a mere acknowledgement of the fact that hidden assumptions about the law inform legal writing. It addresses the underlying conceptions about the workings of the law in a straightforward manner and puts them in the foreground of its analysis. This directness allows for ways of investigating the unarticulated fabric that carries explicit legal reasoning.

A contribution from the judicature to private equality law discourse may serve as an example. In 2021, the German Federal Court of Justice issued a decision in which it held that the organizers of a festival had not violated an equal treatment provision obliging private parties in refusing a man entrance on the grounds of his age.[72] The reasoning rested on the argument that the organizers' commercial activity fell outside the scope of application of the General Equal Treatment Act. The Court stated in particular that organizers contracted with festivalgoers in a way that allowed them to pick and choose the audience for the event.[73] They were found to have the right to decide on the composition of the audience in respect of the participants' age.

From a doctrinal point of view, one may criticize how far the court's interpretation of the equal treatment provision is reconcilable with the wording of the provision or the overall purpose of the General Equal Treatment Act.[74] From the point of view of exploring legal paradigms, the judgment is of interest because it can be read as a manifestation of a prominently held view in private law that the impact of the equal treatment obligation on the relationships between private parties should be kept limited.[75] In this view, the duty to treat persons equally first and foremost obliges the state; private parties should only be bound by equal treatment provisions in so far as their discriminatory behaviour amounts to the violation of personality rights of the person affected. Therefore, even though the judgment makes no explicit reference to the position, it can be read as an expression of a liberal understanding of equal treatment law. Due to the court's 'orientation behavior',[76] the judgment focuses on the freedom of contract aspect of the case while paying less attention to its discriminatory facet.

Apart from investigating the subtext of a text, the approach of exploring legal paradigms has the potential of pointing out path dependencies.[77] By means of borrowing from discourse analysis, it aims to detect lines of references in publications. What information can be extracted from the footnotes? Who is prominently cited? Whose views does the author thoroughly engage with? And whose works are left out? All these questions can offer insights into the course of jurisprudence since the path that legal academia takes is subject to various factors: New legislation, changes in social attitudes, and technological

[72] BGH (2021) NJW 2514.

[73] BGH (2021) NJW 2514 para 19.

[74] Critically Michael Grünberger, 'Anmerkung zu BGH, Urt. v. 5.5.2021, Az. VII ZR 78/20' (2021) NJW 2514, 2517; see also Christian Armbrüster, 'Anmerkung zu BGH, Urt. v. 5.5.2021, Az. VII ZR 78/20' (2021) JZ 1013, 1014.

[75] See eg Thomas Lobinger, 'Perspektiven der Privatrechtsdogmatik am Beispiel des allgemeinen Gleichbehandlungsrechts' (2016) 216 AcP 28, 84.

[76] Wiethölter (n 45) 219.

[77] Bumke (n 57) 48–49, see also Oona Hathaway, 'Path Dependence in the Law: The Course and Pattern of Legal Change in a Common Law System' (2001) 86 Iowa L Rev 601.

innovations play an important role in moving jurisprudence forward. These developments must be critically assessed, rendered intelligible in legal terms, and incorporated into the existing judicial framework. However, processing new material and findings can only partially explain why jurisprudence grows in certain directions and withers in others. The evolution of knowledge is socially contingent.[78] Therefore, scholars' academic environment matters, especially in its influence over their choice of reading. It affects how an author perceives a legal problem and the methods of analysis employed by the author. Given that jurisprudence does not operate with confirmations or falsifications, being aware of intellectual influences, social relationships among scholars, and the ebb and flow of methodological fashions is all the more important.

The approach has another merit, albeit of a less direct nature than that of its potential to reveal hidden assumptions or path dependencies in jurisprudence. The approach forces its users to reflect on the fact that an author's portrayal of a legal topic greatly affects readers' understanding of the topic. It can make readers aware that choices in presentation, structure, style or reference shape how they perceive a text. Even if attention is only sporadically directed towards the discursive mechanisms at play, this exercise can still have an impact on a person's general reading habits. Ultimately, this change may inform profound textual analyses should the doctrinal method be employed. Moreover, reflecting upon the depiction of arguments can enhance authors' self-awareness about their own employment of discursive practices. Authors may become more likely to refrain from using apocryphal aggravations or abbreviations if they have extensively thought about their operation in the past. Alternatively, knowing about the effects of discursive mechanisms may motivate authors to use such mechanisms in a more nuanced or deliberate manner than they would have done otherwise.

5. Potential Pitfalls

Nevertheless, the approach not only comes with benefits but also with associated risks. Two potential pitfalls spring to mind: The danger exists of prematurely ascribing adherence to a paradigm to a legal academic, and temptation may be present to draw too far-sweeping conclusions from the recognition of certain paradigms or discursive mechanisms in legal debates.

The approach of exploring legal paradigms asks its users to go beyond a strict textual interpretation to detect underlying presuppositions or attitudes

[78] Fleck (n 51) 53.

towards the law that guide the text. This move from text to subtext must be approached with caution, as the subtext, by its very nature, does not consist of concrete utterances that can be referred to. Therefore, any analysis of the subtext leaves the solid realm and enters the territory of the intangible. In arguing that a text gives expression to an author's presuppositions, assumptions are made about that author's beliefs. As a result, different critiques of the interpretation of the subtext can be expected: The author, whose statement is analysed, may feel misrepresented. Furthermore, other members of the legal community could conceivably consider the interpretation a false portrayal, arguing that the findings presented fit too smoothly, that intellectual points of reference have been alleged that actually do not exist, or that the analysis of the subtext has paid too little attention to particularities in the author's reasoning.

These points of critique address legitimate concerns, for which there are two possible replies. The first relies on the distinction between text and author. Since a text is a separate entity from its author, the text can be said to be influenced by underlying paradigms even if its author might not be aware of their effects or—going even further—does not associate with the paradigms ascribed. The second answer is more convincing. It states that the critique should be taken seriously. In attempting to trace the origins of ideas or attitudes, there is always the danger of drawing pictures that little resemble real events or pointing out connections where there are none. These possibilities must be addressed by acknowledging the subjective element of the approach. The critique should also compel users of the approach to work cautiously. Disclosing the limitations of the findings and articulating uncertainties are part of good practice.

The approach comes with the additional danger of attaching too much importance to the findings that can be produced with its help. Naming and reflecting upon underlying assumptions in a legal text can help to deepen a person's understanding of it and to position the contribution within the sphere of jurisprudence. However, the approach cannot substitute existing approaches to unpacking the law. Instead, it is intended to complement established doctrinal, philosophical and theoretical approaches to the law.

6. Case Study: Sharenting

The preceding paragraphs have sought to sketch the approach, make its intellectual influences visible, and elaborate on its advantages and drawbacks. For the most part, the explications remained in the abstract due to their theoretical nature. Now, an example of its application is meant to 'bring the approach to life'. The discussion on parents posting pictures of their children online lends itself to reference material.

As in other countries, many parents in Germany post pictures of their children on social media. Under German law, publishing a person's picture and processing that person's data must be lawful. Specifically, the actions are considered lawful if and to the extent that the person who is depicted or whose data are processed has consented to their use.[79] The ability to provide valid consent is subject to the person's ability to reason and power of judgment.[80] Consequently, minors, who have not yet reached the phase in their personal development when they are able to decide on the publication of their pictures on the internet for themselves, need another person to decide on their behalf. Given this setting, the question arises if, and under what circumstances, parents can consent to the posting of pictures of their children. The question is particularly controversial because the parents' consent would legitimize their own actions if they posted the pictures.

In its search for answers, the related discourse focuses on the legal nature of consent. According to one opinion, consent to the publication of pictures on social media is a legal action (*Rechtsgeschäft* or *rechtsgeschäftsähnliche Handlung*). As a result, a provision of German agency law is applicable and bars parents from legitimizing their actions by means of consent.[81] A supplementary curator (*Ergänzungspfleger*) will have to take the decision on consent in their position instead. Especially jurists whose work focuses on data protection law favour this view.[82] In another view, consenting to the publication of pictures online is a factual action and, therefore, falls within the domain of parental responsibility. As such, the decision on whether to post a picture of the child on social media is, in principle, only taken out of the parents' hands in instances of child endangerment.[83] The latter position is particularly prominent among representatives of family law.[84]

[79] Art 6 I 1 a DSGVO.

[80] BGHZ 29, 33, 36.

[81] § 181 BGB prohibits an agent to contract with himself/herself.

[82] Benedikt Buchner, 'Von der Wiege bis zur Bahre? – Datenschutz im Familienrecht unter der DS-GVO' (2019) FamRZ 665, 666–67; Jörg Fritzsche and Jonas Knapp, 'Bildnisse von Kindern im Internet und in sozialen Medien' (2019) FamRZ 1905, 1907–08; Anna Schimke, 'Rechtliche Rahmenbedingungen der Veröffentlichung von Kinderfotos im Netz durch Eltern' (2019) NZFam 851, 853. This insight is adopted from Saskia Lettmaier, 'Die Veröffentlichung von Bildnissen des Kindes durch die sorgeberechtigten Eltern: Rechtsprobleme des „Sharenting"' in S Lorz and others (eds), *Festschrift für Klaus Vieweg* (Duncker und Humblot 2021) 355, 356.

[83] § 1666 BGB.

[84] Anja Amend-Traut, in: BeckOGK, version: 1.2.2022, § 1626 BGB Rn. 111.1; Katrin Lack, 'Grenzen der elterlichen Entscheidungsbefugnis – Wer bestimmt über die Preisgabe persönlicher Daten des Kindes im Internet?' (2017) FamRZ 730, 1731; Lettmaier (n 82) 362–63.

One promising way of analysing the issue is to look at the arguments brought forward in favour of the approaches and ask which arguments are more convincing and conform to existing legislation. Another promising approach is to explore the legal paradigms that underlie the discussion on the nature of consent when it comes to posting pictures on social media. Why is so much attention being paid to classifying consent as either a legal or a factual action? And why does the matter seem to have a dividing line between representatives of data law and representatives of family law?

Examining the subtext of the debate, it appears as if two competing sets of preconceptions and assumptions are operating. The statements that consider consent as a legal action perceive the question in terms of consistency with data protection law and the transfer of rights on data through the institution of consent. The compatibility of the finding with the system of family law is of lesser concern. By contrast, the statements that consider consent to be a factual action perceive the question in terms of consistency with established standards of custody law. Their focus is more centred on the legal understanding of the relationship between parents and their children when it comes to posting pictures online. In addition, the approach that perceives consent to the posting as a factual action can be considered an expression of the view that family relations should remain as free from state interference as possible. If consent is understood as a legal action, and it falls to a supplementary curator instead of the parents to declare or refuse it, a representative of the state makes the decision. Such a transferal of decision-making power would substantially encroach upon the family relationship. Therefore, although the notion of family law as a legal space with as little state intervention as possible is not explicitly articulated in the debate about the nature of consent, it exerts a strong influence over the family law-centred argumentation.

V. Conclusion

The interconnections between legal studies and the humanities are well-known. At the same time, legal research is far from having exhausted the possibilities for analyses that neighbouring disciplines such as hermeneutics, narratology, or literary studies offer. Exploring legal paradigms is one approach that seeks to avail itself of the methods of these disciplines. It emphasizes the subtext of legal texts and asks its applicants to study a legal text with other than the usual questions in mind. Where in the discourse is the contribution located? And where does the author want the contribution to be located? These are but two questions that the approach of exploring legal paradigms poses. In doing so, it does not aim at substituting doctrinal research. Instead, it seeks to complement systematizing analyses of the law. Its ultimate goal is to develop a better understanding of legal discourses and, therefore, of the law with the help of close reading.

Are you convinced? If not (and if so), I suggest this exercise: Read the next legal academic text once for its content and again with your 'exploring legal paradigms' glasses on. Then, let me know if you have experienced a difference. First, I am curious about your experiences, and second, because there is added value in discussing methods.

3

When Private Law Theory is Close Enough

*Andrew S. Gold**

I. Introduction

Private law theorists often adopt concepts that are a close, but imperfect, fit for the concepts actually used in the law. For example, theorists employ concepts that diverge moderately from the legal concepts courts adopt while still resembling those concepts. In other cases, theorists may match the law's concepts as a legal matter, but they employ concepts that diverge moderately from those found in moral reasoning. Such theories diverge to some degree from the moral understanding, but they are still 'in the right ballpark'. This chapter will assess the value in legal theories that come close to a set of target concepts, but which are not quite a fit for them.

What it means to be 'in the right ballpark' varies. Some theories are close but imperfect fits for legal concepts. Others are close but imperfect fits for moral concepts. In some instances, the target concepts at issue are neither legal nor moral. Despite the variations, I will suggest two overarching reasons for the development of legal theories that are close but still a near miss: a) being close enough to a conceptual target supports a goal of interpretive accuracy; or b) being close enough to a conceptual target supports a theorist's prescriptive aims. In short, theories that are in the right conceptual ballpark can help us discern what the law is, or they can guide us in figuring out what the law ought to be. Interpretive and prescriptive theories thus both have reasons to be in the right ballpark, even if their reasons differ.

I will begin with criteria for interpretive theories—that is, theories that seek to replicate the law's 'self-understanding'. In that setting, one reason to seek a theory that is in the right ballpark conceptually is if such a theory is more likely to be an accurate interpretation of existing law than a theory that diverges

* Professor, Brooklyn Law School. I am grateful to Nils Jansen, Paul Miller, Henry Smith, and Sandy Steel for helpful discussion of ideas in this chapter. I am also grateful to participants in the conference on methodology in private law theory held at the Bucerius Law School and co-sponsored by Notre Dame Law School. Any errors are my own.

Andrew S. Gold, *When Private Law Theory is Close Enough* In: *Methodology in Private Law Theory*. Edited by: Thilo Kuntz and Paul B. Miller, Oxford University Press. © Andrew S. Gold 2024. DOI: 10.1093/oso/9780198885306.003.0003

more dramatically. A leading example of such an approach is when private law theorists aim for concepts that are sufficiently close to existing legal concepts that they are plausible for judicial adoption—that is, these concepts may not be the ones courts actually use, but they are concepts which they *could* have used.

As an illustration, consider Stephen Smith's influential account of a moderate transparency criterion. Under this criterion, a theorist should look for concepts that are 'recognizably legal', with the aim of capturing the internal point of view.[1] Some theories, such as efficiency theories of contract law, tend to fare poorly under this criterion. Even so, the criterion is not very strict, for Smith contends that a theorist should adopt concepts that courts could have adopted but that they need not use the concepts that the courts actually employ.[2] Thus, a reliance theory of contract such as Fuller and Perdue's theory is acceptable, given that its chosen concepts are at least remedial, despite their divergence from actual legal reasoning. I will argue that Smith's approach is overly flexible: if we want to match the internal point of view, it is more plausible to adopt the legal concepts courts claim to use rather than those they could have used in a hypothetical world.

A moderate morality criterion fares better for interpretive purposes.[3] Smith's version of the morality criterion is likewise an influential approach. If we seek to match the internal point of view of legal actors, he suggests that a good interpretation of contract law will use concepts that courts could at least think are moral, even if they are not, in fact, moral. He argues for the import of moral concepts in light of the law's claim to authority. At the same time, Smith notes that we need to take into account that courts could be mistaken about what is moral. If we wish to successfully track the internal point of view, we must allow for errors in that point of view. A moderate morality criterion takes into account both of these premises. While I will raise doubts about some aspects of this approach, I think the ultimate conclusion is correct; a moderate morality criterion helps us to locate theories that fit their subject matter, all else equal. Such a criterion requires concepts that are 'recognizably moral',[4] and in doing so, it advances the goal of capturing the internal point of view.

The relevance of these approximations of concepts—legal or moral—shifts if we turn our attention to prescriptive theories. A moderate transparency criterion now *does* accomplish something valuable. Theories that employ recognizably legal concepts can provide a valuable template for legal reform (or an

[1] See Stephen A Smith, *Contract Theory* (OUP 2004) 30 (referencing 'recognizably legal ideas').
[2] ibid 28.
[3] ibid 18 (endorsing a moderate morality criterion).
[4] ibid 20 (referencing 'recognizably moral principles').

argument for retaining the status quo). For example, such theories can facilitate legal reforms that still offer a fit with the conceptual structure of a private law field.[5] This architectural fit may enable the law to function better as a system, to cut down on information costs, or to increase legal compliance. Indeed, similar benefits are available where prescriptive theories incorporate recognizably *moral* concepts. There may be good institutional reasons in some settings for a divergence between the legal and the moral.[6] However, in cases where a divergence is required, it could still be valuable, within the parameters set, to at least approximate what is moral. For example, this could be true if the burden on moral agents would be lessened by narrowing the gap between legal and moral.

There may also be reasons for a theory to approximate concepts that are neither legal nor moral. Loyalty duties provide good examples (as loyalty is not always moral). There is often cause for fiduciary loyalty to diverge from extra-legal loyalty.[7] Among other reasons, fiduciaries need to count as 'loyal' from the instant a fiduciary relationship forms, and the law ought not to mandate the emotional attachments that attend common forms of loyalty.[8] Administrability concerns may also necessitate a standardized version of loyalty that differs from its extra-legal content. Likewise, the law has good reason to cabin the effects of legal loyalty in order to avoid the excessive kinds of loyalty that can emerge in non-legal relationships. Even so, the law may have good reason to adopt versions of loyalty that are 'recognizably loyal' rather than completely foreign to loyalty practices as usually experienced.

Returning to transparency criteria, I will suggest that a shift in how we understand theories that use recognizably legal concepts can open up new avenues of inquiry. In the interpretive setting, a moderate transparency criterion tends to channel a great deal of scholarly energy into highly difficult and contested questions of fit. If, on the other hand, we adopt a stricter transparency criterion for our interpretive theories, our focus may change. Given that such ballpark concepts will be ruled out for interpretive purposes, their usefulness will likely be in the prescriptive realm. And, in figuring out whether a 'close

[5] See Andrew S Gold and Henry E Smith, 'Restatements and the Common Law' in Andrew S Gold and Robert W Gordon (eds), *The American Law Institute: A Centennial History* (OUP 2023).

[6] On the import of such distinctively legal reasons, see Seana Valentine Shiffrin, 'The Divergence of Contract and Promise' (2007) 120 Harvard LR 708.

[7] For helpful discussion focusing on moral loyalties, see Paul B Miller, 'Dimensions of Fiduciary Loyalty' in DG Smith and AS Gold (eds), *Research Handbook on Fiduciary Law* (Elgar 2018).

[8] On the former concern, see Stephen A Smith, 'The Deed, Not the Motive: Fiduciary Law Without Loyalty' in PB Miller and AS Gold (eds), *Contract, Status, and Fiduciary Law* (OUP 2016). On the latter, see Andrew S Gold, 'Accommodating Loyalty' in PB Miller and AS Gold (eds), *Contract, Status, and Fiduciary Law* (OUP 2016).

enough' set of concepts is valuable from a prescriptive perspective, we may have important further questions to ask. For example, if we are 'in the right ballpark' legally, how close does one need to be in order for a new set of concepts to mesh well with existing concepts? How close does one need to be for courts to be open to a reform? If we are approximating moral concepts, how close is necessary to achieve desirable compliance effects? When will any information cost benefits be worth the price of divergence? When will a small divergence from moral concepts overly burden moral agents? These and related questions can move to the fore.

As this chapter develops, the tendency of private law theories to seek concepts that are close enough to their subject matter is justifiable but in a context-dependent way. There are reasons why a moderate transparency or moderate morality criterion makes sense. In each case, however, we must attend to the reasons in favour of these criteria. Much depends on whether our theory is intended to be an interpretation of existing law, tracking the internal point of view, or a prescriptive theory that might endorse changes to that law. Section II of this chapter will discuss theories that are 'close enough' in the interpretive setting. Section III will discuss prescriptive theories. Section IV will offer some thoughts on why it matters if we shift toward a more stringent transparency criterion in the interpretive setting. The likely effect is that theories that are 'in the right ballpark' will have greater relevance as prescriptive rather than as interpretive theories. In turn, a range of interesting questions arise if such theories are offered as prescriptive rather than interpretive. Section V will then conclude.

II. Interpretive Theories that are 'Close Enough'

Much recent private law scholarship is concerned with law's self-understanding, or with the internal point of view.[9] This naturally raises the question of why theorists seek this perspective since many leading theories of private law lack this aim. Why exactly should we wish to know the law's self-understanding?

Smith helpfully illustrates one of the reasons by comparing a non-legal social practice, the seventeenth-century practice of bloodletting. As he indicates,

[9] While theorists often reference the law's self-understanding, the internal point of view is also a common formulation of the goal. See, eg, John CP Goldberg and Benjamin C Zipursky, 'Seeing Tort Law from the Internal Point of View: Holmes and Hart on Legal Duties' (2006) 75 Fordham L Rev 1563. For additional insights, see Paul B Miller and Jeffrey A Pojanowski, 'The Internal Point of View in Private Law' (2022) 67 Am J Jurisprudence 247.

a social scientist might build an account of bloodletting based on its physical consequences alone. But in doing so, something would be lost:

> Such an account might conclude that the practice of blood-letting, which turned out to be a poor medical technique, was basically a practice for making sick people sicker. In purely medical terms, this account is not inaccurate, but as an interpretation of the meaning of blood-letting it is missing something.[10]

Instead, if we want the full picture of bloodletting, we need an account that incorporates the understanding of participants in the practice. A similar academic interest should carry over to legal settings.[11]

Another reason to care is that *stare decisis* and settled expectations often carry weight in our deliberations over what the law should become. We need to know how private law is currently understood before we can adequately make decisions about its reform.[12] And a further reason is that the way the law is currently understood by legal actors can give us insights into law's function that are otherwise obscured. For example, we may better understand how private law fields make use of modularity if we understand what concepts are actually in play.[13] Likewise, we may better understand how private law doctrine guides the behaviour of regulated parties if we understand the concepts actually in use.[14]

There are, of course, multiple internal points of view. Those who focus on the internal point of view tend to privilege legal actors, but that could mean that we need to know the perspective of practising lawyers as much as we need to know the perspective of judges.[15] In some contexts, one might even include legal academics on the list.[16] These perspectives need not perfectly coincide, and it is

[10] See Smith (n 1) 14.

[11] cf John Oberdiek, 'Method and Morality in the New Private Law of Torts' (2012) 125 Harvard LR Forum 189, 202 (noting the value in understanding tort law cannot be reduced to its practical payoff).

[12] This point is convincingly developed in Benjamin Zipursky, 'Pragmatic Conceptualism' (2000) 6 Legal Theory 457. As Zipursky indicates, modifying the law 'will involve a whole range of considerations about precedent, stare decisis, and institutional role that are simply elided by the functionalist account of what law is.' ibid 477.

[13] See Andrew S Gold and Henry E Smith, 'Sizing Up Private Law' (2020) 70 U Toronto LJ 489, 500–01 (discussing the role of modularity in private law).

[14] On this guidance function and its import for utilitarian approaches, see Stephen A Smith, 'The Normativity of Private Law' (2011) 31 Oxford J Legal Stud 215.

[15] See W Bradley Wendel, in this volume (emphasizing the import of lawyers). See also Andrew S Gold, 'Internal and External Perspectives: On the New Private Law Methodology' in AS Gold and others (eds), *The Oxford Handbook of The New Private Law* (OUP 2020). For Smith, the key actors are those who 'participate officially in making and applying the law', which includes judges, lawyers, legislators, and others. See Smith (n 1) 14.

[16] For discussion of how scholarly perspectives have historically related to the law in Germany, see Nils Jansen, in this volume. I am also grateful to Nils Jansen for emphasizing to me that perspectives on what the 'internal point of view' itself means may vary across jurisdictions.

telling that academics often foreground the views of courts. That challenge, however, does not preclude us from thinking that an internal point of view is there to be found, nor does it preclude us from thinking that the endeavour is valuable.

Even if the import of law's self-understanding is granted, this is only a first step. An approach that seeks the law's self-understanding must do more than argue for the import of the internal point of view; it also needs insights into the best methodology for ascertaining that point of view. We not only need to know why the internal point of view is important, we need to know how it should be located.

Smith has suggested several of the leading guidelines. A central methodological starting point is that we should take seriously what courts say they are doing. It is possible to develop accounts of private law fields that look nothing like the internal point of view as that view is expressed in published judicial opinions. All we have to do is imagine that courts are deceitful in their opinions, joined together in a scheme to mislead. Even so, Smith rules out such conspiracy-based theories. As he argues:

> No one doubts that judges and other law-makers occasionally dissemble, but as a general explanation for features of law that have evolved over centuries through the efforts of countless individuals, conspiracy explanations are unrealistic.[17]

For similar reasons, Smith rules out functionalist 'invisible hand' type explanations of law's claim to authority:

> Given the number, variety, and sophistication of the actors involved in making law's claims to authority, the suggestion that these actors have all wildly misunderstood the reasons with which they explain the law is prima facie implausible.[18]

If these claims are right, then only some theories will make the cut. This approach rules out those theories that treat judicial opinions as a cover for the courts' true understanding or as erroneous missteps operating on a large scale.

However, there is much more at issue than these basic constraints. Smith has elaborated in detail on several interpretive criteria, and these criteria helpfully

[17] See Smith (n 1) 16.
[18] ibid 20.

select between theories. These criteria also merit revisiting. This chapter will focus on two of them in particular: transparency and morality.[19] In each case, they provide useful mechanisms for assessing interpretive theories that seek to track the law's self-understanding. Yet, as we will see, they require revision if they are to adequately serve their intended purposes. Once revised, we can more readily prioritize among interpretive criteria in cases where they conflict. Moreover, we can better see why approximations of concepts (legal or otherwise) will sometimes make sense, and sometimes not.

1. The Transparency Criterion

I will begin with the transparency criterion, given its evident concern with the internal understanding of the law. If law is transparent, that internal perspective is accurately expressed: that is, '[l]aw is transparent to the extent that the reasons legal actors give for doing what they do are their real reasons'.[20] Smith suggests (rightly in my view) that law claims to be transparent, and a transparency criterion calls for a legal theory that will explain the reasons judges give for their decision. The question, once again, is whether it is desirable to be 'close enough'. Will a moderate transparency criterion suffice? I will suggest that if our goal is interpretive accuracy, we should adopt a stricter criterion.

Transparency criteria may have various levels of strength. A strong transparency criterion 'holds that a good theory of law will portray legal practice as in fact transparent'.[21] A weak criterion means something much less stringent: 'it is enough that a theory explain why legal actors might claim, sincerely or not, that the law is transparent'.[22] And the moderate criterion that Smith endorses 'holds that a good theory explain the law in a way that shows how legal officials could sincerely, even if erroneously, believe the law is transparent'.[23]

As Smith notes, a transparency criterion can likewise be understood as a component of the fit criterion.[24] It requires theorists to take into account certain facts about the underlying legal phenomena to be explained.[25] If fit is

[19] Other criteria in the private law theory literature have included: fit, coherence, determinacy, predictive force, simplicity, justice, and consilience.

[20] See Smith (n 1) 24.

[21] ibid 25.

[22] ibid.

[23] ibid.

[24] ibid 7, n 8.

[25] See also Ernest Weinrib, *The Idea of Private Law* (HUP 1995) 16 ('Because legal concepts and institutions are indicia of the law's self-understanding, an internal account attempts to make sense of them on their own terms by allowing them to have the meaning they have in juristic thought.').

central to our explanatory account, we might by extension think that this aspect of fit is also central. Theorists may decide that fit concerns need only extend to core features, and it is possible to think that a court's legal reasoning is not a core feature of the data to be explained. Yet this latter option is hard to square with an emphasis on the law's self-understanding if that is one of our goals in interpretation.

Smith's moderate criterion, however, allows for the acceptability of theories that incorporate concepts that differ from the legally adopted ones. As he argues, one may:

> [E]xplain the law using concepts that are recognizably 'legal' (or at least using concepts that, though more abstract than standard legal concepts, work through recognizably legal concepts in their explanation of particular rules and decisions) even if those concepts are not the same legal concepts that were employed by judges.[26]

Thus, a broadly legal realist approach to contract theory like the one espoused by Lon Fuller and William Perdue can meet this requirement. They view expectation damages as a proxy for reliance—a view which is arguably in tension with the concepts courts actually employ—but their remedial picture is at least making use of recognizably legal concepts.[27] It passes the test.[28]

The benefit of this moderate criterion is that it allows for mistaken judicial judgments.[29] Just as judges can be mistaken about what is moral, they can also be mistaken about how to explain the law. Smith's key precondition is this: 'a false, but sincere, claim is perfectly intelligible so long as a plausible (ie non-conspiracy-based) explanation is given for that claim'.[30] Inasmuch as the real reasons for a judicial decision can plausibly differ from what judges think they are, there is no difficulty.

On the other hand, it is not evident that we need such a moderate criterion in order to allow for judicial mistakes. For example, we could adopt a

[26] See Smith (n 8) 28.

[27] See Lon Fuller and William Perdue, 'The Reliance Interest in Contract Damages' (1936) 46 Yale LJ 53.

[28] Quite possibly more radical deviations from traditional legal concepts would also pass the test of this moderate criterion. cf Nathan Oman, 'Unity and Pluralism in Contract Law' (2005) 103 Mich L Rev 1483, 1494–1495 (suggesting the transparency criterion challenge for efficiency theories of contract may not be as severe as Smith indicates).

[29] See Smith (n 3) 29.

[30] ibid 28. From what I can tell, a concern with avoiding conspiracy-based explanations is not identical to a broader idea that we should presume judges are acting in good faith. I thank Paul Miller for suggesting the latter presumption as a possibility.

semi-strong transparency criterion. Perhaps the arguments that judges employ do not always determine the results of cases when correctly understood (because judges sometimes err in thinking that a given set of conceptual premises leads to a given conclusion), *but a theory must understand each legal concept in the manner that judges claim to understand it*. This would be a substantially more stringent transparency criterion than the moderate version, but it would still allow for judicial error.

Granted, the mere fact that other criteria are available is not a sufficient argument in their favour. Why select a stronger transparency criterion, even if it is possible to adopt one while allowing for judicial error? The reason has to do with the plausibility of the theories that a given criterion allows for. The central challenge for a moderate transparency criterion is that it allows for theories that do run afoul of the injunctions against conspiracy and false consciousness explanations.

For Smith, an internal explanation must only comply with the moderate transparency criterion, but this permits a notable gap between a given interpretation and the internal point of view. What Smith sees as an internal explanation may differ from the explanation judges provide for their holdings; indeed, he recognizes as much. As he notes, '[i]n those cases in which the theorist's internal explanation differs from the judicial explanation, the explanation for this difference . . . is simply that those offering the judicial explanation are mistaken'.[31] Even so, the judicial explanation is 'in the right ball park, as it were'.[32] On Smith's view, 'no assumption is made or implied that the judiciary is engaged in a fraud or is in the grip of an unseen force. They simply made a mistake'.[33]

However, the mistakes that Smith's account accepts are not just isolated mistakes in the application of doctrine to a specific fact pattern or failures to get the morality quite right in a complex area. They are more systematic than that.

For example, consider again the claim that Lon Fuller and William Perdue are correct about contract damages. This means that the expectation remedy is properly seen as a proxy for reliance. This also means that if judges fail to see that expectation damages are there to protect the reliance interest, they fundamentally misunderstand the point of contract law remedies. Wouldn't this suggest a false consciousness? Alternatively, if such judges genuinely have in mind the reliance interest but talk as if they were protecting a performance

[31] ibid 29.
[32] ibid.
[33] ibid.

interest, wouldn't that suggest the kind of conspiracy theory that Smith rejects?[34]

True, such an explanation is 'in the right ballpark',[35] for it does use recognizably legal understandings of what a remedy for a wrong is. But we need to know why conspiracy theories or false consciousness arguments are less troubling when one's substantive theory is at least in the right ballpark. It is not obvious why that premise should be accepted. In fact, if our concern is with tracing conceptual inferences—or with predictive force—we might think that even theories like Fuller and Perdue's should be ruled out to the extent they deviate from the reasoning courts actually use. The argument that approaches which are not recognizably legal fail—because they depend on false consciousness or conspiracy theories—would seem to be an equally good argument against recognizably legal approaches which depend on false consciousness or conspiracy theories.

More importantly, the resulting interpretive theory has a questionable claim to be law's self-understanding. If a theory offers different concepts from the ones courts use—albeit concepts they *could* have used—that is another way of saying that it is not the internal perspective on the law. It is, rather, a near miss. We might call such theories *quasi-internal*.[36] Theories of this stripe are internal to the extent they make use of enough central private law concepts to be recognizably legal to courts and litigants, yet external because they do not make use of private law concepts in a way that actually matches the legal reasoning under consideration.[37]

If our objective is to interpret private law fields in a way that reflects the law's self-understanding, our resulting theory should allow for judicial error while nonetheless adopting the legal concepts that courts actually use. Those concepts may not have the features courts think they do, and they may entail

[34] I leave to one side the possibility that judicial language has become so detached from ordinary language that it has a special meaning in such cases. cf Kraus, 'Transparency and Determinacy in Common Law Adjudication: A Philosophical Defense of Explanatory Economic Analysis' (2007) 93 Va L Rev 287, 326–36. While that is a possibility in narrow circumstances, it seems very unlikely to operate on a large enough scale to address the present concerns.

[35] See Smith (n 1) 29 (noting that an external theory 'is not even in the right ball park').

[36] For discussion of this idea, see Gold (n 15).

[37] It is an interesting question how to treat theories that largely match existing legal concepts yet in a simplified version. On such theories, see Paul B Miller, 'Corporations' in AS Gold and others (eds), *The Oxford Handbook of the New Private Law* (OUP 2020) 341, 341–342. Miller is concerned with simplification that takes a relatively radical form. What of minor or de minimis simplifications? It is also interesting to consider cases that adopt a micro-level (or even atomic level) perspective on legal concepts. A sufficiently microscopic perspective—as is sometimes evident in Hohfeldian analysis—might also distort the concepts in use in legal reasoning, if they are unrecognizable when viewed at the mid-level. cf Andrew S Gold and Henry E Smith, 'Scaling Up Legal Relations' in S Balganesh, TM Sichelman and HE Smith (eds), *Wesley Hohfeld a Century Later: Edited Work, Select Personal Papers, and Original Commentaries* (CUP 2022).

results that courts do not yet realize, but absent exceptional circumstances, they should be taken at face value. The question, then, is whether theories that fail such a test yet are in the right ballpark may still retain their value. Before considering that question, I will turn to another way that interpretivists approximate a set of target concepts.

2. The Morality Criterion

Like the transparency criterion, the morality criterion can be understood as a part of a fit criterion.[38] It is a benchmark designed to assist in obtaining the law's self-understanding. Smith argues that the criterion follows from what law claims; in other words, the morality criterion reflects a central feature of the legal practice being explained. The law is commonly thought to claim authority, and he builds on this idea to suggest that a moderate morality criterion is appropriate. I think this view is incorrect: there is no useful morality criterion that can be derived from what law claims.[39] Yet this does not mean that a morality criterion is undesirable, but instead that its justification should change. Changing its justification, however, may also suggest changes to the robustness of the morality criterion.

As with the transparency criterion, a morality criterion can be categorized by its strength. A strong morality criterion will require a theory to show that the law is morally justified. The difficulty is that courts could be wrong in their assessment of morality. A weak criterion recognizes that the law's claim to authority requires an explanation but allows for any explanation to suffice. A weak criterion, however, will allow for conspiracy theories and false consciousness-based explanations, explanations which are implausible given the structural features of common-law adjudication.

As Smith suggests, a moderate morality criterion 'holds that a good legal theory should explain the law in a way that shows how the law *might be thought to be justified* even if it not justified'.[40] Such a criterion makes law's claim to authority intelligible:

> Insofar as the law is, or could be thought to be, supported by recognizably moral principles, law's claim to authority is intelligible. It is intelligible

[38] See Smith (n 1) 7, n 8.

[39] As we will see, a morality criterion could be derived from the law's claim to authority; the difficulty is that the resulting criterion would do almost no work as a filter for private law theories.

[40] ibid 18.

> because we have satisfactorily explained why legal actors might claim the law is morally justified. The explanation is that the actors believe the relevant principles both fit the law and morally justify.[41]

Such a criterion also has the benefit of allowing for legal error without opening the door to conspiracy theories or false consciousness. The moderate morality criterion thus assesses interpretive theories based on the extent to which the principles that they recognize in contract, tort, or other fields are morally justified or at least plausible enough that legal actors could think they are morally justified (that is, even if their justification is mistaken).

There is, however, a major difficulty with this argument for a moderate morality criterion: law's claim to authority may have a different content. And this is precisely what some have argued, for a law's claim to authority need not equate to a claim that its content or reasoning is morally correct. A chapter in John Gardner's work, *Law as a Leap of Faith*, illustrates the difficulty.[42]

Gardner's argument responds to Robert Alexy's contention that the law claims to be both just and moral. Alexy offers two key examples to suggest these claims: a constitutional provision which states that 'X is a sovereign, federal, and unjust republic' and a judge who holds that 'the accused is sentenced to life imprisonment, which is an incorrect interpretation of prevailing law'.[43] Both legal statements admittedly sound odd to the ear. Yet Gardner rejects Alexy's conclusions in each case. As he concludes: 'law does not make either of the moral claims that Alexy ascribes to it – either the claim to be just or the claim to be morally correct'.[44]

The kind of language Alexy points to is not contradictory or unheard of. Gardner notes a prominent example. In a legal opinion, Lord Goff described feeling forced by precedent to reach a decision that he did not prefer. He expressly stated: 'I feel ... that I would be lacking in candour if I were to conceal my unhappiness about the conclusion which I feel compelled to reach.'[45] Lord Goff likewise noted the challenge when authority appears to call for a conclusion that a judge 'senses to be unjust or inappropriate'.[46] As Gardner indicates, judges are sometimes bound by precedent to reach outcomes that they find neither just nor moral, and they may even explicitly note when this has

[41] ibid 20.
[42] See John Gardner, 'How Law Claims, What Law Claims' in *Law as a Leap of Faith* (OUP 2012) 125.
[43] See Robert Alexy, *The Argument from Injustice: A Reply to Legal Positivism* (trans Paulson and Paulson) (OUP 2002) 36.
[44] See Gardner (n 42) 141.
[45] ibid 141 (citing *Elliot v C* [1983] 2 All ER 1005 at 1010, 1012).
[46] ibid.

occurred.[47] It is not an instance of incoherence on the judge's part, nor is it inconsistent with what the law claims.

Law still makes a moral claim, and it makes a claim to authority. But the law's claims are different from Alexy's apparent understanding.[48] Law claims to be morally *binding*, and that is not the same thing as a claim to be just or morally correct.[49] Judges may feel that they must follow statutes and precedents even if they think those statutes and precedents are gravely mistaken. Judges may still contend that such holdings bind the parties and even that they morally bind them. As Gardner emphasizes: 'moral authority is such that abiding by it is morally correct even though the exercise of it was morally incorrect'.[50]

Where does that leave the morality criterion? Recall that the moderate version of the morality criterion 'holds that a good theory should explain the law in a way that shows how the law *might be thought to be* justified even if it is not justified'.[51] Depending on how we apply it, this morality criterion is now open to doubt. Courts could very reasonably determine that some private law doctrines are morally binding given their origins in legitimate precedent while simultaneously concluding that those doctrines ought to be changed because they are not justified.

In short, if we focus on the law's claim to moral authority—rather than a claim to moral correctness—then a moderate morality criterion that focuses on what is morally justified (or what could be thought to be morally justified) is far from obvious. A good interpretive theory should merely have to show how the law might be thought morally *binding*, whether or not it is binding in fact. Legal pronouncements can be morally binding without their content being morally justified, and legal actors are well aware of this unfortunate reality. A morality criterion that takes this into account, however, will have limited usefulness, as it will be the unusual case in which private law mandates could not even *be thought to be* morally binding on the regulated parties. Such a criterion would filter out very few theories.

Still, there are ways to rehabilitate a moderate morality criterion to further our interpretive goals. For example, we might focus on judicial language and

[47] ibid 142.

[48] There is arguably some ambiguity in Alexy's argument. Gardner suggests that '[s]ometimes Alexy explains law's claim as a claim to correctness *simpliciter*, not as a claim to legal correctness coupled with a claim to moral correctness.' See ibid 140, n 33.

[49] ibid.

[50] ibid 143.

[51] See Smith (n 1) 18. Note that lawmakers might also be justified in providing legal rights that they anticipate will be used in immoral ways, in light of moral rights to do moral wrong. That, however, is a different challenge. For discussion, see Andrew S Gold, Book Review (2023) 133 Ethics 320.

predictable features of judicial psychology in support of a moderate morality criterion. Supposing that law only claims to be morally binding (and not justified in its content), it can still make sense to think that a good theory will explain the law in a way that shows how private law principles are justified or might be thought to be morally justified. Judges frequently talk as if the principles described in their opinions are morally justified, and it is not unreasonable to think that—as a matter of psychology—they are drawn to readings of precedent that will square with their sense of what is morally correct.

That said, because judges are also drawn to follow precedents (whether through respect for *stare decisis*, policy reasons, or cognitive biases), we should be hesitant to rely on a moderate morality criterion where there is judicial language that points in another direction. To do otherwise would court the false consciousness and conspiracy theory concerns noted earlier. If the language in a given area of law suggests that courts are following precedents that are hard to square with what is morally justified, then we should focus on what those precedents actually indicate rather than insisting—contrary to the legal evidence—that the principles of private law must be expressible in moral terms (or in terms that could be taken as moral terms). The likely pathways of judicial thought should be our key concern.[52]

Indeed, if this analysis is correct, we may obtain insights into the proper prioritization among interpretive criteria for private law theories. Little has been said about what should happen when these interpretive criteria are in tension.[53] If, however, the reasons for adopting a moderate morality criterion are that this criterion often tracks the likely psychology and reasoning of judges and other legal actors, we should be cognizant of indications in legal language and legal history that point in a non-moral direction. In such cases, it is less realistic to expect that a moderate morality criterion will assist us in accurately discerning the internal point of view. We would still need to know what to make of these indications in the legal language and legal history—it is always possible, for example, to disregard what courts say they are doing. The transparency criterion may then be decisive. So long as false consciousness, judicial conspiracy, or wide-ranging linguistic drift are unlikely, the transparency criterion will make sense as a guideline; it will give theorists reason to disregard

[52] See Andrew S Gold, *The Right of Redress* (OUP 2020) 18–19.

[53] An exception is Allan Beever, *Rediscovering the Law of Negligence* (2009). Beever contends that there is no prioritization among the four main interpretive criteria (fit, coherence, morality, transparency). See ibid 25.

deviations from what is moral (or from what judges would likely think to be moral).

Where a strict transparency criterion would rule out a given private law theory that tracks moral understandings, we will often have reason to adopt a non-moral theory. Granted, exceptional cases may exist where the transparency criterion should not hold sway. For example, if a theory suggests a private law field is morally monstrous or incoherent to the point of incomprehensibility, the transparency criterion's role could be undermined. In that case, conspiracy theories, false consciousness arguments, or linguistic drift merit consideration (for example, if it is easier to imagine a judicial false consciousness than a morally monstrous belief). Persuasive evidence of judicial terms of art may bear on the linguistic drift hypothesis. When we reach the point of absurdity, there is likewise cause to reconsider our interpretation because such things as false consciousness or linguistic drift may be comparatively more plausible. These extreme instances aside, doctrinal fit, and by extension transparency, should be our primary guidelines if we seek the internal point of view.

With these caveats, we have reason to look for theories that are at least in the ballpark, morally speaking, even if the courts' understanding of what is moral turns out to be mistaken. The transparency criterion should usually take priority over the morality criterion, but even a strict transparency criterion will not always tell us which theory to adopt. In those cases, a moderate morality criterion is not only justifiable; it is a valuable rule of thumb for assessing private law theories. The fact remains that adopting recognizably moral concepts will not always indicate a greater likelihood that an interpretive theory has captured the law's self-understanding.

III. Prescriptive Theories

Turning now to prescriptive theories, there is cause to reconsider the importance of recognizably legal concepts or, for that matter, recognizably moral concepts. If our goal is to match the internal point of view, we should reject accounts that make use of concepts that fail to match the concepts courts actually employ. Suppose that we are instead concerned with reforming the law. It might be that our goal is to change the law by filling interstitial gaps, or by creating new causes of action, or by replacing existing legal doctrines with better ones. Or, it may be that our goal is to crystallize underdetermined legal concepts, not replacing them altogether but modifying them so they are more precise.[54] In each of these contexts, it may still be wise to approximate a set of target concepts, legal, moral, or otherwise.

1. The Recognizably Legal

I will begin with legal concepts. Recall Stephen Smith's suggestion in the interpretive setting that a legal theory need not perfectly match its subject matter. Instead, he contends, one might explain the law 'using concepts that are recognizably "legal" (or at least using concepts that, though more abstract than standard legal concepts, work through recognizably legal concepts in their explanation of particular rules and decisions) even if those concepts are not the same legal concepts that were employed by judges'.[55] Such explanations are 'in the right ball park'.[56] From this perspective, the key question to ask is 'whether the theorist's explanation is of the sort that, once translated into legal concepts, could be accepted by a court, even if no court has yet done so'.[57]

That approach is problematic if one adopts Smith's other arguments concerning the internal point of view (for example, avoidance of conspiracy theories or false consciousness arguments). Yet the 'recognizably legal' category is important not only for interpretive theories but also for prescriptive theories that embrace legal reform. One reason has to do with judicial uptake; a recognizably legal account could have a better chance of being adopted by common-law courts. Yet there is also another reason. Employing recognizably legal concepts allows for legal reforms that more closely fit the structure, or architecture, of existing common-law reasoning. And this conceptual architecture is consequential: even where this architecture is an impediment with respect to a given functional goal, significant deviations from its structure can be costly.

Others have noted the importance of structure when assessing how well an explanatory theory fits the law as it currently is.[58] Yet structure also offers a

[54] Indeed, courts sometimes engage in this practice. On the way that courts crystallize existing legal concepts in deciding cases, see Ori Herstein, 'How Tort Law Empowers' (2015) 65 U Toronto LJ 99, 111. Legal shifts between more and less determinate concepts may of course go in either direction. cf Simon Deakin, 'Juridical ontology: the evolution of legal form' (2015) 40 Historical Social Research 170, 173 (discussing shifts in levels of generality of legal concepts).

[55] See Smith (n 1) 28–29.

[56] ibid 29.

[57] ibid 30.

[58] See, eg, Jules Coleman, *The Practice of Principle: In Defense of a Pragmatist Approach to Legal Theory* (OUP 2001) 21 (indicating that the corrective justice account of tort law 'seeks to show how the structural components of tort law are independently intelligible and mutually coherent in the light of a familiar and widely accepted principle of justice'); Benjamin C Zipursky, 'Civil Recourse, Not Corrective Justice' (2003) 91 Geo LJ 695, 708 ('But even to identify when the law is applied, extended, revised, or

dimension of fit that is relevant even when reforming the law. As Henry Smith and I have argued elsewhere, this dimension can be described as 'architectural fit'.[59] Private law's structural features are usually emphasized by theorists who want to understand the law accurately prior to making any changes, but this structure can also matter for designing such changes. It is possible to be 'in the right ballpark' when revising the law, and in particular, it is possible for a reform to be in the right ballpark because it matches the law's conceptual structure. In short, there are reasons for legal reform to make use of concepts that are recognizably legal.

2. The Recognizably Moral

One might think that for purposes of legal reform, it will only make sense to actually match moral concepts as they exist in extra-legal settings. Why be only sort of moral? Yet, that view is not always going to be right. The law will sometimes have good reason to deviate from an exact replication of a moral requirement as it would exist in the absence of the relevant law, while still getting close to the original moral requirement.[60]

Consider an accommodationist approach like the one developed by Seana Shiffrin.[61] This is an approach that calls for limits on the divergence between the norms of contract law and the norms of promissory morality in contexts where both contract and promise are simultaneously implicated. Moral agents that take seriously the rationale of the law in such cases may experience a real burden, and it is one that the law should avoid imposing. As she has emphasized, however, there are distinctively legal reasons for divergence, as when specific performance would be unduly expensive to administer.[62] I think this is right, but it is not an argument against approximation. In such cases, it could be desirable to aim for the recognizably moral as a next best thing (for example, expectation damages in lieu of specific performance) so that the burden on moral agents caused by a divergence is not overly heavy.

rejected, we need to have some idea of what the law is. This requires identifying what concepts and principles structure tort doctrine.').

[59] See Gold and Smith (n 5).

[60] In doing so, the law may even improve upon what morality would otherwise provide, as can sometimes occur when the law provides greater precision in areas that are indeterminate. For variations on the theme, see Tony Honore, 'The Dependence of Morality on Law' (1993) 13 Oxford J Legal Stud 1; John Gardner, *Torts and Other Wrongs* (OUP 2020) 45–46.

[61] Shiffrin (n 6).

[62] ibid 733.

While it is an empirical question, there may also be compliance-based arguments that support legal concepts that are in the right ballpark. Where legally recognized duties diverge from extra-legal moral understandings, this can decrease compliance with the law's commands.[63] If it turned out that near misses were better in compliance terms than more distant conceptual offerings, this would be a reason to at least aim for the near miss. For example, parties to a contract, or potential tortfeasors, might be more inclined to comply with their legal duties if those duties at least approximate what they understand to be their moral duties. Alternatively, there could be delineation cost and information cost justifications for approximating extra-legal, moral concepts.[64] Where there is an actual match, courts can more readily figure out what those concepts require in a new case, and private parties can more easily understand what the law requires of them. Yet, as Henry Smith has indicated, these benefits may not require a precise match with moral concepts; some divergence could be superior from an information cost perspective.[65]

In each of these cases, there is a reason for being close to the moral understanding despite, by hypothesis, a good cause for not seeking an exact match. Why not an exact match? It will depend on context. An accessible understanding of a duty—one that fits into a recognizable structure of rights, duties, wrongs, and remedies—may be easy to apply, but one that is highly particularized, as some moral duties are, could be difficult for courts to set forth accurately or to enforce reliably. In other cases, there may be institutional constraints of a different kind. A duty to remedy the harms that a tortious wrong caused could be recognizably moral, but perhaps a more precise match for what is morally required would also require an apology. Legally forced apologies, however, would involve concerns with sincerity and, in the United States, with the First Amendment.

Note, however, that the reasoning differs in this setting from our earlier discussion of the recognizably moral as a type of fit criterion. The point is not that a moderate morality criterion will help us better discern what the law is.

[63] See Paul Robinson and John Darley, 'The Utility of Desert' (1997) 91 Nw U L Rev 453 (discussing this possibility in the criminal law setting); Janice Nadler, 'Flouting the Law' (2005) 83 Tex L Rev 1399 (indicating that the perceived legitimacy of a law or legal outcome can influence compliance with unrelated laws). See also Robert Cooter, 'Expressive Law and Economics' (1998) 27 J Legal Stud 585, 596 (suggesting that 'law breeds respect by tracking morality').

[64] See Henry E Smith, 'Modularity and Morality in the Law of Torts' (2011) 4 J Tort L 1.

[65] ibid 30, n 134 ('I do not rule out that for information cost reasons, the message of tort law might diverge from that of the best moral theory, because it is easier to communicate.'). See also Gold and Smith (n 13) 500, n 44 (noting that non-moral concepts 'may be simple, accessible, and generalizable in their own right.').

Rather, the point is that a moderate morality criterion will help us develop prescriptive theories with certain desirable features.

3. The Recognizably Loyal

Once we think in these terms, it is natural to wonder if a concern with being 'in the right ballpark' is limited to the recognizably legal and the recognizably moral. These are the two most prominent contexts, yet they are not the only important examples. There are other settings in which it is important for private law theories to be 'close enough' in their account. One notable setting is the setting of loyalty, the central concern for much of fiduciary law. There is much controversy over the moral status of loyalty; without taking a position on that topic here, I will assume for discussion purposes that loyalty obligations are not moral and that loyalty is not a virtue. Here, too, prescriptive accounts still have reason to be 'close enough'.

Note, first, that several reasons for adopting the recognizably moral could likewise play a role in justifying the recognizably loyal. Where it is hard to completely eliminate a divergence, minimizing the gap between legal and extra-legal conceptions of loyalty may lessen the burdens on fiduciaries confronted by simultaneous legal and extra-legal loyalty obligations. Likewise, a sufficiently close match between legal and extra-legal loyalties, even if imperfect, may have compliance effects. Furthermore, delineation and information costs may be limited if legal and extra-legal loyalties are broadly similar in their salient features.

There is, however, another potential angle: even if loyalty is not moral or virtuous, one might also be concerned with what kinds of loyalty are made available to the loyal agent who follows legal guidelines. One potential reason is if the law's conception of loyalty could gradually bleed into how people think about loyalty generally.[66] A valuable culture of loyal behaviour could be eroded by the wrong legal approach, with negative social effects. Our worry about the law's conception of loyalty may, however, take another form. Even if a valuable culture of loyalty is not degraded by exposure to legal conceptions of loyalty, the opportunities for valuable loyalty of a certain type may be severely curtailed if the law's understanding of loyalty is unlike those

[66] cf Shiffrin (n 6) 741–42 (indicating that the law's depiction of promises could corrode the moral culture of promising).

kinds of loyalty that enrich our lives, or that help to constitute our special relationships.[67]

Note that people who take their loyalties seriously may also take seriously the law's conception of what their loyalties ought to be.[68] Where it exists, the obligation to obey the law may draw on citizens' sense of loyalty;[69] some will believe their loyalties to the state call for following its directives. Admittedly, there is no guarantee this will occur, even for those of us who are very conscientious about loyalty. Loyalties can operate on local and society-wide scales, and under the right circumstances, loyal parties will experience both types.[70] Some will prioritize local loyalties while others prioritize community or society-wide loyalties. Even so, the legal perspective on loyalty will sometimes prevail. This means that, on an individual basis, legal norms of loyalty may supplant whatever norms of loyalty a party would otherwise have experienced within a given fiduciary relationship.

We might not be overly concerned by this possibility if loyalty is not moral or virtuous—in that case, why care if legal conceptions of loyalty prevail? And, indeed, some scholars have questioned whether loyalty obligations are moral obligations, or whether loyalty is a virtue. In recent work, Simon Keller and James Penner have each raised doubts about the moral status of loyalty.[71] Yet, even if loyalty is not moral, virtuous, or intrinsically valuable (I leave that question open), there could still be reasons for seeking out occasions to manifest loyalty. Despite reservations about loyalty's merits in general, Keller does not hesitate to conclude that a person who fails to experience loyalty is someone to feel sorry for.[72] Someone who never experiences loyalty might reasonably hope to have such experiences, and someone who never experiences the kind of loyalty felt by fiduciaries could regret the loss. Moral or not, our loyalties often give substantial added meaning to our lives.

[67] Attempting a match is complicated, given that legal loyalties may provide a framework that supports the evolution of divergent extra-legal loyalties. For discussion of this possibility, see Andrew S Gold, 'The Reasonably Loyal Person', in Harris Psarras and Sandy Steel (eds), *Private Law and Practical Reason: Essays on John Gardner's Private Law Theory* (OUP 2023).

[68] See Gold (n 8) 204 ('Under the standard view of legal obedience, citizens should obey the law because it is the law. This obedience may be understood extra-legally as a matter of loyalty, and it often is.').

[69] cf Ronald Dworkin, *Law's Empire* 206 (HUP 1986)(comparing political association to family and friendship).

[70] See Andrew Oldenquist 'Loyalties' (1982) 79 J Phil 173 (discussing local versus society-wide loyalties).

[71] See Simon Keller, *The Limits of Loyalty* (CUP 2007) (esp ch 7); James E Penner, 'Is Loyalty a Virtue, and Even If It Is, Does It Really Help Explain Fiduciary Liability?' in AS Gold and PB Miller (eds), *Philosophical Foundations of Fiduciary Law* (OUP 2014) 157, 162–63.

[72] See Keller (n 71) 159. Keller also notes the possibility that some specific kinds of loyalty may be valuable even if we do not find loyalty in the abstract to be valuable. See ibid 149. I leave that possibility to one side.

Part of loyalty's contribution to what we find meaningful has to do with the way we prioritize the objects of our loyalty. If existing legal conceptions of loyalty replaced our extra-legal understandings, would that meaningfulness be placed at risk? It is reasonable to think the answer is yes. Indeed, legal conceptions of loyalty that lack the classic features are not hard to conjure up. Suppose fiduciary law were to widely adopt a conception of loyalty as a hypothetical bargain in a world of zero transaction costs.[73] That view is now expressed in some jurisdictions, and an adequate interpretation of fiduciary loyalty needs to take it into account. But a hypothetical bargain in a world of zero transaction costs is bereft of various features ordinarily associated with what is meaningful in loyalty. In part, this is because the content of the hypothetical bargain analysis is so protean. Any particular instance of hypothetical bargain analysis can take one far afield from what loyalty seems to call for in common usage. Yet there is also a deeper concern; across the board, there is no evident prioritization of the person to whom the fiduciary is to be loyal. There is nothing that feels like 'taking the side' of the beneficiary, let alone in a robust fashion.[74]

Someone looking for opportunities to be loyal who takes seriously the commands of a hypothetical bargain analysis will miss out on some of what loyalty offers. As an attorney, a trustee, a corporate director, or a guardian, they will not be expected to take the side of their beneficiary; they will instead be expected to perform whatever obligations happen to follow from a hypothetical bargain analysis in a world of zero transaction costs. Even if adopting this approach to fiduciary loyalty will not have spillover effects within the broader culture of loyalty practices, the sheer number of legal fiduciary relationships that affect our lives and careers means that a sizable portion of loyalty-based relationships could be stripped of part of their loyalty-based value. A prescriptive theory of fiduciary law may thus have reason to aspire to an understanding of fiduciary loyalty that is 'recognizably loyal', whether or not it is a perfect match for our extra-legal loyalties.

[73] I am assuming that such legal accounts of loyalty qualify as conceptions of 'loyalty' in the first place. For the classic statement of the hypothetical bargain approach to fiduciary loyalty, see Frank H Easterbrook and Daniel R Fischel, 'Contract and Fiduciary Duty' (1993) 36 J L & Econ 425. For discussion of how Delaware corporate law has adopted that view, see Andrew S Gold, 'Interpreting Fiduciary Law' in DG Smith and AS Gold (eds), *Research Handbook on Fiduciary Law* 37, 41–42 (Elgar 2018).

[74] I draw on Keller's work for the 'taking the side of' formulation. See Keller (n 71) 21. Granted, a hypothetical bargain could call for the very same actions called for by a more traditional loyalty obligation. But, as John Gardner rightly emphasizes, that would not make these obligations identical. John Gardner, *From Personal Life to Private Law* 43 (OUP 2018).

IV. The Benefits for Private Law Theory

I will return now to the question of transparency. If the arguments above in Section II.1 are correct, there is a significant advantage to adopting a strict transparency criterion when assessing interpretive theories—doing so promotes the goal of figuring out private law's self-understanding. Indeed, adopting such an approach for interpretive purposes matters even if we are looking to change the law. As Benjamin Zipursky has emphasized, functionalists should care about the concepts internal to the law because they allow us to derive the law's present-day content: 'a first step in determining the answer to a legal question is determining how the concepts within the law apply to the question at hand'.[75] In many cases, functionalists will then want to modify the application of the law. But, as Zipursky explains, modifying the law 'will involve a whole range of considerations about precedent, stare decisis, and institutional roles that are simply elided by the functionalist account of what law is'.[76] As long as these considerations are relevant, legal concepts will need to be understood on their own terms.

If reform is our goal, we may likewise want to know if a theory is 'close enough' to whatever the law currently is. The reasons why may vary. We may care whether courts are sufficiently likely to adopt a given theory in light of its similarity to what came before. Something that is recognizably legal may more readily track common-law reasoning, reasoning that judges feel pressure to adopt if they want to persuade others in their cohort.[77] Assuming a threshold level of substantive benefits, there are reasons for selecting theories that are in the right ballpark simply based on the probability that they will be adopted by common-law courts reasoning as such courts typically reason.

There is also the question of whether new legal concepts will mesh well with those pre-existing concepts that are left intact following a private law reform measure. Some concepts may produce incoherence when wedded to other pre-existing legal concepts (for example, legal realist conceptions of duties may fit quite awkwardly with the interconnected structure of rights, duties, wrongs, and remedies that preceded them). Legal concepts also tend to carry over from

[75] See Zipursky (n 12) 476.

[76] ibid 477.

[77] For helpful discussion, see Shivprasad Swaminathan, 'What the Centipede Knows: Polycentricity and 'Theory' for Common Lawyers' (2020) 40 Oxford J Leg Stud 265. If, as Swaminathan suggests, there may be an aesthetic component to common law reasoning, it is an interesting question whether this might also support an elegance criterion for interpretive theories of private law. cf W Bradley Wendel, 'Explanation in Legal Scholarship: The Inferential Structure of Doctrinal Legal Analysis' (2011) 96 Cornell L Rev 1035, 1070–71 (discussing an elegance criterion for explanatory legal theories).

one setting to another, sometimes in unanticipated ways. As Simon Deakin notes, 'concepts are transferable across different contexts'.[78] The notion of a wrong in tort law can thus influence the notion of a wrong in contract law, to give one example. And, as Jeremy Waldron notes, it is important to be able to 'keep track' of the way that changes to a legal concept will influence its application elsewhere in the law.[79] It is easier to assess how new concepts will transfer across settings if we have familiarity with how similar concepts have done so in the past.

To make this discussion more concrete, consider Kantian theories of private law. Such theories face significant challenges matching legal doctrine and concepts (such as defamation law in the United States),[80] and indeed, a good case can be made that they fail under a robust transparency criterion. Kantian theories fare quite well as explanations of certain private law features, yet they arguably employ concepts different from the concepts courts actually employ. Under a strong transparency criterion, let us hypothesize such theories are therefore ruled out. It would still be reasonable to think that Kantian theories are in the right ballpark; indeed, they almost certainly are. If a Kantian approach does not make use of concepts that courts employ, it does at least make use of concepts that courts *could* employ, that is, concepts that are 'recognizably legal'. If courts were to shift in the direction of such an account, they could do so with moderate transition costs, and it is not unrealistic to think that a court would be willing to use a broadly Kantian approach.

A large amount of ink has been devoted to debates on whether Kantian corrective justice theories, non-Kantian corrective justice theories, civil recourse accounts, and similar approaches are the best interpretations of private law. I do not think at this stage of the discussion that such debates are winnable. They do, however, create pressure for theorists to carve up a field's boundaries to make the preferred interpretive position more compelling, for example, by taking the position that US defamation law is not genuinely a part of tort law, or that punitive damages fall outside of tort law's ambit, or that strict liability is something other than a core component of tort law doctrine. That does not

[78] See Deakin (n 54) 180. There is an added complexity if such concepts are multi-functional. See ibid. For an example of how remedial concepts can be multi-functional, see Gold (n 52).

[79] See Jeremy Waldron, '"Transcendental Nonsense" and System in the Law' (2000) 100 Colum L Rev 16, 47. Waldron goes further in arguing for the benefits of a 'neutral matrix' by means of the law's conceptual structure. I am hesitant to endorse that view across the board, as it might require giving up the simple moral norms that provide much of the accessibility and modularity of common-law concepts.

[80] The defamation law challenge is recognized in Arthur Ripstein's work. See Arthur Ripstein, *Private Wrongs* (HUP 2016) 190–91. On the significance of this challenge, see AS Gold, 'Private Rights and Private Wrongs'(2017) 115 Mich L Rev 1071, 1072–73.

mean such theories fail in their aims, but it is worthwhile to consider an alternative path.

These taxonomy questions matter. Still, shifting the ground of debate from the interpretive to the prescriptive encourages a different way of looking at these problems. Rather than seek to show that a given theory that is in the right ballpark provides the best interpretation of tort law, we can turn to the question of whether tort law would be improved by employing the theorist's preferred conceptual apparatus (and we may be encouraged to do so by a stricter transparency criterion for interpretive theories).

From this perspective, note also that some interesting new questions arise. Some pragmatic questions are anticipated by this discussion. For example, will a particular set of legal concepts be close enough to prior conceptual structures so that courts will entertain them as an option for legal reform? Will such concepts transfer well across legal settings? Other questions may concern the nature of the private law system itself. For example, is the private law system a loosely connected system, or is it one that deductively calls for specific outcomes to each case?[81] If it is not entirely deductive, to what degree? And institutional design may also be a consideration. Courts may not always be the best institution to implement a prescriptive theory's recommendations. If courts are not the best choice for reform, would another institution, such as a legislature, be in a good position to adopt a theorist's proposed conceptual structure?

The concern could be not merely whether a private law theory is in the right ballpark conceptually but also how close the concepts it employs are to the concepts that courts actually employ. Being in the right ballpark could be a matter of degree. Is a civil recourse account closer than a Kantian corrective justice account, or is it further away? Is the degree of closeness enough to matter? Closer along what dimension? Indeed, such questions may turn out to have different answers in different subparts of a private law field. Is a civil recourse account closer to the legal point of view when it comes to punitive damages yet further away when it comes to make whole remedies?

We may also recognize multiple contexts where our conceptual analysis could be in the right ballpark. Perhaps we will need to balance conceptual fit at the legal level against conceptual fit at the moral level (or, in the case of loyalty, from within another normative system). Prioritizing an approximation of legal concepts will not always help us in our efforts to match moral concepts;

[81] For discussion of loosely interconnected legal systems (as opposed to tightly interconnected, more fully deductive systems), see Gold and Smith (n 5). See also Henry E Smith, 'System Effects: Emergent Private Law' in AS Gold and others (eds), *The Oxford Handbook of The New Private Law* (OUP 2020) 139.

each effort to approximate may involve different goals that we might pursue in considering legal reform. Indeed, the relation between these distinct priorities may vary. It is possible in some cases that being close enough to legal concepts in one's theory is a good proxy for being close enough to moral concepts. That relation, however, is by no means assured.

Lastly, interesting questions arise concerning the theorist's choice of a legal field to explain or, for that matter, reform. For example, imagine that a certain understanding of fiduciary loyalty is a mediocre fit for the legal concepts currently employed by judges in fiduciary cases but that it is a relatively good fit for the legal concepts judges currently employ in contract and tort law cases (and if you like, that judges employ in private law as a whole). From an interpretive point of view, should we focus on what might provide a closer fit with the concepts in use across private law, or instead on what will provide a closer fit with the concepts in use in fiduciary law? Does it matter if a theory uses concepts that are a very close fit for fiduciary law and just a moderately close fit for private law generally?

I do not know the answers to these questions, many of which are partly empirical. They are suggestive of insights to be gained not only from future work in the New Private Law mould but also from the burgeoning field of Experimental Jurisprudence.[82] Pursuit of such questions should not displace the type of research and theoretical work associated with classically interpretive approaches. Indeed, assessment of when a proposed reform is in the right ballpark is, again, dependent on an accurate determination of what the law currently is; it is dependent on what its present self-understanding amounts to. Understanding the significance of being 'close enough' is, nonetheless, a desirable aim.

V. Conclusion

Private law theorists often seek concepts that are 'recognizably legal' or 'recognizably moral'. They make use of approximations of the concepts courts use, or near misses that may not even be approximations. This chapter suggests that if our goal is to figure out the law's self-understanding, we should seek something

[82] See Kevin Tobia, 'Experimental Jurisprudence' (2022) 89 U Chicago L Rev 735, 791–96 (discussing relevance of experimental jurisprudence for the New Private Law); James MacLeod, 'Ordinary Causation: A Study in Experimental Statutory Interpretation' (2019) 94 Indiana LJ 957 (indicating a role for experimental jurisprudence in understanding tort law concepts); Gold (n 36) (discussing the relevance of being in the right conceptual ballpark, and also of empirical work, for the New Private Law); Paul B Miller, 'The New Formalism in Private Law' (2021) 66 Am J Jurisprudence 175 (discussing features of the New Private Law methodology).

more than recognizably legal concepts; we should aim for the legal concepts that courts actually employ rather than those concepts that they might have employed. Put differently, if the law's self-understanding is our goal, we need a stricter transparency criterion than the moderate version commonly used today.

By contrast, the pursuit of recognizably moral concepts may be a good starting point if our aim is to locate the law's self-understanding. Given likely patterns of judicial psychology, and the language of judicial opinions, it is plausible to think that courts tend toward concepts that they could at least believe are moral. That said, the connection between the recognizably moral and the internal point of view is contingent, and it is not a connection that should be premised on what the law claims. In the ordinary case, it will make sense to prioritize compliance with a strict transparency criterion over compliance with a morality criterion. Where legal history or doctrine suggests it, we should even be open to the possibility that private law is employing concepts that are not recognizably moral.

A range of interpretive theories fail under a strict transparency criterion (a good example is Fuller and Perdue's account of contract remedies). It does not follow that such theories are pointless. Private law theories that are 'close enough' to a set of concepts (legal or moral) may be quite useful as prescriptive theories. Thinking in such terms, moreover, opens up a range of new and important questions for private law theory. What counts as close enough to encourage judicial adoption of a theory? When will a theory's concepts be sufficiently close to pre-existing concepts located elsewhere in the law, such that they mesh well together? What counts as 'in the right ballpark' for compliance purposes? When is a concept close enough to substantially lower information or delineation costs? We should be glad to have theories that adopt recognizably legal and recognizably moral concepts, but we should also understand why.

4
Understanding Private Law

*Felipe Jiménez**

I. Introduction

Theories of private law attempt to understand private law—to render private law intelligible.[1] This is true for descriptive, interpretive, and prescriptive theories.[2] It is true, in other words, whether the theory's concern is giving an accurate description of private law; offering a rational reconstruction of the values served by private law as it exists; or offering an argument for what values ought to underlie and guide private law.

In the case of descriptive theories, one cannot accurately describe the rules and institutions that fall within private law unless one has at least a working theory about the criteria that determine what counts as private law. One can draw the boundaries of the practice in myriad ways, including by merely stipulating what one will understand by 'private law'. But, to my mind, the least arbitrary way to draw the line would involve at least a presupposition about what private law 'is about'. In the case of prescriptive theories, at the other extreme, identifying the problems with an existing regime requires understanding the status quo. This understanding is the starting point for normative theorization—even if that theorization leads us to abandon or change the current practice.[3] Finally, interpretive theories attempt to provide an account that fits and justifies the central features of private law. They attempt to improve our understanding by identifying the values served by that area of law as it exists,[4]

* Associate Professor of Law and Philosophy, University of Southern California; Profesor Adjunto Extraordinario, Universidad Adolfo Ibáñez. Many thanks to Paul Miller, Marcela Prieto, Thilo Kuntz, and participants at the Methodology in Private Law Theory Conference at Bucerius Law School in Hamburg, Germany.

[1] See Ernest J Weinrib, *The Idea of Private Law* (OUP 2012) 1–21.

[2] For a canonical account of these distinctions in contract theory, see Stephen Smith, *Contract Theory* (OUP 2004).

[3] Liam Murphy, 'The Practice of Promise and Contract' in G Klass, P Saprai, and G Letsas (eds), *Philosophical Foundations of Contract Law* (OUP 2014) 151–52.

[4] Smith, *Contract Theory* (n 2) 5.

Felipe Jiménez, *Understanding Private Law* In: *Methodology in Private Law Theory*. Edited by: Thilo Kuntz and Paul B. Miller, Oxford University Press. © Felipe Jiménez 2024. DOI: 10.1093/oso/9780198885306.003.0004

by providing the best possible justification that fits the existing practice.[5] Thus understood, interpretive theories are centrally concerned with understanding private law.

But if most theories of private law are concerned, at least partially, with understanding private law, what does this mean? This question will take us, in Section II, into the philosophy of social practices. Section III then offers a brief reconstruction of *comparative jurisprudence* and an account of why we ought to take it seriously as a methodological model for understanding law. Given the diversity of approaches, questions, and styles within contemporary private law theory, in Section IV, I offer a simplified taxonomy of contemporary accounts in terms of three central types: instrumentalism, formalism, and the New Private Law. With this framework in hand, Section V moves on to the implications of comparative jurisprudence for private law theory.

II. Understanding Social Practices

Law is a social practice. Some social theorists argue that fully understanding social practices requires grasping the complex meanings and attitudes that form part of the practice as experienced by its participants.[6] This might be too strong[7]—sometimes, the best explanation of a social practice might be that those engaged in it are deceived,[8] or might diverge from the reasons the participants take themselves to have.[9] But, even in these situations, it seems reasonable to provisionally start from the perspective of participants. We cannot conclude that a social practice involves deception or alienation without first understanding what it looks like for those engaged in it.[10]

This idea is familiar in legal theory. It is connected, for instance, to Hart's adoption of a 'hermeneutic approach'[11] that incorporates the *internal point of*

[5] Regarding the desiderata of fit and justification, see Ronald Dworkin, *Law's Empire* (Harvard University Press 1986) 65–68.

[6] Peter Winch, *The Idea of a Social Science and Its Relation to Philosophy* (Psychology Press 1990) 108.

[7] Which is why Winch ends up committed to—to my mind—a series of implausible views about the possibility of detached reconstruction of social practices. See Jeff Pojanowski, 'Reevaluating Legal Theory' (2021) 130 Yale LJ 1458, 1477–78.

[8] Alasdair MacIntyre and DR Bell, 'The Idea of a Social Science' (1967) 41 Proceedings of the Aristotelian Society, Supplementary Vols 95, 101.

[9] Notably, the opposite extreme might also be true: it could be that the reasons that participants in private law practice understand themselves to have are, from an external or objective standpoint, true reasons for action. See Jeffrey A Pojanowski and Paul B Miller, 'The Internal Point of View in Private Law' [2022] Am J Jurisprudence 10–11. Notably, Pojanowski and Miller go further and argue that the internal point of view cannot be a non-moralized position.

[10] See Dworkin (n 5) 14; Smith, *Contract Theory* (n 2) 13–14.

[11] HLA Hart, *Essays in Jurisprudence and Philosophy* (OUP 1983) 1, 13–14.

view of legal participants—and particularly their acceptance of legal norms as binding standards of conduct[12]—as necessary for the intelligibility of legal discourse.[13] It is also reflected in Dworkin's work—particularly, in his insistence that understanding law as an argumentative practice requires adopting the point of view of its participants.[14] Thus, even those who disagree about how to best characterize legal practice agree that understanding it involves starting from the commitments, attitudes, and actions of those involved in those practices.[15]

At a more general level, this idea is connected to Max Weber's notion of *Verstehen*, under which explaining social practices requires an interpretive grasp of their meaning.[16] For this purpose, 'thin description' in terms of brute observable data is insufficient. What is needed is a 'thick description' that alludes to thoughts, expectations, and intentions.[17]

Part of the reason for this is that the constituent elements of social practices are already pre-theoretically identified and defined by participants.[18] For example, the judge adjudicating a private law dispute is already acting on the basis of an understanding of private rights, duties, and the more specific concepts (like wrong, causation, breach, etc.) involved in private law reasoning. The theorist, then, must theorize an institution for which at least a partial account already exists in the very conceptual and linguistic practices of those involved in it. This internal understanding is something that the theorist needs to account for. Some would go further and claim that the theorist would need to mirror the internal understanding.[19] I do not think mirroring is required[20]—but we can ignore this for now. The relevant point is that understanding a social practice requires understanding its meaning, which is at

[12] HLA Hart, *The Concept of Law* (Clarendon Press 1994); Scott J Shapiro, 'What Is the Internal Point of View?' (2006) 75 Fordham L Rev 1157, 1159. For a recent account of the internal point of view in private law theory, see Pojanowski and Miller (n 9).

[13] Shapiro (n 12) 1166.

[14] Dworkin (n 5) 13.

[15] Grégoire Webber, 'Asking Why in the Study of Human Affairs' (2015) 60 Am J Jurisprudence 51, 53. In legal interpretation, see Friedrich Karl von Savigny, *System of the Modern Roman Law* (Asylum Press 1867) 171.

[16] Max Weber, *The Theory of Social and Economic Organization* (Free Press 1947) 87–98. See also Clifford Geertz, 'Thick Description: Toward an Interpretive Theory of Culture', *The Interpretation of Cultures* (Basic Books1973) 311.

[17] On the distinction between thin and thick description, see Gilbert Ryle, 'Thinking and Reflecting', *Collected Essays 1929–1968* (2009) 489–90; Gilbert Ryle, 'The Thinking of Thoughts: What Is "Le Penseur" Doing?', *Collected Essays 1929–1968* (2009) 501.

[18] Guy Oakes, 'The Verstehen Thesis and the Foundations of Max Weber's Methodology' (1977) 16 History and Theory 11, 20–21.

[19] ibid 21.

[20] See Felipe Jiménez, 'Two Questions for Private Law Theory' (2021) 12 Jurisprudence 391.

least partly constituted by the actions, commitments, and attitudes of those involved in it.[21]

This line of thought can be carried too far. It can assume a too radical distinction between the social world and the physical world.[22] It can deny the legitimacy of explanations that do not simply replicate or assume the same terms used by those involved in the relevant social practice,[23] but instead, attempt to provide general covering laws with predictive power.[24]

Thus, my claim here is limited: understanding what a social practice is—what the social facts that any theoretical explanation must be able to explain are—should start with understanding what the practice means to those involved in it. Adopting this internal perspective is required to understand what the object—in this case, private law—is.[25]

Merely reporting what the internal practices of the participants are, however, does not amount to a full theory. Private law theory seeks not just to report what private law reasoning looks like from the inside. It also seeks to clarify the point of the practice.[26] Arguably, such a clarification is what *fully* understanding private law entails.[27] But the provisional starting point for this understanding is the perspective of the participants,[28] a 'working out' of the concepts and frameworks embedded in the practice.[29]

Different notions of theorization from an internal point of view have been significant in private law theory.[30] These go from the strong internalism of Weinrib's *The Idea of Private Law*[31] to the weaker versions of Stephen Smith,[32]

[21] Oakes (n 18) 22. See also Brian Bix, 'H.L.A. Hart and the Hermeneutic Turn in Legal Theory' (1999) 52 SMU L Rev 167, 186. For a version of this claim in anthropology, see Geertz (n 16) 314. A similar idea underlies Vico's conception of historical understanding, on Berlin's reconstruction in Isaiah Berlin, 'The Divorce between the Sciences and the Humanities' in Henry Hardy (ed), *Against the Current: Essays in the History of Ideas* (2nd edn, Princeton UP 2013) 133.

[22] For criticism, see Paul A Roth, 'Beyond Understanding: The Career of the Concept of Understanding in the Human Sciences' in S Turner and PA Roth (eds), *The Blackwell Guide to the Philosophy of the Social Sciences* (John Wiley 2003).

[23] See Charles L Barzun, 'Inside-Out: Beyond the Internal/External Distinction in Legal Scholarship' (2015) 101 Va L Rev 1203.

[24] See Carl G Hempel, 'The Function of General Laws in History' (1942) 39 Journal of Philosophy 35.

[25] The concern, then, is understanding the *explanandum* 'private law' rather than providing an explanation with predictive power in the scientific sense. Some critics of Hart's methodological positivism and his use of the internal point of view miss this. See, eg, Stephen R Perry, 'Hart's Methodological Positivism' (1998) 4 Legal Theory 427, 436–37.

[26] Gerald J Postema, 'Jurisprudence as Practical Philosophy' (1998) 4 Legal Theory 329, 332.

[27] On the distinction between mere knowledge and genuine understanding, see Neil Cooper, 'The Epistemology of Understanding' (1995) 38 Inquiry 205; Karsten R Stueber, 'The Ubiquity of Understanding: Dimensions of Understanding in the Social and Natural Sciences' (2019) 49 Philosophy of the Social Sciences 265, 266.

[28] MacIntyre and Bell (n 8) 110.

[29] Ernest J Weinrib, 'Can Law Survive Legal Education?' (2007) 60 Vand L Rev 401, 425.

[30] For an overview, see Pojanowski and Miller (n 9).

[31] Weinrib, *The Idea of Private Law* (n 1).

[32] Smith, *Contract Theory* (n 2).

John Goldberg,[33] and Benjamin Zipursky.[34] I think these versions can generate implausibly strong constraints on private law theory.[35] My argument here is weaker: if we want to understand private law, an important first step in the process of doing so is clarifying its meaning for those involved in it. This is entirely compatible with perspectives that seek an external or functional understanding of the practice—as long as those perspectives do not assume an imperialistic ambition.[36] Understanding private law from an internal perspective is necessary to theorize the object 'private law'—but it is not clear to me why, as many private law theorists sometimes seem to assume, this is also the end story of private law theory.

In order to flesh out what I take this notion of understanding to require from private law theorists, I will move away from private law theory for a while and instead borrow from the methodology of comparative law, and particularly from *comparative jurisprudence*.

III. Comparative Jurisprudence

Towards the end of the twentieth century, many scholars of comparative law argued for a focus on the cognitive structure, cultural traditions, and mentalities underlying legal systems.[37] One important contribution to this development was William Ewald's conception of comparative law as a philosophical undertaking, which he presented under the notion of *comparative jurisprudence*, in two influential articles published in 1995—*Comparative Jurisprudence (I)*[38] and *Comparative Jurisprudence (II)*.[39] Understanding a legal system, for Ewald, requires going beyond the surface level of legal texts, towards the shared understandings and philosophical assumptions that constitute the deep structure of the legal system.[40]

Ewald contrasts comparative jurisprudence to the two dominant strands in comparative law at the time he was writing: *contextualism* and *textualism*.

33 John CP Goldberg, 'Pragmatism and Private Law' (2012) 125 Harvard LR 1640.

34 Benjamin Zipursky, 'Pragmatic Conceptualism' (2000) 6 Legal Theory 457.

35 See Jiménez, 'Two Questions for Private Law Theory' (n 20).

36 My thinking on this point has been influenced by Barzun (n 23).

37 See Mark Van Hoecke and Mark Warrington, 'Legal Cultures, Legal Paradigms and Legal Doctrine: Towards a New Model for Comparative Law' (1998) 47 ICLQ 496.

38 William Ewald, 'Comparative Jurisprudence (I): What Was It like to Try a Rat?' (1995) 143 U Penn L Rev 1889.

39 William Ewald, 'Comparative Jurisprudence (II): The Logic of Legal Transplants' (1995) 43 Am J Comp Law 489.

40 Following Ewald, see Catherine Valcke, 'Comparative Law as Comparative Jurisprudence: The Comparability of Legal Systems' (2004) 52 Am J Comp Law 713; Van Hoecke and Warrington (n 37).

Those two strands, according to Ewald, see law from the outside, ignoring the specific position of the legal operator: the contextualist sees law as a product of social forces, while the textualist sees it purely as a matter of formal rules. According to Ewald, both of these approaches lose sight of the fact that neither economic and social phenomena, nor legal texts, can reveal how legal systems think about legal problems.[41] In order to understand this, one has to grasp the underlying ideas that animate and differentiate legal systems.[42] Understanding law is not a matter of accumulating data, but rather of mastering abilities of reasoning: a matter of *learning how* rather than *learning that*.[43] Law, for Ewald, is not just a heap of rules, but 'a social practice that both reflects and constitutes a community's commitment to governing itself in accordance with certain shared ideals'.[44]

The following sections develop the idea of comparative jurisprudence.

1. Against Naïve Universalism

Law is a culturally embedded practice.[45] Because of this, it is reasonable to expect different legal systems to manifest the same plurality that can be observed across cultures. As a consequence, we should be suspicious of a naïve form of universalism that presupposes that all legal systems are fundamentally alike or based on the same normative foundations just because they are legal systems.

Comparative jurisprudence's rejection of naïve universalism is not at odds with a more nuanced universalism. For instance, comparative jurisprudence is open to the possibility of deep-level similarities in underlying principles despite surface differences.[46] But this can only be the end of the inquiry, not the starting assumption. The method of inquiry has to be, according to comparative jurisprudence, one that tries to understand the philosophical and cultural outlook that underlies the surface level of legal systems, the processes of reasoning by jurists over time in each specific legal culture that ultimately lead

[41] William Ewald, 'The Jurisprudential Approach to Comparative Law: A Field Guide to "Rats"' (1998) 46 Am J Comp Law 701, 703–04.

[42] Valcke, 'Comparative Law as Comparative Jurisprudence' (n 40) 717.

[43] Ewald, 'Comparative Jurisprudence (I)' (n 38) 1896.

[44] Catherine Valcke, *Comparing Law: Comparative Law as Reconstruction of Collective Commitments* (CUP 2018) 10.

[45] Van Hoecke and Warrington (n 37) 498.

[46] James Gordley, *Foundations of Private Law* (OUP 2007) 32–42; James Gordley, 'The Universalist Heritage' in P Legrand and R Munday (eds), *Comparative Legal Studies: Traditions and Transitions* (CUP 2011); Konrad Zweigert and Hein Kötz, *An Introduction to Comparative Law* (3rd edn, Clarendon Press 1998) 37. In the case of contract law, see Felipe Jiménez, 'Against Parochialism in Contract Theory: A Response to Brian Bix' (2019) 32 Ratio Juris 233.

to specific legal rules.[47] Whether these philosophical and cultural commitments are constant across different jurisdictions is a contingent question.

This requires focusing on the jurisprudential commitments of the participants in specific legal systems.[48] In this aspect, comparative jurisprudence echoes Charles Taylor's critique of cross-societal comparisons that ignore the specificity of meanings in the practices of different societies.[49] Law is a social practice embedded within specific patterns of social activity, in specific political communities, with specific traditions and histories. Grasping law requires taking those patterns and traditions seriously and letting them, in their specificity, guide inquiry.

2. Beneath the Surface of Legal Systems

One potential response to this cautious attitude towards universalist claims would be that such an attitude would make sense in a world of widespread divergence across legal systems. However, if legal systems tend towards convergence in rules and institutions—at least at a broad level—then perhaps starting from a universalistic assumption makes sense.

It is an open and complex question to what degree the legal rules and institutions of different legal systems converge or tend towards convergence.[50] Independently of that question, comparative jurisprudence argues that understanding a legal system is a matter of understanding the conscious ideas at work in it: the 'principles, concepts, beliefs, and reasoning that underlie... legal rules and institutions.'[51] Convergence at the level of rules is not sufficient to ground the conclusion that entire legal systems converge.[52]

The reason for this is that a legal system is a complex web of historical, cultural, and intellectual traditions.[53] Even the conclusion that a certain legal system has a certain rule is mediated by these historical and intellectual

[47] Ewald, 'Comparative Jurisprudence (I)' (n 38) 1949.

[48] ibid 1958–59.

[49] Charles Taylor, 'Interpretation and the Sciences of Man' (1971) 25 The Review of Metaphysics 3, 34.

[50] Pierre Legrand, 'European Legal Systems Are Not Converging' (1996) 45 ICLQ 52; John Henry Merryman, 'On the Convergence (and Divergence) of the Civil Law and the Common Law' (1981) 17 Stan J Int L 357.

[51] Ewald, 'The Jurisprudential Approach to Comparative Law' (n 41) 705. See also John Bell, 'English Law and French Law—Not so Different?' (1995) 48 Current Legal Problems 63, 69–70.

[52] Incidentally, the opposite is true too: the fact that surface-level rules diverge does not entail that the legal systems as such diverge.

[53] Pierre Legrand, 'How to Compare Now' (1996) 16 Legal Studies 232, 236. See also Felipe Jiménez, 'Legal Principles, Law, and Tradition' (2022) 33 YJLH 59; Martin Krygier, 'Law as Tradition' (1986) 5 Law and Philosophy 237.

practices. A legal rule is, thus, much more than a canonical set of inscribed words.[54] As Ewald explains, a rule is an accretion of cultural elements, a single part of a complex world of meanings.[55]

We cannot understand a legal system without understanding these underlying substantive norms and habits that legal participants adopt as their own.[56] Legal practitioners, scholars, and judges are subject to the history of legal institutions and practices.[57] Legal concepts are historical artifacts,[58] and legal rules are a product of the law's institutional tradition. A grasp of legal rules is, thus, just the beginning of the process of understanding a legal system.

For comparative jurisprudence, then, the law is not just a set of posited rules with formal authority but also a set of discursive practices, normative commitments, and convergent attitudes. Consider the treatment of certain acts of Parliament in the United Kingdom as 'constitutional'. As John Gardner argued, the constitutional effect of those acts is not determined by their enactment but rather by how they are treated by legal officials, and particularly courts.[59] Gardner thought this was peculiar to the UK's constitutional regime—although he was somewhat tempted by the view that this could be true even of written constitutions.[60] He still noted that, while at the moment of enactment a written constitution might be wholly written, as soon as it needs to be applied it begins to be filled out by lawyers and judges. As time passes, more and more of the constitutional law will depend on more than its text.[61]

This is precisely what the familiar distinction between interpretation and construction captures.[62] There is always a potential gap between the communicative content of a legal enactment and the legal content for which it will stand once applied by courts and other legal officials. This gap between communicative and legal content depends, at least in part, on the underlying phenomena comparative jurisprudence recommends focusing on: the legal culture's underlying commitments, attitudes, and values.

[54] Pierre Legrand, 'The Impossibility of Legal Transplants' (1997) 4 MJECL 111, 115.

[55] ibid 116.

[56] Krygier (n 53) 244. See also EP Thompson, *Whigs and Hunters: The Origin of the Black Act* (Allen Lane 1975) 263.

[57] Hans Georg Gadamer, *Truth and Method* (Crossroad 1989) 280. See also Donald R Kelley, *The Human Measure: Social Thought in the Western Legal Tradition* (Harvard UP 1990) 6.

[58] Niklas Luhmann, *Law as a Social System* (F Kastner and R Nobles eds, Klaus Ziegert tr, OUP 2004) 340.

[59] John Gardner, 'Can There Be a Written Constitution?' in L Green and B Leiter (eds), *Oxford Studies in Philosophy of Law: Volume 1* (OUP 2011) 165.

[60] ibid 169–70.

[61] ibid 189.

[62] See Lawrence B Solum, 'The Interpretation-Construction Distinction' (2010) 27 Constitutional Commentary 95; Peter M Tiersma, 'The Ambiguity of Interpretation: Distinguishing Interpretation from Construction' (1995) 73 Washington U L Rev 1095.

I am thinking, for instance, about commitments and attitudes regarding: (i) the relative prevalence or relevance of formal reasoning as compared to substantive reasoning;[63] (ii) the significance of more formal and even deductive practices of reasoning versus the use of imaginative techniques;[64] (iii) the openness to arguments from comparative law;[65] (iv) the relative receptivity to arguments from other disciplines, such as economics;[66] (v) the willingness to consider academic legal scholarship as a legitimate source for judicial decisions;[67] (vi) the role of law in fostering and allowing for political and social change; (vii) the significance and management of the problems generated by legal norms' over- and under-inclusiveness (for instance, by resorting to equity); etc.

3. An Internal Point of View

Comparative jurisprudence, thus, sees law as a complex social practice. And, as we have seen, understanding social practices requires starting from their internal dimension. In the case of law, from the inside, legal practice is an intellectual phenomenon: a set of conceptual activities[68] and cognitive practices through which legal operators interpret and organize the social world.[69] Law is thus not a set of rules but a world of meaning;[70] legal relations not just the upshot of rules but the expression of a cognitive structure.[71]

The methodology of comparative jurisprudence can be used for studying multiple legal issues, such as the concept contract,[72] legal reasoning,[73] and

[63] See PS Atiyah and Robert S Summers, *Form and Substance in Anglo-American Law: A Comparative Study of Legal Reasoning, Legal Theory, and Legal Institutions* (Clarendon Press 1991).

[64] On imagination in the common law tradition, Maksymilian Del Mar, 'Exemplarity and Narrativity in the Common Law Tradition' (2013) 25 Law and Literature 390, 392.

[65] Jeremy Waldron, 'Foreign Law and the Modern Ius Gentium' (2005) 119 Harvard LR 129.

[66] Kristoffel Grechenig and Martin Gelter, 'The Transatlantic Divergence in Legal Thought: American Law and Economics vs. German Doctrinalism' (2008) 31 Hastings Int and Comp L Rev 295; Ronald J Scalise Jr, 'Why No Efficient Breach in the Civil Law: A Comparative Assessment of the Doctrine of Efficient Breach of Contract' (2007) 55 Am J Comp Law 721.

[67] Neil Duxbury, *Jurists and Judges: An Essay on Influence* (Hart Publishing 2001); Nils Jansen, *The Making of Legal Authority: Non-Legislative Codifications in Historical and Comparative Perspective* (OUP 2010); Frederick Schauer, 'The Authority of Legal Scholarship' (1991) 139 U Penn L Rev 1003; Fábio P Shecaira, 'Legal Arguments from Scholarly Authority' (2017) 30 Ratio Juris 305.

[68] Ewald, 'The Jurisprudential Approach to Comparative Law' (n 41) 704.

[69] Ewald, 'Comparative Jurisprudence (I)' (n 38) 1940.

[70] See Robert M Cover, 'The Supreme Court, 1982 Term - Foreword: Nomos and Narrative' (1983) 97 Harvard LR 4.

[71] See, at a more general level, Winch (n 6) 23.

[72] Catherine Valcke, 'Convergence and Divergence of the English, French, and German Conceptions of Contract' (2008) 16 ERPL 29; Catherine Valcke, 'Contractual Interpretation at Common Law and Civil Law: An Exercise in Comparative Legal Rhetoric' in R Bronaugh, JW Neyers and SGA Pitel (eds), *Exploring Contract Law* (Hart Publishing 2009).

[73] Atiyah and Summers (n 63).

statutory,[74] and contract interpretation.[75] In each of these domains, understanding the relevant issue requires understanding what it looks like for those engaged in the practice—what a French judge would think about contracts and the conditions for their enforcement, how a German lawyer would characterize legal reasoning, and how a Supreme Court justice in the United States would define the task of statutory interpretation. Understanding legal reasoning and legal practice is, in this regard, just like understanding Balinese cockfights: we cannot understand either without understanding the cultural web of meanings that make sense for those who take part in the relevant practices.[76]

This means those engaging in comparative jurisprudence need a certain cultural familiarity with the legal practice they are theorizing. This does not mean that we can only engage in comparative jurisprudential analysis of our own legal systems. It does suggest, however, that we should be careful and appropriately humble about the scope of application of our theoretical views and attempt to engage other legal systems with an awareness that knowledge of their surface rules is insufficient for understanding them as legal systems.

3. The Truth in Comparative Jurisprudence

There is still a question looming here. I have given a basic and skeletal account of the claims of comparative jurisprudence. But if the question about the relationship between this approach and private law theory is to have substantive relevance, then comparative jurisprudence ought to be true or at least plausible.

Here, I cannot do justice to the debates regarding the methodology of comparative law. But I believe comparative jurisprudence—whatever its merits or demerits as a methodological approach in comparative research—captures a series of critical substantive truths about the nature of domestic legal systems. Those truths are:

(i) The content of the law in any jurisdiction depends on more than its surface rules and doctrines;

[74] Neil MacCormick and Robert Summers, *Interpreting Statutes: A Comparative Study* (Routledge 2016).
[75] Mark Van Hoecke, 'Deep Level Comparative Law' in Mark Van Hoecke (ed), *Epistemology and Methodology of Comparative Law* (Bloomsbury Publishing 2004).
[76] See Clifford Geertz, 'Deep Play: Notes on the Balinese Cockfight' (2005) 134 Daedalus 56.

(ii) Understanding the law of a jurisdiction requires a deep understanding of the values, commitments, and shared frameworks of legal agents; and
(iii) This deep understanding can only be achieved if one starts from an internal perspective.

Regarding (i), one does not have to look too far to see its plausibility. Independently of its jurisprudential implications, Dworkin's early critique of Hart's legal positivism[77] captured something important: legal reasoning does not exclusively rely on posited rules with a canonical formulation. Instead, legal reasoning is characterized by constant references to norms (which he called *principles*) without canonical formulation or a clear enactment.[78] Moreover, legal reasoning is something that has to be learned: being a lawyer is not so much a matter of knowing certain rules but rather of knowing how to 'think like a lawyer'.[79] Instead of (just) accumulating knowledge about rules and doctrines, law students become lawyers by learning how to reason in certain distinctive ways, how to adopt certain commitments internal to the practice of law, etc.

Precisely because of this reason, (ii) is true: if one wants to understand the law of a certain jurisdiction, one has to understand the values, commitments, and shared intellectual practices of legal agents. Law is a way of making sense of the social world, of institutionally labelling and conceptualizing certain facts and behaviours, etc.

Because of this, empirical knowledge about behavioural regularities and an understanding of the causal mechanisms that lead to certain outcomes are different from understanding law. As point (iii) posits, understanding law requires starting from an internal perspective.

The upshot of this is that the central questions one should ask about a legal culture or a specific area of legal culture go well beyond legal texts. The central questions of comparative jurisprudence are concerned with the values of lawyers and judges, their implicit commitments, the intellectual styles and forms of reasoning they value and adopt, etc. In this aspect, comparative jurisprudence is committed to a picture of law as more than a set of rules, a mechanism for governance, or a coercive apparatus that claims authority. It sees law as an intellectual and cultural phenomenon.

[77] Ronald Dworkin, *Taking Rights Seriously* (Harvard University Press 1978).
[78] ibid 1.
[79] Frederick Schauer, *Thinking Like a Lawyer* (Harvard University Press 2009) 1–2. *But* see Larry Alexander and Emily Sherwin, *Demystifying Legal Reasoning* (CUP 2008).

IV. Three Views of Private Law Theory

What are the implications for private law theory? For this purpose, let me distinguish—somewhat simplistically—between three approaches towards private law theory: instrumentalism, formalism, and the 'New Private Law'. As is the case for any simplified categorization, there is much that this distinction distorts. However, I think these three ideal types characterize three distinct types of contemporary views about private law theory.

1. Instrumentalism

Instrumentalist views see private law as a means for achieving public goals that we can identify independently of private law institutions. For an instrumentalist theory, private law is just a tool that we can use to maximize the achievement of collective goals. The best account of private law as a social practice, for these views, lies in society-wide consequences[80] such as the maximization of overall welfare.[81]

An instrumentalist theory of contract law, for instance, understands it as an institutional device that produces good overall social consequences (such as the maximization of social welfare).[82] The view rejects the claim that contract law is best understood from the perspective of the rights and obligations of the contractual parties, and instead sees the point of contract law in overall social consequences.[83] A conspicuous example of such a view, at least in the United States, is the economic analysis of contract law. Importantly, though, instrumentalists might also be committed to other end goals beyond welfare (understood in the sense of contemporary economics).[84] For instance, one could see the law of contracts as an institution that maximizes the existence of valuable choices for individuals to pursue their goals and life projects.[85]

Instrumentalism can refer to different levels of private law: it can refer to an entire institution and specific rules.[86] It can also refer to specific behaviours. Instrumentalist theories—and particularly, economic theories—have

[80] Murphy (n 3) 154.
[81] Louis Kaplow and Steven Shavell, *Fairness versus Welfare* (Harvard UP 2006).
[82] In this characterization, I follow Murphy (n 3) 153.
[83] ibid 154.
[84] ibid 162.
[85] See Hanoch Dagan and Michael Heller, *The Choice Theory of Contracts* (CUP 2017).
[86] See Lewis Kornhauser, 'Three Roles for a Theory of Behavior in a Theory of Law' (2000) 31 Rechtstheorie 197.

been subject to the criticism that they are not able to transparently account for the practice of private law reasoning.[87] I have addressed these critiques in my previous work by referring to the distinctions between types of instrumentalism, and I will not be concerned with them here.[88] The only point to bear in mind here is that nuanced and moderate versions of instrumentalism are perfectly capable of fitting and transparently explaining the internal practice of private law reasoning. But, admittedly, the most influential instrumentalist claims in the American literature—developed by the first wave of law and economics scholars, such as Posner and Calabresi—are not much like this type of moderate or nuanced view. Instead, the most influential instrumentalist claims have been characterized precisely by their readiness to replace or at least reduce private law reasoning to questions about efficiency, costs, benefits, and incentives.[89]

2. Formalism

Formalist theories are the polar opposite of instrumentalism. They attempt to disclose a specifically legal or juristic perspective towards private law institutions.[90] For formalists, the point of legal theory is to unearth the justificatory structures internal to, and implicit in, legal thought.[91]

Formalist accounts, thus, claim that the theorization of private law does not turn on the identification of the valuable social effects it produces but on the norms and practices internal to private law. Private law, on this view, is—as the conceptual and inferential practices of lawyers and judges suggest—concerned with interactions between private parties and their juridical upshots.[92] For formalist theories, the key to understanding contract law, for instance, is to elucidate the abstract conceptual structure immanent in the materials of contract doctrine.[93]

[87] See, eg, Smith, *Contract Theory* (n 2) 151; Zipursky (n 34) 459.

[88] See Jiménez, 'Two Questions for Private Law Theory' (n 20).

[89] Weinrib, 'Can Law Survive Legal Education?' (n 29) 410.

[90] See Peter Benson, 'The Idea of a Public Basis of Justification for Contract' (1995) 33 Osgoode Hall LJ 273, 306.

[91] See Ernest J Weinrib, 'Legal Formalism: On the Immanent Rationality of Law' (1988) 97 Yale LJ 949; Weinrib, *The Idea of Private Law* (n 1).

[92] Allan Beever, *Forgotten Justice: Forms of Justice in the History of Legal and Political Theory* (OUP 2013) 158.

[93] For a recent example, see Peter Benson, *Justice in Transactions: A Theory of Contract Law* (Harvard UP 2019).

One clear advantage of formalist views like these is that they fit with multiple aspects of the discursive practices of private lawyers and judges, who routinely talk about rights, wrongs, and their normative consequences.[94] This is an important difference with regards to instrumentalist views, which are almost necessarily, given their aggregative and *ex ante* perspective, less consistent with the individualized, *ex post* features of private law adjudication.[95] On the contrary, formalists focus on the correlative structure of the bilateral private law relationship.[96]

Thus, private law formalists tend to take private law reasoning quite seriously. However, the formalist view is not entirely practice-driven. Even though formalists like Benson, Ripstein, and Weinrib start from legal materials, they do not see the systematic reconstruction of legal materials as the end point of their theories. Instead, in each case, the account of private law institutions leads to, or is cabined within (depending on where it starts), a comprehensive philosophical theory about the normative structure of private law. The end product of the theorization is not a contingent reconstruction of the legal institutions that we happen to have, but rather an explanation about why those legal institutions are authoritative determinations that are intelligible without, and can serve to evaluate, legal institutions.[97] While the idea of corrective justice, for instance, is partly indeterminate, and legal institutions can accordingly vary across time and space, it is still *the* idea that must be instantiated in private law institutions.[98]

Because of this, we should not understand formalism as equivalent to the traditional work of doctrinal reconstruction.[99] Doctrinal reconstruction starts from legal materials from which general principles are derived—but it is consistent with the view that the posited legal materials always have the last word. Formalism also takes law seriously—but because it sees law as the instantiation of an abstract notion of right or reason.[100]

[94] See Jiménez, 'Two Questions for Private Law Theory' (n 20) 408.

[95] On these differences, see Jody Kraus, 'Philosophy of Contract Law' in JL Coleman, KE Himma, and SJ Shapiro (eds), *The Oxford Handbook of Jurisprudence and Philosophy of Law* (OUP 2004).

[96] Ernest J Weinrib, 'Private Law and Public Right' (2011) 61 U Toronto LJ 191, 192. See also Benson (n 93) 8, 21.

[97] See, eg, Arthur Ripstein, *Force and Freedom: Kant's Legal and Political Philosophy* (Harvard UP 2009) 86; Weinrib, *The Idea of Private Law* (n 1) 225–26.

[98] Weinrib, *The Idea of Private Law* (n 1) 222–29.

[99] This paragraph expresses an idea I developed in Felipe Jiménez, 'Contracts, Markets, and Justice' (2021) 71 U Toronto LJ 144, 152–54.

[100] Dan Priel, 'Two Forms of Formalism' in A Robertson and J Goudkamp (eds), *Form and Substance in the Law of Obligations* (Hart 2019) 168.

3. The New Private Law

Is there a middle ground between the instrumentalist and the formalist? For some time, in North American private law theory, the answer seemed to be negative. However, recently, many private law theorists—including Paul Miller, Benjamin Zipursky, John Goldberg, and Andrew Gold—have adopted a more intermediate view (following their own usage, I will use the 'New Private Law').

According to the New Private Law, we should take the structure of private law seriously. However, this is compatible with asking functional questions about legal doctrines and concepts.[101] As Goldberg explains, the approach is thus pragmatic while embracing the conceptual complexity of private law and its theorization.[102] Under this type of view, private law theory must appreciate the 'nuances in the conceptual structure of the law'.[103] Because the New Private Law takes law seriously, it also takes legal doctrine as a legitimate starting point for analysis and a structure that deserves serious explication.[104] But legal doctrine, in this picture, is the beginning of the inquiry—an inquiry that can easily lead to more instrumentalist and functionalist analyses.

One central feature of the New Private Law is that it is relatively consistent with what Kevin Tobia has dubbed 'the folk law thesis': the idea that ordinary concepts are at the basis of many important legal concepts.[105] As Goldberg argues, for the New Private Law there is commonly at least a 'family resemblance' between legal and ordinary concepts.[106]

Paul Miller has characterized the New Private Law as a new and distinctive type of formalism in private law, according to which private law provides practically reasonable normative guidance to its addressees.[107] From this perspective, the New Private Law argues that understanding private law requires understanding its attempt to provide normative guidance.[108] As such, as Andrew Gold explains, the New Private Law is committed to adopting an internal point of view.[109] Importantly, the New Private Law sees private law

[101] Andrew S Gold, 'Internal and External Perspectives: On Methodology in the New Private Law' in AS Gold and others (eds), *The Oxford Handbook of the New Private Law* (OUP 2020) 4; Henry E Smith, 'Intellectual Property and the New Private Law' (2017) 30 Harvard JOLT 1, 6.

[102] Goldberg (n 33) 1650.

[103] ibid 1652.

[104] ibid 1655.

[105] Kevin Tobia, 'Law and the Cognitive Science of Ordinary Concepts' in B Brozek, J Hage, and N Vincent (eds), *Law and Mind: A Survey of Law and the Cognitive Sciences* (CUP 2021).

[106] Goldberg (n 33) 1656.

[107] Paul B Miller, 'The New Formalism in Private Law' (2021) 66 Am J Jurisprudence 175, 178.

[108] ibid 198.

[109] Gold (n 101) 3–4.

as a mutable, ongoing practice, which is historically contingent and changes as a consequence of human activity.[110] However, and precisely because private law practices embody traditions that extend over time, the New Private Law starts from a default assumption that, while there might be pockets of practical unreasonableness in private law, it would be surprising if it were pervasively deficient.[111]

V. Private Law Theory as Comparative Jurisprudence

So far, I have offered a brief account of what understanding private law as a social practice requires (Section I); an overview of comparative jurisprudence, its central commitments, and its plausibility as a methodology for understanding private law (Section III); and a brief outline of contemporary North American private law theory (Section IV). With these ingredients, we can move on to discuss how comparative jurisprudence bears on private law theory.

1. Private Law as a Cultural Phenomenon

An instrumentalist view of private law need not be thoroughgoing in its instrumentalism. For instance, in other work I have argued that an instrumentalist view about contract law's foundations is compatible with a formalist approach towards the adjudication of contractual disputes.[112] Earlier, Henry Smith had argued that the formal conceptual structure of property is compatible with—and contributes to—property law's instrumental efficacy.[113] And Liam Murphy has similarly argued for the significance of a public culture that takes the duties of contract law seriously, within an instrumentalist framework.[114]

To the extent that instrumentalism adopts this more nuanced, two- or multi-level structure that makes space for the distinctive character of private law reasoning, it looks a lot like the New Private Law, and particularly like the forms of New Private Law that incorporate functionalist elements.[115]

However, this type of instrumentalism is the exception rather than the rule, at least in American legal culture, where the most influential form of

[110] Miller (n 107) 216.
[111] ibid 219.
[112] Felipe Jiménez, 'A Formalist Theory of Contract Law Adjudication' (2020) 2020 Utah L Rev 1121.
[113] Henry E Smith, 'On the Economy of Concepts in Property' (2012) 160 U Penn L Rev 2097.
[114] Murphy (n 3).
[115] Similarly, Gold (n 101) 4–5.

instrumentalism is the instrumentalism of law and economics: a thorough instrumentalist view about foundations, legal concepts, and duties. I will focus on this thoroughgoing instrumentalist view—although I am aware of, and, in fact, would agree with, more nuanced versions of instrumentalism. I do so both because of its influence, particularly in American legal theory, and because its pitfalls are instructive of the direction in which theorization about private law should go if, as I have argued, comparative jurisprudence captures an important set of truths about law.

The thoroughgoing instrumentalism that I have in mind is well captured by Kaplow and Shavell's normative argument in *Fairness versus Welfare*.[116] According to that argument, social decisions—including all the institutional decisions adopted within private law regimes—should be based exclusively on maximizing individuals' welfare, while ignoring notions of fairness, justice, and rights.[117] If one takes this view seriously, the obvious implication for private law adjudication is that judges should try to maximize social welfare—that is, that they should be what Posner would characterize as a pragmatist judge.[118] Unsurprisingly, an important part of the project of law and economics has been to offer an interpretive theory of the central areas of the common law in terms of efficiency, wealth maximization, and so on.[119]

However, most judges do not seem to act as pragmatists—they use the deontic language of private law as carrying genuine normative implications. Faced with this fact, the instrumentalist appears to need to claim that the actual reasons underlying the practice are hidden from sight in the everyday practice of private law. The critiques to this view are by now familiar.[120] In synthesis, according to the critics, this type of thoroughgoing instrumentalism fails to take law seriously and treats private law reasoning as a duplicitous or alienated form of practical reasoning.[121]

I have some doubts about the ultimate force of this objection.[122] Here, however, I want to focus on specific problems of thoroughgoing instrumentalism that comparative jurisprudence is particularly well-suited to illuminate its tendency to ignore legal culture and its universalist perspective towards the value of private law institutions.

[116] Kaplow and Shavell (n 81).
[117] ibid xvii, 3.
[118] See Richard Posner, 'Pragmatic Adjudication' in M Dickstein (ed), *The Revival of Pragmatism: New Essays on Social Thought, Law, and Culture* (Duke UP 1998).
[119] See, eg, Richard Posner, *Economic Analysis of Law* (Aspen Publishers 2011).
[120] See Zipursky (n 34). But see Jody Kraus, 'Transparency and Determinacy in Common Law Adjudication: A Philosophical Defense of Explanatory Economic Analysis' (2007) 93 Va L Rev 287.
[121] Smith, *Contract Theory* (n 2) 132–36.
[122] Jiménez, 'Two Questions for Private Law Theory' (n 20).

Human beings are 'animals suspended in webs of significance', which we have spun ourselves and which constitute our culture.[123] Legal systems are, in this sense, cultural artifacts: they are structures of meaning that organize social life.[124] Variations across legal systems, from this perspective, are not just variations in rules but also in the structures of meaning that different legal systems constitute and are part of. When a French judge makes a legal decision or announces an interpretation of a legal rule, they are also acting as French lawyers, doing things that only make sense within the mentality of the French legal culture, etc.[125] Understanding this interpretation requires situating it against the backdrop of, and within, a specific historical and cultural practice.[126]

If that is the case, the thoroughgoing instrumentalist faces a problem. They must treat as epiphenomenal[127] something that, if comparative jurisprudence is right, is quite central to what private law is. The problem is not—or not just—that a too blunt economic characterization of behaviour might end up ignoring its legal meaning.[128] The deeper problem is that, in its quest for a single external goal that can fully explain and justify the intricacies of legal doctrine, the thoroughgoing instrumentalist must ignore otherwise important factors about the meanings and expectations that characterize legal reasoning from the inside. The issue is not so much the instrumentalist's justification or interpretation of the goals of legal practice but their deliberately superficial understanding of the legal practice itself.

This is not to deny that instrumentalist explanations of areas of private law can convey something important about it. On the contrary, my view is that instrumentalism expresses significant truths about the functions played by private law and about its value for democratic and pluralistic societies. In fact, they might be adequate theories to justify private law—to connect the internal understanding of private law I have alluded to with the values and concerns of those not directly involved in the practice.[129] The issue is that these truths that instrumentalism conveys can only coexist with the cultural distinctiveness of different private law regimes if it refuses to be thoroughgoing—if it makes

[123] Geertz (n 16) 5.

[124] Gunter Bierbrauer, 'Toward an Understanding of Legal Culture: Variations in Individualism and Collectivism between Kurds, Lebanese, and Germans Cultural Differences and Legal Consciousness' (1994) 28 Law & Society Rev 243, 243.

[125] Legrand, 'The Impossibility of Legal Transplants' (n 54) 115.

[126] ibid 116. See also Van Hoecke and Warrington (n 37) 498.

[127] Nathan B Oman, 'Private Law and Local Custom' in Andrew S Gold and others (eds), *The Oxford Handbook of the New Private Law* (OUP 2020) 160–161.

[128] See, eg, Dan M Kahan, 'Social Meaning and the Economic Analysis of Crime' (1998) 27 J Legal Studies 609.

[129] See Felipe Jiménez, 'Justifying Private Law' in P Miller and J Oberdiek (eds), *Oxford Studies in Private Law Theory* 2 (forthcoming, 2023).

space, in other words, for the meaning that private law reasoning has for those involved in the practice. The reason for this is that one cannot fully understand the object 'private law' without understanding this internal dimension. For instance, the claim that tort law is best understood as an instrument for optimizing the reduction of accident and accident-avoidance costs[130] seems to capture something important about the law of torts. But this perspective can only fully understand tort law if it makes space for the actual conceptual and inferential practices of tort lawyers and judges.

If, instead, the instrumentalist refuses to limit the scope and ambitions of their theory, if—to continue with the example—the claim that the law of torts is an instrument for reducing the total costs of accidents is understood as a claim not just about the institution, but also about the meaning of its specific doctrines and concepts—such as duty, wrong, and causation—then instrumentalism must erase the distinctiveness of the internal culture of (in this case) American tort law. At this point, the thoroughgoing instrumentalist might want to bite the bullet. They might want to argue that the cultural aspect of private law is something that we are better off ignoring. I think this is a mistaken path. As comparative jurisprudence suggests, ignoring the cultural practices and understandings that underlie legal rules and institutions leads to misunderstanding those rules and institutions. It is unlikely that the instrumentalist will be able to provide an adequate account of the object if it refuses to take the object—and its internal dimension—seriously.

There is yet another issue with instrumentalist views—an issue that is particularly significant for thoroughgoing instrumentalists but that even the more limited versions of instrumentalism can face. That issue is a naïve form of universalism that tends to see every instantiation of a legal institution in different jurisdictions as explained by, justified by reference to, or evaluated by, the same value or set of values.[131] There is, again, a modest version of universalism, according to which—given the history and actual evolution of legal institutions—an approach that transcends parochial legal systems to theorize areas of law might be contingently justified.[132] But the instrumentalist is typically not *modestly* universalist. They tend to see all practices of private law everywhere as explainable and measurable by the same criterion—efficiency, wealth maximization, or some such.

130 Guido Calabresi, *The Cost of Accidents: A Legal and Economic Analysis* (Yale UP 2008).

131 See Brian Bix, 'The Promise and Problems of Universal, General Theories of Contract Law' (2017) 30 Ratio Juris 391, 392.

132 As I argue in Jiménez, 'Against Parochialism in Contract Theory: A Response to Brian Bix' (n 46).

This might seem too quick. After all, couldn't the instrumentalist argue that an instrumentalist theory is just a plausible theory of *our* private law or some specific private law regime? I think this alternative is actually open to the instrumentalist. But it is one that most instrumentalists have not been particularly keen on adopting. The reason is, again, that most instrumentalists tend to treat doctrinal language, conceptual practices, and legal culture—precisely what distinguishes one national practice of private law from another—as data of second-order relevance. The real explanatory work is done by the underlying instrumental goals. From this perspective, the linguistic and conceptual divergences between legal practices do not matter much for theorizing private law. What matters is the underlying goal. That goal must be the same because, after all, where would any differences between the goals pursued by different practices be if we deliberately treat the differences in legal discourse as epiphenomenal or of secondary importance? There is, thus, a strong tendency in some forms of instrumentalism to see every practice of private law as guided by the same normative commitment—and that normative commitment as the benchmark for evaluating every legal practice.[133]

What is the explanation for this tendency to treat every instance of, for example, property law as understandable and justifiable in terms of the same goal? I believe the explanation has to do with instrumentalism's conception of law and its relationship to the goals it pursues. Under that conception, the relevant goals pursued by legal institutions—such as maximizing social welfare—can be specified independently of those institutions.[134] The institutions are contingent instruments to achieve those goals. If that is the case, then variability across legal institutions shouldn't have any bearing on characterizing the underlying goals. But if comparative jurisprudence is right, this approach will distort the object we are trying to justify.

To avoid any misunderstanding, I think it is plausible that the moral point of a certain type of legal institution or practice might be the same across different jurisdictions. And I do not think it is necessarily mistaken to believe that we can specify the moral values served by a legal institution independently of the internal structure of that institution. What I do take as a mistake is the naïve assumption of universalism—the idea that private law serves or ought to serve efficiency anywhere it exists, independently of what each private law practice is concerned with from an internal perspective. That assumption is

[133] See, eg, Rafael La Porta and others, 'Law and Finance' (1998) 106 J Political Economy 1113.

[134] This is an idea I take from Martin Stone, 'Legal Positivism as an Idea about Morality' (2011) 61 U Toronto LJ 313.

partly explained by the instrumentalist insistence on seeing legal institutions as a mere contingent instrument of goals that are valuable *qua* independent goals, not *qua* the goals that are significant for—and therefore partly constitute—any specific legal culture.

A better version of instrumentalism—one more compatible with comparative jurisprudence—would instead take its cue from Isaiah Berlin. It would expect different societies and different legal systems to adopt different ideals, aim at different goals, and reflect different commitments.[135] It would see different regimes of private law as characterized by different intellectual styles and cognitive practices that embody different sets of values.[136] That is the instrumentalism we should have, but not the one that the most influential instrumentalism on offer—law and economics—has provided so far.

2. The Contingency of Private Law

While many instrumentalists seem happy to discount the significance of legal discourse, formalists tend to start from the opposite claim: the claim to take law's internal rationality seriously.[137] This certainly seems to bring formalism closer to comparative jurisprudence. In fact, Catherine Valcke has linked formalism to Ewald's account of comparative jurisprudence.[138] However, formalism is at odds with comparative jurisprudence in at least two ways. First, while formalism treats domestic private law seriously, it still sees it as an attempt to approximate an abstract and indeterminate blueprint that can be brought to bear on the evaluation of private law and that determines what it is with at least some independence from the contingent variations across legal cultures. Second, formalism is committed to a specific philosophical framework to understand private law regimes—a philosophical framework that can be quite different from those derived from the more variable, contingent history of the specific legal tradition. In both respects, formalism—while closer in some ways to comparative jurisprudence than instrumentalism—is not sufficiently committed to the intellectual specificity derived from the path dependence and the contingent historical routes followed by each distinct legal

[135] Ella Myers, 'From Pluralism to Liberalism: Rereading Isaiah Berlin' (2010) 72 The Review of Politics 599, 612.

[136] George Kateb, 'Can Cultures Be Judged? Two Defenses of Cultural Pluralism in Isaiah Berlin's Work' (1999) 66 Social Research 1009, 1023–24.

[137] See, eg, Weinrib, *The Idea of Private Law* (n 1).

[138] Valcke, 'Comparative Law as Comparative Jurisprudence' (n 40) 716 fn 22.

system. In other words, formalism tends to obscure the contingency of private law.

Private law formalists are aware of this critique. Arthur Ripstein, for instance, writes:

> A number of people have asked… about the viability of 'turning Kant into a common lawyer.' Students of the history of the common law often note its antitheoretical orientation, its practice of developing one case at a time, and some writers have thought it important to point out the great common law judges of earlier centuries did not read Kant. No doubt they did not, but any felt need to point this out betrays a misconception of Kant's, and indeed any, philosophical project of understanding an area of legal doctrine… I do not put forward a historical hypothesis… I take seriously Kant's own insistence that he would not presume to invent a new moral principle. The point of providing an account of the form of thought in an area of legal doctrine is not to invent that area, or give someone else credit for inventing it. Instead, it is to make it intelligible, to show how the characteristic modes of reasoning, the questions asked, and the inferences permitted or refused fit into an integrated pattern. That pattern is composed of conceptual and normative structures.[139]

Thus, the formalist response to this type of critique is that it misunderstands what it means to render a social practice like private law intelligible. Such a project requires, according to Ripstein, showing 'how the characteristic modes of reasoning, the questions asked, and the inferences permitted or refused [by an area of private law] fit into an integrated pattern.'[140]

The problem with this response is that the characteristic modes of reasoning, the inferential moves allowed, and so on, have a specific and contingent history—a specific genealogy that diverges from system to system at different points in time.[141] While there is certainly a distinction between understanding an area of private law and describing its historical path, the internal dimension of the relevant practices is impacted by, and depends on historical contingency. The problem, from this perspective, is not that common-law judges did not read Kant, but that the intellectual sources from which their practices derived and that give those practices their specific features and make them what they are were quite specific to the common-law tradition.

139 Arthur Ripstein, *Private Wrongs* (Harvard UP 2016) xi.
140 ibid.
141 Making this claim from the perspective of common law theory, Oman (n 127) 174.

Formalists can accommodate variability and contingency, to some extent. In the Kantian account, for instance, the rights protected by private law are not, at the most fundamental level, artificial or fully dependent on legal practices. They are intelligible before conventional institutions and civil society. However, these private rights are—in the absence of legal institutions—provisional because they are unilaterally asserted, and therefore, their status as valid rights-claims is unsettled in the absence of—and until there is—positive law.[142] Private rights in a civil condition are the full realization of the *idea* of rights that, in the state of nature, are merely provisional.[143] Under this view, our private rights are authoritatively determined by the public legal institutions of each specific society.[144] The determinations of these institutions are constitutively required to make each person's rights consistent with the rights of others.[145] The general norms of abstract right that, according to the Kantian formalist, underlie private law, can receive different specific instantiations in different legal cultures.

The limitation, however, is that for formalists the specific questions answered by legal institutions are all derived from a more general, distinctive question that morality demands an answer to, and which explains the need for legal institutions.[146] On this account, there is a straight line—a coherent unity—between the Kantian idea of a will, abstract right, corrective justice, and public legal order.[147] The notion of right 'is comprehensive, unifying, and systematic, encompassing everything from the operation of the will to substantive legal doctrines and institutions'.[148]

Thus, formalism makes space for variation across legal cultures. The notion of right is, after all, *abstract*. However, the formalist sees private law in different societies as aiming to answer a universal moral question. As such, private law theory is, in the eyes of the formalist, primarily a philosophical elucidation of that universal moral question.

In this aspect, comparative jurisprudence is quite different. It sees philosophy as relevant to understand the intellectual underpinnings of specific legal systems, as necessary because we want to understand the intellectual foundations of the legal system and the underlying phenomena that make a specific legal

[142] Alan Brudner, *The Unity of the Common Law: Studies in Hegelian Jurisprudence* (2nd edn, University of California Press 2017) 70.

[143] Martin Stone and Rafeeq Hasan, 'What Is Provisional Right?' (2022) 131 Philosophical Review 51.

[144] Brudner (n 142) 76.

[145] Ripstein (n 97) 9.

[146] See Martin Stone, 'Kant's Apparent Positivism' in M Stone (ed), *Freedom and Force: Essays on Kant's Legal Philosophy* (Hart 2017) 174.

[147] Weinrib, *The Idea of Private Law* (n 1) 100–09.

[148] ibid 109.

practice what it is.[149] What the formalist sees as multiple attempts to answer a universal moral question, then, is to the comparative jurisprude the actual variation that we should expect to observe across different social practices that reflect different cultures, commitments, and histories. What we need, in order to understand private law, is not to connect each specific instance of it to Kant's or Hegel's legal philosophy but rather to see how those different practices represent the offshoots of the philosophical ideas of Ulpian, Coke, Blackstone, Cajetan, Savigny, Ihering, Cardozo, or Pothier. This requires putting the contingent intellectual histories of each legal practice in the driving seat rather than at the service of a general, abstract, and universal legal philosophy.

3. Professional Private Law

The New Private Law seems to be in a better position to capture private law's contingency than formalism. And, unlike thoroughgoing instrumentalism, the New Private Law is more oriented towards capturing how the internal dimension of private law is compatible with its functional analysis.[150]

I think the New Private Law is, thus, a step in the right direction. But some of its commitments (or, at least, some of the commitments of some theorists who see themselves as members of the New Private Law) can be somewhat in tension with comparative jurisprudence and the truths about the law that, as I have argued, it captures.

One of the truths that comparative jurisprudence captures is that law is a cognitive practice in which judges, lawyers, and legal academics engage. Law is the living record of the intellectual activities of legal actors.[151] Thus, the culture that we should try to understand is, primarily, the culture of legal practitioners—the *internal* legal culture, that is, the practices and ideas of legal officials, lawyers, and legal academics.[152]

The New Private Law puts great emphasis on the law's guidance of citizens. Paul Miller, for instance, argues that the law's central role is providing 'practically reasonable guidance' to its addressees, which includes citizens,[153] through

[149] Ewald, 'Comparative Jurisprudence (I)' (n 38) 1960.

[150] Andrew S Gold and others, 'Introduction' in AS Gold and others (eds), *The Oxford Handbook of the New Private Law* (OUP 2020) xv.

[151] Ewald, 'Comparative Jurisprudence (I)' (n 38) 1948–49.

[152] On internal legal culture, see Lawrence M Friedman, *The Legal System: A Social Science Perspective* (Russell Sage Foundation 1975) 223; Sally Engle Merry, 'What Is Legal Culture? An Anthropological Perspective' (2010) 5 J Comp Law 40, 43.

[153] Miller (n 107) 196–97.

the provision of practical reasons.[154] In similar terms, Gold and Smith write that 'implicit in law's claim of authority is the possibility that citizens have the capacity to follow the law's guidance'.[155] Because of this, private law ought to be understandable by ordinary citizens, knowable by parties subject to its rules, etc.[156] John Goldberg argues, in a relatively similar vein, that according to the New Private Law, there is often at least a family resemblance between legal and lay concepts and norms, and this explains private law's authority.[157] This overlap, Goldberg argues, is not a coincidence. Private law is partly designed to make that overlap possible (for instance, through the institution of the jury, standards of reasonableness, trade usages, and interpretive techniques that attempt to align legal and ordinary meaning).[158] Goldberg recognizes there is no perfect fit here between legal and social norms.[159] The point is just that private law strives, in general, to a certain degree of consistency with lay moral intuitions, a fact that should be acknowledged by private law theory.[160] The project of private law adjudication, expressed in the very idea of the 'common law', according to Goldberg and Zipursky, involves drawing the wrongs that the law recognizes from everyday life.[161]

This general orientation towards private law's guidance of ordinary citizens through predictable, scalable, and recognizable standards of conduct that characterize the New Private Law has been recognized by scholars beyond this group. Kevin Tobia, for instance, has noted how—from the perspective of experimental jurisprudence—many legal concepts share features of ordinary concepts and how this overlap is compatible with the New Private Law's commitment to a defeasible preference for this overlap.[162] For both movements, Tobia writes, laypeople are not objects but central members of 'our' legal community, 'poised to contribute meaningfully to legal theory'.[163]

I would certainly accept that there are connections between legal and ordinary concepts. And I agree that an important point of legal institutions is to guide the behaviour of ordinary people. Nevertheless, this should not lead us to downplay something centrally important about private law in contemporary

[154] ibid 199.
[155] Andrew S Gold and Henry E Smith, 'Sizing up Private Law' (2019) 70 U Toronto LJ 489, 511.
[156] ibid 512.
[157] Goldberg (n 33) 1656.
[158] ibid 1657.
[159] ibid 1658.
[160] John CP Goldberg and Benjamin C Zipursky, *Recognizing Wrongs* (Harvard UP 2020) 79.
[161] ibid 208.
[162] Kevin Tobia, 'Experimental Jurisprudence' (2022) 89 U Chicago L Rev 735.
[163] ibid.

Western legal systems—namely, that private law is a peculiarly and particularly *professional* area of law.

As I have argued elsewhere,[164] law is an institutional structure that becomes operational once it is populated by specific agents in charge of interpreting, applying, and enforcing legal norms, operating against a specific social and physical background. A legal system is a social apparatus populated by actual human beings, such as lawyers and judges. Because of this, how any legal system operates depends partly on who populates it and fills out specific institutional positions within it.

This general claim is particularly salient in private law. Private law lawmaking is characteristically driven by professional elites—by judges, lawyers, and law professors—even when it takes place, formally, in democratic venues.[165] The interpretation of private law is characteristically developed by judges in judicial venues. Moreover, unlike other areas of law, in private law doctrinal reasoning seems to drive outcomes much more than 'external' factors. This might explain why formalism—which sees law and politics as radically separated and law as a self-standing and autonomous justificatory structure—found its home in private law theory.

Many of private law's central categories in common-law jurisdictions are creations of professionals—specifically, judges. There is a long tradition that theorizes the common law as following and building upon local social customs.[166] Whether that theory was consistent with reality in the eighteenth and nineteenth centuries is an important question. However, while certainly sensitive to lay practice, common-law reasoning is very much driven by judges—so much so that the way in which common-law standards are ascertained and determined by lawyers does not involve empirical investigation into social practices, but rather legal research involving judicial decisions and legal authorities.

The contribution of law professors is less commonly mentioned, but also significant and important—not just in civil law systems.[167] Features as central to American law as the distinction between the reliance and expectation interests[168] or the right to privacy[169] cannot be understood without reference to law professors' contribution.

[164] Felipe Jiménez, 'Some Doubts About Folk Jurisprudence: The Case of Proximate Cause' [2021] U Chicago L Rev Online <https://lawreviewblog.uchicago.edu/2021/08/23/jimenez-jurisprudence/>.

[165] See Jansen (n 67) 45–49; Arie Rosen, 'The Role of Democracy in Private Law' (2022).

[166] See generally Oman (n 127).

[167] James Gordley, 'The State's Private Law and Legal Academia' (2008) 56 Am J Comp Law 639, 641.

[168] Lon Fuller and William R Perdue, 'The Reliance Interest in Contract Damages: 1' (1936) 46 Yale LJ 52.

[169] Samuel D Warren and Louis D Brandeis, 'The Right to Privacy' (1890) 4 Harvard LR 193.

Private law's professional characteristics might be troublesome from a variety of normative perspectives, including concerns about fair notice, predictability, and democratic legitimacy. But we cannot fully understand private law, its virtues and its potential risks if we ignore this trait.[170] Private law in the Western legal tradition is characterized by the presence of technical terms and terms with specialized meanings.[171] Because of this, there is always a potential tension between the layperson and the lawyer, between ordinary and legal language. This explains why lawyers need to engage in a certain translation to communicate across these two languages.[172]

What all of this entails is that understanding private law requires understanding its specific features, including the professional and technical character of its discourse. The New Private Law's focus on guidance and the provision of practical reasons for ordinary citizens is warranted, but it has to be combined with a deep awareness of the fact that these tasks are mediated by legal professionals and legal culture. New Private Law theorists already recognize the potential divergences between legal and lay views.[173] Yet if it wanted to follow the lead of comparative jurisprudence—and, for the reasons I have alluded to, I think it should—the New Private Law should put the inferential, linguistic, cognitive, and cultural practices of private law professionals (judges, lawyers, and legal scholars) front and centre, and see law's role in supplying practical guidance in connection with the mediation of these legal experts.

VI. Conclusion

Understanding private law requires understanding not just the rules and doctrines of private law but the underlying cultural, ideological, and philosophical ideas that characterize it. Understanding private law, in other words, is a matter of interpreting the cognitive structure that characterizes the practice for those actively engaged in it.

This understanding is necessary for interpretive, normative, and descriptive projects in private law theory. But if it is necessary, then the question is what type of methodology is best suited for understanding private law theory.

[170] This paragraph builds upon Jiménez (n 131).

[171] Frederick Schauer, 'Is Law a Technical Language?' (2015) 52 San Diego L Rev 501, 501–502. See *also* Meir Dan-Cohen, 'Decision Rules and Conduct Rules: On Acoustic Separation in Criminal Law' (1984) 97 Harvard LR 625, 652; Lon Fuller, *Legal Fictions* (Stanford UP 1967) 12.

[172] James Boyd White, 'An Old-Fashioned View of the Nature of Law' (2011) 12 Theoretical Inquiries in Law 381, 388–89.

[173] Goldberg (n 33) 1658.

My view, as I have argued, is that comparative jurisprudence is an attractive model for that methodology. Comparative jurisprudence highlights, precisely, that the content of private law depends on more than its surface rules and doctrines, understanding private requires understanding the values and commitments of legal agents, and this requires the adoption of an internal perspective.

As I have explained, instrumentalism—particularly, the thoroughgoing instrumentalism characteristic of some forms of law and economics—is not well-suited to adopt this perspective. It basically ignores that law is a cultural phenomenon characterized by modes of thought and talk that are not merely epiphenomenal or instrumental. Formalism, while better in this specific aspect, tends to downplay the contingency of private law and the fact that philosophical ideas are made relevant by social practices—not the other way around. The New Private Law is in a better position than both instrumentalism and formalism. But, as I argue, it should move towards a greater insistence on the professional character of private law.

5

Against Essentialism in Private Law Theory

Private Law as an Artifact Kind

*Thilo Kuntz**

I. Introduction

In recent years, scholars on both sides of the Atlantic have reopened a debate about the foundations of private law and private law methodology. Whereas in Germany, a growing number of academics question the mainstream according to which the interpretation of the law should be grounded in a purely legal point of view, US scholars working in the field of New Private Law raise doubts about the validity of a perspective on the law mostly driven by consequentialist aims and frameworks such as law and economics. Notwithstanding the differences in traditions, legal systems and training, German and US scholars share a common interest, namely the place of diverging norms and values in a private law which seems in danger of being torn apart between demands coming from different and opposing camps (for example, efficiency vs corrective justice). Their positions and approaches vary considerably, however. The vantage points range from theories shearing private law from any kind of consequentialist value in the United States[1] through a robust push for efficiency-oriented reasoning in Germany.[2] A growing number of scholars, however, position themselves between the extremes and either enrich morality

* For valuable comments and suggestions, the author would like to thank participants of the Bucerius Law School-Notre Dame Conference on Methodology in Private Law Theory, participants of the 'Aktuelle Stunde' at the Max-Planck-Institute for Private Law in Hamburg, Germany, Daniel Damler, Lukas Daub, Andreas M Fleckner, Lisa Guntermann, Alexander Hellgardt, Alexander von Lützow, Robert Nies, and Sophie Schönberger. Any errors are the author's alone.

[1] See, eg, Charles Fried, *Contract as Promise* (HUP 1981) 17; Ernest Weinrib, *The Idea of Private Law* (HUP 1995) 3–4, 46–48; see also John CP Goldberg and Benjamin C Zipursky, *Recognizing Wrongs* (HUP 2020) 44–48.

[2] See, eg, Hans-Bernd Schäfer and Claus Ott, 'Die ökonomische Analyse des Zivilrechts – Irrweg oder Chance wissenschaftlicher Rechtserkenntnis' (1988) 43 Juristenzeitung 213; Gerhard Wagner, 'Prävention und Verhaltenssteuerung durch Privatrecht – Anmaßung oder legitime Aufgabe?' (2006) 206 Archiv für die civilistische Praxis 352.

Thilo Kuntz, *Against Essentialism in Private Law Theory* In: *Methodology in Private Law Theory*. Edited by: Thilo Kuntz and Paul B. Miller, Oxford University Press. © Thilo Kuntz 2024. DOI: 10.1093/oso/9780198885306.003.0005

with consequentialist points of view and similar considerations of public welfare or offer a model which allows giving pride of place to either of these norms and values, depending on the issue at hand.[3] What unites these perspectives is the argument that 'single-idea' accounts insufficiently describe private law. This is the position underlying this chapter:

Viewing specific private law fields like contract, property, or torts exclusively through the lenses of corrective justice or private autonomy[4] fails just as much as sacrificing them on the altar of efficiency[5] provided that private law theory presents a theory about the makings and workings of private law as it is practised. A sharp delineation between 'internal' and 'external' perspectives on private law, with morality-oriented theories subsumed under the first heading and consequentialist approaches under the second,[6] is doomed to fail as a theory about existing private law or private law 'as it is'. The prevailing division of 'external' and 'internal' reflects essentialist readings of private law, a search for its 'true' nature. Alas, or so this chapter argues, there is none. Private law accommodates and rests on a mixed set of norms and values with weights and relevance changing over time, rendering any partisan account ineffective.[7] Efforts to cleanly sort internal and external views and separate an inside of private law from its outside in terms of moral norms and values must remain futile.[8] The participants of the legal system, those employing the internal point view, do not hold single-value opinions on private law as such or even about areas such as tort or contract. Consequently, a private law theory aspiring to describe and analyse private law 'as it is', that is, aspractised, must acknowledge its ambivalent and multipolar nature. In the end, this strengthens the autonomy of law because private law cannot be pocketed by scholars sailing under the flag of a single-value picture of a multi-value world.

Methodologically, this requires a neutral point of departure, or at least one not already wading knee-deep in the premises of theories about private law.

[3] For Germany: Marietta Auer, *Zum Erkenntnisziel der Rechtstheorie* (Nomos 2018); Thilo Kuntz, 'Recht als Gegenstand der Rechtswissenschaft und performative Rechtserzeugung – zugleich ein Beitrag zur Möglichkeit von Dogmatik' (2016) 21 Archiv für die civilistische Praxis 866; Thilo Kuntz, 'Auf der Suche nach einem Proprium der Rechtswissenschaft' (2019) Archiv für die civilistische Praxis 254. For the United States: Andrew Gold, 'Internal and External Perspectives: On the New Private Law Methodology' in A Gold and others (eds), *The New Private Law* (OUP 2021) 3, 16–17; Paul B Miller and Jeffrey A Pojanowski, 'The Internal Point of View in Private Law' (2022) 67 Am J Jurisprudence 247, 267–77.

[4] See, eg, Fried (n 1) 16; Weinrib (n 1) 19; in the German literature Florian Rödl, *Gerechtigkeit unter freien Gleichen. Eine normative Rekonstruktion von Delikt, Eigentum und Vertrag* (Nomos 2015).

[5] eg, William Landes and Richard Posner, *The Economic Structure of Tort Law* (HUP 1987) 1.

[6] For a recent overview for the United States: Charles L Barzun, 'Inside-Out: Beyond the Internal/External Distinction in Legal Scholarship' (2015) 101 Va L Rev 1203, 1207–09, 1232–33. For Germany Kuntz, 'Performative Rechtserzeugung' (n 3) 867–69.

[7] See also Barzun, ibid 1285: 'The internal/external distinction has outlived its utility'.

[8] For a similar view ibid 1237–42, 1258–85.

This chapter draws on artifact theory. Artifact theory appears attractive because it is, first of all, not a theory about the law in general or private law. At artifact theory's core lies the idea that an 'artifact[] [is an] object intentionally made to serve a given purpose'.[9] This ties into how lawyers and legal theorists think about the law: Brian Leiter claims that a person denying law's artifactual nature 'would be subject ... for psychological, not philosophical investigation.'[10] Even natural-law theorists do not dispute that law is a human creation, or, as John Finnis put it, 'artefact and artifice, and not a conclusion from moral premises ...'[11] Others find artifact theory helpful in building a bridge between 'formalistic legal positivism and ... antiformalistic legal realisms.'[12] In short, both legal positivists and adherents of natural law accept that law is an artifact. Bringing artifact theory to bear upon private law thus appears promising, especially since it does not carry a distinct concept of law as baggage. Artifact theory is a thriving field in various parts of philosophy[13] and, over the past few decades, has gained traction in legal philosophy.[14] Relying on artifact theory as a methodological tool for private law theory has several advantages.

Abstracting from substantive theories about what the law or 'just' about what private law is, artifact approaches shed some new light on ontological interdependencies of materials a positivist considers 'existing law' and the insights of so-called externalists concerning the law's transient character and the importance of outside perspectives.[15] This is especially helpful in private law, one of the starting points of both legal realism, law and economics, and the new wave of internalist approaches. Artifact theory not only offers tools for solving problems within private law but instead provides an analytical grid for questions *about* private law—its structure, content, roots, and creation.[16] It thus allows for private law theory proper, a method of studying how private law's

[9] Lynne R Baker, *The Metaphysics of Everyday Life* (CUP 2007) 49. See also Beth Preston, 'Artifact' in EN Zalta and U Nodelman (eds), *Stanford Encyclopedia of Philosophy* (3 October 2022)beginning of section 1.

[10] Brian Leiter, 'The Demarcation Problem in Jurisprudence' in J Ferrer Béltran, JJ Moreso, and DM Papayannis (eds), *Neutrality and Theory of Law* (Springer 2013) 161, 164.

[11] John Finnis, 'The Truth in Legal Positivism' in RP George (ed), *The Autonomy of Law* (OUP 1996) 195, 205.

[12] Corrado Roversi, 'On the Artifactual – and Natural – Character of Legal Institutions' in L Burazin, KE Himma, and C Roversi (eds), *Law as an Artifact* (OUP 2018) 89, 103.

[13] For an introduction see Preston (n 9).

[14] See Luka Burazin, 'Can There Be an Artifact Theory of Law?' (2016) 29 Ratio Juris 385, and various contributions in the collected volume *Law as an Artifact* (n 12). Kenneth E Himma, *Coercion and the Nature of Law* (OUP 2020) 81. For a critical view see, eg, Miguel Angel Garcia-Godinez, 'Flaws and Virtues of an Artifact Theory of Law' (2019) 32 Ratio Juris 117.

[15] Roversi (n 12) 103.

[16] cf Felipe Jiménez, 'Two Questions For Private Law Theory' (2021) 12 Jurisprudence 391, 400, 412, on the importance of distinguishing these two issues for the purposes of private law theory.

institutional design is to be understood, justified, and evaluated given its underlying purposes.[17] To be clear: Neither is the artifact approach to private law the only game in town nor does it cash out in new fundamental insights into how laws and legal norms are created as law contrary to, say, social norms. It is, however, a valuable tool to evaluate old questions in a new light and emphasize issues that have not exactly stood at the centre of attention of the grand theories of law.

Section II sets out in more detail how private law is created from an artifact point of view. Having hammered out this analytical grid, Section III shows why externalist perspectives fail. They underestimate the significance of the moral norms and values building the deep-level base of private-law norms. Any judge aiming to create private law has to place the new artifact token within an existing framework, or their attempt misses the target. Going forward, the section then demonstrates how internalist perspectives suffer from a similar flaw—they underestimate the relevance of consequentialist leanings already present in much of current private law. Additionally, many, if not most, internal theories are built around an externalist kernel. In the end, combined perspectives share the flaws of both points of view. Moreover, they are unable to solve the problem when a judge may include external views. If they are external to the law, there must be legitimate reasons for doing so, especially in light of the separation of powers.

Section IV then argues against essentialist renderings of private law. Private law rests on a multiplicity of deep-level norms—from morality to efficiency—and is historically contingent. It resists any attempt to reduce it to a single-sided point of view. Legal officials take on a double role in judging and lawmaking. They evaluate the law 'as it is' and apply it to the facts at hand, governed by the criteria of fit and consilience. This implies they must pay attention to what the law 'does'. Given the opacity and vagueness of private-law norms with respect to their *ratio*, the latitude courts and administrators enjoy is wider than especially hard positivists would like. Moreover, the law requires efficient and effective application concerning the aims it serves, covering moral norms with a consequentialist layer. As a result, private law's characteristics are diffuse and unstable. Consequently, legal officials enjoy the discretion to reframe existing legal norms and thereby slowly shift the foundational deep-level structures of private law. The legislator is a special case. Contrary to courts, a legislator has the power to change the whole system of private law. Whenever the legislator aims at incremental change, existing private-law norms work as a constraint. Section V concludes.

[17] ibid 413.

Two limitations must be made explicit beforehand: Firstly, and most importantly, this chapter takes part in the debate about the nature of private law. It is limited to one aspect of the issue, however. The following pages concern the question as to whether it is possible to construe private law through a single-value essentialist reading according to which private law has certain innate and necessary properties.[18] In the course of the analysis, the chapter explains why any attempt at doing so must fail. This has implications for the debate about what private law is (or is not). Exploring this issue on a more general level in greater depth would, however, lead too far away from the general framework of the book it is part of, that is, methodology in private law theory and the attempt to start a dialogue between private-law theorists from both sides of the Atlantic who assume there is such a thing as private law proper. A reader looking for a general theory of private law and whether, and if yes, how it can be distinguished from public and criminal law has to turn elsewhere.[19]

Secondly, this chapter does not cover private customary law and 'law merchant'. Integrating customary law into artifact theory comes with its own set of specific difficulties and, therefore, leads too far away from New Private Law and the methodological debates in Germany surrounding internal and external perspectives.[20]

II. Creating Private Law as an Artifact

1. Private Law as an Artifact

As mentioned above, standard notions of 'artifact' centre on an intention to create something which serves a given purpose.[21] If artifacts are human kinds, that is, made by humans to serve human needs, intention most likely plays a

[18] On the distinction between essential and accidental properties and ways to define essentialism see, eg, Teresa Robertson Ishii and Philip Atkins, 'Essential vs. Accidental Properties' in EN Zalta and UNodelman (eds), *Stanford Encyclopedia of philosophy* (26 October 2020).

[19] This is an issue which, for historical reasons, stood at the heart of many debates about private law and private law theory in Germany and continues to provide the background music of German private law theory today. This debate has never been pursued with the same intensity in the United States (or in any other common-law jurisdiction). For an analysis of the historical background of the sharp distinction between private law and the state/public law in Germany see Hans-Peter Haferkamp, 'The Science of Private Law and the State in Nineteenth Century Germany' (2008) 56 Am J Comp L 667.

[20] For two perspectives on customary law (including international customary law) as artifact: Jonathan Crowe, 'Law as An Artifact Kind' (2014) 40 Monash U L Rev 737, 743–46 (in favour); Dan Priel, 'Not All Law Is an Artifact: Jurisprudence Meets the Common Law' in *Law as an Artifact* (n 14) 239 (against).

[21] See n 9 and accompanying text.

role in their creation.[22] A lawyer could object that this may be true for simple tools like spoons,[23] but not for law. At least in a democracy, the creation of laws does not depend on the intention of its creator(s) alone. Put differently: Not everything a judge wants to be (private) law becomes a legal norm.[24] A leading position on artifacts helpfully espouses a more fine-grained definition according to which—

> [n]ecessarily, for all x and all . . . artifactual kinds K, x is a K if and only if x is the product of a largely successful intention that (Kx), where one intends (Kx) if and only if one has a substantive concept of the nature of Ks that matches that of prior makers of Ks (if any) and intends to realize that concept by imposing K-relevant features on the object.[25]

This definition underlines the interdependence of the creator's intentions and concepts of others, the 'prior makers of Ks'. In terms of lawmaking, the creator needs to have a 'substantive concept' of private law which matches the core features of concepts shared by prior lawmakers, that is, its intension.[26] This means that meeting the concepts of others about the artifact amounts to a success condition.[27] If their work is off target, they begin and end up with a lump of clay rather than a statute. Put differently: Unless the creator wants to design a new artifact that does not resemble a given type, they necessarily have to employ an already existing set of criteria. Newer work convincingly expands and refines this framework and emphasizes the importance of public norms.[28] Individual intentions alone cannot explain how an artifact may be recognized by others.[29] In order to attain the objective of artifact creation, the creator must consider how observers treat and regard that type of artifact, that is, which characteristics they ascribe to it.[30] These features command respect and, in that regard, exhibit normative force. In other words, private-law norms

[22] Preston (n 9) section 2.3.

[23] A closer look reveals, however, that the definition in the text above leaves a lot to explain even with respect to spoons and chairs, see, eg, Amie L Thomasson, 'Realism and Human Kinds' (2003) 67 Phil and Phenom Res 580, 593–95.

[24] See also text after n 31.

[25] Thomasson, 'Realism'(n 23) 600.

[26] Crowe (n 20) 741. For a narrower view Paul Bloom, 'Intention, history, and artifact concepts' (1996) 60 Cognition 1, 10–12, 17; for a critique of that position in the artifact literature see, eg, Thomasson, 'Realism' (n 23) 595–96. Because there already is private law, the case that a law creator produces private law for the first time can be left out.

[27] cf Crowe (n 20) 741.

[28] Amie L Thomasson, 'Public Artifacts, Intentions, and Norms' in M Franssen and others (eds), *Artifact Kinds* (Springer 2014) 45, 54–56.

[29] ibid 55.

[30] ibid.

do not belong here simply because a judge decided so and thereby caused the norms to have private-law properties. Rather, it is because the norms created map on public conventions, which in turn qualify norms with certain properties as private law.[31]

This is of major importance in creating private law: Public norms, in the sense just described, constitute the context of justification[32] for any maker of private law. To be successful and produce an artifact, the creator of private law has to follow a set of procedures established by the constitution. They must consider the existing private law already in existence and as laid out and interpreted by prior creators. If the creator of private law is a court, it has to decide on a specific issue under a specific description. A party claims damages under tort law, sues for performance relying on a contract or demands the return of their property because they are the owner. Even if 'black-letter law' does not determine the outcome of the case in a way a mathematical formula would, and the decision may be surprising for all but Judge Holmes, a court still has to justify its decision in a language and with reasoning recognizable and acceptable to others, especially if the court is not the US Supreme Court or the German Federal Court of Justice.[33]

2. A Brief Digression: Public Norms, Institutions, and the Role of Intention

Two arguments against artifact theory need to be addressed because, if valid, they endanger the whole approach: Firstly, some scholars claim that artifact theory does not apply to law because law is an institution, not an artifact.[34] Others look at the nature of common law and argue that common law is customary law.[35] According to certain critics of artifact theory, this implies that common law cannot be an artifact because contrary to the creation of common law, the production of artifacts requires intention.[36] These arguments do not hold water:

[31] cf Muhammad A Khalidi, 'Three Kinds of Social Kinds' (2015) 90 Phil and Phenom Res 96, 106, in whose model legal norms would fall under the third category described ibid 99–104.

[32] cf Hans Reichenbach, *Experience and Prediction* (University of Chicago Press 1938) 6–7.

[33] cf *Brown v Allen*, 344 US 443, 540 (1953) (Jackson J, concurring): 'Reversal by a higher court is not proof that justice is thereby better done. There is no doubt that if there were a super-Supreme Court, a substantial portion of our reversals of state courts would also be reversed. We are not final because we are infallible, but we are infallible only because we are final.'

[34] Garcia-Godinez (n 14) 127–30.

[35] John Gardner, *Law as a Leap of Faith* (OUP 2012) 70 (2012); Priel (n 20) 248.

[36] Priel, ibid.

Artifact theory is neutral regarding the relevant 'public norms' and the quality they must have to govern artifact creation. Neil MacCormick, well known for his institutional theory of law, defines institutions as formally articulated normative orders.[37] There is nothing about that description which cuts against the notion of public norms. Quite to the contrary: If law consists of rules, that is, 'explicitly articulated norms',[38] then the law as an institution fits the bill. Artifact theory's understanding of public norms is capacious enough to integrate institutional theories of law.

Scholars criticizing the artifact approaches to law by pointing to the 'intention' requirement appear to tacitly conflate a definition of intention in the lawyerly sense with that of artifact theory.[39] The latter is much less demanding. Its core function is to separate human kinds (artifacts) from natural kinds.[40] Natural kinds are not made by anyone *for* something.[41] Judges need not have a complete explicit theory of law in mind when they create new law.[42] But they have to act in their capacity *as* judges. They do have to intend to produce proper *legal* norms, not merely social or fake norms, as part of a theatre play. Judges wishing to succeed will take into account what the institutions of law, the public norms, require. Nothing more, nothing less. In other words, Judges intend to create legal norms pursuant to what the law governing the production of new legal norms requires. This does not happen by accident.

III. Shortcomings of Externalism, Internalism, and Combination through Adoption

1. Shortcomings of Externalist Perspectives

One significant shortcoming of externalism is that its proponents often pay scant attention to differences and distinctions dear and important to internalists, sometimes levelling them altogether. Tort law is a good example of this. Pursuant to a seminal text in the economic analysis of tort law,

[37] See Neil MacCormick, *Institutions of Law* (OUP 2007) 20, 33.

[38] ibid 24.

[39] Or, to be more precise, to those variations of artifact theory requiring intention at all. For an artifact theory with a much more limited role for intention see Ruth G Millikan, *Language, Thought, and Other Biological Categories* (MIT Press 1984). At least direct proper functions, whether biological or artificial, depend on reproductive history and is able to perform a specific function; intention of the/a maker is not required, ibid 17–38. According to Millikan, '[i]ntentionality... admits of degrees' (ibid 126).

[40] Preston (n 9) section 1.

[41] ibid.

[42] This seems to be the assumption of Priel (n 20) 249.

'the common law of torts is best explained as if the judges who created the law … were trying to promote efficient resource allocation.'[43] Proponents of this view typically equivocate a court order to compensate tort damages and criminal sanctions, subsuming both under a general notion of 'sanction' or cost.[44] Indeed, as a matter of first impression, in pecuniary terms, the difference between a fine of EUR 5,000 and a compensation order of EUR 5,000 does not amount to much—the party charged with the fine or order loses EUR 5,000. For the calculating Holmesian 'bad man', the formula looks more or less the same, notwithstanding the legal origin of the price he pays should his actions be uncovered: *probability of being uncovered * amount of sanction*. This picture, however, is woefully incomplete because remedy does not equate to remedy. It ignores the differences in how the judge has to gauge the amount.

The public norms governing this procedure display significantly diverging conventions. Leaving punitive damages aside for a moment, damages under tort law hinge on the victim's loss. Both in US tort law(s) and in Germany, compensation is the reigning principle. Criminal-law fines depend on the delinquent's intent and aims, crimes committed in the past and other factors, the loss or hurt suffered by the victim not being the most important. That is true even for economic offences like theft or property destruction where it would be relatively easy to calculate a monetary loss.[45] Holmesian arguments about tort duties not being relational law because tort law is enacted by the state and duties are owed to the state[46] lack sufficient explanatory power in that regard.

Downplaying the compensation principle as just another form of sanction defined by the state means to dodge the answer to the question of why 'the state' should restrict tort claims. There is at least a good argument that this may be grounded in specific value judgments of past law creators relevant to torts but not to criminal law. The 'wrong' to be offset, or so it seems, has a different quality than that of a crime. Otherwise, there would not be a reason to establish specific criteria depending on the kind of wrong. This is an important point the critics of civil-recourse theory in tort law overlook when they complain that proponents of that school of thought fail to explain how to identify what

[43] Landes and Posner (n 5).

[44] See, eg, Robert Cooter, 'Prices and Sanctions' (1984) 84 Col L Rev 1523, 1524–25: 'A sanction is a detriment imposed for doing what is forbidden, such as failing to perform an obligation. For example, a defendant in a tort dispute may be ordered to pay compensatory damages for an injury caused by his negligence, or a convicted criminal may be sentenced to jail.' (Italics in original suppressed.)

[45] cf sec 46(2) of the German Criminal Code (*Strafgesetzbuch*), United States Sentencing Commission, *Guidelines Manual*, § 2 B 1 (Nov. 2021).

[46] cf John CP Goldberg and Benjamin C Zipursky, 'Seeing Tort Law from the Internal Point of View: Holmes and Hart on Legal Duties' (2006) 75 Fordham L Rev 1563, 1567–68.

constitutes a 'wrong' for which tort law should provide redress.[47] Contrary to what some say,[48] the argument that tort law defines what counts as a wrongful injury and to think that tort law provides redress for wrongful injuries does not suffer from circularity. In order to see that this accusation misses the mark, it is helpful to bring a distinction to mind which concerns social conventions, namely the difference between deep and surface conventions:[49] Offering a fine-grained analysis, Andrei Marmor demonstrates 'that for many surface conventions to be possible at all, a deeper set of conventions must be present.'[50] Deep conventions offer 'normative responses to basic social and psychological needs'[51] and 'typically enable a set of surface conventions to emerge, and many types of surface conventions are only made possible as instantiations of deep conventions.'[52] Moreover, '[d]eep conventions are actually practiced by following their corresponding surface conventions.'[53]

Distinguishing between deep and surface conventions is fruitful for tort law and defining a 'wrong'. Tort law is the surface convention.[54] It is based, however, on a deep-level set of norms, for example, moral norms.[55] Given the openness of most moral norms and the disagreement concerning their concrete content and import with respect to specific cases, for a modern secular legal system to work, their consequences need to be spelled out more clearly and in a manner making them more predictable—which closes the circle to law as surface convention.[56] As concomitant effect, law establishes a public minimum threshold of what the deep-level norms, especially moral norms, require of citizens and market participants.[57]

This bears directly on the starting point—the purported circularity of civil recourse theory. There are two levels of 'wrong': One on the deep level of moral norms, the other on the surface of tort law. It is not wrong to injure someone in their bodily integrity or to damage property belonging to another because tort law says so, but because deep-seated moral norms govern this kind of

[47] eg Richard A Posner, 'Instrumental and Noninstrumental Theories of Tort Law' (2013) 88 Ind LJ 469, 473.
[48] ibid.
[49] Andrei Marmor, *Social Conventions* (Princeton UP 2009) 58–59.
[50] ibid 58.
[51] ibid.
[52] ibid 59.
[53] ibid.
[54] On the normative nature of conventions and law as convention, Marmor, *Social Conventions* (n 49) 155–75.
[55] Note that there is no claim made against efficiency as a deep-level norm. For the purposes of this chapter, this question is not essential. If one regards efficiency as a deep-level norm, the same considerations apply.
[56] cf Miller and Pojanowski (n 3) 268–69.
[57] cf ibid 269.

behaviour. Tort law, in turn, contains a more specific set of—depending on your theoretical preferences—duties or liability rules. In *that* sense, tort law defines wrongness.[58] Consequently, the civil-recourse theorist is correct in arguing that tort law delineates the boundaries of injuries counting as 'wrong' in terms of the law. The reason why these wrongs are wrong in the first place, however, is that they violate deep-level norms. Picking up the definition of surface and deep conventions mentioned above,[59] it is fair to say tort law instantiates deep-level norms. For those undergirding tort law with moral norms and stressing that private law should recognize these,[60] it is thus reasonable to contend that a wrong as defined by the law mirrors a moral wrong.[61] This is also why Holmes' critique of tort law being non-relational falls flat. If deep-level norms structure interpersonal relationships and tort law serves as their instantiation, the latter necessarily has a relational nature.

Following a cursory inspection, this seems like an externalist position: The deep-level norms are, at least to a certain degree, external to the law.[62] At the same time, however, the law contains concretizations which, by virtue of their character as law, may originate in said norms, but stands on its own feet as a set of value judgments. Tort law norms and those of other areas of private law are the result of one possible interpretation of the underlying moral norms. That also means that they have a value and content of their own. Consequently, there are two sets of public norms relevant to the creation of private law as an artifact—those at the surface level but also the broader deep-level norms, at least to the extent they take shape in the law and thus are accessible from an internal point of view.[63] Insofar, the deep-level norms are not external, but part of the internal structure of private law.

As a last point, exclusively externalist perspectives of judges and legislators suffer from incoherence. They can only pursue their aim to create law if they start from an internalist perspective. After all, a judge acts as such in that role,

58 For a similar account (but starting from different premises) Miller and Pojanowski, ibid.

59 n 52 and accompanying text.

60 Miller and Pojanowski (n 3) 262, 264.

61 See, eg, Miller and Pojanowski (n 3) 264. To be clear: this chapter is agnostic about the character of the deep-level norms. They could also relate to efficiency or another content. The only issue of importance for the purposes of the text above is how deep-level norms and surface conventions intertwine.

62 This does not imply a Razian account of law according to which law is an exclusionary reason to refrain from acting for other reasons than those provided by the law, see Joseph Raz, *Practical Reason and Norms* (2nd edn, OUP 1999, reprint 2002) 39. '[T]o a certain degree' refers to the universally accepted character of law to function as a reason for action, not in dispute between positivists and natural lawyers. If law is to fulfil that function, it has to be independent from its deep-level foundations at least insofar as the moral reasons to act are not the relevant guiding motives when it comes to law. In that sense, the deep-level foundations are external to law.' The text does not presuppose that law excludes moral reasons as reasons to act, but only says that law is a sufficient reason to act.

63 cf Miller and Pojanowski (n 3) 264.

not as an actor mimicking a judge. They want to deliver a decision with specific consequences set out by the law. That, however, requires that the judge adopts an internal point of view about the law regarding their own position—as a judge based on existing legal institutions and conventions[64] deciding an actual case in a procedural setting which follows a specific set of rules depending on the issue at hand rooted in a specific legal field, for example, criminal or tort law, in a competent court. Relying on internal perspectives and arguments in order to legitimize and establish one's own authority as a creator of legal norms while at the same time relegating an internal point of view to the fringes when it comes to exercising this exact power is an incoherent position.

2. Shortcomings of Internalist Perspectives

As established in Section 1, there is no escape from internal points of view. Externalism, in its pure form, is doomed to fail. This does not imply, however, a triumph of internalist perspectives, at least not as they have been articulated in influential accounts of private law, namely those of Ernest Weinrib and Jules Coleman.[65]

In his well-known attempt to extricate private law from the grasp of functionalism, Weinrib conceives private law as 'a distinctive setting, and a characteristic mode of reasoning'.[66] His idea of private law is that of an 'immanently intelligible'[67] field resting on 'Aristotle's conception of corrective justice as the unifying structure'[68] with its 'normative force deriv[ing] from Kant's concept of right as the governing idea for relationships between free beings.'[69] For him, private law's purpose is to be private law.[70] Ascribing private law's 'distinctive rationality' to corrective justice[71] is impossible to square with the many forms of private law; just think of corporate law. Even for tort law, Weinrib's idea of private law lacks sufficient explanatory power. Several authors correctly

64 cf Marmor, *Social Conventions* (n 49) 163.

65 Jules Coleman, *Risks and Wrongs* (CUP 1992, reprint 2003); Weinrib (n 1). This is not to say that there are no other important and influential accounts of private law in the English-speaking world. It seems fair to think, however, that Coleman and Weinrib's contributions had the most prominent impact over the years with other scholars' works often 'only' extending or criticizing their ideas, see William Lucy, 'Method and Fit: Two Problems for Contemporary Philosophies of Tort Law' (2007) 52 McGill LJ 605, 609.

66 Weinrib (n 1) 5.

67 ibid 18.

68 ibid 19.

69 ibid. For a similar version of private law in Germany see Rödl (n 4).

70 Weinrib (n 1) 5.

71 ibid.

denounce the unwitting kinship of Weinrib's with externalist perspectives. His reliance on remedies resembles the outcome-oriented vantage point of law and economics.[72] Moreover, Weinrib's interpretive strategy of reducing tort law to a theoretical Procrustean bed despite obvious frictions and dispensing with views of participants of the legal system standing square to his version of the law resembles traditional externalist practice.[73]

But there is more. Recent theories of private law take their cues from currently existing private law. Concentrating on the (private) law 'as it is', they underplay the contingencies of private law. Considering its nature as a surface convention, private law, first of all, is contingent upon deep-level norms and values, as has already been pointed out in sub-section 1. That is especially true given that private law is not a closed system isolated from other areas of the law, most visibly tort law. Arguably, the mark of a good explanatory theory is consilience.[74] Corrective-justice accounts or civil-recourse theory both cut out or are highly sceptical regarding efficiency and regulatory perspectives on tort law, especially those employed by law and economics.[75] This makes it very hard for them to integrate important parts of tort law into their version of tort law, namely all those areas where tort law interlaces with public or criminal law. Examples abound: Section 823(2) of the German Civil Code holds anyone liable who is in breach of a statute intended to protect another person.[76] This section serves as a transmission belt to turn criminal and public law into tort. In the US, the Georgia Code states that a 'tort may also be the violation of a public duty if, as a result of the violation, some special damage accrues to the individual.'[77] English law regards certain abuses of public power as a tort called 'misfeasance in public office' and offers exemplary damages, combining elements of public and private law.[78] One may argue, following a line of reasoning with respect to punitive damages in the United States,[79] that these and similar

[72] Miller and Pojanowski (n 3) 256–57.

[73] Lucy (n 65) 622.

[74] Jules Coleman, *The Practice of Principle* (OUP 2001, reprint 2008) 38, 41.

[75] For corrective justice: Weinrib (n 1); for civil-recourse theory Goldberg and Zipursky, *Wrongs* (n 1) 46: 'economic school ... [is] off-base' (but conceding that 'courts might sometimes legitimately consider the consequences of adopting different possible interpretations of [the] law', ibid).

[76] Sec 823 of the German Civil Code (own translation):

> '(1) A person who, intentionally or negligently, unlawfully injures the life, body, health, freedom, property, or any right of another is liable to compensate the other for any damage arising from this injury.
> (2) The same applies if a person infringes a statutory provision intended to protect another person ...'.

[77] OCGA § 51-1-1 (2022).

[78] Donal Nolan, 'Tort and Public Law: Overlapping Categories?' (2019) 135 LQ Rev 272.

[79] Benjamin C Zipursky, 'Theory of Punitive Damages' (2005) 84 Tex L Rev 105.

provisions entail elements of both private law and criminal or public law, imposing punishment as the state's goal and allocation of a private right to punish. But the lines remain blurry, and the fact remains that tort law integrates public welfare concerns through clauses linking tort and public law.

Moreover, private law is historically contingent. Property law is a good example: In Germany, private-law scholars traditionally draw a sharp line between public law governing property and private property law. Whereas the latter supposedly primarily serves a delimiting function and has to define and delineate the content and extent of property rights, the former carries the regulatory burdens concerning common welfare and the protection of third parties against the use and abuse of property.[80] In this dichotomy, property law appears as apolitical law or at least as autonomous from concerns of public welfare. And yet, it takes no great effort to find examples for deep-level norms that internalists disqualify, without much ado, as external. Section 137 of the German Civil Code prohibits private actors from excluding a party's power to dispose of property.[81] The historical background is the abolishment of feudalism.[82] Section 137 ensures that private parties do not re-establish restrictions of property rights resembling an entailed estate or other arrangements of old. The corollary to this is the protection of free markets for property rights,[83] arguably an efficiency-oriented goal supporting public welfare. Nevertheless, until recently, a vast majority of German scholars have been particularly hostile to the economic analysis of law, execrating a 'legal theory without law'.[84]

What internalist readings of private law should also take into account is that even on a more general level, a private law of property is by no means the historical default. In an intriguing study, Blaufarb showed that for France before the French Revolution, public power and property in land were intertwined. Under the old order, there was no private property regime for real estate, but only a private regime for public power, for example, in the form of

[80] eg Jürgen F Baur and Rolf Stürner, *Sachenrecht* (18th edn, CH Beck 2009) 2–3.

[81] Sec 137 of the German Civil Code (own translation): 'The power to dispose of an alienable right may not be excluded or restricted by contract or any other private transaction. This effectiveness of an obligation not to dispose of such a right is not affected by this provision.'

[82] cf Alexander Hellgardt, *Regulierung und Privatrecht* (Mohr Siebeck 2016) 122–27 (but see also ibid 141–48 on persisting limitations after the German Civil Code entered into force on 1 January 1900).

[83] cf BGHZ 56, 275, 278–79 (German Federal Court of Justice, order of 18 June 1971—docket no V ZB 4/71); Hellgardt (n 82), 137–40; Rüdiger Liebs, 'Die unbeschränkbare Verfügungsbefugnis' (1975) 175 Archiv für die civilistische Praxis 25–26.

[84] Ernst-Joachim Mestmäcker, *A Legal Theory Without Law* (Mohr Siebeck 2007), see also Karl-Heinz Fezer, 'Aspekte einer Rechtskritik an der economic analysis of law und am property rights approach' (1986) 41 Juristenzeitung 817. For a more recent discussion (in favour of law and economics) Gerhard Wagner, 'Privatrechtsdogmatik und Ökonomische Analyse' in M Auer and others (eds), *Privatrechtsdogmatik im 21. Jahrhundert, Festschrift für Claus-Wilhelm Canaris zum 80. Geburtstag* (de Gruyter 2017) 281.

jurisdictional lordship and venal public office, both of which came with rights over property.[85] It was the revolutionaries who excised property from political power and created private property as an institution on its own terms.[86]

Summing up, cutting off efficiency or other reasons outside the canonical morality-oriented norms from internalist views suffers from the same flaws as any externalist manoeuvre—because, in essence, it is one, just executed from the other side of the fence. Reading private law as an expression of moral norms only and banishing welfare concerns such as efficiency from private law's inside rests on implicit assumptions about its nature, which do not withstand scrutiny. It is not only the term 'externalist' which awaits further clarification but also its 'internalist' sibling.[87] Prevalent conceptions of private law, prominent internalist views in the United States as well as traditional constructions of private law in Germany, engage in the same manoeuvre they so vehemently oppose. They start from an external premise about what private law supposedly is and which functions it serves.

3. Shortcomings of Combination Through Adoption

As mentioned earlier in the introduction,[88] a rising number of scholars aver the complementarity of external and internal points of view and suggest integrated approaches. One version of these efforts keeps an internal or external core but adopts arguments and insights from the respective 'other'.[89] Contrary to hybridization, combination through adoptions rests on a lexical ordering of vantage points.[90] Whatever is adopted ranks second from the vantage point of the default set by the (internal *or* external) core. There is an obvious allure of combination through adoption. It allows one to stay true to a strong coherence criterion and to posit private law or at least definable subparts like torts or contracts within the framework of a unified theory,[91] but still tolerate ideas and tools foreign to the preferred theoretical construct. For a Kantian, adopting efficiency-minded arguments opens an avenue to concretize duties where deontic concepts suffer from indeterminacy.[92] The economic analyst of the law

[85] Rafe Blaufarb, *The Great Demarcation* (OUP 2016) 15–47.
[86] ibid 48–81.
[87] But see the recent piece by Miller and Pojanowski (n 3).
[88] See n 3 and accompanying text.
[89] See Gold (n 3) 5–16. The other version relies on hybridization, which will be dealt with below in Section IV.
[90] See Section IV for a hybrid approach.
[91] For such a strong view on coherence Weinrib (n 1) 29–46; on different versions of coherence Stephen A Smith, Contract Theory (OUP 2004, reprint 2007) 11–13.
[92] Kraus, 'Transparency' (n 108) 304, 335–36.

profits from integrating the internal point of view when attempting to evaluate legal consequences as outcomes.[93] A theoretical framework buttressing this specific type of combinatory strategies is missing, however.[94] Three things are amiss:

Firstly, all of these strategies suffer from their carry-on baggage. Authors starting from a unitary theory built around a purified vision of private law fall prey to the same flaws as those pursuing externalist or internalist perspectives as outlined above.[95] At their core, they represent just another variant of single-value worlds of private law.

Secondly, any attempt at enriching or supplementing them by introducing additional arguments drawn from opposing viewpoints runs up against a deep-seated problem of how to legitimize such an interpretive move. An author defending a pure deontic vision of tort law has to explain on the basis of what theory one may turn to for efficiency. As soon as one qualifies efficiency as something external to tort law, one has to legitimize how and to what extent efficiency may play a valid role in any legal argument *as* a legal argument which actually influences the outcome.[96]

Thirdly, just because it is useful to include ideas and concepts from the other side of the fence, it is by no means theoretically or methodologically possible. The creation of law as an artifact requires one to act in accordance with the public norms governing the production of an artifact.[97] Especially with respect to efficiency, the legal official in private law has to regard a very specific set of public norms at play—the constitution and the question whether and, if yes, to what extent legal official may include external norms into their deliberations. From a common lawyer's point of view, with a picture of judges at the centre of lawmaking and a much narrower reading of the scope of codes than civil lawyers are used to,[98] this most likely runs against deeply ingrained intuitions. Therefore, shifting to civil-law systems, such as in Germany, might help to unpack the issue:

As a matter of principle, a code in Germany is a set of legal norms aiming at complete coverage of an area and containing an original statement of the law and not only an amendment or modification of customary law, which thus has to be read narrowly.[99] The German code overrides precedent. This implies

[93] Gold (n 3) 8.
[94] In a similar vein Miller and Pojanowski (n 3) 272.
[95] Sections III.1 and III.2.
[96] And not only as an argument which may be recognized by the law without being incorporated *into* the law, cf Raz, *Practical Reason* (n 62) 152–54.
[97] Section II.1.
[98] Still on point: Ernest Bruncken, 'The Common Law and Statutes' (1920), 29 Yale LJ 516.
[99] ibid 516–17.

that—in the ideal world of a Montesquieu'ian judge reduced to mouthing the law—a judge is bound by the code and thus obligated to interpret it in light of the relevant deep-level considerations set by the legislator. If the provision in question relates to corrective justice, they must not argue from an efficiency perspective, however inefficient or indeterminate they may think the law is.[100] This curbs the possibilities for German judges to take external viewpoints into account. However, to avoid leaving a false impression, the reality of the administration of justice in Germany is much more complicated. German judges are not bookkeepers or accountants of the law. But the general point made here is recognized even by those who are open to an efficiency perspective or other views generally alluded to as 'external'.[101] In those parts of US codes, which amend or modify existing law or create new law where there was none before, the problem appears to be similar, at least for defenders of internalist theories of private law and those who mourn the 'death of common law'.[102] From a German point of view, it would at least merit a more probing analysis from the vantage point of theories of democracy and separation of powers to determine to what extent judges presiding over private-law cases in the United States are precluded from combining internalist and externalist approaches.

US constitutional law offers a docking station. Repeatedly, the US Supreme Court discarded efficiency-oriented arguments and emphasized that '[r]aw consequentialist calculation plays no role in our decision'.[103] North American scholars routinely place this as a problem of constitutional law.[104] But it is a problem for private law as well. A practically reasonable legal official[105] will not and should not include external criteria like efficiency into consideration without good cause. For their model of combination through adoption, this presents a significant obstacle. Whereas it is not impossible to include external consequentialist reasoning,[106] the main question is left unanswered, namely when, how, and to what extent legal officials are allowed to join internal and external norms and values through adoption.

There is, of course, work on the problem of combining external and internal perspectives.[107] One prominent example is a duo of articles Jody Kraus

[100] cf Horst Eidenmüller, *Effizienz als Rechtsprinzip* (4th edn, Mohr Siebeck 2015) 458–59.
[101] eg Eidenmüller, ibid 450–85.
[102] J Lyn Entrikin, 'The Death of Common Law' (2019) 42 Harv J L & Pub Policy 351.
[103] *Niz-Chavez v Garland*, 593 US ___ (2021), 141 S.Ct. 1474, 1486 (2021).
[104] See, eg, David Pozen and Adam Samaha, 'Anti-Modalities' (2021) 119 Mich L Rev 729; Aaron Tang, 'Consequences and the Supreme Court' (2023) 117 Nw U L Rev 971.
[105] In the sense of Miller and Pojanowski (n 3) 272–73.
[106] For examples see Tang (n 104) 985-1007 .
[107] See Gold (n 3).

authored a while ago.[108] He holds vertical integration to be the most promising approach to constructing a comprehensive unified theory encompassing both efficiency and autonomy in contract law.[109] Vertical integration can be achieved by either according efficiency lexical priority over autonomy theories or treating efficiency as normatively derivative of normative foundational autonomy-based theories of contract law.[110] Kraus convincingly lays out how efficiency theories help in overcoming an indeterminacy problem of autonomy-based vantage points which more often than not remain too abstract in order to be applicable in practice whereas the former fail to deliver an explanatory framework for basic features of the idea of right and duty.[111] He also gives examples under which philosophical framework it would be possible to vertically integrate efficiency and autonomy.[112] Kraus unfolds a rich account of how to legitimize the integration of efficiency and autonomy in general. He certainly proves efficiency to be a helpful concept even in a contract-law edifice resting solidly on autonomy as its cornerstone. His theory falls short, however, in that it does not provide criteria in which case and under which circumstances it is legitimate or perhaps even necessary to refer to efficiency-related arguments. Showing that the latter have their uses does not prove they may or must be taken into account from a methodological perspective.

IV. Private Law on the Fence: The Futility of Essentialist Readings

The discomforting consequence of the preceding analysis is that none of the current perspectives presents a satisfying account of the characteristics of private law. Externalist theories fail because they miss the public norms framing the concept of private law, which rests on an abundance of deep-level norms other than consequentialist concerns. Internalist approaches suffer from a truncated methodology excommunicating public-welfare norms, such as efficiency from private law proper. These vantage points lack theoretical foundations in terms of intention—both 'external' and 'internal' are insufficiently fleshed-out terms. This makes it very hard to decide what lies inside or outside

[108] Jody S Kraus, 'Transparency and Determinacy in Common Law Adjudication: A Philosophical Defense of Explanatory Economic Analysis' (2007) 93 Va L Rev 287; Jody S Kraus, 'Reconciling Autonomy and Efficiency in Contract Law: The Vertical Integration Strategy' (2011) 11 Phil Iss 420.

[109] Kraus, 'Reconciling', ibid 437.

[110] ibid 421, 436.

[111] ibid 430, 431–32, 434–35.

[112] ibid 422–23 (Scanlon), 423–24, 426 (Rawls).

their respective boundaries. In extension, this affects the viability of attempts to unfold perspectives which combine through adoption. All of these views share a common core. They embody essentialist readings of the nature of private law. In the following subsections, this chapter shows why any endeavour to unearth an essence of private law is doomed to fail. Private law rests on a broad variety of deep-level norms and is built on shifting ground. Theorizing about private law thus best builds on hybrid accounts, accepting different influences ranging from consequentialist and public welfare values to autonomy and distributive justice as equally important without ordering them lexically.[113] The public norms governing the making of private law artifacts are indeterminate as regards their deep-level foundations (Section 1). They are subject to interpretation and, thus, at least to a certain extent, fluid and open to change. Not only that—the creator also enjoys some leeway to decide which public norms provide the relevant framework for the production ofproducing legal artifacts. As a case study shows, private law is subject to modification not only on its surface but also with respect to the relevant deep-level norms. Because of the feedback any such change generates concerning the public norms governing the process of artifact production, this has important ramifications. Given its position in the architecture of law and the separation of power, the legislator deserves special treatment (Section 2).

1. The Ambivalence of Creating Private Law Artifacts

The successful creation of artifacts depends on whether the creator meets the set of relevant public norms.[114] If one intends to produce a copy or at least a token of an artifact type already in existence, one has to meet the form and substance of the prior model.[115] For a lawyer, this sounds familiar. In a more positivist lawyerly language, the requirement of meeting the form and substance of prior models translates into a duty of at least courts and administrators to apply the law.[116] Private-law norms as artifacts are created successfully only if and when they hew to the composition and structure of existing private law. Theorizing about private law requires 'carrying forth ideas, principles, and norms that are already in the law'.[117] But just as legal theory in general and

[113] As combinatory approaches would do, see text above accompanying n 90.
[114] Section II.1 above.
[115] Section II.1 above.
[116] Raz, *Practical Reason* (n 62), 139. On the legislator Section IV.2.
[117] John CP Goldberg and Benjamin C Zipursky, '*Thoroughly Modern Tort Theory*' (2021) 134 Harvard LR 184, 189.

positivist accounts of the law in particular face the problem of judicial discretion, the leeway courts enjoy and exploit complicates the matter for private law theory, too, when it comes to essentialist readings, irrespective of their colours. In the process of legal artifact creation, legal officials assume a dual role. They identify existing law and use it to address the case at hand. Inevitably, this involves thinking about what the law 'does' (Section a)). Moreover, and notwithstanding whether the deep-level foundations are clear or not, the law calls for efficient application or consequentializing, adding an efficiency-oriented layer to the moral norms of any stripe (b)).

a) Dual role of legal officials in judging and lawmaking

In the process of judging and lawmaking, legal officials assume a dual role. On the one hand, they identify the relevant existing law as, for example, construed by courts (precedent) and parliament (codes and statutes).[118] On the other, judges and administrators have to evaluate the law 'as it is' in terms of fit and coherence with respect to the question at hand and then apply or adapt (develop) it to the case. Both movements leave plenty of room for interpretive manoeuvre. Moreover, in the end, legal officials create new legal artifacts, whether one distinguishes between the mere application of settled law and the development of unsettled law[119] or thinks that every so-called application necessarily entails the creation of new law.[120] Even those holding something like 'pure' application to be possible must recognize that a new judgment or an administrative ruling creates something which was not there before—an explanation that and how a certain fact pattern falls within the ambit of a legal norm or a part of the law, that it belongs to fiduciary, tort, property, or contract law, and a specific rule or provision of that area. For future cases, it serves as a further reference and benchmark and may be used as an argument in legal reasoning.

Especially for legal positivists, it does not seem too far-fetched to put courts and administrators under an obligation to apply this so-called existing law.[121] What appears to be an innocuous procedure, comparable to flipping to the right page in a book, upon closer inspection emerges as something rather rich in content: Creating private-law artifacts without having a jurisprudential or

[118] There are, of course, other sources of existing law, depending on how 'law' is defined. One example would be regulations promulgated by administrative agencies.

[119] eg Andrei Marmor, *Positive Law and Objective Values* (Clarendon 2001) 71–81; Joseph Raz, *The Authority of Law* (2nd edn, OUP 2009, reprint 2011) 49, 183–84; in the German literature, eg, Karl Larenz and Claus-Wilhelm Canaris, *Methodenlehre der Rechtswissenschaft* (3rd edn, CH Beck 1995) 143.

[120] eg Kuntz, 'Performative Rechtserzeugung' (n 3) 876–7.

[121] eg Raz, *Practical Reason* (n 62) 139.

moral normative deep-level justification in mind will fail. Giving private law, on the surface, pride of place as a set of public norms in their own right entails an inferential chain running from the law's language to its justification. Even if the law is in some sense 'just a text' or another form of literature, there is no death of the author.[122] Law's language is fashioned for a specific regulatory purpose. It diverges from texts of law and literature in that the latter are intransitive, that is, not directed at anyone.[123] Legal norms concretize moral and other deep-level norms. They alleviate the indeterminacy problem of moral norms and thus reduce error costs and facilitate coordination.[124] The direction of fit is mind-to-world.[125] In other words, the author's intention has purchase in the world of law, even in the realms of exclusive positivism.[126]

But still, or so critics might argue, this does not matter much: In many cases, a deep dive into law's moral foundations is simply unnecessary for legal practice because the law is settled.[127] If a tort statute says that a person hurt by another in their bodily integrity and health has a claim, a court need not bother about whether compensation is required by corrective justice or efficiency. The standards of interpretation have been developed and tested over a multitude of similar fact patterns so that courts come to acceptable conclusions in compliance with public norms because they can rely on sufficiently robust conventions.[128] In not a few cases, however, judges do not walk on solid interpretive grounds and need to test the waters. To expand on the tort example just given: What if the tort victim suffers not only a broken leg but faces mental impairments as well, or is a haemophiliac who had to go through a life-threatening experience and severe pain caused by the additional blood loss? Now, the court will have to test the limits of tort law and see where the tortfeasor's liability ends under rules on foreseeability and other norms. It is cases like these where legal

[122] Famously declared by the French literary critic and philosopher Roland Barthes (in an English publication!), 'The Death of the Author' in Brian O'Doherty (ed), *Aspen: The Magazine in a Box*, no 5 + 6, item 3 (Aspen 1967) (no pagination available). On the context of this publication, John Logie, *1967: The Birth of 'The Death of the Author'* (2013) 75 College English 493. On the resurrection of the author, eg, Séan Burke, *The Death and Return of the Author: Criticism and Subjectivity in Barthes, Foucault, and Derrida* (Edinburgh University Press 1998).

[123] Barthes, ibid.

[124] Larry Alexander, 'Can Law Survive The Asymmetry of Authority?' (2000) 19 QLR 463, 465–66.

[125] On direction of fit see, eg, John Searle, *Rationality in action* (MIT Press 2001) 36–38.

[126] cf Joseph Raz, 'Intention in Interpretation' in *The Autonomy of Law* (n 11) 249, 280: '[T]he interpretation of statutes, etc., in accord with the author's intentions is a universal feature of legal systems which recognize legislation as a source of law, for it is implied by the very notion of legislation.' This is not to say that purpose necessarily trumps language or text. But even adherents to originalism and textualists in legal interpretation make room for the intention of law's creators, see, eg, Amy C Barrett, 'Assorted Canards of Contemporary Legal Analysis: Redux' (2020) 70 Case W RSRV L Rev 855, 857.

[127] See, eg, Raz, *Authority* (n 119) 184–85.

[128] On the importance of conventions of interpretation Raz, 'Intention' (n 126) 280–81.

officials cannot rely on settled routines and must first construct a deep-level framework as a guide for the interpretation of the law.

Of course, this is something even hard positivists do not dispute.[129] They just call into question the frequency of difficult cases as an empirical matter.[130] What hard positivists like Raz underestimate, however, is the consequences even one hard case may have. When a court breaks new ground in the interpretation of a legal norm, it may lead to a subtle shift in the tectonics of private law or at least in certain areas of private law and instigate a re-evaluation of what was accepted as settled law until then. Even in cases that seemingly belong to an area with long-standing principles, courts always have to keep in mind whether new developments in other parts of the law give cause to question established conventions of interpretation.

b) Opacity and ambivalence of normative foundations

As laid out before, part of a legal official's interpretive analysis necessarily probes into the deep-level foundations of the legal norms at play, whether they are part of the *ratio decidendi* of precedent or a statute's *ratio legis*. Sometimes, legal officials can unearth legal materials offering guidance on what motivated the process, leading to the existing norms. More often than not, however, the analyst runs into trouble because the normative foundations of many legal norms are opaque.[131] At least judges or members of administrative agencies do not typically deal in ethics or jurisprudence. Instead, they justify their actions in juridical language such as 'right', 'wrong', 'duty' or 'obligation'.[132] Parliamentary materials seldom contain essays on moral philosophy. Consequently, legal officials may choose normative foundations as they deem fit, as long as they are able to connect them to deep-level norms, which are generally accepted as a possible grounding for legal norms in that area. If a specific rule of tort law lacks a clear, deep-level foundation, a judge will look to general justifications for tort law which have been accepted by legal officials in the past. This does not solve any problems, however, because the foundations of many norms are vague.

Tort law nicely illustrates how different deep-level norms coalesce in one and the same field, sometimes in a single provision such as Section 823 of the German Civil Code.[133] Moreover, many surface-level norms do not serve a sole

[129] See, eg, Raz, 'Intention' (n 126) 183–84.
[130] Raz, 'Intention' (n 126) 184, with respect to precedent: 'In the main, however, the identification of the *ratio* of a case is reasonably straightforward.' (Italics in original.)
[131] See Alexander (n 124); Jiménez (n 16) 410.
[132] Goldberg and Zipursky, 'Seeing Tort Law' (n 46) 1576–77.
[133] See n 76 and accompanying text.

aim but have non-negligible corollary effects. Even very traditional German tort scholars standing as far from law and economics as possible accept that tort law has a secondary function to regulate future behaviour[134] and thus cannot be wholly separated from instrumentalist and consequentialist frameworks. Tort law and property law are closely related and overlap with public law in several respects,[135] which means that ideas and regulatory concepts governing public law flow into private law. This ambivalence opens up possibilities for a delicate refinement of the deep-level basis of private law. Depending on how they identify, construe, and weigh different deep-level norms and their expression on the surface, courts can put emphasis on different aspects.

It is at this point that lawmakers decide what counts as 'internal' or 'external'. There is no way to define beforehand what lies within the law and what lurks beyond its borders. To the contrary: In interpreting the law and identifying the relevant deep-level norms, a legal official creates an inside and an outside. 'Internal' and 'external' are notions which become clear only *after* the fact.

Additionally, over time, aspects which traditionally may have been considered secondary can gain importance because they become more prominent. Whereas the first decision emphasizing a secondary aspect to be decisive in *this* case could be interpreted as a maverick, the third or fourth building on it already looks like settled law, especially if higher courts follow that strategy.[136]

c) Methodological struggles

If the existing law provides the starting point of a search for justifications for private law and theories about private law, disentangling what the law is and what the law does may prove to be more complicated than assumed by not a few interpretivists.[137] Reconstructing the law implies a concern about what the—until now—existing law *would* do, assessed in comparison to what the law *should* do given its purpose as an artifact[138] and therefore necessarily a hypothesis about the likely effects of an application of existing norms and doctrine to the present case. Consequently, the inquiry entails a perspective on what the law does. Courts going back to remedies fashioned in the past may conclude that these remedies did not serve their purpose well and, therefore,

134 Karl Larenz and Claus-Wilhelm Canaris, *Schuldrecht, Besonderer Teil Vol II/2* (13th edn, CH Beck 1994) para 75 I.2.i).

135 See n 76 and accompanying text.

136 For an example Section IV.1.e).

137 Insisting on this distinction, eg, Jules Coleman, *Practice* (n 74) 14; Benjamin C Zipursky, 'Pragmatic Conceptualism' (2000) 6 Legal Theory 457, 482.

138 Section II.1.

need remodelling. Because legal officials must ask different questions, they must employ different methodologies.[139] Construing the law 'as it is' requires a methodological apparatus that economic theory and instrumentalist views on private law do not offer. Internalist points of view do not provide the tools for evaluating the real-world effects of law legal officials consider when moulding law into form. The data they look at are not the same.[140] Depending on which questions they ask about the law and to what end they create novel legal artifacts, they (should) employ a different methodology.[141]

Additionally, extrapolating normative foundations from the language of law is an inductive endeavour. Legal officials creating new legal artifacts lack the capacity to investigate every norm and precedent governing specific areas such as torts or contracts. They have to select a moral norm based on a small sample of private-law norms and then generalize.[142] By scaling up, the micro-level analysis of a concrete case or a specific issue transforms into a macro-level conjecture.[143] This, though, entails a change of the issue. What started as a question of legal interpretation now becomes a problem of ethics: Generalizing a moral norm and subsuming big chunks of private law under a monistic ethical framework requires philosophical reasoning and, therefore, a methodology which keeps an eye on the law but fundamentally centres on the moral problem.[144] Cutting off punitive damages from private law because of a corrective justice rendering of tort law[145] does not follow from legal (surface) rules, but from a jurisprudential move after tying tort law as surface norms to corrective justice as the foundational moral deep-level norm. There is no way out of this problem. Even civil-recourse theorists who emphasize law's autonomy as an argument against both corrective justice and instrumentalist views concede that theirs 'is a philosophically informed account'.[146]

[139] Assuming that methodology must be suitable to the issue.

[140] Jody S Kraus, 'Philosophy of Contract Law' in J Coleman, KE Himma, and S Shapiro (eds), *Oxford Handbook of Jurisprudence and Philosophy of Law* (OUP 2002) 687, 689.

[141] cf Kraus, ibid.

[142] On the importance of generalizable simplicity for internalist theories Andrew S Gold and Henry E Smith, 'Sizing Up Private Law' (2020) 70 U Toronto LJ 489, 510–12.

[143] On scaling up in private law and the problem of the relation of micro- and macro-level analysis Gold and Smith (n 142) 490, 494.

[144] Assuming for a moment that it is really possible to solve this problem rationally on the basis of theory and methodology. However: For the purposes of this text, the relevant point is a different one; namely that the issue is not one of legal methodology, but that anyone dealing in these questions has to rely on a rather different conceptual and methodological framework.

[145] See, eg, Weinrib (n 1) 135 n 25.

[146] Goldberg and Zipursky, 'Tort Theory' (n 117) 188.

d) Consequentializing legal norms

A similar problem occurs with respect to what modern moral philosophers dub 'consequentializing', that is, the reconstruction of a non-consequentialist theory in consequentialist terms.[147] As has been pointed out in tort law, norms of corrective justice have 'to do a good job of regulating whatever it regulates. There needs to be an adequate case for regulating the subject matter by that norm.'[148] '[T]o fulfill its morally constitutive role, tort law's norm of corrective justice *must* be evaluated as an instrument.'[149] In sum, a deontological or rights-based rendering of private law does not preclude efficiency-oriented or instrumentalist analysis. A nice example can be found in the German law of damages for infringements of intellectual property. The German Federal Court of Justice argues that given the specific challenges of enforcing intellectual property rights, the law must be oriented towards prevention and consequences ('what the law does') to fulfil the redistributive aims of the German law of damages.[150]

Consequentializing has a serious impact on the justification of private law. Whereas the old norms the legal official found to be wanting in terms of their instrumental adequacy may have been based on corrective justice or autonomy, the new legal artifacts engendered to improve the instrumental quality of private law take this purpose as part of their normative deep-level foundation. This has ramifications for the whole of private law and what private law is about—and thus for private law theory. Firstly, ascribing unitary values to private law writ large becomes even more unconvincing. Secondly, the contours of private law change over time. This is all the more true given the reverse strategy of limiting instrumentalist norms through a combination of consequentialism and Kantian thought,[151] 'deontologizing',[152] or

[147] For an introduction Douglas W Portmore, 'Consequentializing' (22 August 2022) in EN Zalta and U Nodelman (eds), *The Stanford Internet Encyclopedia of Philosophy*; for a more extensive treatment Douglas W Portmore, *Commonsense Consequentialism: Wherein Morality Meets Rationality* (OUP 2011) 84–117; for a critical view, eg, S Andrew Schroeder, 'Consequentializing And Its Consequences' (2017) 174 Philos Stud 1475; Mark Schroeder, 'Teleology, Agent-Relative Value, and "Good"' (2007) 117 Ethics 265.

[148] John Gardner, 'What is Tort Law For? Part 1. The Place of Corrective Justice' (2011) 30 Law & Phil 1, 14 (original italics suppressed).

[149] ibid 19 (italics in original). This is the reason why the critique of consequentializing in general moral philosophy does not apply (or at least not fully) to the issues discussed in the text above. The argument in favor of consequentializing has its roots in the normative foundations of private law, even if the latter should be anchored in corrective justice or autonomy.

[150] More on this in Section IV.2.

[151] See Douglas W Portman, *Kantsequentialism: A Morality of Ends*, available at https://sites.google.com/site/dwportmore/kantsequentialism-a-morality-of-ends (last accessed 25 January 2023).

[152] Paul Hurley, 'Consequentializing and Deontologizing: Clogging the Consequentialist Vacuum' in M Timmons (ed), *Oxford Studies in Normative Ethics*, Vol 3 (OUP 2013) 123; Benjamin Sachs,

a scheme of prioritization with second-order rank allocated to functionalist values.[153] To give an example:

Even where the German Federal Court of Justice qualifies certain areas of private of law as efficiency-driven, the prevailing view on constitutional law is that the protection of human dignity enshrined in the German constitution excludes certain results flowing quite naturally from a consequentialist view, such as sacrificing the life of an innocent to save twenty innocents.[154] Though German law accords consequentialist arguments, the constitution draws boundaries in deontological terms. It is only within this framework a legal official may refer to efficiency.

e) Shifting contours of private law: a case study

German private law, or, more specifically, the German law on compensation for damages in tort and contract, offers a nice example for the argument developed in the preceding subsections a)–e). A line of decisions by the German Federal Court of Justice concerning compensation for the infringement of intellectual property rights shows how legal officials promote secondary deep-level foundations to primary concerns and thereby modify the general normative justificatory basis of private law over time.

As a matter of general German private law, damages are limited by the compensation principle.[155] The German Federal Court of Justice refrained from enforcing a US judgment granting punitive damages because, to the mind of the judges, punitive damages violate the principle of corrective justice and therefore stand in opposition to core principles of German private law.[156] What is interesting for the purposes of this chapter is the court's approach to infringements of intellectual property rights. At the time of the court's decision concerning punitive damages, it was well established that efficiency was part of the normative grounding of the law governing the compensation of damages resulting from violations of intellectual property rights, precedent with a (relatively) long tradition:

'Consequentialism's Double-Edged Sword' (2010) 22 Utilitas 258. For a critical view see, eg, Schroeder (n 147) 1485–87.

153 See Kraus, 'Reconciling' (n 108) 430–31.

154 See BVerfGE 115, 118, 159–60 (German Constitutional Court, judgment of February 15, 2006—docket no 1 BvR 357/05).

155 Jens Ekkenga and Thilo Kuntz, 'Vor § 249' in Hans Th Soergel (founder), *Commentary on the German Civil Code*, Vol 3/2 (13th edn, Kohlhammer 2014), para 26.

156 BGHZ 118, 312, 338–40 (judgment of 4 June 1992—docket no IX ZR 149/91).

Early on, German courts pointed out that, given the immaterial character of intellectual property rights, holders of such rights encounter difficulties in proving infringements, making it hard for them to enforce their rights. As a result, the courts allowed to either disgorge profits made by the party violating the holder's rights or to claim payments in the amount of a reasonable royalty.[157] Later on, the German Federal Court of Justice rephrased its reasoning and underlined that the law on damages 'sanctions and compensates'.[158] Reviewing the issue again after roughly twenty years, the court relied on these earlier decisions and explained that to levy illegal profits 'also serves the sanctioning of violating behaviour … and in this way the prevention against a violation of intellectual property rights requiring special protection …'.[159] In the following years, the German Federal Court of Justice's judges routinely cited prevention as one of the decisive elements in their opinions on violations of intellectual property rights.[160]

Put differently: Notwithstanding its adage of the limits of the compensation principle, the court regards as settled that sanctions and prevention—at least the latter a classic consequentialist argument—operate as foundational principles in an important area of German private law. It used an argument most German scholars regard as a secondary aim of the law on damages and efficiency[161] to cast a supporting pillar for a practically significant area of private law. Even if the judges have only sown a pocket and not a whole new mantle for the German private law governing damages, the consequences reach beyond intellectual property law. The precedent on intellectual property offers a point of departure for reasoning by analogy and, thus, for an extension in other areas of the law. The German Federal Court of Justice already transferred the regime developed for intellectual property rights to certain violations of the law on unfair commercial practices more than forty years ago.[162] Given that the decisions on intellectual property law served as a template, it would be easy for the judges also to apply the new justification for the principles governing damages.

[157] RGZ 156, 65, 67–69 (German *Reichsgericht*, judgment of 13 October 1937—docket no I 262/36).

[158] BGHZ 68, 90, 94 (German Federal Court of Justice, judgment of 30 November 1976—docket no X ZR 81/72).

[159] BGHZ 145, 366, 372 (German Federal Court of Justice, judgment of 2 November 2000—docket no I ZR 246/98), author's translation.

[160] See BGHZ 181, 98, 125–26 margin no 76 (German Federal court of justice, judgment of 14 May 2009—docket no I ZR 98/06); BGHZ 221, 342, 348 margin no. 20 (judgment of 26 March 2019—docket no X ZR 109/16); BGH GRUR 2022, 229, 238 margin no 87 (judgment of 16 December 2021—docket no I ZR 201/20).

[161] On this issue Ekkenga and Kuntz (n 155) para 28, 34.

[162] BGHZ 57, 116, 120–21 (German Federal Court of Justice, judgment of 8 October 1971—docket no I ZR 12/70).

This example shows that even as courts stress basic structures of private law, such as compensation and corrective justice, as deep-level moral norms, they have enough room to promote principles thought secondary to a more prominent role. The result is a shift in the values private law reflects and enforces. Through general principles like 'good faith', the duties of care and loyalty in fiduciary law and similar mechanisms, private law incorporates changing social norms[163] and becomes a platform for balancing tradition and innovation in society at large. Changing times force judges to develop new answers to what may appear as an old question. Inevitably, courts will interpret the existing private law in a different light and, in the process, re-evaluate the relative importance of various deep-level norms for the relevant surface norms to come up with a reasonable solution.

f) Two possible objections from legal theory

aa) The exclusive positivist's objection

The procedure described in subsections a)–e) is an evaluative endeavour. According to the argument developed in these sub-sections, determining the content of private law necessarily involves value judgments.[164] At least at first glance, this is not only a conjecture concerning private law and private law theory but rather a claim about the nature of law going against the views of hard positivists. Raz, to provide the obvious and most famous example, emphasized that at least where judges apply 'settled' law and do not develop 'unsettled' law,[165] 'the content and existence of the law can be determined by reference to social facts and without relying on moral considerations'.[166] '[I]dentifying the content of the law and determining its existence depend exclusively on facts of human behavior capable of being described in value-neutral terms and applied without resort to moral argument.'[167] Of course, Raz allows the law to refer to morality. But this reference does not transform morality or moral norms into law; it only permits recognizing moral norms just as it is possible to recognize foreign law.[168]

Luckily, there is a way out, even for hard positivists, building on the distinction of primary and secondary rules.[169] For exclusive positivism, it is important

[163] For good faith see Marietta Auer, *Materialisierung, Flexibilisierung und Richterfreiheit* (Mohr Siebeck 2005) 166–76, for fiduciary law and social norms Matthew Harding, 'Fiduciary Law and Social Norms' in EJ Criddle, PB Miller, and RH Sitkoff (eds), *Oxford Handbook of Fiduciary Law* 797 (2019).

[164] cf Gerald J Postema, 'Law's Autonomy and Public Practical Reason' in *The Autonomy of Law* (n 11) 79.

[165] On this distinction Raz, *Authority* (n 119) 49–50.

[166] ibid 52.

[167] ibid 39–40.

[168] ibid 46.

[169] See Scott Shapiro, 'On Hart's Way Out' (1998) 4 Legal Theory 469.

to validate primary legal norms as law according to a secondary rule of recognition, which does not include morality. 'Unenacted' moral norms may never count as law.[170] That does not preclude primary rules from integrating value-laden terms and concepts. Their validity depends on the rule of recognition, and so does the nature and content of moral criteria relevant for interpretation.[171] Which moral or welfare norms demand respect in the process of determining the content of law and the application of the law 'as it is' to new cases, therefore, is a question of social pedigree.[172]

bb) The natural lawyer's objection

Whereas natural lawyers do not take offence when it comes to moral language and value-laden rules of recognition, they may have other problems with the picture drawn in subsections a)– e), especially with respect to the view on consequentialist arguments being part of private law. If and when law existentially depends on its accordance with morality, understood as something other than consequentialism, interpreting legal norms by drawing on efficiency-oriented notions appears highly problematic. Such ideas seem to run counter to what the (private) law demands. Taken in this absolute form, this critique overreaches. First of all, even from the vantage point of natural law, consequentializing is a necessary and unavoidable feature of law.[173] Additionally, it is far from clear that natural law theory necessarily implies that all arguments in identifying the content of legal norms have to be arguments following the route of moral philosophy in method and substance. After all, natural lawyers take the law not to equate law and morality. They take the law seriously on its own terms as reasons for action[174] and work with it on the basis of a distinctly legal—that is, not ethical—methodology.[175] As long as the results of an efficiency-oriented interpretation stay within the outer boundaries drawn by moral norms, it is dubious whether the differences of consequentialist and deontological reasoning

170 ibid 497.

171 ibid 498.

172 What this means in metaethical terms and for claims about the ontology of moral norms is a question for hard positivism in general and thus outside the scope of this chapter. For analyses concerning the general problem see, eg, the essays in Brian Leiter (ed), *Objectivity in Law and Morals* (CUP 2000). With respect to the text above, there is no need to delve into that problem as the text deals with a possible objection by a hard positivist.

173 See Section IV.1.d).

174 That the law or legal norms provide reasons for action does not stand in dispute between legal positivists and defenders of natural law. Finnis, to name but one member of the latter group, has written: 'So one begins to see the sense of the term 'natural law': reasons for actions which will instantiate and express human nature precisely because they participate in and realize human goods.' John Finnis, 'Natural Law and Legal Reasoning' (1990) 38 Clev St L Rev 1, 2.

175 See, eg, Miller and Pojanowski (n 3), who propose to integrate consequentialist arguments in private law theory based on ideas developed by John Finnis.

matter much for private legal theory, even though they may still be significant philosophically.[176]

g) Conclusion: private law's shifting contours

Both interpretive and constructive strategies cause a constant latent instability of private law's deep-level foundations. In sum, private-law theorists tracking what happens within private law, how courts argue and decide cases, how the law develops, and how precedent undergoes incremental change face an ever-changing object with inherently ambivalent features regarding its normative deep-level structures. As others pleading for a 'social-welfare' approach to private law have already pointed out, private 'law ... is a messy business'.[177] Shoehorning private law into a single-value frame and pinning down an essence, however defined, is impossible. Private law does not rest on solid ground but floats on a swamp. The German Federal Court of Justice's approach to damages for infringement of intellectual property provides an illustrative example.

2. The Legislator as a Special Case

Until now, the chapter has mainly focused on courts and judges as creators of private law. The doctrine of separation of powers binds these actors—at least from a theoretical starting point, judges follow the law enacted by parliament. Leaving all the difficulties of legal methodology aside for a moment, most scholars would most likely agree that when a judge, after careful consideration, concludes that the law aims at promoting corrective justice, one at least needs very good reasons to turn to efficiency. In the common-law world, judges are also bound by precedent.[178] Parliament, however, has the power to create new law and, to echo an old adage in German legal scholarship, to discard whole

[176] See Allen W Wood, *Kantian Ethics* (CUP 2008, reprint 2011) 259–69, and ibid 268: 'Kantians and optimizing consequentialists may or may not ... reach the same decisions. But Kantian ethics will not reach them by the same route, or on the same ultimate value basis, as the optimizing consequentialist.' For a position more sympathetic towards the possibility of combining Kantian thought and consequentialism see, eg, Richard M Hare, 'Could Kant Have been A Utilitarian?' (1993) 5 Utilitas 1, 2: '[T]he story that Kant and utilitarians have to be at odds is now regularly told to all beginner students of moral philosophy. But is it true? My own hesitant answer would be that it is not. The position is more complicated. Kant, I shall argue, could have been a utilitarian, though he was not. His formal theory can certainly be interpreted in a way that allows him—perhaps even requires him—to be one kind of utilitarian. To that extent what J. S. Mill says about the consistency of his own views with Kant's Categorical Imperative is well founded.' For an even stronger position that Kant's ideas necessarily lead to consequentialism see David Cummiskey, *Kantian Consequentialism* (OUP 1996).

[177] Goldberg and Zipursky, 'Tort Theory' (n 117) 186 (on tort law).

[178] Again: To the extent possible.

libraries with three correcting words.[179] If the German *Bundestag* adopts a reform of the law governing damages in private law and includes punitive damages as well as efficiency as a general principle, what a vast majority of scholars deems to be the essence of German law concerning damages, namely the compensation principle and corrective justice,[180] is overturned. This is neither surprising nor new.

Why bother with the legislator when everything seems obvious, a reader could ask. Because of the catch. Whereas the legislators in theory are (almost) omnipotent in a legal sense, in the reality of lawmaking they are not. They seldom drive groundbreaking reforms such as the property reform enacted by the French revolutionaries.[181] Instead, the creation of new legal norms in private law occurs within an already existing framework, typically aiming at incremental change only. Even a relatively far-sweeping reform of tort or contract law will concentrate on selected issues such as product liability or sales contracts. Consequently, there is no complete reframing of 'tort' or 'contract' in general. This implies that the deep-level structures of private law, by and large, remain intact. At best, the lawmaking process introduces new elements into the edifice's structure or strengthens components.

V. Conclusion, or Moving Beyond the Internal/External Divide

Private law is a humankind, an artifact created to serve a purpose. This purpose, however, evades any attempt at capture. Scholars trying to cultivate a single-minded rendering of private law underplay the historical contingency of private law and its multi-value deep-level structure as much as they overstate their case. Private law provides footholds for internal and external theories because it has roots in morality and public welfare, thus offering points of reference for each vantage point. And yet, internalism and externalism suffer from a similar general flaw. The private-law surface conventions reflect and concretize the various deep-level norms and provide public norms relevant for creators of new private-law tokens, at least for judges. If these public norms entail morality and public welfare, monistic approaches like 'externalism' and 'internalism' lack

[179] Julius von Kirchmann, *Die Werthlosigkeit der Jurisprudenz als Wissenschaft* (J Springer 1848) 23: 'drei berichtigende Worte des Gesetzgebers und ganze Bibliotheken werden zu Makulatur', roughly translatable as 'three correcting words of the legislator and whole libraries are reduced to shambles.'

[180] On this issue Ekkenga and Kuntz (n 155) para 26–28, 34.

[181] See n 85 and accompanying text.

sufficient explanatory power for private law. On closer inspection, internalist theories are just a masked version of externalism—if private law also rests on consequentialist values, enunciating a theory with morality at its centre glosses over core concerns like externalist positions ignore moral norms. In light of the profusion of deep-level norms and values private law incorporates, efforts to distil an essence of private law appear fruitless. That is all the more true given the powers of a legislator to change the system of private law or to introduce new deep-level norms.

The lack of an essence does not imply a lack of autonomy. On the contrary, private law is autonomous in that it is not restricted to one specific vantage point and may develop based on the deep-level norms and values it integrates. It does not hinge on any particular concept of private law and, by providing the public norms for making New Private Law, governs the creation of new tokens. That is the real autonomy of private law.

II

NEW PRIVATE LAW AND *RECHTSDOGMATIK*: FORMALISM AND CONCEPTUALISM IN PRIVATE LAW THEORY

6

In Defence of Ambiguity

Towards a Shandean Way for Legal Methodology

Ino Augsberg

I. Circumscribing the Way

At a certain point in his (fictitious) autobiography, Tristram Shandy sighs and complains (as he so often does) to the reader about the difficulty of his task: 'so much unfixed and equivocal matter starting up, with so many breaks and gaps in it'.[1] However, as every reader of 'Tristram Shandy' knows, these breaks and gaps do not simply exist by chance or due to misfortune. For the most part, they are the result of Tristram's own doing. In contrast, those intellectual efforts that we call scholarship, rationality, or scientific methodology, all seem to be moving in exactly the opposite direction. Apparently, they are all means to the end of closing the gaps, of putting together what seems broken, of fixing and clarifying that strange 'matter' which gives us so much trouble.

Yet could it be also the other way around? Could there be another way around it? Is there such a thing as a methodology which does not aim for the *hodos* in the sense of the straight line, the clear-cut argument which ends all further debates? A methodology that does not aim to avoid digressions and deviations, but that tries to find them, thus moving, at best, in 'a tolerable straight line'?[2] Hence a methodology, which, rather than being merely prescriptive—'What shall we do?'—or mainly descriptive—'What do we do, in fact?'—might be characterized as circumscriptive, in the literal sense of writing in circles, more around something than directly about it? A writing that, moving in this peculiar circular way, inevitably always already writes also about itself and not only about a certain object? In a word, a more Shandean type of methodology? This is what I would like to discuss in the following.

[1] Laurence Sterne, *The Life and Opinions of Tristram Shandy, Gentleman*, vol VI, ch XXXIII (here quoted from: *The Florida Edition of the Works of Laurence Sterne*, vol II (ed by Melvyn New and Jane New, The University of Florida Press 1978) 558).

[2] Sterne (n 1), vol IV, ch XC (at 570).

Ino Augsberg, *In Defence of Ambiguity* In: *Methodology in Private Law Theory*. Edited by: Thilo Kuntz and Paul B. Miller, Oxford University Press. © Ino Augsberg 2024. DOI: 10.1093/oso/9780198885306.003.0006

II. The Promise of Legal Methodology

If one asks what legal methodology—not only private law methodology, but legal methodology, more generally speaking—is actually all about, my guess is that the typical answer will be: it is about securing the rationality of legal decision-making. Rationality, in this view, is not only understood in classical Weberian terms, that is to say, as a certain technique, a formalization, which serves to demystify or disenchant the world. Rather, it indicates a certain transfer process, a kind of '*Umbesetzung*',[3] in which one of the classical divine attributes, the capacity of *providentia*, is passed on to human beings and social institutions. Rational thinking in this context is understood in an almost mathematical sense as a certain form of *calculus* that enables us to predict the outcome of a process that is either still in progress or has not even begun yet. It means doing the maths, taking into account certain preconditions and general laws of development, in order to calculate the future. It enables us to know what to expect from the course of events. Legal rationality, then, apparently follows the exact same strategy of combining a concrete individual situation with a more generalized background, except that its laws are not the scientifically explained concepts of causality, etc., but normative constructions, be it in the form of statutes or precedents.

Accordingly, the legal methodology is something like the law of the laws, namely a technique which tells us how we have to combine the circumstances of an individual case with the general prescriptions of the law in order to arrive at a solution that is not only one possible outcome but the inevitable consequence of this precise combination—or at least presents itself as such. Legal methodology tells us what the law has to say with regard to a specific situation. It provides the 'predictability of legal dispositions'.[4] In doing so, legal methodology presents itself as the specifically juristic way of operationalising the *providentia*, thereby constructing a system of decisions which are supposed to be just, and that is to say, in this context: equal decisions.[5] Because of the appropriate methodology, no legal decision is arbitrary or ambiguous. It is the power of legal methodology that overcomes the contingencies of individual points of view, characterized by subjectivist, spatial, and temporal limitations, and turns

[3] See Hans Blumenberg, *Die Legitimität der Neuzeit. Erneuerte Ausgabe* (2nd edn, Suhrkamp 1988) esp 75, 541.

[4] Antonin Scalia and Bryan A Garner, *Reading Law: The Interpretation of Legal Texts* (Thomson/West 2012) xxvi.

[5] See on this understanding of equality as a specific form of juristic justice Niklas Luhmann, *Die soziologische Beobachtung des Rechts* (Alfred Metzner 1986) 42 f.

them into a comprehensive perspective in which everyone who reads the law must have a share and play their part accordingly.[6]

Moreover, the methodology has another significant effect. It reduces the burden of responsibility for the individual decision-maker. 'Legal interpretation', Robert Cover tells us in the very first sentence of his essay on 'Violence and the Word', 'takes place in a field of pain and death'.[7] Notwithstanding the maybe somewhat exaggerated, overblown pathos of the formulation, the sentence is completely justified in terms of its content. Legal interpretation is not a game. Its outcomes matter in a very direct, literal or even physical sense. The established rules of legal interpretation take this situation into account.[8] Because of them, that is to say, because of an elaborated legal methodology, it is not the individual judge who decides (and hence is personally responsible for this decision) what cruelties may happen in this field, for instance, that a defendant is sent to prison for several years, a plaintiff is no longer allowed to see his children, or an asylum application is not only rejected but the applicant and her family are also sent back to their home country. The legal methodology enables us to conceive of as responsible, instead of those individuals, that peculiar impersonal entity we call 'the law'. Accordingly, it is not the individual judge who gives orders and thus provides 'authoritative normative guidance for the resolution of conflict and coordination issues'.[9] It is 'the law' that tells the judges what they have to do in the first place. Legal methodology helps us to understand this internal injunction. It makes it clear to legal decision-makers what 'the law' has to say. This is the promise that legal methodology gives. Given the 'field of pain of death' in which legal interpretation takes place, it ought to be clear that this promise is not just a somehow old-fashioned idea that could and should be replaced by fancier, more modern, and more interdisciplinary concepts. By contrast, it is of existential importance for all those working in and on the law. Hence, the fundamental test for any reasonable replacement of or addition to the traditional legal method must be the extent to which it can, in turn, help deliver on that promise.

[6] See eg Scalia and Garner (n 4) 31: 'Through accurate knowledge of language and proper education in legal method, lawyers ought to have a shared sense of what meanings words can bear and what linguistic arguments can credibly be made about them.' For a quite different take on this supposedly in itself unambiguous method of 'reading (the) law' Peter Goodrich, *Reading the Law. A Critical Introduction to Legal Method and Techniques* (Basil Blackwell 1986).

[7] Robert Cover, 'Violence and the Word' in M Minow, M Ryan, and A Sarat (eds), *Narrative, Violence, and the Law. The Essays of Robert Cover* (University of Michigan Press 1993) 203–38, 203.

[8] See for the benefits as well as the limits of insights about other forms of interpretation, outside the legal sphere, Kent Greenwalt, *Legal Interpretation. Perspectives from Other Disciplines and Private Texts* (OUP 2010).

[9] Paul B. Miller, 'Formalism, Legality, and the Rule of Law', in this volume, at 206.

III. Legal Methodology and Its Discontents

Yet despite its enormous importance, it is easy to see that this promise is never truly fulfilled, at least not in practice. Obviously, the transfer of *providentia* has not worked properly. If it had, there would be no need for lawyers.[10] Nor would we need a fully developed, complex judicial system. At most, we would need a sufficient number of well-trained investigators to provide us with the specific facts for each case and a corresponding yet relatively small number of equally well-trained judges to decide on these cases. Accordingly, if this observation were true, the very existence of a complex judicial system could arouse some suspicion: it could be regarded as a symbol that the law distrusts its own methodology. Why else all the institutional effort?

What remains to be determined, then, is the answer to the question of whether this apparent malfunction of legal methodology is only an individual, subjective deficit of those practising the law. If the broken promise of legal methodology was just the result of individual inabilities, it could be overcome by less faulty, more godlike creatures, such as someone who is at least a half-god, like Hercules. Similarly, though with a different focus, one might suggest that, if not a single person, then perhaps a certain collective form of intelligence, gradually emerging from a crowd rather than from a single mind, could solve the problem. In both cases, the inadequate practical implementation of legal methodology would not affect its general idea. Reading the law would still imply that there is a distinct inherent meaning to it, even though, due to our finite existence and respective incapacities, we might not be able to grasp it so very easily. Despite all these difficulties, uniform meaning would remain the goal for all those involved in and dealing with the law, although, admittedly, a practically unattainable one.[11]

IV. A Literary Critic's Perspective

Hence, with regard to this process in which legal methodology makes a promise but cannot deliver on it, the next question to ask and answer is whether, when looking at the inability to keep that promise, we are indeed talking of something

[10] See on the specific role and relevance of lawyers for the legal system and the corresponding specific legal regulations W Bradley Wendel, 'How Can You Have Law Without Lawyers? Legal Formalism, Legality, and the Law Governing Lawyers', in this volume.

[11] See Scalia and Garner (n 4) 31 ff, who try to present an unambiguous concept of ambiguity by confronting (unintentional) ambiguity with (intentional) vagueness: 'True ambiguity[!] is almost always the result of carelessness or inattention.'

like human faults, which as such could be overcome, at least theoretically (or maybe even practically, by relying on new, algorithm-based technology), or whether there is something more to it. Are there possibly structural reasons that necessitate this strange double-bind situation?

Indeed, for instance, the literary critic Werner Hamacher has not only raised and specified this question but also answered it in the affirmative, stating that it is:

> one of the trivia of literary criticism that every text is open to an illimitable abundance of interpretations, applications, and reactions; but most crucially, this manifold of interpretive possibilities does not indicate a lamentable insufficiency of the interpreters that could be healed in a messianic moment; rather, it is a structural effect of the constitution of language itself ... The structure of language does not simply make different interpretations of texts possible, but it does so with necessity. Polysemy is a necessary possibility of linguistic utterances.[12]

The task, then, would be to elaborate on a closer methodological reflection which takes these said structural effects and the insufficiency of classical legal methodology into account and analyses them in more detail, thus explaining that and for which reasons the 'necessity' which Hamacher talks about is relevant not only from a literary critic's point of view but also from the legal perspective. Along these lines of argument, one might come to an understanding in which the promise of legal methodology had to be conceived of in the double sense in which Paul de Man relates to the promise of language. De Man writes, in German, '*Die Sprache verspricht (sich)*',[13] thus indicating that the promise of the language is not only a promise of itself but also a parapraxis, a Freudian slip.

V. Two Examples from the Jurisdiction of the German Federal Constitutional Court

Yet instead of trying to explain the situation along these lines of literary criticism and philosophy of language (which I have tried to do elsewhere in

[12] Werner Hamacher, 'LECTIO: de Man's Imperative' in L Waters and W Godzich (eds), *Reading de Man Reading* (University of Minnesota Press 1989) 171–201, 189.

[13] Paul de Man, 'Promises (*Social Contract*)' in *Allegories of Reading. Figural Language in Rousseau, Nietzsche, Rilke, and Proust* (Yale University Press 1979) 246–77, 277. De Man continues: 'to the extent that is necessarily misleading, language just as necessarily conveys the promise of its own truth'.

more detail[14]), one could also—if only because of a certain propensity for digressions—take a different turn, walk in another direction. Rather than confronting legal methodology with insights derived from other disciplines, we can try to take a more subjective or internal point of view, asking how the law itself looks at the problem and reacts to it.

If we take this perspective and proceed further in this direction, the first remarkable finding is that the aforementioned idealization of legal procedures remains largely ignorant of what one might call legal facts, that is, the characteristic structures and elements that form the legal system in modern societies. A closer look at these facts reveals that the legal system accepts said deficit as an inevitable fate. What is more, at least some of its mechanisms deliberately undermine the rationality of the law in the initially explained sense. Rather than support the ideal of unity and clarity, these mechanisms tend to subvert the fundamental assumption that there ought to be only one right answer to every legal question. They even openly contradict it. Yet if the law deliberately proceeds in this way, then one might assume that what first looks like a mere deficit could, at a second closer glance, reveal a different side of the story, telling us that the ambiguity of the law might have a certain function of its own.

As my key witness for the internal observation that legal methodology is structurally unable to reach its own objectives, that is, an observation carried out and expressed by the legal system itself, I would like to call the German Federal Constitutional Court to the witness box. The Court has, in various decisions, explicitly stated that even legal reasoning based on a perfectly well-elaborated methodology does not necessarily lead to the one right answer—quite the contrary.

The first example of this kind of observation is the well-known and much-debated Honeywell decision. In this decision, the Court basically deals with its relationship with the jurisdiction of the European Court of Justice. In doing so, it emphasized that 'questions of interpretation of Union law', even if they are 'interpreted methodically within the usual framework of jurisprudential discussion, can lead to different results'.[15] Two things in this statement should catch our attention: first, when it comes to the question what legal methodology actually means, the Court does not try to give its own, authoritative

[14] See Ino Augsberg, *Die Lesbarkeit des Rechts. Texttheoretische Lektionen für eine postmoderne juristische Methodologie* (2nd edn, Weilerswist 2020). For a short version of the argument Ino Augsberg, 'Reading Law. On Law as a Textual Phenomenon' (2010) 22 Law Lit 369–93.

[15] *Entscheidungen des Bundesverfassungsgerichts* (ie official collection of the decisions of the German Federal Constitutional Court) vol 126, 286–331, 307.

account. It refers, albeit in a rather diffuse way, to a different kind of authority, namely to legal scholarship. Second, while this legal scholarship may indeed determine—in a strong, normative sense—certain boundaries of what may be called a proper or appropriate legal methodology, keeping within these boundaries, that is to say, following the established rules of legal methodology, does not prevent ambiguity. Different results remain possible. So basically what the Court tells us is that the classical legal methodology, even in its most elaborated scholarly form, does not work—at least not in the way it is supposed to do.

A second example from the Federal Constitutional Court's jurisdiction stresses this point even more explicitly. In order to explain its concept of a 'constitution-conform' interpretation, the Court makes once again quite remarkable claim with regard to the limited function of traditional legal methodology. It states:

> The requirement of interpreting the law in a way that is consistent with the Constitution requires that of several possible interpretations of the law, some of which lead to an unconstitutional result and some of which lead to a constitutional result, the one that is consistent with the Basic Law be preferred. A norm is therefore only to be declared unconstitutional if no interpretation is possible which is permissible according to recognised principles of interpretation and which is compatible with the constitution. If the wording, the history of origins, the overall context of the relevant provisions and their meaning and purpose permit several interpretations, one of which leads to a constitutional result, the latter is required.[16]

Once again, the statement is quite clear. What the Court talks about is not just a flawed methodology that, as such, has to be corrected in a certain way. Quite the contrary. What the decision states is that even a professional, from a methodological point of view, flawless interpretation will not present us with the one right answer. Reading the law, therefore, does not mean finding the true meaning of the law. While legal methodology may not be completely useless in this regard, it is also not sufficient to solve this task. We need additional techniques.

At first glance, what the Court does is exactly just this: to explain such an additional technique, thus leaving the main objective of legal methodology untouched and unimpaired. However, a second, closer glance reveals that the

[16] ibid vol 119, 247–92, 274.

Court, perhaps unintentionally, points to a more fundamental dilemma. In some way, the explanation is self-contradictory. The Court does not address and explain the question of how we can get to an unambiguous understanding of those constitutional rules that are supposed to serve as criteria for the so-called constitution-conform interpretation. Yet, if legal methodology cannot guarantee a uniform understanding of the law, this problem inevitably also affects our interpretation of the Constitution. Thus, what the Court initially mentions rather casually as a prerequisite for a specific kind of interpretation is, in fact, a far more disturbing statement which undermines the possibility of interpretation in general. Consequently, a certain problem left by the traditional methodology is not remedied by the 'constitution-conform' interpretation. Instead, this interpretation is itself infected by the very disease it was supposed to cure.

VI. Preserving Ambiguity in Law

In this perspective, ambiguity still appears as a structural deficit, albeit an unavoidable one. Yet the movement does not stop here. Several mechanisms in the legal system go one step further. They do not only accept ambiguity but deliberately produce it. In this sense, one could indeed distinguish between mere vagueness and 'true' ambiguity,[17] however ambiguous this distinction may be. Of course, the law may use deliberately vague formulations, for example, in legal texts, which, as such, may allow some room for interpretation. 'True' ambiguity, however, refers to something more. To accept ambiguity means to allow for and even support entirely divergent points of view. It thus points to something else than the mere idea of a plurality, at least insofar as with this idea, one primarily emphasizes the possibility of peaceful coexistence and does not refer at least as much to the immanent conflicts. Ambiguity does not only mean the harmonious coexistence of different meanings. It includes a possibly painful awareness of the tensions and contradictions between them.

The first, rather obvious example of an acceptance of ambiguity in this sense is dissenting votes. The very possibility of these votes indicates a certain distrust of the idea that there can be only one correct decision, for if there were that answer, why bother with an alternative? Nevertheless, the law explicitly guarantees this peculiar kind of legal alternative truths, at least in certain areas,

[17] See, once again, Scalia and Garner (n 4) 31 f.

namely in the jurisdiction of the Supreme Courts. It not only allows for differences of opinion but even makes internal disagreements visible to the public, thereby undermining the idea of a homogeneous, purely rational legal apparatus.

The second example is the independence of judges. While it is quite obvious why judges need to be able to decide their cases without being subject to political pressure, it is far less clear why the same kind of independence should be granted within the judiciary itself. Why should a lower court whose decision has not been upheld by the higher court be allowed to invoke its own independence vis-à-vis that higher court, in the sense that it may decide the next case entirely in the spirit of its former, then overturned judgment? Considering that the reversal itself can only be based on legal reasons, which means that the overruling must actually assert that the previous decision is legally wrong, why, then, should the lower court be allowed to proceed with this particular kind of legal wrongdoing? Yet once again: still, that is precisely what is happening. The independence of the judiciary is all at once also an independence from and against the judiciary. Thus, the legal system allows for internal self-contradictions.

Of course, one could say that these mechanisms are only means to a certain common end, namely means to operationalise a certain 'crowd wisdom', in the sense of an incremental process of generating the knowledge and skills we need to solve our cases. Accordingly, it may seem too harsh to speak of 'self-contradictions' since all participants and decisions generally aim in the same direction as a 'right' or 'just' decision-making. On the other hand, however, one may also ask where such confidence in continuous development leading to the better comes from and whether its somehow crypto-teleological character might not seem too optimistic. What if the fundamental legal goal was not to find an ever-better solution but merely to keep the wheel turning? In any case, the assumption of a larger overarching framework should not lose sight of the finding that the law not only allows but encourages contradictory decisions. Consequently, the law is characterized by an internal structure that makes such self-contradictions possible.

VII. Lexibility

If we understand 'reading' in the traditional sense as a process which tracks down and detects the meaning inherent in a text—and this text is to be understood in a very broad sense, encompassing the spoken word, of course, but also every other kind of symbols, signs, etc—then as an interim result of the considerations so far one could conclude that the law, *lex*, lacks legibility. Accordingly, if we were not too afraid of strange neologisms, we could say that one of the law's characteristics is its 'lexibility'. Apparently, the law is, at least to a certain extent, illegible or unintelligible since no reading of the law will provide us with an unambiguous meaning.[18] Moreover, this illegibility is not just the result of an unconscious bias or a certain pathology, which as such is recognized as unintentional but unavoidable by the law itself. The illegibility is something that the law both implicitly and explicitly accepts and even embraces.

This illegibility of law (or, as I would be inclined to say, its lexibility) undermines an understanding of legal methodology, which not only points to a specific methodology for the legal sphere but to a legal or juridical element in the very heart of methodology itself, namely the hermeneutical idea that to understand something means to 'get it', to grasp it, and to transform it from something that used to be strange or foreign into something which one can now rightly call one's own.[19] In this perspective, a proper understanding is an understanding in which an insight has to be acquired in order to belong to the person who seeks to understand.

The illegibility of law, however, points in the opposite direction. If we can never fully grasp the meaning of a legal norm—which, as mentioned before, means more than a statute—if, by contrast, every attempt to catch this meaning only demonstrates that there is a multiplicity of different meanings which as such inevitably escape from this attempt, then we will never arrive at a proper understanding. Properly understood, our understanding—and that includes, of course, our understanding of understanding—will never be truly ours in the strict sense of property law.

Hence, a legal methodology conceived in this way undermines its own legal character. Yet it does not do so by ignoring the legal character because it mistakes the law as something else, such as literature. Quite the contrary. It does so

[18] See for the specific ambiguity of this particular process, ie the possible different readings of 'reading', ibid, on the one hand, and Goodrich (n 6), on the other.

[19] See on this traditional understanding of understanding eg Friedrich Schleiermacher, 'Über den Begriff der Hermeneutik mit Bezug auf F. A. Wolfs Andeutungen und Asts Lehrbuch' in M Frank (ed), *Hermeneutik und Kritik* (Suhrkamp 1977) 309–46, 315; and in a similar vein Georg Wilhelm Friedrich Hegel, '*Grundlinien der Philosophie des Rechts*, § 69' in Hermann Glockner (eds), *Sämtliche Werke. Jubiläumsausgabe in zwanzig Bänden, Siebenter Band* (3rd edn, Frommann und Holzboog 1952) 126. Hereunto in more detail Ino Augsberg, '*Diaspomenos*. Hermeneutics of Exile' in L Feierstein and D Weidner (eds), *Diaspora and Law: Culture, Religion, and Jurisprudence beyond Sovereignty* (Walter de Gruyter 2023) 37–47.

because it emphasizes and insists on the legal element in the methodology. It presents the bill for paying too much, not too little, attention to the characteristics or, to use a more suitable term, the properties of law.

What remains to be answered, then, are two questions: first, the reason for this kind of movement, which leads to the acceptance of ambiguity, and second, why formalism—possibly a renewed idea or understanding of formalism[20]—could play a decisive role in supporting this function.

VIII. Why Ambiguity?

The answer to the first question is so evident that it hardly seems to require broader attention. Faced with a final unambiguity, only a couple of days before he eventually lost consciousness and died, Paul Feyerabend has summarized the entire argument in a single and quite paratactic (and indeed rather unambiguous) sentence: 'Without ambiguity, no change, ever.'[21] Thus, to accept ambiguity means moving away from what Heinz von Foerster has called a trivial machine, that is to say, a machine which, given the same input, constantly produces the same output, hence a purely mechanical device, and turning instead to a non-trivial machine where the input does not necessarily imply the output.

Yet, of course, ambiguity itself is ambiguous. To talk about change does not mean that everything can happen—despite a persistent prejudice which claims otherwise, even a very superficial reading of Feyerabend's texts shows that 'anything goes' was never his motto. Quite the opposite. The preface of 'Against Method' explicitly emphasizes that Feyerabend only made use of this expression in an ironic way.[22] Unluckily, this irony has been lost on most of his readers, or rather on those who have not read him. Irony, however, is also an ambiguous technique. The same, namely ambiguity, applies to Feyerabend's sentence: not only this sentence but change itself is ambiguous. Change always implies that there is something that changes—pure chaos does not change; it is change. Therefore, against this background, no particular change could ever be recognized as such. Accordingly, change necessarily contradicts itself, and that

[20] See Paul B Miller, 'The New Formalism in Private Law' (2021) 66 Am J Jurisprudence 175–238.

[21] Paul Feyerabend, *Killing Time: The Autobiography of Paul Feyerabend* (The University of Chicago Press 1995) 180.

[22] See Paul Feyerabend, *Against Method. Outline of an Anarchistic Theory of Knowledge* (4th edn, Verso 2010) xvii.

is to say, it contradicts its own apparently contradictory character. If change is the opposite of unity and stability, then this does not mean it is simply something else. Rather, its own position remains shaped and characterized by this opposition. Change implies not only something that changes but also something that does not change. Otherwise, the act of transformation could never be perceived as such. Change presupposes and includes both, all at once: continuity and transformation.

A legal methodology based on ambiguity thus means, on the one hand, to enable the legal system to internal adaptations and transformative processes. On the other hand, it does not necessarily mean that we must give up the systemic or even systematic character of law altogether.

IX. Formalism as a Counterposition?

That leaves us with the question of what something like a 'new formalism'[23] might have to say in this context. Is there something that formalistic approaches and a position which attempts to argue 'in defence of ambiguity' might have in common?

Apparently not. Formalism, be it in its classical or renewed form, obviously moves in the exactly opposite direction. It seems to be interested in a closed, systemic form of law, clearly distinguished from other forms of normativity and other social systems.[24] Thus, the formalistic existence that the law is said to wish for is the wish to have an independent existence.[25] Uninfluenced by the contingencies of the rest of the society, like economic interests, political ideas, religious beliefs, etc, the law is supposed to follow only its own, internal norms. On this account, the wish to have a formal existence points in the same direction as the promise that the legal methodology makes. It aims at a law of the law that safeguards the legal sphere as a clearly marked territory. Instead of insisting on a certain blurring of boundaries, it emphasizes the distinctiveness and uniqueness of law. If we want to argue 'in defence of ambiguity', a reference to formalism will, therefore, hardly support our claim.

[23] See Miller, 'The New Formalism in Private Law' (n 20).

[24] See also, however, Miller, 'Formalism, Legality, and the Rule of Law' (n 9), defending a broader normative perspective within the formalist view. On a similar topic, albeit with a different result, John Gardener, 'The Supposed Formality of the Rule of Law' in *Law as a Leap of Faith. Essays on Law in General* (OUP 2012) 195–220.

[25] See Stanley Fish, 'The Law Wishes to Have a Formal Existence' in *There's No Such Thing as Free Speech, and It's a Good Thing, Too* (OUP 1994) 141–79, esp. 141 ff.

X. Two Other Attempts to Eliminate Ambiguity

Yet perhaps this assessment is premature. Maybe to emphasize the 'lexibility' does not necessarily mean that we have to 'go down the anti-formalist road'.[26] At least in a specific negative respect, we might find something like a certain consensus between the attempt to defend ambiguity and a formalistic approach. It could be that both approaches have common opponents in the form of two recent methods, both of which are directed against formalistic perspectives but at the same time also want to combat ambiguity.

Indeed, there are two new approaches in legal methodology which deliberately distance themselves from the classical procedure. While they acknowledge the impossibility of discovering the one true meaning of a legal norm through interpretation alone, they also do not abandon the old promise of rationality and predictability but hold on to it. They suggest that we need additional methodological tools to reach this goal, techniques that at least complement, if not completely substitute, the old procedures. Ambiguity, for these approaches, is therefore still something that has to be fought against and replaced as far as possible by an unambiguous account of the so-called legal reality.

The first and rather evident way to maintain the traditional ideal of legal rationality by introducing additional techniques that are supposed to guarantee the one right answer is the concept of balancing. First introduced and widely applied in the case law on fundamental rights, in particular in the jurisdiction of the German Federal Constitutional Court (whose trust in and reliance on legal methodology is, as we have seen, quite limited), this technique has later been theorized as a necessarily complement to traditional interpretation.[27] This theory echoes Dworkin's classic distinction that the law consists of two different types of norms, rules, and principles.[28] It further asserts that, just as interpretation is needed for rules, balancing of principles is a second, indispensable part of legal methodology.[29] Where the interpretation of at first glance clear-cut rules fails, as it does not lead to an unambiguous result, the seemingly rather diffuse balancing of principles steps in and fills the gap, offering a rational explanation how to resolve the conflict.

[26] See Stanley Fish, 'Introduction: Going Down the Anti-Formalist Road' in *Doing What Comes Naturally. Change, Rhetoric, and the Practice of Theory in Literary and Legal Studies* (Duke UP 1989) 1–33.

[27] See Robert Alexy, *A Theory of Constitutional Rights* (OUP 2002).

[28] See Ronald Dworkin, 'The Model of Rules' in *Taking Rights Seriously* (Duckworth, 1977) 14–45.

[29] See Robert Alexy, 'The Weight Formula' in *Law's Ideal Dimension* (OUP 2021) 154–74.

This specific technique has recently found its way from constitutional to private law.

The second way of substituting or at least complementing classical legal methodology is less obvious but has found increasing attention in the last couple of years. Its basic claim is that in order to arrive at predictable decisions, we may not only look at the legal norms. We have to take into account the empirical facts of reality and consider law as a part of this greater empirical environment.[30] Hence, while the general goal of predictability is once again left by and large untouched, the methodology that ought to be used has changed. Rather than rely on a particular technique of reading norms, we shall refer to the social sciences. Their knowledge of empirical facts and the (causal) connections between them is supposed to supplement in its most radical form, even to substitute, the traditional legal methodology.

While both techniques or approaches converge in their claim that legal methodology is incapable of delivering on its promise of rational decision-making and yet hold on to the idea of this rationality as such, the implications of the respective approaches are quite different. Whereas balancing tends to expand the field in which legal decisions play a decisive role, the so-called 'New Legal Realism'[31] narrows this field to the point of doubting that there is such a thing as a distinct legal field at all. Balancing not only offers a one-size-fits-all solution to the legal problem, thanks to which we can apparently dispense with a specifically private law methodology. What is more, the balancing process allows the law to consider almost any aspect of life as a legal problem, as it no longer needs to rely on fairly precise, well-defined norms to do so. Instead, a few general principles, whose existence as rather diffuse background assumptions is easily asserted, suffice for legal evaluation.

In contrast, the new legal realism tends to ignore that there could be such a thing as an *eigen*-rationality of law. Accordingly, while one technology tends to colonize the rest of society, the other seeks to dissolve law as a distinct social sphere. In both cases, it is the unwillingness to accept ambiguity, or to be more precise, the ambiguity inherent in the legal system, that creates the problem.

[30] See with regard to international law the contributions in (2015) 28 Leiden J Int L 185–281; with respect to constitutional law eg Niels Petersen, 'Avoiding the Common-Wisdom-Fallacy: The Role of Social Sciences in Constitutional Adjudication' (2013) 11 I-Con 294–318; and with a focus on private law Kevin Tobia, 'Private Law Theory From an Empirical Perspective', in this volume.

[31] See eg Gregory Shaffer, 'The New Legal Realist Approach to International Law' (2015) 28 Leiden J Int L 189–210.

XI. Formalism and Ambiguity

Against the background of this first negative consideration, we can perhaps take another step, which now also asks about the possible positive correspondence between formalism and ambiguity. Maybe formalism itself has to be understood ambiguously, in the sense that it emphasizes the distinctiveness of law, but without claiming that this distinctiveness must lead to a concept of law based on systematic unity, that is to say, a concept of law as a self-contained social sphere, separated from its environment.[32] Reading and interpreting the law may not lead to the one and only true meaning inherent in the text. However, this does not mean that the reading has to stop or that the process itself cannot be regarded as a distinct movement. Quite the opposite. A formalist understanding could focus on this process and emphasize that it does not have to end with a single outcome. It can go on and on. Yet, in doing so, it preserves a particular character. In consequence, ambiguity does not only concern a specific problem within legal methodology. It refers to the very existence of the law.

XII. 'Digressions are the Sunshine'

Let me conclude with a final comment on why we may need to move in circles rather than in a straight line when dealing with these methodological issues. To defend ambiguity is obviously a paradoxical endeavour. If we truly and wholeheartedly believe this is the right thing to do, we already contradict our approach. Any support for ambiguity remains, as such, ambiguous in itself. In other words: There is no such thing as 'true ambiguity', hence no chance to fight for it. Consequently, in order to defend ambiguity, we may never put the lingering doubt to rest whether this is a really fruitful goal.

Yet perhaps these lingering doubts could be understood, once again, not only as the sign of a defect or as the symptom of a pathological situation. Maybe it can also be seen from a different angle. It might be possible to take another turn, thus giving a different ring to the initial talk of 'breaks and gaps'. Tristram Shandy, at least, would deny that necessary detours around those 'breaks and

[32] See for a corresponding effort, though with a different focus, Miller, 'Formalism, Legality, and the Rule of Law' (n 9).

gaps' are nothing but a waste of time. Quite the contrary: 'Digressions, incontestably, are the sun-shine;—they are the life, the soul of reading.'[33] A proper reading, therefore, in the Shandean sense, is a reading that wanders around, and that is to say, it is a reading that coincides with the process, or maybe the art, of *ambi(ge)re*.

[33] Sterne (n 1) vol II, ch XXII (at 81).

7

The Nature and Value of Conceptual Legal Scholarship

Christian Bumke and Fritz Schäfer

I. Goal of the Chapter

In this chapter, we pursue two goals. First, we want to compare how German legal dogmatics, on the one hand, and the group of approaches, which in the United States is labelled the New Private Law theory, on the other hand, think about and work with the law. We argue that while there are considerable differences between the two, they can be understood as two variants of the same general approach towards legal scholarship, which we will call conceptual legal scholarship. By examining the commonalities and differences between legal dogmatics and New Private Law, the first part of the chapter sets out what is characteristic of this way of engaging with the law.

Our second goal is a reflection on methodology. For this purpose, we examine the differences within conceptual legal scholarship. Our goal is to point out that—notwithstanding the commonalities described in the first part of the chapter—very different activities are pursued both within legal dogmatics and New Private Law scholarship. To this end, we introduce a distinction between two different kinds of conceptual legal scholarship. We distinguish between approaches which aim to explain a certain legal phenomenon on the one hand and approaches which aim to understand law's normative content on the other hand. This distinction is relevant both for the German and the American discussion. Differentiating between the two perspectives is, in our view, important because they respond to different expectations and have to conform to different standards.

Christian Bumke and Fritz Schäfer, *The Nature and Value of Conceptual Legal Scholarship* In: *Methodology in Private Law Theory*. Edited by: Thilo Kuntz and Paul B. Miller, Oxford University Press.
DOI: 10.1093/oso/9780198885306.003.0007

II. Commonalities and Differences between Legal Dogmatics and New Private Law Scholarship

1. Commonalities

Legal dogmatics[1] (*Rechtsdogmatik*) is a way of thinking about and working with the law which is characteristic of German legal scholarship and legal practice.[2] As an academic discipline—and this is what our reflections will be about—it examines the law and develops concepts and tools which help to order it, to make it operable and to guide legal practice. With New Private Law scholarship, it shares three main attributes: First, it is oriented towards the existing positive law, second, it employs the perspective of a participant in the legal system, and third, it is based on the idea of the law as an ordered whole. Together, those attributes make up what we call conceptual legal thinking.

a) Orientation towards the existing positive law

The first element of conceptual legal thinking, shared by legal dogmatics and New Private Law scholarship concerns its object. This object is the positive law of a particular legal system. Conceptual legal thinking is concerned neither with some ideal law nor with the law 'as such' but with the questions and phenomena which arise in the context of the positive law in existing legal systems.[3]

[1] The term legal dogmatics, which we use to translate the German term *Rechtsdogmatik*, is rarely used in the international discussion. In the American discussion it basically does not appear at all. This has not always been the case. At the beginning of the twentieth century, when American scholars were still engaging heavily with the German discussion, one can find authors who use the term in a way that is reminiscent of German *Rechtsdogmatik*. See for example John Chipman Gray, *The Nature and Sources of the Law* (Col UP 1909) 1, 4; Roscoe Pound, 'Vinogradoff, Outlines of Historical Jurisprudence book review' (1922) 35 Harvard LR 774; Roscoe Pound, 'The History of Conspiracy and Abuse of Legal Procedure' (1922) 1 CLJ 156. There were also foreign authors publishing in American Law journals who used the term, see for example Paul Vinogradoff, 'Aims and Methods of Jurisprudence' (1924) 24 Col L Rev 1; Mario Rotondi, 'Dogmatic and Comparative Law' (1933) 8 Tul L Rev 83.

[2] For a comprehensive account of German legal dogmatics see Christian Bumke, *Rechtsdogmatik* (Mohr Siebeck 2017). From the more recent German discussion see also Gregor Kirchhof, Stefan Magen and Karsten Schneider (eds), *Was weiß Dogmatik?* (Mohr Siebeck 2012); Horst Dreier (ed), *Rechtswissenschaft als Beruf* (Mohr Siebeck 2018); Matthias Jestaedt, 'Wissenschaft im Recht' (2014) 69 Juristenzeitung 1; Nils Jansen, *Recht und gesellschaftliche Differenzierung* (Mohr Siebeck 2019) 297–330; Philipp Sahm, *Elemente der Dogmatik* (Velbrück 2019); Jannis Lennarz, *Dogmatik als Methode* (Mohr Siebeck 2017); see also the contributions in the first issue of Archiv für die civilistische Praxis (2014) 214, 1-308. In the international discussion similar issues are discussed under the label of 'legal doctrinal scholarship'. From this discussion see for example Jan Smits, 'What is Legal Doctrine?' in R van Gestel, HW Micklitz and EL Rubin (eds), *Rethinking Scholarship: A Transatlantic Dialogue* (CUP 2017); Mátyás Bódig, *Legal Doctrinal Scholarship* (Elgar 2021).

[3] The problems with which conceptual legal thinking is concerned can be limited to a particular jurisdiction but may also arise in the same or similar ways in a variety of jurisdictions, as for example questions about the nature and functions of property. (We will examine this discussion more closely in the final section of the text.)

In this, conceptual legal scholarship distinguishes itself from moral philosophy or political theory but also from general jurisprudence.

There are different ideas about what the basic characteristics of positive law are. However, all phenomena discussed under that label can be captured by the term 'rule'. This term applies to general norms like statutes as well as individual norms like court decisions or provisions in a contract. Legal rules can be issued by a state authority or private actor. They can be authoritative texts or unwritten rules recognized in practice. They can also have very different contents and addressees. Rules of conduct, fundamental rights, and competence norms are all covered by this category.[4] In addition to the term rule, we use the term 'legal act' to refer to legal objects such as statutes, court decisions or contracts. Legal acts are created on the basis of rules, and they also contain rules. However, they are not identical to those rules. Legal acts are the components that make up legal practice and the legal system, whereas rules represent a step of abstraction from that practice. Conceptual legal thinking is directed at the legal material thus circumscribed.

b) Participant perspective

Law is not only a collection of rules but also an institutionally constituted social practice.[5] Conceptual legal scholarship studies the law and engages with it from the perspective of a participant in this social practice. This participant perspective is the most important common denominator among the various approaches within legal dogmatics and New Private Law scholarship. It refers to a particular stance towards law and legal scholarship. Those who participate in law as a social practice presuppose the authority, normativity, and legitimacy of the law. They assess questions of validity and legality solely on the basis of existing rules and articulate arguments in a specifically legal way. For the participant, the relevant justifications for legal decisions are contained exclusively in those legal arguments.

Legal scholars who employ this participant perspective can pursue a variety of goals. They might attempt to determine the legal reasons that are decisive for a particular judgment or work out suggestions as to how certain difficult cases should be decided. In this respect, they can engage with the law in much

[4] The structural equality of all these different kinds of rules (or, in his terminology, norms) has famously been posited by Hans Kelsen, *Pure Theory of Law* (2nd edn 1960, Max Knight tr, The Lawbook Exchange 1967) 3–23.

[5] In this vein, James Boyd White, *The Legal Imagination* (45th anniv edn, Wolters Kluwer 2018) xxii writes: 'Law has its own materials, its own life and its own way of being.'

the same way as courts or attorneys would.[6] However, the participant perspective includes more than that. Conceptual legal scholars can engage with legal phenomena—be it rules, legal acts or individual legal arguments—in other ways as well. They can analyse, describe, explain, historicize, interpret or create them. In particular, the participant perspective includes approaches which attempt to explain the functions of a certain legal phenomenon. Since the participants in a legal practice know about and take into account the functions of the law (law jobs), it would be surprising if those functions were not also a viable topic for conceptual legal scholarship. As long as these functional explanations do not aim to replace the realm of legal rules and arguments but instead complement them, they are perfectly compatible with the participant perspective.

This openness towards different research interests is also why the participant perspective is not identical to what is in the American discourse often referred to as the internal perspective. While this term is notoriously ambiguous,[7] in the context of the New Private Law. It is usually taken to be synonymous with an *interpretive stance* towards the law and contrasted with functional accounts.[8] Understood in this way, the term 'internal perspective' is narrower than what we mean by 'participant perspective' which includes both interpretative and functional approaches. We believe that a sharp distinction between internal and external accounts distracts from the commonalities shared by the various approaches that we label conceptual legal scholarship.[9] Functional and interpretive approaches do not have to reflect fundamentally different perspectives on the law and can, in fact, often supplement each other. The participants of a legal practice are interested in more than only the interpretation of legal rules, and functional explanations do not have to disregard the self-understanding

[6] This is neither thwarted by the uncertainty which comes with interpreting and applying legal rules, nor by the influence of extralegal factors on those activities. The participant perspective presumes neither that the law is neutral nor that there is only one right answer in hard cases. Similarly, the parts of the law whose meaning is unclear do not make it impossible to understand rules as reasons, guidelines, and criteria. It suffices that legal scholars know and take into account how different the reliability of their statements, assessments, and insights can be.

[7] A helpful overview over different understandings is offered by Charles L Barzun, 'Inside-Out: Beyond the Internal/External Distinction in Legal Scholarship' (2015) 101 Va L Rev 1203. From the New Private Law discussion see for example Andrew S Gold, 'Internal and External Perspectives: On the New Private Law Methodology' in Andrew S Gold and others (eds), *The Oxford Handbook of the New Private Law* (OUP 2020); John CP Goldberg and Benjamin C Zipursky, 'Seeing Tort Law from the Internal Point of View: Holmes and Hart on Legal Duties' (2006) 75 Fordham L Rev 1563; Paul Miller and Jeffrey Pojanowski, 'The Internal Point of View in Private Law' (2022) 67 Am J Jurisprudence 247. From the German discourse see Leonard Hoeft, *Normen im Labor* (Duncker & Humlot 2022) 23–56.

[8] Andrew S Gold and Henry E Smith, 'Sizing Up Private Law' (2020) 70 U Toronto LJ 489.

[9] This seems to be also a common view within New Private Law theory; see for example Gold and Smith (n 8); Gold, 'Internal and External Perspectives' (n 7); Felipe Jiménez, 'Understanding Private Law' in this volume; see also Thilo Kuntz, 'Against Essentialism in Private Law Theory: Private Law as an Artifact Kind' in this volume.

of the participating legal actors.[10] This last aspect is the crucial point. What all approaches which employ the participant perspective have in common is that they think and work within legal practice; that is, they presuppose and take seriously the practice as a legal practice.

Even though the participant perspective encompasses a great number of approaches, it also has limits. Because it can be employed for a variety of different goals and contexts, these limits are not easy to set out in the abstract. However, two important ones can be identified. First, the participant perspective does not include approaches which aim to identify the 'true reasons' for a certain legal phenomenon as opposed to those that the law itself deems relevant. A good example of an approach that leaves behind the participant perspective and addresses this fact explicitly is Paul Kahn's 'cultural study of law'. Kahn understands law as a social practice, just like any other social practice. He wants to study the 'culture of law' in the same way as other cultures.[11] Therefore, the categories he introduces are not specifically tailored towards law as a legal practice but can be used to explain all sorts of social practices. From the perspective of participants in the law, this approach has little to offer. By studying it, they might be able to better understand the practice that they are a part of, but it does not help them engage with the legal material.

Second, the participant perspective does not include approaches that aim to either justify or criticize legal phenomena using criteria that those approaches themselves regard as lying outside of the law. In general, the justification or critique of specific legal acts or parts of legal doctrine is a central part of conceptual legal scholarship. Conceptual legal scholars frequently criticize the prevailing understanding of the law and work out alternative accounts[12] or, correspondingly, defend and justify the status quo.[13] As long as this critique or justification operates with criteria which are part of the legal realm of argumentation, this does not mean that they depart from the participant perspective. Actually, the fact that the law itself provides such criteria is one of its characteristic features.

[10] This idea takes centre stage in the work of Henry E Smith, which we will have more to say about in the final section.

[11] Paul W Kahn, *The Cultural Study of Law* (Chicago UP 1999) 1.

[12] Two of many examples from German legal dogmatics are the works of Ralf Poscher, *Gefahrenabwehr* (Duncker & Humblot 1999) who offers an alternative concept of 'danger' to the one dominant in German police law and Werner Flume, *Allgemeiner Teil des Bürgerlichen Rechts*, vol 1 (Springer 1977)chs 4, 5 who pioneered the view that the partnership under civil law (GbR) can be an independent subject of rights and duties. On legal dogmatics' critical function see also Paul Krell, 'The Critical Potential of Doctrinal Analysis' in this volume.

[13] On the ways in which—in his terminology—interpretive approaches to private law can also make justificatory claims about private rights see Paul Miller, 'Juridical Justification of Private Rights' in Michael Crawford and others (eds), *Justifying Private Rights* (Hart Publishing 2021).

In the democratic constitutional state the most important and ultimately authoritative standard for the justification of legal acts is the constitution. Beyond that, many conceptual legal scholars also try to obtain evaluation criteria from the particular area of law they are concerned with.

Now, which criteria exactly are part of the legal realm of argumentation and which are not is, of course, subject to dispute. In this respect, the participant perspective is open to a wide range of different understandings. However, the participant perspective is abandoned when scholars point to a realm of arguments that they themselves view as distinct from the legal realm of arguments. In particular, this concerns approaches which refer to considerations of 'morality' not only as being connected with or embedded in the law but instead as a yardstick against which all legal arguments have to be measured if they are to be taken into account.[14] This pointing towards the outside of the law, is incompatible with the participant perspective. It does not take the distinctly legal character of law as a social practice seriously.

c) The law as an ordered whole

Conceptual legal scholarship assumes that law can be understood and engaged with as an ordered whole. In this context, two aspects have to be differentiated. The first aspect concerns the extent to which the *rule-making actors* within a legal system let themselves be guided by the idea that law is an ordered whole. This guidance can be the result of certain rules which aim to create such unity, like, for example, constitutional requirements of consistency in legislation and adjudication, but it also, to a large extent, manifests itself in an attitude those legal officials take towards the law. At least in German legal practice, this attitude is still very much shaped by the belief in law as an ordered whole. The idea of unity and order in law continues to prevail despite changing democratic legislatures, the federal structure of government, ever-new changes in the law due to European legislation and the constant creation of new legal acts by courts, administrative agencies and private parties.

[14] Whether references to morality run against the participant perspective therefore depends on the specific nature of these references. The critical question is whether authors start with the law or with morality. If they start with a legal question and make reference to morality only in order to resolve interpretive uncertainties, this does not run against the participant perspective (even though we do not think that this is a helpful way to think about these situations (text to n 45)). If, however, authors take as the starting point a particular conception of morality and then in a second step use this conception to evaluate and reinterpret the law, they leave behind the perspective of a participant. See as an example for the first alternative and about this distinction generally Ernest J Weinrib, *The Idea of Private Law* (OUP 1995) 50.

The second and, for our purposes, more interesting aspect concerns the question as to how the belief in law as an ordered whole shapes the way *legal scholars* engage with the law. It does so in two ways; on the one hand, it serves as a premise and, on the other hand, as a goal. Because law is an ordered whole, systematizing and unity-building efforts are worthwhile, and those efforts, in turn, contribute to the fact that law is an ordered whole. Beyond this point, there are different and partly contradictory ideas about what the idea of law as an ordered whole entails. On the one hand, there are monistic approaches which aim to structure an area of law with the help of only one guiding principle.[15] These approaches are much more prevalent in the American discussion than in the German discussion, where the vast majority of scholars favour pluralistic approaches, which work with multiple different principles or elements. The main problem with monistic approaches is that an area of law is made up of rules and concepts that serve a variety of purposes. Monistic approaches have to assume such a high degree of coherence that it is hard to reconcile with the rules and the legal practice in the relevant area of law.[16] Furthermore—as will be shown later in the chapter—conceptual legal scholarship includes so many different activities and goals that it is hard to see how one principle or concept can do all of these tasks at once. Therefore, what emerges as the systematic order of a field of law is usually a meshwork (*Geflecht*) composed of disparate elements.

2. Differences

While the relationship between legal dogmatics and New Private Law theory is characterized primarily by the commonalities just described, there are also important differences to which we now turn. There are three differences which we want to highlight. First, legal dogmatics and New Private Law scholarship differ with respect to their status within their respective disciplines. Second, they engage differently with the legal material. The New Private Law theory, being part of the common law tradition, thinks about the law starting from concrete cases. Meanwhile, German legal dogmatics focuses exclusively on rules. Third, the two approaches relate differently to legal practice.

[15] See eg Weinrib (n 14) 32–36.

[16] For more detailed criticism see Felipe Jiménez, 'Two Questions for Private Law Theory' (2021) 12 Jurisprudence 391, 393–400; Hanoch Dagan, *A Liberal Theory of Property* (CUP 2021) 19–23. On the role of coherence in theory building generally Stephen A Smith, *Contract Theory* (OUP 2004) 11–13.

a) Status within the discipline

In German legal scholarship, legal dogmatics is the dominant approach.[17] While it has found a significant number of critics—a first big wave of criticism taking place at the turn of the twentieth century, a second one in the late 60s and 70s, and a third one within the last two or three decades[18]—this critique has not impeded its dominance. However, not everything has remained the same. Legal dogmatists today are not as naive anymore when it comes to legal theory, philosophy of language, and philosophy of science as they were a few decades ago. There is now widespread knowledge about the openness of hermeneutic endeavours, and the majority of scholars accept that extralegal approaches like economic or feminist analysis of the law can provide valuable insights. What has, however, remained firm is the conviction in the autonomy of law. This belief, which is fundamental to legal dogmatics, is still the starting point for the overwhelming majority of legal scholarship in Germany.

This contrasts sharply with the situation of the New Private Law movement in the United States. In the American scholarly discourse, the idea that law is an autonomous discipline is far from universally accepted. On the contrary, a great number of American scholars believe that there is no distinctive legal way of thinking but that questions of law can be reduced to questions of morality, politics, power or economics. The New Private Law wants to overcome that understanding, but it is only one of many approaches in the US discourse. For that reason, New Private Law theorists often feel the need to explain why systematic and conceptual engagement with the law is a fruitful task in the first place. Meanwhile, their German counterparts typically view this as self-evident and just proceed to do it.

b) Material—cases or rules

The second difference we were able to identify is of a more fundamental nature. It concerns a difference not only between legal dogmatics and the New Private Law but between American and German legal thinking in general. Law is a social practice that can be described and approached in many different ways. It consists, on the one hand, of certain rules and legal acts and, on the other, of a variety of legal actors and institutions (for example, parliaments, courts or administrative agencies) and their practices. When legal scholars engage with the law so understood, they can therefore focus on different aspects. Against this

[17] It is basically impossible to obtain a professorship at a German law school without having published at least one major dogmatic study.

[18] For an historical overview see Bumke, *Rechtsdogmatik* (n 2) 16–43.

background, we believe that Anglo-American and German legal thinking can be understood as two approaches towards the law that highlight different elements. Roughly speaking, the difference consists of a focus on concrete decisions on the one hand and a focus on abstract rules on the other hand.

As a result of the common law tradition, Anglo-American legal thinking starts with the concrete case. The courts decide a concrete case and bind themselves for the future with regard to the judgment and the relevant circumstances of the respective case. Cases that distinguish themselves from the decided case can be decided differently.[19] Over time, a growing meshwork of case-related legal determinations develops. During this process, rules that span over a whole range of cases can emerge, which are then called doctrines. These doctrines correspond roughly to the court-generated general rules, characteristic of German legal thinking. When American legal scholars attempt to systematize a certain area of law, they have to put both of these things together. Both concrete decisions of certain focal cases and general rules, spanning over a range of cases (this also includes the relevant statutes), are integrated into a conception of a particular area of law. Accordingly, the typical form in which an area of law is presented is the casebook. Closely related to this perspective focused on the decision of a concrete case is the idea of the legal dispute. The decisions are the result of legal disputes.

In contrast, at the heart of German legal thought are general rules. Those can be enacted by the legislature or generated by a court while deciding a particular case. Courts postulate—be it explicitly or implicitly—general legal rules in order to connect the concrete case with the legislative rule covering that case.[20] The general rules so created point beyond the individual case at hand and supplement the legislative rules, without, however, having the same binding force as the latter.[21] Over time, a meshwork evolves which—contrary to those in the American system—only consists of these general rules. The typical way in which an area of law is presented in the German context is the legal commentary. Its purpose is to connect the legislative and the court-generated rules. Relatedly, the legal dispute is not as significant as it is for American legal

[19] The binding effect is, of course, limited. Past decisions which are deemed incorrect can be overruled. Whether that happens or not depends not only on the extent to which the past decision is incorrect but also on the amount of trust which has developed in the previous legal situation.

[20] For a more detailed analysis of this interaction see Christian Bumke, 'Abstrakt-generelle Hinweise des Gerichts—(k)eine judikative Handlungsform' (2021) 74 Neue Juristische Wochenschrift, 1366, 1369.

[21] About the phenomenon of judge-made law from a German perspective see Christian Bumke, 'Einführung in das Forschungsgespräch über richterliche Rechtsarbeit' in Christian Bumke (ed), *Richterrecht zwischen Gesetzesrecht und Rechtsgestaltung* (Mohr Siebeck 2012); Mehrdad Payandeh, *Judikative Rechtserzeugung* (Mohr Siebeck 2017).

thought. It is the trigger for decisions in which courts generate general rules. However, the focus does is not on that particular dispute but on the existing meshwork of general rules, which provides the basis for the decision. Judges ask whether the meshwork in its present state gives them sufficient guidance on how to decide the case or whether they need to introduce a new general rule to justify their decision.

The difference between starting from a decision and starting from a rule may seem insignificant at first. However, we believe it to be important because it affects the possibilities of systematic engagement with the law. Decisions, understood as resolutions of concrete legal disputes, are much less suited than general rules to serve as the basis for systematic work. For that reason, we believe that the different perspectives we described shape the way legal scholarship is conducted in Germany and the United States and, therefore, also impact the relationship between legal dogmatics and the New Private Law.

c) Relationship towards legal practice

The third difference between legal dogmatics and New Private Law scholarship concerns their respective relationships towards legal practice. When it comes to legal dogmatics, the relationship is traditionally relatively close.[22] In fact, many see the close connection between legal dogmatics as an academic discipline and legal practice as its defining characteristic.[23] There are others who are very critical of this and believe that this connection is precisely what must be overcome if legal dogmatics is to be a truly scientific discipline. Either way, the assessment that, in its present state, legal dogmatics is closely intertwined with legal practice is shared by most German scholars.[24]

The fact that legal dogmatics is typically oriented towards questions about the practical application of the law also gives rise to a second kind of criticism, which has to do with the status of dogmatic sentences. Traditionally, legal dogmatics is seen as a normative discipline. Because it aims to offer guidance for deciding difficult cases, its claims have to be normative in nature. In recent times, this self-understanding is increasingly under attack. Some authors have started to question whether legal dogmatics should aim to answer these kinds

[22] Since legal dogmatics encompasses a great variety of approaches, there are a variety of different ways in which dogmatic approaches can relate to legal practice. See in more detail Bumke, *Rechtsdogmatik* (n 2), 101–07.

[23] For a recent formulation of this view see Wolfgang Kahl, *Wissenschaft, Praxis und Dogmatik im Verwaltungsrecht* (Mohr Siebeck 2020) 65.

[24] See for example Jansen, *Recht und gesellschaftliche Differenzierung* (n 2) 321–30 and for further references Anna-Bettina Kaiser, 'Juristische Methode, Dogmatik und System' in Wolfgang Kahl and Markus Ludwigs (eds), *Handbuch des Verwaltungsrechts*, vol 1 (Otto Schmidt 2021) ch 24 para 46.

of questions at all. They want to establish a sharp distinction between descriptive claims about what the positive law is and prescriptive claims about how the positive law should be altered or adjusted.[25] What these authors worry about is, once again, the scientific nature of legal dogmatics as an academic discipline. In contemporary discussions about legal dogmatics, this is one of the biggest points of contention, and the reason why it is problematic is the close connection legal dogmatics has with legal practice.

In New Private Law theory, the situation seems to us to be different. As its name indicates, it evolved and is part of a theoretical discussion in which large parts are relatively detached from legal practice. By detached, we do not mean that these theoretical approaches do not have implications for legal practice but rather that it is relatively easy to see in what sense they are different from what actors in legal practice do.[26] The problem is how the academic discipline can distinguish itself from legal practice does not arise in the same way.

This difference is also reflected in how the different kinds of private law scholarship are categorized. In the United States, private law theory is often distinguished from doctrinal legal scholarship.[27] An approach within private law theory may touch on doctrinal questions, and it may even have direct doctrinal implications, but private law theory and doctrinal work are not the same thing. When it comes to New Private Law theory, many authors emphasize the importance of legal doctrine and the need to engage with it.[28] However, even this emphasis on the connection between the two presupposes the distinction. Doctrinal work is seen as one part of private law theory, but the starting points are questions of private law theory.[29]

[25] Oliver Lepsius, 'Kritik der Dogmatik' in Kirchof (ed) (n 2) 43; Jestaedt (n 2) 3; Patrick Hilbert, *Systemdenken in Verwaltungsrecht und Verwaltungsrechtswissenschaft* (Mohr Siebeck 2015) 109–18. For a detailed critique of this position see Christian Bumke, 'Erzeugung und Gebrauch von Wissen in der Rechtsdogmatik' in I Augsberg and GF Schuppert (eds), *Wissen und Recht* (Nomos 2022) 475–77; see also text to n 44.

[26] A good example for this is the prominent theoretical account offered by Ernest J Weinrib (n 14). This theory has wide-ranging doctrinal implications (eg the rejection of strict liability (ibid 171–203)). However, Weinrib is nevertheless detached from legal practice in the sense that his work is clearly part of a theoretical and not of a practical discourse about law.

[27] On the relationship between legal or private law theory and doctrinal scholarship see for example Stephen A Smith, 'Taking Law Seriously' (2000) 50 U Toronto LJ 241, 241–42; Felipe Jiménez, 'Contracts, Markets, and Justice' (2021) 71 U Toronto LJ 144, 152–54; Mátyás Bódig, 'Legal Theory and Legal Doctrinal Scholarship' (2010) 23 Can J L & Jurisprudence 483.

[28] See for example John CP Goldberg and Benjamin C Zipursky, *Recognizing Wrongs* (HUP 2020) 7; John CP Goldberg, 'Pragmatism and Private Law' (2012) 125 Harvard LR 1640, 1655–56; Smith, 'Taking Law Seriously' (n 27) 241–42.

[29] A good example of this can be found in Smith, *Contract Theory* (n 16). Smith emphasizes the importance of doctrinal work and the third part of the book contains an examination of the most important doctrines in contract law. However, this is only one part of the book. In its entirety his account is one in contract *theory*.

In Germany, the situation is different. Here, there is also a distinction between private law dogmatics and private law theory.[30] However, this distinction is not identical to the distinction between doctrinal work and private law theory in the American discourse. Legal dogmatics is a broader field than doctrinal work and encompasses much of what in the United States goes by the name of private law theory. This is not just a question of terminology but also has important implications for the questions the respective approaches are concerned with. Because legal dogmatics includes questions that an American scholar would allocate with doctrinal work, it is often—not always—heavily involved with the many micro-level issues[31] which arise in the process of applying the law, whereas approaches in New Private Law theory typically deal with more abstract, overarching questions.

III. Variants of Conceptual Legal Scholarship

In the remaining parts of the chapter, we would like to take up the topic of methodological reflection because we believe it to be equally relevant for legal dogmatics and New Private Law theory as they are both part of conceptual legal scholarship. We would like to draw attention to a point that is practically and theoretically significant. In the first part of the chapter, we have described what unites the perspectives of legal dogmatics and New Private Law theory, the most important uniting feature being the belief in law as an autonomous discipline. What we now want to stress is that even when one accepts this fundamental premise, there are various ways to engage with the law, which are fundamentally different from each other. If we do not pay attention to these differences, that can lead to our using unsuitable standards to evaluate concepts, raising irrelevant objections and having pointless disputes.

It is not possible for us here to cover all the variants of conceptual legal scholarship in all their complexities. There is so far very little explicit knowledge about the different ways in which we engage with the law to draw on. Therefore, we want to concentrate on only one distinction. That distinction concerns the difference between understanding what the normative content of the law is—that is, figuring out what the law says in general or with respect to a certain

[30] See eg Stefan Grundmann, Hans-Wolfgang Micklitz, and Moritz Renner (eds), *Privatrechtstheorie*, 2 vols (Mohr Siebeck 2015)who offer a very heterogenous compilation of what they believe to be major texts in private law theory.

[31] Jiménez, 'Contracts, Markets and Justice' (n 27) 154 calls this the 'nitty-gritty of legal materials'.

case—on the one hand and explaining a particular legal phenomenon on the other hand.

We first want to illustrate this distinction by analysing a discussion from German constitutional law in which we can see both of these different perspectives at work. Following that, we will ask whether the distinction can be fruitfully applied to discussions in New Private Law theory. For that, we will discuss the 'architectural approach' towards property that Henry Smith has developed.

1. Explaining and Understanding in German Constitutional Law

a) Explaining a legal phenomenon

The discussion from German constitutional law we want to focus on concerns the relationship between fundamental rights and private law.[32] Specifically, it concerns the question of whether and in what way fundamental rights influence civil legal disputes between private parties. For a long time, private and constitutional laws were seen as completely separate areas of law. Until about the middle of the twentieth century, most legal scholars in Germany discussed problems of private law without any regard to questions of constitutional law. After the Second World War, however, a discussion about the impact of fundamental rights on civil legal disputes began to emerge. This debate first arose in private and constitutional law scholarship but then received a decisive impulse from the Federal Constitutional Court. In 1958, it issued its *Lüth* decision—one of the most famous decisions in the history of German constitutional law.[33] In this decision, the Court developed a conception of the impact of fundamental rights on civil disputes, which shaped the discussion until the present day.

The decision was prompted by Erich Lüth calling for the boycott of a recently published movie. The reason for this was that the movie had been directed by Veit Harlan, one of the leading film directors of the Nazi era. In reaction to this call to boycott, Harlan's production company sued Lüth in front of a civil court and was victorious. The court declared the call to boycott a tortious act and awarded damages to the production company. Lüth then appealed this decision in front of the Federal Constitutional Court and argued that it violated his freedom of speech.

[32] For an overview of the approach the Federal Constitutional Court takes see Christian Bumke and Andreas Voßkuhle, *German Constitutional Law* (OUP 2019) 80–86.

[33] BVerfGE 7, 198 (1958).

The problem presented to the court was therefore whether Article 5 of the Basic Law, which guarantees freedom of speech, requires that the relevant norms of tort law be understood as not covering Lüth's call to boycott. That is, in fact, what the court decided. It ruled that opinions which aim to influence the general discourse in matters of public interest enjoy priority over the interests of conflicting private parties unless there are exceptional circumstances.[34] In order to come to that result, the court first had to establish how fundamental rights can impact questions of private law generally. It did so by introducing the concept of 'indirect third-party effects' of fundamental rights. According to this concept, fundamental rights are directly binding only for the state in its dealings with its citizens. However, they can indirectly affect other private citizens (or third parties) because they 'radiate' out onto the norms of private law that govern the respective civil disputes. In particular, they guide the interpretation of general provisions like, for example, Section 242 of the civil code, which stipulates the principle of good faith.[35] This—essentially metaphorical—talk of fundamental rights 'radiating' on to private law constitutes the starting point for the scholarly discussion until today. In contemporary discussions, this conception is, on the one hand, continually reproduced.[36] On the other hand, it is and has always been seen as an object of critique as many see it as an unsatisfying solution to the problem.

This is the point at which the first variant of conceptual legal scholarship comes into play: the explanation of a legal phenomenon. The unspecific and metaphoric nature of the Constitutional Court's conception has led many legal scholars to propose alternative ways in which the impact of fundamental rights on private law can be operationalized.[37] For example, some scholars have suggested that we do not need the concept of fundamental rights, 'radiating effect' at all.[38] They argue that we can conceptualize the impact of fundamental rights

[34] ibid 212.

[35] ibid 207.

[36] See for example Hans-Jürgen Papier, 'Drittwirkung der Grundrechte' in *Handbuch der Grundrechte*, vol 2 (CF Müller 2006) ch 55 para 11; Michael Kloepfer, *Verfassungsrecht*, vol 2 (CH Beck 2010) ch 50 C.

[37] On the historical development of that discussion see Christian Bumke, 'Die Entwicklung der Grundrechtsdogmatik unter dem Grundgesetz' (2019) 144 Archiv des öffentlichen Rechts 1, 59–61.

[38] There are different variations of this line of critique. Some argue that all constellations in which fundamental rights impact private law can be dealt with on the basis of the traditional understanding of fundamental rights as defensive rights against the state (for this view see Jürgen Schwabe, *Die sogenannte Drittwirkung der Grundrechte* (Goldmann 1971); Ralf Poscher, *Grundrechte als Abwehrrechte* (Mohr Siebeck 2003) 245–89). Others believe that this works only in some cases, namely those in which the court orders the party in question to do or refrain from a certain action (as was the case in the *Lüth* decision, where the court ordered Lüth to pay damages and refrain from his calls to boycott). In other cases, those authors believe, we have to conceive of the way fundamental rights impact private law in a different way. This concerns namely those cases where the situation is reversed and the possible fundamental rights violation does not lie in the court imposing duties on the rights holder in question, but instead in the court refraining from imposing certain duties on the opposing party. Had Lüth won in

on civil disputes in just the same way in which we conceptualize their impact on disputes between the state and its citizens. The reason for this is that the civil court is a state actor. If it imposes an obligation on one of the parties, this act can, in principle, be thought of in just the same way as we think about other state actors imposing obligations on citizens (like, for example, administrative agencies or criminal courts). When it comes to operationalizing the impact of fundamental rights, the fact that there is another private party involved does not make a difference.[39]

This example shows, in our view, what is characteristic of conceptual legal scholarship, which aims to explain a certain legal phenomenon. The authors who argue that the concept of fundamental rights' radiation effect is superfluous are not interested in the specific normative content of the fundamental rights in question or, for that matter, of constitutional law generally. They are not concerned with the question of to what extent constitutional law should impact problems of private law and to what extent private law should stay autonomous. Instead, they are interested in how to make sense of a certain phenomenon—which is the impact of fundamental rights on civil disputes—and ask whether the conception of the 'radiation effect' is the best way to do so. If it can be shown that another approach is better suited to fulfil that purpose, the conception should be abandoned.

This concern with the explanation or operationalization of a particular phenomenon is, in our view, typical for quite a significant part of dogmatic scholarship. Highlighting it as a specific way of conducting conceptual legal work is important because it has to conform to standards different from those that apply to other kinds of legal scholarship. A good or useful explanation should conform to the following criteria:

First, it should allow easy handling of the phenomenon.[40] It should provide clear criteria and distinctions with which one can approach and talk about the

the civil court and the production company claimed a fundamental rights violation because of that, that would constitute an example of this kind of situation. Here, it is argued, the defensive dimension of fundamental rights does not help, because the impairment in question does not originate from the state. Instead, many authors in those cases refer to a different dimension of fundamental rights which is the state's duty to protect the rights bearer from their fundamental rights being impaired not due to state interference, but for other reasons. This duty to protect is today a widely recognized dimension of fundamental rights, but its relationship towards the concept of 'radiation effect' is not clear. The authors we are referring to here believe that once one realizes that the effect of fundamental rights can be conceptualized by using the defensive and the duty-to-protect dimension of fundamental rights, there is no longer any need for the doctrine of 'radiation effect'. One prominent formulation of this view is offered by Claus-Wilhelm Canaris, 'Grundrechte und Privatrecht' (1984) 184 Archiv für die civilistische Praxis 201.

[39] Jürgen Schwabe, *Probleme der Grundrechtsdogmatik* (1977) 211–17.

[40] Gold and Smith (n 8) also highlight the importance of simplicity as a criterion for theory-building.

phenomenon in a coherent and precise way. The Constitutional Court's rather diffuse conception of a 'radiation effect' does not score well with respect to this criterion.

Second, a good explanation should fit well into the existing body of doctrine. If it is necessary to significantly modify existing conceptual structures in order to integrate the explanation, that constitutes an argument against the account. If, on the contrary, an approach can explain a phenomenon with the help of concepts and criteria that already exist—as the authors who believe that the concept of radiation effect is a superfluous claim—that speaks in favour of it.

Third, a good explanation has to be able to accurately capture the relevant legal practice. This criterion might seem odd at first, given that in the example we just gave, the scholars advancing explanatory approaches are proposing them explicitly as an alternative to the Constitutional Court's account. However, they want to distance themselves only from the court's conceptualization of its own practice, not from the practice itself. They do not claim that the court should decide the relevant cases differently, but only that what the court does in these decisions can be explained in a different, more precise way.

b) Understanding law's normative content

A very different perspective on legal practice is taken when scholars employ the second mode of conceptual legal scholarship, that is when they attempt to understand law's normative content. The object of this interpretive approach can be a concrete decision, a rule or a complex of rules. Again, the discussion centring around the *Lüth* decision can help to illustrate this kind of legal scholarship. In this decision, the Constitutional Court not only established in what way fundamental rights can impact private law generally. It also developed a new substantive understanding of the right to free speech. It ruled that the right to free speech not only and not even primarily serves to protect the opportunity to freely express oneself in a private sphere. Instead, it emphasized the significance of the right to free speech for a democratic society. For the court, protecting citizens' rights to speak freely is an important instrument to ensure an open, pluralistic, and non-violent public discourse.[41] Balanced against this interest is the protection of the opposing party's civil honour, which had traditionally constituted an important limit for free expression, has to take a back seat. Over several decades, the court has been heavily criticized for reorienting the right to free speech in this way. Many scholars accused it of illegitimately

[41] BVerfGE 7, 198, 208–12 (1958).

privileging political over other kinds of opinions.[42] They argued that the functional considerations the court took into account contradicted what is characteristic of fundamental rights.[43]

These scholarly criticisms constitute a different type of legal scholarship than the explanatory approaches described in the last section. They aim directly at understanding the normative content of Article 5 of the Basic Law. The scholars in question are engaged in an act of legal interpretation. They claim to understand Article 5 better than the Federal Constitutional Court and believe it has decided at least some of its cases incorrectly. They put forward a much stronger normative claim than the scholars in our first example, who want to explain fundamental rights' impact on private law differently. Because of this, their approach also has to conform to different, normatively more demanding standards. Where can one find these standards?

Pointing to the meaning of the legal provision in question does not help. Figuring out this meaning is precisely the goal of interpretive understanding. There is no second instrument other than interpretation which can help us grasp the meaning of a legal text against which we can then judge the adequacy of an interpretation. This is also why a sharp distinction between the law and the dogmatic interpretation of the law[44] is unworkable. There simply is no such thing as a law that exists before its interpretation. That does not mean that there are no limits on interpretation. Various factors can serve as obstacles to a certain interpretation. These include historical materials or the specific phrasing of a rule. Furthermore, juristic forms of argumentation, fundamental doctrinal structures or established legal practices can provide some guidance. However, these criteria only get you so far. They cannot resolve the uncertainties that come with interpretation.

For this reason, many have suggested that we look for guidance outside of the law. In particular, many authors in the American discussion refer to 'morality' as a standard which can be used to evaluate interpretive theoretical accounts.[45] We are very sceptical whether this is helpful. First, it is unclear what

[42] See for example Hans H Klein, 'Öffentliche und Private Freiheit' (1971) 10 Der Staat 145, 159–68.

[43] For a general critique of this functional approach towards the interpretation of fundamental rights see Ernst-Wolfgang Böckenförde, 'Grundrechtstheorie und Grundrechtsinterpretation' (1974) 27 Neue Juristische Wochenschrift 1529, 1534–35.

[44] See text to n 25.

[45] Ronald Dworkin, *Law's Empire* (Fontana Press 1986) 285; Weinrib (n 14) 230; from the German discussion see Robert Alexy, *Begriff und Geltung des Rechts* (Alber 1992) 126–29; see also Smith, *Contract Theory* (n 16) 13–24 who offers a detailed discussion of the morality criterion and advocates for a weaker understanding of the criterion than the one offered by Dworkin and Weinrib. For another sceptical view on the usefulness of the morality criterion for interpretive theories in private law theory see Andrew Gold, 'When Private Law Theory is Close Enough' in this volume.

exactly the term 'morality' means in this context. Is a moral argument a specific kind of argument that can be distinguished from, for example, aesthetic, economic, or policy arguments? Does morality refer to some ideal dimension of the law? Or does it simply mean 'all things considered'? Second, referring to morality as a standard for interpretive claims about the law seems to imply the existence of a different realm of argumentation in which the same questions are debated as in the legal discussion only without the constraints of positive law. We do not believe such a realm of argumentation exists (at least with respect to most difficult legal questions). If one takes away the specific legal context in which a difficult interpretive question is posed, one is no longer dealing with the same question. Third, it is unclear how the reference to morality is supposed to reduce the interpretive uncertainties in question. Engaging with questions of morality—however one understands the term—is an enterprise no less uncertain than the interpretation of open-ended legal provisions. To conceive of these uncertainties as moral uncertainties only reframes the problem but does not contribute to its solution.

However, despite these objections, we believe that there is a sense in which this reference to morality contains a kernel of truth. While we cannot resolve interpretive uncertainties by pointing to a specific realm of arguments called morality, it is true that understanding law's normative content is not, in the same way, an exclusively legal enterprise as the dogmatic explanation of a legal phenomenon. Questions which are interpretive in the sense just described are open towards arguments from extralegal realms of argumentation in a way that questions explanatory approaches deal with are not. This can be illustrated by looking, once again, at the two examples we just gave. With regard to the question of whether expressions of opinion in public affairs should be privileged over other expressions of opinion, it is not hard to imagine how arguments from other fields, such as political theory, can be integrated into the discussion.[46] This is not all there is to the discussion, and one can argue about how helpful it is to refer to these 'extralegal' arguments, but it is not nonsensical from the outset to refer to policy or morality in this context.

In contrast, the question of how we can best conceptualize the impact of fundamental rights on private law cannot possibly be recast as a question of morality or policy. Arguing that one way of operationalizing this phenomenon is morally superior to another would not only be questionable but incomprehensible. Because approaches that merely aim to explain a certain legal

[46] See on this point in more detail Bumke, 'Wissen in der Rechtsdogmatik' (n 25) 447–48, 454–55.

phenomenon[47] are not directly concerned with law's normative content, normative arguments from other fields do not play a part in them.[48] That does not mean that those problems are easier to solve than problems which concern the understanding of law's normative content. It does, though, seem easier to identify evaluative criteria for explanatory approaches which do not depend on strong normative premises. The resulting difference in reliability is, in our view, one of the most important insights that the distinction between the two approaches provides.

If we were to consider not only these two modes of legal scholarships but instead look at conceptual legal scholarship in a more encompassing way, an even fuller and more nuanced picture would emerge. However, even just looking at this distinction illustrates how diverse the approaches towards conceptual legal scholarship are and how important it is to be aware of their different properties and standards.

2. Explanatory Approaches in New Private Law Theory—the Example of Property Theory

In the final part of the chapter, we turn from German legal dogmatics to the New Private Law. We look at the discussion in property theory, particularly at the 'architectural theory' of property developed by Henry Smith. This theory constitutes, in our view, an example of an approach that aims to explain a certain legal phenomenon—albeit a different one than in the previous example we gave. By analysing this approach and how it relates to others in property theory, we try to show first the distinctions laid out in Section C.I apply not only to German legal dogmatics but can also be fruitfully applied to the New Private Law and, second, attempt to get a better idea of the different kinds of explanatory approaches there are.

a) Constructive and essentialist explanations

The term 'property' can refer to different objects. It can refer to a particular area of law, it can refer to an element of a particular provision like, for example, the

[47] There are, of course, approaches which aim both at explaining a certain legal phenomenon and at understanding law's normative content. In this case they are confronted with all the problems and uncertainties that come with the latter.

[48] Note that this difference cannot be captured by the internal versus external distinction. In both examples the authors in question deal with questions which are directly relevant for legal practice in the sense that they both offer categories and distinctions which can be applied by actors in legal practice. Neither approach can plausibly be described as external. Still, they ask very different kinds of questions.

term 'property' in the fifth amendment of the US Constitution, or it can be used as a *concept* within legal theory or legal dogmatics. This third option is at the centre of the theoretical controversy and interests us here. Initially, arguably, all conceptions of property can, in a broad sense, be understood as explanatory approaches. They all refer to the concept of property in order to explain a certain phenomenon. However, not all explanations are of the same kind. Rather, there are fundamental differences between them, which can essentially be reduced to three factors: First, the perceptions about the object to be explained; second, the aspiration or the goal of an explanation; and third, the elements included in the respective explanatory approach. For our purpose, it suffices to concentrate on the second aspect. In particular, we want to use the example of property theory to illustrate how explanatory approaches differ with respect to how closely they are tied to a specific explanatory context.

On one side of the spectrum, there are explanatory approaches which are completely independent of specific explanatory contexts. To use a term which appears quite often in property theory—even though in very different ways[49]—we might call these explanations 'essentialist'. Essentialist explanations want to reveal the essence, the idea, or the substance of the object of explanation. They claim to offer the correct understanding of that object. An essentialist is not concerned with the different contexts in which such an explanation might be relevant but argues that one simply cannot grasp what the object of the explanation is if one does not proceed from what the theorist identifies as its essence. On the other side of the spectrum, there are explanatory approaches which we might call 'constructivist'. Constructivist approaches do not claim to offer a 'correct' explanation of their object. Instead, they are developed relative to a particular explanatory context and claim for themselves only to be a useful or productive explanation within that context. This distinction is not a clear-cut or binary one. Most approaches are neither completely indifferent to the relevant explanatory contexts nor are they continually linked back to them.

[49] The term is used for example by Katrina M Wyman, 'The New Essentialism in Property' (2017) 9 J Legal Analysis 183; Shane N Glackin, 'Back to Bundles: Deflating Property Rights, Again' (2014) 20 LEG 1, 6 and Thomas W Merrill, 'Property and the Right to Exclude' (1998) 77 Neb L Rev 730, 734–39. However, we do not use the term in the same way as those authors. When we speak about an approach being essentialist, we refer neither to a particular substantive position like for example property having a 'stable core' (that is Wyman's understanding) nor to a claim about the ontological status of property. Instead, we refer to a specific, namely a decontextualized, way of framing the explanatory problem. Understood in this way, even conceptions which vehemently oppose the idea that property has a definable essence can be described as essentialist. A good example for this is the position of Thomas C Grey, 'The Disintegration of Property' in JR Pennock and JW Chapman (eds), *Nomos XXII: Property* (NYUP 1980). This, in our view, constitutes an extreme example of an essentialist problem-framing because it pays basically no attention to different explanatory contexts.

However, not only can the range of contexts to which a certain concept claims to be relevant differ considerably, but there are also more essentialist and more constructive ways of framing the problem a certain approach responds to.

This can be illustrated by looking at the discussion in property theory. Much of the discussion there is framed as an argument about what property *is*.[50] What—if anything—is the 'actual nature'[51] of property? Is it characterized by one key feature like, for example, the right to exclusion[52] or can it only be properly understood as a composite of several heterogenous features?[53] In this description of the problem, there is no reference to a specific goal or context in which the explanation is supposed to prove useful. It allows for a very diverse set of property conceptions to be conceived of as different answers to the same fundamental question. That is why this problem framing can be described as generally essentialist. One feature which some—not all—approaches that figure on this side of the spectrum exhibit concerns the distinction we laid out in the previous section. A number of property conceptions connect conceptual questions about how property works with normative questions about how far property rights should extend. In particular, essentialist concepts of property are sometimes used on the level of constitutional law to determine what constitutes a taking of private property under the fifth amendment. This is not limited to one particular strand in property theory. The attempt to answer questions of constitutional law by referring to explanatory conceptions of property can be found in the work of authors who believe that there is a stable core to property[54] as well as in the work of those who proceed from the bundle of rights picture.[55] This mingling together of questions of explanation with questions of interpretation is one example of how explanatory can be decontextualized. However, it is not the only one. Even leaving aside the

[50] See for example Jeremy Waldron, 'Property Law' in J Patterson (ed), *A Companion to Philosophy of Law and Legal Theory* (2nd edn, Blackwell 2010) 9–11 who distinguishes between an analytic and a justificatory question and calls the former a question about the 'ontology' of property.

[51] See James Penner, 'The Bundle of Rights Picture of Property' (1996) 43 UCLA L Rev 711, 713 who describes much of the property discussion as being concerned with this question.

[52] James Penner, *The Idea of Property in Law* (OUP 1997) 68–104; Merrill (n 49).

[53] See famously Tony Honoré, 'Ownership' in AG Guest (ed), *Oxford Essays in Jurisprudence* (OUP 1961). For a more recent formation of this position see Dagan (n 16) 79–113.

[54] See for example Eric R Claeys, 'Bundle-of-Sticks Notions in Legal and Economic Scholarship' (2011) 8 Econ Journal Watch 223; Leif Wenar, 'The Concept of Property and the Takings Clause' (1997) 97 Col L Rev 1923. Wenar's approach in particular provides an interesting contrast to Henry E Smith's. At first glance, they appear to be quite similar. Both Smith and Wenar conceptualize property as something that is not just a bundle of rights but rather refers to a thing. However, the explanatory context in which Wenar is interested is completely different from the one Smith refers to. Wenar is interested primarily in the interpretation of the takings clause, which plays no role in Smith's writings.

[55] See for example Richard Epstein, *Bundle-of-Rights Theory as a Bulwark against Statist Conceptions of Private Property* (2011) 8 Econ Journal Watch 223.

determination of law's normative content, there is still a great variety of explanatory goals one can pursue.

b) The 'architectural theory' of property

One example of a property theory with a rather specific explanatory goal is the 'architectural theory' of property developed by Henry Smith. His approach, which has sometimes been described as essentialist[56] (albeit in a different sense than we use the term), represents, in our view, an example of a relatively contextualized or constructivist approach. While Smith also often talks about what property is—namely the 'the law of things'—he is not interested in the nature of property 'per se' but in a more specific question. He wants to explain how property can best be conceived of from an—as he calls it—functional perspective. He distinguishes between the purposes property serves and the means with which it achieves those purposes. Those means are at the centre of his theory. Specifically, Smith is interested in how the concepts within property law serve as a device to reduce the complexity of interactions among legal actors. They do that, according to Smith, by serving as modules that are semi-autonomous elements which interact with other elements within the same system only in a limited way. For the system of property law, Smith identifies the in rem character of property rights and the exclusion rights which come with them as the most significant modules. Those and other modules furnish important baselines for the participants in the legal system by walling off interactions with other modules. They prevent changes in one part of the system from affecting the rest of the system and thereby reduce its complexity.

The first thing to notice about this approach is that Smith is not interested in understanding law's normative content.[57] He does not attempt to resolve

[56] See Wyman (n 49). For Wyman, essentialist conceptions of property stipulate that property has a 'stable core' (ibid 185). This definition is very different from our own since it refers to the substantive content of the approach in question. However, her definition is not unconnected to our understanding, because Wyman also presupposes that all the conceptions she categorizes as essentialist attempt to answer the same essential problem. She groups approaches with quite different explanatory goals together. In this regard, her approach can itself be described as essentialist. This is also the reason why Smith himself is ambivalent about this categorization (Henry Smith and Thomas Merrill, 'The Architecture of Property' in H Dagan and B Zipursky (eds), *Research Handbook on Private Law Theories* (Elgar 2020) 154).

[57] In this regard, Smith's approach stands in contrast to another prominent approach from New Private Law theory which at first glance shares a lot of similarities with it: John Goldberg's and Benjamin Zipursky's civil recourse theory. Like Smith, Goldberg and Zipursky want to identify the basic structural features of the area of law they are concerned with and build a theoretical account on that basis. While for Smith the central category is the thing, for Goldberg and Zipursky it is the wrong. They argue that American tort law should be understood as that area of law which provides a damaged party with an avenue of recourse against the wrongdoer in response to the wrong inflicted on her (see Benjamin C Zipursky, 'Civil Recourse, Not Corrective Justice' (2003) 91 Geo LJ 695). However, unlike Smith, they attempt to do more than merely explain the phenomenon that is the law of torts. They also want

interpretive questions about the scope of constitutional protection for property. When it comes to questions like whether there is an ownership interest in taxicab licences which enables the holders of these licences to sue local or state governments if they diminish in value[58] an explanatory approach like the one offered by Smith may be able to point out the differences that exist between ordinary objects of private property and a state licence. However, it cannot and does not seek to determine whether those reasons should lead to a different treatment of these cases. It makes no sense to criticize Smith for his approach being malleable in this regard. When Katrina Wyman faults Smith's approach for being unable to 'offer definite prescriptions for resolving live legal controversies'[59] she imposes an explanatory context on the theory which is alien to it.

This separation of interpretive and explanatory questions is not the only respect in which Smith's theory is tailored towards a specific explanatory context. His sensitivity to different explanatory tasks can also be illustrated by his discussion of alternative approaches, particularly the Hohfeldian bundle of rights picture of property. Unlike other scholars who are sceptical of this approach,[60] he does not claim that the bundle of rights picture is wrong or can never be useful. Rather, he views it as unhelpful for the kind of property theory he aims to provide.[61] According to Smith, the bundle of rights picture provides a helpful analytical device, but it tells us nothing about what is specific about the institution of property. Correspondingly, he also continually stresses that his own theory has to be judged only by its usefulness to its specific explanatory context. He defends himself against critics who fault him for failing to highlight features of property which might be important from their theoretical perspective but

to establish a theory that can be applied when deciding a difficult case. According to Goldberg and Zipursky, the civil recourse principle can provide normative guidance for the courts. While on the one hand they draw the civil recourse principle from legal practice, on the other hand they use it to criticize particular decisions and interpretations of the common or statutory law of torts (for examples see Goldberg and Zipursky (n 28) 293–339). For this reason, we would classify their concept as one which attempts to understand the normative content of the law even though, like most interpretive approaches on this level of abstraction, it possesses explanatory elements as well. This means that when it comes to identifying the standards on which their theory can be shown to be superior, they are confronted with all the difficulties described in Section III.1.b). Their conception of 'pragmatic conceptualism' (see Benjamin C Zipursky, 'Pragmatic Conceptualism' [2000] 6 LEG 457) constitutes, we believe, an attempt to react to these specific uncertainties, which for Smith do not arise in the first place.

[58] The example is used by Wyman (n 49) 228–36.

[59] ibid 237.

[60] A significantly more scathing critique of Hohfeld is offered by Penner, 'The Bundle of Rights Picture' (n 51); James Penner, *Property Rights: A Re-Examination* (OUP 2020) 3–56. Even though Smith is in many ways indebted to this critique, he is less categorical in his criticism of the bundle of rights approach.

[61] Henry E Smith, 'Property as the Law of Things' (2012) 125 Harvard LR 1691, 1694–1700; Henry E Smith, 'Property is not just a Bundle of Rights' (2011) 8 Econ Journal Watch 279.

which are, in Smith's view, uninteresting from a functional perspective.[62] In sum, Smith's approach can be understood as an attempt to disentangle different explanatory contexts and define the criteria on which theoretical accounts are to be measured relative to these contexts.

3. Categorizing Conceptual Legal Scholarship

One might ask how much Smith's approach or the discourse of property theory more generally has to do with the discussion from German constitutional law, which we addressed in Section C.I. The question of whether the 'radiation effect' of fundamental rights is the best way to conceive of their impact on private law seems to be structurally quite dissimilar from the question of how we can best conceptualize the law of property. This is true in a way. While both discussions are concerned with explaining a legal phenomenon, the objects of that explanation differ significantly. The German authors who want to reconceptualize the 'radiation effect' of fundamental rights address a relatively specific and limited phenomenon, whereas Smith and other property theorists are concerned with systematizing an entire area of law, which entails very different challenges.

However, this difference becomes much less poignant if we shift the focus on the German discussion a bit. For that, we have to look at the discussion about the impact of fundamental rights on private law not as one centred around an isolated problem but as part of a more general discussion about the nature, the organizing principles, and the functions of fundamental rights. In this larger discussion, similar questions are asked, and similar conflicts arise, as in American property theory. Like in property theory, some scholars investigate the 'actual nature' of fundamental rights in a highly decontextualized manner, whereas others tie their conceptions more closely to a specific explanatory context. While for some scholars, the different dimensions in which fundamental rights operate are closely tied to different conceptions of liberty, others try to disentangle the technical and substantive aspects of the problem. If we look at how we can best operationalize the way fundamental rights impact private law as one of several puzzle pieces in this discussion, the objects of the two explanatory approaches we examined no longer appear so dissimilar.

This, in the end, shows once again that conceptual legal thinking can be looked at from many different angles and categorized in many different ways.

[62] Henry E Smith, 'On the Economy of Concepts in Property' (2012) 160 U Pa L Rev 2097, 2106.

The distinctions we focused on are just one way to approach it. Distinguishing between explanatory approaches and approaches that aim to understand law's normative content and between constructive and essentialist explanatory approaches helps to make sense of some features of conceptual legal scholarship but leaves others unexplored. If one were to focus on a different aspect—say, the difference between the operationalization of rules or micro-level phenomena more generally on the one hand and system building on the other—one would have to introduce other distinctions and start anew.

8

The Point of View of Doctrinal Legal Science

Nils Jansen

I. A Crisis?

There is today a general feeling of crisis among German legal scholars. Many fear that doctrinal legal science (*Rechtsdogmatik*)[1] is in danger of fragmentation and marginalization, that the German law faculties are losing the status and influence which gave them prominence well into the twentieth century, and that the law faculties and legal education are thus in need of reform. The resulting discussions,[2] which have been overheating since the beginning of this century, may themselves be seen as a symptom of this crisis. In addition,

[1] For the German concept of *Rechtsdogmatik*, see N Jansen, 'Rechtsdogmatik im Zivilrecht' in Enzyklopädie zur Rechtsphilosophie (EzR), http://www.enzyklopaedie-rechtsphilosophie.net (2011) and the references therein. In particular, the concept refers on the one hand to legal doctrine, ie the body of legal knowledge, namely the conceptual and systematic tools used to describe, and give expression to, a legal system. On the other hand, *Dogmatik* also refers to doctrinal jurisprudence, ie to those activities by which doctrinal knowledge is produced and by which the relevant conceptual and systematic tools are designed. In this paper, I translate this latter concept of *Rechtsdogmatik* with 'doctrinal (legal) science' where I refer to specifically academic contributions. Whether a distinction between doctrinal legal science and practical jurisprudence actually makes sense is one of the questions addressed in the paper.

[2] See C Engel and W Schön (eds), *Das Proprium der Rechtswissenschaft* (Mohr Siebeck 2007); M Jestaedt and O Lepsius (eds), *Rechtswissenschaftstheorie* (Mohr Siebeck 2008); G Kirchhof, S Magen, and K Schneider (eds), *Was weiß Dogmatik?* (Mohr Siebeck 2012); E Hilgendorf and H Schulze-Fielitz (eds), *Selbstreflexion der Rechtswissenschaft* (Mohr Siebeck 2015; 2nd edn, 2021); H Dreier (ed), *Rechtswissenschaft als Beruf* (Mohr Siebeck 2018). Recent monographs: C Schönberger, *Der 'German Approach'. Die deutsche Staatsrechtslehre im Wissenschaftsvergleich* (Mohr Siebeck 2015); O Lepsius, *Relationen. Plädoyer für eine bessere Rechtswissenschaft* (Mohr Siebeck 2016); C Bumke, *Rechtsdogmatik* (Mohr Siebeck 2017); J Lennartz, *Dogmatik als Methode* (Mohr Siebeck 2017); M Flohr, *Rechtsdogmatik in England* (Mohr Siebeck 2017); M Auer, *Zum Erkenntnisziel der Rechtstheorie. Rechtsphilosophische Grundlagen multidisziplinärer Rechtswissenschaft* (Nomos, 2018). Articles *inter alia*: R Stürner, 'Das Zivilrecht der Moderne und die Bedeutung der Rechtsdogmatik' [2012] Juristenzeitung 10; ibid, 'Die Zivilrechtswissenschaft und ihre Methode' (2014) 214 Archiv für die civilistische Praxis 7; M Jestaedt, 'Wissenschaft im Recht. Rechtsdogmatik im Wissenschaftsvergleich' (2014) Juristenzeitung 1; M Klatt, 'Integrative Rechtswissenschaft' (2015) 54 Der Staat 469; N Jansen, 'Rechtsdogmatik, Rechtswissenschaft und juristische Praxis' (2018) 143 Archiv des öffentlichen Rechts 623.

Nils Jansen, *The Point of View of Doctrinal Legal Science* In: *Methodology in Private Law Theory.* Edited by: Thilo Kuntz and Paul B. Miller, Oxford University Press. © Nils Jansen 2024. DOI: 10.1093/oso/9780198885306.003.0008

scholars usually point to two 'alarming' developments, namely, a decline in the international reputation of German doctrinal science[3] and its diminishing influence on the judiciary.[4]

While German doctrine[5] is still esteemed highly in some parts of the world, such as East Asia and South America, it, unfortunately, seems that the best explanation for this present reputation is the splendour of the German legal tradition rather than the originality and international influence of present publications. Gone are the days when German textbooks were translated as a matter of course into leading international languages and when a textbook on French law in Germany (*Zachariä von Lingenthal*) could become a leading authority in France (*Aubry & Rau*).[6] International law students are no longer seen in great numbers in German lecture halls (apart from, of course, Erasmus students). Only the *Max Planck Institutes* are still attractive to foreign scholars, but those institutes do not normally focus on issues of legal doctrine but instead on foundational legal research.

The second development troubling many traditional scholars is the diminishing influence of doctrinal science[7] on judicial practice in Germany. This decline is an expression of legal science's loss of its leading position in the legal system:[8] Judges confronted with a difficult legal issue no longer look to law professors; they do not orientate themselves based on what scholars write (as was common practice during the nineteenth and large parts of the twentieth century). Instead, German doctrinal science has begun to follow the French example by subordinating itself to the courts.[9] Indeed, ever more

[3] H Koziol, 'Glanz und Elend der deutschen Zivilrechtsdogmatik' (2012) 212 Archiv für die civilistische Praxis 1, 3 f and *passim*; cf also Stürner, 'Zivilrecht der Moderne' (n 2) 16 ff.

[4] Scholars commonly criticize a 'Rechtsprechungspositivismus (case -law positivism)' of doctrinal science; see B Schlink, 'Die Entthronung der Staatsrechtswissenschaft durch die Verfassungsgerichtsbarkeit' (1989) 28 Der Staat 161, 163 f, 168 ff; M Jestaedt, 'Verfassungsgerichtspositivismus. Die Ohnmacht des Verfassungsgesetzgebers im verfassungsgerichtlichen Jurisdiktionsstaat' in O Depenheuer and others (eds), *Nomos und Ethos. Hommage an Josef Isensee* (2002) 183–228, 188 ff; T Lobinger, 'Perspektiven der Privatrechtsdogmatik am Beispiel des allgemeinen Gleichbehandlungsrechts' (2016) 216 Archiv für die civilistische Praxis 28, 68, 103 f, 106; similarly F Bydlinski, *Juristische Methodenlehre und Rechtsbegriff* (2nd edn, Springer 1991) 507; S Martens, *Methodenlehre des Unionsrechts* (Mohr Siebeck 2013) 288 f. However, such complaints are not really new; see P Oertmann, *Bürgerliches Gesetzbuch. Allgemeiner Teil* (2nd edn, Heymann 1908) vi, and cf D Kästle-Lamparter, *Welt der Kommentare, Struktur, Funktion und Stellenwert juristischer Kommentare in Geschichte und Gegenwart* (Mohr Siebeck 2016) 279 f.

[5] For the concepts used in this paper, see above n 1.

[6] Oliver Decamps, 'Handbuch des Französischen Civilrechts' in S Dauchy and others (eds), *The Formation and Transmission of Western Legal Culture* (Springer 2016) 336, 338.

[7] For the concepts used in this paper, see above n 1.

[8] cf also W Twining, W Farnsworth, S Vogenauer, and F Tesón, 'The Role of Academics in the Legal System' in P Cane and M Tushnet (eds), *The Oxford Handbook of Legal Studies* (OUP 2005) 920, 940: 'de-academization of legal culture'. In 2005, the authors perceived only some early signs of such a development, however.

[9] See JP Dawson, *The Oracles of the Law* (University of Michigan Law School 1968) 375–415.

scholars accept the judiciary's leading role in the legal system and, accordingly, see their task in explaining case law to other lawyers.[10] Whether this development is best explained in terms of a diminishing 'quality' of academic writing, or whether it is instead a result of other factors, will need closer examination (Section II.1).

In what follows, I will first analyse in more detail the current state of doctrinal science in Germany and thereby explain the factors and developments that have led to the present crisis (Section II). In a second step, I will then develop new perspectives for contemporary doctrinal science; here, I will draw some lessons from the German past and take some inspiration from contemporary Anglo-American jurisprudence (Section III).

II. Transformations of Doctrinal Science

In current discussions concerning the state of doctrinal science, it is often assumed that it is possible for contemporary scholars to simply continue the tradition of learned law. Many scholars accordingly argue that doctrinal science today is, and should be, similar to nineteenth-century models, such as the works of Friedrich Carl von Savigny[11] or Rudolf Jhering.[12] Doctrinal science today would thus serve similar functions and take the same place in the legal system as it did during the nineteenth century and in pre-modern times. Whether this assumption is actually correct is very rarely discussed.[13] Yet, since the nineteenth century, legal systems—in particular, the German legal system—have undergone significant changes, and it is important to understand those changes when reflecting on the role and the specific perspective of doctrinal science.

1. The Centre of the Legal System

Many jurists today believe that the most fundamental development in German legal history in the nineteenth and twentieth centuries was the codification of large parts of the legal system, including the Constitution.

[10] Thus, the critique of case law positivism; see above n 4.
[11] Thus Bumke, *Rechtsdogmatik* (n 2): hermeneutic systematisation of the law.
[12] Thus Lennartz, *Dogmatik* (n 2): construction of doctrinal 'figures' (structures); cf also the contributions by Stürner cited above (n 2).
[13] For exceptions, see below, n 14.

Equally fundamental, though perhaps less visible, transformations of other features of the legal system often remain unnoticed.[14] One of them is the shift in the centre of gravity from the law faculties to the courts. This shift has changed practical jurists' modes of thinking and perceptions of the legal system perhaps more fundamentally than the fact that the Digest was replaced with the Civil Code.

This development had started before the end of the nineteenth century.[15] Whereas in that century, the legal system centred on the major faculties and leading scholars, today this centre has shifted to the Federal Constitutional Court, the Federal Court of Justice (*Bundesgerichtshof*), and other superior courts in Germany, or the Court of Justice of the European Union. Obviously, this shift is the main factor explaining why doctrinal science no longer centres on itself but instead revolves around the authoritative judgments of the highest courts. Thus, in Germany, judge-made law (*Richterrecht*) today occupies the place formerly held by learned 'professors' law' (*Juristenrecht*). Citizens asking for legal advice will be directed to or informed about precedential cases. Daily newspapers report on decisions of the Federal Constitutional Court and other supreme courts, just as they report on new legislation. Doctrinal textbooks, in contrast, have been reduced to tools of legal education. They are written for student readers; hence, they are short, usually follow a descriptive approach, and often confine themselves to rather basic information. If the important dogmatic innovations of the nineteenth century were the product of leading scholars,[16] comparable progress in the twentieth century originated primarily in leading decisions of the highest courts.[17] Those decisions increasingly 'determine the horizon of thought, the language, the doctrinal "figures" (structures)'

[14] For apt observation, though rather casual discussion, see Lennartz, *Dogmatik* (n 2) 16 f, 114 ff; M Eifert, 'Zum Verhältnis von Dogmatik und pluralisierter Rechtswissenschaft' in: Kirchhof, Magen, and Schneider (eds), *Was weiß Dogmatik?* (n 2) 79, 84. For discussion, see Schönberger, *German Approach* (n 2) 18–37, arguing that the Federal Constitutional Court had taken over 'the old future-oriented role of constitutional jurisprudence' (ibid 29); the latter, as the 'maid' of the court, 'only carries the train behind it ... instead of shining ahead with the torch' (ibid 31). See, in more detail, N Jansen, *Recht und gesellschaftliche Differenzierung* (Mohr Siebeck 2019) 297–305.

[15] R Jhering, 'Ist die Jurisprudenz eine Wissenschaft?' in O Behrends (ed), *Ist die Jurisprudenz eine Wissenschaft* (Wallstein-Verlag 1998) 47, 80 ff. Jhering had welcomed this development: The courts should take the lead in the further development of the law, because they possess much better and more precise knowledge about the 'needs of practice' than professors; the task of doctrinal science consists in 'taking that which, in concrete form, judicial decision delivers to it and elevating it to a generality of concept (*das, was der Richterspruch ihr in concreter Gestalt entgegengetragen hat, zur Allgemeinheit des Begriffs erheben*)' (ibid 90).

[16] See Lennartz, *Dogmatik* (n 2) 140 ff and below at n 72 ff.

[17] Here, Lennartz primarily refers to decisions of the Federal Constitutional Court: *Dogmatik* (n 2) 157 ff, 160, 175: *Lüth*, *Apotheken*-decision. He does, however, also acknowledge academic innovation; see *loc cit*, 175.

of the German legal system.[18] They constitute what citizens and lawyers perceive as 'the law'.

The shift in the legal system's centre has not been caused by a decline in academia but has instead resulted from two other factors. The first is the professionalization of the judiciary.[19] While even in the eighteenth century, many judges in Germany still did not hold a university degree;[20] since the beginning of the nineteenth century, practising lawyers and judges have been required to pass a truly academic education, including a serious examination. Thus, in accordance with Savigny's programme to fill judicial benches with scholars,[21] they have been trained on the high methodological standards of the *Historical School*[22] and have possessed the same knowledge and abilities as legal scholars. Professors are no longer better jurists than judges.

The second factor is the publication of judicial decisions. Wherever legislation does not provide an unambiguous answer to a legal issue, jurists tend to assume that courts will follow prior decisions; hence, wherever courts have their decisions published, they unofficially become lawmakers.[23] Yet, while English judges from early on had reported cases and treated them as sources of the law,[24] such reporting was not practised on the continent before the seventeenth century[25] and the courts did not themselves publish their decisions before 1800.[26] In view of the increasing complexity of society and of the law, judges have felt it necessary for the courts to take a more active role.[27] With

[18] See, with a focus on constitutional law, M Stolleis, 'Zur Bedeutung der Rechtswissenschaft für die Dynamik der Rechtsordnung im 19. und 20. Jahrhundert' in S Dauchy, J Monballyu, and A Wijffels (eds), *Auctoritates. Xenia R.C. Van Caenegem Oblata* (1997) 118–32, 130 f.

[19] Such professionalization had been part of the reform programme of the Historical School; see H-P Haferkamp, *Die Historische Rechtsschule* (Vittorio Klostermann 2018) 269 ff.

[20] E Döhring, *Geschichte der Deutschen Rechtspflege seit 1500* (Duncker & Humblot 1953) 50 ff, 59 ff; R Wendt, *Die bayerische Konkursprüfung der Montgelas-Zeit* (Uni-Druck 1984) 13 ff, 30 ff: Even if most Bavarian judges were expected to pass a few years of legal education, their employment did not depend on their legal abilities. Positions in the administration could be bought and inherited; hence, they remained a privilege of the nobility and a few bourgeois families.

[21] FC von Savigny, *System des heutigen Römischen Rechts* (Veit 1840–49) vol 1, 89.

[22] P Krause, 'Geschichte der Justiz- und Verwaltungsausbildung in Preußen und Deutschland' in C Baldus, T Finkenauer, and T Rüfner (eds), *Juristenausbildung in Europa zwischen Tradition und Reform* (Mohr (Siebeck) 2008) 95–125, 100 ff.

[23] Jansen, *Differenzierung* (n 14) 280; id, 'Methoden, Institutionen, Texte' (2011) 128 Zeitschrift der Savigny-Stiftung für Rechtsgeschichte (Germanistische Abteilung) 1, 35 ff.

[24] On the bureaucratization of the King's court, see J Hudson, *The Oxford History of the Laws of England, vol 2, 871–1216* (OUP 2012) 523, 851; for the early reporting of cases, see J Baker, *An Introduction to English Legal History* (5th edn, OUP 2019) 188 ff.

[25] For detail, see H Coing, *Europäisches Privatrecht, vol 1: Älteres Gemeines Recht (1500–1800)* (CH Beck 1985) 125 f; F Ranieri, 'Kasuistik und Regelbildung bei der Rechtsfindung im europäischen Ius Commune des 16.–17. Jahrhunderts' in G Essen and N Jansen (eds), *Dogmatisierungsprozesse in Recht und Religion* (2011) 153, 174 ff.

[26] Dawson, *Oracles* (n 9) 432 ff; Ranieri, 'Kasuistik' (n 25) 174 ff.

[27] Jansen, *Differenzierung* (n 14) 281 f.

the creation of a German Supreme Court in 1869 (*Reichsoberhandelsgericht* viz *Reichsgericht* or *Bundesgerichtshof*),[28] the judiciary took a leading role in the unification of German law;[29] at the same time, influential scholars such as Bernhard Windscheid began to include the analysis of relevant case law in their textbooks on national (Roman) German law.[30] The judiciary assuming a more active role in the progress of the law is, hence, a fairly recent development.[31]

2. The Distance between Legal Practice and Legal Science

German scholars often assume that the 'brand core' of legal doctrine is its 'exclusive orientation' towards the applicable law of a concrete legal system,[32] yet rarely notice that, with this assumption, they adopt a position opposite to what has long been self-evident. Indeed, from the end of the eighteenth century, scholars developed a specifically academic 'structural preference for universalistic knowledge systems';[33] this habitus significantly distinguished them from the learned *usus-modernus* professors of the eighteenth century. Legal science—both in private and constitutional law—was oriented towards the—somewhat artificial, though nevertheless vivid—idea of a national German law.[34] Even after the collapse of the Old Empire in 1806, German law faculties continued to teach the same law, treating it not only as a school of thought but also as a common national law.[35] Where common (Roman) sources were lacking, as in conflicts of laws, textbooks were written on the basis of broad comparative surveys, including American, French, and Dutch sources.[36]

[28] In 1869, the *Reichsoberhandelsgericht*, a supreme court for commercial cases, was established in Leipzig (originally as the *Bundesoberhandelsgericht*); in 1878, when a decision was made to unify all private law and criminal law, it was replaced with, or rather transformed into, the *Reichsgericht* (which later became the *Bundesgerichtshof*).

[29] M Payandeh, *Judikative Rechtserzeugung* (Mohr Siebeck 2017) 86 f.

[30] B Windscheid, *Lehrbuch des Pandektenrechts* (7th edn, Rütten & Loening 1891).

[31] H-P Haferkamp, 'The Science of Private Law and the State in Nineteenth Century Germany' in N Jansen and R Michaels (eds), *Beyond the State? Rethinking Private Law* (Mohr (Siebeck) 2008) 245, 257 f; cf K Kroeschell, *Deutsche Rechtsgeschichte, vol 3. Seit 1650* (5th edn, Böhlau 2008) 171 f.

[32] Jestaedt, 'Wissenschaft im Recht' (n 2) 4 ff, 8, 12; H Dreier, 'Rechtswissenschaft als Wissenschaft. Zehn Thesen' in id (ed), *Rechtswissenschaft als Beruf* (n 2) 1, 7; cf Lennartz, *Dogmatik* (n 2) 119 ff; Bumke, *Rechtsdogmatik* (n 2) 56–99.

[33] R Stichweh, 'Motive und Begründungsstrategien für Wissenschaftlichkeit in der deutschen Jurisprudenz des 19. Jahrhunderts' (1992) 11 Rechtshistorisches Journal 330, 332.

[34] Jansen, 'Rechtsdogmatik' (n 1) 634 f.

[35] AFJ Thibaut, *System des Pandekten-Rechts* (4th edn, Mauke1814) vol 1, 11 (§ 13). See, for the discussions on the idea of a *Volksgeist*, Haferkamp, *Historische Rechtsschule* (n 19) 62 ff: 'Why teach dead laws?'

[36] Von Savigny, *System* (n 21) vol 8, *passim*.

All this, however, changed fundamentally after 1900, though apparently not as a result of the codification of the law, but rather in accordance with a new self-definition of the 'cultural sciences (*Kulturwissenschaften*, humanities)' as individualizing (ideographic), rather than generalizing (nomothetic) academic disciplines.[37] This self-perception of the humanities was a reaction to philosophical debates concerning the nature of sciences in general, and of history in particular. Although there was never any general agreement on the issue, this perception soon determined the legal point of view. Yet, as far as I can see, legal scholars never thought about the eventual consequences of such a turn towards one single legal system. One reason may be that the idea of the law as a system helped to preserve a specifically academic point of view. Scholars were concerned with the abstract system of the law rather than with particular issues related to specific legal provisions.[38] Academic legal literature was therefore clearly distinguishable from practitioners' commentaries: While commentaries were supposed to reconnect legal practice to established doctrine,[39] legal science was believed to flourish in the form of treatises.[40] The form of the commentary, which had specifically been designed for the needs of practice by attorneys and judges, such as Hermann Staub and Adolf Baumbach,[41] generally seemed 'inconvenient' as far as doctrinal science was concerned.[42] Doctrinal innovation was to be found not in a commentary, but in academic treatises.[43] Thus, despite their focus on the positive law of Germany, scholars maintained a genuinely academic distance from daily legal practice—a distance necessary for the production of new and innovative knowledge.

Since the second half of the twentieth century, however, trust in the systematic nature of the law has been declining.[44] Various factors have contributed

[37] I have analysed those discussions in much detail in N Jansen, 'Hermann Kantorowicz' Concept of Legal Science and the Social Role of Legal Scholarship, Today' (2022) 26 Edinburgh LR 321, 330 ff; id, 'Der Gegenstand der Rechtswissenschaft' (2020) Juristenzeitung 213, 217 ff.

[38] See, in more detail, N Jansen, 'Vom Aufstieg des Kommentars und Niedergang des Lehrbuchs' in D Kästle-Lamparter, N Jansen, and R Zimmermann (eds), *Juristische Kommentare. Ein Internationaler Vergleich* (2020) 25, 28 f.

[39] Kästle-Lamparter, *Kommentare* (n 4) 236 f.

[40] Kästle-Lamparter, *Kommentare* (n 4) 238 with further references.

[41] While Staub was an attorney in Berlin, Baumbach acted as a presiding judge in Berlin's Court of Appeal; see J Thiessen, '"Ein ungeahnter Erfolg". Zur (Rezeptions-) Geschichte von Hermann Staubs Kommentaren' in T Henne, R Schröder, and J Thiessen (eds), *Anwalt—Kommentator—'Entdecker'. Festschrift für Hermann Staub zum 150. Geburtstag* (2006) 55, 59 ff, 86 ff; Kästle-Lamparter, *Kommentare* (n 4) 224 ff; D Willoweit, 'Juristische Literatur des 20. Jahrhunderts' in id (ed), *Rechtswissenschaft und Rechtsliteratur* (n 45) 3, 28 ff.

[42] M Stenglein, *Kommentar zur Strafprozessordnung für das Deutsche Reich* (Beck 1884)III (preface).

[43] C Crome, *System des Bürgerlichen Rechts, vol I: Einleitung und Allgemeiner Teil* (JCB Mohr 1900) 59; E Rabel, Review of 'Staudingers Kommentar zum BGB' (1915) 7 Rheinische Zeitschrift für Zivil- und Prozeßrecht 508, 510.

[44] See O Lepsius, 'Kritik der Dogmatik' in Kirchhof, Magen, and Schneider (eds), *Was weiß Dogmatik?* (n 2) 39, 54 ff; Auer, *Erkenntnisziel der Rechtstheorie* (n 2) 64 f; cf also Stürner, 'Zivilrechtswissenschaft'

to this decline, including the thick glosses of case law, which today overlay the codifications' provisions, and the integration of national legal systems into international, and especially European, multi-layer systems. Such integration is often at odds with systematic conceptions of national law and, in effect, even breaks them up. Only a few scholars today are still convinced of the law-forming potential of legal systematization on the one hand and, on the other, of the possibility of systematically reconstructing larger areas of law. It is a consequence of this development that scholars have been losing their last remaining device for distancing science from practice. Since the second half of the twentieth century, professors have thus been pushing into the market for commentaries.[45] While professors after 1900 had avoided this form of publication, they nowadays even characterize the commentary 'as the most characteristic publication format of doctrinal science'.[46] Meanwhile, the commentary has even replaced traditional treatises as the leading form of academic writing.

Now, the purpose of standard commentaries, such as the *Grünberger* (formerly *Palandt*) or the *Münchener Kommentare*, is to map the fabric of statutory and case law within the regulatory framework of a codification—and that means in a contingent legislative, rather than in a scientific, theoretical framework (traditionally: the system).[47] Scholars contributing to such commentaries apparently see their task primarily in making case law accessible to legal practitioners. Indeed, those commentaries are usually not meant to reflect systematically on progress in other disciplines or otherwise to offer new theoretical insights, to present new concepts, ideas, or models for system building or a better, deeper understanding of doctrinal problems.[48] They are thus not

(n 2) 22 f; T Lobinger, 'Perspektiven' (n 4) 68. See also J Gernhuber (writing as general editor), in H Lange (ed), *Schadensersatz* (1979) v (preface): 'Anyone who is looking for the contemporary law of obligations will hardly find it in the text of §§ 241-853 BGB. Case law has overgrown the norms in often unrestrained diversity; new types of contracts have found their way into legal transactions ...; contractual relationships have arisen which the thinking prescribed by the BGB ... is unable to cope with. Of the basic assumptions that dominated the doctrinal science of the law of obligations at the beginning of the century, none has ultimately been able to stand firm: ... everything is gone.'

[45] Jansen, 'Aufstieg des Kommentars' (n 38) 38 ff, for the *Münchener Kommentar zum BGB*, in particular, FJ Säcker, 'Münchener Kommentar zum BGB' in D Willoweit (ed), *Rechtswissenschaft und Rechtsliteratur im 20. Jahrhundert. Mit Beiträgen zur Geschichte des Verlages C.H. Beck* (Beck 2007) 405. This work was conceived as a professors' commentary (loc cit, 408); it owes its creation not to the plan of a publisher, but to the initiative of a university professor, the later co-editor Säcker (loc cit, 405 f).

[46] Jestaedt, 'Wissenschaft im Recht' (n 2) 6.

[47] W Hassemer, 'Dogmatik zwischen Wissenschaft und richterlicher Pragmatik. Einführende Bemerkungen' in Kirchhof, Magen, and Schneider (eds), *Was weiß Dogmatik?* (n 2) 3–15, 8 f. See also Eifert, 'Dogmatik' (n 14), 87 ff, describing the courts as active players in the doctrinal making of the law, in contrast to scholars merely acting as observers.

[48] For a philosophical discussion of the criteria for 'science', cf P Hoyningen-Huene, *Systematicity: The Nature of Science* (OUP 2013) 14 ff and *passim*.

innovative and do not contribute to the production of new legal knowledge; instead, they present the established knowledge of the courts in an easily accessible format and thus offer an overview of current legal debates. Where such commentaries define the standards of doctrinal writing, science orients itself around the expectations of legal practice and thus becomes indistinguishable from practical jurisprudence.[49] Scholars thus become (relatively poorly paid) professional collaborators in the administration of the law. From the academic system's perspective, it accordingly becomes difficult to perceive doctrinal literature of this sort as scientific research[50]—despite its undoubtedly high value for legal practice.

At the same time, doctrine has been divorced from other legal disciplines, such as legal history, legal philosophy, and comparative law.[51] Although such narrow conceptions of legal doctrine have been criticized by leading institutions in the academic system,[52] many jurists today believe that the philosophical, historical, or sociological analysis of a legal issue is irrelevant as far as actual legal doctrine is concerned.[53] It is indeed not easy to see why that should be untrue. It has become unclear in what sense historical, philosophical, sociological or comparative knowledge might be relevant when jurists look for information about the actual fabric of case law and legislation.

III. The Academic Perspective

The preceding analysis (Section II) naturally leads to the following three conclusions. These conclusions are normative; I do not mean to say that German legal science is, in fact, gravitating away from doctrinal analysis towards

[49] Bumke, *Rechtsdogmatik* (n 2) 50; Jansen, 'Rechtsdogmatik' (n 1) 635 f.

[50] It is accordingly impossible to find research funding, eg, for the project of a doctrinal commentary, even if such a commentary would be highly desirable from the point of view of legal practice; see U di Fabio, 'Systemtheorie und Rechtsdogmatik' in Kirchhof, Magen, and Schneider (eds), *Was weiß Dogmatik?* (n 2) 63, 64; H Rottleuthner, 'Methodologie und Organisation der Rechtswissenschaft' in Hilgendorf and Schulze-Fielitz (eds), *Selbstreflexion* (n 2; 2nd edn) 241, 250 ff; cf also G Samuel, 'What is the Role of a Legal Academic' (2022) 2/3/2 Amicus Curiae 305, 308 ff.

[51] Jansen, 'Rechtswissenschaft' (n 37) 219. On the emancipation of legal history and comparative law from doctrinal science, see R Zimmermann, *Roman Law, Contemporary Law, European Law. The Civilian Tradition Today* (OUP 2001) 9 ff, 22 ff; R Michaels, 'Im Westen nichts Neues? 100 Jahre Pariser Kongreß für Rechtsvergleichung – Gedanken anläßlich einer Jubiläumskonferenz in New Orleans' (2002) 66 Rabels Zeitschrift für internationales und ausländisches Privatrecht 97, 100 ff.

[52] Wissenschaftsrat, *Perspektiven der Rechtswissenschaft in Deutschland. Situation, Analysen, Empfehlungen* (2012).

[53] But see N Jansen, 'Gesetzliche Schuldverhältnisse: eine historische Strukturanalyse' (2016) 216 Archiv für die civilistische Praxis (AcP) 112; M Auer, 'Eigentum, Familie, Erbrecht. Drei Lehrstücke zur Bedeutung der Rechtsphilosophie im Privatrecht' (2016) 216 AcP 239; L Klön, 'Minderheitenschutz im Personengesellschaftsrecht. Rechtsökonomische Grundlagen und Perspektiven' (2016) 216 AcP 281.

alternative forms of scholarship. Such a reorientation of German private law as a whole seems unlikely, at least as far as the near future is concerned. Nevertheless, there are scholars exploring new perspectives,[54] and the conclusions may serve as a starting point for further discussions concerning the necessary reorientation of doctrinal science.

(1) In modern society, legal academia and the judicial administration of the law have been clearly differentiated. Therefore, merely contributing to the making of new law (*Rechtsfortbildung*) cannot be a function of doctrinal legal science. Scholars are not in a position to control the development of the law effectively; nor are they legitimized to do so.

(2) Scholars should no longer see their profession in stabilizing the law doctrinally by means of commentaries and other forms of practical legal literature. Ultimately, this leads to a conflation of the academic and the legal perspectives and, in the end, threatens to undermine doctrinal science as a whole.

Note: This is not to say that legal scholars should not contribute, in their role as legal experts, to the legal system. The point is merely that scholars should distinguish legal science from contributions to the legal system (practice). Indeed, the interconnection between practice and academia is even closer in medicine, but at university hospitals nobody regards patient care as an academic activity. Here, science is generally understood as research: as the effort to gain new knowledge (which may, of course, be related to patient care). To this end, researchers analyse disease processes, test new treatment methods and conduct studies on the effectiveness of certain diagnostic and therapeutic methods. Only what is new can be published as scientific. It is not clear why such a differentiation should not also be possible, and also be meaningful, in law.[55]

(3) The task of scientific research is to formulate new legal knowledge of any sort in the form of meaningful, generalizing statements about some given object (this is also true in history, etc). This must also hold true for doctrinal science if it wants to maintain its place in academia. The task of doctrinal science must therefore be to generate new legal knowledge,

[54] cf the contributions to M Grünberger and N Jansen (eds), *Privatrechtstheorie heute. Perspektiven deutscher Theoriebildung* (Mohr Siebeck 2017) and the references in the preceding n 53.

[55] Jansen, 'Rechtsdogmatik' (n 1) 652 f. But see, more sceptically, C Möllers, 'Vorüberlegungen zu einer Wissenschaftstheorie des öffentlichen Rechts' in Jestaedt and Lepsius (eds), *Rechtswissenschaftstheorie* (n 2) 151, 158 f.

which does not exhaust itself in the description of the norms of an individual legal system.

Note: This does not mean that doctrinal science should formulate, in the same way as other sciences, truth-apt, viz. falsifiable, statements.[56] Such objectivity is possible only from the external perspective of comparative law or legal history (describing the law, for example, as systems of communicative actions). Legal doctrine, in contrast, is concerned with the intellectual structure of law, as well as with the design of legal concepts. In this respect, legal doctrine is always the result of legal argumentation. Doctrinal constructions are not true or false, but rather more or less appropriate or inappropriate.

The basic question, in view of those three propositions, is whether generalizing statements are producible as far as legal doctrine is concerned and whether such statements actually make sense. As has been shown above, many scholars assume that doctrinal science is necessarily concerned with the positive law of a single legal system[57] and that generalizing statements are, therefore, of no doctrinal interest. Yet, as we have further seen, this is not necessarily the case. When Kantorowicz argued that the object of doctrinal science was the law as a 'system of valid norms (*Inbegriff geltender Normen*)',[58] he knew quite well that this had become the prevailing opinion in Germany only during the previous few decades.[59] Similarly, it is a matter of course for common lawyers that doctrine need not be narrowly bound to the positive law of a single legal system.[60] New private law theories often describe principles of private law, viz 'the' common law in quite general terms.[61] Even in twentiethth-century German

[56] The hope that legal theory could be falsified with 'test propositions' (C-W Canaris, 'Funktion, Struktur und Falsifikation juristischer Theorien' (1993) Juristenzeitung 377, 385 ff) would presuppose that legal theories could conclusively determine the limits of what is said with a legal norm. Yet, this is implausible; see Jansen, 'Dogmatik, Erkenntnis und Theorie im europäischen Privatrecht' (2005) Zeitschrift für Europäisches Privatrecht 750, 771 ff.

[57] Above, at n 32 ff.

[58] H Kantorowicz, 'Was ist uns Savigny?' (1911/12) 1 Recht und Wirtschaft 47 and 76, 51, 76.

[59] Kantorowicz, 'Was ist uns Savigny?' (n 58), 51, arguing that it was due to the infelicitous influence of Savigny that the common German law (*Gemeines Recht*), rather than Prussian law, had been taught in Prussia.

[60] EG Hosemann, '"The New Private Law": Die neue amerikanische Privatrechtswissenschaft in historischer und vergleichender Perspektive' (2014) 78 Rabels Zeitschrift für internationales und ausländisches Privatrecht 37; cf also, for common law in general, M Flohr, *Rechtsdogmatik in England* (Mohr Siebeck 2017) 239 ff and *passim*.

[61] Here, not least for the American Restatements, there continues to exist a uniform American doctrinal science, although it goes without saying that special, sometimes strongly divergent laws apply in individual states; N Jansen, *The Making of Legal Authority. Non-legislative Codifications in Historical and Comparative Perspective* (OUP 2010) 52 ff; cf, as an example, SA Smith, *Contract Theory* (OUP 2004) ix, 5. Smith refers to 'present law', specifying this as 'common law ... in particular the English common law', yet he maintains that 'much of what is said applies equally to the civil law tradition'.

law, legal doctrine received its most innovative impulses through historically and comparatively informed doctrinal contributions.[62]

The object of such contributions is not the specific positive law of an individual legal system, but rather the conceptual and systemic tools for legal thinking. Such analyses do not simply describe legal rules. In fact, they put them in perspective and, for that purpose, construct concepts and intellectual models which may then be used for the doctrinal description of individual legal systems in the context of legal practice.[63] Usually, such analyses combine a functional analysis with the design, viz construction of concepts and models. The assumption that different legal systems and their rules often serve similar functions[64] allows doctrinal science to formulate generalizing statements and design models and concepts independently of individual legal systems. Yet, as law is a social institution, it would be unwise to assume that the functions of legal institutions are necessarily of a universal, viz eternal nature; hence, doctrinal analysis is relative to the plausibility of functional assumptions.

1. Lessons from the Past?

It has been shown above that, for German scholars, such a perspective has long been a matter of course.[65] The basis of nineteenth-century science was the—somewhat fictitious—idea of a national German law on which the many different positive laws in Germany were modelled. As this national German law was (then) 'today's' Roman law, the Digest could normally serve as the starting point for doctrinal analysis.[66] With this as the object of legal

[62] Examples include not least the authoritative opinions on the reform of the law of obligations in the late 1970s (Bundesminister der Justiz (ed), *Gutachten und Vorschläge zur Überarbeitung des Schuldrechts*, 3 vols, 1981/1983), which became highly influential in the reform of the law of obligations in 2002; and the law of unjustified enrichment, which has gained its modern shape not from the meagre provisions of §§ 812–22 Civil Code, but from a series of historically comparative studies, namely W Wilburg, *Die Lehre von der ungerechtfertigten Bereicherung* (Leuschner und Lubensky 1934) and E von Caemmerer, 'Bereicherung und unerlaubte Handlung' in *Festschrift für Ernst Rabel* vol 1 (1954) 333; see Jansen, 'Gesetzliche Schuldverhältnisse' (n 53) 148 ff. A well-known public-law example is the construction of the administrative act based on French models; see Lennartz, *Dogmatik* (n 2) 136.

[63] cf H Kantorowicz and EW Patterson, 'Legal Science – A Summary of its Methodology' (1928) 28 Col L Rev 679, 682 ff; id, 'Staatsauffassungen. Eine Skizze' (1925) 1 Jahrbuch für Soziologie 101, 102 f: rational sciences concerned with the scientific construction of objective meaning (mathematics, doctrinal sciences). Later, in particular H Heller, *Staatslehre in der Bearbeitung von Gerhart Niemeyer* (VA 1934; 6th edn, 1983) 54 ff, 60 ff. Today, Schönberger, *German Approach* (n 2) 50 f: Development of models, function types and typologies, informed by comparative experience.

[64] For detail, see R Michaels, 'The Functional Method of Comparative Law' in M Reimann and R Zimmermann (eds), *The Oxford Handbook of Comparative Law* (2nd edn, OUP 2019) 345, 354 ff, 362 ff.

[65] Above at n 33.

[66] FC von Savigny, *Vom Beruf unserer Zeit für Gesetzgebung und Rechtswissenschaft* (Mohr und Zimmer 1814) 151 ff and *passim*.

doctrine, there was no problem of distancing science from the many different positive laws of the German territories, or otherwise of gaining a generalizing perspective.

Today, there is no way back to the legal sources of an ancient culture. Already during the nineteenth century, it was obvious that those texts gave expression to pre-modern values—lawyers working with those texts always had to distinguish the 'living' from the 'extinct law'—and that they could not be applied like modern legislation. What is more, nineteenth-century models of private law were highly political in that they were designed to protect bourgeois society in its independence from governmental regulation.[67] Scholars therefore built their systems on the fiction that society consisted of free and equal citizens and that distributive considerations had to be disregarded as far as private law was concerned—this was necessary to keep governmental policies out of the private law. They conceived of legal transactions (*Rechtsgeschäfte*) as an embodiment of liberal notions of private autonomy and regarded the Roman *actiones poenales* (penal actions in private law) as good law,[68] although those actions had long been out of use.[69] Hence, the fault principle became an 'axiom' of tort law.[70] Citizens could even be granted the power to give effect to non-assignment clauses vis-à-vis third-party assignees. Leading authorities reasoned that an obligation could come into existence as a non-transferable claim.[71] Today, such a political approach, in open opposition to a legislature's intervention, is inappropriate.

Nevertheless, there are at least two lessons for modern legal science to learn from nineteenth-century experiences. The first positive lesson is the academic benefit of distancing doctrinal science from practice. Pandectist doctrines are clear proof of the fact that such distance facilitates conceptual and systematic doctrinal progress. The Pandectists did not have to collect

[67] See Haferkamp, *Historische Rechtsschule* (n 19) 111 ff, with a thorough discussion of nineteenth-century sources.

[68] FC von Savigny, *Das Obligationenrecht als Theil des heutigen Römischen Rechts* (Veit 1851/1853) vol 1, 312 ff, 317 ff, 321 ff; Thibaut, *System* (n 35) §§ 66–68; GF Puchta, *Lehrbuch der Pandekten* (9th edn, Ambrosius Barth 1863) §§ 230, 261; Windscheid, *Pandektenrecht* (n 30) vol 2, § 326. As far as the law of delict was concerned, German scholars argued remarkably close to the Roman actions; see W Ernst, 'Negligence in 19th Century Germany' in E Schrage (ed), *Negligence. The Comparative Legal History of the Law of Torts* (2001) 341, 343 ff; more generally R Zimmermann, *Roman Law, Contemporary Law, European Law* (2001) 11 ff.

[69] G Hugo, *Lehrbuch des heutigen Römischen Rechts* (7th edn, August Mylius 1826) 282 ff. For further discussion and references, see N Jansen, *The Structure of Tort Law* (OUP 2021) 271 ff.

[70] R Jhering, *Das Schuldmoment im Römischen Privatrecht* (Emil Roth 1867) 40 ff and *passim*; further, among many others, Thibaut, *System* (n 35) § 250.

[71] Windscheid, *Pandektenrecht* 2 (n 30), § 335; see N Jansen, in N Jansen and R Zimmermann (eds), *Commentaries on European Contract Laws. Foundations, Commentaries, Synthesis* (2018) Art 11:301, [3].

court judgments in their textbooks on Roman law; accordingly, they were interested more in the facts of cases brought before the courts than in the decisions. Clearly, they felt bound to the law but not to precedents. This distance was the basis for their inventing entirely new constructions and concepts, such as the subjective public right (*subjektives öffentliches Recht*);[72] the idea of abstract legal transactions,[73] including a grant of authority, distinguished from the mandate giving rise to it;[74] and the invention of the law of enrichment.[75]

The second, negative lesson is to say farewell to political, normatively dense legal doctrine. While scholars may, of course, feel called to criticize existing rules and inherited institutions normatively, they should not hide such claims in thick doctrinal constructions. Instead, doctrine should be conceived as normatively as thin as possible. Of course, doctrine can never be innocent; doctrinal concepts and constructions connect descriptive, normative, and conceptual elements.[76] They unavoidably embody implicit normative assumptions. In that respect, legal doctrine resembles language, which likewise gives expression to underlying social norms, as shown by sociolinguistics in general and the discussions on gender and language in particular. Nevertheless, scholars can reflect upon the normative content of doctrine; they should keep doctrinal concepts and constructions as flexible as possible. Doctrine has to respond to legislation; hence, its function cannot be conceptually to stabilize contested values and policies.[77] Constructions should, therefore, no longer *embody* possibly contested values and policies but rather *give expression to* them as clearly and appropriately as possible. Well-designed constructions should fit divergent rules and regulations; there must not be normative 'tensions' between doctrine and legislation.[78] Transparent and normatively thin forms of doctrine should be preferred to thick conceptions.

[72] G Jellinek, *System der subjektiven öffentlichen Rechte* (JBC Mohr 1892) 63 ff; see Lennartz, *Dogmatik* (n 2) 140 ff.

[73] Von Savigny, *System* (n 21) vol 3, 312 ff; id, *Obligationenrecht* (n 68) vol 2, 254, 256 ff.

[74] P Laband, 'Die Stellvertretung bei dem Abschluß von Rechtsgeschäften nach dem allgem. Deutsch. Handelsgesetzbuch' (1866) 10 Zeitschrift für das gesamte Handelsrecht, 183, 203 ff; cf R Zimmermann, *The Law of Obligations* (Juta 1990) 57 f.

[75] Von Savigny, *System* (n 21) vol 5, 109 ff, 507 ff, 526; see N Jansen, 'Die Korrektur grundloser Vermögensverschiebungen als Restitution. Zur Lehre von der ungerechtfertigten Bereicherung bei Savigny' (2003) 120 Zeitschrift der Savigny-Stiftung für Rechtsgeschichte (Romanistische Abteilung) 106,149 ff.

[76] R Alexy, *A Theory of Constitutional Rights* (2002) 6 ff.

[77] Jansen, 'Rechtsdogmatik' (n 1) 650 f.

[78] cf Stürner, 'Zivilrechtswissenschaft' (n 2) 20: '*Spannungsverhältnis*' between doctrinal science and democratic legislation.

2. Conceptual Linguistic Analysis?

Some authors in Germany today argue that legal theory can serve as a neutral, academic perspective on legal doctrine.[79] The exact meaning of this claim is not quite clear, as every (good) science formulates theoretical statements, and there exists no such clearly defined discipline as 'legal theory'. Thus, 'theory' may first be understood as analytical jurisprudence, viz conceptual analysis; here, the science gains distance from its object by means of conceptual abstraction. Classic examples of such approaches include Hohfeld's theory of rights,[80] Kelsen's *Rechtslehre*,[81] Hart's *Concept of Law*,[82] Wright's NESS formula for causation,[83] or Alexy's principles-theory of constitutional rights.[84] All of these theories are formulated in abstract terms; they do not describe a specific legal system, but rather analyse general legal concepts, such as 'right', 'duty', 'legal system', or 'causation'. Hence, they may be normatively thin: they are not constructed to embody specific policies or values but instead describe the 'pure' structure of the law (Kelsen), independent of its normative contents.

The fact that those works are still read and cited in most parts of the world shows that analytical jurisprudence can indeed formulate lasting legal knowledge; hence, it may serve as a starting point for doctrinal analysis.[85] Unfortunately, such a view has a rather narrow focus; as far as doctrine is concerned, its explanatory power is limited. Conceptual linguistic analysis does not in itself generate doctrinal insights, as it does not explain the normative—as opposed to the logical—structure of a legal field or institution. It may explain the distinction between first- and second-order rules, between powers, claims, and liberties, or between principles and rules, but it does not normatively explain the distinctions between legislation, administrative action, and

[79] Auer, *Erkenntnisziel der Rechtstheorie* (n 2). Auer locates this 'new legal theory (*neue Rechtstheorie*)' 'between' legal doctrine on the one hand, and legal history, sociology of law, and legal philosophy on the other, describing it as an 'amalgam' of different theoretical elements from the humanities, sociology, and economics. What holds those elements together seems to be a comparatively high level of abstraction.

[80] WN Hohfeld, 'Some Fundamental Legal Conceptions as Applied in Judicial Reasoning' (1913/14) 23 Yale LJ 16; id, 'Fundamental Legal Conceptions as Applied in Judicial Reasoning' (1916/17) 26 Yale LJ 710.

[81] H Kelsen, *General Theory of Law and State* (Harvard University Press 1945); id, *Reine Rechtslehre* (2nd edn, Franz Deuticke 1960).

[82] HLA Hart, *The Concept of Law* (2nd edn, Clarendon Press 1994).

[83] R Wright, 'Causation in Tort Law' (1985) 73 Cal L Rev 1735. In 1980, Ingeborg Puppe had formulated, independently of Wright, a very similar theory; see Puppe, 'Der Erfolg und seine kausale Erklärung im Strafrecht' (1980) 92 Zeitschrift für die gesamte Strafrechtswissenschaft 863.

[84] Alexy, *Constitutional Rights* (n 76).

[85] For an illuminating discussion of some methodological issues, in particular the underlying philosophical assumptions (Austin vs Wittgenstein, viz Oxford vs Cambridge), see N Lacey, 'Analytical Jurisprudence Versus Descriptive Sociology Revisited' (2006) 84 Tex L Rev 945, 965 ff.

judicial decision, or strict liability and fault.[86] It therefore does not provide the synthesis necessary to understand legal institutions, such as assignments of claims, contracts or torts. From a doctrinal perspective, analytical jurisprudence can only represent a first step.

3. Philosophical Foundations?

A more normative conception of legal theory[87] is the search for what Anglo-American scholars often describe as the 'philosophical foundations' of a particular field of the law.* A well-known, early example was Hart and Honoré's *Causation in the Law* (1959),[88] which still presented itself in large part as linguistic philosophical analysis.[89] Meanwhile, more normative contributions to this discussion, by scholars such as George P Fletcher,[90] Jules L Coleman,[91] Ernest J Weinrib,[92] Tony Honoré,[93] and Charles Fried,[94] have long since become classics.

While the rather specific political background of this branch of private law theory was a counter-attack against overly instrumental conceptions of private law in general and critical legal studies[95] and law and economics in particular,[96] the academic objective of such theories is to reduce the apparent complexity of a given field of law; to provide better normative explanations than other theories;[97] or to identify moral inconsistencies in the law and suggest solutions to overcome them.[98] Usually, they integrate interpretive or hermeneutic with

[86] cf Jansen, *Tort Law* (n. 69) 32 ff, 58–110.

[87] The concept of normativity is notoriously contested, and I do not wish to contribute to those discussions. I do not use, or otherwise refer to, the noun in this article. By 'normative' I simply mean 'relating to' or 'implying norms'; a 'more normative' conception is thus a conception which more directly addresses evaluative, rather than purely conceptual, issues.

[88] HLA Hart and T Honoré, *Causation in the Law* (2nd edn, OUP 1985) lxxxviii f; 62–83 and *passim*. See Lacey, 'Analytical Jurisprudence Versus Descriptive Sociology' (n 85) 963 ff.

[89] See Hart and Honoré, *Causation* (n 89) 1: the purpose of the book was to 'identify the sources of the uncertainties and confusions which continue to surround the . . . use of' some legal 'language'. Similarly, today, S Steel, *Proof of Causation in Tort Law* (CUP 2015) 2: 'conceptual problems, problems of consistency, and normative problems'.

[90] GP Fletcher, 'Fairness and Utility in Tort Theory' (1972) 85 Harvard LR 537.

[91] JL Coleman, *Risks and Wrongs* (CUP 1992).

[92] Weinrib, *Private Law* (n 97).

[93] T Honoré, 'Can and Can't' (1964) 73 Mind 463–79; id, *Responsibility and Fault* (1999).

[94] C Fried, *Contract as Promise. A Theory of Contractual Obligation* (Harvard University Press 1981).

[95] Fried, *Contract as Promise* (n 94) 3.

[96] EJ Weinrib, *The Idea of Private Law* (Harvard UP 1995) 3 f, 46 ff.

[97] cf Weinrib, *Private Law* (n 96) 2 ff, 29–55, arguing that only 'formalist', non-functional theories could provide a coherent explanation of private law, because only such theories could explain (make intelligible) the bi-polar structure of private law relationships. It is obvious that Weinrib thus understands coherence in a particularly strong, though ultimately not convincing way; cf Smith, *Contract Theory* (n 61) 11 ff.

[98] cf Smith, *Contract Theory* (n 61) 14 ff, claiming that this accords with 'the law's self-understanding'.

normative perspectives,[99] regarding the law, in accordance with traditional conceptions of the common law,[100] as a positive expression of reasonable moral convictions. Hence, they analyse legal institutions and doctrines from the point of view of private or 'political morality',[101] claiming that 'complex legal institution(s)' such as contract 'can be traced to and (are) determined by a small number of basic moral principles'.[102] The basic elements of such theories are usually common-sense notions of moral duties;[103] thus, torts are described as moral wrongs, that is, as 'the breach of a moral duty',[104] and the law of contract is explained in terms of the morally binding force of promises.[105]

In all of those theories, seemingly self-evident principles of common-sense morality serve to define a specific academic perspective for legal doctrine. This is a rather intuitive starting point. Nevertheless, many such theories provide important normative insights. Legal doctrine based on a limited set of basic principles makes jurists understand, rather than merely know, the law.[106] It is true that such theories embody strong normative assumptions, but the claim is usually that those assumptions are uncontested or self-evident even in modern society. They may thus be political, but not in an inappropriate way. At first sight, common-sense moral intuitions, therefore, offer an appropriate perspective for academic legal doctrine. Nevertheless, I am sceptical of whether such intuitions may serve as a sufficiently solid foundation for legal analysis. There are two main reasons for scepticism.

The first is that moral intuitions are reliable only as far as two-person relationships are concerned. Clearly, one should keep one's promises, and people are responsible for loss caused by their fault, but things get more difficult when three or more persons are affected. Imagine a rather simple case: Bank B erroneously pays C some money on the basis of a transfer order that has, in fact, been revoked. Is C obliged to return this money to bank B or to A, who had placed this order? Who is thus to bear the risk of C's insolvency? Of course, the mistaken transfer falls within the responsibility of the bank where the error

[99] Smith, *Contract Theory* (n 61) 4 ff.

[100] W Blackstone, *Commentaries on the Laws of England*, vol 1 (Clarendon Press 1765) 70, describing the common law as 'the perfection of reason'. Blackstone's formulation was quite representative of his age; for discussion and references on other authorities, such as Coke, see S Banner, *The Decline of Natural Law. How American Lawyers Once Used Natural Law and Why They Stopped* (OUP 2021) 46 ff, 58 ff, 63 ff.

[101] S Steel, 'On the Moral Necessity of Tort Law: The Fairness Argument' (2021) 41 OJLSt 192.

[102] Fried, *Contract as Promise* (n 94) 1.

[103] cf Steel, *Causation* (n 89) 110 ff.

[104] cf, as an example, S Steel, 'Compensation and Continuity' (2020) 26 Legal Theory, 250.

[105] Fried, *Contract as Promise* (n 94) 8, 16 f, and *passim*.

[106] cf Smith, *Contract Theory* (n 61) 5 f on interpretive theories.

occurred. But what if A had announced the transfer to C and did not correct this information? In this case, C would have relied on A's behaviour.

Even more complex considerations apply where the legislature uses private law as a means of public regulation: here, moral intuitions are certainly not an appropriate basis for legal analysis; it would be implausible to assume that jurists usually understand such rules in moral terms.[107] Thus, European consumer contract law is an instrument for market regulation—indeed, according to Article 114 of the Treaty on the Functioning of the European Union, the Union's legislative power is based on and limited by the intention to promote the establishment and functioning of the internal market.[108] Such legislation is not formulated as an expression of corrective justice or some other moral principle, but rather on the basis of public policy. The best one could say about such rules in moral terms is that it was morally acceptable to include such policies in the law, but that does not transform public policy into moral principles.

Even long-established doctrines like the acquisition of property in good faith can only be explained by reference to public commercial interests,[109] which are sometimes difficult to square with moral intuitions. Thus, the acquisition of another's property in good faith expropriates the innocent former owner, often without compensation.[110] It is not based on moral principle but on commercial policy. Since the times of the Roman emperors, jurists have nevertheless developed a habitus of ignoring such policies in the context of private law.[111] During the nineteenth century, ignoring public policy was even a means to protect society against governmental regulation.[112] Today, such ignorance is illegitimate. Scholars may regret the resulting complexity of the law,[113] but they must not ignore it. Relying on moral intuitions alone is, therefore, no longer appropriate. This is true not least for pure corrective justice conceptions of tort

[107] But see Smith, *Contract Theory* (n 61) 15 f for such a 'morality thesis'.

[108] B Heiderhoff, *Europäisches Privatrecht* (5th edn, CF Müller 2020) [185] f.

[109] cf D Mevius, *Commentarii in Jus Lubecense Libri Quinque* (4th edn, Wildius and Richterus 1700) *pars* 3, *titulus* 2, *articulus* 2, n 5: 'Prospectum enim hâc in re est commerciorum utilitati & securitati, cui Lubecensis Jurisprudentia contra merum jus laxè opitulatur, quia nempe ad summum Reipublicae, cui Leges conduntur, pertineat'.

[110] F Peters, *Der Entzug des Eigentums an beweglichen Sachen durch gutgläubigen Erwerb* (JCB Mohr 1991) 6 ff, 117 f,123 f, and *passim*.

[111] N Jansen, 'Staatliche Gesellschaftspolitik und juristische Argumentation im römischen Privatrecht' in H Altmeppen, I Reichart, and M Schermaier (eds), *Festschrift für Rolf Knütel* (2009) 493; N Jansen and R Michaels, 'Private Law and the State. Comparative Perceptions and Historical Observations' in id (eds), *Beyond the State?* (n 31) 17 ff.

[112] Above, at n 67.

[113] cf, in particular, Weinrib, *Private Law* (n 96) 38 ff, 42 ff, dismissing functional perspectives on private law as unavoidably 'incoherent'.

law, which often ignore the fact that distributive concerns have become pervasive in modern law.[114]

A second reason for scepticism is that we have seen such searches for philosophical foundations before, with eighteenth-century natural law theories (private law scholars even describe their approach in terms of a natural law tradition, without, however, explaining whether it actually makes sense to continue with this tradition).[115] Even if natural law theory was formulated in normative, rather than in interpretive terms, those theories similarly started from 'evident' moral principles and developed them into complex doctrinal systems. Indeed, much of what is currently presented as private law theory bears strong similarities with those theories. Thus, Fried's analysis of promises[116] looks very similar to what Hugo Grotius wrote on the issue,[117] and his analysis of the risks of mistakes and errors[118] simply repeats a classic argument by Christian Thomasius.[119] Yet, one should not forget that natural law theory fell into decline for good reasons.[120] At the end of the eighteenth century, the discussion had become so polyphonic that it was obvious that natural law theory would never agree on either basic principles or specific rules.[121] An observer remarked, rightly: 'If the progress of a science may be measured by the speed with which its textbooks follow one another, then natural law stands well above all other disciplines.'[122] Even common-sense principles of private law turned out to be deeply political. Many natural lawyers had forcefully argued that tort law should be based on the fault principle,[123] but others had likewise plausibly

[114] Jansen, *Tort Law* (n 69) 94 ff, 336 f, 468 ff, and *passim*.

[115] P Benson, 'Abstract Right and the Possibility of a Nondistributive Conception of Contract' (1988/89) 10 Cardozo L Rev 1077–1196, 1089f; id, 'Contract' in D Patterson (ed), *A Companion to Philosophy of Law and Legal Theory* (2nd edn, Wiley-Blackwell 2010) 29, 48 f, 61 f; H Unberath, *Die Vertragsverletzung* (2007) 1 and *passim*.

[116] Fried, *Contract as Promise* (n 94) 8 ff.

[117] H Grotius, *De iure belli ac pacis libri tres* (Jansson Waesberg, 1735) *liber* 2, *caput* 11, §§ 1–4.

[118] Fried, *Contract as Promise* (n 94) 66 f.

[119] C Thomasius, *Institutionum jurisprudentiae divinae libri tres* (7th edn, Halle/Magdeburg 1720) *liber* 2, *caput* 7, §§ 39 ff.

[120] N Jansen, 'Das Recht und seine Vernunft. Eine Geschichte universeller Gerechtigkeit' in N Jansen and S Meier (eds), *Iurium Itinera* (Mohr Siebeck 2022) 121, 138 f.

[121] cf, for the US discussion, S Banner, *The Decline of Natural Law* (OUP 2021) 137 ff: 'two-sidedness of natural law'.

[122] Anonymous review of Johann Christoph Hoffbauer, *Naturrecht aus dem Begriffe des Rechts entwickelt* (1793) in (1794) Gothaische gelehrte Zeitungen, 260. For this development, see D Klippel, 'Das deutsche Naturrecht am Ende des 18. Jahrhunderts' in V Fiorillo and F Grunert (eds), *Das Naturrecht der Geselligkeit, Anthropologie, Recht und Politik im 18. Jahrhundert* (2009) 301, 310ff. Thus, between 1790 and 1799, seventy-five such treatises were published (loc cit, 304).

[123] S Pufendorf, *De officio hominis et civis juxta legem naturalem libri duo* (Cambridge 1682) *liber* 1, *caput* 1, §§ 18 ff and *caput* 6, § 9; id, *De iure naturae et gentium libri octo* (Frankfurt and Leipzig 1759) *liber* 1 *caput* 5, § 5: fault as 'axioma in moralibus'; Weinrib, *Private Law* (n 96) 134 f, 145 ff, 151 f, 171, 177 ff. For discussion, see Jansen, *Tort Law* (n 68) 76 ff, 253 ff.

defended a principle of strict liability.[124] Similarly, I regard Thomasius as convincing in his claim that each party to a contract is responsible for their misstatements, unless the error results from a misrepresentation by the other party, or is at least shared by the other party.[125] Yet, many natural lawyers agreed on the contrary approach, according to which mistaken declarations could not bind a party, as they found that there was no sufficient basis in that party's will.[126] There is apparently no sufficient basis in common moral intuitions to design legal rules on which at least all reasonable jurists would agree.

4. Widening the Horizon

In view of those findings, it is remarkable that private law theorists from England regularly base their analyses on—often very thorough—comparative findings. An early example is, again, Hart and Honoré's *Causation in the Law*, with its strong basis in both common law and German law.[127]

The first advantage of such an approach is that it takes the idea of the 'philosophical foundations' of the law seriously, as this idea implies some element of universality and thus a commitment to transcend one's narrow horizon.[128] Philosophical and moral arguments are not limited to the boundaries of legal systems. As long as there are no plausible reasons to assume that one specific legal system is generally a better expression of moral values than other legal systems, all legal systems should likewise reflect morality, and moral values are universal. Thus, if there are good philosophical arguments to conceive of non-contractual liability in terms of corrective justice, those arguments apply not only in the common law,[129] but also in civilian legal systems.[130] Yet, despite agreement in many, often important, aspects, legal systems differ from one another. Often, although many legal systems agree on a specific issue, some legal systems depart from the international consensus. It is thus implausible to assume that a legal system, with all its principles and rules, is an exemplification

[124] N Jansen, 'The idea of legal responsibility' (2014) 34 OJLSt 221.

[125] N Jansen and R Zimmermann, 'Contract Formation and Mistake in European Contract Law: A Genetic Comparison of Transnational Model Rules' (2011) 31 OJLSt 625, 645 ff.

[126] Grotius, *De iure belli ac pacis* (n 118) *liber* 2, *caput* 11, §§ 6 f. cf M Schermaier, 'Europäische Geistesgeschichte am Beispiel des Irrtumsrechts' (1998) 6 Zeitschrift für Europäisches Privatrecht 60–83, 71 ff; R Zimmermann, 'Heard melodies are sweet, but those unheard are sweeter ...' (1993) 193 AcP 121, 146 ff.

[127] Hart and Honoré, *Causation* (n 88) 7, 431 ff; more recently, Smith, *Contract Theory* (n 61); Steel, *Causation* (n 89) 12 ff.

[128] cf Lacey, 'Analytical Jurisprudence Versus Descriptive Sociology' (n 85) 980 ff.

[129] Weinrib *Private Law* (n 96); A Ripstein, *Equality, Responsibility, and the Law* (CUP 1999).

[130] Jansen, *Tort Law* (n 69) 68–110.

of moral values. 'To the extent that, say, an English lawyer has a firm conviction as to the moral value of some principle, the fact that the same principle has been explicitly rejected by German Courts gives at least some reason to pause and consider whether the conviction should be as firmly held.'[131]

Nevertheless, where a broad majority of legal systems accords on a specific issue, one might presume that such a common core (or, in Roman terms: *ius gentium*) is more likely to conform with basic moral principles than the *Sonderweg* of one single legal system.[132] In contrast, where no such common core is discernible, for example with strict liability in tort law, one might presume that different moral principles collide or that there is for some other reasons serious moral disagreement.[133] Searching for the philosophical foundations of such a legal institution would then mean reconstructing the moral issue and identifying relevant moral arguments. Of course, presumptions of moral reasonableness are rebuttable: there may be good reasons for introducing a rule not (yet) acknowledged in many legal systems, and there may be good reasons to reject a rule that is widely accepted. Thus, European lawyers have always known that slavery is contrary to natural law,[134] although it was acknowledged as an institution of the *ius gentium*.[135] Nonetheless, comparative findings determine the burdens of relevant moral argument; hence, the search for the philosophical foundations of some legal institution naturally triggers an interest in comparative information.

A second advantage of relating legal analysis to the findings of an appropriate comparative survey is that it helps describe the law in transparent, normatively thin concepts. Thus, where the comparative survey reveals significant differences between legal systems, the search for philosophical foundations may identify a common moral or intellectual framework in which different, possibly contested, principles apply. Doctrinal concepts describing such a structure may well embody the weak moral assumptions underlying the general framework, though not the more contested moral principles applying within it. They are not normatively empty, though they are necessarily rather thin.

[131] Steel, *Causation* (n 90) 13.

[132] cf also Steel, *Causation* (n 90) 12 f, describing such an approach as a 'wider process of "reflective equilibrium"'. Along ultimately similar lines, J Waldron has suggested squaring natural law ideas with the old idea of a *ius gentium*, ie the common legal convictions of all nations: 'Foreign Law and the Modern Ius Gentium' in M Andenas and D Fairgrieve (eds), *Courts and Comparative Law* (OUP 2015) 536; id, 'Treating Like Cases Alike in the World' in S Muller and S Richards (eds), *Highest Courts and Globalisation* (Hague Academic Press 2010) 99; see also Jansen, 'Das Recht und seine Vernunft' (n 120) 141 ff.

[133] This is what I have done with my *Structure of Tort Law* (n 68) 403 ff and *passim*.

[134] Inst 1,2,2; Florentinus, D 1,5,4,1; Ulpian, D 1,1,1,4; ibid, D 50,17,32.

[135] Inst 1,2,2; cf also Ulpian, D. 1,1,4; *Decretum Gratiani*, Dist 1,9; Isidorus Hispalensis, *Etymologiarum sive originum libri XX*, ed by WM Lindsay (1911) V,6.

One example may be my suggestion to keep the corrective justice framework of tort law open for distributive concerns and accordingly reconceptualize the notions of wrongs and fault with Tony Honoré's concept of 'outcome responsibility'.[136] Through such an approach, it becomes possible to put a single legal system's rule in perspective; to reflect normatively on assumptions embodied in traditional doctrinal concepts; and mutually to reconnect nationally isolated doctrinal sciences.

In this approach, doctrinal science's focus on the positive law of one legal system is relativized by its broader comparative horizon. Scholars thus proceed from explaining the specific rules of a single legal system doctrinally to understanding those rules in view of other doctrinal options or solutions. Methodologically, this means crossing the comparative perspective with doctrinal or philosophical ones; in effect, it emancipates science intellectually from established normative and intellectual frameworks. The task of scholars is not to develop traditional constructions in further detail but rather to formulate spectra of alternative models, that is, consider alternative paths for the future development of the law and evaluate different options.[137] More specifically, this means, *inter alia*, comparing different concepts, or different possibilities for constructing a legal institution such as an assignment,[138] or even different rules and outcomes. It is then for judges and legislators to make the necessary choices and decisions. Scholars no longer have to pretend that there is one right answer to a legal issue but can see their task in empowering judges and legislatures to make well-considered decisions. Legal scholarship transcends the borders of legal systems; its task is to formulate doctrinal concepts and constructions designed to integrate the rules of different legal systems intellectually.[139]

One classic example of such an approach is the concept of 'indicia of seriousness', which makes it possible to describe and understand quite different legal institutes, such as formal requirements, the English consideration, the French *cause*, and the German *Rechtsbindungswille*, as doctrinal alternatives.[140] Another is the concept of assignments of claims. While such assignments

[136] Jansen, *Tort Law* (n 68). This approach acknowledges that the basic structure of tort law is defined by a framework of corrective justice, in which, however, there is room for a number of different considerations of distributive justice.

[137] It would be absurd, of course, to consider all *possible* alternatives here. It suffices to focus on reasonable alternatives, ie those which are superior to current practice in at least one respect, or which have been successfully applied in other legal systems.

[138] cf below at n 142 ff.

[139] cf N Jansen, 'Comparative Law and Comparative Knowledge' in M Reimann and R Zimmermann (eds), *The Oxford Handbook of Comparative Law* (2nd edn, OUP 2019) 291, 301 f.

[140] H Kötz, 'Indicia of Seriousness' in MaxEuP (n 150) (https://max-eup2012.mpipriv.de/index.php/Indicia_of_Seriousness). More examples can be found in the *International Encyclopedia of Comparative Law* (IECL) and in the non-legislative codifications of European and global private law.

have often been described as transfers,[141] such an analysis does not fit well with the rules of many legal systems. Indeed, with the assignment of future claims, the metaphorical idea of a 'transfer of a thing' is clearly overstretched—how can one 'transfer' a 'thing' which does not yet exist? More importantly, the idea ties together the effects of an assignment between the parties vis-à-vis the debtor and other third parties (this is the basic understanding underlying the civilian systems of Germany, Austria, and Switzerland). Yet, from a comparative perspective, it is not obvious why the transfer of an item of wealth between the assignor and the assignee should follow the same rules as the effects of this transfer against third parties—in particular with the substitution of creditors.[142] On the one hand, debtors can obviously not be forced to render performance in favour of the assignee unless they have consented to the assignment, or at least received reliable notice of the assignment. Some legal systems therefore make assignments dependent upon the debtor's agreement or on receiving formal notification.[143] Yet, on the other hand, the need to protect debtors is no reason for the relationship between assignor and assignee to depend on such formality. Moreover, priority conflicts between the assignee and creditors of the assignor should not be determined by the doctrinal construction of such 'transfers', nor by other considerations of conceptual consistency. The French *Code civil* and other codifications[144] therefore separate the effects of assignments 'entre les parties' from the effects vis-à-vis the debtor and third parties;[145] similar rules can be found in Scots law[146] and under transnational

[141] F Terré, P Simler, and Y Lequette, *Les obligations* (11th edn, Dalloz 2013) [1274] f, [1286] f; Art 3:83 Dutch BW; s 136 (1) English Law of Property Act (1925); J Beatson, A Burrows, and J Cartwright, *Anson's Law of Contract* (30th edn, OUP 2016) 696; D Looschelders, *Schuldrecht Allgemeiner Teil* (15th edn, Carl Heymanns 2017) [1164]–[1166].

[142] On what follows, see G Lubbe, 'Assignment' in H MacQueen and R Zimmermann (eds), *European Contract Law: Scots and South African Perspectives* (Edinburgh UP 2006) 307, 312–21. Some legal systems, in particular those of Nordic countries, have replaced the traditional 'unitary' approach to the passing of ownership with such a 'functional', fragmentary approach. For a critical evaluation of advantages and disadvantages of this approach, cf L van Vliet, 'Acquisition and Loss of Ownership of Goods – Book VIII of the Draft Common Frame of Reference' (2011) 19 Zeitschrift für europäisches Privatrecht 292, 293 f.

[143] See Jansen, in: *Commentaries on European Contract Laws* (n 70) Art 11:303, [5]–[8].

[144] H Kötz, 'Rights of Third Parties. Third Party Beneficiaries and Assignment' in R David and others (eds), *International Encylopedia of Comparative Law*, vol 7, ch 13, [58]–[105], [86].

[145] Arts 1323, 1324 *Code civil*. The debtor can only be forced to perform in favour of the assignee if they were notified or otherwise have knowledge of the assignment. Until 2016, the claim could likewise not be attached by the assignee's creditors, unless the assignment had been solemnly notified to the debtor (Art 1690 *Code civil*[1804]). Since 2016, however, the effects vis-à-vis third parties have been tied to the effects between the parties: Art 1323(2), (3) *Code civil*.

[146] P Nienaber and G Gretton, 'Assignation/Cession' in R Zimmermann, D Visser, and K Reid (eds), *Mixed Legal Systems in Comparative Perspective* (OUP 2005) 787–818, 790 f; K Luig, 'Assignation' in K Reid and R Zimmermann (eds), *A History of Private Law in Scotland*, vol 1. *Introduction and Property* (OUP 2000) 399, 403.

legal principles.[147] It may thus be concluded that an assignment should merely entitle the assignee to proceeds received by the assignor from the debtor[148] and 'vest(s) in the assignee a power to effect substitution of the creditor'.[149] Such a doctrinal analysis of assignments is much more precise and transparent than the notion of a transfer; in particular, it is normatively thin and thus makes it possible to reflect on assumptions and rules, for example, on priority conflicts, which have traditionally been taken to be implied in the concept of assignment as a transfer of a thing.

IV. Conclusion

One difficulty with such an approach is how to define the doctrinal horizon appropriately. Nineteenth-century scholars, with their idea of a national German legal system, were in a privileged position in this respect. They had common reference texts that determined an overarching legal system and, thus, a common perspective from which all the particular legal systems of the different state territories could be analysed. The same is true for common-law scholars, who can still today argue on the basis of a common common law; moreover, the common law has always been more open to foreign influence than civilian legal systems, with their legislation-oriented habitus. For civilian jurists, such a broader perspective, which would be equally plausible in scientific and political terms, is more difficult to find. One option, as far as private law is concerned, is European law, broadly understood, that is, including both the regulatory *acquis communautaire* and the comparative *acquis commun*.[150] Such a perspective means 'thinking together' the European Union's regulations and directives and the many European non-legislative codifications, such as

[147] See, in more detail, Jansen, in *Commentaries on European Contract Laws* (n 71) Introduction before Art 11:101, [15].

[148] SV Bazinas, 'Key Policy Issues of the United Nations Convention on the Assignment of Receivables in International Trade' (2003) 11 Tul J Int Comp L 275, 289.

[149] Lubbe, 'Assignment' (n 142), 327; cf also Nienaber and Gretton, 'Assignation/Cession' (n 146), 790 f, 796; H Kötz, 'Assignment' in J Basedow, KJ Hopt, and R Zimmermann (eds), *Max Planck Encyclopedia of European Private Law* ([*MaxEuP*] OUP 2012) (https://max-eup2012.mpipriv.de/index.php/Assignment), 75–78, 76, describing the 'effects of assignment' as an entitlement of the assignee against the assignor 'to deliver to him all documents evidencing the debt assigned and provide the information needed for its collection'. See also UNCITRAL, *Legislative Guide on Secured Transactions* (2010), Recommendations 115 and 119.

[150] See, in more detail, N Jansen and R Zimmermann, 'European Contract Laws. Foundations, Commentaries, Synthesis' in *Commentaries on European Contract Laws* (n 71) 1–18, 13 ff.

the PECL,[151] the DCFR,[152] or the Acquis Principles,[153] as well as comparative findings. Here, European jurists are confronted with an extensive plurality of legal sources. From a practical lawyer's perspective, such plurality appears frightening. From the academic perspective, it seems attractive, as it makes jurists think in alternative options.

One should not over-emphasize the question of the right horizon. Widening one's horizon does not necessarily require scholars to refer to an overarching or even universal legal system. Including comparative perspectives may suffice to learn from other legal systems and thus gain the academic distance necessary for thinking in alternative models rather than looking for the single best interpretation. It is then a pragmatic decision which legal systems to include in one's analysis. Thus, as far as human rights are concerned, South African law may be particularly interesting (besides German and the US law), while South African law may be less interesting as far as torts or contracts are concerned.

What is the purpose, or the social function, of such legal science? While former generations of academics worked on the assumption that their views of the law would eventually become the law, this is quite clearly no longer the case. Judges have become the 'oracles of the law',[154] even in civilian legal systems. Scientific legal knowledge will increasingly be detached from individual legal systems; at the same time, it assumes a role similar to the knowledge of other disciplines. It is of general societal value, as it helps jurists to better understand the law in general, and thus their legal system in particular; moreover, its relevance for legal decision-making, including legal reform and (European) harmonization, is obvious. Academics will continue to speak to judges, not in order to convince them, but rather to put them in a position to make better decisions. Only such legal knowledge enables jurists—including legislators and judges—to leave the established paths of the law where those paths lead astray.

[151] O Lando and H Beale (eds), *Principles of European Contract Law*, Part I (1995), Parts I and II (Kluwer Law International 2000); O Lando, E Clive, A Prüm, and R Zimmermann (eds), *Principles of European Contract Law*, Part III (Kluwer Law International, 2003).

[152] C von Bar and E Clive (eds), *Principles, Definitions and Model Rules of European Private Law: Draft Common Frame of Reference (DCFR)* (Sellier de Gruyter 2009).

[153] Research Group on the Existing EC Private Law (Acquis Group) (ed), *Principles of the Existing EC Contract Law (Acquis Principles): Contract II* (Sellier 2009).

[154] Blackstone, *Commentaries I* (n 100) 69; Dawson, *Oracles* (n 9).

Note

* cf, as examples, DG Owen (ed), *Philosophical Foundations of Tort Law* (OUP 1995); J Oberdiek (ed), *Philosophical Foundations of the Law of Torts* (OUP 2014); JS Kraus, 'Philosophy of Contract Law' in J Coleman and S Shapiro (eds), *The Oxford Handbook of Jurisprudence and Philosophy of Law* (2002) 687–751; R Chambers, C Mitchell, and J Penner (eds), *Philosophical Foundations of the Law of Unjust Enrichment* (OUP 2009). The discussion long seemed to focus on private law; yet, in recent years, it has clearly exceeded those boundaries; cf T Endicott, S Lewis, and HD Kristjánsson (eds), *The Philosophical Foundations of Precedent* (OUP 2023) and the other overviews in Coleman and Shapiro, *loc cit*.

9

Formalism, Legality, and the Rule of Law

*Paul B. Miller**

I. Introduction

I have elsewhere argued that New Private Law scholarship evinces an implicit commitment to a new formalist methodology of legal analysis.[1] The new formalism is *new* in that it rejects many views prominently associated with other formalisms, serious and pejorative (for example, the view that practical deliberation in adjudication is paradigmatically deductive and mechanistic). It is *formalistic* in that it asserts—contra the sort of nominalism about legal concepts fomented by legal realism—that law is meant to be an authoritative source of normative guidance, supposes that law can supply effective normative guidance, and attends to the structural formality of law as well as the deliberative formality of legal reasoning.

I have also said that the new formalism treats the formality of law—structural and deliberative—as an implication of legality and the rule of law.[2] I will here offer further argument in support of that suggestion. I will also explain the values served by the formality of law while highlighting important moral limits of legal form and corresponding moral and methodological limits of legal formalism.

I shall have to cover wide terrain with economy. In order to establish that the formality of law (structural and deliberative) is entailed by legality and the rule of law, Section II offers an analysis of the relationship between the formality of law, legality, and the rule of law. In order to establish that the rule of law evinces a morality that is served by structural and deliberative formality, in Section III, I explain the value of a community's achievement of legality in comportment with the rule of law. In Section IV, I underscore the thin and limited nature of this achievement, canvassing other measures of the morality of law.

* Professor, Associate Dean for International and Graduate Programs, and Director of the Notre Dame Program on Private Law, Notre Dame Law School.

[1] Paul B Miller, 'The New Formalism in Private Law' (2021) 66 Am J Jurisprudence 175.

[2] Miller, 'New Formalism' (n 1) 196.

Paul B. Miller, *Formalism, Legality, and the Rule of Law* In: *Methodology in Private Law Theory*. Edited by: Thilo Kuntz and Paul B. Miller, Oxford University Press. © Paul B. Miller 2024. DOI: 10.1093/oso/9780198885306.003.0009

In Section V, I trace implications, cautioning against analyses of the value of legal form and formalism that lash it exclusively to legality and the rule of law. I also note limitations of formalist methodology, noting that a formalistic interpretive posture can and should make room for methodologies aimed at analysing the objective moral value of law and/or predicting or assessing its moral impact relative to its aims.

II. New Formalist Methodology

New formalist methodology is a method of scholarly interpretation of private law doctrine aimed at surfacing the structural and deliberative formality of private law.[3] Its practice unites a movement that is otherwise eclectic. Most New Private Law scholars combine formalistic interpretive analysis of law with methodologies derived from other disciplines (for example, philosophy, history, and the social and behavioural sciences). We also have different and sometimes conflicting views on the substantive morality of law.

Central to the new formalist methodology is the proposition that the central function of law is that of provision of authoritative normative guidance for the resolution of conflict and coordination issues and the related proposition that the law guides primarily by directing or otherwise shaping the practical deliberation of its addressees.[4] An implication is that legal form, legality, and the rule of law are mutually constitutive: the generality of legal form (relative context invariance) is essential to the realization of legal order and to the manifestation of key indicia of the rule of law.

The association of legal form and legal formalism with legality and the rule of law is not new.[5] Proponents of other varieties of legal formalism have invoked these notions in defending their views.[6] But some of these authors espouse implausible substantive conceptions of legality and the rule of law.[7] As I will explain, new formalist methodology works with more conventional—and,

[3] Miller, 'New Formalism' (n 1). See also Andrew Gold, 'Internal and External Perspectives: On the New Private Law Methodology' in AS Gold and others (eds), *The Oxford Handbook of the New Private Law* (OUP 2021) 3.

[4] Miller, 'New Formalism' (n 1). On the guidance function of law, see Joshua Pike, 'How the Law Guides' (2021) 41 OJLS 169.

[5] See, eg, Jeremy Waldron, 'The Concept and the Rule of Law' (2008) 43 Ga L Rev 1.

[6] Antonin Scalia, 'The Rule of Law as a Law of Rules' (1989) 56 U Chicago L Rev 1175.

[7] Richard Epstein, *Property Rights and the Rule of Law* (HUP 2011). For criticism of substantive conceptions of the rule of law, see Jeremy Waldron, 'Legislation and the Rule of Law' (2007) 1 Legisprudence 91.

importantly, normatively thin—conceptions of both concepts. This allows one to appreciate (a) the sense in which the formality of law is answerable to moral criteria that include but reach beyond ideals of legality and the rule of law and (b) the moral limits of all varieties of formalism, scholarly, and otherwise.

1. The New Formalism in Private Law

In order to understand the new formalist methodology, one ought to bear in mind a distinction between *legal form* (or the structural formality of law) and *legal formalism(s)* (or: the deliberative formality of legal reasoning, especially by participants in social practices meant to be immediately influenced by law[8]). *Legal form* is a property of posited law, and more specifically, its expression: law is given formal expression to the extent that it is posited by way of norms and enabling doctrines formulated so as to be general in application and, hence, relatively invariant to context.[9] Laws find formal expression as standalone norms (for example, simple duty-imposing or liability-generating rules) and through compound structures that are composites of different norms and/or enabling doctrines. In respect of the latter, *legal form* is synonymous with distinctive *legal forms* of action, transaction, relationship, holding, and association (for example, 'the corporate form').

Legal formalism, by contrast, is a deliberative posture toward law. Deliberatively formalistic legal reasoning aims for *responsiveness* toward law by way of clarification of, and/or comportment with, the guidance it law supplies. Formalism is popularly associated with certain kinds of scholarship and judicial philosophies.[10] But deliberative formalism here denotes the practical reasoning of anyone who intends to be and is deliberatively responsive to the form and content of applicable law. So, for example, it characterizes the deliberations of a Board of Directors aiming at abidance of procedural rules on shareholder meetings, much as it characterizes judicial decision-making meant to be intelligible as giving effect to posited law.

[8] For example, practices of lawyering, judging, forming a corporation, negotiating a contract, terminating a lease, making out a will, and so on.

[9] See Henry E Smith, 'On the Economy of Concepts in Property' (2012) 160 U Penn L Rev 2097, 2105, citing Francis Heylighen, 'Advantages and Limitations of Formal Expression' (1999) 4 Found Sci 25, 26–27. The formality of law, so understood, does not exclude contextual specification of general norms or enabling doctrines, such as is involved in the derivation of actionable practical reasons from norms, enabling doctrines, or combination(s) thereof.

[10] Miller, 'New Formalism' (n 1) 179–95.

Returning to the new formalism: it is a lawyerly method of scholarly interpretation focused on elucidating legal form in private law; clarifying and critically evaluating deliberatively formalistic engagement with private law; and delineating limits of legal form (the structural formality of law) and deliberative formalism (deliberative formality in legal reasoning). It is *lawyerly* in that it presupposes the knowledge and craft of one learned in law. It is *interpretive* in that its aims are primarily explanatory and exegetical in relation to posited law and its posited morality.

The new formalism is lawyerly, but it also adopts widely-held general jurisprudential positions on the nature and normativity of law.[11] Of these, the most important is the emphasis on the law's guidance function. The notion that all law, including private law, is meant to provide authoritative normative guidance informs each of the new formalism's ancillary tenets; notably, those that treat *legal form* and/or *legal formalism* as: i) a matter of deliberating, arguing, deciding or acting otherwise in good faith according to law; ii) an implication of legality and the rule of law; iii) manifested in doctrine, including in the organization of norms and/or enabling doctrines in legal forms of interaction; and iv) reflected in the formal systematicity of legal systems.[12]

2. Legal Form, Formalism, and Legality

I have pledged to elaborate here on one of these tenets: namely, that the structural formality of law and deliberative formalism in legal reasoning are entailed by the idea of *legality*. The relationship of entailment reflects a mutually constitutive relationship between legal form, formalism, and legality. One would have no reason for legal form, and no occasion for formalistic deliberative engagement with law were political communities to be governed other than by law (for example, informally, via non-legal social norms). In turn, conditions of legality are generated by both the formal articulation of law and its impact in guiding, and hence in shaping, behaviour. The structural formality of law and deliberatively formalistic legal reasoning are thus the mechanisms through which the law generates and maintains order, even as the relationships between the content of law, responsive deliberative engagement with law, and behavioural manifestations of order are neither fixed nor linear.

[11] See generally, Miller, 'New Formalism' (n 1) and works cited therein.
[12] Miller, 'New Formalism' (n 1) 196.

A few points by way of further elaboration:

First, 'legality' as an *idea* denotes the realization of social order through law,[13] achieved through the ordering of human conduct by way of legal norms and enabling doctrines. Legality as an *ideal* is the more perfect realization of order, bearing in mind that the over-extension of law into spheres of life best left to informal order will mean an inversion of the ideal (that is, the realization of the vice of 'legalism', commented upon by Green).[14] Loci of legality are practices of governing as well as interactions between individuals and intermediate institutions in civil society. Legality is realized primarily through: lawmaking, policy formation, and social planning; reliance on law as a guide to deliberation and conduct by government, intermediate institutions and individuals (evidenced via deliberatively formalistic engagement with law); and law enforcement action and dispute resolution. The effects of legality are often diffuse; indeed, notwithstanding that the achievement of legality entails deliberative formalism, the guidance supplied by law can be so familiar as to go unnoticed.

Second, legality as an idea and ideal is premised on the supposition that law is meant to produce social order.[15] If law is to produce order, it must be practically efficacious. That is, it must be capable of generating and sustaining order in virtue of its social impact *directly* when properly seized upon for guidance in occasions calling for it and *indirectly* by shaping social habits and conventions. The practical efficacy of law as an instrument of legality is a matter of the form (generality), content, and quality of the normative guidance it provides, *as well as* the adequacy of provisions made for impartial dispute resolution and enforcement.

Finally, notice that, as implied by the suggestion that they are mutually constitutive, the new formalist methodology takes the nexus between form, formalism, and legality to be tight. For the new formalist, deliberative formalism is as important to legality as is the structural form of law. Legal form is itself inert: it makes a promise of legality made real only where taken up in the deliberative practices of participants in a legal system.

[13] As contrasted with accounts in which legality is understood to denote legal validity and/or legal criteria of same, or the quite different usage according to which it denotes the legitimacy of legal authority and criteria for same. See generally HLA Hart, *The Concept of Law* (3rd edn, OUP 2012) 100–23 and David Dyzenhaus, 'The Legitimacy of Legality' (1996) 46 U Toronto LJ 129.

[14] Leslie Green, 'Legality and Community' (1985) 5 OJLS 463.

[15] In other words, it is premised on the notion that resulting order (social conditions manifesting realization of legality) is *planned*. But the significance of planning does not imply that order achieved must have, or is even customarily, anticipated in detail. On planning and legality, see Scott J Shapiro, *Legality* (HUP 2011), Scott Hershovitz, 'The Model of Plans and the Prospects for Positivism' (2014) 125 Ethics 152 and Martin J Stone, 'Planning Positivism and Planning Natural Law' (2012) 25 Can J L & Jurisprudence 219.

3. Legal Form, Formalism, and the Rule of Law

I have also pledged to elaborate on the suggestion that the structural formality of law and deliberative formalism are entailments of the *rule of law*, understood in a thinly normative Fullerian sense.[16] Here, too, the claim of entailment follows from the conviction that legal form, formalism and the rule of law are mutually constitutive; indeed, in ways that track the interrelationship of legal form, formalism, and legality. The rule of law, being premised on the law's generality, assumes extensive structural formality in legal systems, even as it can accommodate informality (for example, in equity). In turn, the rule of law implies deliberative formalism, most obviously in the supposition that law functions as an authoritative source of normative guidance and so must be fit for use as such.

The existence and prevalence in a given political community of mutually constitutive relationships between legal form, formalism, and the rule of law are important to the extent, but only to the extent that the community aspires to legality. There is no need for formal articulation of norms and enabling doctrines through familiar lawmaking mechanisms where a community accepts being ruled (governed) other than by law or wishes to achieve social order other than by rule.[17] In such contexts, certain elements of the rule of law—recast as elements of a normative economy of social norms—might remain salient (for example, one might say that informal sanctions that arise upon violation of social norms ought to be premised on a norm being made known, being reliably enforced, and so on) but the rule of law *as such* would have no purchase for reason of having no object (no law, or craft of lawmaking, for which to serve as a measure). Similarly, one would have no occasion for deliberatively formalistic engagement with law in a community ordered other than by law.

With this summary in place, I will briefly elaborate upon three points: the conception of the rule of law with which I associate new formalist methodology, the relationship between the structural formality of law (or legal form) and the rule of law, and the relationship between deliberative formalism (or legal formalism) and the rule of law.

As Jeremy Waldron has observed, the rule of law is an idea under strain.[18] It has been saddled with implications that it cannot readily bear, many robustly

[16] Lon L Fuller, *The Morality of Law* (Revd edn, Yale UP 1969).

[17] See generally Robert C Ellickson, 'The Aim of Order Without Law' (1994) 150 J Inst & Th Econ 97

[18] Waldron, 'Legislation and the Rule of Law' (n 7) 120: 'There is a constant temptation to read too much into the rule of law, as though it were supposed to be the sum total of our political philosophy.' See also Paul Craig, 'Formal and Substantive Conceptions of the Rule of Law: An Analytical Framework' in R Bellamy (ed), *The Rule of Law and the Separation of Powers* (Routledge 2005).

normative. For example, some equate the rule of law with support for the conclusions of libertarian political morality.[19] Like Waldron, I am inclined to view these renderings as corruptions. Hence, by the 'rule of law' I mean to invoke the normatively modest, influential account provided by Lon Fuller.[20] The rule of law, so understood, identifies a morality of law focused on formal elements of the fitness of law for the provision of authoritative normative guidance. With Fuller, I take it that a law or legal system comports with the rule of law to the extent that it consists in general norms or enabling doctrines, the latter being prospective in application, sufficiently clear, reasonably stable, promulgated and enforced publicly, generally consistent by reason of being non-contradictory in their permissions and demands, amenable of intentional conformity, and supported by adjudication and enforcement congruent with guidance derived from the law's content.

The close connection between the structural formality of law and Fuller's rendition of the rule of law should be plain. The first desideratum of the rule of law, and the one presupposed by the rest, is that laws are of general application in terms that are relatively invariant to context. Hence, the seemingly banal cornerstone of general jurisprudence: the nature of law is such that it consists, in part, of *rules*. The rule of law is a testament to law's status as the preeminent example of *rule through social rules*.[21] The law would be incapable of supplying authoritative normative guidance for entire political communities other than through general rules that enable like treatment of like cases. Generality denotes the breadth of application of law and distinguishes the latter from the specificity of command and, in turn, grounds the supposition that legal sanctions are responsive to rule violations and are not mere expressions of personal disapproval channelled through the coercive apparatus of a state.

Of course, the achievement of structural formality and, where a legal system is mature, a relatively high level of formal intricacy, does not imply that a legal system otherwise fares well as a matter of the rule of law. The 'generality' desideratum implies structural formality but failure to satisfy other desiderata will usually be suggestive of avoidable defects of legal form.

The contingent nature of the law's formal rationality underscores the importance of formalistic deliberative engagement with law. One cannot begin to see, much less work constructively toward the resolution of defects in the received form of law if one fails to recognize its form *as such*.

[19] Epstein, *Property Rights* (n 7).
[20] Fuller, *Morality of Law* (n 16).
[21] For discussion, see Frederick Schauer, 'Rules and the Rule of Law' (1991) 14 Harv J L & Pub Policy 645.

Thus, we come around again to deliberative formalism and the rule of law. To be *guided* by law as an authoritative source of normative guidance is necessarily to engage with it in a deliberatively formalistic way. One is guided by law in this sense to the extent that one's deliberation and action are intelligible as aiming at compliance or conformity with the law (that is, with practical reasons derived from applicable law).[22] The rule of law is impossible absent deliberatively formalistic legal reasoning and, in turn, formalistic engagement with the law is impossibly absent the law's minimal fitness for guidance as judged by the rule of law.

I would emphasize, in closing, that structural formality does not exhaust modes of expression used in law, nor does deliberatively formalistic legal reasoning exhaust the practical judgment invited by law, even where formally intricate law casts long shadows. In deciding cases, judges must make findings of fact that shape formalistic analyses and will often have to dispense equity rather than render verdicts. In turn, legislators and judges must make value and empirical judgments in setting purposes for and predicting the moral impact of, contemplated laws. In these and other respects, we encounter moral and practical limits of received legal form and of the prospects for our deliberative engagement with it.

III. The Morality of Legality and of the Rule of Law

To this point I have suggested that the relationships between legal form, formalism, legality, and the rule of law are normatively consequential insofar as they are linked to the capacity of law to serve its core function: providing authoritative normative guidance. The desiderata of the rule of law evince a *formal* morality—emphasized by Fuller—tethered to the law's formal suitability for the provision of authoritative guidance. But I have not yet explained the sense in which legal form manifests in ways that implicate legal formalism, the *substantive* morality of law (for example, the morally sound means, ends, and impact in relation to which law may prove worthy of its claim of moral authority).[23] As I will explain here and in Section IV, the substantive morality of law—and, by implication, of legal form—encompasses values associated with legality and of the rule of law. But resorting to these values does not get one

[22] Miller, 'New Formalism' (n 1).

[23] On the law's claim of moral authority, see Joseph Raz, 'Hart on Moral Rights and Legal Duties' (1984) 4 OJLS 123, 131 and Leslie Green, 'Positivism and the Inseparability of Law and Morals' (2008) 83 NYU L Rev 1035, 1048.

very far in determining whether a law or legal system is all-things-considered practically reasonable. One must have resort to other moral considerations that mark our need for law, constrain the use of law as a means for the realization of morally sound ends, and contemplate the law's moral impact.

1. Background

General jurisprudence of the mid-to-late twentieth century witnessed intense debate on whether legality should be understood in a positivistic way or as a moral achievement. The skirmish—fomented partly by an extended exchange between HLA Hart and Lon Fuller—drew on wider debates over the concept of law and the rule of law. In favour of positivistic renderings, some offered observations about the advanced structural formality of certain wicked legal systems as support for inferences that legality and the rule of law are neutral as indicators of the overall moral quality of a legal system.[24] The achievement of legality and the rule of law, Hart observed, is 'unfortunately compatible with very great iniquity'.[25] Against insistence on value neutrality were pressed arguments, first by Fuller,[26] and subsequently by Waldron,[27] that realization of legality and the rule of law might be inherently morally valuable even if neither ensures the moral soundness of a legal system and its laws.

A frustrating feature of the debate between Hart and Fuller was that both failed to recognize the other's insights. Hart said many things that reflect attributions of value to legality even if the attributions were made indirectly and in passing.[28] Furthermore, Hart strained to avoid commenting on the rule of law, and where he relented, he ended up taking contradictory positions.[29]

[24] See the debate between Hart and Fuller: HLA Hart, 'Positivism and the Separation of Law and Morals' (1958) 71 Harvard LR 593 and Lon L Fuller, 'Positivism and Fidelity to Law—A Reply to Professor Hart' (1958) 71 Harvard LR 630. See also Joseph Raz, 'Authority, Law and Morality' (1985) 68 The Monist 295. For critical perspective, see David Dyzenhaus, *Hard Cases in Wicked Legal Systems: Pathologies of Legality* (2nd edn, OUP 2010).

[25] HLA Hart, *The Concept of Law* (3rd edn, OUP 2012) 207.

[26] Fuller, *Morality of Law* (n 16) 200–24.

[27] Jeremy Waldron, 'Positivism and Legality: Hart's Equivocal Response to Fuller' (2008) 83 NYU L Rev 1135, 1167.

[28] For instance, in various passages in *The Concept of Law*, Hart suggests that the stability and security realized by law have value as a matter of liberty and welfare interests (as where Hart contrasts the authority claimed for law with the power asserted by a gunman, implies that the maturation of a legal system through the development of secondary rules is good in that the latter underlie the system's capacity to generate and sustain order, and argues that the order produced by law is responsive to universal human interests in survival and in predicting and planning for one's life and commitments).

[29] Waldron, 'Positivism and Legality' (n 27) 1157 ('Hart's discussion of legality … often seems to be motivated by a desire to say nothing more than is necessary to dispatch Lon Fuller's critique.').

Equally, Fuller did not acknowledge Hart's insight that realization of legality and the rule of law are compatible with the moral wickedness of a law or legal system.

All of this being allowed, like Waldron, I think that Fuller got the better of the debate with Hart. Hence, I here offer a loosely Fullerian account of the morality of legality and the rule of law, subject to a Hartian insistence that, as moral achievements, neither are decisive of the overall (all-things-considered) morality of law. I shall address the morality of legality in subsection B, taking up that of the rule of law in subsection C.

2. The Morality of Legality

Legality consists in the achievement of social order through law, encompassing practices of government and social practices in civil society. The achievement of legality may be inferred where human conduct is intelligible as evincing comportment with applicable law in ways that reflect the design of lawmakers (that is, the order sought to be achieved through law).

I suggested earlier that legality is an idea and an ideal. As an idea, legality denotes the efficacy of law as an instrument of social order. This idea has empirical and normative dimensions, insofar as it contemplates a causal role for law in bringing about a state of affairs (social order) to which we attach normative significance. As an ideal, legality denotes the quality of social order per se as realized by law (that is, the existence, scope, and stability of order attributable to law). The ideal also has empirical and normative dimensions insofar as one thinks that the quality of social order is amenable of empirical observation and assessment and insofar as elements of the ideal are genuinely *qualitative* (that is, *ceteris paribus*, are indicative of improved social conditions). Legality, in both senses, presupposes the instrumental significance of law to the formation and maintenance of political community (that is, that law is, or can be, partly constitutive of communities by supplying some of the requisites of a community's survival and flourishing).

That legality has normative significance can be appreciated by considering how the idea and ideal figure in practices of praise and blame. Consider the invocation of the ideal in: the celebration of the achievement, maintenance or improvement of social order generally through a given legal system, or of the effectiveness of a particular framework of laws; identification and critique of disorder in government and civil society as reflecting want of legality; law reform efforts aimed at producing more well-ordered social practices; and criticism of perversions of legality that arise when government slips the bonds of reciprocal constraint.

If one grants that legality is normatively freighted, what moral value(s) do or ought we to associate with it? I suggest that the value of legality *as such* lies in the positive moral impact that is attributable to the generation and maintenance of social order, whatever ends make social order intelligible (that is, as planned) and whatever means are devised through law for the achievement of these ends.[30] The direct moral advantages of well-ordered government and civil society are so commonly taken for granted, and collective memories of perversions of legality are so searing, that it is easy to get turned around in one's thinking and suppose that the moral benefits of legality are too trifling to mention.[31] As Hobbes memorably chides, one need only contrast the lot of those within well-ordered communities with the lot of those whose lives are beset by civic and political disorder to see that legality is a significant moral achievement. Hobbes construed the value of legality in terms of freedom from wanton violence and exalted this over other values.[32] But one need not fetishize order as Hobbes did in order to appreciate that, in addition to its promise of security, legality generates reserves of freedom that enable us to plan our lives, even if the freedom might be limited and prospects around which one can plan might be grim.

3. The Morality of the Rule of Law

As Fuller recognized, desiderata of the rule of law serve as baselines *and* ideals for laws and the craft of lawmaking. Serious rule-of-law deficiencies imperil legality in that their presence means that a law or legal system will be impaired in its ability to generate or to maintain social order. To adapt Fuller's turn of phrase, the rule of law encompasses criteria that make law possible (serving as functional baselines).[33] And the same criteria establish indicia of excellence (serving as functional ideals), the thought being that above-baseline comportment will, *ceteris paribus*, mean the law's improved fitness for guidance and hence for generation and maintenance of social order.

[30] As suggested by Thomas Hobbes, *Leviathan* (CB MacPherson ed, Penguin 1986).

[31] Trifling in comparison with the moral advantages of good (practically reasonable) laws and the moral disadvantages of bad (practically unreasonable) ones.

[32] Hobbes also asserted the indirect value of legality in enabling commerce, industry, knowledge, and the arts. Hobbes, *Leviathan* (n 30). However, we may set these claims to one side, for the realization of these valued states of affairs depends on choices made by lawmakers in setting particular ends for particular laws.

[33] Fuller, *Morality of Law* (n 16) 33.

As was true of legality, we might acknowledge that the rule of law is a normative idea, yet wonder in what *sense* it is normative. Might not the rule of law be normative in an *exclusively* functional sense, for example, encapsulating criteria of the effectiveness of law as a guide to conduct, whatever is to be said morally for or against the guidance supplied?

Here, too, we must revisit old controversies. As noted earlier, positivists, including Hart and Raz, have suggested that the rule of law should be understood in an exclusively functional sense.[34] The function of law, framed positivistically, is to serve as a dispositive guide to conduct; legality marks the law's fulfilment of that function in a municipal legal system; and the rule of law explains how the law effectively guides.

By contrast, Fuller treats the rule of law as normative in a functional *and* moral sense, such that satisfaction of rule of law baselines should be counted as a morally good thing, holding all else equal, and likewise above-baseline comportment with the desiderata.[35] Notwithstanding my general alignment with Fuller, I have a slightly different view of the morality of the rule of law.

I begin with common ground. Fuller suggests that desiderata of the rule of law delineate a formal morality of law's fitness for the guidance of persons; this formal morality is underlain by a substantive morality that consists in the rule of law's implicit assertion of the equal dignity of persons as rational beings[36] and its assumption that government and citizens are joined in a moral bond of mutual constraint (these constraints calling for fidelity to law, through deference to the law's rule).[37] As Waldron explains, for Fuller, the rule of law implies that law generally is meant 'to respect human dignity and secure a certain equality or reciprocity between ruler and ruled'.[38] Legal officials live up to that commitment by promulgating law and by enforcing or otherwise upholding it through conduct manifestly congruent with the guidance supplied by law. Citizens reciprocate by treating the law as a presumptively authoritative guide to their conduct and by respecting the decisions of legal officials as lawful, where they are lawful (for example, a judicial decision is intelligible as giving effect to law). All of this is, in my view, sensible.

Now for three points of departure. First, I take leave of Fuller in drawing the morality of the rule of law into closer proximity with the general jurisprudential

[34] HLA Hart, 'Review of *The Morality of Law* by Lon Fuller' (1965) Harvard LR 1281; Joseph Raz, 'The Rule of Law and its Virtue' in his *The Authority of Law* (OUP 1979).

[35] Fuller, *Morality of Law* (n 16) 157–59.

[36] Lon L Fuller, 'A Reply to Professors Cohen and Dworkin' (1965) 10 Vill L Rev 655.

[37] Fuller, *Morality of Law* (n 16) 209–10.

[38] Waldron, 'Legislation and the Rule of Law' (n 7) 116.

position on the nature of law that I noted earlier. That position, again, is that the core function of law is one of provision of authoritative—and, hence, practically reasonable—normative guidance to persons joined in political community. The rule of law matters not because we require effective guidance, whatever its moral upshot(s), but because we require *practically reasonable* guidance, and the achievement of same is contingent on satisfaction of norms of formal *and* substantive morality. Second, this allows us to better appreciate the *necessarily* limited moral significance of the rule of law. Comportment with the rule of law enables but cannot secure the law's provision of practically reasonable guidance. That is because the all-things-considered practical reasonableness of law turns on the morality of its ends, the suitability of means devised to realize its ends, and its actual moral impact.

IV. The Wider Morality of Law

I have thus far explained the sense in which legal form and legal formalism are entailments of legality and of the rule of law. The account of the relationship between form, formality, legality, and the rule of law in Section II was partly conceptual. But I have emphasized that it is also normative in that it reflects the normativity of law (that is, the fact that law consists in normative constructs meant to guide, and so shape, normative social practices). Hence, while one can *practice* the new formalism as a method of scholarly interpretation in a normatively agnostic way, one's *motivation* for doing so is answerable to demands for justification. To take legal form seriously through formalistic reasoning is to engage with the guidance the law supplies *as* normative guidance. It would be odd to think that one should reason formalistically without querying the moral requisites of the law's assertion of authority to supply binding guidance and its associated expectation of reasoning of this sort.

Thus, our relatively modest conclusions to this point: that the morality of legality (marked by values of relative freedom and personal security) and of the rule of law (characterized by the values of equal dignity of all persons and of reciprocity in the relationship of government and governed) supply practical reasons that contribute positively to the overall morality of law. By extension, these reasons also provide normative motivation for sophisticated scholarly formalism.

I have emphasized, too, though, that the practical reasonableness of law turns on a variety of substantive moral considerations. In order that we might more clearly grasp the moral limits of legal form and the moral and methodological limits of legal formalism, I outline some of these considerations in what follows.

1. Practical Reason and Practical Reasonableness

We may begin with the normative significance for law of the fact that humans are endowed with a capacity for practical reason and, in turn, that practical reasonableness is a moral good meant to be manifested in persons and mirrored in and supported by law.[39]

One might think that we should, for clarity's sake, keep these facts and our teasing out of their implications separate. One might think this because practical reason is a characteristic of being human, while practical reasonableness is a matter of evaluating human motivation and behaviour. Certainly, their loci are different in that the law assumes (takes for granted, even) practical reason, while practical reasonableness is a matter of judgment on the objective moral soundness of laws, moral and legal decision-making, and other outcroppings of our sociality.

Consistent with this, one might also think that whether a law or legal system respects persons by respecting our capacity for practical reason is but a procedural matter going the means deployed through law for the realization of lawmakers' ends, while practical reasonableness is a matter of the morality of those ends or of there being consilience in the morality of the means, ends and impact of law. On this view, one might suppose that the moral significance of practical reason is captured in the rule of law and its morality. It is, after all, in the various desiderata that one finds specific indications of how laws prove fit for the guidance of persons endowed with a capacity for practical reason.

While the morality of the rule of law seems most responsive to practical reason, and the morality of the law's ends (or moral consilience in the law's ends, content, and impact) seems most pertinent to the law's practical reasonableness, the distinction is not analytic. A law can prove practically unreasonable insofar as it elides or impairs our capacity for practical reason, even as it comports with the rule of law. Consider, for example, laws that ignore or bypass reasoned deliberation by the law's addressees in leveraging cognitive biases or distortions, aiming to achieve effective social control by way of 'nudges' and

[39] John Finnis, *Natural Law and Natural Rights* (2nd edn, OUP 2011) 88 and 100–26. For contextualization and discussion, see George Duke, 'The Aristotelian *Spoudaios* as Ethical Exemplar in Finnis's Natural Law Theory' (2013) 58 Am J Jurisprudence 183.

other manipulations of 'choice architecture'.[40] While perhaps not inherently objectionable, these strategies are practically unreasonable to the extent that they ignore, subvert, or circumvent human capacity for practical reason. This is true no matter how well-intentioned or beneficial they might be and no matter how well-crafted they are by light of the rule of law.[41] When lawmakers treat citizens as dupes, they deny that part of our dignity that is bound up in the expectation that law ply its trade in the space of public reason.

2. Moral Rights and Duties, Powers, and Liabilities

Reflecting the wisdom of Hart's distinction between duty-imposing and power-conferring rules, for several decades, the work of interpretive private law theory has placed right-duty and power-liability relationships at its centre.

Relatedly, more recent interest amongst interpretivists in the Hohfeldian logic of jural relations in private law has been mostly innocent.[42] Less so, however, when paired with the conviction that the normative structure of private law simply embeds or replicates deontic ethics. It may be that legal duties are a species of (presumptive) moral duties, that legal powers belong within the genera of normative powers, and so on, but this does not imply direct correspondence or derivation (for example, that legal rights replicate or involve the specification of cognate moral rights). In a Hartian spirit, we should be prepared to recognize that some jural relations have no direct moral counterparts. Likewise, we should be prepared to recognize that ends other than securing respect for moral rights or enabling the improved exercise of moral powers might ground legal rights and powers.

However, one can be wary in these ways while recognizing that the morality of right and duty is pertinent to law. As Fuller emphasized, members of diverse political communities might disagree on moral ideals yet find consensus on genuine moral rights and duties and on the importance of their being protected by law.[43] Similarly, with normative powers generated by or embedded

[40] Richard H Thaler and Cass R Sunstein, *Nudge* (Penguin 2009).

[41] *Pax* Cass R Sunstein, *Why Nudge? The Politics of Libertarian Paternalism* (Yale UP 2015). For criticism of these practices, see Heidi M Hurd, 'Fudging Nudging: Why "Libertarian Paternalism" Is the Contradiction It Claims It's Not' (2016) Geo J L & Pub Pol'y 703. For an attempted defence, see Cass R Sunstein, 'The Ethics of Nudging' (2015) 32 Yale J Reg 414.

[42] Wesley N Hohfeld, 'Fundamental Legal Conceptions as Applied in Judicial Reasoning' (1917) 26 Yale LJ 710; Shyam Balganesh, Henry E Smith, and Ted Sichelman, *The Legacy of Wesley Hohfeld* (CUP 2022).

[43] Fuller, *Morality of Law* (n 16) 5–9 and 19–27.

within facilitative legal forms of transaction, relationship, or association (for example, of contract or incorporation). Put otherwise, while the deontic features of our moral landscape do not warehouse legal forms for off-the-rack adoption, they *do* supply moral learning from which we may (and may have) derived practical reasons that motivate and justify some norms and enabling doctrines in private law.

3. Public Goods and Human Goods

The substantive morality of law also encompasses considerations that liberal political theorists are wont to denote matters of *public good* as well as matters that natural law theorists analyse in terms of the *common good*[44] but which—for the avoidance of confusion with recent work in American constitutional theory—I shall call matters of *human good*, personal and communal.

Public goods encompass amenities provided in satisfaction of public needs that can only or best be addressed through governmental expenditure, coordination and/or oversight.[45] Examples include the establishment and maintenance of critical infrastructure (for example, public roads and works), resources (for example, parks and museums), services (for example, universities, schools, and hospitals), utilities (for example, electrical and water supply), and emergency services (for example, policing).

As should be evident, much law—public *and* private– is aimed, in part, at enabling or securing the realization of public goods. Consider laws enabling the formation and administration of governmental or quasi-governmental organizations as trusts or corporations (for example, the incorporation of school boards or public hospitals). Or consider the role of conservation servitudes in preserving land for public benefit. To the extent that legal forms are made available at private law for the realization of a public good, their moral value shares in that of the good itself.

Human goods encompass facets of personal and communal human flourishing, or else conditions requisite to flourishing, that require or benefit from governmental provision through law.[46] Judgments about *human goods* are value judgments about what it means to live well (that is, to flourish), and

[44] See Thomas W Smith, 'Aristotle on the Conditions for and Limits of the Common Good' (1999) 93 Am Pol Sci Rev 625.

[45] Vincent Ostrom and Elinor Ostrom, 'Public Goods and Public Choices' in E Savas (ed), *Alternatives for Delivering Public Services* (Routledge 1979).

[46] Finnis, *Natural Law and Natural Rights* (n 29) 81–96.

mixed judgments of fact and value about material conditions requisite to human flourishing. The notion encompasses *primary, intrinsically valuable, goods* (which are often difficult, if not impossible, of being secured directly by law) and *secondary, derivatively valuable, goods* (more readily secured or promoted directly by law) which are instrumental to the realization of primary goods.[47] Primary goods include life, good health, filial love, loving companionship, friendship, peace, solidarity, the pursuit of truth, and aesthetic appreciation.[48] Secondary goods include personal and economic security, access to employment on fair terms, freedom of worship, expression, and assembly, access to health care and education, and access to credible news and information about science, the arts, law, economics, politics, and other matters of general public interest.[49]

One need not reach a settled view on the relationship between public goods and human goods or about how to discern the value of goods in order to recognize their salience for law. Indeed, even in work critical of natural law theory,[50] it is commonplace that law is answerable for its effectiveness in channelling debate over and in promoting the realization of human and public goods.[51] These goods figure as ends toward which particular laws are to be oriented—and their impact assessed—subject to political accountability mechanisms meant to ensure that lawmakers' decisions reflect proper public deliberation and justification.

Nicholas McBride has recently argued that much of private law is best interpreted as oriented toward the enhancement of human flourishing.[52] In credit to him, one might wonder how it could be thought otherwise.[53] If we are to enjoy economic security, we will need to be able to make and enforce contracts. If we are to pursue truth, we must be able to form and administer organizations that foster and safeguard that pursuit. If we are to enjoy the security of our person and property, we will need tort law or its equivalent.

[47] For discussion, see Nicholas J McBride, *The Humanity of Private Law: Part I: Explanation* (Hart 2018). See, too, Nicholas J McBride, *The Humanity of Private Law: Part II: Evaluation* (Hart 2020).

[48] Some of which are recounted in McBride, *The Humanity of Private Law—I* (n 47).

[49] cf McBride, ibid.

[50] Leslie Green, 'Law, Coordination and the Common Good' (1983) 3 OJLS 299, 324 (criticizing Finnis' coordination model of the law's responsiveness to human goods and adverting to 'other and perhaps better ways of making the common good the ground of legal life'). See also Joseph Raz, 'Rights and Individual Well-Being (1992) 5 Ratio Juris 127 (rejecting the conventional opposition of the presumed individualism of deontic ethics and the morality of the common good).

[51] A theme emphasized in Jeremy Waldon, *Law and Disagreement* (OUP 1998).

[52] McBride, *The Humanity of Private Law—I* (n 47); McBride, *The Humanity of Private Law—II* (n 47).

[53] Notwithstanding that the morality of human goods is frequently ignored in private law theory.

4. Political Morality

Contemporary private law theorists mostly overlook considerations of political morality, including those bearing on the form and structure of government, the relative political authority of different branches of government, the relationship between legal and political judgment, the morality of office and procedure, and the like.[54] There would seem to be an implicit belief that *status quo ante* arrangements are sound.

But one need not press hard to find difficult questions of political morality involving private law. In contract law, there are concerns about corrupting political influences on fundamental private law and on contracting practice, reflected in the prevalence of one-sided boilerplate.[55] Arguments for tort reform are often rooted in concerns of political morality about unequal access to justice.[56] And in equity, there are questions about the political legitimacy of courts deviating from equity's traditional corrective function in acting quasi-legislatively.[57]

5. Justice

Finally, the substantive morality of law reserves a prominent place for justice. As Fuller haltingly recognized when pressed by Hart, moral baselines and ideals of justice are not reducible to, nor can their realization be taken to move in tandem with, those of legality or the rule of law.[58] A legal system might achieve legality in a manner consistent with rule of law baselines yet prove unjust or else admit of significant injustice; likewise, a given law might be substantively unjust yet be effective in guiding behaviour, hence contributing to the realization of legality. This makes it misleading, if not dangerous, to say that particular forms of justice are 'immanent' within law: for example, corrective justice within private law or distributive justice within public law. That

[54] Exceptions include Matthew Harding, *Charity Law and the Liberal State* (CUP 2014); Joseph Singer, 'Property as the Law of Democracy' (2014) 63 Duke LJ 1287; Martijn Hesselink, 'Democratic Contract Law' (2015) 11 Eur Rev Contract L 81; and Arie Rosen, 'The Role of Democracy in Private Law' in PB Miller and J Oberdiek (eds), *Oxford Studies in Private Law Theory, Volume II* (OUP 2022).

[55] Margaret Jane Radin, *Boilerplate* (Princeton UP 2012).

[56] Deborah L Rhode, *Access to Justice* (OUP 2004); Frederick Wilmot-Smith, *Equal Justice* (HUP 2019).

[57] Paul B Miller, 'Equity as Supplemental Law' in D Klimchuk, I Samet, and HE Smith (eds), *Philosophical Foundations of the Law of Equity* (OUP 2020).

[58] Fuller, *Morality of Law* (n 16) 157–59.

law is apt for justice,[59] and that it sometimes—perhaps reliably—demonstrates this in achieving justice, is not to say that justice inheres in law. Rather, it is a promise made through law that is ever awaiting fulfilment. The flipside, emphasized by Les Green, is that law is inherently morally risky; there is an ineliminable risk of injustice generated or tolerated by law.[60]

In understanding justice and the extent of the law's aptness for realizing it, I shall here take my lead from Aristotle, introducing, first, his general characterization of justice; second, the significance of the fact that he left normative criteria of justice unspecified; and third, the implications of his account of equity for our understanding of the limits of law's aptness for justice.

First, there is lost wisdom in Aristotle's treatment of justice as a matter of political and personal virtue. Contemporary work on justice tends to focus on the political at the expense of the personal and positions justice as an abstract normative ideal rather than a constitutive element of the moral character and condition of persons and communities. From Aristotle, we inherit a more holistic and demanding conception of justice as a measure of the excellence of the character of political communities *as political communities* and the excellence of persons in their *civic personage*. The virtue of justice consists in reliably rendering to others what is morally their due. Justice is thus an inherently other-regarding virtue: it reflects a proper moral ordering (one might say: practised integrity) of communities and persons made evident in a pervasive way in politics and in ordinary social interactions. As Aristotle recognized, justice is realized through *authentic social performance*: through deliberative conduct through which one discerns and delivers to others their due acting personally and (as pertinent) in an official capacity. To *be just* is to *see to it that justice is done* (that is, to take responsibility for justice in one's person and for one's community). Consistent with the fact that virtues are stable characteristics of the moral constitution of persons and polities, it follows that justice is most perfectly realized where habituated. A just person is one who is habitually just. Likewise, the just polity is one that is arranged and administered so as to reliably dispense justice.

Second, Aristotle sensibly distinguished natural and legal justice.[61] *Natural justice* signifies what universal moral principles require of us in our treatment of one another. Thus, the realization of natural justice is a matter

[59] Green, 'Positivism and the Inseparability of Law and Morals' (n 23) 1050–52; see also John Gardner, *Law as a Leap of Faith* (OUP 2012).

[60] Green, ibid 1052–54.

[61] See generally George Duke, 'Aristotle and Natural Law' (2020) 82 Rev Politics 1.

of a person or polity treating others as they ought in full recognition of what they are due. Natural justice is inherently perfectionistic: in satisfaction of its demands, one finds the achievement of justice in its most complete sense. *Legal justice*, by contrast, is a matter of the existence and—by the light of natural justice—sound operation of general laws and legal institutions in the public dispensation of justice. Legal justice involves (a) the public articulation of general rules that aim successfully at rendering others their due and (b) the public enforcement of these rules (including public provision for redress of legal injustices). For Aristotle, legal justice is answerable to natural justice as a matter of ends *and* means: the justice of law and its public administration.

Moral reasons of natural justice constrain and inform without determining the content of laws or the design of legal institutions. Furthermore, these reasons support distinctions between varieties of legal justice without specifying how they are to be made operational. As others have emphasized, one finds in Aristotle's work a distinction between corrective and distributive justice.[62] These varieties of legal justice reflect, in a more focused way apt to the specification of the moral content and aims of certain kinds of legal rules, what we owe to one another interpersonally and what the state owes to all members of a political community. Norms and mechanisms of corrective and distributive justice might thus be viewed as different *modalities* for the properly contextualized realization of natural justice through law. Note, though: each assumes but does not supply normative *criteria* of justice;[63] that is, norms of natural justice that indicate what we owe to one another interpersonally and through soundly governed political communities. These criteria are, obviously, debatable. However, they must be expected to encompass values germane to the moralities of right and duty, of political morality, and of public and human goods, each being facets of the moral landscape that are proper objects of legal justice and hence not to be left to one's personal answerability in conscience to the demands of natural justice.[64] Certain efforts to give justice more definite content (for example, to equate justice with fairness or equal freedom) point beyond the varieties of justice as *modalities* to *criteria*, something that is easy to

[62] See, eg, Jules Coleman, 'Corrective Justice and Wrongful Gain' (1982) 11 J Legal Studies 421; Ernest J Weinrib, 'Aristotle's Forms of Justice' (1989) 2 Ratio Juris 211; and Peter Benson, 'The Basis of Corrective Justice and its Relation to Distributive Justice' (1992) 77 Iowa L Rev 515.

[63] For discussion, see Ernest J Weinrib, 'Corrective Justice' (1992) 77 Iowa L Rev 403, 419.

[64] A separate question is that of the relative normative priority of matters of right, political morality and the good. For discussion, see John Rawls, 'The Priority of Right and Ideas of the Good' (1988) 17 Phil & Pub Aff 251.

miss but ought not to be. One might, for instance, agree that corrective justice is a modality of legal justice for which private law is especially apt and yet deny that equal freedom is its sole criterion.[65]

Finally, as Aristotle recognized, laws and institutional arrangements for their administration might be perfectly just as a *general* matter—hence realizing *legal justice*—and yet still fail to produce just outcomes (that is, to render to each their due as a matter of *natural justice*). This is because the very generality of law—its structural formality—generates a risk of *particular injustice*.[66] This risk manifests in different ways, including through opportunistic abuse or misuse of the law.[67] Thus, Aristotle emphasized the importance of equity to natural justice and, in turn, to the perfection of legal justice.[68] The truly just person, Aristotle says, is one who will act equitably though the law permits inequitable conduct. In turn, the truly just polity will provide suitably for the public dispensation of equity, entertaining the perfectionistic demands of natural justice to the extent possible without undermining legal justice.

V. The Moral Limits of Form and the Methodological Limits of Formalism

In Section I, I noted that the new formalism is a methodology of interpretive legal scholarship that takes legal form seriously, attending to the structural formality of law as well as to deliberatively formalistic legal reasoning by participants in social practices in which law figures as a guide to right conduct. I noted that new formalist methodology treats legal form and formalism as entailments of legality and the rule of law. And, while these relationships may be understood in a purely positivistic way, I explained that in recognition of the normativity of law, new formalists should be interested in the sources and limits of the morality of the structural form of law as well as attendant moral and methodological limits of deliberative formalism. I shall say more now about these limits.

[65] See John Gardner, *Torts and Other Wrongs* (OUP 2019) 51–55.

[66] Dennis Klimchuk, 'Aristotle at the Foundations of Law and Equity' in D Klimchuk, I Samet and HE Smith (eds), *Philosophical Foundations of the Law of Equity* (OUP 2020).

[67] ibid; Henry E Smith, 'Equity as Meta-Law' (2021) 130 Yale LJ 1050.

[68] As discussed in Samuel L Bray and Paul B Miller, 'Christianity and Equity' in J Witte, Jr and R Domingo (eds), *The Oxford Handbook of Christianity and the Law* (OUP 2023).

1. The Moral Limits of Legal Form

One point has already been made but bears repeating: sophisticated scholarly formalism ought to be carried out in a way that is mindful of the moral limits of legal form. Scholarly formalisms of old have been criticized—sometimes justifiably—for assuming the moral soundness of received law and hence for seeming to celebrate form for its own sake.[69] As I have explained elsewhere, the new formalism in private law resists apologia for settled law, considering its practical reasonableness something to be tested rather than assumed.[70]

One can assess the moral limits of the structural form of extant law in a stepwise way, descending from general justificatory considerations to more particular ones.

One should begin by ascertaining object(s) of inquiry: is the concern with the general morality of an entire system of private law (for example, that of New York), a bounded framework or category of legal rules (for example, New York corporate law), a particular legal form of interaction (for example, a donative express trust), or a standalone rule (for example, the rule against perpetuities)? If one's object of interest is an entire system, there is likely little to be identified by way of its posited morality other than banal trivialities that are not meant to and do not play a significant role in public practical deliberation and justification. However, with a narrower focus, one is ordinarily able to elucidate a posited morality or a composite of the same. Consider, for example, reference to the values of freedom of association, free enterprise, and wealth maximization as justifying the shape given by Delaware law to the corporate form. Or consider reference to norms of promissory morality as that which justifies, morally, the law's treatment of contracts and gifts as legally binding. One could give countless examples. But the basic point is that the posited morality of law will ordinarily be inextricable from its form if a positivistic rendering of received law is meant to capture not just doctrine but public justification(s) given for it. Furthermore, it is from this starting point that one ought to assess the moral limits of legal form if one means to address not abstract representations of jural relationships but rather the moral justification claimed for the legal forms we have.

By way of identifying limits, one might begin in respect of a given *system* of private law with the most general of considerations: those that bear on the system's functional and normative integrity. Inquiries rooted in concerns about

[69] Miller, 'The New Formalism' (n 1) 190.
[70] ibid 218–19.

legality and the rule of law might be raised: does the system predictably generate order, and in doing so, does it meet rule of law baselines? Closely related are questions drawn from the morality of practical reason: whether a system of private law mostly respects our capacity for practical reason or instead tends to neglect or to undermine it. Given that institutional design and operation are especially prominent objects of analysis of entire legal systems, one might naturally also query whether private law in a system as presently administered is sound as a matter of political morality (for example, considering the need for democratic legitimation). It will be more difficult to come to a capacious yet well-informed general assessment of the soundness of systems of private law as a matter of the more intricate, retail-level moralities of right and duty, public and human good, and justice.

In respect of given features of the structural form of law (for example, a legal rule or form composed of rules), inquiries can be more precise. One can ask of a given legal rule or legal form (for example, an offshore express trust or an LLC) whether it expresses well the morality of legality by generating and sustaining planned order. One can ask whether, and if so, to what extent, it is adequate as a matter of rule of law baselines, for example, in respect of its clarity or coherence. One might query whether it respects the morality of practical reason, for example, by enhancing or undermining the exercise of that capacity.[71] One might question the law's failure to recognize certain moral obligations as legally binding or its creation of legal obligations that have no discernible moral justification. One might argue that certain human goods are unreasonably ignored by law or that a legal form meant to serve a human good does so poorly. And, of course, one might think that a legal form by design or result inscribes or tolerates injustice.

Even this exceedingly brief summary of interrogatories suffices to show how one might assess the actual practical reasonableness of the structural form of law and its posited morality.

Our emphasis has been on the moral limits of legal form. But it should be noticed that attention to these limits matters precisely because of the moral promise of law. The moral authority claimed by law is meant to be more than pretence.[72] Again, as Green has put it, law is necessarily *apt* for justice.[73] More specifically, it is apt in its capacity to prove robustly responsive to moral reasons

[71] As is asked of contract law in Seana Valentine Shiffrin, 'The Divergence of Contract and Promise' (2007) 120 Harvard LR 708.

[72] An emphasis on pretense over promise is evident in Green, 'Positivism and the Inseparability of Law and Morals' (n 23).

[73] ibid 1050–52.

that can only or best be acted upon by lawmakers and legal institutions. The aptness of law for justice is bound up with formal expression, and we can acknowledge that while also acknowledging that the structural formality of law means that it may be bent to unjust ends (that is, that legal form can produce legal injustice) and that it is inherently susceptible of generating particular injustice (that is, that legal form can produce inequity).

2. The Methodological Limits of Legal Formalism

The methodological limits of formalism follow, in part, from recognition of the moral limits of legal form. The new formalism is an interpretive methodology that is modestly normative and otherwise positivistic. It is positivistic insofar as it aims to supply synthetic representation of the structural form of private law and to account for how it generates order through deliberatively formalistic legal reasoning. The positivistic ambition is to present the structural form of law as found in law and downstream in social practices in which the law's guidance is taken up. The modestly normative ambition lies in (a) engaging with private law in a manner mindful that legal practices are normative practices, and likewise the law's form of address (the claims it makes and enables to be made); and (b) elucidating the posited morality of legal form.[74]

Given moral limits of legal form, it follows that an interpretive methodology that hews to it and its posited morality will be limited in its power to shed light on the normative and functional adequacy of private law (that is, whether it is practically reasonable and otherwise fit for its function of supplying authoritative normative guidance). These limits point in two directions. First, the supplementation of formalist methodology by methods drawn from normative moral and political theory. And second, supplementation by empirical methods drawn from the social sciences.

Some positivists have, of late, come to find common ground with natural lawyers on certain necessary connections between law and morality,[75] namely that law necessarily: claims moral authority; makes use of normative modes of address; aims to supply practically authoritative normative guidance; assumes that persons have a capacity for practical reason; claims moral authority; is

[74] On the interpretive task of elucidating the posited morality of law, see Paul B Miller, 'Juridical Justification of Private Rights' in M Crawford, S Degeling, and N Tivieros (eds), *Justifying Private Rights* (Hart 2020).

[75] Green, 'Positivism and the Inseparability of Law and Morals' (n 23); John Gardner, 'Nearly Natural Law' (2007) 52 Am J Jurisprudence 1.

morally fallible, and so on. Understanding these connections is essential to understanding the nature of law. But they are not illuminated by legal formalism; indeed, they might go unnoticed by the scholarly formalist interested only in providing a faithful interpretation of received legal form and its posited morality. If the claims of morality on private law are to be understood, one must take leave of formalistic analyses of law. One must turn to moral philosophy to analyse of practical reason and reasons, the morality of right and duty, theories of the good, and such. One must turn to political philosophy for analysis of political morality and justice. The point is not that in doing so one will find definite answers capable of winning consensus on hard questions; it is, rather, that the questions lead there.

Then, there are questions that neither lawyers nor philosophers can answer unaided. If one supposes that law's guidance function underlies various necessary links between law and morality, one will invariably encounter a surfeit of empirical questions about precisely how the law functions, and might function more effectively, in supplying normative guidance. Questions like: How is practical reason engaged by law in different social practices in which the law figures as a guide to right conduct? What are the psychological and socio-contextual variables that influence the effectiveness of guidance supplied by law, and how might lawmakers anticipate these? How do linguistic practices and constraints influence the effectiveness of law? Answers to these and similar questions are important to our assessment of the ultimate practical reasonableness of law, for law must perform its functions in the real world.[76]

This survey of the methodological limits of formalism is not meant to diminish the value of formalist methodology. It is instead a plea for humility and encouragement of interdisciplinarity: inquiry grounded in serious scholarly engagement with the received structural form of law and the deliberative formalism invited by it, supplemented by a willingness to take questions about the practical reasonableness of law where they lead, beyond private law as such and into the humanities and other social sciences.

VI. Conclusion

In other work, I have argued that the structural formality of law and deliberatively formalistic legal reasoning are closely associated with legality and the

[76] Paul B Miller and Jeffrey A Pojanowski, 'The Internal Point of View in Private Law' (2022) 67 Am J Jurisprudence 247.

rule of law. The association is conceptual and normative. The very ideas of legality and the rule of law are such as to imply the formality of law and the necessity of deliberatively formalistic engagement with the guidance it supplies. In turn, the values that belong per se to legality and the rule of law—for example, those of relative social stability, personal security, and freedom from arbitrary interference—attach by implication to legal form and legal formalism. Should a case need to be made for the law's reliance on form, for its expectation of deliberative formalism, and/or for sophisticated scholarly formalism, one can build it through appeal to the values advanced by the achievement of legality in comportment with rule of law baselines.

That said, all varieties of formalism—including the new formalism in the New Private Law—engage with extant law and its posited morality. As a matter of methodological choice, sophisticated scholarly formalists focus on interpreting the law as found and on the public justification(s) given for posited law by lawmakers. This means one must be mindful of taking the bad with the good. The practical reasonableness of our laws and the reasons given in public justification for them is a contingent thing. It turns on more than the law's responsiveness to the values of legality and of the rule of law. One ought to be aware of the moral limits of legal form as well as the moral and methodological limits of legal formalism. I have argued that the moral limits of legal form can only be discerned if due attention is paid to the values of practical reason, of moral right and duty, of political morality, of justice, and of the good. I have suggested that the methodological limits of scholarly formalism are (a) implied by awareness of the moral limits (relative to the moral promise) of legal form, and (b) recognition of the ways in which assessment of the soundness of law points beyond the juridical to normative moral and political theory, as well as empirical examination of the likely or actual effectiveness of the normative guidance supplied by law.

10

Private Law Formalism and Jurisprudential Method

Jeffrey A. Pojanowski

I. Introduction

A rich vein of contemporary scholarship looks to general jurisprudence to answer questions about the proper means to understand and theorize about private law.[1] Many scholars pursuing these methodological questions operate within the 'New Private Law' movement, which takes traditional legal categories and the internal point of view more seriously than legal realist or standard law-and-economics approaches to private law.[2] By contrast, Kantian private law scholarship,[3] whose formalist critiques of private-law externalism and functionalism helped lay the intellectual groundwork for the New Private Law, stands more aloof from general jurisprudence. This reticence by leading formalists like Ernest Weinrib raises questions about this important approach's methodological grounds. Such questions are interesting in their own right, and answering them may help clarify the relationship between Kantian formalism and New Private Law approaches that share its critique of externalism and strong functionalism.

That latter question is also important because, despite their similarities, Kantians and New Private Law scholars working in general jurisprudence often

[1] See, eg, Jules Coleman, *The Practice of Principle, In Defence of a Pragmatist Approach to Legal Theory* (revd edn, OUP 2004); Andrew Gold, 'A Moral Rights Theory of Private Law' (2011) 52 William and Mary L Rev 1873, 1882–85; John CP Goldberg and Benjamin C Zipursky, 'Seeing Tort Law from the Internal Point of View: Holmes and Hart on Legal Duties' (2006) 75 Fordham L Rev 1563; Paul B Miller, 'The New Formalism in Private Law' (2021) 66 Am J Jurisprudence 175.; John Oberdiek, 'Method and Morality in the New Private Law of Torts' (2012) 125 Harvard LRForum 189; Benjamin C Zipursky, 'Pragmatic Conceptualism' (2000) 6 Legal Theory 457.

[2] See 'Introduction' in AS Gold and others (eds), *The Oxford Handbook of the New Private Law* (OUP 2020).

[3] Weinrib's formalism is quite different to the rule-based formalism of ethical positivists like Fred Schauer or Larry Alexander. See Frederick Schauer, 'Formalism' (1988) 97 Yale LJ 509. It is also different from the natural law-inflected new formalism in private law that Paul Miller has recently and ably theorized. See Miller (n 1).

Jeffrey A. Pojanowski, *Private Law Formalism and Jurisprudential Method* In: *Methodology in Private Law Theory*. Edited by: Thilo Kuntz and Paul B. Miller, Oxford University Press. © Jeffrey A. Pojanowsk 2024.
DOI: 10.1093/oso/9780198885306.003.0010

seem to speak different conceptual languages, or even reside in different philosophical countries with merely superficial resemblances. This chapter, then, is in part a work of translation between two scholarly dialects. It will seek a fresh understanding of the grounds of Kantian formalism by situating the work of Ernest Weinrib in terms of the methodological debates in contemporary general jurisprudence. This study provides some surprises, including closer-than-expected resemblances between contemporary methodological legal positivism and Kantian formalism. To suggest that Weinrib's formalism shares significant features with contemporary positivist methodology sounds bizarre, misguided, or even intentionally provocative. Those who criticize his theory of private law—and Kantian private law theory in general—often contend that the approach is too ethereal, abstract, or metaphysically elaborate; hardly the kind of thing that comes to mind when we think of legal positivism's hard-headed, just-the-facts approach to legal theory.[4] Weinrib himself states that his theory 'is not positivist, because corrective justice and distributive justice are conceptual categories that inform the content of the law without themselves being posited by legal authority'.[5] His approach is not 'detached' from posited norms, but rather 'claims to render them juridically intelligible'.[6]

But to see a yawning gap between Weinrib's formalism and positivist methodology may be to overestimate the thickness of Weinrib's substantive commitments while understating the abstractness and sophistication of contemporary positivist legal thought. It is plausible and illuminating to consider Weinrib's idea of private law as a cousin of sorts of the indirectly evaluative legal positivist method.[7] While such positivists as Joseph Raz and Julie Dickson apply this method at the highest level—to the institution of law in general—a conceptual formalist like Weinrib deploys *similar* tools at lower levels of generality, namely to the distinction between public law and private law, and to subfields of private law like tort. And, to the extent that a theory like Weinrib's wants to escape the grasp of methodological positivism, it must more directly embrace on substantive, evaluative grounds the Kantian concepts it often portrays as merely immanent, organizing principles.

[4] cf John CP Goldberg, 'Introduction: Pragmatism and Private Law' (2012) 125 Harvard LR 1640, 1648 (arguing that theories like Weinrib's have 'fertile sources of arguments against brass-tacks pragmatism, but they have also required embracing controversial foundational assumptions about the rights individuals have qua individuals'); Zipursky (n 1) 458 (rejecting Weinrib's defence of corrective justice because it is 'metaphysically elaborate and antipragmatic').

[5] Ernest J Weinrib, *The Idea of Private Law* (OUP 1995) 229.

[6] ibid.

[7] See generally Julie Dickson, *Evaluation and Legal Theory* (Hart Publishing 2001).

Nevertheless, even without such amendment, Weinrib's approach differs importantly from the positivist's indirectly evaluative legal theory, particularly with respect to meta-theoretical values like unity, coherence, and form. This features of Weinrib's formalism, in turn, can illuminate debates between directly evaluative theorists (like natural lawyers and Dworkinians), on one hand, and methodological positivists like Hart, Raz, and Dickson on the other. Weinrib's approach shares some of the same shortcomings of methodological positivists' attempts to detach interpretation of legal practices from moral judgment. At the same time, his discussion of form and his insights on the role that coherence and unity play in justification capture important truths and highlight the limits of methodological positivists' attempts to engage in value-neutral theorizing.

II. The Methodology Debate in Contemporary General Jurisprudence

This section provides a brief overview of arguments about methodology between legal positivists and critics who believe general theorizing about the nature of law requires moral evaluation. This summary sketch will set the stage for contextualizing Kantian private law formalism.

Contemporary legal positivism has, for the most part, eschewed Austinian arguments that law is simply the command of a sovereign and has sidelined Hobbesian and Benthamite ethical arguments about the benefits of treating law as a command of the sovereign.[8] HLA Hart's *The Concept of Law* initiated this internal turn, in which positivist theorizing about the nature of law focuses on the beliefs and understandings of a legal system's participants. This is true of so-called 'exclusive' or 'hard' positivists like Joseph Raz and Scott Shapiro, who believe law can only be grounded in social facts. It is also true of 'inclusive' or 'soft' legal positivists like Hart, who believe that non-posited moral norms can be law, so long as the legal system incorporates them. What unites these positivists is their commitment that the master rule of recognition determining which norms are part of the legal system is itself a social fact that we can identify without moral criteria. More importantly for present purposes,

[8] Fred Schauer has offered scepticism in both respects. Frederick Schauer, *The Force of Law* (Harvard University Press 2015); Frederick Schauer, 'Positivism as Pariah' in RP George (ed), *The Autonomy of Law: Essays in Legal Positivism* (OUP 1996). On the difference between Benthamite positivism and the later conceptual positivism of Hart and his heirs, see Dan Priel, 'Toward Classical Legal Positivism' (2015) 101 Virginia L Rev 987.

their understanding of what counts as a good understanding of the legal system looks to the *beliefs* of those who participate in the system. These beliefs, not sanctions or external patterns of behaviour, are the social facts a sound jurisprudential method must focus on.

In response, non-positivists have argued that such neutral description of law as a social institution is impossible. John Finnis argued in his seminal critique of Hart that no one 'can give a theoretical description and analysis of social facts without also participating in the work of evaluation, of understanding what is really good for human purposes, and what is required by practical reasonableness'.[9] This is not a matter of sheer dogmatic preference for moralism, but rather an argument about how coherent theory about human practices is possible. There are lots of things in the world that people label 'law', and those things, even if they are indisputably part of legal institutions, have lots of features. To pick out which of that welter of phenomena count as 'law' and which features of those phenomena are relevant and salient, Finnis argues, one first needs a 'principle of selection', and in understanding human practices, that principle of selection will turn on the reason(s) for having the practice in the first place.[10] Jurisprudence, like other kinds of social theorizing, 'aspires to be more than a conjunction of lexicography with local history' or, more ambitiously, 'a juxtaposition of all lexicographies conjoined with all local histories'.[11] In selecting the viewpoint about law's purpose(s), Finnis argues further, one must therefore adopt the standpoint of the practically reasonable person, which is an irreducibly evaluative inquiry.[12] In a similar vein, Ronald Dworkin also challenged the positivist's belief in the distinction between description and evaluation at the level of theory construction. He argued that because we have deep disputes about the 'grounds of law' that are not reducible to arguments about the facts of social practice, we have no choice but to adopt an interpretive argument that understands the facts of the practice in their best light.[13]

Some legal positivists responded by conceding evaluation of a type was necessary for a sound jurisprudential method, while denying that this necessary evaluation was moral. Building on the work of Joseph Raz, Julie Dickson

[9] John Finnis, *Natural Law and Natural Rights* (2nd edn, OUP 2011) 3.

[10] ibid 4.

[11] ibid 4.

[12] ibid 15. For a concise and illuminating discussion about the difference between Finnis and Hart about the nature of legal philosophy and the possibility evaluatively neutral theory construction, see Brian Bix, 'On the Dividing Line between Natural Law and Legal Positivism' (2000) 75 Notre Dame L Rev 1613.

[13] See Ronald Dworkin, *Law's Empire* (Harvard University Press 1986) 3–6, 52–53.

has defended this approach most extensively. Following an important line of modern methodological positivism, she explained that the task of general jurisprudence is to identify features that are 'necessarily true' and 'adequately explain the nature of law'.[14] She recognized, however, that one cannot identify these 'essential properties'[15] of law by compiling lists describing things that people believe about law. Legal theory needs to elucidate, organize, and clarify the data the theorist gathers about people's beliefs about law as a practice.[16]

General jurisprudence can do this in two ways, neither of which is moral. First, Dickson argued, in response to Finnis's worries about a principle of selection, that theorists can rely on 'purely meta-theoretical values' like 'simplicity, clarity, elegance, comprehensiveness, and coherence'.[17] One should assemble the data with an eye toward explanations that clearly, coherently, and elegantly describe wide swathes of the practice. Theories that are idiosyncratic, muddled, or narrow are not good candidates for identifying crucial features of legal practices. Similarly, Brian Leiter, in responding to Dworkin's argument from disagreement about the 'grounds of law', offered a list of meta-theoretical criteria for resolving disagreement, namely: simplicity, consilience, and methodological conservatism (in that explanations leave other 'well-confirmed beliefs and theories intact').[18] None of these values, which are just as crucial for theorizing about solar systems as they are for social practices, require a purposive or teleological filter.

Dickson pressed further beyond what she called such 'banal' meta-theoretical values to argue that a sound approach requires thicker criteria that are nonetheless not directly evaluative. She argued that a theorist needs to identify which features the participants in the practice consider to be 'important', 'significant', or 'illuminating'.[19] She analogized to an agnostic who wants to understand a Catholic mass.[20] The theorist will understand that, for the practitioners, kneeling and the Eucharist are important, significant, and illuminating in ways that the inevitable shuffling of feet and fidgeting of children are not. In parallel, we should regard as central to a sound legal theory features like law's claim of moral authority, officials who resolve disputes about law's content, or

[14] Dickson (n 7) 17.
[15] ibid.
[16] See Julie Dickson, 'Methodology in Jurisprudence: A Critical Survey' (2004) 10 Legal Theory 117, 132.
[17] Dickson (n 7) 32.
[18] Brian Leiter, 'Explaining Theoretical Disagreement' (2009) 76 University of Chicago L Rev 1215, 1239.
[19] Julie Dickson, 'Ours is a Broad Church: Indirectly Evaluative Legal Philosophy as a Facet of Jurisprudential Inquiry' (2015) 6 Jurisprudence 207, 221; Dickson (n 7) 52.
[20] Dickson (n 7) 68–69.

the fact that violating law requires an explanation.[21] This is not because law's claim of moral authority is in fact justified, or that it is good to have authoritative resolution of legal disputes, but rather because those who participate and reflect on the practice *believe* as a matter of fact that those features are significant and make sense of it. Her legal theory is 'indirectly evaluative' because it draws on the evaluations of the practice's participants without endorsing their moral worth.[22]

To synthesize, we can see mainstream analytical positivists like Dickson understanding general jurisprudential explanation to (a) capture law's essential nature, (b) based on the participants' beliefs and self-understandings about what is important about law, (c) while avoiding direct moral or political evaluation of law so conceptualized.[23] As noted, a leading competitor to this framework is the evaluative approach to social theorizing most prominently articulated in recent decades by natural law theorist John Finnis. This approach is not parochial to self-proclaimed natural lawyers or their particular moral theorizing within the framework. Forms of this argument have been adopted by evaluative scholars like Stephen Perry, and its strength has been conceded even by positivists like John Gardner.[24] This approach also holds that human practices are to be understood in terms of their practitioners' beliefs or understandings about the practice. The principle of selection for sifting data about the practitioners' views, however, is the practically reasonable person's beliefs about the purpose(s) or point(s) of the practice. Like methodological positivism, it is internal, evaluative, and transcends mere reportage. Unlike methodological positivism, it recognizes that, at least at higher levels of theorization, direct moral evaluation is impossible to avoid in selecting which point of view is central for understanding the practice. Its essentialism, moreover, does not resemble an inquiry into natural kinds or a search for empirical regularities; rather it is grounded in the evaluative criteria that identify the purposes or points of the practice that are stable and enduring features of moral reality.[25]

This approach, whose soundness is presupposed here, rather than defended extensively, identifies flaws or incompleteness at each point of the methodological positivist's programme. Although the proper point of theorizing is

[21] See Jeff Pojanowski, 'Reevaluating Legal Theory' (2021) 130 Yale LJ 1458, 1469 (synthesizing Dickson's argument).

[22] Dickson (n 7) 53.

[23] Pojanowski (n 21) 1487 (summarizing the project as such).

[24] See Miller and Pojanowski (n 50) 265–67 (detailing the extent of the approach's acceptance).

[25] For a more detailed summary and defence of this approach, as well as an excavation of its implicit philosophy of social science, see Miller and Pojanowski (n 50) (detailing the approach and applying it to private law theory); Pojanowski (n 21) (contextualizing theory in philosophy of social science).

internal, the sheer variety of internal perspectives render this orientation alone insufficient for identifying the proper standpoint. We have to choose among internal points of view, which leads us to the question of *evaluation*. Indirectly moral evaluation suffers from the same problem of identifying the internal point of view without moral judgment. We have to decide *whose* claims of significance and importance are worth crediting, and what counts as an elucidation rather than a distortion of the practice.[26] Furthermore if, as Dickson argues, compilation of linguistic usage and 'banal' meta-theoretical values are insufficient for making sense of the primary data, it is not clear why those more 'neutral' criteria can sort out meta-level disagreement about significance, importance, and elucidation. If so, Dickson is wrong and directly evaluative theorists are right, unless naturalist positivists like Leiter are correct, that more austere criteria like simplicity, consilience, and methodological conservatism will do the trick. Finally, an evaluative philosophy of social science holds that it is a mistake to look for universals in human practices in the way we look for them in natural kinds. Any *essentialism* must refer to more enduring features of moral reality.[27] Enduring, necessary features would operate the level of law's anchoring or orienting ideals.

The competing positivist and evaluative approaches to jurisprudential methodology make universal claims about the nature of law. New Private Law scholars have drawn on these resources for their arguments about how to understand and theorize about private law. Kantian formalists like Weinrib, however, are less inclined to situate their approaches to private law in a general jurisprudential framework—or at least are less are likely to do so on the terms of these contemporary debates about method. The next section will try to situate the Kantian philosophy of private law in that broader framework.

III. The Methodology of Weinrib's *Idea of Private Law*

Weinrib's theory understands private law as a practice informed (in the classical sense of form) by the 'direct linking of plaintiff and defendant institutionally through litigation and adjudication and doctrinally through causation and

[26] This point is made especially well in Dan Priel, 'Description and Evaluation in Jurisprudence (2010) 29 Law and Philosophy 633, 653–656.

[27] A more deeply hermeneutical approach to social science would agree with me on the first two points, but deny any kind of essentialism, moral or otherwise. See Pojanowski (n 21) 1479–82. This approach, exemplified by theorists like Peter Winch, has its own problems, including worries about moral relativism and the impossibility of understandings between cultures.

the other appurtenances of correlative rights and duties'.[28] Aristotle's 'conception of corrective justice' offers the unifying structure that renders this relationship of liability 'intelligible', while Kant's 'concept of right as the governing idea for relationships between free beings' provides the normative underpinning of corrective justice.[29] Whether the substance of this theory of private law is correct is, of course, a matter of great dispute. More interesting for present purposes is how Weinrib gets there.

As discussed in Section II, contemporary methodological positivism seeks to (a) capture law's essential nature (b) based on the participants' beliefs and self-understandings about what is important about law, (c) while avoiding direct moral or political evaluation of law. In reply, critics contend that such essential features and participant understandings must ultimately draw on evaluative judgment about the point or purpose of the practice. Using those duelling methodological frames, this section will explore the implicit methodological commitments of Weinrib's formalism.

1. The Autonomy of the Internal Point of View

The most striking resemblance between Weinrib's work and methodological positivism is its focus on an internal point of view that it professes to describe or characterize on its own terms. This is in contrast with evaluative theorist who contends that any construction of an internal point of view of such a legal institution must be grounded in the overarching point or purposes of the practice.

a) Internalism

Weinrib seeks to understand 'private law as an internally intelligible phenomenon by drawing on what is salient in juristic experience and by trying to make sense of legal thinking and discourse on their own terms'.[30] Like Dickson and Raz, Weinrib theorizes the practice from the internal point of view and, rather than just assembling a list of features, draws on meta-theoretical values and the evaluative attitude of the practitioners. By contrast, he criticizes what he calls functionalist theories of private law for failing 'to take seriously the features expressive of private law's inner character'.[31]

[28] Weinrib (n 5) 28.
[29] ibid at 19; see also Ernest Weinrib, 'Private Law and Public Right' (2011) 61 University of Toronto LJ 191, 192–93.
[30] Weinrib (n 5) 2–3; see also ibid 16 (stating that 'an account that flows from and captures the law's self-understanding assumes the perspective internal to juristic activity').
[31] ibid 2.

For Weinrib, 'one must understand private law from a perspective internal to it'.[32] Theorizing about private law is a matter of 'reflecting on the juristic experience of private law and on the presuppositions of that experience'.[33] It is not, moreover, the experience of theorists qua theorists. What matters is 'our experience of the law, especially the experience of those who are lawyers'.[34] Nor is it the raw, undigested experience of lawyers. Amid the complex body of legal materials, the theorist recognizes that 'certain features have a special significance. . . .are salient in our conception of private law, in the sense that their systematic absence would mean the disappearance of private law as recognizable mode of ordering'.[35] The careful theorist thus identifies 'a set of concepts, a distinctive institutional setting, and a characteristic mode of reasoning'.[36] Using this 'ensemble of institutional and conceptual features salient in juristic experience' as a baseline, the theorist then 'works back to the justificatory framework presupposed in the ensemble, all the while preserving the tendency toward coherence that characterizes both theorizing in general and private law in particular'.[37] This method of 'regression' in private law uncovers the structuring features of 'corrective justice' and then identifies the 'Kantian concept of right' as the normative framework immanent in the structure.[38]

In short, Weinrib's primary data for theorizing are the evaluative attitudes and understandings of its practitioners, or at least of theorists understanding the practice from within. Private law 'is not merely an emanation of external power' one can observe; 'it is a mode of moral association that attaches decisive importance to the justification of norms that constitute it'.[39] Yet one must understand that form of moral association and its justifications 'from within the law', interpreting things like a 'right of action simply as what it purports to be'.[40] Like Dickson, he is not satisfied to compile a mere list of things people label 'private law' or beliefs that people have about the practice. His formalism 'is not a semantic or lexicographical project', but is rather 'concerned with the intelligibility of juridical relationships'.[41] His 'exercise demands a selection of those attributes so decisive of the thing's character that they can truly be said

[32] ibid.
[33] ibid 19.
[34] ibid 9.
[35] ibid 9.
[36] ibid 5.
[37] ibid 19.
[38] ibid 19.
[39] ibid 39.
[40] ibid 11. See also ibid 12 ('[A]n internal account respects the dynamism of private law, *as understood from the standpoint of those who think about the law in its own terms*') (emphasis added).
[41] ibid 31.

to characterize it'.[42] Thus, one looks to the beliefs of reflective practitioners, focusing on those features that they find salient, significant, or characteristic of the practice—without those features, the practice would be unintelligible or simply something else.

Meta-theoretical values also play an important role in Weinrib's project. In fact, these values are so crucial to informing the internal standpoint that he would resist Dickson's labelling them as merely 'banal'. Unity and coherence are central in Weinrib's account, both as a descriptive and structural matter. (Even more important is 'form', of which unity and coherence are important features. At the risk of artificially splitting up the unity of Weinrib's formalism, I will address that aspect later when I discuss essentialism.) He observes that 'private law values and tends towards its own coherence'.[43] Thus, reflective lawyers understand private law's features as 'the interconnected aspects of a single complex of ideas that illuminates the continuing elaboration of legal doctrine'.[44] Coherence is also necessary for any such understanding. The potential coherence of the legal materials 'supplies the internal standpoint from which to understand the doctrines, concepts, and institutional processes of private law'.[45] It is not enough to identify the central features of private law seriatim. The demand of coherence 'points to the existence of some sort of internal connection between the various features that cohere', recognizing 'the primacy of unity over character and kind'.[46] In fact, juridical intelligibility of legal relationships is possible 'only from the standpoint of their possible coherence'.[47] This coherence, moreover, makes private law's 'self-understanding' as a 'justificatory enterprise' possible.[48]

b) Evaluation

Weinrib states that private law 'is the public repository of our most deeply embedded intuitions about justice and personal responsibility'.[49] He does not, however, seek to warrant the moral worth of those ('our') intuitions, nor does he contend that we should understand private law in light of a quest to pursue justice or enforce personal responsibility. Weinrib, like Dickson, realizes that sophisticated legal theorizing requires evaluation, but only insofar as it seeks

[42] ibid 27.
[43] ibid 12; see also ibid 13 ('[T]he striving of coherence is a characteristic of private law and is thus internal to it'.).
[44] ibid 12.
[45] ibid 42.
[46] ibid 30.
[47] ibid 31.
[48] ibid 32.
[49] ibid 1.

to understand and elucidate the evaluative standpoint of those within the practice. But moral evaluation of *those evaluations*, or the ascription of moral purposes beyond the internal logic of the practice so understood by its practitioners, is *not* part of that theorization. 'If we *must* express this intelligibility [of private law] in terms of purpose, the only thing to be said is that the purpose of private law is to be private law'.[50] To view private law as serving external purposes, or to make external moral values necessary criteria for grasping the nature of private law, is to fail to understand it, or even to deform it.

Weinrib's theoretical *bête noire* is functionalism in private law theory. He links functionalism with approaches that understand law in the light of purposes external to the practice itself.[51] His central target is usually economic analysis of law. His arguments that, as an interpretive matter, economic theories cannot explain important features of tort law are compelling; many other legal philosophers who do not embrace his method as a whole have taken them on board. But his argument against external evaluation ranges wider. He argues that 'even noninstrumental moral ideas that are external to private law' can suffer the same flaws.[52] Now, if moral ideas happen to track the internal logic of private law—as he believes the Kantian philosophy of right does—it is permissible to deploy that framework in elaborating private law.[53] But there is no question of going beyond the immanent framework. Theorists 'cannot start with morality—even noninstrumental morality--and consider law merely a means to implementing it. Rather, the moral notions must themselves reflect the character of private law as a distinctive and coherent mode of ordering'.[54] In this respect, even those theorists who understand private law to have roughly the same structure as Weinrib, but who view the ultimate purpose of the practice as promoting human flourishing and securing human rights in the natural law tradition,[55] make the same mistakes as the most bloodless legal economist.

One could, of course, first grasp private law as practised and understood and *then* offer an external critique, but that is a very different enterprise. At the level of general jurisprudence, Dickson sees indirectly evaluative theorizing as a necessary precondition to critique.[56] Weinrib, while less interested than Dickson

50 ibid 5.

51 ibid 3–6.

52 ibid 49. See also Ernest Weinrib, *Corrective Justice* (OUP 2012) 307 and (n 20) (rejecting John Finnis's theory of basic human goods as the grounds of tort law).

53 Weinrib (n 5) 49–50.

54 ibid 50.

55 See John Finnis, 'A Grand Tour of Legal Theory' in *IV Collected Essays: Philosophy of Law* (OUP 2011) 138–40; Paul B Miller and Jeffrey A Pojanowski, 'The Internal Point of View in Private Law' (2022) 67 Am J Jurisprudence 247; Michael P Moreland and Jeffrey A Pojanowski, 'The Moral of Torts' in Robert F Cochran, Jr and Michael P Moreland (eds), *Christianity and Private Law* (Routledge 2021).

56 Dickson (n 7) 63–64, 137.

in taking the next, directly evaluative step, recognizes a similar distinction. His formalism 'does not directly assess the substantive merits of particular legal determinations' in a body of law. Rather, it 'first elucidates a legal relationship's internal principle of organization. Only in light of this formal principle does it then evaluate considerations of substance.'[57] The arrangements the formalist elucidates, to be sure, will have 'political antecedents and effects', but 'the juridical aspect of those arrangements reflects formal considerations that are in some significant sense anterior to judgments about what is substantively desirable'.[58] In that respect, any 'functionalist' criticisms based on an external standpoint are therefore 'irrelevant to the particular enterprise' of capturing and elucidating 'the law's self-understanding'.[59]

For that reason, his quarrel with compensation-and-deterrence theories of tort law, for example, is 'not due to an antipathy toward these goals considered on their own'.[60] Rather it is because such explanations cannot satisfy formalism's requirements of internal coherence.[61] Indeed, if 'compensation were conjoined to doctrinal and institutional features that reflected the same justificatory impulse', then the 'the demands of formalism would be fully met'.[62] In the end, what matters is not 'the substantive desirability of any legal arrangement, but the coherence of the justificatory considerations that support its component features'.[63] We can take or leave our private law, but we have to do so on *its own* terms.

Weinrib believes private law's impermeability from purposes beyond its internal logic is necessary to maintain the autonomy of private law as a discipline. His 'notion of autonomy excludes extrinsic purposes' when theorizing about the nature of the practice.[64] This does not mean, of course, that private law theorizing closes its eyes to other disciplines; rather, it regards 'their insights from its own perspective and assimilates them to its own immanently rational purpose'.[65] Nor does it mean that formalists like Weinrib are committed to the belief that that adjudication is mechanical deduction without discretion; rather it is *legal* judgment pursuant to the direction of the

[57] Weinrib (n 5) 25.
[58] ibid 25.
[59] ibid 16.
[60] ibid 45.
[61] ibid. Weinrib argues, compellingly, that deterrence only looks at one half of the bilateral relationship of liability, while compensation looks at the other, without explaining how the plaintiff's injury and the defendant's action are linked in a unified relationship of accountability.
[62] ibid 46.
[63] ibid.
[64] ibid 214.
[65] ibid.

justificatory structure immanent in the practice.[66] Even if a question of application is hard, the uncertainty operates on the terms and within the confines of a normative structure the theorist identifies independent of extrinsic goals or purposes.

c) The limits of the non-evaluative internal perspective

Like indirectly evaluative legal theory in general jurisprudence, Weinrib maintains that good theorizing about private law is a matter of 'attending to the legal practice, eliciting its inner structure, and enquiring into that structure's normative presuppositions'.[67] We see here, then, a family resemblance between Weinrib's formalism and methodological positivists' theorizing in general jurisprudence. We have also seen the evaluative theorists' critique of such approaches. Attending to that critique—that any sound construction of the internal point of view must draw on the point of the practice and therefore evaluate—helps diagnose some of the difficulties with Weinrib's approach to private law theory.

Take the jarring assertion that from the theorist's perspective, private law serves no end but itself. What the evaluative theorist understands as selecting the proper, orienting point of view for a normative practice, Weinrib writes off as a kind of external instrumentalism that goes beyond the purpose of private law being private law. This strikes many, myself included, as mysterious, possibly misguided, or at least as a distension of the often-admirable goal of understanding legal doctrine on its own terms. Human law, after all, does not exist for its own sake, but rather is a practical discipline with an important impact in our lives. Weinrib's theorization of private law excludes that orienting standpoint. Yoking the internal point of view to external purposes—or, put another way, holding that the internal point of view interpenetrates moral considerations—makes sense of the intuition that we have legal practices and institutions for the good of persons, and builds it into the theory.

Furthermore, directly evaluative criteria for the internal point of view provide more theoretical resources for sorting out conflicting data about private law. Although Weinrib's corrective justice can explain many features of private law, it is less clear what it can do about features that do not fit as nicely, or judicial decisions that depart from his vision of private law besides excluding them. Part of that exclusion flows from Weinrib's thick understanding of form, which I will discuss soon. Beyond that, to the extent the data conflict,

[66] ibid 225–29.

[67] Weinrib (n 52) 303.

one needs a principle of selection to decide what is in or out, central or aberrational, taken for granted or in need of further explanation. And if that selection does not look to the internal point of view of the practically reasonable observer, we are left relying on more austere meta-ethical criteria, lexicography, statistical frequency, or mere stipulation. Far more promising are morally thicker conclusions about the suitability of providing the institutional forms and doctrines of corrective justice or civil recourse when one person is wronged by another. In other words, Weinrib's theory makes more sense if we recognize Kantian commitments to corrective justice animated by equal freedom as the implicit evaluative criteria for sorting the data or constructing the internal point view of the practice. In that respect—and despite his insistence that the morality of law inheres in, rather than transcends, private law—on this more compelling reconstruction, Weinrib would differ from natural lawyers like John Finnis or Paul Miller only in his substantive vision of private law's ends, which is more monist and Kantian. (Indeed, a natural law theorist who views private law as serving plural, often incommensurate moral aims would worry that Weinrib's transcendentalist reconstruction is so abstract that he loses the ability to claim fidelity to participant perspectives on such complex legal practices.)

This is not to say that the evidentiary case for Weinrib's bipolarity critique of law or economics or compensation/deterrence is equivocal or unpersuasive. Rather it is to give reasons why it makes sense to have *and maintain* the structure of private law that Weinrib's critique points toward, while also allowing one to remain open to reform and further development of the practices in light of sound moral reasons. This is also not to say that private law doctrine should always be transparent to background moral reasons. In a reasonably healthy system, the moral value of doctrinal stability and the underdetermined nature of the moral questions private law addresses will usually point its practitioners to ordinary doctrinal science and incremental development and pruning, rather than raw moral reasoning and radical reformation.[68] It is to say, however, that private law has a double life in which overarching considerations of justice are the taproot, the quietly vitalizing source, of a healthy body of private law.[69]

[68] See Miller (n 1). The orienting moral framework can also be more pluralist in orientation than the monism Weinrib sees as immanent in private law's structure.

[69] cf John Finnis, 'Adjudication and Legal Change' in *IV Collected Essays: Philosophy of Law* (OUP 2011) 397.

2. Essentialism

Methodological positivists in general jurisprudence, like Raz in his earlier work, John Gardner, Scott Shapiro, and Julie Dickson, seek to identify the necessary, essential features of legal systems.[70] The plausibility of this essentialism about law has come under attack by positivists and non-positivists alike.[71] A problem with this form of essentialism is that human practices like law are not natural kinds; the project of discovering what 'makes water *water*' (H_2O), is different from looking for 'what makes all and only instances of law instances of *law* and nothing else'.[72] This is because, the objections continue, law is either an artifact without enduring essences or, alternatively, any essence has to be understood in terms of its enduring moral purposes that are its measuring ideal.[73] Methodological positivism like Dickson's, the argument concludes, is an unstable combination of interpretive and positivistic philosophies of social science.[74]

Weinrib's private law formalism offers a similar kind of high-level essentialism, but the form of his argument—indeed his formalism—may be less vulnerable to the methodological-mismatch critique. For Weinrib, the theoretical goal is to 'comprehend the thing in question as what it is; in classical terminology, we grasp its nature or essence'.[75] 'Elucidation of the thing's form therefore entails differentiating between the attributes that are definitive of the thing and those that are merely incidental.'[76] His theoretical quest is to discover what makes private law *private law*. To be sure, his is not the (caricatured) version of formalism which is said to hold that enduring, transcendent rules or principles dictate the particular substantive doctrines of tort law everywhere and anywhere. He notes that 'deduction of the particularities of private law is unavailable'.[77] Tort law, for example, can accept *respondeat superior* or reject it on the grounds that fault is a necessary criterion for legal liability.[78] Rather, his

[70] Dickson (n 7) 17–18; John Gardner, 'Law in General' in *Law as a Leap of Faith: Essays on Law in General* (OUP 2012) 270, 296–97, 296 n 75; Joseph Raz, *Morality of Freedom* (OUP 1986) 55–56; Scott J Shapiro, *Legality* (Harvard University Press 2011) 9.

[71] Brian Leiter, 'The Demarcation Problem in Jurisprudence: A New Case for Skepticism' (2011) 31 OJLS 663, 666; Schauer (n 8) 35–41; Stephen R Perry, 'Hart's Methodological Positivism' in Jules Coleman (ed), *Hart's Postscript: Essays on the Postscript to the Concept of Law* (2nd edn, OUP 2011) 311.

[72] Shapiro (n 70) 9.

[73] Pojanowski (n 21) 1487.

[74] See Perry (n 71); Pojanowski (n 21).

[75] Weinrib (n 5) 27.

[76] ibid.

[77] ibid 228. See also ibid 206 (repudiating the 'myth that the formalist's conceptualism commits private law to a deductive moral geometry').

[78] ibid 228 and n 37.

far more plausible essentialism links private law with the form of corrective justice, as opposed to distributive justice.

Formalism, he explains, does not display a preference for distributive or corrective justice. Rather, 'it requires only that whatever mode of ordering a jurisdiction adopts conforms to the rationality immanent in that mode of ordering'.[79] And the immanent rationality of private law 'presupposes the structure of corrective justice and its grounding in Kantian right'.[80] This immanent rationality also gives private law its juridical character, as well as autonomy from public law and *its* form of distributive justice in the realm of the political.[81] This 'morally differentiated world, marked by different kinds of justification' provides the deep structures of private and public law. If carving up the world of justification in this fashion is a kind of metaphysical or transcendent truth and if private law is necessarily correlated with and in-formed by corrective justice, Weinrib seems to be arguing that he has picked out the essential character of private law.

One possible problem with this interpretation is his argument elsewhere that formalism is not 'an invitation to essentialism', which he identifies with the view that 'an entity's essential properties supply the ultimate measure for understanding what the entity is'.[82] He rejects this approach to essentialism because it ignores 'the primacy of unity over character and kind'.[83] It is not enough to identify a list of essential features; they have to mutually cohere and provide a unity in explanation and justification.[84] The most plausible reading of this dismissal of 'essentialism', especially in light of later discussion of grasping the 'nature or essence' of private law, is that Weinrib is rejecting a kind of essentialism inappropriate to the character of law. Unlike understanding a natural entity, in which summarizing features may be enough to grasp its nature, understanding human practices like law requires identifying their immanent justificatory features and seeing how they hang together. This more demanding

[79] ibid 228.

[80] ibid 207. See also ibid 207 at ('[C]orrective justice requires only that private law realize its own immanent rationality.').

[81] ibid ('The claim that private law is autonomous rests on the immanence of this rationality both in private law and in itself.'); ibid 210 ('Distributive justice is home to the political.'); ibid 219 (distinguishing between 'two public functions—one political, the other juridical—that formalism ascribes to the positivity of law' and identifying distributive and corrective justice with those respective forms). Weinrib, of course, recognizes that private law has 'public' dimensions in that it requires positive law and legal institutions to actualize corrective justice and this practice may have political consequences. See ibid 212 and 218. He contends, plausibly, that those facts alone are not enough to collapse the practice into 'public law'.

[82] ibid 30.

[83] ibid.

[84] ibid 31.

essentialism is suitable for the nature of the phenomenon the theorist is trying to understand. Echoing Kant's method, one sees private law's essential features not so much as 'in' the practice as pre-theoretical data to be discovered, but rather as intertwined with, or identical to, the perceptual forms or categories that make understanding of the practice possible. This is an important difference from methodological positivists like Dickson and, while it is more metaphysically robust (or promiscuous, to the sceptic), its approach to essentialism draws a sharp distinction between human practices and natural phenomena. It regards the former as requiring a different kind of understanding appropriate to their character.

In this respect, Weinrib's formalism stands ready as a striking example of what essentialism in legal theory would have to look like. Scholars like Dickson, Raz, and Shapiro are aware that law is not a natural kind like gold, but nevertheless have held that analogous methods of analysis can apply to both the natural sciences and human practices like law. Given the variability and contingency of human practices, however, the character of such necessity is either narrow ('our concept of law') and thus less theoretically interesting as a form of essentialism, or requires ambitious empirical statements about legal systems everywhere, and thus less plausible. The theoretical entities that are necessary are somewhat mysterious. In the context of private law, however, Weinrib's formalism offers metaphysical grounding to this necessity in the form of corrective justice and the Kantian philosophy of right.

Now, it does not follow that the right kind of essentialism in legal theory requires Weinrib's particular hybrid of Aristotelian and Kantian metaphysics. Weinrib's account of private law's essential features here is not without its challenges. There are scholars even in the Aristotelian tradition who maintain that the distinction between corrective justice (or, as they call it, 'commutative justice') and distributive justice is not sharp in private law,[85] or even in principle.[86] What is of interest here is that Weinrib is offering the kind of essentialism that is available for theorizing about variegated human practices like law, namely one that transcends facts and mere beliefs that people happen to have. In short, Weinrib's idea of private law assumes, along with natural lawyers, that essentialism about human practices will be neither metaphysically austere nor normatively inert.

Nor is it obvious that such essentialism will be value neutral. An indirectly evaluative interpretation of Weinrib's account could claim that our idea of

[85] See James Gordley, Foundations of Private Law (OUP 2006) 12–13.
[86] See Finnis (n 9) 179.

private law only just happens to understand itself as a justificatory practice, and justificatory practices require form, coherence, and unity. This presumes something about the nature of persons, reason, and justification that comes from 'outside' private law, but (the metaphysical deflator would argue) we are bringing it 'in' only because the participants regard this feature to be important about private law. But, as with the response to the methodological positivists, here too we need selection criteria for deciding which views about private law are worth placing at the centre, and there are strong arguments that *that* principle of selection cannot avoid direct evaluation. The reasonable, more directly normative reconstruction of Weinrib's position here is that it is simply *better*, all things being equal, for a practice law to be coherent, unified, and presenting itself in a recognizable form of social practice and action. And while one can try to cordon off this formal, 'internal' morality of law from judgments about the benefits of having private law and its doctrines, even Lon Fuller could not help but believe there was some latent connection between such procedural or formal justice and substantively good rules.[87]

IV. Conclusion

This chapter sought to understand the methodological grounding of Kantian formalism as presented in Weinrib's *Idea of Private Law*. His important and illuminating approach to understanding private law shares a number of the methodological features of indirectly evaluative legal positivism. The limitations of that method of legal theorizing are reflected in some of the most troublesome features of Weinrib's philosophy of private law, which would be a more plausible account if reconstructed along directly evaluative lines. At the same time, Weinrib's understanding of what it means for law to have essential features differs from and is, at least at the level of method, superior to theories that seek law's necessary features while prescinding from direct evaluation of the practice.

[87] Lon L Fuller, 'Positivism and Fidelity to Law: A Reply to Hart' (1958) 71 Harvard LR 630, 636 (musing that 'coherence and goodness have more affinity than coherence and evil').

11

How Can You Have Law Without Lawyers?

Legal Formalism, Legality, and the Law Governing Lawyers

*W. Bradley Wendel**

I. Introduction: Formalism and Method

In an excellent recent article on methodology and the New Private Law, Paul Miller argues that New Private Law is a distinctive variety of legal formalism.[1] Formalism is of course a highly contested concept in jurisprudence. It is often used as a caricature of positions that no sensible theorist has ever held. But formalist methodologies can be deeply interesting to the extent they connect with underlying accounts of practical reasoning and its relationship with legal normativity. The trouble is interesting theoretical positions that might be labelled as formalist coexist in legal scholarship with some fairly silly views. Early in his article Miller provides a list of fifteen characteristics that have been ascribed to legal formalism. As a reader it is obvious that one is expected to accept some and reject, or even scoff at others. This is a clever rhetorical move, for it forces readers to engage with their own preconceptions about what counts as formalism. To the point of this chapter, it also allows a theorist to use silly versions of formalism as a foil for sensible ones.

Consider the following four items from Miller's list. According to some legal scholars, formalism is committed to theses including:

- [T]he prioritization of form over substance in legal argument and decision-making, or … preoccupation with form to the exclusion of substance (substance understood as a matter of the justice or injustice of a law and/or its application);

* Edwin H Woodruff Professor of Law, Cornell Law School. I gratefully acknowledge the research funding provided by the Judge Albert Conway Memorial Fund for Legal Research, established by the William C and Joyce C O'Neil Charitable Trust.

[1] Paul B Miller, 'The New Formalism in Private Law' (2021) 66 Am J Jurisprudence 175.

W. Bradley Wendel, *How Can You Have Law Without Lawyers?* In: *Methodology in Private Law Theory.* Edited by: Thilo Kuntz and Paul B. Miller, Oxford University Press. © W. Bradley Wendel 2024. DOI: 10.1093/oso/9780198885306.003.0011

- The deductive or 'mechanical' application of legal rules in adjudication;
- [T]he notion that the primary role and obligation of the judge is to uphold, and not to make, law;
- [A]contextual interpretation of legal texts, whether sources of law (for example, written constitutions) or mere instruments (for example, wills, contracts, and trust deeds) . . . .[2]

These four points describe to a T the naïve beliefs about the law that many first-year students bring with them to the beginning of their legal education. Much of the task of a first-year course is getting students to see that rules do not determine the scope of their own application, and so there is no such thing as the mechanical application of rules in adjudication; that legal formalities only make sense against a background of understanding of what their point or purpose must be; that no case (or statute, or contract) can be interpreted in isolation but takes on meaning in relation to similar sources of law dealing with analogous problems; and that judging involves a tremendous amount of creativity, not merely calling balls and strikes, as Chief Justice Roberts notoriously asserted in his confirmation hearing.

In this chapter, however, I intend to use Miller's list to make a different, and I think relatively unappreciated point: The naïve, easily mocked jurisprudential views included on Miller's list are those that describe a system of law that could, in theory at least, be operationalized in a world in which there are no lawyers. One could imagine a ruler who wanted to operate as a law-giver nailing a legal code to the palace door; the ruler's subjects could go read the provisions of the code and set out trying to comply with them. We sophisticated legal thinkers of course find this ridiculous, for the same reason we regard our first-year students as naïve. The big learning objective in a first-year course, or so I assume to be the case at most law schools, is to develop the capacity for the exercise of judgment. By the end of the first semester Torts course, a student should be able to consider a hypothetical fact pattern that is somewhere out in HLA Hart's penumbra of a legal rule and be able to appreciate how one might argue to subsume it within that rule, but on the other hand how it might also be possible to contend for the situation to fall outside the rule. This judgment is informed by the purposes underlying the rules and the policies that the area of law is traditionally thought to serve. It also demonstrates awareness that what lawyers refer to as the facts of cases become 'facts' for the purposes of legal analysis only because the field of law picks them out as considerations that bear on the

[2] ibid 180–81.

resolution of disputes. Legal judgment is also sensitive to the administrability of rules by different institutional decisionmakers—what Hart and Sacks referred to as institutional competence considerations—and the way the rule laid down in one case might be applied or misapplied in future cases. Students can therefore appreciate why rules on the recovery of damages for emotional distress or pure economic losses have the limitations they do.

What we teach as 'law' in law schools, therefore, is more aptly characterized by five different theses on Miller's list. Some of the non-silly qualities of legal formalism he considers are:

- A matter of acting, arguing, deliberating, and deciding in good faith according to law, on the supposition that one's practical deliberations and behaviour can evince compliance with guidance supplied by law, on the basis of practical reasons derived from law;
- An implication of legality as such (that is, the very idea of law, and thus of legal ordering of civil society and government) and of the rule of law, understood as 'the law's own virtue';
- Manifested in close attention to doctrine, especially the content and evolution of norms and enabling doctrines (reflected in the development of lines of authority at common law, and in the history and text of legislated law);
- The organization and presentation of norms and/or enabling doctrines in modular or formal legal-conceptual structures (for example, that of the fee simple absolute, corporation, or express trust); and
- A concern with systematicity, and the taxonomical elucidation of same, in legal systems (especially in the treatment of precedent at common law).[3]

If these claims about law ring true, however, it is hard to imagine the law working by being printed in a legal code and nailed to the palace door. For example, it is difficult to understand a written document, or a legal precept loudly proclaimed by the law-giver, as being capable of supporting the idea of deliberating and deciding in good faith, or being guided by law and not something else, such as the fear of sanctions, and affecting the practical reasoning of the law's subjects—that is to say, something corresponding roughly with HLA Hart's internal point of view.[4] Similarly, if considerations like systematicity and

[3] ibid 180–81.

[4] HLA Hart, *The Concept of Law* 90–91 (2nd edn, OUP 1994); see also Gerald J Postema, *Legal Philosophy in the Twentieth Century: The Common Law World* § 7.3.2 (Springer 2011).

coherence, or larger doctrinal structures, are essential to law, it is difficult to see how they could figure into a simplistic picture of law as given by a sovereign.

In many ways these are familiar observations, having much in common with Hart's devastating critique of Austin's account of law. What I do not think has been noticed, or least given enough emphasis in legal theory, however, is the constitutive role lawyers must play in any theoretical explanation of law. Everyone knows the story of Lon Fuller's King Rex.[5] Rex aspired to be a great legal reformer, but was stymied by his own failures to recognize the importance of numerous formal features of law. He began with the method of case-by-case adjudication, but it soon became clear that there was no pattern whatsoever to his decisions. So he set himself to the task of drafting a code that would deal with issues in more general terms, but kept it locked away in his desk, treating it as a state secret. When his subjects complained that the needed to know the rules, Rex agreed to publish the reasons for his decisions, but make them retrospective only. In response to a public outcry for rules that could be known in advance, Rex reluctantly published the document, which was immediately criticized for its obscurity—no one could make heads or tails of it, and so had no idea what they were expected to do—and for its many contradictions. A subsequent revision of the code included numerous legal requirements that were incapable of being complied with, and when Rex endeavoured to revise that version, he spent so long on the task that social circumstances changed dramatically in the interim.

No one seems to notice the absence of lawyers from Rex's kingdom.[6] Maybe Rex should have thought about the role of the legal profession because it was his aim to make law, and it is the nature of law that it claims authority over its subjects.[7] That is to say, the law affects the practical reasoning of citizens. In order to do this, it is necessary for citizens to grasp the way in which the law has an impact on what they have reason to do. One of the conceptual challenges for legal positivism is to explain how legal norms that have no necessary connection to morality can *obligate* citizens. This is the puzzle of legal normativity,[8] which

[5] Lon L Fuller, *The Morality of Law* (revd edn, Yale UP 1964) 33–38.

[6] One exception is a Canadian legal ethics scholar (now a judge on the Court of King's Bench), Alice Woolley, from whom I have learned a great deal. She asks: 'How does the individual citizen exercise his or her capacity to "grasp and grapple with the rationale" of the law, or to voluntarily comply with it, when he or she knows almost nothing about its content or how it ought to apply to the circumstances that he or she faces?' Alice Woolley, 'The Lawyer as Advisor and the Practice of the Rule of Law' (2014) 47 UBC L Rev 743, 767. In jurisprudential terms, Woolley is describing Hart's 'puzzled man'. See Hart (n 4) 40. Woolley's question is rhetorical, and the answer to how the individual is supposed to grasp and comply with the law is 'talk to a lawyer'.

[7] Joseph Raz, 'Authority, Law and Morality' in *Ethics in the Public Domain* (OUP 1994) 210.

[8] Very nicely set out in Scott Shapiro, *Legality* (Harvard UP 2011)40–49.

seems particularly tricky in connection with positivist theories of the nature of law. How can social facts alone—a descriptive statement about the world—underwrite a normative conclusion that one has a reason to do X? Lawyers would have been able to help Rex address law *authoritatively* to his subjects.

One approach to the problem of legal normativity is that there is a shared social understanding that (1) certain norms count as *law*, and not something else, like etiquette, morality, or useful ways of predicting when sanctions will be imposed, and (2) these norms are to be complied with—it is demanded and expected of well-socialized members of the community that they do the things required by law.[9] On one understanding of Hart's internal point of view (IPOV), the normativity of law depends on participating competently in a social practice of evaluating, claiming, justifying, and making demands on each other with reference to the community's law:

> To take the IPOV is to engage competently in those activities that constitute the group's practice of the rule ... Those who take the IPOV use the rules in their deliberating, making claims and demands against each other, in evaluating their conduct or the conduct of others, criticizing others, vindicating or justifying themselves to them.[10]

My suggestion is that, for law to function in this way, lawyers are necessary. It is fairly obvious that lawyers are *epistemically* necessary for ordinary citizens to be able to ascertain the content of their legal rights, duties, permissions, powers, liberties—the whole Hohfeldian apparatus. The law is notoriously inaccessible to regular folks.[11] The language of law can be esoteric, but in addition, non-lawyers lack the specialized training necessary to determine the precise holding of a case, interpret statutory language, understand the interaction of common law, statutes, regulations, and constitutional provisions, and the like. In addition, however, the authority of law relies on its being used as a way of guiding and evaluating conduct.[12] The law functions as a reason that

[9] See the very helpful reconstruction of Hart's internal point of view and account of legal obligation as essentially conventional in Benjamin C Zipursky, 'Legal Obligations and the Internal Aspect of Rules' (2006) 75 Fordham L Rev 1229, 1243–45.

[10] Postema (n 4) 295–96 (following Zipursky (n 9)).

[11] Various codification movements, and recently enthusiasm about digital information technology, have been motivated in part by a hope that access to legal information, including full-text statutes, regulations, and case law, would make lawyers unnecessary for relatively routine legal matters. A couple of decades into the information revolution, this optimism appears to have been unwarranted. The raw information may be available, but to understand and interpret the law—to grasp it from the point of view of an affected citizen—requires quite a bit of legal training.

[12] Scott Shapiro, 'What is the Internal Point of View?' (2007) 75 Fordham L Rev 1157.

may be given by one citizen to another, for instance as a justification for having done something that affects the interests of another. As moral agents, all citizens must be prepared to act in ways they can justify to others. What the law does, in my view, is to provide a distinctive way citizens can explain and justify their actions to those who are affected by them, and also to coordinate and plan with others. Scanlon employs a nice turn of phrase when he refers to interpersonal morality as a system of 'co-deliberation'.[13] In a highly legalized society, the co-deliberation about what we owe to each other will frequently make reference to what the law permits or requires. The idea of participating in a social practice suggests that lawyers do not perform merely an epistemic function but, in fact, constitute the relevant social practice along with citizens.

In order to carry out this role, certain things must be true of lawyers, their ethical obligations, and the law governing the lawyer-client relationship. Sociologists from Émile Durkheim in the nineteenth century to Talcott Parsons in the twentieth century have maintained that lawyers are intermediaries between citizens and the state, whose professional judgment can be exercised to meld disputatious individuals and groups into a common social order.[14] A version of this type of thinking about professionalism, associated with the civic republican tradition, contends that lawyers are in a better position than their clients, or for that matter official legal institutions like legislatures and courts, to exercise civic virtue—that is, an impartiality among private interests, with due concern for the public good or general welfare of society.[15] Not only is this view uncomfortably elitist, but it overlooks the intermediating function of law. The law is not just a way for the governing class to manage the activities of those subject to official authority. It is also a way of manifesting respect for the intelligence, rationality, agency, and self-originating value of others.[16] Individuals are entitled to make their own judgments about what conduces to the general well-being of society.

However, although it is a cliché, it is nevertheless the case that one Robinson Crusoe does not make up a society, and the role of political practices and institutions is to determine, from the point of view of society as a whole, what is in the public interest. I believe it is also generally accepted that the naïve version of formalism is not an apt description of the law, so lawyers cannot function like King Rex's law code nailed to the palace door, and simply transmit the law directly to

[13] TM Scanlon, *What We Owe to Each Other* (Harvard UP 1998) 268.

[14] Rebecca Roiphe, 'The Decline of Professionalism' (2016) 29 Geo J Legal Ethics 649, 652, 659–60.

[15] Robert W Gordon, 'The Independence of Lawyers' (1988) 68 BU L Rev 1, 14–15 (quoting Alexander Hamilton, *Federalist* No 35).

[16] Jeremy Waldron, 'The Concept and the Rule of Law' (2008) 43 Ga L Rev 1, 24–25.

clients. The regulation of the legal profession must therefore respond to conceptual beliefs about the law, which, in turn, are grounded in normative views about the role of the law in human societies. Something like Miller's sophisticated formalism is responsive to the needs and capacities of reasoning moral agents who desire to live alongside others in communities—as Hugo Grotius memorably put it, disputatious yet sociable creatures.[17] Understood correctly, law permits co-deliberation about what members of a political community owe to each other. That is why sophisticated formalism is appealing as a theory of law but simplistic formalism is not. What is needed is an approach to the legal and ethical regulation of lawyers that similarly responds to human interests and capacities.

One methodological question this raises, perhaps of interest only to participants in abstruse debates about the New Private Law, is whether the law governing lawyers is best understood as a branch of private or public law.[18] (A follow-up question would be why it matters.) The lawyer-client relationship is governed by some core private law doctrines. For example, a default rule is that an attorney-client relationship arises where the parties have expressly or impliedly consented to its formation—a principle of agency and contract law.[19] Lawyers have tort duties to use reasonable care in the representation of clients, contract duties to comply with agreed-upon obligations, and agency duties to follow the reasonable instructions of clients, keep them reasonably informed about the matter, refrain from disclosing or misusing confidential client information, and avoid conflicts of interest.[20] All of this fits comfortably within the category of private law. But what principles regulate what might be thought of as a tripartite relationship between the lawyer, the client, and the law? Lawyers are in an interesting position when they counsel their clients that the law permits or requires X, when they assert in a negotiation with another party that their client has a right to X, or when they structure a legal relationship with another party on the assumption that the law recognizes a liberty to X. Lawyers interpret and apply the law in the course of representing clients, which seems like a core public law function.[21]

[17] JB Schneewind, *The Invention of Autonomy: A History of Modern Moral Philosophy* 71–72 (CUP 1998)(citing Hugo Grotius's recognition of this fact about human nature as one of the distinctively modern insights in moral philosophy).

[18] Alice Woolley, 'The Lawyer as Fiduciary: Defining Private Law Duties in Public Law Relations' (2015) 65 U Toronto LJ 285.

[19] *Westinghouse Elec. Corp v Kerr-McGee Corp* 580 F.2d 1311 (7th Cir 1978).

[20] Restatement (Third) of the Law Governing Lawyers §§ 16, 18, 20–24, 59, 121, 132 (2000).

[21] In a previous paper I considered the sense in which a lawyer's duties could be aptly described as duties of loyalty, as that concept is understood in fiduciary law. W Bradley Wendel, 'Understanding the Complex Loyalty of Lawyers: Dual-Commission, Governance Mandate, and Intrinsic-Limit Analyses' in J Oberdiek and PB Miller (eds), *Oxford Studies in Private Law Theory* vol II (OUP 2022) 159. Here

Perhaps one contribution the New Private Law approach can make to the law of lawyering is in its pragmatic method. John Goldberg has offered the label 'brass-tacks pragmatism' to describe a hard-headed, practical-minded approach that eschews highly abstract conceptual reasoning in favour of solving practical problems.[22] Holmes and Llewellyn, for example, both wrote as if the task of judging was to cut through all the lawyerly BS and decide what should be done, either from the standpoint of the practical requirements of the exercise of official power (Holmes) or the policies that underlie all the potentially applicable precedents (Llewellyn). They, in turn, came in for criticism from Duncan Kennedy, who argued that appeals to judicial craft and 'situation sense' were merely makeweights for subjective policy judgments made by individual judges (which must be subjective because the law attempts to harmonize two ultimately irreconcilable worldviews). In what Goldberg nicely refers to as a mood of cheerful scepticism,[23] a brass-tacks pragmatist might be willing to jettison much of the conceptual apparatus of private law in order to accomplish a worthwhile end, such as a reduction in the social costs of accidents. Perhaps the generation of legal ethics scholars discussed in the next section, who are willing to junk much of the doctrinal apparatus of the law governing lawyers in order to accomplish the end of harmonizing private interests with the public good, can be viewed as brass-tacks pragmatists.

As Goldberg notes, however, brass-tacks pragmatism is not the only way to be pragmatic, and New Private Law scholars take a different approach. One reason for this, as he notes, is that legal philosophers have focused renewed attention on the problem of legal normativity.[24] Law must have the property of 'ought to be doneness' about it, or it fails at being law. This seems like an important insight to build into the regulation of the legal profession, which serves as the interface between ordinary citizens—the clients of lawyers—whose views about what ought to be done may be reducible to their own private interests, and the law which seeks to represent a normative position from the point of view of the political community as a whole. This is also one of the commitments Miller ascribes to sophisticated formalism. The question is what other concepts, sets of concepts, or larger doctrinal structures are essential to the law of lawyering (a concern for systematicity being another one of the

I will not be concerned directly with loyalty or fiduciary law, but with the relationship between the duties lawyers have, as a matter of law or professional ethics, and law more generally.

[22] John CP Goldberg, 'Introduction: Pragmatism and Private Law' (2012) 125 Harvard LR 1640.
[23] Goldberg (n 22) 1646–47.
[24] Goldberg (n 22) 1649.

characteristics of sophisticated formalism). The answer, I will contend, is that the law and ethical regulation governing the legal profession must be structured to support the first of the positions Miller associates with sophisticated formalism:

> A matter of acting, arguing, deliberating and deciding in good faith *according to law*, on the supposition that one's practical deliberations and behavior can evince compliance with *guidance supplied by law*, on the basis of practical reasons *derived from law*.[25]

The emphasized language here must be foundational to the regulation of lawyers. When people look to the law for guidance, they necessarily consult lawyers. The law can only fulfil its guidance function with the assistance of a specialized profession of law-interpreters and law-appliers. The lawyer-client relationship is part of private law insofar as clients retain lawyers, enter into contractual relationships with them, and are the principals in an agency relationship in which lawyers are obligated to follow the instructions of clients. But if law is to function in the way sophisticated formalists believe, it must also be possible to obligate lawyers to represent clients only according to law, pursuant to guidance supplied by law, and advise them on the basis of considerations derived from law.

Section II begins with a simple story to illustrate how law functions in the practical reasoning of members of a political community. Section III will then take up the question of what must be the case about the norms governing the legal profession in order that the law be capable of fulfilling this guidance function and serving as an authority with respect to the practical reasoning of its subjects.

II. Legal Obligation, the Internal Point of View, and Lawyers

A classic English case[26] involved two neighbouring properties—a doctor's house and a candy factory. The candy factory ran noisy machines during the day, but this never bothered the doctor, who went to work at his office in town. When the doctor added an examination room and started seeing patients at

[25] Miller (n 1) 9 (emphasis added).
[26] *Sturges v Bridgman* 11 Ch D 852 (CA 1879).

his house, however, he found the pounding and grinding of the machines to be an intolerable interference with his use of his property. In the actual case he filed a nuisance action against the candy factory, seeking an injunction to prevent the operation of the machines during the day. For our purposes here, however, let us start the story before any litigation was commenced. Suppose the doctor and the owner of the factory had a sit-down. The doctor explained that the noisy machines made it impossible to see patients at his house. The factory owner responded that the doctor had never complained before, that the factory was not out of character with the neighbourhood (it being a mixed-use commercial and residential district), that the doctor had the option to continue to use his office in town to see patients, and that the factory always ceased operations by 5:00 pm. Despite their best efforts at reaching an accommodation, the neighbours were unable to agree, so they each consulted a lawyer. The lawyers, being equally competent and well-informed, each informed their respective clients that under the law of nuisance, the candy factor's activity did not constitute a legal nuisance, and thus the doctor did not have a cause of action against the factory owner.[27] Being somewhat jurisprudentially inclined, the lawyers also noted that the candy factory has a legal *right* to operate its machines during the day which, according to Hohfeld, is correlated with a no-right on the part of the doctor to shut down the factor's operations.[28]

Here is the important part for the analysis that follows: Imagine that the doctor is still upset about the activities of the candy factory. He once again has a conversation with the owner to complain about the noise, to which the owner responds, 'I'm sorry for your inconvenience, but what we're doing is *lawful*, so I'm afraid you just have to deal with it, either by soundproofing your examination room or seeing patients in your office downtown.' What is the role of the law, and the assertion of a legal right, in the relationship between two neighbours—or any citizens of a political community—who disagree about what each owes to the other? According to Goldberg, New Private Law is an 'effort to recapture the normative dimensions of private interactions'.[29] A promising approach would therefore be to attempt to link the law with the existing landscape of norms—what we owe to each other simply in recognition of others as free and equal.

27 The opposite result from the actual case, but this version works better for the discussion to follow.

28 Wesley Newcomb Hohfeld, 'Fundamental Legal Conceptions as Applied in Judicial Reasoning' (1917) 26 Yale LJ 710, 723–24.

29 Goldberg (n 22) 1661.

As the Scanlonian allusion suggests, morality can be understood as mediating relationships of mutual recognition or reciprocal respect.[30] The idea of justifiability is basic to morality in this way of thinking about it. Someone whose actions affect another must offer reasons in justification, and these reasons are based on principles that no one may reasonably reject.[31] Brute domination is not a reason that others may not reasonably reject. If the factory owner said to the doctor, 'I'm bigger and stronger than you, and anyway I own a 12-gauge shotgun, so if you try to stop my factory from operating you'll be sorry', that would be a 'reason of the wrong kind',[32] because it is not addressed to the doctor as a moral agent, capable of understanding and responding to reasons. It is not a contribution to co-deliberation about what the parties owe to each other.

I am assuming, with Scanlon, that the characters in our story have reasons to want to act in ways they can justify to each other.[33] Rather than intimidating the doctor, the factory owner is seeking a principled justification that takes those who are similarly situated to the doctor into account. The permissibility of operating the factory during daytime hours must rest on considerations such as the distribution of benefits and burdens of various economic activities, the nature of the harm involved, the importance of the activities to the community as a whole, the actions of the parties in moving to this neighbourhood, the available alternatives (the doctor installing soundproof insulation, for example, or the factory owner shifting production to another location), and any prior agreements, promises, or undertakings between the parties.[34] The normative attractiveness of law is, therefore, related to its capacity to serve as an alternative to brute domination that takes into account the reasons that parties to a dispute would otherwise regard as relevant to what ought to be done under the circumstances.[35]

The invocation of the law by the factory owner is meant to be a reason that the doctor cannot reasonably reject. The norm's status as law plays a role in its not being reasonable rejectable by the doctor. Finishing our little

[30] TM Scanlon, *What We Owe to Each Other* (Harvard UP 1998); see also Stephen Darwall, *The Second-Person Standpoint* (Harvard UP 2006); R Jay Wallace, *The Moral Nexus* (Princeton UP 2019).

[31] Scanlon (n 30) 189.

[32] Darwall (n 30) 101.

[33] Scanlon (n 30) 154. Making this assumption means setting aside, at least for the time being, various challenges that have are part of the heritage of moral philosophy, such as what one would say to the amoralist, who demands a reason to act in ways that can be justified to others, or establishing a connection between moral and nonmoral considerations. ibid 148–51.

[34] ibid 202–10.

[35] Joseph Raz, 'The Problem of Authority: Revisiting the Service Conception' (2006) 90 Minn L Rev 1003, 1012–20.

story, the doctor is supposed to listen to the owner's assertion of a legal right and accept it as a justification for interfering with the 'quiet enjoyment' of his property. Why? Because *the law* permits the operation of the candy factory. For that to make sense as an explanation and justification of the factory owner's actions in terms the doctor cannot reasonably reject, we need to understand how the law in general is supposed to function as a reason for those it affects. This is where the concept of the IPOV comes in. The IPOV is the perspective 'of committed participants, persons who engage with, and participate in' a social practice; it is to treat the practice as giving them reasons for action.[36] It is also an aspect of the concept of law that it provide reasons to those who disagree about the merits of the underlying dispute, such as whether one's neighbour should be permitted to operate a candy factory during daytime hours.[37] Thus, members of a political community become committed participants in a social practice of giving legal norms as justifying reasons because they perceive that the law provides a means to treat others as free and equal.

It is central to Hart's positivism, of course, that one cannot have a *moral* reason for regarding laws as authoritative. It is essential to Hart's position, and to his critique of Austin, that the law be capable of giving rise to reasons for action that do not reduce to prudential considerations, such as the desire to avoid sanctions.[38] It cannot be the case, therefore, that one has a moral obligation to adopt the IPOV. Social practices, including the law understood along Hartian lines, have the authority they do from the point of view of committed participants.[39] So a route to the normativity of law might begin with the observation that we find ourselves thrown together in a group, inevitably interacting with others with whom we sometimes find ourselves in conflict. Then, when we play by 'group rules', we necessarily accept the authority of those rules. As Postema argues, something being convergent behaviour *in a group* is not separable from the attitude one takes toward it—the group is constituted in part by the convergent behaviour *and* the IPOV:

> [T]he fact that behavior is convergent in the group is not accidental or something added to the IPOV; it is convergent in part because those who take the IPOV on the rules see themselves *as members of the group* ... [T]he social dimension is internal to the distinctive normative attitude; indeed, it is not

36 Gerald J Postema, 'Jurisprudence as Practical Philosophy' (1998) 4 Legal Theory 329, 336.
37 Postema, 'Practical Philosophy' (n 36) 352.
38 See David Lyons, *Ethics and the Rule of Law* (CUP 1984) 70–71.
39 Postema, 'Practical Philosophy' (n 36) 335.

possible to grasp the behavior in the right way apart from its relation to the critical reflective attitude.[40]

But why would anyone have any particular critical reflective attitude toward group rules? Why not simply regard them from the Holmesian bad man point of view, as at best a nuisance to be evaded or planned around, and at worst something to be actively resisted? It is certainly conceivable that a relatively stable system of social ordering could exist as an alternative to, or alongside, or in competition with, a regime of formal law.[41] But experience tells us that people do offer justifications based on the positive of a state legal system, and they are accepted by those who are affected by the legally authorized actions of others. A radical Holmesian bad man stance is similar to the amoralist challenge in moral philosophy. It is possible to deny that the law has any reason-giving force, and maybe for those 'denialists', there is no alternative to backing legal norms with coercive force.[42] For most people, most of the time, however, the legal authorization of something, such as the conclusion of the common law of nuisance in our hypothetical case that the candy factory may operate during daylight hours, is accepted as a reason from the point of view of the affected person—here, the doctor. The doctor can see that the factory owner is not attempting to dominate him by brute force but to appeal to a rational process of reconciling the neighbours' competing demands into a type of jointly acceptable resolution of the dispute. Rather than worry about hardcore denialists, a more fruitful jurisprudential project would begin with the attitudes that are expressed when people rely on the law as a way of structuring and regulating relationships with other members of their community. This is one way to understand Goldberg's point above, about New Private Law seeking to recapture the normative dimension of private interactions.[43] Then the issue becomes, how should *lawyers* function within a system that has such as functional end?

The first observation that must be made about a jurisprudence that includes lawyers is that the norms governing lawyers, including positive law and norms regarded as part of the ethics of the profession, must be sensitive to the function that law is intended to serve within the political community. Imagine that one of the parties in our story has retained a lawyer who has taken to heart the civic republic idea that the role of lawyers is to maintain a studious impartiality

[40] Postema, *Legal Philosophy in the Twentieth Century* (n 4) 292–93.
[41] Robert C Ellickson, *Order Without Law: How Neighbors Settle Disputes* (Harvard UP 1994).
[42] Fredrick Schauer, *The Force of Law* (Harvard UP 2015).
[43] Goldberg (n 22) 1661.

among private interests, with the objective of harmonizing them within a coherent conception of the public interest or the common good. William Simon has argued that Louis D Brandeis, in his private practice career before his appointment to the US Supreme Court, exemplified features of the traditional conception of professional practice in his day.[44] These include attempting to dissuade powerful institutional clients from 'unjust or antisocial projects' and considering the interests of third parties with whom their clients were dealing. Brandeis was an example of a lawyer who saw his job as establishing 'frameworks of fair and mutually beneficial cooperation',[45] not merely pressing for the private advantages of his clients. Simon's valorization of Brandeis is not an idiosyncratic position within legal ethics scholarship. In the academy, the dominant theoretical view seems to be that a lawyer should serve as a 'wise counselor' who does not merely manipulate legal rules for the benefit of clients, but nudges powerful individuals and corporations in the direction of socially responsible behaviour.[46]

I have argued against the 'wise counselor' conception of legal ethics based on political considerations such as the duty of civility and the idea of public reason.[47] From the point of view of methodology, however, there is a different version of that argument that should concern not only legal ethics scholars but legal philosophers. To put it starkly, the concern is that professional ethicists may be telling lawyers to act in ways that muck up the operation of law, as law and the legal system are understood in jurisprudence. At the same time, however, there is no way to remove lawyers from jurisprudence because there is no straightforward way for the law to enable a social practice of guiding and evaluating conduct with respect to legal rules without a profession of legally trained agents of clients. Somehow the problem of legal normativity, to which the IPOV is offered as a solution, must make room for a profession of law-applying representatives of citizens. Methodologically, therefore, a feedback loop exists between ideas in general jurisprudence, such as formalism or the IPOV, the law and ethics governing lawyers, and back again to jurisprudence.

[44] William H Simon, *The Practice of Justice* (Harvard UP 1998) 128–29.

[45] ibid 131.

[46] Deborah L Rhode, *In the Interests of Justice* (OUP 2000); Anthony T Kronman, *The Lost Lawyer* (Yale UP 1993); Robert W Gordon, 'Why Lawyers Can't Just Be Hired Guns' in DL Rhode (ed), *Ethics in Practice: Lawyers' Roles, Responsibilities, and Regulation* (OUP 2000) 46; Geoffrey C Hazard, Jr, 'The Lawyer as Wise Counselor' (2003) 49 Loy L Rev 215; Russell G Pearce, 'Rediscovering the Republican Origins of the Legal Ethics Codes' (1992) 6 Geo J Legal Ethics 241; Thomas L Shaffer, 'The Legal Ethics of Radical Individualism' (1987) 65 Tex L Rev 963; Robert A Kagan and Robert Eli Rosen, 'On the Social Significance of Large Law Firm Practice' (1985) 37 Stan L Rev 339, 410.

[47] W Bradley Wendel, 'Pluralism, Polarization, and the Common Good: The Possibility of Modus Vivendi Legal Ethics' 131 Yale LJ Forum (24 October 2021).

Hart's concept of the IPOV, as elaborated by Zipursky and Postema, is a normative stance taken by citizens with respect to the law, although not necessarily one adopted for moral reasons.[48] Postema favours Zipursky's interpretation of the IPOV, emphasizing its social dimensions, over Shapiro's reading of Hart which sees as the IPOV as a matter of individuals internalizing legal norms:

> Those who take the IPOV use the rules in their deliberating, making claims and demands against each other, in evaluating their conduct or the conduct of others, criticizing others, vindicating or justifying themselves to them . . . the interior approach [Shapiro's reading] seriously risks effacing this social dimension.[49]

In either case, however, one important aspect of the IPOV is the engagement between citizens themselves and the law. All of this scholarship about the IPOV, however, appears to assume that it is possible for citizens to engage in an unmediated way with the law. Given the technical complexity of law, the esoteric language in which legal materials are sometimes presented, and the specialized interpretive techniques needed to make sense of legal materials, lawyers are indispensable to the process of using the law in deliberation, making claims and demands upon others, and evaluating, criticizing, vindicating, and justifying with reference to the law. There is a risk, however, that client engagement with the law might be distorted by the involvement of lawyers who see themselves as ethically obligated to advise clients based on their understanding of what the public interest requires. The lawyer representing the candy factory owner, for example, might advise the owner that the public's true interest is in maintaining the character of quiet, residential neighbourhoods without noisy machinery. While this could be one way of understanding the public interest, it also may be that economic development through the encouragement of industrial manufacturing could be in the best interests of the community. The point is that these questions are to be resolved by the legal *system*, not by individual lawyers who believe themselves to have a mandate to act directly in the public interest.

A jurisprudentially minded theorist of legal ethics and the law governing lawyers would therefore conclude that it must be possible to design a regime of regulation of the legal profession that would facilitate the social practice by members of a political community of 'deliberating, making claims and

[48] Postema, 'Practical Philosophy' (n 56) 332 fn 10.
[49] Postema, *Legal Philosophy in the Twentieth Century* (n 4) 295.

demands against each other, ... evaluating their conduct or the conduct of others, criticizing others, vindicating or justifying themselves to them' with reference to positive law enacted by legislatures, administrative agencies, and courts. This brings us back to Miller's sophisticated formalism, with its commitment to it being possible for members of a political community to act, argue, deliberate, and decide in good faith according to law.[50] My contention in the next section is that the law governing lawyers is already well designed to support this functional understanding of formalist law. Given the commitment of New Private Law to take seriously existing doctrinal structures, there are good grounds to reject many of the critiques levelled by legal ethics scholars against the existing law of lawyering.

III. Legal and Ethical Regulation of the Lawyer–Client Relationship

One of the most arresting claims in Daniel Markovits's *A Modern Legal Ethics* is that the law of lawyering requires lawyers to lie and cheat on behalf of their clients.[51] This interpretation of the law of lawyering depends on an idiosyncratic definition of lying and cheating: '[T]o deceive others by asserting a proposition that one privately (and correctly) disbelieves is to lie; and to exploit by promoting claims or causes that one privately (and correctly) thinks undeserving is to cheat.'[52] Assuming that (i) one accepts this way of understanding these concepts, (ii) one is persuaded that the law of lawyering in fact requires lying and cheating, and (iii) all are agreed that lying and cheating are vices, a brass-tacks pragmatist might conclude that radical revision of the law is required to eliminate these vices from our legal system.[53]

A New Private Law approach, on the other hand, would take into account some of Miller's characteristics of sophisticated formalism, including close attention to doctrine, the significance of formal legal-conceptual structures, and a concern with systematicity. It would seek to reveal the normative concepts

[50] Miller (n 1) 10.

[51] Daniel Markovits, *A Modern Legal Ethics: Adversary Advocacy in a Democratic Age* (Princeton UP 2008) 3–4, 13–17.

[52] ibid 34.

[53] I don't think Markovits would describe himself as a brass-tacks pragmatist, or a pragmatist of any sort, and in any event he has a very different critical and reconstructive project in mind. I have used his book as the foil for my argument here because, somewhat unusually for a theoretical legal ethics scholar, he spends quite a bit of energy, and devotes the first third of the book, on a constructive interpretation of the law of lawyering.

that are immanent within the doctrine by taking the doctrine seriously. I believe it is fair to characterize Markovits's approach in *A Modern Legal Ethics* as faithful to New Private Law methods, not only because in other work he has taken a similar approach,[54] but also because he claims in *AMLE* to be seeking the immanent rationality of the law governing lawyers. The normative core he finds is one that is profoundly threatening to the integrity of lawyers, who are then required to salvage some integrity-preserving description of their activities, as set out in Section II of his book. Agree with that conclusion or not, I believe it is a good example of the New Private Law approach in action.

How would one go about arguing that Markovits got it wrong? A first cut at the argument would be to present an alternative account of the doctrine, either denying that the law requires lawyers to lie and cheat, resisting Markovits's definition of those concepts, or de-emphasizing the occasional requirements of lying and cheating in the overall legal scheme—that is, to again invoke Miller's sophisticated formalism, leaning hard on coherence and systematicity to banish purported outlier rules. I have done something along those lines, although not explicitly aimed at Markovits's account, for a volume celebrating the 100th anniversary of the American Law Institute,[55] and I will briefly summarize my constructive interpretation of the doctrinal law of lawyering here. A deeper and more interesting critique, however, would attempt to link up with general jurisprudence. If it is impossible to conceive of the law, or at least a legal system, without lawyers then our understanding of the concept of law should feed into an inclusively pragmatic or pragmatically conceptualist understanding of the law governing lawyers.

First on the alternative view of underlying coherence of the American law governing lawyers. As I argued in the chapter on the ALI Restatement of the Law Governing Lawyers, the most concise encapsulation of the entire field is in Section 16(1) of the Restatement:

> To the extent consistent with the lawyer's other legal duties ... a lawyer must, within the scope of the representation ... proceed in a manner reasonably calculated to advance a client's lawful objectives, as defined by the client after consultation.

[54] Daniel Markovits, 'Sharing Ex Ante and Sharing Ex Post' in AS Gold and PB Miller (eds), *Philosophical Foundations of Fiduciary Law* (OUP 2014) 209; Daniel Markovits, 'Good Faith as Contract's Core Value' in G Klass, G Letsas, and P Saprai (eds), *Philosophical Foundations of Contract Law* (OUP 2014) 272.

[55] W Bradley Wendel, 'Constructing a Legal Field: The Restatement of the Law Governing Lawyers' in AS Gold and RW Gordon (eds), *The ALI at 100: Essays on Its Centennial* (OUP 2022) 237.

This section neatly captures the agency and fiduciary structure of the lawyer-client relationship, which recognizes a separation of decision-making authority, with client empowered to determine the objectives of the representation and lawyers having a duty,[56] grounded in tort and agency law, to proceed in a manner reasonably calculated to achieve those objectives. Importantly, it denies any sort of 'wise counselor' role for lawyers. The lawyer's duty is not to determine whether the client's objectives are consistent with the common good of the community, but to ensure that they are lawful. Although a rule of professional conduct expressly prohibits lawyers from counselling or assisting a client only in conduct that the lawyer knows to be criminal or fraudulent.[57] the Restatement provides, by negative implication from the duty to act in furtherance of a client's lawful objectives, that a lawyer must determine whether the law permits the client to do something, even if it would not be a crime or fraud to do so. As the Reporter to the Restatement project explained, lawyers had come to see themselves not as 'law guardians' but instead as 'client guardians'.[58] Lawyers may have understood their role in that way, but the Restatement sought to incorporate a role for lawyers as law guardians, with emphasis on the (positive) law, not the public interest. Lawyers remain 'client guardians', which is to say agents with fiduciary duties of loyalty and care, to the extent that their representation is oriented around the promotion of the lawful objectives of the client, as defined by the client after consultation.

It may be that my interpretation of the law of lawyering differs from Markovits's because I am more interested in how lawyers counsel clients on compliance with the law and use the law in negotiations and transactional planning with others, while Markovits focuses on adversarial litigation. Even in the litigation context, however, the law does not decisively favour the client guardian role over duties as law guardians. As we were unfortunately reminded after the 2020 presidential election, some lawyers take their role as client guardian to extremes, filing lawsuits without a sufficient factual and legal foundation.[59] One happy side effect of this litigation, however, was a highly visible public reminder that lawyers have a duty not to file frivolous lawsuits,

[56] Deborah DeMott, 'The Fiduciary Character of Agency and the Interpretation of Instructions' in AS Gold and PB Miller (eds), *Philosophical Foundations of Fiduciary Law* (OUP 2014) 321.

[57] ABA Model Rules of Professional Conduct, r 1.2(d).

[58] Charles W Wolfram, 'Toward a History of the Legalization of American Legal Ethics – II: The Modern Era' (2002) 15 Geo J Legal Ethics 205, 208.

[59] *Wood v Raffensperger*, 981 F.3d 1307 (11th Cir 2020); *Donald J Trump for President v Secretary for Pennsylvania*, 830 Fed. Appx. 377 (3d Cir. 2020); *Wisconsin Voters Alliance v Pence*, 514 F.Supp.3d 117 (D.D.C. 2021); *Gohmert v Pence*, 510 F.Supp.3d 435 (E.D. Tex. 2021); *Bowyer v Ducey*, 506 F.Supp.3d 699 (D. Ariz. 2020).

delivered in the form of sanctions orders issued by the courts supervising this litigation.[60] Both the lawyer disciplinary rules and rules of civil procedure prohibit the bringing of meritless claims and the assertion of groundless contentions.[61] To the extent cheating consists of misusing the legal process to gain a private advantage not supportable by the client's legal entitlements, the election litigation shows that there are at least some limits. As for lying, courts take an extremely dim view of lawyers knowingly making false statements of fact or knowingly introducing false testimony or documentary evidence into the record of a litigated proceeding.[62]

Court supervision of litigation tends to deter the most egregious Holmesian bad man conduct from lawyers,[63] except perhaps for those like Sidney Powell, Lin Wood, and Rudy Giuliani who are so ideologically committed (or merely crazy) that they do not respond rationally to incentives. But notice the jurisprudential difficulty that would arise if lawyers did not have a duty to represent clients within the law, or with respect to the legal entitlements of clients. The existence of lawyers as agents would have the ironic effect of severing, not maintaining, the connection between citizens and the law. A client who retained a lawyer would instruct the lawyer that their interests were X—let's say, to run their candy factory for 18 hours a day. Deborah DeMott has argued that the most basic obligation characteristic of a fiduciary relationship is for the agent to follow the instructions of the principal.[64] Now imagine the lawyer is the worst kind of Holmesian bad man, willing to engage in scorched-earth litigation tactics, delay and obstruction, and other tactics designed to run up the neighbour's litigation costs in order to force him to settle the lawsuit on unfavourable terms. (Assume that none of these acts constitutes a crime or fraud and further, that courts in the jurisdiction are overworked and disinclined to impose sanctions on lawyers who engage in these sorts of shenanigans.) Practically speaking, of course, the result is that the factory owner would get its way, even though on the facts and applicable law the factory's operation would be deemed a nuisance. Theoretically speaking, what is interesting here is the way the interposition of a lawyer with this attitude toward the law tends to alienate the factory owner from any non-instrumental understanding of law as

[60] *King v Whitmer*, 556 F.Supp.3d 680 (E.D. Mich. 2021).
[61] Model Rule 3.1; Fed. R. Civ. P. 11.
[62] *US v Shaffer Equip. Co.*, 11 F.3d 450 (4th Cir. 1993).
[63] The image of the bad man comes from the argument by Holmes that a sufficient theoretical account of law could proceed from the point of view of a hypothetical 'bad man' who was concerned only to avoid legal sanctions. Oliver Wendell Holmes Jr, 'The Path of the Law' (1897) 10 Harvard LR 457, 459–62.
[64] DeMott (n 56).

a system of norms established in the name of the political community.[65] A social practice of evaluating, claiming, justifying, and making demands on each other with reference to the community's law would be impossible to sustain if lawyers simply acted on the basis of their clients' interests.

But this type of social practice would also be impossible without lawyers to operationalize it. Suppose the protagonists in our story, the doctor and the factory owner, were interested in resolving their disagreement with reference to norms that are general, impartial, capable of principled application, and therefore are a fair basis for coming to an agreement. In other words, they are looking to the law for guidance. But look at what we are assuming about the law. In his recent article on formalism and private law, Miller describes the features of law that enable it to perform its guidance function and affect the practical reasoning of citizens:

> (a) personal, official, and wider social deliberative practices and behavior evincing advertent or knowing conformity with private law norms (whether or not based on compliance; that is, reasoned endorsement of the practical reasons that the law provides); (b) personal, official, and wider social deliberative practices and behavior evincing advertent conformity with enabling doctrines, including validity conditions governing the acquisition, exercise and alienation of privileges; and (c) judicial enforcement of norms and upholding of validity conditions and other features of enabling doctrines.[66]

Understood this way, it seems extremely unlikely that the law would be perspicuous from the point of view of even a reasonable, well-disposed member of the community lacking extensive specialized training. When, then, are lawyers from the point of view of legal theory? Deborah DeMott, the Reporter for the Restatement of Agency, concedes that lawyers are not agents of the usual sort because the client-lawyer relationship is not simply about the agent following the instructions of the principal.[67] Rather, there is an additional dimension, which DeMott refers to as arising from 'duties the lawyer owe the court, as well as the court's inherent sanctioning powers [which are] grounded in the nature of judicial institutions'.[68] That aspect of the lawyer-client relationship, she says, is beyond the explanatory framework of the law and theory of agency. As it

[65] Robert W Gordon, 'Law as a Vocation: Holmes and the Lawyer's Path' in SJ Burton (ed), *The Path of the Law and Its Influence* (CUP 2000) 7, 13; see also Waldron (n 15) 20, 24, 31.

[66] Miller (n 1) 206.

[67] Deborah A DeMott, 'The Lawyer as Agent' (1998) 67 Fordham L Rev 301.

[68] ibid 306.

happens, that is what I regard as the interesting dimension of the law of lawyering and the feature of the lawyer-client relationship that has an important methodological connection with general jurisprudence.

As legal theorists, we understand Miller's reference to 'wider social deliberative practices and behaviour evincing advertent conformity with enabling doctrines'. A more concise term for that would be 'the stuff we learned in law school'. I don't mean to be glib. In order to advertently conform to the doctrine of, say, nuisance law, one must grasp the social, interpretive, and rhetorical practices through which lawyers determine whether A's use of land constitutes an interference with B's quiet enjoyment of land. This passage from a nineteenth century American case is a pretty good summary of the difficulty in generalizing about nuisance cases or reducing the doctrine to simple rules:

> No rule can be framed which will accurately define what acts or facts will constitute a nuisance in every possible contingency. Each case must be decided on its own peculiar facts. There can be no doubt that a lawful business, which is not inherently a nuisance on account of its offensive character, may be so conducted as to render it a nuisance which equity will restrain. The maxim sic *utere tuo ut alienum non lædas*, undoubtedly expresses the general fundamental rule, but it is also true that the law does not regard every trifling injury or annoyance as an actionable nuisance. Things merely disagreeable, which simply displease the eye, or offend the taste, or shock an over-sensitive or fastidious nature, no matter how irritating or unpleasant, are not nuisances. No man is under a legal duty to consult the taste or preferences of his neighbor in the use of his property, but he is bound to respect his neighbor's legal rights. He cannot fill his neighbor's house with smoke, nor the air, which his neighbor has a right to breath pure and unpolluted, with nauseous or deleterious odors, nor can he throw soot or cinders into his neighbor's house or door-yard to such an extent as to deprive him of the free and full enjoyment of his property.[69]

An implication of the conjunction of legal formalism and the IPOV is that the non-lawyers in our case, the factory owner and the doctor, somehow have to engage in a social practice of treating the reasons given by law—because they stand in for the view of the political community as a whole about what ought to be done in cases like this—as reasons for themselves.

[69] *Demarest v Hardham*, 34 NJ Eq 469 (NJ Ct Ch 1881).

Now it should be clear why I regard the lawyer's duty to 'proceed in a manner reasonably calculated to advance a client's *lawful* objectives, as defined by the client after consultation'[70] as the pivotal section of the Restatement of the Law Governing Lawyers. It underscores the importance of autonomy in the lawyer-client relationship, with the client having the right to define the objectives of the representation, after consultation with the lawyer. It also reinforces the intersection of tort and agency law in the duty to proceed in a manner reasonably calculated to advance the client's objectives. These are both core private law duties. But notice the italicized word 'lawful'. This suggests that the lawyer's role may require, at least in some cases, interpretation of the law in light of the client's situation. Interpretation of the law would not be required on a silly formalist understanding of law, where in principle it could be nailed by King Rex to the palace door. On any sensible, sophisticated version of formalism, however, it is unrealistic to expect non-legally-trained citizens to contend with the systematicity, historicity, modularity, and the complexity of the social sources of law. One of the themes of Susan Koniak's work, for example, is the relationship between law and narrative, and in this article, she reminds readers that 'the meaning of a legal rule in a particular situation almost always demands a conscious act of interpretation, the creation of a story about the rule. Stories connect legal rules to facts, and in the process give meaning to both the law and the facts'.[71] If she is right that lawyers do more than just read rules, but also 'must use the stories embodied in court opinions, legislative debates, and executive agency pronouncements to assess their client's proposed or past conduct',[72] then it seems very difficult to imagine non-legally-trained citizens engaging with the complex social practice of elaborating the meaning of legal rules through complex narratives woven through cases, statutes, and regulations. This practice of interpretation and story-creation almost by definition will be committed to a specialist occupational group.

As for the regulation of that specialized occupational group, otherwise known as lawyers, it is an adequacy condition of either the law or the internal norms (which lawyers refer to as 'ethics rules') governing the profession that these norms require lawyers to facilitate their clients' engagement with the social practice of guiding conduct by rules, doctrines, and interpretive stances that reflect the position of the political community regarding a particular situation. This condition, grounded in general methodological considerations, has

[70] Restatement (n 20) § 16(1) (emphasis added).

[71] Susan P Koniak and George M Cohen, 'In Hell There Will Be Lawyers Without Clients or Law' (2001) 30 Hofstra L Rev 129, 134.

[72] ibid 134–35.

significant normative implications, bearing on how we think about issues such as the following:

1. Commonplace game-playing by lawyers that is difficult to detect and deter, but can seriously interfere with the capacity of the legal system to resolve disputes on the legal and factual merits. Discovery abuse, depressingly familiar to all litigators, is an example,[73] as is 'woodshedding' or coaching witnesses to tell a story that happens to align with elements of a claim or defence.[74] Lawyers often defend these tactics by arguing that they are within the rules. Sometimes that is not true and they have crossed the line into conduct prohibited by the rules. In other instances, however, the conduct may be within the rules but would tend to interfere with a social practice of using law for guidance.
2. The 'wise counselor' conception of the lawyer's role that contemplates that lawyers may, or should, interpose their own views about the wisdom of their clients' proposed course of action or steer their clients into what the lawyers personally believe to be socially beneficial actions. There is nothing at all impermissible about offering advice to clients based on the lawyer's own views about the 'moral, economic, social and political factors' implicated by the client's situation.[75] However, it is extremely important—and admitted a difficult job—for the lawyer to keep these views separate from a good faith interpretation of what the law permits or requires in the situation.
3. Drafting, transactional structuring techniques, the use of overseas shell corporations, and other means that undermine the capacity of law to serve as a framework for guidance. This is the most controversial proposal, I think, and the most difficult to nail down. I have written for most of my career about episodes like the role of lawyers in transactions that brought down Enron Corporation, the design and marketing of bogus tax shelters, the internal Justice Department memos used to justify torture during the Bush Administration, and the activities of law firms revealed in the Panama Papers leak.[76]

[73] For a well-known example of discovery abuse that was actually uncovered and litigated fully, see *Haeger v Goodyear Tire and Rubber Co.*, 906 F. Supp. 2d 938 (D. Ariz. 2012), aff'd as amended on denial of rehearing en banc, 813 F.3d 1233 (9th Cir. 2016), rev'd, 137 S.Ct. 1178 (2017).

[74] See, eg, William W Hodes, 'The Professional Duty to Horseshed Witnesses–Zealously, Within the Bounds of Law' (1999) 30 Texas Tech L Rev 1343.

[75] ABA Model Rules of Prof'l Conduct, r 2.1.

[76] W Bradley Wendel, 'The Rule of Law and Legal-Process Reasons in Attorney Advising' (2019) 99 BU L Rev 107; W Bradley Wendel, 'The Craft of Legal Interpretation' in M Yasutomo, M Stolleis, and J-L Halpdrin (eds), *Interpretation of Law in the Age of Enlightenment: From the Rule of the King to the Rule of Law* (Springer 2011) 153; W Bradley Wendel, 'Executive Branch Lawyers in a Time of Terror' (2008)

All of these problems are difficult in practice, involving problems of definition, line-drawing, administrability, and enforcement. However, as I have argued here, in methodological terms the connection between legal normativity and interpretation is central to understanding the regulation of lawyers.

IV. Conclusion: Private, Public, or Quasi-Public?

One who is inclined to see law interpretation and application as a quintessential function of judges, perhaps also administrative agencies, but certainly public officials, might wonder whether the law governing lawyers must necessarily have one foot in public law while it has one foot in the private law duties arising out of contract, agency, and tort law. I have long advocated for what might be called at least a quasi-public approach to regulating the conduct of lawyers, both by positive law and by ethical norms that are internal to professional practice. This description has always seemed right to me:

> The less compromising forms of free market liberalism must rely on the civic virtue of at least some actors in the system, such as those who administer the sanctions ... [E]ven private lawyers committed to unswerving loyalty to client interests still must assume a quasi-public responsibility for honest observance of the basic rules and procedures of the framework, even in the face of the many opportunities they have to ignore the rules with impunity.[77]

Notice, however, that the quasi-public responsibility placed on lawyers is to maintain the rules and procedures of the framework. The lawyer's most basic obligation is still to follow the instructions of the client and to further the client's lawful objectives, as defined by the client after consultation. The lawyer-client relationship is not structured by a governance mandate, which would give the lawyer the authority to pursue some general end, such as the common good of the community.[78] Rather, the rules and procedures of the framework function as internal limits on the duties owed by the lawyer to the client.[79] I am

31 Dalhousie LJ 247 (2008); W Bradley Wendel, 'Professionalism as Interpretation' (2005) 99 Nw U L Rev 1169.

[77] Robert W Gordon and William H Simon, 'The Redemption of Professionalism?' in RL Nelson and others (eds), *Lawyers' Ideals/Lawyers' Practices: Transformations in the American Legal Profession* (Cornell UP 1992) 230, 235.

[78] Paul B Miller and Andrew S Gold, 'Fiduciary Governance' (2015) 57 Wm & Mary L Rev 513.

[79] Andrew S Gold, 'The Internal Limits on Fiduciary Loyalty' (2020) 65 Am J Jurisprudence 65.

not persuaded that the public vs private distinction matters all that much when the question is what norms should govern the lawyer's professional role, but to the extent it does make a difference, there is a way to see the law governing lawyers as firmly rooted within private law.

What matters more than the public/private distinction is that there be some methodological connection between general jurisprudential accounts of the concept of law and our understanding of the role of the legal profession and its guidance norms. I favour a functionalist approach, emphasizing the law's capacity to enable co-deliberation among members of a political community. Adopting the IPOV, by participating in a social practice of guiding behaviour by law, is a way of respecting other members of the community and treating them as free and equal. The factory owner's invocation of nuisance rules is different in an important sense from forcing the doctor to acquiesce. I hope this pattern of argument can provide a theorist of legal ethics with resources to use when evaluating conduct rules for lawyers. But I also hope that the presence of lawyers in Rex's kingdom provides resources to scholars of general jurisprudence. An understanding of the function performed by lawyers can feed back into an account of law suggesting, for example, what features of sophisticated formalism may be instantiated in a political community in a way that provides guidance for law's subjects. If nothing else, I hope that general jurisprudence makes more room for lawyers alongside all the talk about law. It takes more than a piece of paper nailed to the palace door to make a functional legal system.

III

EMPIRICAL, PHILOSOPHICAL, AND NORMATIVE APPROACHES TO PRIVATE LAW THEORY

12

The Place of Philosophy in Private Law Scholarship

John C.P. Goldberg and Benjamin C. Zipursky[1]

I. Introduction

Why is so much private law scholarship in the United States *philosophical*? While it seems apparent that doctrinal and policy analysis are important to understanding and reforming private law, the relevance of philosophical analysis is perhaps less obvious. And, while hardly the norm, one can occasionally find in the law journals evidence supporting Chief Justice Roberts' sarcastic quip that contemporary legal scholarship is useless for the bench and bar because it is filled with obscure articles about Kant.[2]

We start, in Section I, by addressing two questions. The first, more general question asks why so much private law scholarship in the United States over the past fifty years has been *theoretical*? The second narrows the inquiry by considering why a significant slice of this theoretical writing has involved philosophizing. Answering the second question leads us to distinguish different motivations that appear to have encouraged philosophical analysis of private law. Sometimes, it has been invoked to critique the utilitarian or welfarist instincts that tend to dominate the elite American legal academy and to develop alternatives that focus on rights, duties, fairness, and justice. Other times, philosophy is harnessed to fend off the sort of aggressively reductionistic thinking by lawyers, judges, and academics (welfarist or deontological) that has long been associated with American Legal Realism. Like the efforts of philosophers to challenge non-cognitivism in ethics and logical positivism

[1] Thanks to Martin Gelter, Paul Miller, and conference participants for very helpful feedback.

[2] Chief Justice of the United States John G Roberts, Jr, Interview at Fourth Circuit Court of Appeals Annual Conference, available at http://www.cspanvideo.org/program/FourthCi (see at approx. 30:30 (on 25 June 2011): 'Pick up a copy of any law review that you see and the first article is likely to be, you know, the influence of Immanuel Kant on evidentiary approaches in 18th-century Bulgaria, or something, which I'm sure was of great interest to the academic that wrote it, but isn't of much help to the bar.').

John C.P. Goldberg and Benjamin C. Zipursky, *The Place of Philosophy in Private Law Scholarship* In: *Methodology in Private Law Theory*. Edited by: Thilo Kuntz and Paul B. Miller, Oxford University Press.
 DOI: 10.1093/oso/9780198885306.003.0012

in metaphysics, the aim here is to defend the ordinary against attacks from the scepticism of those who claim to be sophisticates. In private law, philosophical anti-reductionism involves defending the intelligibility and integrity of common-sense lawyerly knowledge of and about the law.[3]

Section II offers two examples drawn from torts scholarship that are illustrative of the main points of Section I. The first is Gregory Keating's work on the proper criteria for evaluating what level of precaution certain parts of tort law should set for persons or firms engaged in profitable activity that risks physical harm to others. The second is John Finnis's analysis of the concept of intent in intentional torts such as assault and battery. Keating's work has at its main target economic interpretations of tort law, and, in that respect, it exemplifies the first category of philosophical argument mentioned in the preceding paragraph. Finnis's work better exemplifies the second: it is addressed to any jurists inclined to reduce the core legal concept of 'intent' to other ideas.

In Section III, we take a different tack, using recent legal analysis of the law of private nuisance not to describe or display philosophical thinking about law in action but rather to demonstrate some of the value that has come from modern efforts to philosophize about law. In the mid-twentieth century, Realist-inspired scholars had—through a reductive, sceptical approach—so vigorously attacked the cogency of the concept of a nuisance that they have largely shorn it of content. Today, by contrast, there is a healthy body of work demonstrating that nuisance law is not best understood as an empty vessel that can be filled with whatever content will achieve a desired policy goal. In some commonwealth jurisdictions, particularly the United Kingdom and Canada, where law-sceptical jurisprudence has had less of a dramatic impact on legal scholarship, work of this sort, which is at once doctrinal and analytic, tends to come naturally. In the United States, however, philosophizing about private law has played an important role in making the legal academy 'safe' for this sort of analysis.

As the preceding description of this chapter already indicates, we are interested in explaining certain features of the scholarship produced by law professors based in the United States. We do so mainly because that is the scholarly world with which we are most familiar. While academic culture, values, and practices surely differ among nations, there is also a long and happy tradition—one to which this conference belongs—of legal scholarship across national

[3] The distinction drawn here between philosophical analysis in the service of deontological legal analysis and philosophical analysis as a response to law scepticism does *not* track neatly onto other, more familiar distinctions, such as the distinction between descriptive or interpretive theory, on the one hand, and prescriptive or normative theory, on the other.

boundaries. We thus expect that some of what we say about legal scholarship in the United States will apply to scholarship in other jurisdictions, while some will not.[4]

II. Philosophical Analysis as a Kind of Theorizing

1. Theory

Theorizing about private law—a category that includes but is not limited to philosophical analysis of the law—has been a particularly popular pastime among law professors in the United States. Why? Part of the explanation is that private law in the United States is, at its core, common law. And common-law reasoning involves abstracting from a set of decisions to rules or principles that can guide persons and other courts. At times, scholars have relied on theory to isolate a unifying commitment running through an entire field of common law or even through common law as a whole. Richard Posner's torts scholarship fits this description: it purports to find across all of tort law a commitment to efficient deterrence. At a meta-level, Ronald Dworkin famously argued that common-law reasoning, done right, requires judges to identify principles in case law and use those principles to organize the law in a manner that will make it the best it can be, morally.[5]

Another reason for the prevalence of theory in US Private Law scholarship has to do with private law being state law. The rules of contract, property, restitution, and tort are determined by the courts and legislatures of fifty different states and the District of Columbia. They thus vary, sometimes significantly. Yet law professors tend to regard themselves as training students to practice law anywhere in the nation and as writing for a national audience. Those who aim to teach and write about predominantly state law as if it were national law need a way of analysing law that bridges variations among jurisdictions.

[4] Indeed, one of the two scholars whose work we use to exemplify trends in US legal scholarship—John Finnis—is English. However, he has often written with a US audience in mind, and for more than twenty-five years has been a member of the faculty of the law school at the University of Notre Dame in Indiana. Some of the most influential modern philosophical scholarship on private law has been published by Canadian legal scholars, including Peter Benson, Arthur Ripstein, Steve Smith, and Ernest Weinrib. In some instances, their work reflects influences that have also been at work in the United States. Weinrib, for example, quite clearly developed his 'formalist' approach to private law in reaction both to economic and critical accounts. In others, it reflects influences that appear to have played a less significant role in the United States. For example, although the work of Kant and Hegel has figured in American private law scholarship, it has not played anything like the central role that it plays in the work of scholars such as Ripstein and Benson (respectively).

[5] Ronald Dworkin, *Law's Empire* (HUP 1986) 239–54.

Because identifying such commonalities often requires abstracting away from specific rules or decisions, theory can help identify them.

A third factor relates to the previous one but is worthy of separate treatment. It comes with a case name attached to it: *Erie Railroad v Tompkins,* decided by the US Supreme Court in 1938.[6] Some background is required to understand this point.

In part to promote impartial resolution of disputes with an interstate dimension, US federal courts have jurisdiction over civil suits between citizens of different states. For example, if a New York resident is injured by the negligent driving of a Florida resident, she can bring her negligence suit against the driver in federal rather than state court. In the nineteenth century, federal judges hoped that federal courts could use this 'diversity jurisdiction' to promote greater uniformity across state common law. The most notable decision in this regard was *Swift v Tyson*, decided by the US Supreme Court in 1842.[7]

Tyson had purchased land in New York State from two sellers by means of a bill of exchange. The sellers, who were indebted to Swift, endorsed the bill over to Swift. However, when Swift presented the bill to Tyson for payment, Tyson refused. Swift then sued Tyson in federal court. In defence, Tyson argued that, under New York common law, he had no obligation to pay Swift because there was a defect in the original transaction between him and the sellers. (Specifically, Tyson claimed that the sellers had defrauded him.) Justice Joseph Story, writing for the Court, acknowledged that Tyson's defence might be valid under the rules of New York common law. Story nonetheless insisted that the federal courts were not bound to follow state law and could instead apply 'general principles' of commercial law. According to these principles, he reasoned, any defects in the transaction between Tyson and the sellers did not affect Swift's entitlement to collect from Tyson, given that Swift had no notice of them.

Justice Story's articulation of the idea of general law was premised on two suppositions: that there was already a fair measure of consistency across states' commercial law and that the federal courts could promote still greater consistency by settling on a rule in those instances where there was divergence among the states (and perhaps also in cases in which some state courts happen to have settled on a perverse rule). His expectation was that the exercise by the federal courts of this power to make general law would promote the development of nationally uniform law for commercial transactions and in other

[6] 304 US 64 (1938).
[7] 41 US 1 (1842).

areas where national consistency was desirable. In particular, it allowed for the possibility that important questions of common law would, sooner or later, receive a single, authoritative answer in the decisions of the Supreme Court of the United States, though for the answer to become truly authoritative, state courts would have to accept in their own decisions the Supreme Court's rendering of the general law.

For various reasons, Story's aspiration was never realized: the efforts of federal judges to guide the state courts toward the development of uniform national common law failed. In turn, the divergences between the substance of the general-law rules that federal courts applied in diversity cases and the rules of state common law that state courts applied gave rise to unseemly forum shopping. Thus, roughly a century after it was launched, the general-law experiment was terminated: *Erie* overruled *Swift* and announced that, henceforth, in diversity cases, federal courts would apply state substantive law rather than attempting to fashion a general law. This is why, today, a federal court entertaining a negligence suit brought by a New York resident against a Florida resident will typically apply the tort law of New York or Florida (depending on certain facts, such as where the accident occurred). In announcing the death of *Swift*'s idea of general law, *Erie* made clear that lawyers and scholars in the United States would be denied the benefits of working within a system in which a single apex court is available to settle disputes about the content of private law. The absence of a Supreme Court for private law, in turn, has created a positive-law vacuum that scholars have sometimes attempted to fill with theory.[8] One could argue, for example, that the rise to dominance of economic accounts of contract law is in part explicable as an effort to bring about by other means the uniform commercial law that Story had sought.

A fourth relevant consideration is more sociological than legal and thus relies on our impressions of academic culture. Law in the United States is taught to college graduates and has long been considered training in a profession comparable in some ways to medical training. In the early part of the twentieth century, legal scholarship reflected this orientation and was heavily historical and doctrinal. The Legal Realists' assault on doctrine, however, left many law professors and law faculties, particularly those affiliated with research universities, feeling defensive about whether they could claim to have distinctive

[8] However, as we have noted elsewhere, the US Supreme Court has not been ruthlessly consistent in adhering to *Erie*. For example, under the aegis of interpreting the free-speech guarantee of the federal constitution's First Amendment, it has fashioned an elaborate federal common law of defamation that has partially supplanted state libel and slander law. John CP Goldberg and Benjamin C Zipursky, 'The Supreme Court's Stealth Return to the Common Law of Torts' (2016) 65 DePaul L Rev 432.

expertise or whether law is anything more than a technical, shallow field of study. Among the responses adopted by legal scholars to this state of affairs was embracing the methods of other disciplines, including those of history, political science, economics, and philosophy.

Finally—and also by way of impressionistic sociological remarks—the culture of the American legal academy reflects a particular understanding of the role of judges within our political system: one that has implications for legal scholarship. Starting with *Brown v Board of Education*,[9] the US Supreme Court has taken centre stage in various areas of American politics. Ever since (and even before), law professors in the United States have been captivated by the idea that our courts have a distinctively robust role to play in setting the rules for our polity. Not coincidently, they have been further captivated by the image of themselves as experts who can advise the judiciary on how to go about this important work. Because this conception of the judicial role is expansive and aspirational, it is unsurprising that legal scholarship—starting with constitutional-law scholarship but then expanding outward to other areas—has become increasingly theoretical. In short, the 'theoretical turn' in American Private Law scholarship has partly been a matter of Private Law scholars keeping up with their constitutional law colleagues. This also helps to explain the timing of that turn, which seems to have occurred around 1970.

2. Kinds of Philosophical Theorizing Within Private Law Theory

We have thus far spoken of 'theory'. As we use that term, it covers many different forms of scholarship, of which philosophical analysis is but one example. Others include economic, psychological, sociological, and critical theories. And indeed, each of these other forms of theory, particularly economic but also critical theories, have featured prominently in Private Law scholarship in the United States. It is thus incumbent on us to push further. Even if we have offered the beginnings of an explanation of why theory has been central to academic, Private Law discourse in the United States since roughly 1970, we have not yet explained why it so often has taken the form of *philosophical* analysis.

The first and most obvious explanation is that philosophical theory in private law emerged partly in reaction to the academic dominance of economic theories of private law in the 1970s and 80s. One could say that early

[9] 347 US 483 (1954).

law-and-economics scholars such as Richard Posner and Guido Calabresi were themselves engaged in a kind of philosophical analysis—one that descended from the utilitarianism developed by Bentham and others. However, even if their work was, in a sense, philosophical, it created a framework for further scholarship that involves the application of economic expertise, not legal or philosophical expertise. As economic analysis increasingly gained cache as the preferred way to bring rigour and order to common law, some Private Law scholars deployed philosophical analysis to critique economic interpretations of doctrine.

There is another answer to the 'why philosophical analysis?' question, and it goes somewhat against the grain of the point we have just made. A good deal of philosophical work in private law has not been a response to economic or critical theory, but instead to a body of dogmatically anti-theoretical scholarship that flourished in the United States in the first half of the twentieth century and is still well-represented in the legal academy today, even though it is not the sort of scholarship most valued by elite law faculties.

One way to grasp the role of anti-theoretical scholarship in the development of Private Law scholarship is to appreciate that Posner and Calabresi were themselves reacting to it. Among their main claims on behalf of economic analysis is that it promised to introduce rigour to the 'soft', unscientific versions of utilitarianism that characterized the work of scholars in the generation that proceeded theirs. Already in the 1940s and 50s, many scholars—the eminent torts scholar William Prosser is an excellent example—had openly embraced an instrumentalist approach to law. According to this approach, the job of high-court judges and scholars is to figure out whether or how legal rules can help achieve some desirable social objective. Yet, unlike the economic instrumentalists who followed them, scholars such as Prosser were deeply suspicious of theory, favouring instead lawyerly judgment about which rules will best serve which ends. In other words, they took to heart Oliver Wendell Holmes's admonition that progress in thinking about private law required lawyers, judges, and scholars to refuse to take its moral concepts (right, duty, etc) at face value and instead to think about law instrumentally, as a means to some social end. At the same time, they had faith that lawyers, judges, and scholars could 'muddle through' on the basis of their experience and judgment.

The philosophical reaction to mid-century anti-theoretical instrumentalism has overlapped with but also extended beyond the philosophical reaction to economic analyses of the law. It has *not* primarily or exclusively aimed to identify deontic content in the law that economists cannot explain or justify. Instead, it is an effort to push back against impatience with familiar legal concepts that tend to have counterparts in ordinary English discourse ('right', 'duty', 'cause', 'intent', 'reasonableness', 'thing', 'possession', and the like). In other words, some legal scholars embraced philosophical analysis primarily to salvage features of the law that supposedly sophisticated jurists had diagnosed as empty and unhelpful—to give a careful account of why it is a reductionist mistake to infer from ambiguities and difficulties in applying these concepts that lawyers will do best not to use them, or to treat them as empty vessels .

III. Examples of Philosophical Work in Tort Law

1. Keating on Justified Precautions

Gregory Keating's article 'Pressing Precaution Beyond the Point of Cost-Justification',[10] nicely illustrates the anti-economic, normative version of philosophizing about private law. He begins by noting that, according to the theory of negligence law developed by law-and-economics scholars, the 'due care' standard at the centre of the negligence tort is and ought to be given content by reference to cost-benefit analysis. In particular, assuming that negligence law's standards of conduct principally address which precautions against harm ought to be taken, economic scholars maintain that the expected costs of taking the precaution ought to be weighed against the aggregate expected savings of taking the precaution (treating injury, damages, pain, and other displacements as costs), and the precaution should be taken only when it costs less than the accident costs its adoption can be expected to avert. Keating argues that considerations of urgency and fairness demand that the law ought, in many instances, to require a higher level of precaution than a cost-benefit analysis would yield.

As he acknowledges, Keating's work on this and other topics reflects the influence of the political-philosophical writings of John Rawls and Thomas Scanlon. Keating contends that the selection of a required precaution level (in much of negligence law) involves a decision about the degree to which some person's (or firm's) liberty to engage in activity that risks bodily harm to others should be constrained or curtailed in light of the interests of others in avoiding such harm (security). With this understanding of what the precaution level of negligence law is, he sketches the following argument (as we have liberally interpreted it):

10 (2003) 56 Vand L Rev 653.

A. A required precaution level ought to be fair.
B. A fair required precaution level is one that could be justified (*ex ante*) to each person; any diminution in potential victims' security against harm posed by others' activities must be justifiable in principle.
C. In some circumstances, because there are significant risks of devastating or fatal injuries to others that can be reduced by feasible precautions, no level of aggregate economic cost serves as an adequate (*ex ante*) justification to potential victims for a failure to take these feasible precautions.
D. Under cost-benefit analyses of 'due care', the aggregate economic costs of feasible precautions sometimes yield the conclusion that due care does not require such precaution level.[11]

Because of C and D, the law's failure to require feasible-but-very-expensive precautions against devastating injuries in some cases is not justifiable to those potentially imperilled; their security at this level is a Rawlsian primary good. In light of B, the law's precaution level would not be fair; under A, it would not be what it ought to be. This line of argument thus leads to the conclusion that:

E. In some circumstances, actors ought to take precautions that are in excess of what a cost-benefit analysis of due care would require (because those precautions are feasible and the failure to require them would not be fair).

Keating analyses in detail what a 'feasibility' standard would look like, and does the same for an even more stringent 'safety' standard. Somewhat ironically, he derives these alternative standards from federal statutes concerning precaution-taking in certain highly regulated areas of the economy. That is, Keating identifies what might count as a genuinely justified precaution level by drawing from federal statutory law, and his ultimate point is that the common law of negligence ought to be interpreted to employ such standards in large domains of its application.

While Keating's article is descriptive and analytical—of the economists' positions, the way tort law works, and a few American statutes—it is also normative. It takes a position on what tort law's standard for precaution-taking *should be* and provides a contractualist framework drawn from contemporary

[11] While D is sometimes true because of the large size of aggregate markets and populations, and while one might think this undercuts the 'significant risk' or 'feasibility' premises built into C, Keating argues in great detail and by reference to real cases and real statutes that the market or population size that generates the E premise *often does not undercut* the 'significant risk' and 'feasibility' premises.

political philosophy to justify its conclusions. At its core is a Rawlsian insistence on the moral separateness of persons: persons or firms who advisedly undertake activities for profit must bear the burden of taking sufficient precaution to protect others whose lives and basic wellbeing are being put at risk because the benefits to the those who stand to profit *do not* offset certain significant risks to others. Interestingly, Keating contends that his contractualist-based conception of the content of a due care norm matches the moral intuitions of the average person (and juror), which tends to hit a point at which the cost-benefit framework is morally repugnant. But he does not merely assume empirical claims about the moral intuitions of the average person, nor does he simply indulge himself in an intuitive argument about the content of 'fairness'. Rather, he invokes an elaborate Rawlsian framework to construct a philosophical account of fairness that is both rigorous and tied to principles that leading courts have put forward.

2. Finnis on Intention

For an example of philosophical analysis that is less normative and more a matter of anti-reductionist concept-salvaging, we turn to John Finnis's deservedly influential essay *Intention in Tort Law*.[12] In it, he uses a philosopher's expertise in parsing concepts to contest Richard Posner's reductive approach to intention in tort law. In particular, Finnis is critical of Posner's treatment of the famous 1828 English 'spring gun' case of *Bird v Holbrook* as fundamentally concerned with striking a utilitarian balance between the value of two conflicting land uses (growing tulips and raising peacocks).

In *Bird*, the defendant had set a trap so that anyone who came into his tulip patch would be shot. A nineteen-year-old boy retrieving a peacock that had wandered away from its owner was seriously injured when he triggered the trap. In Finnis's view, it was of fundamental importance to the court that the defendant had posted no warning of the spring gun's presence: this demonstrated that the defendant clearly had intended entrants to be shot, and the presence of such intent was critical to the imposition of liability. Posner, by contrast, deemed intentionality irrelevant to the resolution of the case. In the spirit of Holmes, Posner refused to take the tort law concept of 'intent' at face value, instead treating it as the law's indirect and clumsy way of setting as a

[12] John Finnis, 'Intention in Tort Law' in David G Owen (ed), *Philosophical Foundations of Tort Law* (OUP 1995) 229.

requirement for liability that a defendant *act with the knowledge that some result has a likelihood of occurring that is higher than it would have been had the defendant taken some precaution.* While clearly revisionary, Posner's seemingly awkward reconstruction could claim support from the Second Restatement of Torts. Section 8A of that document states: 'The word "intent" is used throughout [this] Restatement ... to denote that the actor desires to cause consequences of his act, *or that he believes that the consequences are substantially certain to result from it*.'[13]

Deftly deploying philosophical analysis, Finnis had no trouble establishing that 'substantially certain' and 'desire' are patently untenable interpretations of the idea of intent. As to 'substantially certain', he offered simple examples of instances in which certainty and intent come apart. To give our own (inspired by his): a person who takes an overnight transatlantic flight from New York to Hamburg is substantially certain to have jet lag but does not intend it. Likewise, a torts professor can be substantially certain that some students will be confused by the concept of proximate cause but does not intend for them to be confused. The same goes for 'desire'. One may intend to stay up until 4 am to work on the edits to a manuscript without desiring to do so.

Moving from the critical to the constructive, Finnis argues that to intend to do something necessarily involves trying to do it. Relatedly, forming intentions involves forming a plan or a proposal, however instantaneous and informal, which one then—in the ordinary case—carries out in action. An intention is, in this sense, the first step of an intentional action.

> When one intends some harm to (an)other human person or persons—when one's proposal includes, however reluctantly, some damage to (for example) their bodily integrity, or to their participation in knowledge of reality, or to their means of sustenance—one is shaping oneself as one who, in the most straightforward way, exploits others.[14]

Finally, Finnis shifted his analysis from a more analytic to a more normative inquiry, comparable in some ways to Keating's, though different in substance. According to Finnis,

> [c]ommon, non-utilitarian morality's principle that one must never choose (intend) harm to the person of any human individual both expresses and

[13] Restatement (Second) of Torts §8A (Am L Inst 1965) (emphasis added).
[14] Finnis (n 11) 244.

> preserves the understanding that each human individual is more than just a locus of utility or wealth (to be measured at some arbitrarily chosen future moment), or a channel or conduit for maximizing that wealth or utility (again, a maximum as measured at some *chosen* future moment). It expresses and preserves each individual person's *density*, so to speak, or *dignity*, if you will, as an equal of *everyone* else in basic rights. To choose harm to the person is the paradigmatic wrong, the exemplary instance of denial of right.[15]

As noted, Finnis's critique is partly aimed at making sense of important English tort decisions. But its larger points relate to grand theorizing in the manner of Posner and utilitarian theorizing in private law more generally. While Finnis discusses considerations of justice and the importance of duties of repair that flow from intentional wrongdoings, his larger point is explanatory and descriptive. It is that the law regarding intentional torts *cannot be understood or correctly interpreted* from within a framework that fails to take a choice-dignity perspective seriously. Finnis used both the characteristic modes of argument of philosophical analysis and deontological philosophical theorizing to make his point, which is that other prominent jurists were mischaracterizing an important part of tort law.

We have offered examples drawn from the work of Keating and Finnis as exemplars, respectively, of two ways in which philosophical analysis has informed modern private law scholarship. Whereas Keating was more focused on making a moral- and political-philosophical argument for what level of care negligence law should require of actors, Finnis was more concerned with offering an analytic and interpretive argument about the meaning of the concept of intent, as used in tort law. In fact, most philosophical work in tort law includes both interpretive and normative dimensions. Among scholars based in the United States, this includes the work of Richard Epstein, George Fletcher, Scott Hershovitz, Nate Oman, Stephen Perry, and Richard Wright, among others. Perhaps more surprisingly, it also includes scholars who embrace some version of legal positivism and the idea of a separation between law and morality, including Jules Coleman, Paul Miller, and John Oberdiek. It is also true for our own work, which has been described as adopting 'pragmatic conceptualism' as a methodology, and the work of other prominent scholars, including Andrew Gold.[16]

[15] ibid.

[16] See generally Andrew S Gold and others, *The Oxford Handbook of the New Private Law* (OUP 2021).

IV. Private Nuisance

In Section II, we sketched work by Professors Keating and Finnis to illustrate different types of philosophical analysis of topics in tort law. In this section, we consider a particular corner of Anglo-American private law, namely, the tort of private nuisance. Although we will offer some of our own thoughts about nuisance law, our primary aim is to show how philosophical work of the sort we have described in Section II has allowed scholars to develop traditional understandings of Private Law subjects that were prematurely rejected by sceptically oriented legal scholars writing in the mid-twentieth century. We do not go so far as to say that American-style philosophical, legal scholarship was necessary or sufficient for this scholarly space to 'open up'. As noted, scholarship in other common law jurisdictions that were not so badly scarred by law scepticism has been able to proceed in this manner largely uninterrupted. And practitioners of other methodologies, including second-generation legal economists, have displayed greater receptivity to the thought that sound economic analysis of law requires that doctrine be taken seriously. But it surely has been helpful.

'Nuisance' has been recognized as a legal concept or category in Anglo-American law for centuries. And private nuisance has a pedigree in Anglo-American tort law comparable to torts such as assault, battery, and trespass to land. Still, it has long stood apart from other torts because of the extent to which it is defined by the setback or interference experienced by the plaintiff and the relatively lesser importance of any determination of independently designated wrongful or rights-invasive conduct of the defendant. At the core of private nuisance is the idea of one person causing an unreasonable interference with another's right to use and enjoy land in her possession. Notably, in this formulation, the adjective 'unreasonable' in the first instance characterizes *the nature of the interference experienced by the victim*. This is in contrast to how reasonableness operates in the law of negligence, where it is typically invoked to identify the standard of care to which an actor is obligated to adhere. A car driver who is found to have exercised reasonable care to avoid collisions is one who has driven with due care (non-negligently). By contrast, a property owner who is found to have exercised reasonable care to prevent sickening odours from his basement workshop from invading his neighbour's land can still be found to have committed a nuisance. The gravamen of a claim of private nuisance is *not* unreasonable behaviour that interferes with another's use and enjoyment, nor is there a boundary crossing, contact, or near-contact as found in many intentional torts. It is behaviour that generates an unreasonable interference with another's use and enjoyment of their property.

It is clear that, in nuisance law, the modifier 'unreasonable' is meant to exclude trivial interferences.[17] But what, more affirmatively, can be said about when an interference counts as unreasonable? And are the determinants of unreasonableness, in this context, entirely a function of the impact on the victim? Or does the idea of 'unreasonable interference' implicitly reference a standard of conduct the defendant must fail to meet before being subject to liability? In other words, is private nuisance best understood as a true strict liability tort—one that allows for liability if the effect on the victim is serious enough, irrespective of how the actor who caused the interference conducted himself? Or does it contain within it some notion of wrongful conduct that must be present, along with the effect on the victim, before liability can be imposed?

Questions of this sort were left largely unanswered in pre-modern law. Jurors and judges would determine liability in particular cases, and commentators seemed not to worry too much about the bases on which they did so. About the most they ventured on this topic was to associate nuisance law's idea of unreasonable interference with the Latin phrase *sic utere tuo ut alienum non laedas*, which translates, roughly, as 'use what is yours so as not to harm what is another's'. They also characterized the private nuisance tort as an expression in the law of a moral principle of neighbourly reciprocity—a rule of 'give and take, live and let live'.[18] Roughly speaking, the idea seemed to be that each possessor of land in a community is expected to put up with certain inconveniences stemming from their neighbours' use of their land, but not more than is normal or standard given the nature and customs of the community.

In the late nineteenth and early twentieth centuries, loose and vaguely moralistic renderings of nuisance such as these were natural targets for scholars imbued with Holmesian-style scepticism. Indeed, Holmes himself denounced their vacuity. In several writings, Holmes developed the view that modern tort law was coalescing around a single general principle. According to it, a person who causes tangible harm to another, where the person had a reasonable opportunity to avoid causing it, is subject to liability—they must indemnify the victim for the harm.[19] At the same time, he claimed that courts had carved out exceptions to this principle, each of which identified a special legal 'privilege' to harm where harm could have been avoided. In his view, when courts

[17] Some formulations of nuisance require for liability both a substantial and an unreasonable interference, with 'substantial' doing the work of excluding trivial interferences. In these formulations, it is even clearer that the modifier 'unreasonable' is meant to set a condition of liability beyond nontriviality.

[18] JE Penner, 'Nuisance and the Character of the Neighbourhood' (1993) 5 J Envt'l Law 1, 6 n 29 (quoting *Bamford v Turnley* (1862) 3 B & S 66, 83–84 (Bramwell, B)).

[19] See, eg, Oliver Wendell Holmes, 'The Path of the Law' (1897) 10 Harvard LR 453, 471.

recognized these privileges, they did so out of an intuitive sense that, in the case before them and others like it, it would advance some important public policy to depart from the general principle of liability for causing avoidable losses. However, because judges, by training and ideology, were averse to acknowledging that they made 'policy' decisions, they presented their decisions recognizing these privileges:

> as hollow deductions from empty general propositions like *sic utere tuo ut alienum non laedas*, which teaches nothing but a benevolent yearning, or else ... as if [the privileges] themselves embodied a postulate of the law and admitted of no further deduction, as when it is said that, although there is temporal damage, there is no wrong; whereas the very thing to be found out is whether there is a wrong or not, and if not, why not.[20]

In sum, courts in nuisance cases—as in tort cases generally—had failed entirely to explain what counts as unreasonable interference and what does not.

Roughly fifty years later, William Prosser took Holmes's scepticism about nuisance one step further. According to Prosser, the effort to identify a standard of conduct contained within the tort of nuisance was doomed from the start—a fool's errand. It was doomed because, in Anglo-American law, the legal term 'nuisance' had never been, and was never intended to be, the name of a tort.[21] In modern legal parlance, terms such as 'trespass' and 'negligence' serve as the names of distinct torts because they refer both to an act component (actions that an actor is obligated to avoid taking or must take) and a setback component (the detrimental effect of the actor's conduct on the victim). Prosser maintained that the word 'nuisance' cannot identify a tort because it refers only to a particular type of harm or setback, not a standard of conduct. In this respect, it is analogous to phrases such as 'bodily harm', 'reputational damage', or 'diminished privacy'. Each identifies a type of detriment that can, in principle, support a tort claim, but none identifies a tort as such.

Prosser's 'solution' to the puzzle of nuisance law's apparent failure to specify a standard of conduct was characteristically hyper-sceptical. No less characteristic was his willingness, in his capacity as a Reporter for the American Law Institute, to write his revisionary understanding of nuisance into a document

[20] Oliver Wendell Holmes, Jr, 'Privilege, Malice, and Intent' (1894) 8 Harvard LR 1, 3.

[21] William L Prosser, 'Private Action for Public Nuisance' (1966) 52 Va L Rev 997, 997 ('*Nuisance* is a French word that means nothing more than harm') (italics in original); William L Prosser, 'Nuisance Without Fault' (1942) 20 Tex L Rev 399, 416 ('Nuisance ... is ... a field of tort liability, a kind of damage done, rather than any particular type of conduct').

that purported to 'restate' the American law of torts. Indeed, a comment in the Second Torts Restatement (for which Prosser served as the primary Reporter) puts the point quite bluntly:

> as it is used in [this] Restatement, 'nuisance' does not signify any particular kind of conduct on the part of the defendant. Instead, the word has reference to two particular kinds of harm—the invasion of two kinds of interest—by conduct that is tortious only if it falls into the usual categories of tort liability.[22]

So, according to the Second Restatement, a lawyer who wants to know *which* interferences with another's use and enjoyment of land are unlawful (tortious) cannot find the answer to that question by applying the elements of the nuisance tort or the concept of unreasonable interference. Still, it did not follow for him that nuisance was a full-blown strict liability tort—that any interference with use and enjoyment that passes a certain threshold of significance permits the imposition of liability. Instead, he suggested that liability for nuisances—where, again, 'nuisances' simply refers to instances of harm of a certain sort—turns on the violation of standards of conduct *found elsewhere in tort law*. For example, if a 'nuisance' results from conduct by an actor that lacks *due care*—the standard of conduct employed in negligence—then there is liability. Likewise, if a 'nuisance' is intentionally or knowingly inflicted on the victim—a standard found in certain intentional torts—then there is liability. And if a 'nuisance' results from the defendant engaging in an abnormally dangerous activity—a separate category of strict tort liability—then there is liability. Otherwise, there is no liability for 'nuisances'.

Stepping back, one can appreciate the radicalism of Prosser's proposed 'solution' to the problem of giving content to the idea of an 'unreasonable interference'. It gives up entirely on any hope that 'unreasonable', in this context, sets a standard of conduct. Instead, lawyers are told to look to conduct standards from other parts of tort law. While not unheard of in tort law, this sort of 'borrowing' is quite unusual: lawyers are not told to look to negligence law's

[22] Restatement (Second) of Torts §821A, cmt. *c* (Am L Inst 1977). This passage refers to two kinds of harm because the relevant Restatement provisions aimed to address liability for both 'Public Nuisance' and 'Private Nuisance'. That distinction is not important for purposes of the present analysis. Prosser's use of 'nuisance' to refer to a certain kind of harm was novel to the Second Restatement. However, the prior Restatement also displayed concerns about confusions attending the word 'nuisance'. Restatement (First) of Torts, Division 10, Ch 40: Scope and Introductory Note (1939). It dealt with those concerns by avoiding altogether using the word nuisance, referencing instead the tort of 'non-trespassory invasion of another's interest in the private use and enjoyment of land'. ibid §822.

standard of due care to determine when a loss of privacy is tortious or when reliance on a misrepresentation counts as deceit.

What drove Prosser to this extreme position? Several factors were at work. In part, he was operating under the influence of prior scholars who had concluded that it would be helpful to organize tort law by reference to the tripartite framework of intentional torts, negligence, and strict liability.[23] This, after all, is the framework Prosser deployed in explaining what standards of conduct could be borrowed from other parts of tort law to join to the particular harm of nuisance so as to generate the sort of act-setback combination characteristic of other torts. Second, and more fundamentally, there is Prosser's judgment that there was no hope of finding a conduct-guiding standard within the concept of 'unreasonable interference' that has always figured centrally in judicial formulations of nuisance law.

One last iteration of scepticism about nuisance law is important to mention in this context. It is the scepticism expressed by some members of the modern law-and-economics movement.[24] Their preferred solution to the riddle of private nuisance law's liability standard is to treat the word 'unreasonable' in the phrase 'unreasonable interference' as if it is aimed at characterizing the defendant's behaviour, rather than the degree or type of interference experienced by the plaintiff. By this manoeuvre, they essentially render nuisance a special case of the tort of negligence, understood as liability for harm caused by conduct that lacks due care.[25] Legal economists tend to find this move congenial because, in their view, the idea of 'unreasonable' conduct in negligence is best understood as incorporating into tort law a cost-benefit standard. To act without due care, in this view, is just to fail to take a precaution against harming others that costs less than the harm that can be expected to result from not taking the precaution. Reducing nuisance to a special case of negligence, in turn, jibes with a reductively economic account of the purpose of nuisance law: namely, courts arranging property rights so that land is put to its highest-value use. Thus, if a highly profitable factory cannot operate without causing nauseating smoke regularly to invade a nearby resident's property, there should be no nuisance liability because the economic value of the factory renders the operation of the factory reasonable from a cost-benefit perspective.[26]

[23] See Robert Stevens, 'Professor Sir Frederick Pollock' in JamesGoudkamp and Donal Nolan (eds), *Scholars of Tort Law* (Hart 2019) 75, 78–81.

[24] Here we leave aside Ronald Coase's influential economic analysis of nuisance law.

[25] Henry E Smith, 'Exclusion and Property Rules in the Law of Nuisance' (2004) 90 Va L Rev 965, 967.

[26] ibid 968. Or, on Guido Calabresi's alternative economic framing of this issue, the factory should face liability for monetary damages only (not injunctive relief), because the factory is likely in the best position to determine whether it is cheaper to find a way to stop or ameliorate the interference or instead pay for the damage associated with it. ibid.

Now, finally, to the role of philosophical analysis in responding to sceptical views of nuisance. While some courts in the United States have, wittingly or unwittingly, signed on to Prosser's hyper-sceptical view, and while the economic reconstruction of unreasonable interference has been highly influential with legal scholars, there has been significant pushback against both in the last twenty years. Prominent among the scholars who have pushed back are Chris Essert, Donal Nolan, James Penner, Henry Smith, and Richard Wright. Not all of these scholars are American, and perhaps only Penner would self-identify as a legal philosopher. Nonetheless, they approach nuisance from an anti-reductive perspective that, in the United States, has long been nearly unavailable but now is re-emerging.[27] Some of these scholars maintain that it is a significant overreaction to the ambiguity of 'unreasonable interference' to conclude that the concept provides no standard of conduct. (These interventions are illustrative of the analytic side of philosophical analysis of private law.) Others, including ourselves, argue that it is a mistake to cash out the idea of unreasonable interference in terms of cost-benefit analysis, as opposed to some version of a reciprocity or fairness idea.[28] (These interventions are illustrative of the normative side of philosophical interventions in private law.) Most combine these analytic and normative points, though, strictly speaking, they are severable.[29]

On the analytic side, what we are treating as philosophically inspired interventions combine two ideas. The first involves the embrace of a 'deflationary' strategy for responding to scepticism of various sorts: a strategy deployed in the work of Ludwig Wittgenstein and Richard Rorty, among others. The basic idea is that sceptical arguments illegitimately draw much of their plausibility by setting an implausibly high standard for what it takes to avoid sceptical conclusions. (For example, moral scepticism is sometimes grounded in an indefensibly strict notion of what counts as a justified moral belief.) Applied to nuisance law, a deflationary approach suggests that this particular tort's failure to articulate a crisply defined standard of

[27] John CP Goldberg, 'Introduction: Pragmatism and Private Law' (2012) 125 Harvard LR 1640.

[28] See John CP Goldberg and Benjamin C Zipursky, *The Oxford Introductions to U.S. Law: Torts* (OUP 2010) 244–47 (explaining unreasonableness in nuisance law in terms of harmonization and reciprocity, not in cost-benefit terms); Benjamin C Zipursky, 'Reasonableness in and out of Negligence Law' (2015) 163 U Pa L Rev 2131, 2142, 2169 (describing and developing a 'mutuality' conception of reasonableness and indicating its applicability to nuisance law).

[29] A relevant example here is Keating, who agrees with Prosser that much of private nuisance law involves the recognition of a form of liability that does not hinge on the violation of a standard of conduct. Yet he also argues that, when liability is imposed, it comports with a deontological principle of justice holding that losses caused by permissible conduct should be borne by an actor who benefits from causing them. Gregory C Keating, 'Nuisance as a Strict Liability Wrong' (2012) 4 J Tort L 1.

conduct does not warrant the Prosserian thought that no standard can be identified.[30]

A second related move involves rejecting the inclination of many modern scholars to make sense of an area of law by simplifying or 'flattening' it. Indeed, the instinct of these scholars is precisely the opposite. In order to understand nuisance law, they argue, one must delve into its particular applications and appreciate its complexities. This is precisely what will enable the scholar to make sense of the area because law responds to and reflects the complexity of human interactions and the norms that govern them. One will not be able to make sense of negligence law by boiling it down to the idea of a failure to exercise due care: when and why one person is subject to liability for negligence turns on a host of other considerations contained in distinct legal concepts and doctrines such as 'duty', 'cause', 'proximate cause', 'injury', 'comparative fault', and the like. The same is true of private nuisance. The key to understanding it is to immerse oneself in its applications, to appreciate rather than to ignore its contours.[31]

Also relatedly, scholars of this sort tend to argue that it is a mistake to suppose that the standards of conduct contained in different torts reduce down to a single standard (eg reasonableness) or a few (as in Prosser's suggestion that the standard of conduct in nuisance must be one of three options: intentional interference, carelessness as to the risk of interference, or engagement in an abnormally dangerous activity). There is little reason to suppose that this trio exhausts the universe of conduct standards, and once other possibilities are allowed for, it is possible to identify a distinctive one embedded in private nuisance—one that, unsurprisingly, was regularly alluded to in judicial opinions from the pre-sceptical era.

As noted at the outset of our discussion of nuisance law, Anglo-American courts have sometimes invoked the *sic utere* maxim to express the idea that private nuisance incorporates a principle of reciprocity—of 'give and take, live and let live'. While the determination of whether an actor has adhered to or violated this notion of reciprocity is surely fact-intensive and admits of close cases, it is not so vague as to be contentless or unable to guide conduct. To return to our example, it is easy enough to identify the difference between a homeowner in a residential neighbourhood being kept up at night on one occasion by a

30 Smith (n 24) 970 (suggesting that descriptions of nuisance as a 'mess', '"wilderness" of law', and 'legal garbage can' are overblown and that careful attention to particular cases, combined with attention to information costs, reveals a coherent understanding of when interferences are deemed unreasonable).

31 Donal Nolan, '"A Tort Against Land": Private Nuisance as a Property Tort' in Donal Nolan and Andrew Robertson (eds), *Rights and Private Law* (Hart 2014) 459, 459–60 (arguing that private nuisance law's coherence can be revealed by close attention to doctrine).

neighbour's barking dog and a homeowner regularly being kept up at night because a neighbour has decided to operate a dog kennel from her home. Absent a rule against it, ownership of a domesticated dog (or even several) is a customary and ordinary feature of residential living, and it is in the nature of dogs that they will sometimes bark at inconvenient times. Anyone who lives in such a neighbourhood is expected to—and, so far as the law is concerned, required—to put up with such things. The operation of a kennel out of a residence could easily be a different matter altogether. Depending on the number and breed of the dogs being kennelled, their tendencies to bark or otherwise create annoyances for neighbours, and the conditions under which they are kept, it may well exceed the liberty a possessor in a residential neighbourhood enjoys with respect to the use of her property. If its operation, in turn, regularly interferes with another resident's use and enjoyment of his property, it is an unreasonable interference that, as such, constitutes a private nuisance.

Thus far, our review of attempts to rehabilitate the concept of a private nuisance has partaken of an anti-reductive approach similar to Finnis's in dealing with reductive accounts of 'intent'. But the same kind of argument can also provide a counterweight to the economist's inclination to interpret nuisance law's notion of unreasonable interference as requiring or inviting cost-benefit analysis.[32] Thus, as does Keating in his treatment of precaution levels, the same scholars who have argued against a 'flattened' account of private nuisance have also argued that there is no reason to suppose that the term 'unreasonable', applied to conduct or conditions, always or even typically references ways of acting that generate more costs than benefits.[33] Indeed, as Essert, Penner, Smith, and Wright each has argued in different ways, 'unreasonableness' can—and in the nuisance context—should be understood to have independent content.[34] Properly construed, they argue, there is nothing in nuisance law which says that an activity's large profitability or social value renders 'reasonable' the

[32] See also Zipursky (n 27).

[33] Penner (n 17) 7–10 (emphasizing the extent to which reasonableness in nuisance, as defined by English decisions, is meant to leave all property owners in a locality free to engage in common and ordinary uses, rather than to invite a judicial balancing of the relative value of disparate activities).

[34] Christopher Essert, 'Nuisance and the Normative Boundaries of Ownership' (2016) 52 Tulsa L Rev 85 (arguing that consideration of nuisance law's particular concept of reasonableness and courts' application of that concept reveal that it instantiates a principle of fair and equal normative control over property); Smith (n 24) 997–1005 (arguing that, in several classes of cases, nuisance law recognizes a general right to exclude noises, odours, and vibrations rather than balancing the costs and benefits of the invasive activity); Richard W Wright, 'Private Nuisance Law: A Window on Substantive Justice' in Nolan and Robertson (n 29) 491, 507 (arguing that private nuisance 'articulates, and implements the basic principles of justice and right', and that, as used in the First and Second Torts Restatements' private nuisance provisions, 'unreasonableness' is best understood as incorporating Baron Bramwell's 'give and take, live and let live' principle).

interferences it causes with other's use and enjoyment of their lands. Nuisance law's principle of reciprocity instead ties unreasonableness to norms and legitimate expectations of what makes for a fair use of one's property.

Readers may regard the foregoing analysis as falling on the interpretive and explanatory side (rather than the normative and justificatory side) of the classification set forth earlier. While this may be true, it is misleading for at least two reasons. One is that the rehabilitation of the concept of a private nuisance is done in a manner that integrates an understanding of the normative basis of nuisance law. But a second is that the Prosserian view of nuisance law, in important respects, invited a normative recasting of the law in overtly instrumentalist ways. At a minimum, the rebuttal of the alleged analytic clarity of the Prosserian view requires the advocates of a transformed normative view to provide entirely different kinds of arguments for it.

V. Conclusion

Although this chapter began with a sharp and self-critical challenge, it ended up proffering something more than a set of external or 'causal' explanations for why philosophical analysis has played a significant role in modern Private Law scholarship in the United States. Instead, we have offered an apology (in the philosophical sense) for the philosophical orientation and methods many of us have brought to this area of law. Ironically, one of our central messages is the opposite of what many from the anti-philosophical camp might have expected. Philosophers have aided the cause of understanding not by replacing legal concepts with preferred abstractions from their field but rather by *shielding* those concepts from the radically reductive approaches of scholars who, from a variety of perspectives, insist on the hollowness of legal concepts and the misguidedness of careful legal analysis.

13

The Minimal Morality of Private Law

Lorenz Kaehler

I. The Unspecific Reference to 'Morality'

Hardly any question has attracted as much attention in legal theory as the relationship between law and morality. Could the moral merits of a legal rule, at least in some cases, by themselves influence its validity (dependence-thesis) or is this excluded (independence-thesis)?[1] Although a plurality of positions such as inclusive and exclusive legal positivism and non-positivism have been developed in this regard,[2] there is widespread agreement that morality does play a role for legal decisions. The disagreement mainly concerns the question of whether this is due to a conventional rule of recognition,[3] a necessary feature of the law,[4] the authorization of judges[5] or some other reason. However, little regard has been paid throughout these debates to the question of which moral rules one is talking about.

This question could only be left open if both theses were independent of the content of morality. In this case, moral rules by themselves could either, in principle, not influence the law or could, independently of their content in principle, impact the validity of legal norms. Although opposed to each other, the dependence-thesis and the independence-thesis thus agree that the relationship between law and morality is independent of the specific content of the latter. Whether morality contains only a few basic principles or a detailed array

[1] Conventionally this is conceived of as a question about a necessary connection between law and morality. For a critique see John Gardner, *Law as a Leap of Faith* (OUP 2012) 48; Joseph Raz, *The Authority of* Law (2nd edn, OUP 2009) 314–16.

[2] eg Andrei Marmor, 'Exclusive Legal Positivism' in J Coleman and S Shapiro (eds), *The Oxford Handbook of Jurisprudence and Legal Philosophy* (OUP 2002) 104–23; Kenneth Einar Himma, 'Inclusive Legal Positivism' in ibid 125; Robert Alexy, 'On the Concept and the Nature of Law' (2008) 21 Ratio Juris 284. Some own ideas are sketched in 'What Constitutes the Concept of Law? A Search Beyond Positivism and Non-positivism' in AF Leite de Paula and A Santacoloma (eds), *Law and Morals* (Steiner 2019) 195.

[3] HLA Hart, *The Concept of Law* (2nd edn, Clarendon Press 1994) 97.

[4] Alexy (n 2) 289.

[5] Hans Kelsen, *Reine Rechtslehre* (2nd edn, Verlag Österreich 2000) 57.

Lorenz Kaehler, *The Minimal Morality of Private Law* In: *Methodology in Private Law Theory*. Edited by: Thilo Kuntz and Paul B. Miller, Oxford University Press. © Lorenz Kaehler 2024. DOI: 10.1093/oso/9780198885306.003.0013

of rules, whether it demands only minimal respect or maximal care for others would not matter, as far as the concept of law is concerned. Without looking at its content, one could, without further ado, specify the relationship of morality with law.

However, such an independence seems, at least at the outset, hardly plausible. This can be seen by looking at the extreme cases of an utterly thin and an utterly thick version of morality. Let us start with an extremely thin version of morality. Suppose that morality contains only one minimal rule according to which disputes shall be decided, as far as possible, on the basis of reasons. Legal positivism would then claim it is a contingent question of whether a particular legal system incorporates such a moral norm.

If this were not the case, disputes could, in this positivist perspective, as far as the law is concerned, be decided arbitrarily. There would neither be a necessity to provide reasons for a decision nor the need for the existence of such reasons. If the rule of recognition allows arbitrary decisions and a society would regard them as law, then they would be law. According to positivism, 'whatever counts as law in a given society is law in that society'.[6] The fact that judges are currently not allowed to throw a dice or look into the stars in order to reach a decision would be based not on some necessary feature of law but on the contingent fact that, fortunately, current legal systems prohibit this.

One might object that positivists do not have such a thin version of morality in mind when they deny the validity of legal rules might depend on their moral merits unless provided for by law. Rather, they refer to conventional rules of morality, which encompass much more, such as the rules that one shall not kill, steal, lie, etc. Their claim would then amount only to denying that these conventional rules do not impact the law's validity. However, thereby, they would severely restrict their thesis. It would only entail the view that law does not depend on a particular morality. Hence, whether there is such a relationship with other kinds of morality, for instance, with a minimal version of it, would remain open.

Moreover, even if one qualifies the reference to morality with the help of conventional rules, one has to state precisely which conventional rules one means. There are varying rules of greater or lesser intensity, from conventions among neighbours to duties inside intimate relationships. Therefore, one needs a qualification of these rules in order to avoid ambiguity. Both the independence-thesis and the dependence-thesis have to provide this to be meaningful. But so far, this qualification has been missing in the debate.

[6] Andrei Marmor, 'What's left of general jurisprudence? On law's ontology and content' (2019) 10 Jurisprudence 151, 163.

A similar picture emerges if one looks at the opposite extreme, namely, an utterly thick version of morality. Such a version contains not only basic rules that one shall not kill, not steal, etc., but broad general rules that could affect almost every aspect of life. Such rules are, for instance, requested by the utilitarian principle that one has to optimize the overall utility.[7] This would have far-reaching consequences as it concerns almost any action. It hardly leaves a place for neutral acts because one could always further one's or another's well-being and thus increase the overall utility. Even the decision whether one orders pizza or pasta in a restaurant would turn into a moral question because it would have, at least, a small impact on one's or another's well-being, considering the differences in taste, usage of energy, etc.

Similar far-reaching consequences could be reached on the basis of other conceptions of morality. Many traditional versions argue for a duty to develop one's talents.[8] Such a duty also has huge repercussions because almost any action has at least slightly different consequences for one's development. Whether one goes to the cinema or a museum would not be a question of desire but a moral question concerning how to best develop one's personality. Thus, almost all actions would be determined by a moral duty. Rest and leisure would only be allowed in order to further virtuous activities. In Kant's words, one would demand 'phantastic-virtues' which would have thus far-reaching consequences that he plausibly characterized as leading to tyranny.[9]

Yet, even within Kant's ethics, it is difficult to avoid such conclusions and to account for morally neutral practical decisions. Not only does Kant accept a duty to make oneself perfect,[10] which raises the question of why this duty, at least, should not always be furthered. Moreover, Kant generally understands the realm of freedom as consisting of a realm of ends[11], the fulfilment of which is, to him, a duty.[12] Duties and ends are, therefore, intimately connected in his theory. This has the radical consequence that one acquires a duty as soon as one sets an end for oneself. Not acting according to a self-given end would mean that one acts on the basis of passion, which, according to him, has an animalistic character[13]. Within his theory, it is also difficult to find actions and practical decisions which are morally neutral.

[7] John Stuart Mill, 'Utilitarianism' in J Gray (ed), *On Liberty and Other Essays* (OUP 1991) 137.

[8] eg Immanuel Kant, *Grundlegung zur Metaphysik der Sitten* (de Gruyter 1968) AA IV 424; Georg Wilhelm Friedrich Hegel, *Philosophische Propädeutik, Gesammelte Werke*, vol 3 (Herrman Glockner ed, Frommann-Holzboog 1961) 82.

[9] Immanuel Kant, *Metaphysik der Sitten* (de Gruyter 1968) AA VI 409.

[10] Kant (n 8) 423, 429; (n 9) 386, 419.

[11] Kant (n 8) 433.

[12] Kant (n 10) 239, 384–85.

[13] Kant (n 10) 420.

Many, if not all, moral theories thus have the tendency to determine almost any action. Interestingly, this cannot be said about the law. No existing legal system determines every action, notwithstanding its fairly comprehensive[14] character. Even totalitarian regimes that are defined by all-encompassing and, in this sense, total norms leave at least some room for privacy. This holds even more for the many states that recognize fundamental rights, the idea of which is to create a space of freedom protected but not determined by law. Despite its complexity and a huge number of norms, the law thus differs from thick morality by having a limited range. Any theory that wants to explain the relationship between law and morality has to account for this difference. This poses little difficulty for positivist theories that endorse a separation between them.[15]

By contrast, the explanation of this difference creates difficulties for non-positivist theories that deny the separation of law and morality. For once, there is a connection between them; it becomes unclear why not all moral norms could possibly influence the law. Even the decision of whether one chooses pizza or pasta could impact law if it were unrestrictedly linked to an all-encompassing morality. Such a far-reaching connection of law and morality is implausible, however, given that virtually any legal system allows at least some immoral acts. Even the most fervent supporters of natural law do not claim that it is legally determined whether one shall order pizza or pasta.

The dependence-thesis thus needs to qualify which kind of morality it refers to. Although, in comparison to positivist theories, it has no difficulty accounting for basic moral rules, it must make sure that its reference to morality does not become too strong. Once moral rules and reasons play a role within the law, it has to explain why not all of these rules are relevant to it. In this regard, non-positivist theories, similar to their positivist counterparts, must develop a qualification of the morality to which they refer.

An intriguing example in this regard is Ronald Dworkin. He endorsed, on the one hand, a comprehensive idea of morality by claiming that one can say 'of almost any action, that it is morally required or wrong'.[16] On the other hand, he fervently argued for a union of law and morality by denying their separation and endorsing a 'one-system-picture'.[17]

[14] Raz (n 1) 116.
[15] For qualifications of this thesis see n 1.
[16] Ronald Dworkin, *Justice for Hedgehogs* (Harvard UP 2011) 181.
[17] Dworkin (n 16) 405.

> Law is a branch of political morality, which is itself a branch of a more general personal morality, which is in turn a branch of a yet more general theory of what it is to live well.[18]

This suggests that law is not only connected to public morality but also to personal morality—and even to questions about what constitutes a good life. Consequently, there is nothing of practical importance left to which law is not connected. Due to this holism,[19] it is difficult for his theory to distinguish within morality rules which are relevant to law from those which are not. If moral judgment plays a role within the law, for which Dworkin argued throughout his work,[20] an 'indefinite number of other moral judgments' would be relevant for it as well. Once one opens Pandora's Box of moral reasoning for law, it becomes difficult to stop its flow into it.

The result, however, that legal questions are inseparably mixed with moral questions about almost every aspect of life is hardly convincing. There are many decisions, such as the choice between pizza and pasta, which are not connected to law. Similarly, in many cases, legal decisions do not all depend on moral issues. For instance, whether one has to pay one's rent does not depend on intricate moral questions such as to what extent the rented buildings should be climate-neutral. The very purpose of the law is, in part, to have rules that avoid such moral controversies.

This is not to say that there is no connection between law and morality and that legal arguments cannot, at times, depend on moral arguments. Rather, it is to claim that these arguments must be qualified because not just any moral reason can be used in legal reasoning. Both the complete denial of the influence of moral reasons on the law and their complete incorporation into it seem too extreme to provide a realistic picture of the law. It is equally implausible that not even a single moral rule could be part of the law without an act of incorporation—as well as that every moral rule is connected to the law. It might not be an accident that the countervailing radical theories were developed in the twentieth century, which has also been called the 'age of extremes' in other aspects.[21] At first glance, this extreme character might make these theories rigorous and thus intellectually attractive. However, further analysis shows they provide a one-sided picture by missing a central qualification.

[18] Dworkin (n 15) 5, 405.

[19] Dworkin (n 15), 117: 'The truth of any true moral judgment consists in the truth of an indefinite number of other moral judgments.'

[20] eg Ronald Dworkin, *Law's Empire* (Fontana Press 1991) 260.

[21] Eric J Hobsbawm, *Age of Extremes: The Short Twentieth Century, 1914–1991* (Abacus 1995).

It is, therefore, important to take a closer look at the kind of morality that is typically realized and referred to in law. As I will argue, in both aspects, the law relies only on a minimal version of morality. Especially private law shows that important aspects of life are not legally determined and that certain kinds of moral reasons do not, in principle, play a role in its decisions. First of all, this is a descriptive claim about the character of the prevailing private law. In the following, this will be looked at more closely (III–IV). In addition, this is also a prescriptive claim that private law shall rest and operate on minimal moral reasons (IV). In order to better understand this minimal morality thesis, I shall discuss its relationship to other theses (V).

II. Minimalism of Private Law Institutions

When looking at the morality that is realized and referred to in private law, it seems useful to distinguish two areas. The first concerns the foundation of legislative acts and the second gaps in the law. Both areas are different because the role of morality is obvious in the first case but not so in the second one. Let us start with the first area of positive law. It is revealing to look at its foundation because this helps to understand its character. This shows that the main private law institutions, such as contracts, property, and torts, rest on reasons that are either self-evident or need little argumentative support and hence have a minimal character in either case.

1. Contract Law

To demonstrate this thesis, let us first briefly consider contract law. Its basic idea is that the parties have to fulfil what they have agreed about. Therefore, contract law formulates rights and duties which the parties can foresee in their contract. The enforcement of these rights and duties relies ultimately on the consent to the contract. The same holds for remedies if the contractual rights and duties are infringed. Although parties frequently do not agree about them, these remedies nevertheless rest on the parties' consent because they shall, as far as possible, ensure that the agreement is fulfilled by either protecting the expectation or reliance interest. Thereby, contract law holds the parties accountable for their own decision. Unlike in other situations, the parties cannot complain that they did not consent to the rules that are applied against them because the application of these rules is the consequence of their own decision. This provides a better legitimation than one has in most other cases.

For the bindingness of contracts, one might refer to the Latin formula '*pacta sunt servanda*' and give the justification thereby a traditional, solemn flavour. But one does not need such a reference in order to explain why one shall not act contrary to one's agreements. It is not just a historical insight or a hard-acquired experience that contracts shall be kept. This is a natural part of any social cooperation, which would break down or, at least, be severely hampered if no binding agreements were possible. Being bound by one's agreements is a necessary condition of taking people and oneself seriously. If there is a disagreement about what shall happen and one side can successfully refer to a promise made without duress and deception, disputes usually take on another character and concern, mainly its interpretation. The question of why one shall be bound by one's own words is not accidentally perceived as academic because this is usually taken as self-evident.

One main reason for this bindingness of contract is consistency. If one agrees to something and acts otherwise, one contradicts oneself because one deviates from what one has promised. Such a contradiction is hardly ever a convincing position. If there were reasons not to carry out an agreed-about action, then these reasons should have prevented the parties from making the agreement in the first place. The fact that the agreement has to be carried out later and that the situation might then be different is no counter-argument against this, save for extreme cases of force majeure, because this possible difference is known in advance.

In this regard, the principle that agreements shall be kept resembles the logical law of non-contradiction. Despite difficult philosophical questions about its origin,[22] it is easier to understand than, for instance, the Pythagorean theorem. Even small children understand that promises must be kept and insist on it. For this purpose, they need not learn Latin or history or need to acquire even a primary education. All of this shows that the founding idea of contract law is quite simple.

The same cannot be said about other areas of law and their moral foundation. Take tax law, for instance, which requires for its justification extensive reasons for how the burdens and profits of social cooperation shall be distributed. Any justification of the existing level of taxation cannot refer to a simple idea such as that promises must be kept but has to consider a huge number of reasons for and against it. Among these are considerations about who has the

[22] eg Aristoteles, *Metaphysics*, vol IV 3 (Reclam 1976) 1005b.

greatest needs, who is best capable of bearing the burdens, who deserves the advantages of certain actions, etc. The answer to each of these questions is hotly disputed and depends on complex assessments of the existing situation as well as elaborate arguments of political philosophy.

The same holds for the decision about the basic structure of society as regulated in constitutional law. The problem here is that, in contrast to a contract, one cannot justify it by the actual consent of all those concerned. Tellingly, many theories of political philosophy nevertheless try to base their rules on consent on a hypothetical agreement reached in the state of nature, under ideal circumstances, under a veil of ignorance or similar conditions. This presupposes not only that agreements are binding but also that the bindingness of agreements is less controversial than norms that shall be justified on their basis.

For illustration, let us look at the difference principle that, following Rawls,[23] people would agree about under a veil of ignorance. According to this, social and economic inequalities are of the greatest benefit to the least-advantaged members of society. At this point, it is not important whether such an agreement would indeed be reached but that the bindingness of agreements is thereby presupposed. Otherwise, there would be no point in looking for an agreement. This shows that the bindingness of a contract is more basic and less controversial than the decisions reached under a veil of ignorance. Unlike the latter, it does not require controversial assumptions that people would be risk-averse and therefore insure themselves with the difference principle against the lotteries of life.

The same holds for traditional contract theories that justify basic institutions of governance. They also rely on the assumption that agreements bind and extend this to hypothetical agreements. For that, they need to make elaborate, controversial arguments about what people would agree on in a state of nature. Take, for instance, Hobbes' claim that people in such a situation would give up 'the right of defending another; but not of defending himselfe'.[24] Again, it is not important at this point whether this argument is convincing or whether, at least for some people, the defence of their loved ones is at least as important as their own life. Instead, it is decisive that such arguments require many more assumptions about what people hypothetically would agree about than justifications of why one shall obey agreements. If one could refer to an actual agreement, no such theory would be needed. As far as contract law builds on consent, it rests on firmer moral foundations than any so-called contract theory.

[23] John Rawls, *A Theory of Justice* (Harvard UP 1971) 53.
[24] Thomas Hobbes, *Leviathan* (Richard Tuck ed, CUP 1991) 161.

All of this does, of course, not mean that no dispute about the foundation of contracts is possible. On the contrary, one can find interesting disagreements about it, for instance, between reliance, promise, and transfer theories.[25] The same holds for whether and why persons can bind themselves, although their interests, feelings, and characteristics change over time. This presupposes that an earlier act of the promising person shall have preference over their later wishes, although the person then knows much better what they really need. Not accidentally, there is an extensive philosophical debate about this.[26]

Yet, these questions and disputes should not blur the bigger picture that they concern a point that is hardly controversial and relies, if not taken as self-evident, only on a few assumptions, such as the contradictory nature of a breach of agreement. Being minimal does not mean being unquestionable or philosophically uninteresting. The claim that contract law rests on less controversial, more easily defensible ideas than other norms is a matter of comparison. That hardly anything is uncontroversial and unproblematic in philosophy does not mean that everything is, to the same extent, controversial and problematic. One cannot understand the difference between contract law and other areas of law without noticing that their foundations differ in the degrees to which they need argumentative support. This is not a happy coincidence but a main feature that explains what reasons are needed to justify contract law.

One might object that contract law entails much more than just norms that implement the parties' agreement. And indeed, one can find default rules that are not exclusively modelled after the question of what the parties implicitly agreed about or what they would have agreed about, if they had negotiated the underlying question. Instead, the law also pursues, in part even with obligatory norms, other aims, such as a fair balance of rights and duties between the parties and the protection of consumers, tenants, and employees, all of which have only a loose connection to the consent of the parties to a particular agreement.

However, these supplementary reasons come into play only if an agreement has been made. Consent thus remains foundational. If contract law were to negate the aim of the concluded agreements by supplementing them with its own rules that subvert the parties' intentions, people would no longer conclude contracts. The consent of the parties thus creates a border, which can only, to a limited extent, be transgressed by additionally imposed rules of contract law. The argument is, hence, not that all contract law rules rest on consent

[25] Stephen Smith, *Contract Theory* (OUP 2004) 54–105.

[26] See Allen Habib, 'Promises', *The Stanford Encyclopedia of Philosophy* (Winter edn, 2014) <https://plato.stanford.edu/Archives/win2021/entries/promises/> accessed 10 January 2023.

but that consent provides their main justification and rests on minimal moral assumptions.

2. Property Law

A second area in which such minimalism can be observed is property law. Its main purpose is to clarify to whom the individual chattels and real estate belong. Thanks to its norms relating to the acquisition as well as the transfer of property, one can distinguish between the 'external Mine and Yours'.[27] Thereby, one knows which things one might use and for the usage of which things one needs permission. Without such information, social cooperation would be impossible. A world where everybody was allowed to use everything, and one would not need property, is as unreal as a world in which property would be superfluous because one would not need the things demarcated thereby anyway. All of this is so trivial that the distinction between 'Mine and Yours' is among the first things children learn. Property law does little more than elaborate this basic insight. For this purpose, it makes only some minimal assumptions. The most important among them are, first, that something that belongs to one person shall, in principle, remain their property until they give it up, and second, that the transfer of property has to proceed on a voluntary basis, save some well-explainable exceptions.

In contrast to this, the difficult and, therefore, more controversial question as to whom things shall belong is not the subject of property law. It remains neutral in regard to the distribution of property in a society, especially whether 'the means of production' are in the hands of a few people or owned by the state. These questions are crucial to characterize the social set-up of society but are not dealt with in property law. Its rules remain the same, regardless of whether they are applied only to a few personal belongings or to almost all material things, including public goods. Therefore, the same rules of property law can be used for different and even opposing purposes. For instance, whether an old-timer belongs to a private person who wants to crash it, a museum that wants to save it, or a political party that wants to abolish cars altogether does, as far as property law is concerned, not play a role. Its main purpose is reached as soon as it is clear to whom which things belong and which rights and duties this entails.

[27] Kant (n 10) 261.

This explains why, for instance, the property law of the German BGB could be used without major changes in five politically quite different systems: the monarchical German Empire, the Weimar Republic, the Nazi regime, the socialist German Democratic Republic, and the current Federal Republic. There were changes, as property law, even nowadays, undergoes some reforms. But overall, the same rules are in place as in the beginning. The main reason for this seems to be that property law leaves the purposes open for which it is used and remains neutral as to the distribution of property. It is confined to a very basic idea, namely, that it shall be clear to whom which things belong.

In order to justify property law, one needs, therefore, only a few assumptions, not an elaborate theory. It seems obvious that society is worse off if one, due to the absence of property law, cannot tell to whom which things belong. In such a state of nature, one cannot be sure whether others take what one has produced oneself. Rules about the acquisition and the transfer of property are therefore inevitable. This almost sounds too trivial to be explained. But this triviality is the very point which often goes unnoticed. Because the justification of property law is much more obvious than that of other areas of law and less discussed, its character does not draw much attention. It can already be justified with minimal morality and does not need elaborate theories. Of central interest are, therefore, not the reasons why one needs rules of property but the fact that these reasons are, in contrast to the reasons that justify other areas of law, rather simple.

At first glance, one might object that property is foundational for the economic system and, therefore, property law is the topic of far-reaching theories, of which Marxism and other socialist theories are the most notorious examples. Especially Proudhon's sentence 'Property is theft'[28] seems to refute the thesis that property stands on comparatively uncontroversial grounds. However, at a closer look, even these critics did not dispute that one needs property and did not question the then-existing property law. In particular, Marx did not argue for the total abolition of property (but against the exploitation which is realized via it) and explicitly criticized Proudhon's slogan.[29] Similarly, Proudhon explained later that his slogan was not supposed to abolish property and equally true as the slogan 'Property is freedom'.[30] One would need an extremely radical version of anarchism if one were to argue that all laws of property should

[28] Pierre-Joseph Proudhon, *Property is Theft!, A Pierre-Joseph Proudhon Anthology* (Iain McKay ed, AK Press 2011) 87.

[29] Karl Marx, *Das Elend der Philosophie* (3rd edn, Dietz 1895) 26.

[30] Pierre-Joseph Proudhon, *No Gods, No Masters: An Anthology of Anarchism* (Daniel Guerin ed, AK Press 2005) 55.

disappear and no property could be acquired even where personal belongings are concerned. Nevertheless, such a radical version is imaginable. Therefore, the argument here is not that property is a natural, neutral, apolitical institution that nobody could question. Rather, the point is that property rests on only a few rather simple assumptions and excludes more controversial questions about its distribution.

As for contract law, one might point out that contract law is not just founded on one idea only, namely, that there should be clear rules about the acquisition and the transfer of property. In addition, property law is influenced by considerations of trust, especially when it comes to good faith acquisition and fairness, which can be seen in the limits for the usage of property. But, the fact that these considerations play a role does not show that they have the same impact on the character of property law. They rather supplement the rules, the main purpose of which is to create a clear classification of what is 'mine and yours'. Without such a classification, the additional considerations would not have a place at all. It does not make sense to state limits of fair use if there is no property, which could thereby be limited.

The less demanding the foundation of property is, the more likely it is that people could agree about it. This indicates the minimal character of the underlying decision. In this regard, a comparison of different models of decision-making might help to understand the point. Lasting disagreements among people are frequently solved via voting, in which the majority has the say. In the case of controversial questions such as abortion, taxation, or the level of criminal sanctions, there is hardly another reasonable way of decision-making because there is almost no prospect of solving these disagreements consensually.

But interestingly, not every disagreement necessitates a majority vote. For instance, in open-source software programming, a majority rule is frequently avoided, and a rough consensus model is adopted instead.[31] According to this, a decision can only be adopted if almost everybody agrees with a particular solution. Until then, the debate has to be continued. The idea behind it seems to be that, on the one hand, there will most of the time be some controversy so that radical naysayers could block the development of a common project if consensus is required. One can never exclude that even minimal assumptions are negated as, for instance, philosophical anarchists[32] deny the legitimacy of

[31] See the 'unofficial motto' of the Internet Engineering Task Force: 'We believe in rough consensus and running code', <www.ietf.org/how/runningcode/> accessed 10 January 2023.

[32] Discussion and references in Richard Dagger and David Lefkowitz, 'Political Obligation', *The Stanford Encyclopedia of Philosophy* (2021) <https://plato.stanford.edu/entries/political-obligation/> accessed 10 January 2023.

any political obligation. Therefore, in most areas, it would be too demanding to make decisions based on consent.

On the other hand, this does not always necessitate a majority vote, which would allow to outvote substantial minorities of almost 50 per cent. Instead, super-majorities are sometimes required, of which a rough consensus is only one example. If such a consensus is reached, it is highly likely that a reasonable solution will be found. Such a procedure suggests itself if there are typically obvious reasons to reach a certain decision in one way or the other. This seems possible in some areas, such as software development, whereas in other areas, such as the mentioned political debates about taxation, this is unrealistic. The more a decision can be based on minimal assumptions, the more likely a rough consensus can be reached.

Similarly, among legal norms, one might distinguish those with hotly debated moral foundations and those with comparatively uncontroversial foundations. For instance, it would be illusory to discuss the level of taxation until a rough consensus is reached. There will always be numerous opponents to a proposed solution as there are radically different visions about who deserves which income. When it comes to property law, things are different. For its major principles and foundation, a rough consensus seems possible. For instance, nobody in his right mind would give up the distinction between possession and property. Therefore, property law can be and indeed is[33] in many instances developed by courts which do not, at least openly, pursue a political agenda. This presupposes the possibility of reaching a rough consensus among the deciding judges of various courts in situations where they are not bound due to hierarchy or a doctrine of precedent. Such a consensus indicates that the opinion in question can build on minimal assumptions that are widely shared. Among them is the necessity to have, due to the rules of property law, clarity about the belonging of things.

To deny this thesis, it would be insufficient to find controversial questions of property law. Admittedly, there are, at least in German law, a lot of them. This is not surprising because in applying agreed-upon principles, one can frequently find reasons that demand different answers. But a refutation of the developed thesis would demand showing in addition that either the foundation of property law is more controversial than the foundation of most other areas of law or that the foundation of all legal norms is equally controversial. Considering the relatively uncontroversial aim of a clear demarcation of things, this seems implausible.

[33] For the acquisition of property in Germany eg BGHZ 50, 45.

3. Torts

Let us finally have a short look at the foundation of torts. Hardly any other area of private law generates as many cases and disputes, which is why it seems at first glance far-fetched to regard its foundation as uncontroversial. For instance, one finds extensive disputes about its aims of prevention and compensation, the possibility of alternative liability, and the justification of punitive damages.[34] Nevertheless, the basic idea of torts is quite simple and rests as well on minimal assumptions, namely that one shall not harm others ('*neminem laedere*') and shall compensate them if one has done so.

One might further explain tort liability by a basic respect one owes to other people or by the equality of men, which prohibits giving some of them the privilege to harm others. If one does not already regard the compensation of harm as a natural consequence of commutative justice, one might also justify tort law with the assumption that the prohibition of harm is only effective if the tortfeasor has to compensate his victims and has, therefore, an incentive not to injure them in the first place. Rights to property and life would lack any importance if there were no remedies such as damages in tort law.

All these assumptions and explanations are not very demanding and, therefore, comparatively uncontroversial. Not accidentally, children from an early age onwards are legally responsible for the harm they cause to others.[35] This shows that the law regards the prohibition of injury as so obvious that tort liability does not even presuppose the capacity to read and write for it. One might argue about the limits of this responsibility, for instance, when calculating damages or the precise limits of the duties of care. But the principle that tortfeasors shall be liable hardly needs an elaborate justification to be convincing.[36]

In this regard, tort differs from other areas such as constitutional law, the norms of which are the outcome of hard choices, for instance, whether one shall have a presidential or a parliamentary system, a unitary or a federal state, first-past-the-post voting or proportional representation. The reasons for these decisions point in different directions, are complex and demand an elaborate justification of political theory. They concern not only borderline cases but the very core of the norms in question. That is why children, unlike in tort law, are not expected to understand these norms, let alone follow them. What is

[34] eg Arthur Ripstein, 'Philosophy of Tort Law' in J Coleman and S Shapiro (eds), *Jurisprudence and Philosophy of Law* (OUP 2002) 656; Hanoch Dagan, *A Liberal Theory of Property* (CUP 2021).

[35] eg in Germany, seven years, § 828 BGB.

[36] But see Stephen Sugarman, 'Doing Away with Tort Law' (1985) 73 Cal LR 555, 617, arguing for alternative schemes of compensation.

interesting about the foundation of tort law is hence less the reasons for it but the fact that they are, due to their minimality, different from the reasons for other norms.

At first glance, this might sound like a version of natural law theory, according to which there is a natural set of norms that shall be realized in each legal system. The legislator would, in this case, not have a choice and could only adopt the predetermined natural norms of tort law. However, such a claim is by far exceeding the thesis that tort law rests on minimal assumptions. This thesis does not deny that there are choices to be made and that one can reasonably disagree about the design of tort law. Instead, it merely maintains that these choices are less controversial than other decisions because they rest on fewer and more plausible assumptions.

The minimality thesis does not exclude that one can also find norms that rest on minimal moral foundations outside private law. The prohibition of murder and rape, and the establishment of a police force and an army, are candidates for this. However, if one connects the characterization of contract, property, and torts as the central institutions of private law, one cannot help but notice that, to a great extent, private law relies on an easy-to-defend minimal foundation.

This difference to other areas of law, such as constitutional law, is overlooked if one regards, from a positivist perspective, the law merely as an outcome of legislative or judicial fiat and morality as a private matter about which nothing reasonable could be said.[37] In this perspective, law is exclusively a set of social facts so that it does not matter on which moral foundations it stands. Whether these foundations are controversial or common sense, demanding or simple, complicated or easy, would not play a role as far as the law is concerned.

If one takes the contrary position that law is inseparably connected to morality, a similarly undifferentiated picture might emerge. Unless one specifies the kind of morality to which tort and other areas of law are connected, it would appear that all moral considerations have a place in legal decisions so that law would become politics[38]. Once again, the degree to which these considerations are controversial, demanding, or complicated would be irrelevant and thus, a crucial characteristic of large areas of private law goes unnoticed.

For instance, it is a difference whether one accepts that the one who beats another has to pay for their care or whether one accepts, in addition, that descendants of mistreated people can, after several generations, equally demand

[37] eg Carlos Alchourrón and Eugenio Bulygin, *Normative Systems* (Springer 1971) 1–2.

[38] cf Duncan Kennedy, *A Critique of Adjudication* (Harvard UP 1997) 36: 'There is no metacriterion for choosing between political theories ... other than the judge's conviction that a given theory is the best.'

compensation. Both positions might be justified on the balance of reasons. Possibly, no categorical difference allows calling the one moral and the other political. But this does not mean that they have the same degree of disputability and that, on the balance of reasons, the scales will tip in the same way. As mentioned before, focusing on the extremes might blur the full picture. Part of this is that some assumptions need, due to their minimal character, less justification than others do. The questions underlying private law are neither outside morality nor politics but nevertheless less controversial than in other legal areas. The focus on the extremes, a complete separation of law and morality, and their unlimited connection might have distracted from this crucial characteristic of private law, which lies between them.

III. Minimalism in the Filling of Gaps

Of uttermost importance in law, in general, is the question of how gaps shall be filled. This question not only arises if neither statutes nor precedents determine whether a particular action is legal or illegal. In addition, gaps also occur in the methods with which norms are to be interpreted.

The extent to which gaps play a role in everyday legal arguments becomes visible if one tries to trace each sentence of a Supreme Court decision to a particular statute or precedent. In many cases, this succeeds very well, for instance, for references to a certain statutory norm. But almost any Supreme Court decision also contains sentences for which such a reference is impossible. These sentences are either supposed to be self-evident or need supporting arguments outside the formal sources of law.

Many legal theories of the last century differ in their answer to what to do in this situation. While Kelsen denied that there are gaps in the law, he admitted that some questions are not determined by statutes and assumed that judges are authorized to determine the issue themselves in these cases.[39] Later positivists such as Raz did not deny that there are gaps, but equally assumed that judges mostly have discretion to fill them out.[40] Dworkin disputed that there is much leeway and argued that in these cases judges have to take resort to principles which in turn are connected to political philosophy.[41] Law and economic scholars[42] plead for adopting the most efficient answer in such cases. All

[39] Kelsen (n 5) 253.
[40] Raz (n 1) 70.
[41] Ronald Dworkin, *Taking Rights Seriously* (Duckworth 1977) 107.
[42] Richard Posner, *Economic Analysis of Law* (6th edn, Aspen 2003) 539.

of them agree that once the legal norms do not provide an answer, one has to look for other sources, be they moral or economic arguments.

Thereby, the impression emerges that once there is a gap, all considerations could be used to fill it out and that there are no filters due to which only reasons with a certain level of plausibility are admissible. If economic reasons about the efficiency of a norm could, in principle, be used for a legal decision, so the argument goes, then there is no limit in regard to their complexity, empirical soundness, and disputability. Similarly, if moral reasons are indeed admissible to fill a gap, then, it is argued, one should look for 'the best conception of what justice requires'.[43] Again, it does not seem to matter for such a view how complicated and demanding a moral argument is in order to be used to fill out a legal gap. It suffices that it has a slightly greater argumentative force than the counterarguments against it.

However, if one looks at the legal practice of dealing with gaps, a different picture emerges. There, not all morally sound reasons play a role, but predominantly reasons with which almost everybody agrees—at least in the abstract. While one does find occasional references to justice or even to Rawls' idea of a 'veil of ignorance'[44] in decisions of the highest courts, they predominately do not adopt whole moral or economic theories. Rather, they try to use simpler arguments that are understandable even in the absence of a worked-out theory. These arguments can nevertheless be disputed as they are moral in nature, but are more plausible than elaborate theories that rest on a great number of assumptions.

Similarly, courts occasionally use economic arguments, for instance, by referring to the incentives one or the other solution to a legal question would bring about.[45] But tellingly, judgments hardly ever use or discuss elaborate economic models. In comparison to the advanced mathematical models and the extensive statistical analysis that one finds in journals of economics, the arguments in court decisions are comparatively simple. They build on basic insights, which most of the time could be formulated even without a mathematical apparatus, and rely on commonsensical knowledge rather than an extensive statistical analysis. This minimalism is not just a matter of lawyers' limited competence in economics but part of the *modus operandi* of private law. Arguments usually have to pass a comparatively high threshold of plausibility in order to be admitted into law.

[43] Dworkin (n 16) 352.
[44] German Constitutional Court, BVerfGE 101, 158 para 272; Rawls (n 23) 118.
[45] eg BVerfG, NVwZ 2006, 559, 571.

This minimalism can also be seen in the arguments used in equity and good faith. These concepts require a concretization for which, at first glance, all kinds of arguments could be used. But interestingly, one mainly finds arguments that are either self-evident or rely on only a few assumptions. For instance, hardly anybody denies that one who seeks equity must do equity, or that one shall not profit from one's own wrong, etc. These maxims go back to Roman law and are still applicable despite radical historical changes because they do not rest on changing circumstances but on minimal assumptions. Therefore, these maxims are, in their substance (but not necessarily their name), accepted in most legal systems.[46]

The cause for this convergence seems to lie not necessarily in a common history[47] or similar norms of statutory or customary law. Instead, it has also to do with the high plausibility of these maxims. This makes it possible to base a legal decision on them without a specific foundation in statutory law or another legal source. Therefore, arguments of equity and good faith differ in at least two regards from moral considerations that play a role in political theory and practice. First, in contrast to the latter kind, they are part of a minimal morality for which a higher epistemological confidence seems in reach. For instance, one can be sure that others should not act in a contradictory way and therefore allow a good-faith-objection against such behaviour ('*venire contra factum proprium*') than one usually is with regard to the question of how society shall compensate for the inequality of income. Although moral considerations play a role in both cases, only in the first one is the certainty high enough to be easily applied to private law decisions.

Second, apart from the epistemology, the ontology of these reasons is also different. Reasons used to concretize the idea of equity or good faith are either basic assumptions, which do not need further justification, or rest on only a few of such basic assumptions. That is why no elaborated theory is needed to justify them. For instance, the objection against contradictory behaviour is not only easier to understand but also, in its foundation, simpler than, for instance, rules why and to which extent one needs the limitation of responsibility in corporate law.

In many cases, the reasons used in good faith are not only minimal, but also basic, that is not reducible to more basic reasons. However, the minimality thesis does not rest upon the basic character of the reasons decisive for private

[46] Overview in Reinhard Zimmermann and Simon Whittaker (eds), *Good Faith in European Contract Law* (CUP 2000).

[47] For China see eg Simona Novaretti, 'General Clauses and Practice: The Use of the Principle of Good Faith in the Decisions of Chinese Courts' (2010) 18 ERPL 953, 970.

law. Being minimal does not necessarily mean being basic. It is at least conceptually possible that there are non-minimal basic reasons, for instance, complicated assumptions about an optimal behaviour. Equally, there might very well exist minimal reasons that are not basic because they could be reduced to other reasons, for instance, if one explains the prohibition of contradictory behaviour by its lack of efficiency or its detrimental effect on human relations. The minimality thesis concerns the degree to which reasons and foundations of private law are controversial and parsimonious in their assumptions and not the question of whether they are reducible to more basic ideas.

Minimalism only has relevance in filling gaps if it excludes reasons that do not have such a minimal character, as only in this way may it come to other conclusions than theories that allow all reasons to fill out gaps. Therefore, it is most interesting to look for cases in which, with moral minimalism, another solution would be optimal than the one demanded without it. In such cases, the answer the law gives would differ from what would be morally or economically best. This is possible in an abstract way if the morally or economically optimal decision rests on reasons that are not compatible with the law's minimalism and would hence have to be excluded from the law.

To illustrate this possible divergence in the reached results, let us look at a case of neighbour law about which the German Supreme Court had to decide some years ago.[48] Two terraced houses were built at the beginning of the twentieth century in such a way that they were attached and shared therefore a great part of one wall. One house was longer than the other, which is why they did not share all of the wall. A part of the longer house was, therefore, directly exposed to the neighbouring lot. As usual at the time of the construction, this wall had only one layer of bricks and not any additional isolation. A hundred years later, the owner of the longer house wanted to insulate the open part of the wall to save heating costs. For this purpose, he needed to put an insulating material on it, which then would protrude 14 cm into the neighbouring lot. By German law, he would be allowed to do so if he 'exercised reasonable discretion'.[49] At first glance, this rather vague standard opens the gates for all kinds of considerations and allows judges to decide what they hold optimal. Yet, the Supreme Court abstained from such a standard and asked instead what would be 'in the interest of every reasonably thinking co-owner'[50]. It assumed that this would include the wall being brought up to the current general standard.

[48] BGH NJW 2008, 2032.
[49] §§ 922 p 4, 745 s 2 BGB.
[50] BGH NJW 2008, 2032 p 15.

This reference to a general standard as well as to 'every reasonably thinking co-owner' entails a significant limitation as, according to it, overwhelming but still disputed reasons would not be sufficient. These higher standards could, on the balance of reasons, be morally preferable but not legally obligatory. For instance, let us suppose that the owner chooses a thicker insulation of 30 cm, which consists of organic material instead of an artificial poisonous one. Then, its usage might be morally preferable due to its lesser impact on the environment. Nevertheless, as long as there can be reasonable disagreement on whether the thinner insulation is preferable, the neighbour does not have to tolerate the thicker one.

The same holds if the thicker insulation were preferable because of its slightly lower price or because of its origin from an African producer that is vital for a rural community. Under the standard used by the court, there would not be a right to put such insulation on the wall because this would accord neither with a general standard nor with that which 'every reasonably thinking person' would agree to. Others could, for instance, argue that the neighbour is not responsible for the protection of the environment or that there are superior means to support the African economy.

All of this shows that the threshold of minimal morality might entail other standards than the ones required by optimal moral, economic, or ecological standards. It is a truism that law frequently imposes a minimal and not a maximal number of duties.[51] However, it is less obvious that this refrainment from maximal duties holds even if one deals with vague standards such as 'reasonably exercised discretion' which allows, at first glance, to demand more than a minimum.

Contrary to this, theories that incorporate without any limitation all kinds of economic or moral reasons into the law would come to a different conclusion. They would allow all such reasons to determine the decision and grant the judge full freedom to fill a gap. For instance, they would allow the usage of non-standard isolations because of their overall beneficial effect. Hence, they could not explain why a solution that is, taken separately, morally or economically optimal should nevertheless not be required by a discretionary decision of private law. The lower standard chosen by the Supreme Court can thus be justified only if one allows minimal but not maximal moral arguments to supplement the law. This case shows that minimal morality can bring about other results than approaches that do not limit the discretion of judges. The difference

[51] cf Georg Jellinek, *Die socialethische Bedeutung von Recht, Unrecht und Strafe* (Hölder 1878) 42: 'the law is nothing else than the ethical minimum' [my translation].

between minimal and maximal morality matters. The fact that there is a sliding transition between them does not prevent their distinction or relevance.

IV. The Necessity of Minimal Morality in Private Law

The look at central institutions of private law as well as how gaps are filled out, was supposed to demonstrate the minimality thesis in its descriptive dimension. What was left out insofar was the prescriptive dimension, that is, the question of whether private law shall operate in this way. There are at least, three reasons which are fairly general and thus hardly dependent on the particular legal system and historical situation but can nevertheless acquire throughout time a different weight:

1. Law's Coercive Character

The first reason is connected to the possibility to enforce private law via the state's coercive apparatus. Debtors who do not pay can be forced to do so by the confiscation of their property. People who do not leave one's flat might be expelled with the help of the police, who are authorized to use violence for this purpose. The same holds for virtually every other private law obligation. This connection to physical force is not specific to private law but crucial for the arguments employed in it. If they are based on morality, they shall be minimal in character because otherwise, the certainty about their justifiability would be too low.

While the uncertainty about non-minimal moral arguments does not make them wrong, the considerable likelihood that one is mistaken about them makes their usage for the legitimization of state force problematic. The fewer steps one needs to develop an argument and the more basic its assumptions are, the lower the risk of being wrong. One crucial argument for minimalism in law is that legal arguments contribute to decisions which are, if necessary, implemented by force.

To justify the usage of violence, not all arguments seem therefore appropriate. Rather, they shall have a statutory basis and thus rest on a democratic decision or be so convincing that there can hardly be a reasonable doubt about them. For violence intrudes on the freedom of others to such an extent that the intervening person or institution must be quite sure that they do not make a mistake thereby. There shall hence be a difference between views about which ones are so certain that it seems appropriate to impose them, if necessary, by force, and views which one regards as plausible but which nevertheless stand epistemologically or ontologically on such weak foundations that one shall abstain from this kind of enforcement. Where exactly this border runs is not important at this point. It suffices to see that there is such a border.

One might object that private law institutions such as contract, property, and tort are frequently codified so that they enjoy the same level of legitimation as all other statutes. Therefore, it seems to be merely a decision of the democratic legislator to make high or low demands on private parties via private law. Indeed, one can find statutory decisions in labour, tenancy, and consumer law for which one needs more than just minimal morality. However, this does not alter the fact that the main private law institutions were developed mostly by courts and the academia, both of which relied in this regard mainly on reasons and not on their institutional authority. The norms were adopted because they seemed reasonable and not because they were part of a political programme. One might ridicule this image as naïve and try to prove its ideological underpinnings. But even such a critique could not obfuscate the fact that these foundations are minimal compared to the foundation of other norms. The argument that there are no apolitical, merely technical rules.[52] does not show that there are no differences in the degree of disputability among the rules one has. The less norms are disputable, the more their enforcement via violence is legitimate.

This is even more true for decisions not determined by statutory law and, instead, have to be made by courts who, in comparison to parliament, have less democratic legitimacy. This is, for instance, when abstract concepts such as negligence or causation have to be concretized and rules about their interplay be developed. In this concretization of abstract concepts and the development of norms, judges must rely on reasons. Their legitimacy is the higher the more minimal their foundations are.

2. Private People as Law's Addressees

A second reason why private law shall have a minimal character is connected to the characteristics of private law's addressees. The central institutions of private law, such as contracts, property, and torts are important for almost everyone. There is hardly any adult who never concludes contracts, has no property at

[52] cf Kennedy (n 38) 292.

all or does not have to exercise proper care in regard to other people's life and property.

In this aspect, private law differs from other norms, the application of which one can avoid by not engaging in the activity that they regulate. For instance, as long as one does not run a nuclear power station, one does not have to know the detailed requirements for its operation; as long as one does not produce medical pills, one does not have to know which information has to be provided with them, etc. While the law can presuppose that producers of pills hire professionals familiar with these requirements, it cannot equally presuppose a high level of legal information among those for whom the ordinary rules of contract, property and torts apply. Instead, it must rely on their ability to obey these rules without ever reading them. Private law applies to addressees regardless of their education or intellectual capacity. That is why it is in some languages called 'citizen's law',[53] which makes clear that it is for all citizens and not just for lawyers, officers, consultants, or other specialists.

These differences in the addressee's characteristics have repercussions for the design and content of private law and the arguments one can use in its application. As far as possible, its norms have to meet social expectations.[54] Only thereby can it minimize the surprises about what the law requires. Private law must not require a thorough legal analysis before its commands can be known. Hence, there is a great need to keep its rules simple. One way for this is to base them on simple foundations, which have foreseeable consequences in the form of the particular rules of private law. This also explains why many private law norms rest on easily understandable principles such as realizing contractual promises as far as possible, safeguarding stability in the demarcation of property, or holding tortfeasors responsible. These principles are intuitive and can be applied more easily than a set of complicated rules, which are the outcome of a highly differentiating theory. Private law's minimalism has partly to do with the limitations of what it can demand from its addressees. Even if one ignores that moral rules are already by their content, often surprisingly simple, private law needs such simplicity to fulfil its function.

In this regard, a comparison with the requirements for designing a computer program might illustrate the point. This design also depends not only on the abstract task it shall fulfil but also on the abilities of the potential users. If they are unwilling or unable to cope with complicated procedures, one has to limit

[53] German: *Bürgerliches Recht*; Russian: гражданское право.

[54] cf Andrew Gold and Henry Smith, 'Sizing Up Private Law' (2020) 70 U Toronto LJ 489, 504–05 referring to the 'local morality' as a starting point for contract law.

the complexity of the user interface—even if this compromises the program's functions. Therefore, programs for consumers differ from programs for professionals, even if similar tasks are to be performed by them. For instance, accounting software to track revenues and expenses inside companies is much more detailed and more complicated than programs that do the same for private people. This does not necessarily have to do with the amount of money and the number of accounting entries involved but also the different readiness to study detailed rules before applying them. In a similar way, private law norms that address virtually everybody are to be as simple as possible and shall thus be based on minimal foundations that are easy to grasp.

The same holds for reasons courts use to decide private law disputes. These reasons shall not state what one has to do once one is acquainted with all scholarly arguments for and against a certain action. Instead, these reasons shall justify what the parties should have known before without studying dogmatic treatises. The task of the courts is, hence, not to invent rules that the parties would have the best reason to adopt in future once they become acquainted with the court's opinion but to explain which rules they should have applied even before coming to court. It is only because of this that the loser shall pay for the court's as well as opponents' expenses—unless the American rule applies. The rationale behind this is that the loser could have avoided this payment if he had acted properly before.

Therefore, there are limits as to the kind of arguments that judges shall use in private law disputes. Although their arguments will unavoidably surprise the parties many times, they should meet as far as possible the reasonable expectations of laypeople. Given the differences in a pluralist society, they can do so only if these arguments are minimal in character.

3. Law's Generality

A third reason for private law's moral minimalism goes back to its generality. It is designed not only for specific cases but for all situations in which its highly abstract rules apply. Hence, many circumstances play no role in it. Whether one buys an apple or a rocket is immaterial as far as the law of sales is concerned. Whether one destroys a skyscraper or a screw is irrelevant to the tort rules that shall be applied. Similarly unimportant are the characteristics of the parties involved. Whether one deals with a Fortune 500 company or the craftsman next door does not play a role. Admittedly, in recent decades, this generality was reduced by introducing consumer law that provides some privileges for them. But even according to this law, there is no difference whether a Supreme Court judge or a constable at the court orders something via the internet and whether the order goes to Amazon or an artist who only occasionally sells his works online.

This generality has huge repercussions for the content and justification of private law. For it, the characteristics of the people and situations involved have to be ignored unless private law rules refer to them. One can merely ask in the abstract which rights and duties the parties to a contract or the owners of a certain property shall have and cannot investigate the particular situation they are in. Therefore, in many respects, one does not need the above-mentioned 'veil of ignorance' for the design of private law. Already, its generality prevents only a certain group of people from benefitting from it. For instance, the rights and duties of sellers and buyers, tortfeasors and victims do not depend on the age, history, or financial capacities of the involved parties. The lack of knowledge of their characteristics constitutes a natural 'veil of ignorance' that helps to filter reasons of minimal morality from more demanding reasons. Asking what 'a buyer' or 'an owner' should do or could expect makes it difficult to pay attention to morally relevant circumstances such as the experience of the people involved.

This partial ignorance of morally relevant factors contributes to the described minimalism. Once a considerable number of possible considerations has to be left out, one has to concentrate on reasons that hold independent of them. They have to be so robust that they cannot be refuted by reasons that come into play only if one pays attention to the particular circumstances of the situation. For instance, the experience of a party with a certain product becomes immaterial if a party has accepted it. The prohibition of contradictory behaviour is so robust that it does not depend on previous knowledge or similar factors. This justifies ignoring many other factors. The generality of private law hence contributes to its moral minimalism.

V. Relationship to Other Concepts

In order to understand the idea that private law rests and operates on moral minimalism, it seems finally useful to relate it to two other theses. At least in name, it has a superficial resemblance to Sunstein's description of judicial minimalism, according to which decisions in the courts extensively use incompletely theorized agreements.[55] He thereby refers to the phenomenon that

[55] Cass Sunstein, *One Case at a Time: Judicial Minimalism on the Supreme Court* (Harvard UP 1999) 249.

judges frequently agree about the outcome of a case or mid-level principles but not a theory behind them. In this way, he suggests that these decisions operate without a sufficiently worked-out theory.

Although this kind of minimalism also prevents deep moral disagreements from affecting the law, it nevertheless differs from the moral minimalism described here in at least one important respect. The claim that Supreme Court decisions rely on incompletely theorized agreements suggests a lack of theory and that the accepted mid-level principles are not defendable unless one works out a full theory for them. Although the minimality thesis does not exclude that such a phenomenon occurs in Supreme Court decision-making, it denies such a lack of theory for the phenomenon it aims to describe, that is, private law works with minimal moral assumptions. It is a theoretical statement and not an abandonment of theory to claim that private law builds to a significant extent on minimal assumptions which are either self-evident or need only little argumentative support. Moreover, these statements themselves are theoretically sound according to moral minimalism and not incompletely theorized.

A parallel to architecture might help to understand this point. In comparison to baroque churches and Italian palazzos, modernist buildings might, at first glance, appear as lacking architecture. They neither have small towers nor stucco, nor decorations, nor frontispieces. Their form shall follow function, which basically means that there is almost no form that is not functionally necessary. To some, such buildings might, therefore, indeed appear as empty and 'incompletely architectured'. But this radical elimination of opulence constitutes just another style of architecture. Minimalist buildings have their own appeal. Therefore, these buildings are indeed 'fully architectured'—although their minimalism diverges considerably from other styles. Similarly, the moral minimalism thesis defended here claims that private law embodies a special kind of theory and not a deficiency of it.

Due to its openness to moral arguments, moral minimalism might also be confronted with the practical difference thesis advanced by many positivists.[56] According to this, morality provides no sufficient guidance, which is why one needs the law. Only its authority could make a practical difference compared to a situation where one would be merely guided by moral considerations. If one were to incorporate morality into the law, this practical difference would disappear. Moral considerations could hence not be part of the law.

The minimal morality thesis denies this conclusion for two reasons. First, incorporating moral considerations into a legal argument does not mean that

[56] See Jules Coleman, *The Practice of Principle* (OUP 2001) 69.

they fully substitute all legal norms contained in it. Even with such an incorporation, one can take positive law seriously: Which means, first and foremost, that norms of statutory or customary law are a central and almost always binding part of any legal argument. These norms alone can make all the practical difference one needs. But this does not exclude that moral considerations play some additional role, especially if it comes to interpreting vague concepts or filling out gaps.

Second, incorporating or recognizing *some* moral considerations within the law does not mean that morality, thereby through and through, becomes part of the law. As seen, large parts of it should not play a role within the law because they are too demanding and not sufficiently robust to justify enforcement by police power. The questions of how to optimally develop one's talents or best contribute to the overall utility of mankind are barred from shaping a legal argument, although they might very well have moral significance. But this does not exclude the use of minimal moral arguments for private law altogether. Therefore, the choice between incorporating morality in total or abstaining from it in total is a wrong alternative.

There is a third possibility, namely, to use minimal moral arguments. They help to fill out gaps and justify its foundations, although they might still be disputed and not verifiable by the laws of formal logic, statistics, or other methods of the natural sciences. Nevertheless, they provide a much better justification than if there were no arguments at all or only equally disputed ones. Insofar they resemble statutes, which, despite all interpretive quarrels, also provide a better foundation for a decision than one would have if there were no statutes at all. When it comes to filling in the gaps in private law and reaching a discretionary decision, minimal moral arguments are all one can hope for—and all one needs.

14

Rights Without Standing

On the Nature of Equitable Rights

*Larissa Katz**

I. Introduction

Across a wide range of theories of private law, the idea of a private law right is closely connected to the idea of standing. In many such theories, a private law right exists only if one has the standing to enforce it.[1] And in other theories of private law, standing in a broader sense defines the very substance of a right: a right is just the standing to decide some questions, to the exclusion of others.[2] Standing in this broader sense gives the nature or content of the

* Professor and Canada Research Chair in Private Law Theory, University of Toronto, Faculty of Law. Research assistance was funded by Social Sciences and Humanities Research Council. I am very grateful to Paul Miller, John Goldberg, and other participants at the Private Law Methodology workshop at Bucerius Law School for insightful comments and discussion. I would also like to thank Manula Adhihetty, Jared Barkman, and Michael Law-Smith for research assistance and comments on various drafts of this chapter, and Arthur Ripstein, Matt Shapiro, and especially Malcolm Thorburn for comments on earlier drafts.

[1] See Arthur Ripstein, *Private Wrongs* (HUP 2016); Ernest Joseph Weinrib, *The Idea of Private Law* (revd edn, OUP 2012). For others, a moral principle, such as a principle of civil recourse, connects the idea of a right in private law and standing. See John CP Goldberg and Benjamin C Zipursky, *Recognizing Wrongs* (HUP 2020). See also Andrew S Gold, *The Right of Redress* (OUP 2020) and John Oberdiek, 'It's Something Personal: On the Relationality of Duty and Civil Wrongs' in P Miller and J Oberdiek (eds) *Civil Wrongs and Justice in Private Law* (OUP 2020) 301. John Goldberg and Benjamin Zipursky offer an account of equity outside of private law, which they understand as the scheme of civil recourse. See John CP Goldberg and Benjamin C Zipursky, 'From *Riggs v Palmer* to *Shelley v Kraemer*: Judicial Power and the Law–Equity Distinction' in D Klimchuk, I Samet, and HE Smith (eds) *Philosophical Foundations of the Law of Equity* (OUP 2020). Even those who think that private rights do not entail the standing to enforce recognize strong institutional reasons for allocating enforcement rights to the holder of a private law right. See Larissa Katz and Matthew Shapiro, 'The Role of Plaintiffs in Private Law Institutions' in H Psarras and S Steel (eds) *Private Law and Practical Reason: Essays on John Gardner's Private Law Theory* (OUP 2023)(on whether the standing to enforce private rights should presumptively be allocated to right-holders).

[2] See eg Ripstein (n 1). For a jurisdictional account of property rights, see Larissa Katz, 'Exclusion and Exclusivity in Property Law' (2008) 59 U Toronto LJ 275; Larissa Katz, 'Spite and Extortion: A Jurisdictional Principle of Abuse of Property Right' (2013) 122 Yale LJ 1444; Larissa Katz, 'Blowing Hot and Cold: The Role of Estoppel' in P Miller and J Oberdiek (eds) *Civil Wrongs and Justice in Private Law* (OUP 2020). See also Avihay Dorfman, 'Private Ownership and the Standing to Say So' (2014) 64 U Toronto LJ 402.

Larissa Katz, *Rights Without Standing* In: *Methodology in Private Law Theory*. Edited by: Thilo Kuntz and Paul B. Miller, Oxford University Press. DOI: 10.1093/oso/9780198885306.003.0014

right. For example, ownership (at least on some accounts) is defined in terms of the standing to resolve the question of who can do what with respect to a particular thing.

In common-law jurisdictions, however, there is an important doctrinal category of rights[3] in private law—equitable rights—that lack this deep connection to standing in either the broad or narrow sense. Equitable rights, such as the beneficiary's interest in a trust, a restrictive covenant or a mortgagor's equity of redemption, emerge from concepts and principles developed historically by specialized courts of equity. These rights do not convey standing in the narrow sense: courts doing equity retain discretion over *whether* to intervene in the name of equity.[4] Equitable rights are associated, instead, with a pale reflection of standing: the power merely to commence judicial proceedings that invite, rather than require, a court to do equity. Equitable rights also do not convey standing in the broad sense because they do not put the right-holder in charge of anything; instead, equitable rights are defined by reference to what a court thinks that conscience, in a civil or political sense—the integrity of the system of private law rights—requires in the particular case.[5]

Equitable rights are rights without standing because they have a public dimension that can never be fully within private control: it is never a matter for private actors but is for courts only to decide whether to do equity in a particular

[3] While for reasons I advance in this chapter we may prefer the term 'interest', courts and commentators routinely describe equitable interests as a private 'right'.

[4] The discretionary nature of equity is not controversial. See also Peter M McDermott, *Equitable Damages* (Butterworths 1994) 54–55. Not only does it mean that a private actor cannot require a court to do equity, but it also means that they cannot require a court *not* to do equity. See *Burgess v Rawnsley* [1975] Ch 429 (one cannot waive an equitable right by insisting *ex ante* that equity does not obtain; courts will determine the existence of an equitable right *ex post facto*). See also Larissa Katz, 'Pathways to Legal Rights: The Function of Equity' in D Klimchuk, I Samet, and HE Smith (eds) *Philosophical Foundations of the Law of Equity* (OUP 2020) (discussion on the discretionary nature of equity). But see Hanoch Dagan and Avihay Dorfman, 'Substantive Remedies' (2020) 96 Notre Dame L Rev 513 (highlighting that 'equitable remedies do not invite "free-floating discretion"' (561) and that 'remedial adhocery', in which significant discretion is exercised to tailor the remedy to each case, 'breeds indeterminacy into primary rights, thus undermining relational justice' (540).

[5] See *Cook v Fountain*, 3 Swan 585 (Ch 1733), 600: 'The conscience by which I am to proceed is merely *civilis et politica*'. See discussion of conscience in Katz (n 4) 171. See also Irit Samet, *Equity: Conscience Goes to Market* (OUP 2018) (developing the idea that equity's function is to ensure that legal accountability tracks the requirements of morality). But see Larissa Katz, 'Conscience with a Filter: Comments on *Equity: Conscience Goes to Market*' (2020) 1 Jerusalem Rev L S 21, 22 (raising doubts that equity follows conscience in the familiar moral sense) and Paul B Miller, 'Equity as Supplemental Law' in D Klimchuk, I Samet, and HE Smith (eds) *Philosophical Foundations of the Law of Equity* (OUP 2020) 111 (outlining the challenges of establishing whether equity is '*uniquely* grounded in conscience' and noting its insignificance in certain equitable doctrines). See also Nyuk Y Chin, 'Relieving Against Forfeiture: Windfalls and Conscience', (1995) 25 W Australia L Rev 110, 111 (offering doctrinal grounds for the view that '"improper" or "shabby" behaviour on the part of the party against whom relief is sought has much less to do with relief than is believed'); Alan Brudner, *The Unity of the Common Law* (2nd edn, OUP 2013), 132–43, 170–74, 204–36 (Brudner offers a unified account of common law and equity by invoking something like this idea of a conscience with a filter).

case. Equitable rights are thus what Kant considered to be ambiguous rights:[6] they are private rights with a public dimension that ordinary private law rights lack. Equity and equitable rights, thus, present a challenge for private law theories organized around the concept of standing.

One way to resolve the challenge posed by equitable rights might be to rethink the central importance of standing in private law theory. Another approach might be to allow the idea of standing a central place in a theory of private law but to treat equity as something apart from private law.[7] However, a theory of private law that excludes equity would do a disservice to our understanding of private law and its institutional requirements. It would also do a disservice to a full understanding of equitable rights, which depends on understanding their connection to private law. In this chapter, I propose a third track which recognizes that ordinary private law rights regulate certain spheres of interaction between private parties, involving standing, while equity regulates another sphere of human interaction that arises out of private law: the way that one person uses a private law right to trigger a forfeiture of another's valuable interest.[8] By guarding against injustice in this sphere, equity preserves the integrity of the private law order.

The nature and structure of equitable rights in common-law systems prompt methodological reflection about how we frame our thinking about private law rights and institutions.[9] All private law theory aims to understand how private law rights fit in the legal system and in relation to public authority. Making sense of equity within a theory of private law raises a number of important questions. Most obviously, it raises anew an old and enduring question about

[6] Kant used this term to describe equitable rights as he understood them, as rights not coupled with a right of coercion. I will have more to say on Kant's view later. See n 26 below and accompanying text. In short, he takes this perspective on equitable rights because of his view of courts as adjudicating rights. See n 19 below and accompanying text. As adjudicators, courts would not be able to coercively enforce equity as a matter of right: what equity requires is not within or outside of anyone's private law right. I will argue that courts have another role in the context of disputes between private actors, in which they are not adjudicators, but agents of equity or guardians of the legal order.

[7] A version of this approach would be a theory of private law unified around a principle, such as civil recourse, which accounts for ordinary private law rights, but excludes equity. See eg Goldberg and Zipursky, 'From *Riggs v Palmer* to *Shelley v Kraemer*' (n 1) 296–97 (contrasting equity with private law as a scheme of civil recourse).

[8] I develop a more robust account of this distinctive sphere of human interaction in other work. The gist of my account is that courts of equity fulfil the role of the state to preserve the integrity of the legal order by regulating the pathways in and out of private law rights. A person who is on a completable but as yet incomplete path to acquire legal rights is vulnerable to interruption by someone with legal rights, triggering the forfeiture of her valuable position. See Katz (n 4); Larissa Katz, 'Equitable Remedies: Protecting "What We Have Coming to Us"' (2021) 96 Notre Dame L Rev 1115.

[9] This, I think, is of significance to the civilian as well as the common-law lawyer. And I say this not just because Kant, the quintessential civilian, was interested in the nature of equitable rights. He might have been motivated to take account of equitable rights by his love of a good inversion: equitable rights for him were rights without coercion, the inverse of necessity, coercion without right.

why common-law systems define ordinary private law rights at one stage, adding equitable constraints at a second stage, while civilians seem to do just as well without a formal system of equity.[10] Whether or not to have a formal system of equity is clearly an institutional choice.[11] But reflecting on the nature of equitable rights also draws attention to two quite distinctive roles that private law courts come to play: as adjudicators of private rights claims, and as guardians of the system of rights as a whole.[12] A one-step approach risks collapsing the distinction between these two quite distinct roles and so may fail to explain why courts of equity should intervene in the exercise of private law rights. Flattening law and equity into a single one-step definition of rights with built-in limits conceals the nature of the problem that equity solves and the considerations appropriate to it.

In what follows, I begin by clarifying the different senses of standing in law in order to reveal an ambiguity in the nature of (some) rights in private law: equitable rights, I will argue, are private rights without standing because they are private rights with a distinctively public dimension. I then offer a reflection on the methodological insights to be gained from accounting for equity and equitable rights in a theory of private law. A two-step approach to analysing private law rights (first defining legal rights, then grafting equitable constraints on to them) yields a clearer, more compelling, and more complete theory of private law: it brings into view some distinctive institutional requirements of a system of private rights, including the role of guardian of the legal order (filled by judges in common-law jurisdictions) alongside the role of adjudicator (filled by judges in both common-law and civil-law jurisdictions).

[10] Henry Smith has offered a vigorous defence of the second-order nature of equity. See eg Henry E Smith, 'Fusion of Law and Confusion of Equity' in D Klimchuk, I Samet, and HE Smith (eds) *Philosophical Foundations of the Law of Equity* (OUP 2020) (arguing that equity functions as 'meta-law', handling in particular problems of opportunism and multipolar disputes). See also Henry E Smith, 'Equity as Meta-Law' (2021) 130 Yale LJ 1050; Henry E Smith, 'Fusing the Equitable Function in Private Law' in K Barker, K Fairweather, and R Grantham (eds) *Private Law in the 21st Century* (Hart Publishing 2017). But see Miller (n 5) 98–102 (arguing that Smith's theory of equity as a 'safety valve' is predominantly a remedialist account, and that equity should move beyond remedialism and be understood as *supplemental* law).

[11] To be clear, these two roles need not take the institutional form of law and equity. Even within the common law it was understood that the common-law courts could and sometimes did take on this institutional role of guardian of the legal order, ensuring the basic conditions for legitimacy in the administration of justice. See *Alcock v Cooke* [1829] 5 Bingham 340, 348: '[T]he common law has no object that is dearer to it than to preserve [the Crown's honour].' The separation between law and equity, however, serves to emphasize what is distinct about these concerns.

[12] See Katz (n 4). The theme that judges doing equity are in some respects more like executive officials than adjudicators also emerges in the work of two other contributors to the same book: see Goldberg and Zipursky, 'From *Riggs v Palmer* to *Shelley v Kraemer*' (n 1) and Evan Fox-Decent, 'The Constitution of Equity' in D Klimchuk, I Samet, and HE Smith (eds) *Philosophical Foundations of the Law of Equity* (OUP 2020).

II. The Idea of Standing and Ordinary (Private Law) Rights

The idea of standing in law is the idea that something is a matter for you to decide. The two basic kinds of standing in private law—standing to enforce and standing to decide a substantive matter—are connected to the idea of a private law right in many theories of private law. That something is a matter for you to decide—over which you have standing—has downstream, normative implications. Your standing to decide a question makes it permissible for you to take it upon yourself to decide that question. The standing to decide a question also gives that decision a force that changes the normative situation of others in a variety of context-specific ways. For example, an owner's standing to refuse others entry makes their entering a wrong should the owner decide to exclude them.[13] The standing of a court to order the defendant to pay damages in a tort action generates a duty on the part of that defendant to pay any damages so ordered. Equitable rights lack standing in either of these senses, conveying only a pale reflection of standing in the form of a power to commence a proceeding.[14] (The power to commence a proceeding is allocated to equitable right-holders for largely pragmatic, institutional reasons that I will explain in Section III.

Standing, in a broad sense, defines the substance of a private law right: the matter over which the right-holder has control. Our rights to our person and to property, for example, put us in charge of our person and things. Standing makes a person's decision about who can do what with respect to a thing binding on others. Take the example of property rights. Imagine that an owner, A, invites C to swim in the owner's pool, and B, A's neighbour, invites D and E to do the same. The invitation from A, the owner of the pool, has a normative effect that the invitation from neighbour B lacks: C is privileged to be there because of A's invitation, but D and E have a duty to exclude themselves despite B's 'invitation'. Standing makes the difference: it is the very essence of ownership

[13] Of course, not all standing to decide a question is *exclusive* standing. Co-owners may both have standing to decide a question, etc. But the sort of standing associated with private law rights is normally exclusive.

[14] The power to commence a proceeding can be understood itself as a very thin kind of standing that is non-exclusive (anyone can bring a proceeding, even in the absence of a juridical foundation) and defined very narrowly (it does not amount to the standing to enforce). I opted for the language of power over 'very thin kind of standing' because the power to commence proceedings is not necessarily entailed by the standing to enforce and the standing to decide a substantive matter, associated with ordinary private law rights (eg where an action is barred by a statute of limitations) and may exist independently by them (which I argue is the case in respect of equitable rights and individualized public rights protected by public nuisance law). For helpful accounts of public nuisance as private rights with public dimensions, see Ripstein (n 1); Arthur Ripstein, 'Public and Private in the Tort of Public Nuisance', University of Toronto, Working Paper; Jason Neyers, 'Reconceptualizing the Tort of Public Nuisance' (2017) 76 CLJ 87.

that only the owner of a thing has the standing to decide who gets to do what with respect to it.[15] In short, having the standing to decide a question has two normative implications: first, the decider with standing does no legal wrong in making that decision: it is theirs to make. Indeed, those without standing commit a wrong in taking a decision reserved for someone else (someone with the exclusive standing to decide that question). Secondly, standing gives normative force to a decision that decisions without standing lack: a decision made with standing changes the normative situation of others, creating new privileges, powers, rights or duties.

A second, narrower kind of standing is the standing to *enforce* a right through self-help or civil action. Standing in this sense gives control over whether to bring the coercive force of the state (in the form of justified self-help or a judicial remedy) to bear in response to a right violation. Thinking of plaintiffs as in charge of enforcement may not be intuitive. After all, the courts have the authority to decide whether plaintiffs have met their burden of proving that they have a right and that the defendant violated it. But courts do not have the discretion to refuse a remedy if they find that the plaintiff has established the existence of a right and made out its violation.[16] Both kinds of standing confer control over some matter, although they concern different kinds of questions and relate to each other in a sequenced way.[17]

Standing in these two senses figures centrally in the idea of a private law right in many theories of private law in both the natural law and legal positivist traditions. For civil recourse theorists like John Goldberg and Benjamin Zipursky, a principle of civil recourse connects substantive private law rights and the standing to enforce private law rights through civil action.[18] For

[15] See sources referenced above in n 2.

[16] See Goldberg and Zipursky, 'From *Riggs v Palmer* to *Shelley v Kraemer*' (n 1) 293 ('In areas of private law such as tort and contract, if a complaint is properly pleaded and its allegations proven, the plaintiff is *entitled* to have a judgment against the defendant'). Of course, a plaintiff may not be allowed to bring an action (the Statute of Limitations) or to adduce certain facts required to establish either the existence of a right or its violation. See Katz, 'Blowing Hot and Cold' (n 2). That is just to say that the plaintiff in these circumstances lacks or has impaired standing to enforce the right.

[17] This point is important to counter a cogent argument sometimes made in doctrinal terms that wrongs, not rights, are the central node of legal analysis in the common law tradition—a claim that collapses the standing to enforce and the standing to decide a question. See eg John Anthony Jolowicz, *The Judicial Protection of Fundamental Rights Under English Law*, 2nd ser. (Heidelberg: The Cambridge-Tilburg Law Lectures, 1979), 9: 'So far as systematisation of the law and the statement of general principle are concerned — and both are to be found today in the judgments of the courts as well as in the writings of legal scholars — attention is generally concentrated on the circumstances in which a judicial remedy is available to a complainant, that is on "wrongs" rather than on "rights." And, though a "wrong" may be no more than a correlative of a "right", this means that an analysis and account of the "rights" that are protected by English law, whether "fundamental" or not, still appears to most English lawyers to involve a reversal of his customary mode of thought.'

[18] See Goldberg and Zipursky, 'From *Riggs v Palmer* to *Shelley v Kraemer*' (n 1).

Kantians, the idea of standing connects both substance (the standing to decide a question) and procedure (the standing to enforce) in private law.[19] For some legal positivists, there may not be a deep normative connection between a right and standing to enforce but the connection is forged nonetheless on contingent institutional grounds and in legal practice. Kelsen thought it was a stable feature of capitalist legal systems to leave it to the right-holder to decide whether to trigger sanctions for wrongdoing.[20] John Gardner thought along Kelsenian lines about rights-holders' standing to enforce their rights: it was theirs as a result of institutional choices we make and not because rights-holders have a moral claim to it for reasons personal to them.[21] Legal positivists have thus recognized that the standing to enforce is at least a *possible* feature of private law rights: private law rights are the kind of rights that a private actor *could* have the standing to enforce through court action, even if, for contingent institutional reasons, they sometimes do not.

III. Equitable Rights: Rights Without Standing?

Equitable rights lack both the broad and narrow forms of standing typical of private legal rights. They neither confer jurisdiction over some substantive question the way other (private) legal rights do, nor do they entail standing to enforce the right, as private law rights do. A court of equity may do various

[19] Kant, *The Metaphysics of Morals* (Mary J Gregor ed and trans, CUP 1996) AK 6:232, 26: 'Right and authorization to use coercion therefore mean one and the same thing'; Goldberg and Zipursky, *Recognizing Wrongs* (n 1); Ripstein, *Private Wrongs* (n 1); Stephen Darwall and Julian Darwall, 'Civil Recourse as Mutual Accountability' (2011) 39 Florida S U L Rev 17, 24 (an obligee has the individual authority to hold a wrongdoing obligor accountable because the obligation is owed to the victim obligee: 'bipolar moral obligations, that is, directed duties whose violation entails that the violating obligor has injured *and*, at least other things equal, *wronged* his obligee, also conceptually entail an authority to address claims and demands').

[20] See Hersch Lauterpacht, 'Kelsen's Pure Science of Law' in E Lauterpacht (ed) *International Law: Being the Collected Papers of Hersch Lauterpacht, Volume 2, The Law of Peace, Part I: International Law in General* (CUP 1975). Kelsen at least understood that if we opt for a subjective right as a technique for determining whether sanctions will be applied, we have opted for standing—to leave it up to the plaintiff to determine whether the defendant's duty is enforced. 'Every legal rule necessarily lays down a legal duty. It may contain a legal right if the putting into effect of the consequence of the disregard of the legal rule is made dependent upon the will of a person who has an interest in the sanction of the law being applied ... The subjective right is one of the possible and by no means necessary tools of legal technique. It is the specific technique of a society which is built upon the basis of private property and therefore pays particular attention to individual interests' (ibid 409–10).

[21] See John Gardner, *From Personal Life to Private Law* (OUP 2018) 204–05. Gardner argued that it is a 'legalistic fallacy' to suppose that a person cannot have a right unless they also have the power or standing to sue for violations of that right. A legal right-holder's standing to enforce their right requires independent justification, which he thought could be given in terms of institutional considerations, not in terms of considerations personal to the right-holder as the victim of a rights-violation. See Katz and Shapiro (n 1).

things (to compel creditors with a legal right to the payment of a sum of money not to sue their debtors to enforce that right in circumstances where the creditors were paid but did not formally discharge the debt;[22] require the mortgagee to allow the mortgagor the opportunity to continue loan payments so as to redeem the property; compel the trustee to execute the trust; and so on).[23] And a court of equity may decide to exercise its discretion to do equity (by giving an equitable remedy in a dispute or recognizing an equitable right) only in respect of people in certain positions: the beneficiary of a trust, the mortgagor, etc.[24] But the equity-seeker lacks the standing to *demand* or require that the court do any of these things even if they have an equitable right in the circumstances. The power to intervene remains inherently within the discretion of the courts.[25]

The conventional view that rights always come with the standing to enforce them raises the question of whether and in what sense equitable rights are rights at all. Kant drew attention to one version of this question: equitable rights, he thought, are rights without coercion.[26] His central example concerned a contract for wages between an employer and employee:

[22] There are other examples of the pathways in and out of legal relations protected by equity. One such equitable principle is *res judicata*, which has evolved into a more flexible principle, referring to courts' power to bar a right of action pursuant to the doctrine of repose. See *Henderson v Henderson* [1843–60] All ER Rep 378 (Eng V-C), 381–82: 'the plea of *res judicata* applied...not only to points upon which the court was actually required by the parties to form an opinion and pronounce a judgment, but to *every point which properly belonged to the subject of litigation and which the parties, exercising reasonable diligence, might have brought forward at the time*' (emphasis added). See also Lord Devlin in *Connelly v Director of Public Prosecutions*, [1964] 2 All ER 401 (UKHL), 445; *Arnold v National Westminster Bank Plc (No 1)*, [1991] 3 All ER 41 (UKHL) (*res judicata*, preventing abuse of process); *Hoque v Montreal Trust Co of Canada*, 1997 NSCA 153.

[23] These ideas are developed in Katz (n 4); Katz, 'Equitable Remedies' (n 8); JH Baker, *An Introduction to English Legal History* (4th edn, Butterworths LexisNexis, 2002) 102–03.

[24] As befits the discretionary nature of equity, a court has the discretion to give an equitable remedy or recognize an equitable right where equity requires it, for the benefit of people who do not fit within any previously recognized categories of equity-seekers. See eg *Schmidt v Rosewood Trust Ltd* [2003] UKPC 26.

[25] See John Gardner, *Torts and Other Wrongs* (OUP 2019), defining 'civil recourse' as the 'legal power for someone who holds herself to have been on the receiving end of a tort (a "plaintiff") to summon the alleged tortfeasor (a "defendant") before the courts, and to do so unilaterally (without the leave of any official), with a view to obtaining a court-imposed or court-approved remedy against the defendant' (ibid 3). Elsewhere, Gardner writes that in private law, 'public authority (the authority of the court) is put at the disposal of the wronged person … The wronged person, in short, is given a right not only against the wrongdoer but also against the court, a right to conscript the court (and its officers) in [their] quest for corrective justice against the wrongdoer' (ibid 86).

[26] See Johann Friedrich Vigilantius, 'Notes on the Lectures of Mr. Kant on the Metaphysics of Morals' in Immanuel Kant, *Lectures on Ethics* (P Heath and JB Schneewind eds, P Heath trans, CUP 1997): 'Equity is in itself a genuine right, but has no right of coercion coupled with it, because owing to want of imputation the condition of coercion is not encountered there', 27:573, 326. The contrast that Kant draws is between the idea of right without coercion (equity) and the idea of right that simply is an authorization to use coercion. See Kant (n 19) AK 6:232–34, 25–27.

> Now [the employee's] wages are fixed, but the value of the currency is declining. The *quaestio* is: whether he can demand an increase in a fixed wage during his period of service? Equity looks to the disposition and aims of the contracting parties; strict right, however, to the content of the contract.[27]

The equitable right—essentially to what the employee had coming to him through the contract, that is, a living wage—was not, in Kant's view, coercively enforceable either by the employee *or* by a judge acting within their proper role. By contrast, the legal right to fixed wages was, in his view, a coercively enforceable right. Kant grasped that equitable rights raise a puzzle because they lack a central feature of ordinary private rights in a legal system. But Kant's idea of equity as a right without coercion mischaracterizes the puzzle. Kant's account implies, wrongly, not only that the equitable right-holder lacks the standing to enforce the right but that the court, too, lacks the coercive power to give effect to equitable rights: 'It is thus a contradiction, to decide according to equity, and yet to be a judge.'[28]

A very different problem arises when we see equitable rights not as rights without coercion (for the reasons I give subsequently, courts do have a normatively justified power to intervene coercively),[29] but rather as rights without standing. Explaining how and why equitable rights are rights without standing requires an appreciation of their public dimension.

The public dimension of equitable rights emerges most clearly in the core, animating concern of equity to safeguard the integrity of the system of private law rights (property, contract, tort). The legitimacy of public authority in setting out and maintaining a system of private law rights requires that these rights not be used *in themselves* as instruments of oppression and injustice. Equitable intervention generally aims to ensure precisely that: to prevent the use of ordinary private law rights as instruments of oppression and injustice.[30] But the integrity of a system of private law rights should be seen as a matter of shared

[27] Vigilantius (n 26) 27:573, 326.

[28] See ibid. Kant wanted to explain that courts of chancery are somehow outside of the private law, an acknowledgement of the public dimensions of equity but note the tie in with the private law order.

[29] This power is grounded largely in the idea that equity acts *in personam* and so can require a person, on pain of contempt of court and ultimately imprisonment, to bear the burden of seeing equity done.

[30] This is an argument I develop in more detail in other work. See Katz (n 4) (the problem that equity is especially attuned to is the potential for forfeiture or interruption along a completable but as yet incomplete pathway to legal rights). For other accounts of the function of equity, see generally Dennis Klimchuk, Irit Samet, and Henry E Smith (eds) *Philosophical Foundations of The Law of Equity* (OUP 2020). Henry Smith has developed an account of equity as guarding against opportunism (see Smith (n 10)) and Irit Samet has argued that equity serves to align law with the requirements of conscience (see Samet (n 5)).

concern.[31] Equitable rights can be seen, then, as individualized offshoots of public responsibility to safeguard the integrity of a system of private law rights.[32] The distinction between equitable rights and ordinary private law rights—rights without standing and rights with standing—tracks the two distinctive institutional roles of the court: first, as adjudicator, and second, as guardian of the legal order. The court, as adjudicator, resolves private disputes by determining whether a matter falls within or outside the object of a person's right. Courts *would* lack a justified power to give effect to equitable rights coercively if they had only an adjudicative function. A court that conceives of its role as only a calculator of correct private law outcomes would not take any perspective but that of the litigants and so could not justify its power to reconcile the exercise of private rights with the legitimacy of public authority in setting up a system of private rights. This is, of course, exactly how Kant thought of the role of the judge—hence his attempt to explain away the courts of chancery as operating outside of private law entirely, imposing limits on the government's rights or powers for the benefit of the subject rather than as imposing limits on one private actor's rights for the benefit of another.[33]

However, courts have a second role in the administration of a system of private law and that is the role of guardian of the legal order. In this capacity, courts have the mandate to reconcile legal rights with the integrity of the system of rights, which is meant to protect against injustice and the oppression of others. The basis of the courts' power to intervene in equity is the discharge of the court's mandate as guardian of the legal order. Unlike courts in the role of adjudicator, whose powers are defined narrowly by the legal suit between the parties (*lis inter partes*),[34] courts of equity have broad powers to do equity in the matter. Their mandate to do equity, activated by the petitioner's suit, is to determine not only the petitioner's rights but also the equities of the situation

[31] William L Prosser, 'Private Action for Public Nuisance' (1966) 52 Va L Rev 997, 1107. See also Ripstein (n 1) and Neyers (n 14).

[32] Some interactions between private actors, it turns out, are regulated as matters of individualized public right: *Dwyer v Staunton* [1947] 4 DLR 393.

[33] See Vigilantius (n 26) 27:573–74, 326: 'In England, to be sure, the court of chancery decides between subjects and the government, but it judges and also disposes, as it were, over the rights of the latter to the advantage of the former; for example, goods are to be levied from the countryside at a certain time, but a mishap prevents this; if the confiscation is now suspended, and the Chancellor thus grants exemption from a governmental requirement, rather than having to decide the matter according to strict right, he is no longer solely a judge; for the latter, on the other hand, the only verdict is: *fiat justitia et pereat mundus*.'

[34] See Herbert Felix Jolowicz, *Lectures on Jurisprudence* (Athlone Press 1963) 339–41 (*lis inter partes* is the distinguishing feature of judicial power). See also Jeremy Waldron, 'Do Judges Reason Morally?' in G Huscroft (ed) *Expounding the Constitution: Essays in Constitutional Theory* (CUP 2008)(priority of the basic institutional role of courts).

overall.[35] Courts thus retain the discretion to consider the effects on others, including third parties, of recognizing and giving effect to an equitable right.

Because the court's power and responsibility in equity are so broad, the petitioner cannot have the standing to enforce a right that equity be done. Only the courts, acting as guardians of the legal order, can have the standing to decide how to exercise this broad responsibility and whether to intervene for the petitioner's benefit. This public dimension of equitable rights leads to an inherent indeterminacy in the object of those rights. The object of an equitable right is the discharge of a public mandate: that the court ensure the integrity of the system of private law rights in a particular case. The court's mandate in doing equity involves an exercise of judgment about what equity requires in a specific case.[36] In this way, it is radically different from the object of a common-law private right. The object of a common-law right—say, the right to contractual performance—is reducible simply to the duty of the other party to perform the contract as specified in the contract. The object of an equitable right, by contrast, is itself another's (the court's) mandate to do equity, requiring the exercise of judgment. Equitable rights have an indeterminate object because the mandate itself involves the further exercise of discretionary power that is beyond the right-holder's control.

Private standing to enforce equitable rights would treat the court's mandate as an object within the control of the right-holder, in the same way that a thing, as an object of a property right, and the performance of the contract, as the object of a contract right, are within a legal right-holder's control.[37] But an

[35] See *Chippewas of Sarnia Band v Canada (Attorney General)* [2000] OJ No 4804, 195 DLR (4th) 135, 264 (a claim of equity must be considered in relation to the rights of others: 'The complaining party cannot claim entitlement to the mechanical grant of an automatic remedy without regard to the consequences to the rights of others that might flow by reason of the complaining party's own conduct, including any delay in asserting the claim. It is for this reason that the established principles governing the availability of public law remedies require that, before a remedy is granted, consideration be accorded to the rights and interests of others who may have had every reason to rely upon the apparent validity of the impugned act.').

[36] I will explain in normative terms why a system would have a planned indeterminacy in the formulation of rights. I will give a longer answer as the chapter progresses when I talk about doing equity as a public responsibility. The short answer is that there are normative reasons for formulating equitable rights this way: equitable rights are indeterminate in this way because the mandate to see equity done remains a matter for the courts to decide directly. Of course, the reader will want to know *why* a legal system would formulate equitable rights as a right to the discharge of a mandate to do equity, rather than taking a one-step approach that defines prohibitions or limitations into the legal right itself and avoids the indeterminacy. I will return to this question later in the chaper.

[37] There is no self-help in equity for equitable remedies. See Peter Birks, *An Introduction to the Law of Restitution* (Clarendon Press 1989) 66; Janet O'Sullivan, 'Recission as a Self-Help Remedy: A Critical Analysis' (2000) 59 CLJ 509, 514 (citing Birks); *Commercial Union Life Assurance Co. of Canada v John Ingle Insurance Group Inc* [2000] OJ No 3289, 328–35 (as a matter of trust law, a trustee does not have a right of self-help by which the trustee can collect a debt from a beneficiary through set-off against the trust property).

equitable right-holder cannot have the standing to enforce the right without thereby assuming control over the mandate itself: to control the object of an equitable right would amount to control over the court's inherent discretion to do equity. To transform equity into just a limit on another's legal rights would deny equity's public dimension and the exercise of public judgment it requires. It would also deny equity's public dimension to put the court's mandate to do equity within the control of private actors by conveying the standing to enforce equitable rights.[38]

Equitable rights, therefore, *are* rights authorizing the use of coercion—just not rights with (private) standing.[39] Indeed, equity's coercive nature is fundamental to its function within the legal order: to reconcile the exercise of private law rights with the integrity of a system of private rights. Within common-law jurisdictions, equity is an offshoot of one of the most coercive forms of state power, the prerogative power.[40] Throughout its history, equity expressed itself through commands (in the form of 'because I said so') and disobedience to those commands were punished as contempt of court. The subpoena, an important and early tool of equity, commanded a person to appear under threat of penalty but contained neither the reason for the appearance nor even the name of the petitioner who would have initiated the process.[41] Today, even after courts of law and equity have merged in most common-law jurisdictions, equitable remedies still take the form of particularized commands.[42] Equity's coercive quality supports its public dimension: the use of private law rights as instruments of injustice and oppression, unchecked, would threaten the integrity of a system of private rights.[43] The court's purpose in equity is in this way

[38] John Gardner describes plaintiffs enforcing their legal rights as *conscripting* courts into their personal quest for justice. See Gardner (n 25) 86. Whether or not this accurately captures the role of courts as adjudicators, it is certainly antithetical to the relation between petitioners and courts of equity: courts of equity, as guardians of the legal order, discharge a public mandate.

[39] Even if the judicial discretion to determine whether to intervene, and so to enforce the petitioner's right, is only triggered by the petitioner's decision to commence a proceeding.

[40] See Thomas Poole, *Reason of State: Law, Prerogative and Empire* (CUP 2015) 53. See also Mark D Walters, *A. V. Dicey and the Common Law Constitutional Tradition: A Legal Turn of Mind* (CUP 2020) 162–225 (concerns about prerogative power and arbitrary use of power). See Larissa Katz, 'Ownership and Offices: The Building Blocks of the Legal Order' (2020) 70 U Toronto LJ 267; Katz and Shapiro (n 1) 245: 'The power to decide a matter of concern to others for any reason or no reason at all amounts to arbitrary discretion—the very nightmare that, for liberals generally, law and legal institutions are meant to dispel.'

[41] See WM Ormrod, 'The Origins of the *Sub Pena* Writ' (1988) 61 Historical Research 11, 11, 15.

[42] See Samuel L Bray, 'The System of Equitable Remedies' (2016) 63 UCLA L Rev 530. See also John H Langbein, 'The Disappearance of Civil Trial in the United States' (2012) 122 Yale L J 539 (quoted by Bray: '[N]o society can tolerate a legal system that lacks the power to grant specific remedies.') See Supreme Court of Judicature Act 1873 (36 & 37 Vict c 66); Supreme Court of Judicature Act 1875 (38 & 39 Vict c 77).

[43] See Katz (n 4) 171 (discusses 'equity as an institution' with the state attending 'to the potential for oppression and injustice')

like the purpose of criminal law[44] but with a narrower focus: the reconciliation of the uses of private law rights with the integrity of the system of private law rights.

IV. The Power to Commence Proceedings

One challenge to the account I have given of equitable rights as rights without standing is a simple institutional one: petitioners seeking equity have the power to commence a proceeding wherein equity is done. But we can and should peel the power to initiate a proceeding apart from the standing to enforce. It is possible to have one without the other: a power to commence a proceeding without the standing to enforce (as in equitable rights) and the standing to enforce a right without the power to commence a proceeding (as where the holder of an ordinary private law right is caught by a statute of limitations).

The power to commence a proceeding refers *just* to the power to launch a proceeding. In common-law jurisdictions, there is a wide latitude to commence an action even without a valid cause of action. One must only file documents correctly to commence a proceeding; no other form of standing is required in fact at that stage.[45]For example, I could commence a proceeding that complains that you failed to hold the door for me when I entered a building behind you. Of course, proceedings like this—ones that rely *solely* on the power to commence a proceeding[46]—will be thrown out swiftly. In the common law, the standing to enforce a legal right provides the normative justification for the power to commence a legal action. An unjustified proceeding (in common law, one that is not grounded in the standing to enforce a right) will be dismissed.[47] The function of a motion to dismiss is to trigger the court's jurisdiction to identify and dismiss a proceeding as unjustified if brought only based on the power to commence an action; that is, without a juridical basis. A motion to

44 See Malcolm Thorburn, 'Criminal Law as Public Law' in RA Duff and S Green (eds) *Philosophical Foundations of Criminal Law* (OUP 2011).

45 Gardner (n 21) 201 (noting that the rights-holders' powers to enforce their rights are 'radically discretionary' in that 'the conditions for the[ir] valid exercise ... are few and proforma, and that there are scant legal duties regulating their exercise'). See Katz and Shapiro (n 1).

46 Black's Law Dictionary offers multiple definitions of 'cause of action', one of which is the *right* which a party has to institute a judicial proceeding. Here I think the emphasis should be on a right: if one has the standing to enforce a right, then one could be said to have a right to institute judicial proceedings, where that right has as its subject-matter the standing to enforce a right. The standing to commence legal proceedings, however, is at best a privilege, but confers no right.

47 The lack of standing to enforce is a reason to dismiss a suit a person has the power to bring. See Gardner (n 21) 202; Benjamin C Zipursky, 'Substantive Standing, Civil Recourse, and Corrective Justice', *Florida State University Law Review* 39, no. 1 (2011) 299, 304.

dismiss is a claim that the plaintiff *lacks* the standing to enforce a right. But it also presupposes that the plaintiff had the narrower power to commence a legal proceeding even without that cause of action: a motion to dismiss only makes sense as a step *after* the start of a judicial proceeding.

Why allow the power to commence proceedings even when there is no underlying enforceable private law right? There is a good institutional reason for that: it is hard for a court to know before seeing a statement of claim and the defendant's response whether the action is baseless. We need a process for that! But after a successful motion to dismiss, we do not look back at a baseless proceeding and say it was never commenced. We recognize instead that it was initiated, the defendant responded with a motion to dismiss, and the proceeding came to its proper terminus: dismissal.

Equity seekers also have the power to commence a proceeding and, together with the court, to make decisions that shape how the proceeding goes, even in the absence of standing in the narrow or broad senses I have previously introduced.[48] Equitable right-holders have the power to commence a proceeding for both institutional and personal reasons: they are the direct beneficiaries of the court's discharge of its mandate to do equity in particular cases, and best placed to bring the particulars of the case to the court's attention given their knowledge and personal interest to see equity done.[49]

While private actors have the power to commence proceedings in equity, it would be normatively and conceptually coherent to allocate the power to commence proceedings to public officials.[50] Consider, by analogy, the move from private to public prosecutions in criminal law. Historically, individuals who were victims of crime had the power to commence criminal actions.[51] We have chosen to have a director of public prosecutions for the past hundred or

[48] See Gardner (n 21): Gardner noted the extensive power of plaintiffs in private law actions ('[t]he special feature of private law, procedurally speaking, is that the most extensive legal powers to determine the powers of the court, those most akin to those of a criminal prosecutor, lie with the very person who claims to have been wronged' (ibid 200) and '[t]he court has narrow legal powers and many legal duties in dealing with whatever proceedings I may launch, whereas I have wide legal powers and few legal duties in launching them' (ibid 201–02)).

[49] See Katz and Shapiro (n 1) 247 (the strength of an equitable rights-holder's interest to commence a proceeding may vary). See *Schmidt v Rosewood Trust Ltd* [2003] UKPC 26 on the standing of a mere object of a power of appointment (described as a mere hope or expectation, not even an equitable right) to trigger the court's power to require the trustee to render account and share information about the trust; and the denial of standing to the beneficiary of a trust with a defeasible remote interest.

[50] This is something we already find in equity in common law jurisdictions: charitable purpose trusts are sufficiently advantageous to the public that the dangers they pose to the integrity of public authority that backstops property rights is managed by appointing a public trustee to ensure the trust is performed according to its terms.

[51] Clive Emsley and Robert D Storch, 'Prosecution and the Police in England Since 1700' (1993) 18 IAHCCJ Bull 45, 46.

so years for institutional reasons. Private individuals (that is, the victim of a crime or the equitable petitioner) unusually affected by a situation that calls out for a public response may have the power to commence a proceeding, but we could just as well opt to move that power into the hands of a public official. While there are circumstances in which it may be expedient to enable and incentivize affected private citizens to bring certain proceedings with a public dimension—such as public nuisance actions, actions under legislative regimes like the *Clean Water Act*, and criminal proceedings—the ultimate responsibility for those public matters rests with the state. We might say the same is true of equitable rights. The state has the primary responsibility to safeguard the integrity of the system of rights: to carry out that responsibility requires that inequity be brought to its attention. Whether equity is better served if public officials have the power to commence proceedings, rather than those immediately affected by the inequitable exercise of legal rights, is an empirical question. The experience of the common law suggests a complaints-driven process works: private actors most affected by unjust and oppressive uses of legal rights are best placed to identify those threats and to activate the court's inherent jurisdiction to see equity done. But it could be otherwise.

V. A Methodological Reflection

The explicit treatment of equity in common-law jurisdictions raises an important methodological question: if it is possible to conceive of a system of private rights without equitable rights, as civilian jurisdictions have done, what is gained by taking the two-step approach we find in common-law jurisdictions, first defining private rights in law, and then subjecting these private law rights to an additional layer of equitable constraints?[52]

A two-step approach to private law offers a number of advantages for theoretical inquiry: it leads us to a much clearer view of the roles that courts have to play in private law disputes and the reasons why each of these roles matter in the administration of justice. Kant's view of the role of the judge in private law disputes follows from his view about the nature of private law rights, according to which having a right entails standing in the broad and narrow sense I set out

[52] There is an analogous set of questions about how to define constitutional rights. We could think of the *Charter* as setting out constitutional rights and then subjecting them to a limit: see Jamal Green, 'Rights as Trumps?' (2018) 132 Harvard LR 28; Malcolm Thorburn, 'Proportionality' in D Dyzenhaus and M Thorburn (eds) *Philosophical Foundations of Constitutional Law* (OUP 2016); Jacob Weinrib, *Dimensions of Dignity: The Theory and Practice of Modern Constitutional Law* (CUP 2016).

in this essay. Courts, in Kant's view, are only adjudicators resolving disputes from the perspective of the private litigants, determining whether and to what extent the defendant stepped into the plaintiff's sphere of jurisdiction. Courts, in their role as adjudicators, also ensure that the jurisdiction accorded to each litigant in the form of a right is consistent with the requirements of reciprocity (whatever jurisdiction is claimed for one person must be consistent with a like jurisdiction for everyone else).

Reflecting on equitable rights as rights without standing reveals a second role that judges can have in private disputes (and do have in common-law jurisdictions): the role of guardians of the system of private law rights. In this role, courts doing equity are not (as Kant thought) disposing of the rights of government for the benefit of the subject.[53] Rather, equitable rights constrain other private law rights for the benefit of a particular subject, in the name of the system as a whole. In equity, courts do not resolve disputes from the perspective of the private litigants but from their own standpoint as the guardians of the legitimacy of the system of private rights. The judge in deciding private disputes does not simply (as Montesquieu would have it) calculate correct answers, determining what is or is not within one or the other party's right.[54] Rather, in the course of resolving private law disputes, the judge also attends to the reconciliation of legal rights with the legitimacy of public authority.

As a branch of public law relating specifically to private law, equity not only limits injustice and oppression in the exercise of particular legal rights. It also aims at fulfilling a requirement for the administration of justice. Having rights within a *system* of rights requires at least two things beyond the clear definition

[53] This is, however, the common law's understanding of the court's role in interpreting grants of public rights in the form of licences, land patents, monopolies, and charters: every public grant is a diminution of prerogative power and ought to be interpreted so as to be consistent with the public power to govern in *salus populi*. According to ancient common law principles, public grants of rights or licences should be construed favourably to the government for the reason that any such rights would constrain public power. See *Lieding v Ontario* [1991] CarswellOnt 557 (ONCA), 22 ('This practice [of construing in favour of the Crown] was adopted because of the view that while the public might be indifferent to the construction of a grant between subject and subject, it would not be similarly indifferent with respect to grants from the Crown because the Crown essentially represents the public interest (*R v Meyers* [1853] 3 UCCP 305 (CA) 350–51)'). See also *Feather v Regina* [1865] 122 ER 1191, 1201 (where the court had to determine whether a patent for an invention conferred an exclusive right vis-à-vis the Crown as well as private parties. The court noted the rule of construction, according to which: 'Nothing passes except that which is expressed, or which is matter of necessary and unavoidable intendment in order to give effect to the plain and undoubted intention of the grant. And in no species of grant does this rule of construction more especially obtain than in grants which emanate from, and operate in derogation of, the prerogative of the Crown ... "All grants of the Crown are to be strictly construed against the grantee, contrary to the usual policy of the law in the consideration of grants; and upon this just ground, that the prerogatives and rights and emoluments of the Crown being conferred upon it for great purposes and for the public use, it shall not be intended that such prerogatives, rights and emoluments are diminished by any grant".').

[54] David Dyzenhaus, 'The Very Idea of a Judge' (2010) 60 U Toronto LJ 61.

of rights in law. The first is the accommodation of other, potentially conflicting rights.[55] This is the function that the law of nuisance performs in property law. This requirement concerns how rights are configured within a system of reciprocal rights. A second and distinct requirement is the reconciliation of legal rights with legitimate public authority in the administration of justice. This is the function equity performs in the context of private law.[56] A two-step approach—defining legal rights and then subjecting their use to the demands of equity —reveals the normative underpinnings of a system of rights and the importance of this second requirement. What is at stake in distinguishing between ordinary private rights and equitable rights is a clearer view of the two distinctive roles for courts in relation to a system of rights: the adjudication of disputes (defining rights and reconciling rights with other rights) and safeguarding the integrity of the system (reconciling legal rights with the legitimacy of public authority).

VI. Conclusion

Standing is a legal concept that frames theoretical inquiry into the nature, structure, and normative underpinnings of private law. A methodological limit of some theories of private law is to view it through the lens of standing, bringing into focus ordinary private law rights and the role of judges as adjudicators enforcing the boundaries between right-holders' separate spheres of jurisdiction. In this essay, I have argued that taking account of equity leads us to adjust that frame and develop clearer, more complete theories of private law that reveal a second role for courts, distinct from their role as adjudicators: the courts as guardians of the legal order.

[55] See eg Jamal Greene, *How Rights Went Wrong: Why Our Obsession with Rights Is Tearing America Apart* (Houghton Mifflin Harcourt 2021).

[56] See James Edelman, 'The Equity of the Statute' in D Klimchuk, I Samet, and HE Smith (eds) *Philosophical Foundations of the Law of Equity* (OUP 2020).

15

The Critical Potential of Doctrinal Analysis

Paul Krell

I. Introduction

In 2018, Rob van Gestel, Hans-Wolfgang Micklitz, and Edward L Rubins published a book titled 'Rethinking Legal Scholarship' with a distinct focus on doctrinal analysis. In the introduction, the authors emphasize certain significant differences between European and US legal thinking: 'European and American legal scholarship have tended to function as two self-contained traditions ... While legal scholars on both sides of the Atlantic have devoted serious attention to the globalization of legal issues and legal systems, they have done so by relying on their separate methodological approaches ... not only providing different answers to problems they now inevitably share, but they are asking different questions for example, with regard to the relationship between theory and practice.'[1] The authors also indicate that one reason for the discrepancy could lie in the differences between the legal systems themselves: 'One factor that may contribute to these divergent attitudes regarding the scientific nature of legal theory is the difference between a code law and a common-law regime. If a legal system is based on comprehensive codes, the aspiration to draft those codes according to systematic and coherent principles will be strongly felt and sometimes associated with a 'legal science' in which law is seen as a coherent system of written and unwritten rules.'[2]

Rechtsdogmatik undoubtedly plays a fundamental role in German legal scholarship. In fact, many think that *Rechtsdogmatik* is unique to German legal scholarship, and some even claim that nothing remotely comparable can be found in the legal systems of other countries.[3] Others dispute this and see

[1] R van Gestel, H-W Micklitz, and E Rubin, 'Introduction' in R van Gestel, H-W Micklitz, and E Rubin (eds), *Rethinking Legal Scholarship* (CUP 2017) 1.

[2] R van Gestel, H-W Micklitz, and E Rubin, 'Introduction' in R van Gestel, H-W Micklitz, and E Rubin (eds), *Rethinking Legal Scholarship* (CUP 2017) 6.

[3] M Jestaedt, 'Rechtsdogmatik als gemeinsames Kommunikationsformat von Rechtswissenschaft und Rechtspraxis' in G Kirchhof, S Magen, and K Schneider (eds), *Was weiß Dogmatik?* (Mohr Siebeck 2012) 118; O Lepsius, 'Kritik der Dogmatik' in G Kirchhof, S Magen, and K Schneider (eds),

Paul Krell, *The Critical Potential of Doctrinal Analysis* In: *Methodology in Private Law Theory*. Edited by: Thilo Kuntz and Paul B. Miller, Oxford University Press.DOI: 10.1093/oso/9780198885306.003.0015

no significant difference between *Rechtsdogmatik* and, for example, doctrinal analysis.[4] Some allege that the focus on *Rechtsdogmatik* isolates German legal scholarship, making international discourse more difficult.[5] Others claim that, on the contrary, it facilitates such discourse.[6] Some even go so far as to say that the alleged high reputation of doctrinal analysis in German private law is evidenced by the fact that it is enthusiastically taken up worldwide.[7] For the time being, I will use 'doctrinal analysis' as a generic term, so when I refer to it I do not distinguish it from what we call *Rechtsdogmatik*.

I would like to approach the meaning and the role of doctrinal analysis with a particular question in mind: To what extent can we resort to doctrinal analysis to criticize the law? The question can be illustrated by a 1998 paper by Richard G Bone titled 'A New Look at Trade Secret Law: Doctrine in Search of Justification', in which the author critically examines the theoretical foundations of trade secret law. I do not intend to deal with these foundations or the criticism in too much detail. However, the example is well suited to illustrate my subject for multiple reasons. The protection of trade secrets in the United States was established by case law (most importantly, *Kewanee v Bicron* and *Peabody v Norfolk*) and is thus prototypical for common law.[8] In Germany, on the other hand, it was regulated by statute (originally in the late nineteenth century) and only recently fundamentally overhauled by a new statute in 2019 and is therefore prototypical for civil law. Moreover, it is an area of law belonging to private law, which fits the framework of this workshop better than the examples from criminal law, on which I must rely otherwise. I will, therefore, return to certain issues of trade secret law later, but again, I intend to do so without getting lost in the details. For now, it is sufficient to point out that Bone considers all current theories concerning the foundation of trade secret law to be insufficient. 'Simply put, the thesis is that there is no such thing as a

Was weiß Dogmatik? (Mohr Siebeck 2012) 46–47. See also C Möllers and A Voßkuhle, 'Die deutsche Staatsrechtswissenschaft im Zusammenhang der internationalisierten Wissenschaften' (2003) 36 Die Verwaltung 321, 327.

[4] P Sahm, *Elemente der Dogmatik* (Velbrück Wissenschaft 2019) 26–29. See also A Peczenik, 'Scientia Juris' in E Pattaro and A Peczenik (eds), *A Treatise of Legal Philosophy and General Jurisprudence* (Vol 4, Springer 2005) 1; P Windel, 'Ist das rechtsdogmatische Zeitalter vorbei?' (2019) 69 Anwaltsblatt 447.

[5] F Schorkopf, 'Dogmatik und Kohärenz' in G Kirchhof, S Magen, and K Schneider (eds), *Was weiß Dogmatik?* (Mohr Siebeck 2012) 140.

[6] G Kirchhof and S Magen, 'Dogmatik: Rechtliche Notwendigkeit und Grundlage fächerübergreifenden Dialogs – eine systematisierende Übersicht' in G Kirchhof, S Magen, and K Schneider (eds), *Was weiß Dogmatik?* (Mohr Siebeck 2012) 165–166.

[7] See H Koziol, 'Glanz und Elend der Zivilrechtsdogmatik' (2012) 212 Archiv für die civilistische Praxis 1, 2–3.

[8] *Kewanee v Bicron* 416 US 470 (1974) and *Peabody v Norfolk* 98 Mass 452 (1968).

normatively autonomous body of trade secret law.'[9] Underlying this finding is a compelling analysis that has greatly stimulated discussion on trade secret law in the United States.

There is something else remarkable about Bone's analysis, and that is another reason why it is interesting as a starting point for general considerations of doctrinal analysis. Bone concludes: 'I have argued that this muddle is due to the absence of a convincing normative theory capable of making coherent sense of trade secret doctrine ... the way out of the muddle is to recognize trade secret law for what it is: A collection of contract and tort theories grouped together by the nature of the subject matter they regulate. On this view, it is clear that trade secret law should be narrowed.'[10] In concrete terms, this means: 'Courts and legislatures should reject broad trade secret torts.'[11] This is obviously a very sweeping critique. From a traditional German point of view, however, it is unusual for a doctrinal analysis to cast such extensive doubt on the *legitimacy* of an area of law. It is even claimed that the question of legitimacy is beyond the scope of doctrinal analysis.[12] Although I am addressing a specific issue (the critical potential of doctrinal analysis), in doing so I will address potential differences in the role of doctrinal analysis in common law and case law.

In the first section of this chapter, I will show that although we find a common and undisputed definition of doctrinal analysis that does not differ significantly between Germany and the United States, a great deal of controversy is concealed behind this alleged consensus. In Section II, I will categorize doctrinal analysis based on its point of reference. This will enable me to point out in Section III why we find it so hard to elaborate on the methodology of doctrinal analysis. Section IV distinguishes doctrinal analysis from the economic analysis of law. This distinction is important because doctrinal analysis has a critical potential, for which, in my opinion, an economic analysis cannot compensate. Finally, Section V examines the critical potential specific to doctrinal analysis. Here, I address the limits arising from referring doctrinal analysis to the applicable law. Subsequently, I will deal with the authority of doctrinal analysis.

[9] RG Bone, 'A New Look at Trade Secret Law: Doctrine in Search of Justification' (1998) 86 CLR 241, 245.

[10] ibid 304.

[11] ibid 302.

[12] J Schulz, 'Die Strafrechtsdogmatik nach dem Ende der vor- und außerjuristischen Gerechtigkeit' in C Engel and W Schön (eds), *Das Proprium der Rechtswissenschaft* (Mohr Siebeck 2007) 137.

II. Why Doctrinal Analysis is More Than a Bridge

In the book by van Gestel and others on legal scholarship, in one of the chapters, Jan M Smits explores the question of what doctrinal analysis is: 'It is probably best described as research that aims to give a systematic exposition of the principles, rules and concepts governing a particular legal field or institution and analyses the relationship between these principles, rules and concepts with a view to solving unclarities and gaps in the existing law.'[13] It is perhaps safe to assume that this understanding is widely shared. At least, we find similar descriptions of *Rechtsdogmatik* in Germany.[14] However, these similarities should not obscure the fact that several controversial issues lie dormant behind this basic consensus.[15] It would be impossible to address all these issues here, let alone cover them in detail. I will address only a few issues that are significant for the critical potential of doctrinal analysis.

In advance, it is important to emphasize that it seems neither reasonable nor promising to take a specifically German understanding of doctrinal analysis as a reference and, from that specific standpoint, to ask whether and to what extent such an understanding can be found in US legal thinking.[16] For one matter, this would be problematic because, beyond the consensus previously mentioned, it is to a large extent unclear precisely what constitutes doctrinal analysis. More importantly, such comparative considerations are often based on certain presuppositions about the Anglo-American legal tradition that are controversial and sometimes even stereotypical. Therefore, I do not intend to base my reflections on such grounds but rather to show that the meaning of doctrinal analysis depends more on whether it relates to written or judicial law.

In the Anglo-American discussion, it is said that doctrinal analysis 'sets the terms for future resolution of cases in an area'.[17] Again, we find similar

[13] J M Smits, 'What is Legal Doctrine?' in R van Gestel, H-W Micklitz, and E Rubin (eds), *Rethinking Legal Scholarship* (CUP 2017) 210; See also L Alexander, 'What We Do, and Why We Do It' (1993) 45 Stan L Rev 1885, 1886.

[14] R Alexy, *Theorie der juristischen Argumentation* (9th edn, Suhrkamp 2019) 307–08; C Bumke, *Rechtsdogmatik* (Mohr Siebeck 2017) 1–2; J Harenburg, *Die Rechtsdogmatik zwischen Wissenschaft und Praxis* (Steiner 1986) 42–47; U Diederichsen, 'Auf dem Weg zur Rechtsdogmatik' in R Zimmerman (ed), *Rechtsgeschichte und Privatrechtsdogmatik* (CF Müller 1999) 66; C Waldhoff, 'Kritik und Lob der Dogmatik' in G Kirchhof, S Magen, and K Schneider (eds), *Was weiß Dogmatik?* (Mohr Siebeck 2012) 26–28.

[15] P Sahm, *Elemente der Dogmatik* (Velbrück Wissenschaft 2019) 41; F Schorkopf, 'Dogmatik und Kohärenz' in G Kirchhof, S Magen, and K Schneider (eds), *Was weiß Dogmatik?* (Mohr Siebeck 2012) 140.

[16] See also M Flohr, *Rechtsdogmatik in England* (Mohr Siebeck 2017) 24.

[17] E Tiller and F Cross, 'What is Legal Doctrine?' (2006) 100 Northwest U L Rev 517.

statements in Germany.[18] A metaphor used by Rolf Stürner illustrates this. He pictures doctrinal analysis as an *intermediate layer* ('*Zwischenschicht*') between written law and the application of that law.[19] Nils Jareborg illustrates doctrinal analysis in a very similar way: as a *bridge* between legislation and adjudication.[20] Both metaphors, in my opinion, aptly describe the function of doctrinal analysis for the most part. Moreover, they allow me to emphasize some other important points. However, it should be noted that both metaphors depict doctrinal analysis only to a certain degree. In other respects, they are even misleading. If I nevertheless continue to use them here, it is precisely because of this partial inaccuracy. Indeed, the images allow us to draw out both certain differences and similarities between common law and civil law that should not be neglected.

It should also be mentioned that doctrinal analysis has various meanings unrelated to the individual issues yet to be discussed (and those not discussed here). Doctrinal analysis can refer to (1) a discipline that produces rules, (2) a method of producing those rules, (3) the rule-producing activity, and (4) the product of that activity (provided it meets certain requirements).[21] To take up the metaphors again, doctrinal analysis is the art of building a bridge or an intermediate layer in a certain way, but also the bridge and the layer themselves (if built in that way). This raises the question of what constitutes this specific art: What is the method of doctrinal analysis? If my impression is correct, this is precisely where a particularly great need for research is presumed. Smits states: 'It has even become a truism that most jurists know how to do doctrinal

[18] W Hassemer, 'Dogmatik zwischen Wissenschaft und richterlicher Pragmatik' in G Kirchhof, S Magen, and K Schneider (eds), *Was weiß Dogmatik?* (Mohr Siebeck 2012) 11; P Sahm, *Elemente der Dogmatik* (Velbrück Wissenschaft 2019) 21, 60; T Würtenberger, 'Grundlagenforschung und Dogmatik aus deutscher Sicht' in R Stürner (ed), *Die Bedeutung der Rechtsdogmatik für die Rechtsentwicklung* (Mohr Siebeck 2010) 5.

[19] R Stürner, 'Das Zivilrecht der Moderne und die Bedeutung der Rechtsdogmatik' (2012) 67 Juristenzeitung 10, 13; R Stürner, 'Die Zivilrechtswissenschaft und ihre Methodik' (2014) 214 Archiv für die civilistische Praxis 7, 11; R Stürner, 'Die Rolle des dogmatischen Denkens im Zivilprozessrecht' (2014) 127 Zeitschrift für Zivilprozessrecht 271, 276; see also M Eifert, 'Zum Verhältnis von Dogmatik und pluralisierter Rechtswissenschaft' in G Kirchhof, S Magen, and K Schneider (eds), *Was weiß Dogmatik?* (Mohr Siebeck 2012) 81, 90.

[20] N Jareborg, 'Legal Dogmatics and the Concept of Science' in G Freund and others (eds), *Grundlagen und Dogmatik des gesamten Strafrechtssystems. Festschrift für Wolfgang Frisch zum 70. Geburtstag* (Duncker & Humblot 2013) 54; see also M Jestaedt, 'Rechtsdogmatik als gemeinsames Kommunikationsformat von Rechtswissenschaft und Rechtspraxis' in G Kirchhof, S Magen, and K Schneider (eds), *Was weiß Dogmatik?* (Mohr Siebeck 2012) 136, who, however, relates the image of the bridge to the connection between legal scholarship and legal practice.

[21] B Burkhardt, 'Geglückte und folgenlose Strafrechtsdogmatik' in A Eser, W Hassemer, and B Burkhardt (eds), *Die deutsche Strafrechtswissenschaft an der Jahrtausendwende* (CH Beck 2000) 114; A Peczenik, 'Scientia Juris' in E Pattaro and A Peczenik (eds), *A Treatise of Legal Philosophy and General Jurisprudence* vol 4 (Springer 2005) 2; B Rüthers, C Fischer, and A Birk, *Rechtstheorie mit Juritischer Methodenlehre* (10th edn, CF Müller 2018) 196; P Sahm, *Elemente der Dogmatik* (Velbrück Wisenschaft 2019) 41; see also A Stark, *Interdisziplinarität der Rechtsdogmatik* (Mohr Siebeck 2017) 7–8, 25, 77–80.

work but are not able to tell how they do what they do.'[22] Similar statements are made by German legal scholars.[23] We are apparently capable of building bridges in a specific way, but for some reason cannot precisely describe how we do this.

I do not intend to deal with the methodology of doctrinal analysis in depth; however, I will return to the subject later. For now, it should have become clear why it is doubtful that Bone's criticism can be classified as doctrinal. Bone did not build a bridge; moreover, he disputed that it was even possible to do so. However, it would be premature to conclude that his criticism should not be regarded as doctrinal. While both metaphors seem to fit civil law, they obviously do not fit common law insofar as it deals with case law. It could be argued that there was no trade secret law prior to *Peabody v Norfolk*. This could indicate that doctrinal analysis has a different role in common law from that in civil law. In the case of the former, doctrinal analysis cannot be meaningfully characterized as either a bridge or an intermediate layer; it is rather the very foundation of the law.

But it is not that simple, and at this point, it becomes apparent how both metaphors are inaccurate in some respects. First, they are based on simplification. The idea of a bridge fits when you think of a specific legal problem, especially a rather simple one. Here, doctrinal analysis guides the way, helping to bridge the gap. It functions as a kind of user's manual.[24] However, as soon as more complex problems are encountered, we cannot simply think of one single path but rather a way through a labyrinth where different issues must be resolved. More importantly, doctrinal analysis is more than a mere guideline to solve specific problems.[25] This is where another popular metaphor comes into play. In Germany, doctrinal analysis is often referred to as a *building* (*Gebäude*).[26] This image better reflects the fact that doctrinal analysis is usually

[22] J Smits, 'What Is Legal Doctrine?' in R van Gestel, H-W Micklitz, and E Rubin (eds), *Rethinking Legal Scholarship* (CUP 2017) 221; see also A Peczenik, 'Scientia Juris' in E Pattaro and A Peczenik (eds), *A Treatise of Legal Philosophy and General Jurisprudence* (Vol 4, Springer 2005) 3.

[23] C Bumke, 'Rechtsdogmatik' (2014) 69 Juristenzeitung 641, 642, 645; C Bumke, *Rechtsdogmatik* (Mohr Siebeck 2017) 116; A Oeter, 'Responsive Regulierung und das Verhältnis der Rechts-, Wirtschafts- und Sozialwissenschaften in der Politikberatung' in K Bizzer, M Führ, and C Hüttig (eds), *Responsive Regulierung* (Mohr Siebeck 2002) 201; A Stark, *Interdisziplinarität der Rechtsdogmatik* (Mohr Siebeck 2017) 23.

[24] cf J Harenburg, *Die Rechtsdogmatik zwischen Wissenschaft und Praxis* (Steiner 1986) 234; E Rubin and M Feeley, 'Creating Legal Doctrine' (1996) 69 S Cal L Rev 1989, 1999.

[25] See O Behrends, 'Das Bündnis zwischen Gesetz und Dogmatik und die Frage der dogmatischen Rangstufen' in O Behrends and W Henckel (eds), *Gesetzgebung und Dogmatik* (De Gruyter 1989) 14–15, 36; T Vesting, *Rechtstheorie* (2nd edn, CH Beck 2019) 21.

[26] W Hassemer, 'Dogmatik zwischen Wissenschaft und richterlicher Pragmatik' in G Kirchhof, S Magen, and K Schneider (eds), *Was weiß Dogmatik?* (Mohr Siebeck 2012) 11; K Langenbucher,

built on a multitude of principles, concepts, and interrelationships, which ideally form a system. Here, the image of a bridge is rather misleading because when we construct this building, we usually do so without specific legal problems in mind; instead, we need a certain level of abstraction.[27]

The image of an intermediate layer remains adequate in this regard. But it, too, fails when doctrinal analysis does not refer to concrete written law. By definition, an intermediate layer exists between two things, just as a bridge connects two sides. Where no written law exists, we cannot think of doctrinal analysis this way. The notion of doctrinal analysis as a building does not have this drawback. Its shortcoming is that it reflects an important function of doctrinal analysis less clearly. But it is highly illustrative when doctrinal analysis fills a void that results from a lack of written law. It should be mentioned that this different meaning of doctrine is not necessarily related to presumed differences between common law and civil law. Such a void might be less common in civil law, but it also exists there. Common examples in Germany are collective labour law, the law of leasing, or (for a time) plea bargaining (which I will come back to later). Obviously, I have used various metaphors and been on the verge of mixing them. My goal has not been to find the most appropriate metaphor but to show that several exist, and each has its advantages and deficiencies. Indeed, this is no coincidence. A major problem we encounter when trying to better understand doctrinal thinking is that doctrinal analysis is supposed to be many things: a guide to resolving cases, a method of mapping out whole areas of law, and the result of both.

III. The Point of Reference of Doctrinal Analysis

The difference I have dealt with in the previous section depends on whether doctrinal analysis attaches to written law. It might appear to stand to reason that this is easy to say, but that is not true at all. Sometimes, the written law treats a certain aspect so sparingly that it becomes questionable whether doctrinal analysis still refers to it. For example, in the German Criminal Code, omission is only rudimentarily regulated, intention and negligence are only

'Dogmatik, Falsifikation und zwei Perspektiven auf die Rechtswissenschaft' in M Auer and others (eds), *Privatrechtsdogmatik im 21. Jahrhundert. Festschrift für Claus-Wilhelm Canaris zum 70. Geburtstag* (De Gruyter 2017) 220; P Sahm, *Elemente der Dogmatik* (Velbrück Wissenschaft 2019) 17, 71.

[27] P Sahm, *Elemente der Dogmatik* (Velbrück Wissenschaft 2019) 65–66; G Virgo, 'Doctrinal Legal Research' in P Cane and J Conaghan (eds), *The New Oxford Companion to Law* (OUP 2008).

mentioned in passing, and causality is not referred to. In all these cases, one can nevertheless assume an intermediate layer because doctrinal analysis closes gaps in the Criminal Code. But one could also argue that, for example, the doctrine of causation was constructed in a void—much like the trade secret law in the United States. And even where we think we are interpreting more expressive statutes, the boundaries between them and case law have long been blurred in view of the detail-loving doctrinal analysis in Germany. Anyone who has ever had to answer whether criminal fraud has occurred in complicated economic contexts will almost exclusively utilize doctrinal considerations that have little to do with the wording of the statute on fraud. This is another reason one should not overestimate the differences between case and common law. Either way, it is probably fair to say that there is a correlation between the density of the written law and the need for doctrinal analysis: the more questions a statute does not clearly answer, the greater the need for doctrinal analysis.[28]

All this is worth mentioning because it suggests doctrinal analysis plays a vital role even when it does not refer to a statute—and that this role is partially neglected. Martin Flohr, who studied the role of doctrinal analysis in England, conjectures that the reason it has not spread there as it has in Continental Europe is in part because there were significantly fewer written laws in that jurisdiction.[29] Where bridges are not needed, no one learns to build them. Gerhard Wagner argues similarly in respect of the United States.[30] Such assumptions seem to be based on a premise that Winfried Hassemer advocates: that a statute is essential for doctrinal analysis even to exist.[31] On the other hand, van Gestel and others point out that doctrinal analysis may still be important for understanding the law *even in areas where common law has been replaced by statute*.[32] The incompatibility of the two positions is unmistakable: some believe that there must be a sufficient set of statutes for doctrinal

[28] See also W Frisch, 'Wesenszüge rechtswissenschaftlichen Arbeitens – am Beispiel und aus der Sicht des Strafrechts' in C Engel and W Schön (eds), *Das Proprium der Rechtswissenschaft* (Mohr Siebeck 2007) 162; M Maiwald, 'Dogmatik und Gesetzgebung im Strafrecht der Gegenwart' in O Behrends and W Henckel (eds), *Gesetzgebung und Dogmatik* (De Gruyter 1989) 122.

[29] M Flohr, *Rechtsdogmatik in England* (Mohr Siebeck 2017) 135–41, 147–49.

[30] G Wagner, 'Privatrechtsdogmatik und ökonomische Analyse des Rechts' in M Auer and others (eds), *Privatrechtsdogmatik im 21. Jahrhundert. Festschrift für Claus-Wilhelm Canaris zum 70. Geburtstag* (De Gruyter 2017) 282–83.

[31] W Hassemer, 'Dogmatik zwischen Wissenschaft und richterlicher Pragmatik' in G Kirchhof, S Magen, and K Schneider, *Was weiß Dogmatik?* (Mohr Siebeck 2012) 8. It must be emphasized that he nevertheless acknowledges the significance of doctrinal analysis for judicial law.

[32] R van Gestel, H-W Micklitz, and E Rubin, 'Introduction' in R van Gestel, H-W Micklitz, and E Rubin (eds), *Rethinking Legal Scholarship* (CUP 2017) 9. They attribute this to R Posner, *How Judges Think* (HUP 2008) 111. However, while Posner does stress the value of doctrinal thinking, he does not deal with its importance in a legal system in which statutes are increasingly prevalent.

Table 1 Categories of doctrinal analysis

Constituent doctrinal analysis		**Constituted doctrinal analysis**	
The law is based on doctrinal analysis		**Doctrinal analysis is based on the law**	
(1) law = statute	(2) law = judicial law	(3) law = statute	(4) law = judicial law

analysis to have any significant meaning. Others assume that with an increasing number of statutes, the importance of doctrinal analysis diminishes (even if they consider this problematic). Apparently, there are different dimensions to doctrinal analysis. We can resort to it when we create statutes and work with already existing statutes—but also when we work without reference to written law. It is important to distinguish these dimensions. Doctrinal analysis plays a different role in each of them, and the distinction allows for an important categorization. A distinction can be made between doctrinal analysis as the basis of law or, vice versa, law as the basis of doctrinal analysis. The first is when we rely on doctrinal analysis to create new laws, whether statutory or judicial. The latter is when we rely on doctrinal analysis to make sense of that law (again, be it a statutory or judicial law). In Germany, doctrinal analysis is sometimes described as a loyal servant.[33] This is accurate only regarding the second category. We can describe the first category as constituent doctrinal analysis and the second as constituted doctrinal analysis. Within these categories, further distinctions can be made as to whether doctrinal analysis relates to statutes or judicial law.

It is possible to attribute different statements about doctrinal analysis to different (sub) categories displayed in Table 1. When van Gestel and others suggest that doctrinal analysis is particularly important as the foundation of codes, this corresponds to category (1). Flohr's assumption that in England, doctrinal analysis was of little importance because there was so little written law that could have been systematized clearly correlates to category (3). And those who claim that the US and German legal scholarship do not differ much as far as doctrinal analysis is concerned thus correspond to categories (2) or (4). But again, in the German legal system, it is also possible to recognize categories (2) and (4) because there is also judicial law, which relies on doctrinal reasoning.

[33] cf W Hassemer, 'Dogmatik zwischen Wissenschaft und richterlicher Pragmatik' in G Kirchhof, S Magen, and K Schneider (eds), *Was weiß Dogmatik?* (Mohr Siebeck 2012) 12; P Sahm, *Elemente der Dogmatik* (Velbrück Wissenschaft 2019) 81.

Apparently, if one claims (like Hassemer does) that the existence of a statute is vital for doctrinal analysis,[34] that seems to exclude the possibility of accepting categories (2) and (4). If we accept all categories, on the other hand, this suggests that we are not dealing with significantly different perceptions of doctrinal analysis in Germany and the United States. Of course, it may be true that one category or another is more typical in common or civil law.

At this point, it is important to emphasize that while the distinction between constituent and constituted doctrinal analysis is analytically insightful, in practice, the transition between the two is fluid. For doctrinal thinking never starts at some sort of zero hour; it usually refers to existing figures, principles or constructions.[35] Plea bargaining is a perfect example of this. Until 2009, the German Code of Criminal Procedure did not contain a provision for plea bargaining. In the 1980s, legal scholars began to discuss whether it was doctrinally justifiable. The Federal Court of Justice then set out the legal framework for plea bargaining in a fundamental ruling. In doing so, it drew substantially on the doctrinal groundwork laid by scholars. Later, the legislature incorporated this case law almost without any significant changes into a statute. However, what at first glance seems like a textbook example of constituent doctrinal analysis did not start at ground zero. Rather, the doctrinal groundwork was built on existing doctrinal knowledge, which, in turn, was distilled from the German Code of Criminal Procedure and thus constituted doctrinal analysis. Either way, once the statute is in place, the constituent doctrinal analysis assumes the role of an intermediate layer (without in this respect differing from constituted doctrinal analysis).[36]

The creation of law is a fluid process, and doctrinal analysis therefore oscillates between yesterday's, today's, and tomorrow's law. We are dealing with *recursive interactions*. This applies to constituted doctrinal analysis, too, when it becomes the basis of new law (be it case law or a statute) and then appears as constituent doctrinal analysis. This recursiveness is also the main reason Julius von Kirchmann's famous dictum about the three pen strokes of the legislator making entire libraries obsolete is vastly exaggerated. This may be true in very rare cases, but usually, doctrinally cultivated legal knowledge does not lose its significance.[37]

[34] See again W Hassemer, 'Dogmatik zwischen Wissenschaft und richterlicher Pragmatik' in G Kirchhof, S Magen, and K Schneider (eds), *Was weiß Dogmatik?* (Mohr Siebeck 2012) 8.

[35] R Wahl, 'Entwicklungspfade im Recht' (2013) 68 Juristenzeitung 369, 372; see also C Gusy, 'Das Mehrheitsprinzip im demokratischen Staat' (1981) 106 Archiv des öffentlichen Rechts 329, 352.

[36] See C Starck, 'Rechtsdogmatik und Gesetzgebung im Verwaltungsrecht' in O Behrends and W Henckel (eds), *Gesetzgebung und Dogmatik* (De Gruyter 1989) 113.

[37] H Sendler, 'Zur Makulaturproduktion des Gesetzgebers' in D Wilke (ed), *Festschrift zum 125-jährigen Bestehen der Juristischen Gesellschaft zu Berlin* (De Gruyter 1984) 758–63; C Starck,

IV. Doctrinal Analysis and Methodology

I have dwelt on the different dimensions of doctrinal analysis for some time because the pertinent distinctions yield insights into the question of which method is used by doctrinal analysis. Of course, this question is far too big to deal with in depth here. I will be content to emphasize an important distinction that ties in with my previous thoughts. In Germany, a traditional legal methodology goes back to Friedrich Carl von Savigny. This is a method we use when we deal with the written law. When we *interpret* the law, we do it in a certain way, and there is a broad consensus on that way, at least in Germany (albeit some details are disputed). Assuming doctrinal analysis relies on this methodology when it comes to interpretation,[38] it is at first glance surprising if the method of doctrinal analysis appears to us nevertheless as a kind of black box. The simple yet important reason for this is that doctrinal analysis is more than the mere interpretation of law.[39] It is sometimes aptly referred to as *both* interpretation *and* the production of doctrinal statements not based on interpretation.[40]

I am convinced that the uncertainties surrounding the methodology of doctrinal analysis are rooted in the second category (the non-interpretative method). This is not only but also because this category is only negatively delimited and not positively defined. It is easier to develop specific rules on how written laws should be interpreted, but it is more difficult to develop similarly clear rules on how doctrines can be developed without a comparable

'Rechtsdogmatik und Gesetzgebung im Verwaltungsrecht' in O Behrends and W Henckel (eds), *Gesetzgebung und Dogmatik* (De Gruyter 1989) 114.

[38] See H Koch and H Rüßmann, *Juristische Begründungslehre* (CH Beck 1982) 185. See also W Frisch, 'Wesenszüge rechtswissenschaftlichen Arbeitens – am Beispiel und aus der Sicht des Strafrechts' in C Engel and W Schön (eds), *Das Proprium der Rechtswissenschaft* (Mohr Siebeck 2007) 158; M Maiwald, 'Dogmatik und Gesetzgebung im Strafrecht der Gegenwart' in O Behrends and W Henckel (eds), *Gesetzgebung und Dogmatik* (De Gruyter 1989) 122; A Peczenik, 'Scientia Juris' in E Pattaro and A Peczenik (eds), *A Treatise of Legal Philosophy and General Jurisprudence* vol 4 (Springer 2005) 11; E von Savigny, 'Methodologie der Dogmatik: Wissenschaftstheoretische Fragen' in E von Savigny, U Neumann, and J Rahlf (eds), *Juristische Dogmatik und Wissenschaftstheorie* (CH Beck 1976) 7–13. However, some argue, even though Rechtsdogmatik is close to methodology, both are competitors, see W Hassemer, 'Juristische Methodenlehre und richterliche Pragmatik' (2008) 39 Rechtstheorie 1, 15.

[39] C Bumke, *Rechtsdogmatik* (Mohr Siebeck 2017) 113; J Lennartz, *Dogmatik als Methode* (Mohr Siebeck 2020) 40–41, 137. See also W Krawietz, 'Juristische Methodik und ihre rechtstheoretischen Implikationen' (1972) 2 Jahrbuch für Rechtssoziologie und Rechtstheorie 12, 32–33; K Larenz, *Methodenlehre der Rechtswissenschaft* (6th edn, Springer 1991) 226.

[40] J Harenburg, *Die Rechtsdogmatik zwischen Wissenschaft und Praxis* (Steiner 1986) 270. See also R Poscher, 'Rechtsdogmatik als hermeneutische Wissenschaft' in J Nolte, R Poscher, and H Wolter (eds), *Die Verfassung als Aufgabe von Wissenschaft, Praxis und Öffentlichkeit. Freundesgabe für Bernhard Schlink zum 70. Geburtstag* (CF Müller 2014) 208–11, who argues that we are dealing with interpretation in both cases.

reference point. How we do the latter is beyond the scope of the traditional legal methodology.[41]

However, the distinction between these two categories (interpretative and non-interpretative) should not obscure that the line between them is blurry. Even where doctrinal analysis relates to written law, it is usually not merely interpretation. For private law in Germany, the typical method of doctrinal analysis has been described as follows: first, we identify the fundamental idea of a certain statute, then the basic terms and categories, and then we distinguish these terms from each other or other terms in different areas.[42] The same could be said for criminal law, and the description can probably be generalized beyond that.

Even when dealing with a particular question, the boundaries between the interpretative and the non-interpretative method may become blurred. Let me illustrate this with a specific question from trade secret law. For over 100 years, there has been controversy in Germany about whether someone divulges a trade secret when they disclose that illegal conduct has taken place in a company (something we nowadays call 'whistleblowing').[43] At first glance, this is clearly a matter of interpretation. We just need to determine what a trade secret is. The traditional methodology starts with the wording of the law. Now, it is apparent that a secret is known only to a limited group of people. But what exactly is a trade secret, and how does it differ from other secrets, such as state secrets or attorney-client privilege? Like in many cases, it all comes down to the so-called teleological method (originally not included by Savigny): we ask ourselves, what is the purpose of trade secret law? Sometimes, a statute elaborates on its purpose. But where it does not, we have to identify that purpose ourselves. To make this a little more descriptive, one possible explanation of trade secret law adapts John Locke's labour theory of property. In *Peabody v Norfolk*, the Massachusetts Supreme Court essentially paraphrases Locke: 'If a man establishes a business and makes it valuable by his skill and attention, the good will of that business is recognized by the law as property … If he invents or discovers, and keeps secret a process of manufacture … he has a property in

[41] W Ernst, 'Gelehrtes Recht' in C Engel and W Schön (eds), *Das Proprium der Rechtswissenschaft* (Mohr Siebeck 2007) 39–40; J Lennartz, *Dogmatik als Methode* (Mohr Siebeck 2020) 133; see also W Frisch, 'Wesenszüge rechtswissenschaftlichen Arbeitens – am Beispiel und aus der Sicht des Strafrechts' in C Engel and W Schön (eds), *Das Proprium der Rechtswissenschaft* (Mohr Siebeck 2007) 162; W Frisch, 'Zur Bedeutung der Rechtsdogmatik für die Entwicklung des Strafrechts' in R Stürner (ed), *Die Bedeutung der Rechtsdogmatik für die Rechtsentwicklung* (Mohr Siebeck 2010) 172–73.

[42] M Flohr, *Rechtsdogmatik in England* (Mohr Siebeck 2017) 33.

[43] The question can be dated back to G Freudenstein, 'Ueber den Schutz gewerblicher und technischer Geheimnisse durch die Gesetzgebung' (1884) 32 Goltdammer's Archiv für Strafrecht 265, 274.

it.'[44] We can on this basis now ask whether it is appropriate also to protect the knowledge that illegal conduct takes place in an enterprise as a trade secret.

I am certain that if the same question (are we dealing with trade secrets where whistleblowing is concerned) were discussed in the United States, very similar considerations would be made, even if there were no statutes to be interpreted. As a matter of fact, I have elsewhere relied heavily on the doctrinal analysis in the United States on this very issue.[45] I did so because there was no similar discussion in Germany about the purpose of trade secret law. But everyone seems to agree that we can easily rely on the doctrinal analysis from the United States. If true, it is another indicator that doctrinal thinking in the United States and Continental Europe may not be so different after all. Of course, this is no coincidence, but again, it is dependent on the fact that the boundary between the two categories (interpretative and non-interpretative) is fuzzy. And so it is within the teleological interpretation that we find rather similar obscurity concerning the method of doctrinal analysis we have previously identified with the non-interpretative method.[46]

We can now see even more clearly why it would have been premature to conclude that Bone's reflections on trade secret law had nothing to do with doctrinal analysis. This becomes particularly evident when one imagines that he would have allowed even one of the justifications discussed to stand. In this case, there would be no doubt that they were doctrinal considerations. However, it does not seem very plausible to make the classification of the considerations dependent on the result.

V. Doctrinal Analysis and the Economic Analysis of the Law

This is probably a good time for a side note on an issue that should not go unmentioned in a transatlantic workshop. I am talking about the economic analysis of the law. The following considerations should be seen in the light of the fact that doctrinal analysis is often perceived to be in crisis.[47] We find an example in Rubin's contribution to the book mentioned at the outset of this

[44] *Peabody v Norfolk* 98 Mass 452, 457 (1968).

[45] P Krell, 'Grund und Grenzen des (neuen) Schutzes von Geschäftsgeheimnissen – am Beispiel des Whistleblowings' (2021) 133 Zeitschrift für die gesamte Strafrechtswissenschaft 714, 722–36.

[46] See also G Lübbe-Wolff, 'Expropriation der Jurisprudenz?' in C Engel and W Schön (eds), *Das Proprium der Rechtswissenschaft* (Mohr Siebeck 2007) 284–85, 288.

[47] See J Smits, *The Mind and Method of the Legal Academic* (EE Publishing 2012) 1–7; see also N Luhmann, *Rechtssystem und Rechtsdogmatik* (Kohlhammer 1974) 12–14.

chapter: 'Legal scholarship must wake from its coherentist reveries. The world has changed, and the legal system has changed with it. Law is no longer limited to a system of normatively grounded rules designed to maintain public order. Rather, it is now a means by which democratic society carries out the varied and extensive purposes that are characteristic of an administrative state. As a result, internal or doctrinal coherence is no longer a sufficient criterion for law.'[48]

Such statements are, among other things, an expression of a consequentialist view for which doctrinal analysis and the accompanying need for coherence are no longer contemporary.[49] The economic analysis of the law is a prominent manifestation of such a consequentialist view. In Germany, economic analysis is conventionally regarded as a different discipline (and thus, in some ways as a competitor) to doctrinal analysis, but while the two seem to coexist peacefully in the United States, economic analysis in Germany was initially opposed by legal scholars, though they have recently become increasingly receptive to it.[50] The discussion here revolves around the question whether economic analysis can play a role alongside (or be integrated into) doctrinal analysis when we interpret the law.[51] The importance of a consequence-based approach (which the economic analysis of the law clearly is) has long been cited as a possible reason why the importance of doctrinal analysis is waning in Germany as well.[52]

I believe that doctrinal analysis assumes a function in the application of law that cannot be substituted by a consequentialist view. This can be illustrated by revisiting the question of whether knowledge of illegal conduct in companies is to be considered a trade secret. A common justification of trade secret law is based on an economic analysis of the law. The basic idea is this: if we do not legally protect such secrets, competing companies will invest a lot of money to obtain them. The owners, on the other hand, will invest money to protect the secret. Because on one of the two sides, the investments are inevitably in vain, this state of affairs is ultimately inefficient.[53]

[48] E Rubin, 'From Coherence to Effectiveness' in R van Gestel, H-W Micklitz, and E Rubin (eds), *Rethinking Legal Scholarship* (CUP 2017) 349–50.

[49] See also W Krawietz, 'Juristische Methodik und ihre rechtstheoretischen Implikationen' (1972) 2 Jahrbuch für Rechtssoziologie und Rechtstheorie 12, 36–42.

[50] See G Wagner, 'Privatrechtsdogmatik und ökonomische Analyse des Rechts' in M Auer and others (eds), *Privatrechtsdogmatik im 21. Jahrhundert. Festschrift für Claus-Wilhelm Canaris zum 70. Geburtstag* (De Gruyter 2017) 282–91.

[51] H Eidenmüller, 'Rechtsanwendung, Gesetzgebung und ökonomische Analyse' (1997) 197 Archiv für die civilistische Praxis 80, 81.

[52] N Luhmann, *Rechtssystem und Rechtsdogmatik* (Kohlhammer 1974) 13.

[53] D Friedman, W Landes, and R Posner, 'Some Economics of Trade Secret Law' (1991) 5 J Econ Perspectives 61, 67–71; see also V Chiapetta, 'Myth, Chameleon or Intellectual Property Olympian? A normative Framework supporting Trade Secret Law' (1999) 69 Geo Mason L Rev 69, 86, 94–96.

Like I have argued elsewhere, I am not at all suggesting that such considerations are unimportant or should be overlooked; however, they do not help very much in determining the scope of trade secret law.[54] If one follows the efficiency-based approach, one will also have to protect the knowledge of illegal conduct. There is simply no room for teleological considerations, and, therefore, such an approach tends to blur the boundaries of a legal area. I know too little about the economic analysis of the law to be sure that this is a structural problem, but I strongly suspect it is. Doctrinal analysis and economic analysis can both be valuable and possibly complement each other. Nevertheless, they are different ways of thinking.

If the economic analysis of the law is a different discipline (and thus possibly uses another method) to doctrinal analysis, one can most likely also garner insights into what distinguishes doctrinal from non-doctrinal criticism. Indeed, just as we know implicitly what doctrinal thinking is, we can say what is not. The prohibition of drugs is a very good example. Apart from maybe the objection that other drugs are unfairly regulated and differently from alcohol, it is hard to name doctrinal objections to this prohibition. Nevertheless, more and more legal scholars are making a strong case against this prohibition, arguing in a consequentialist manner. While drug prohibition might well be justified in theory, it cannot be enforced efficiently: it creates black markets and promotes organized crime, thus having disastrous effects on countries where drugs are grown on a large scale, and it pushes addicts into illegality—and all this costs a huge amount of money every year, while the state misses out on tax revenues.[55] The example shows that the consequentialist view has its justification, and in extreme cases can even be superior to doctrinal reasoning. Nevertheless, doctrinal analysis has a function that a consequentialist view cannot make up for.

VI. The Critical Potential of Doctrinal Analysis

Because of our implicit knowledge, we seem to be able to distinguish doctrinal and non-doctrinal criticism, at least to a certain degree. However, the question remains: How far can doctrinal criticism go? In fact, the question even arises whether such criticism can exist at all. This has to do with another controversy over doctrinal analysis: To what extent is doctrinal analysis bound by the

[54] P Krell, 'Grund und Grenzen des (neuen) Schutzes von Geschäftsgeheimnissen – am Beispiel des Whistleblowings' (2021) 133 Zeitschrift für die gesamte Strafrechtswissenschaft 714, 727–28.

[55] See L Böllinger, 'Strafrechtsprofessoren für eine Reform des Betäubungsmittelstrafrechts: ein Projekt' (2014) 26 Neue Kriminalpolitik 115.

authority of existing law? I will deal with this question in the first subsection. In the second section, I will address a topic I feel is a little neglected: in Germany, many assume that the authority to criticize judgments or statutes is bestowed upon doctrinal analysis. But where is this authority supposed to come from?[56] This issue is closely related to the discussion surrounding the constraint of doctrinal analysis, which is traditionally highly valued in Germany, but viewed with some suspicion in the United States.

1. The Self-restriction of Doctrinal Analysis to the Applicable Law

It is often emphasized that doctrinal scholarship can and should make a critical contribution—for example, by identifying dysfunctional rules or developing alternatives.[57] Even though most doctrinal scholars would probably agree with that proposition, the question remains concerning how this aligns with the assumption that doctrinal analysis is a servant discipline, one that stabilizes rather than problematizes. Gustav Radbruch defines the actual science of law (by this he explicitly means doctrinal analysis) as the science of the objective sense of existing legal systems—as a science of the *applicable* law, not of the *right* law.[58] Entirely along these lines, Arthur Kaufmann describes doctrinal analysis (as distinct from legal philosophy) as follows: the legal doctrinist thinks *ex datis*, he starts from presuppositions which he accepts as true without examination.[59] And for Josef Esser, doctrinal analysis is characterized by the fact that it is determined by the authority of binding texts (for example, statutes), while it is left to other disciplines (such as legal philosophy) to question these texts.[60]

It stands to reason that such statements primarily concern the dimension I have called constituted doctrinal analysis. It is difficult to say how rigorously

[56] See also T Kuntz, 'Recht als Gegenstand der Rechtswissenschaft und performative Rechtserzeugung' (2016) 216 Archiv für die civilistische Praxis 866, 904; E von Savigny, 'Methodologie der Dogmatik: Wissenschaftstheoretische Fragen' in E von Savigny, U Neumann, and J Rahlf (eds), *Juristische Dogmatik und Wissenschaftstheorie* (CH Beck 1976) 9.

[57] See W Hassemer, 'Dogmatik zwischen Wissenschaft und richterlicher Pragmatik' in G Kirchhof, S Magen, and K Schneider (eds), *Was weiß Dogmatik?* (Mohr Siebeck 2012) 12; N Jansen, 'Making doctrine for European Law' in R van Gestel, H-W Micklitz, and E Rubin (eds), *Rethinking Legal Scholarship* (CUP 2017) 243; R Stürner, 'Die Zivilrechtswissenschaft und ihre Methodik' (2014) 214 Archiv für die civilistische Praxis 7, 11; G Virgo, 'Doctrinal Legal Research' in P Cane and J Conaghan (eds), *The New Oxford Companion to Law* (OUP 2008).

[58] G Radbruch, *Rechtsphilosophie* (8th edn, KF Koehler 1973) 205.

[59] A Kaufmann, *Rechtsphilosophie* (2nd edn, CH Beck 1997) 11–12.

[60] J Esser, 'Möglichkeiten und Grenzen des dogmatischen Denkens im modernen Zivilrecht' (1972) 172 Archiv für die civilistische Praxis 97.

doctrinal analysis is limited here to the perception of current law and whether and to what extent there is room for a critique of that law because the context of all these statements is the distinction of doctrinal analysis from legal philosophy. It is obvious that, for example, theories of justice are outside the scope of doctrinal analysis. But the question remains of how strongly doctrinal analysis is restricted by the authority of existing law or whether and how much room there is for criticism of that law. Obviously, a narrow view that essentially limits doctrinal analysis to description leaves less room for innovative potential.[61]

When doctrinal analysis is tied to the existing law, this can mean one of at least two things. Some say that considerations *de lege ferenda* have nothing to do with doctrinal analysis (but rather belong in the domain of legal policy).[62] This is a formal restriction of doctrinal analysis. On the other hand, in his distinction from legal philosophy, Kaufmann emphasizes that doctrinal thinking need not necessarily remain uncritical, but that where doctrinists critically examine the law, they must always do so in a way that is immanent to the system, as the system must remain unchallenged.[63] This is a substantial restriction of doctrinal analysis. The two restrictions (formal and substantial) are not necessarily the same. One can, for example, raise demands to change the law based on a system-immanent critique. This would be in line with the substantial restriction but not the formal one. I do not believe a formal restriction to the current law makes much sense. If I criticize this law in a system-immanent manner, this usually implicitly suggests that the law should be changed—regardless of whether I explicitly say so. Furthermore, the idea that considerations *de lege lata* and *de lege ferenda* can be clearly separated is deceptive.[64] Doctrinal analysis oscillates between *lex lata* and *lex ferens*.

While the formal restriction is fairly clear, it is much harder to say how far the substantive restriction goes. It is often emphasized that doctrinal analysis must always accept the current law as valid.[65] The general idea behind this restriction is plausible at first glance. It is said that doctrinal analysis is supposed

[61] W Frisch, 'Zur Bedeutung der Rechtsdogmatik für die Entwicklung des Strafrechts' in R Stürner (ed), *Die Bedeutung der Rechtsdogmatik für die Rechtsentwicklung* (Mohr Siebeck 2010) 170.

[62] P Reimer, *Verfahrenstheorie* (Mohr Siebeck 2015) 118.

[63] A Kaufmann, *Rechtsphilosophie* (2nd edn, CH Beck 1997) 12. See also A Stark, *Interdisziplinarität der Rechtsdogmatik* (Mohr Siebeck 2017) 136.

[64] A Peczenik, 'A Theory of Legal Doctrine' (2001) 14 Ratio Juris 75, 76; C Bumke, *Rechtsdogmatik* (Mohr Siebeck 2017) 103–05; S Simitis, 'Die Bedeutung von System und Dogmatik' (1972) 72 Archiv für die civilistische Praxis 131, 151; see also N Luhmann, *Rechtssystem und Rechtsdogmatik* (Kohlhammer 1974) 18–19; T Kuntz, 'Recht als Gegenstand der Rechtswissenschaft und performative Rechtserzeugung' (2016) 216 Archiv für die civilistische Praxis 866, 872–73.

[65] C Bumke, 'Rechtsdogmatik' (2014) 69 Juristenzeitung 641, 647; P Sahm, *Elemente der Dogmatik* (Velbrück Wissenschaft 2019) 54.

to stabilize, but it does not problematize.[66] In a similar manner, it is said that doctrinal work is productive (or constructive) per se.[67] But it is obviously not that simple. Sometimes, a certain part of a building does not work or does not work as intended. We must recognize this as a problem before we can repair the building.[68]

This, too, can be illustrated by an example from trade secret law. Some argue that trade secret law, much like patent law, is about protecting innovation.[69] In the German discussion, it is pointed out that this approach can be used to justify the protection of know-how but that it is then implausible that for example, secret information about customer bases is protected.[70] Since under current German trade secret law that information is protected as well, the innovation-based approach would consequently have to argue for restricting trade secret law to the protection of know-how. This would be a criticism of the current law. I suspect, however, that it would be widely assumed that the boundaries of doctrinal analysis have not yet been crossed in this instance. It can be said that merely a (allegedly) dysfunctional room was removed from the building here.

But where is the line? Philipp Sahm draws it where the authority of the law in question is fundamentally challenged.[71] We can destroy individual parts of a building if it is purposeful, but we cannot tear down the whole building. At first glance, this makes sense, and one would be inclined to say that Bone's critique of trade secret law is such a fundamental challenge. But again, it is not that simple. Indeed, when we think of the legal system or individual areas as buildings, it depends on which building we refer to. If we think solely of trade secret law, Bone has torn down the whole building. But if we see trade secret law as part of a larger building (for example, intellectual property), there is an argument to be made that, much like in the previous example, merely a dysfunctional room has been removed from the bigger building. It is obviously very difficult to determine which criticism is still within tolerable bounds and which is too fundamental.

66 S Simitis, 'Die Bedeutung von System und Dogmatik' (1972) 72 Archiv für die civilistische Praxis 131, 132–33.

67 M Flohr, *Rechtsdogmatik in England* (Mohr Siebeck 2017) 27; P Sahm, *Elemente der Dogmatik* (Velbrück Wissenschaft 2019) 20–21.

68 See also I Augsberg, 'Lob der Dogmatik' (2014) 4 rescriptum 63.

69 *Kewanee v Bicron* 416 US 470, 481 F (1974); *Peabody v Norfolk* 98 Mass 452, 457–58 (1968); D Friedman, W Landes, and R Posner, 'Some Economics of Trade Secret Law' (1991) 5 J Econ Perspectives 61, 64; M Lemley, 'The Surprising Virtues of Treating Trade Secrets as IP Rights' (2008) 61 Stan L Rev 311, 331.

70 B Kalbfus, *Know-how-Schutz in Deutschland zwischen Strafrecht und Zivilrecht* (Carl Heymanns 2011) 45–46.

71 P Sahm, *Elemente der Dogmatik* (Velbrück Wissenschaft 2019) 53, 76–82.

I thus come to the somewhat unsatisfactory conclusion that it is not always possible to say conclusively when a criticism can be classified as doctrinal. The main reason for this lies again in the ambiguity of doctrinal analysis, and specifically in its multiple meanings as an activity (discipline or method) and a product. Another reason is that we cannot clearly distinguish constituent and constituted doctrinal analysis.

2. The Authority of Doctrinal Analysis

This leaves the question of the status of doctrinal critique. In Germany, doctrinal analysis has a remarkable self-perception, for which there are several reasons. One of them is the alleged (albeit not undisputed)[72] importance of the development of the big codifications. Another reason is the close relationship between legal science and practice in Germany. This self-perception concerns both the relationship of doctrinal analysis to the legislature and that branch of government to the courts. German legal scholars maintain that the legislature on its own can only handle routine matters; for greater achievements, it must allegedly rely on the contribution of legal scholarship.[73] And when courts disregard sufficiently prominent doctrinal analysis, German legal scholars sometimes perceive this as an affront. But even in international discourse, we find statements concerning doctrinal analysis providing that '[i]f a rule does not fit into the system, it is not law'.[74] Aleksander Peczenik refers to doctrinal analysis not only as a 'source of law', but also assumes it has authority 'because of the quality of argumentation it typically produces'.[75]

However, even if a discipline thinks so much of itself, authority does not derive from (assumed) expertise. In this respect, legal scholarship differs significantly from statutes and rulings.[76] The former has authority because of the legislative process, and the latter because judges, by law, may rule on behalf of the people. Let us assume that Bone criticized trade secret law in Germany and

[72] See P Noll, *Gesetzgebungslehre* (Rowohlt 1973) 216.

[73] C Roxin, 'Die Strafrechtswissenschaft vor den Aufgaben der Zukunft' in A Eser, W Hassemer, and B Burkhardt (eds), *Die deutsche Strafrechtswissenschaft vor der Jahrtausendwende* (CH Beck 2000) 388.

[74] J M Smits, 'What is Legal Doctrine?' in R van Gestel, H-W Micklitz, and E Rubin (eds), *Rethinking Legal Scholarship* (CUP 2017) 219.

[75] A Peczenik, 'Scientia Juris' in E Pattaro and A Peczenik (eds), *A Treatise of Legal Philosophy and General Jurisprudence* vol 4 (Springer 2005) 17.

[76] H Kelsen, *Reine Rechtslehre* (2nd edn, Deuticke 1960) 351–52; see also H Albert, 'Erkenntnis und Recht' (1972) 2 Jahrbuch für Rechtssoziologie und Rechtstheorie 80, 88; M Bodig, 'Legal Theory and Legal Doctrinal Scholarship' (2010) 23 CJLJ 483, 501.

demanded that an entire statute be abolished because the doctrinal basis was insufficient. Is that not asking too much of the legislature?

There is a famous dictum in Germany by Willi Geiger from 1979 according to which the legislation owes the people the statute but not the rationale behind it.[77] Since then it has been repeatedly discussed whether a duty for the legislator to give reasons can be established.[78] In the 1970s, a discussion about a legislative doctrine (*Gesetzgebungslehre*) evolved in Germany.[79] However, the expectations that went along with this were quite divergent. Some saw the *Gesetzgebungslehre* as an accommodation of rules of wisdom.[80] Others went so far as to derive a duty from the constitution to legislate optimally.[81] Today, at least, this idea is probably outdated. It has become increasingly accepted that statutes draw not only their authority but also their rationality and their legitimacy from the democratic process—and thus from the majority principle and compromise.[82] Of course, this is a bounded rationality that falls short of the standards of elaborated understandings of rationality (such as those established by discourse ethics).[83] This lower standard of rationality is expressed, for example, in the insight that statutes, as well as rulings, are 'incompletely theorized agreements'.[84] Therefore, the high standards of rationality and coherence of doctrinal analysis are also hardly compatible with the democratic concept of rationality.[85] There is thus a structural risk of wanting to

[77] W Geiger, 'Gegenwartsprobleme der Verfassungsgerichtsbarkeit aus deutscher Sicht' in T Berberich, W Holl, and K Maaß (eds), *Neue Entwicklungen im öffentlichen Recht* (Kohlhammer 1979) 141; see also K Schlaich, 'Verfassungsgerichtsbarkeit im Gefüge der Staatsgewalten' (1981) 39 Veröffentlichungen der Vereinigung der Deutschen Staatsrechtslehrer 99, 109.

[78] See H Gart, *Begründungspflicht des Gesetzgebers* (Nomos 2015); T Hebeler, 'Ist der Gesetzgeber verfassungsrechtlich verpflichtet, Gesetze zu begründen?' (2010) 63 Die Öffentliche Verwaltung 754; C Waldhoff, 'Der Gesetzgeber schuldet nichts als das Gesetz' in O Depenheuer, M Heintzen, and M Jestaedt (eds), *Staat im Wort. Festschrift für Josef Isensee* (CF Müller 2007) 325–43.

[79] See esp P Noll, *Gesetzgebungslehre* (Rowohlt 1973).

[80] M Kloepfer, 'Gesetzgebung im Rechtsstaat' (1982) 40 Veröffentlichungen der Vereinigung der Deutschen Staatsrechtslehrer 63, 88–89.

[81] See esp G Schwerdtfeger, 'Optimale Methodik der Gesetzgebung als Verfassungspflicht' in R Stödter and W Thiema (eds), *Hamburg, Deutschland, Europa. Festschrift für Peter Ipsen zum 70. Geburtstag* (Mohr Siebeck 1977) 173–88.

[82] See V Büchler-Tschudin, *Demokratie und Kompromiss* (Helbing und Lichtenhahn 1980); M Greven, *Kontingenz und Dezision*, (Leske & Budrich 2000) 51–62; H Homann, *Demokratie und Rationalität* (Mohr Siebeck 1988); H Kelsen, *Allgemeine Staatslehre* (Springer 1925) 324; H Schulze-Fielitz, *Theorie und Praxis parlamentarischer Gesetzgebung* (Duncker & Humblot 1988) 375–513.

[83] K Meßerschmidt, *Gesetzgebungsermessen* (Berlin-Verlag Spitz 2000) 802; H Schulze-Fielitz, *Theorie und Praxis parlamentarischer Gesetzgebung* (Duncker & Humblot 1988) 407.

[84] C Sunstein, 'Incompletely Theorized Agreements' (1994) 108 Harvard LR 1733; see also L O'Hara, *Konsistenz und Konsens* (Mohr Siebeck 2017) 155–56.

[85] P Dann, 'Verfassungsgerichtliche Kontrolle gesetzgeberischer Rationalität' (2010) 49 Der Staat 630, 640; K Gärditz, 'Strafbegründung und Demokratieprinzip' (2014) 53 Der Staat 331, 346, 353; W Hoffmann-Riem, 'Gesetz und Gesetzesvorbehalt im Umbruch' (2005) 130 Archiv des öffentlichen Rechts 5, 30–34; O Lepsius, 'Rechtswissenschaft in der Demokratie' (2013) 52 Der Staat 157, 184; N

implant the strict rationality standard of doctrinal analysis into the democratic process.[86]

In my opinion, Bone's criticism of trade secret law has succumbed to precisely this risk. It is here where we find the valid essence of the statement that the legitimacy of law lies outside the scope of doctrinal analysis. This legitimacy derives from the democratic process and all its undeniable rationality deficits, but it does not depend on legal scholars being able to make full sense of the law. Therefore, anomalies in doctrines are no reason to abandon them completely (at least if there is no good alternative).[87] A compelling example from criminal law concerns the abandonment of an attempted crime. The German Criminal Code provides for non-punishment in such cases. Nevertheless, we traditionally find it difficult to develop a rationale for this provision, and we make do with what we can come up with. What Wolfgang Stegmüller has repeatedly pointed out in the discussion of paradigm shifts in scientific theory applies here, too: we prefer a roof with holes in it to no roof at all and, if shipwrecked, we would rather have a broken rudder than no rudder at all.[88]

So, while I think it is fair to say that Bone threw the baby out with the bathwater, the question again arises concerning what critical contribution doctrinal analysis can make. In my estimation, this contribution lies primarily in pointing out alleged contradictions, conflicts with other statutes, or other systematic inadequacies. However, it is important that the self-conception remains sufficiently moderate. In most cases, the critique will result in suggestions that the legislature can, but need not, take up. So, it falls to doctrinal analysis to facilitate discourse.[89] Doctrinal analysis can thus assume the role of partially compensating for the rationality deficits of the democratic process. This is in line with its task, which it normally fulfils by making sense of the law, and where it is unable to do this, it may encourage changes to that law. Beyond extreme cases, however, doctrinal analysis is not called upon to question the legitimacy of the law based on its high standards of rationality. In this respect, I strongly disagree with Smits, who not only claims that doctrinal analysis can provide 'a justification of the existing law', but furthermore disputes

Petersen, 'Gesetzgeberische Inkonsistenz als Beweiszeichen' (2013) 138 Archiv des öffentlichen Rechts 108, 110.

[86] N Petersen, 'Gesetzgeberische Inkonsistenz als Beweiszeichen' (2013) 138 Archiv des öffentlichen Rechts 108, 110; see also A Steinbach, *Rationale Gesetzgebung* (Mohr Siebeck 2017) 220.

[87] See C Canaris, 'Funktion, Struktur und Falsifikation juristischer Theorien' (1993) 48 Juristenzeitung 373, 388.

[88] See W Stegmüller, *Theorie und Erfahrung, Zweiter Halbband. Theorienstruktur und Theoriendynamik* (Springer 1973) VIII, 246, 282.

[89] See also M Bodig, 'Legal Theory and Legal Doctrinal Scholarship' (2010) 23 CJLJ 483, 498.

that rules that do not fit should be considered law at all.[90] Doctrinal analysis thus facilitates discourse and can thereby increase rationality. As a matter of fact, Bone's analysis is again an excellent example because it has greatly stimulated the discourse on trade secret law. The critical potential is not dependent on the criticism ultimately prevailing. If one accepts this, it also means that the claim that doctrinal analysis does not problematize but stabilizes is beside the point. Problematization can also have a stabilizing effect and an important one at that.

These considerations also allow for a side note on the much-heralded crisis of doctrinal analysis.[91] I think this crisis has been exaggerated. The importance of doctrinal analysis has not waned severely, nor will it do so soon. Even if one assumes that legislators have a great deal of leeway and should be guided only by efficiency (and not, for example, by coherence), laws come into being that we need to make sense of to apply them.[92] I have already indicated that economic analysis is of only limited help here. It can even be argued that the more the legislator is primarily focused on other criteria, the greater the need to create coherence after the fact. It is possible to assign the critical potential of doctrinal analysis to the various dimensions I categorized earlier. With prototypical constituent doctrinal analysis, the criticism occurs mainly in the discussion *before the law comes into force*—that is, in discussing legislative proposals and counterproposals. In the case of constituted doctrinal analysis, on the other hand, the critical potential lies in pointing out systematic frictions in the law already in force. In response to the assertion that a consequentialist view renders doctrinal analysis less important, I would therefore counter that the importance merely shifts from constituent to constituted doctrinal analysis.

This brings me to a final point of particular interest for a transatlantic workshop. We have just pretended that Bone's criticism was directed at German trade secret law and, therefore, at a statute. But what changes if this criticism is directed against case law? Obviously, things become more complicated. The dictum that the legislator owes only the statute is no longer pertinent. On the contrary, we expect courts to give reasons, as their absence makes accepting judgments difficult and their rationality doubtful. For one thing, there is the problem of whether there are specific minimum standards that judicial rulings

[90] See again J M Smits, 'What is Legal Doctrine?' in R van Gestel, H-W Micklitz, and E Rubin (eds), *Rethinking Legal Scholarship* (CUP 2017) 219.

[91] See J Smits, *The Mind and Method of the Legal Academic* (EE Publishing 2012) 1–7. See also N Luhmann, *Rechtssystem und Rechtsdogmatik* (Kohlhammer 1974) 12–14.

[92] See also M Auer, 'Selbstreflexion der Privatrechtswissenschaft' in E Hilgendorf and H Schulze-Fielitz (eds), *Selbstreflexion der Rechtswissenschaft* (2nd edn, Mohr Siebeck 2021) 323.

must adhere to. This is not yet a question directly relevant to doctrinal analysis. But it is probably fair to say that we have certain standards of argumentation, and this is where a link to doctrinal analysis arises. The issue is obviously closely related to a topic discussed as the constraint of doctrinal analysis.[93] In my estimation, this matter is much more controversial in the United States than in Germany. Legal realists traditionally argue that judicial decisions are political decisions. From their point of view, the notion that judges are guided by doctrinal analysis is more of an illusion. Some even argue that doctrinal analysis is problematic because it allows judges to give the appearance of rationality to their rulings, which they, in fact, do not have.[94] It should be mentioned, however, that controversy surrounds the extent to which legal realists disdain doctrinal analysis.[95]

From a German point of view, such scepticism may appear cynical at first. Our belief in the constraint of doctrinal analysis is traditionally quite strong. However, there are also sceptics in Germany who emphasize that result-oriented arguments are often made under the guise of methodology.[96] I think both points of view are excessive. If the legal realists' disdain could be considered cynical, our great confidence seems somewhat naive. First, I would like to outline why the constraint of doctrinal analysis is limited. To this end, it must be remembered once again that doctrinal analysis is more significant the vaguer the law and, therefore, the more complicated the case. If we do not believe in someone like Ronald Dworkin's Hercules, who is able to find the only right solution to a problem, we are left with the insight that there are several correct answers.[97] If we think of doctrinal analysis as a bridge, we must refine that metaphor. It is more precise to say that doctrinal analysis constructs several bridges, and when a problem is somewhat thought out, the court must then choose only among these bridges.[98]

[93] See S Balganesh, 'The Constraint of Legal Doctrine' (2015) 163 U Penn L Rev 1843; B Leiter, 'Legal Realism and Legal Doctrine' (2015) 163 U Penn L Rev 1975.

[94] F Cohen, *Ethical Systems and Legal Ideas* (Great Seal Books 1959) 237; J Frank, *Law and the Modern Mind* (Coward-McCann Books 1930) 130.

[95] See H Dagan, 'Doctrinal Categories, Legal Realism and the Rule of Law' (2015) 163 U Penn LRev 1889, 1898–99.

[96] See M Jestaedt, 'Öffentliches Recht als Disziplin' in C Engel and W Schön (eds), *Das Proprium der Rechtswissenschaft* (Mohr Siebeck 2007) 254; see also R Alexy, *Theorie der juristischen Argumentation* (9th edn, Suhrkamp 2019) 333.

[97] cf C Bumke, *Rechtsdogmatik* (Mohr Siebeck 2017) 134; see also K Langenbucher, 'Dogmatik, Falsifikation und zwei Perspektiven auf die Rechtswissenschaft' in M Auer and others (eds), *Privatrechtsdogmatik im 21. Jahrhundert. Festschrift für Claus-Wilhelm Canaris zum 70. Geburtstag* (De Gruyter 2017) 224.

[98] See also H Dagan, 'Doctrinal Categories, Legal Realism and the Rule of Law' (2015) 163 U Penn L Rev 1889, 1891–92.

To get a better grasp of the significance of doctrinal analysis, we need to acknowledge the important distinction between rationale and cause.[99] To underestimate the importance of the cause would be too optimistic, but to play down the importance of the rationale would be too sceptical. Allow me to illustrate this with an example. A law student once told me that if she was going to be an attorney one day, she could never, in good conscience, represent an employee. When I asked, puzzled, why that was, she explained that her parents had told her too many stories about unreliable, dishonest employees. Now, what if this student had later become a judge rather than an attorney and had to decide the problem, already addressed here several times, of whether the disclosure of illegal conduct is the violation of a trade secret? A legal realist would argue that she would naturally rule against the employee. A traditional German doctrinist would probably say that doctrinal analysis would protect the judge from making the decision based on her biases. Although I would not go that far, I find it hard to deny that doctrinal analysis has a constraining effect. It at least compels the judge to provide a rationale that meets certain standards and thereby enables a discourse that would otherwise not be possible. This factor should not be underestimated.

This is true even if the reasoning is then influenced by a bias (that is, if the judge chooses the 'fitting' doctrine, so to speak). For example, some claim that trade secret law is all about confidentiality: 'The starting point for the present matter is not property or due process of law, but that the defendant stood in confidential relations with the plaintiffs.'[100] If we follow the premise of the legal realists, it will stand to reason that the judge would embrace this specific doctrine. The common objection to the confidentiality-based doctrine is that it cannot explain why external espionage is also prohibited.[101] I do not consider this a sufficient reason to completely banish the trust aspect from the doctrine of trade secret law, for this aspect may help us better understand what conduct that emanates from employees trade secrets are protected from.

However, the focus on confidentiality is unsuitable to give trade secret law sufficiently clear shape, for confidentiality is not protected per se, but only with reference to trade secrets.[102] This becomes clear if one imagines

[99] See T Kuntz, 'Recht als Gegenstand der Rechtswissenschaft und performative Rechtserzeugung' (2016) 216 Archiv für die civilistische Praxis 866, 897.

[100] *Du Pont De Nemours Powder Company v Masland* 244 US 100, 102 (1917); see also H Ortloff, 'Zum Schutz der Geschäftsgeheimnisse' (1883) 7 Schmollers Jahrbuch der Gesetzgebung, Verwaltung und Volkswirtschaft 229, 235.

[101] M Lemley, 'The Surprising Virtues of Treating Trade Secrets as IP Rights' (2008) 61 Stan L Rev 311, 323.

[102] P Krell, 'Grund und Grenzen des (neuen) Schutzes von Geschäftsgeheimnissen – am Beispiel des Whistleblowings' (2021) 133 Zeitschrift für die gesamte Strafrechtswissenschaft 714, 723–24, 730; J Stedman, 'Trade Secrets' (1962) 23 OSLJ 4, 24.

a company spying on a competitor because it (correctly) assumes that the latter regularly obtains orders through bribery. If the betrayed trust was the decisive point, a trade secret would exist in one case but not in the other. This is a compelling reason to keep the trust aspect out of the question of what constitutes a trade secret. The example is supposed to show that the constraining effect of doctrinal analysis is not negligible even where bias takes hold.

Of course, one might object that the court could have found a better rationale. But if it had done so, it would have made a defensible decision on an undetermined question that meets the standards of doctrinal analysis. Whether it did so for reprehensible reasons is irrelevant from the perspective of doctrinal analysis,[103] as it is not the task of doctrinal analysis to guarantee completely unprejudiced decisions.

Here, too, the critical potential of doctrinal analysis becomes apparent. Doctrinal analysis is not merely (expressed positively) a guideline to judges in unclear situations, and nor (expressed negatively) does it make discretionary decisions more difficult. Much like the discussion of statutes, it can also help to maintain an ongoing discourse on the application of law in decisions. This can also alleviate a rationality deficit. It is often emphasized that courts—which are, after all, obliged to decide—must make concessions to bounded rationality.[104] We cannot reasonably expect them to cover the entire status quo of the doctrinal discussion. This is especially true because German jurisprudence tends to make things exceptionally complicated. This is reflected both in a quantitatively unmanageable number of proposed solutions and a degree of complexity that courts cannot seriously accommodate. What we can do is point out serious alternatives or substantial arguments that have been presumably neglected. We can also claim that certain problems in a case have not been sufficiently identified. Here, however, I think doctrinal analysis must be content with such a stimulating role. If one takes the assumption seriously that, as a rule, several solutions to a legal problem are justifiable, one will rarely be able to accuse courts of having reached the wrong conclusion.

[103] See also I Augsberg, 'Rechtswirklichkeiten, in den wir leben' (2015) 46 Rechtstheorie 79–81; T Kuntz, 'Recht als Gegenstand der Rechtswissenschaft und performative Rechtserzeugung' (2016) 216 Archiv für die civilistische Praxis 866, 898.

[104] See M Shapiro, 'Stability and Change in Judicial Decision-Making: Incrementalism or Stare Decisis' (1965) 2 Law in Transition Q 134; C Sunstein, *One Case a Time. Judicial Minimalism on the Supreme Court* (HUP 1999); see also K Bybee, 'The Jurisprudence of Uncertainty' (2001) 35 L & Soc'y Rev 943; N Snortland and J Stanga, 'Neutral Principles and Decision-Making Theory: An Alternative to Incrementalism' (1973) 41 Geo Wash L Rev 1006.

VII. Conclusion

Whether we look at definitions of doctrinal analysis or specific legal arguments, there are no crucial differences between doctrinal thinking in the United States and Germany. If, nevertheless, it is often claimed that these differences exist, this is because the various conceivable dimensions of doctrinal analysis are not sufficiently considered. Of course, a conception of doctrinal analysis inappropriate for case law is possible. But it is not compelling. This is mainly due to the recursiveness of recourse to doctrinal analysis in processing law-making.

Doctrinal analysis has a very high standard of rationality that is not fully consistent with the standard of rationality for legislation or court rulings. For the latter, the procedural dimension also plays an important role. Moreover, doctrinal analysis has no authority equal to that of legislatures or judges. It is, therefore, problematic when legal scholars require laws or rulings to live up to the rationality standards of doctrinal analysis. However, this does not mean that doctrinal analysis has no critical potential. The critical potential of doctrinal analysis is that it promotes discourse about both statutes and judicial law and thus has a rationalizing effect. It is merely more modest criticism than is often assumed. Doctrinal analysis is no panacea. It does not necessarily enable us to create flawless statutes. It cannot always make full sense of the law. Nor does it give us the right answer to a certain legal problem or prevent prejudice or political views from affecting a ruling (consciously or subconsciously). It rarely puts us in the position of declaring a court decision to be wrong. Nevertheless, the restraint of doctrinal analysis and its rationalizing effect should not be underestimated or disregarded.

16

Private Law Theory from an Empirical Perspective

*Kevin Tobia**

I. Ordinary Concepts in Private Law Theory

A central part of private law theory is the analysis of legal concepts.[1] Consider, as an initial example, Antony Honoré and John Gardner's framing of their handbook entry on 'Causation in the Law':

> The basic questions dealt with in this entry are: (i) whether and to what extent causation in legal contexts differs from causation outside the law, for example in science or everyday life, and (ii) what are the appropriate criteria in law for deciding whether one action or event has caused another.[2]

Question (i) asks whether and how causation in law (for example, causation in tort law) differs from causation in everyday life, and question (ii) asks what are the appropriate legal criteria for causation. Honoré and Gardner categorize both questions as ones of jurisprudence or legal theory.[3]

Honoré and Gardner are not alone in posing questions like (i) about the relationship between legal concepts and ordinary concepts (for example,

* Associate Professor of Law and Philosophy (by courtesy), Georgetown University. Thanks to Thilo Kuntz, Paul Miller, and participants at the Methodology in Private Law Theory Conference at Bucerius Law School. Special thanks to Paul Miller and Ben Zipursky for generous written comments.

[1] eg Ernest J Weinrib, 'Legal Formalism: On the Immanent Rationality of Law' (1998) 97 Yale LJ 949, 962 ('Legal formalism postulates that the law's content can be understood in and through itself by reference to the mode of thinking that shapes if from the inside. For the formalist, law is *constituted* by thought: Its content is made up of the concepts (e.g., cause, remoteness, duty, consideration, offer and acceptance) that inform juridical relationships. Law is identical to the ideas of which it is comprised, and the intelligibility of law lies in grasping the order and connection of these ideas.').

[2] Antony Honoré and John Gardner, 'Causation in the Law' (2010) Stanford Encyclopedia of Philosophy Archive.

[3] In this chapter, I use 'jurisprudence' and 'legal theory' synonymously and as broader than 'legal philosophy.' See, eg, Lawrence Solum, 'Legal Theory Lexicon: Legal Theory, Jurisprudence, and the Philosophy of Law' (6 May, 2018) <https://lsolum.typepad.com/legaltheory/2018/05/legal-theory-lexicon-legal-theory-jurisprudence-and-the-philosophy-of-law.html> accessed 12 January 2023.

Kevin Tobia, *Private Law Theory from an Empirical Perspective* In: *Methodology in Private Law Theory.* Edited by: Thilo Kuntz and Paul B. Miller, Oxford University Press. © Kevin Tobia 2024. DOI: 10.1093/oso/9780198885306.003.0016

legal and ordinary cause). Legal theorists regularly assess legal concepts, like cause, reasonableness,[4] and consent,[5] in relation to their ordinary language counterparts (that is, ordinary reasonableness and consent). Theorists also analyse legal concepts in relation to related ordinary concepts that do not share the same name. For example, Weinrib analyses tort duty in close connection to society's (ordinary) intuitions about obligation and liberty,[6] and Shiffrin endorses an essential relationship between legal contract and ordinary promise.[7]

Legal philosophy is a 'broad church',[8] and so is legal theory. Nevertheless, the preceding remarks may not characterize all theories, such as those that entirely reject legal concepts' significance.[9] But—this chapter proposes—any legal theory that takes legal concepts seriously should take facts about the relevant ordinary concepts seriously.

The 'New Private Law' carefully evaluates legal concepts. As the introduction of the theory's handbook states: 'The New Private Law takes law seriously on its own terms; it recognizes a distinct sphere for private law; and it also shows

[4] Gregory C Keating, 'Reasonableness and Rationality in Negligence Theory' (1996) 48 Stan L Rev 311 ('Latent in our ordinary moral consciousness, and manifest in philosophical reflection, is a distinction between reasonableness and rationality').

[5] Heidi M Hurd, 'The Moral Magic of Consent' (1996) 2 Legal Theory, 121, 143 ('What should we do in the face of our conflicting intuitions . . .? One possible solution is to grapple with our intuitions some more in the hope that further thought experiments will help us to determine which set of intuitions misleads us').

[6] Ernest J Weinrib, 'The Case for a Duty to Rescue' (1980) 90 Yale LJ 247, 275 ('The legal argument for a duty to rescue in emergencies, however, is not one of deduction but one of coherence. Recognizing that the central concepts are those of obligation and liberty, the argument looks for the common law's concrete manifestation of society's general intuitions about these concepts. Examining instances of the operation of these concepts, the argument extracts general features from the instances, searching for and shaping a coherent pattern that fits as much of the law as possible while respecting the underlying ethical intuitions.').

[7] Shiffrin's article is well known for emphasizing the *divergence* of contract and promise, but footnote 1 describes the crucial relation between the two concepts: 'Although this Article discusses those aspects of contract that diverge from promissory norms, other parts of contract law depend fairly explicitly upon a variety of moral judgments and concepts, not to mention the concept of a promise itself . . . [A] partial convergence between morality and contract would call for justification if one took the position that contract and promise are entirely separate domains.' Seana Valentine Shiffrin, 'The Divergence of Contract and Promise' (2007) 120 Harvard LR 710, 710 fn 1.

[8] Julie Dickson, 'Ours Is a Broad Church: Indirectly Evaluative Legal Philosophy as a Facet of Jurisprudential Inquiry' (2015) 6 Jurisprudence 207, 209; see also Dan Priel, 'Evidence-Based Jurisprudence: An Essay for Oxford' in G Battista and others (eds), *Analisi e Diritto*, vol 2 (2019) 87, 88.

[9] The proposition that legal concepts have *no* significance for law or legal theory is a very strong view. Even proponents of critical legal studies aim, as a part of their jurisprudential method, to understand and describe legal concepts. See, eg Robert Gordon, 'Unfreezing Legal Reality: Critical Approaches to Law' (1987) 15 Florida S U L Rev 195, 197 ('We hoped also to begin to build up a number of descriptions of legal practices—concepts, doctrines, institutions, routines, underlying structures—that would seem more real, more resonant with our experience.'). Even theorists that are skeptical about the merit of law's concepts see the value in interrogating and understanding those concepts.

an openness to new methodologies, insights, and subject areas.'[10] Moreover, it 'takes private law concepts and categories seriously'.[11]

Additionally, the New Private Law attends to the relationship between legal and ordinary concepts. As Professor John Goldberg explains, 'there is often at least a family resemblance between legal and extralegal concepts and norms that bear on questions of personal interaction'.[12] The New Private Law recognizes the significance of Honoré and Gardner's framing of jurisprudential analysis: In legal conceptual analysis, it is methodologically essential to interrogate legal concepts in relation to their ordinary counterparts and delineate the shared features and the legal concept's unique features, which helpfully sets the stage for further jurisprudential analysis.

A brief aside: Nothing I have said so far implies that legal concepts *should* generally reflect features of corresponding ordinary concepts or that there are benefits to such convergence. However, some theorists have suggested as much.[13] As Professors Andrew Gold and Henry Smith put it: 'The set of legal concepts benefits from its congruence with relatively simple local forms of conventional morality ... Certainly, contract law can diverge from the morality of promising, just as legislation can go beyond corrective justice. Nevertheless, the ability to draw on simple local morality is an important starting point.'[14]

This section's claim (thus far) is merely that private law theory regularly evaluates ordinary concepts. This is a methodological claim about private law theory, not a substantive claim that law should reflect ordinary concepts. An investigation into legal concepts and their ordinary counterparts may uncover a host of surprising facts, any of which might support that the law adopts the ordinary concept *or* rejects it.

[10] 'Introduction' in AS Gold and others (eds), *The Oxford Handbook of The New Private Law* (OUP 2020) xv.

[11] ibid xvi.

[12] John CP Goldberg, 'Introduction: Pragmatism and Private Law' (2012) 125 Harvard LR 1640, 1650.

[13] See, eg, Gideon Yaffe, 'Criminal Attempts' (2014) 124 Yale LJ 92, 106–07 ('It is a closely related project in the philosophy of law to identify the necessary and sufficient conditions that must be met for a person to intend a particular event or condition in the sense of relevance to intentional torts, or in the sense of relevance to formation in contract, or in the sense of relevance to intentional discrimination, or in the sense of relevance to criminal responsibility. However, it is a hypothesis worth exploring that all of the various senses of the legal term "intention" circle around a core notion that has its natural home in ordinary discourse. The law is better when it uses ordinary terms in ordinary ways and employs concepts that bear a close resemblance to those used in everyday life by citizens asked to conform their behavior to law. It is the core notion of intention that has been investigated by philosophers of mind and action. If indeed such a core notion informs the law, then it is important for those interested in criminal responsibility to understand what philosophers of mind have discovered about the nature of intention.').

[14] Andrew S Gold and Henry E Smith, 'Sizing Up Private Law' (2020) 70 U Toronto LJ 489, 504–05.

To drive the methodological point home, consider a few more excerpts from *Recognizing Wrongs*, a tour de force in tort theory.[15] The authors, Professors Goldberg and Zipursky, describe the book's task:

> We come to the job of explaining the common law somewhat like one trying to explain how the members of a community use their language. The goal is to make explicit the various patterns of thought and conduct that animate this area of the law. If it turns out that many of the concepts and principles utilized in this area have the same character as, or a character very similar to, those which are utilized in non-legal discourse about how one ought (morally) to conduct oneself—indeed, if it turns out that some of the concepts are identical—that is something to be acknowledged, not hidden from view.[16]

A principal part of the project is to 'make explicit' the patterns that animate law. This view takes seriously law's language. Legal concepts like duty, cause, or reasonableness do not simply stand in as vessels for external theory (whether Posnerian efficiency or Kantian morality). Rather, there is an internal logic of these concepts, which the private law theorist seeks to uncover.[17] In Goldberg and Zipursky's words:

> Holmes's … understandable disdain for the pedantic moralist unfortunately led him to pose a false dilemma between the pedant and the bad man. Missing from his analysis is the ordinary person, the lawyer who counsels this person, and the judge who understands, applies, and crafts the law imagining that her legal community expects her to take this perspective seriously.[18]

This call—for legal theorists to attend to the 'ordinary person'—is distinct from similar-sounding calls for law to attend to the 'good man'. Professor Rebecca Stone has argued that consequentialists should drop the 'bad man' and instead contemplate legal design for the 'good man'.[19] Building on empirical

[15] John CP Goldberg and Benjamin C Zipursky, *Recognizing Wrongs* (Harvard UP 2020).
[16] ibid 79.
[17] See also ibid 207–08 ('Publicity, notice, generality, prospectivity, and the other values that Fuller emphasized seem lacking in a system that relies on judges to articulate rules and principles on a case-by-case basis instead of stating them in canonical form in a code or statute book … There is another way in which tort law achieves a kind of fairness in operation by means apart from Fullerian methods … Part of what it means for tort law to be "common law" … is that the wrongs recognized by tort law are, in their substance, drawn from everyday life rather than constructed *de novo* by judges in aid of some sort of social engineering project.').
[18] ibid 109.
[19] Rebecca Stone, 'Legal Design for the "Good Man"' (2016) 102 Va L Rev 1767.

research in psychology and behavioural economics, Professor Stone persuasively argues that laypeople have complex motivations to comply with law. In short, the bad person is not the real person. Ordinary people are not purely-self-interested rational actors, and thus consequentialist theories should consider a more empirically accurate 'person'.[20]

This 'good man' account is ultimately instrumental, accepting a consequentialist premise. Goldberg and Zipursky's 'ordinary person', however, is not a legal fiction designed for greater efficiency; rather, it is a legal fiction designed to help understand the internal logic of (tort) law.

The appeal to the 'ordinary person' might seem strange. When inquiring into the structure of legal concepts, why should we contemplate the perspective of someone with no legal training? One answer is that most (nearly all) important legal concepts are plausibly related to ordinary ones. It is no accident that legal concepts share names with ordinary ones: cause, consent, duty, injury, intent, knowledge, reason. 'It is not only judges and lawyers who interact with the law of torts, directly or indirectly. Everyone does.'[21]

Again, this observation (that legal concepts stand in relation to ordinary ones) does not imply that legal concepts do or should equate to ordinary ones. Many important works of private law theory elaborate on the interesting and surprising ways legal concepts *diverge* from ordinary ones. For example, recall Shiffrin's famous account of the divergence of contract from promise.[22] These 'divergence' projects, emphasizing legal concepts' distinctiveness, support that legal concepts do not *equate* to ordinary ones. But they also demonstrate the enormous significance of ordinary concepts to legal concepts. The divergence of contract from promise is so exciting and surprising because of our background understanding that legal contract plausibly shares many of the features of ordinary promise. For nearly any other *X*, 'the divergence of contract from *X*' would be a less informative project than 'the divergence of contract from promise'.

[20] For a helpful summary of empirical research that further supports this argument, see Tess Wilkinson-Ryan, 'Psychology and the New Private Law' in AS Gold and others (eds), *The Oxford Handbook of The New Private Law* (OUP 2020).

[21] Goldberg and Zipursky (n 15) 364. Of course, as a general matter, that we all interact with *X* does not imply the methodological relevance of the ordinary understanding of *X*. We all interact with chemicals, but the ordinary view of chemistry is generally irrelevant to chemist's methodology. Goldberg and Zipursky's analysis helpfully outline some reasons for the distinctiveness of legal methodology: 'We all need to know what to expect of the persons, businesses, offices, and organizations around us, and we all need to know what is expected of us. That is why the wrongs recognized by courts as torts cannot be the wrongs that Judge Hercules would endorse for being those whose recognition would make the law the best it can be from the perspective of aspirational political or moral theory.'

[22] Shiffrin (n 7).

In sum, the analysis of legal concepts is a longstanding part of private law theory and a central part of the New Private Law. Moreover, legal conceptual analysis involves the careful comparison of legal concepts to corresponding or related ordinary ones. That method does not imply that legal concepts do or should generally equate to ordinary concepts. Instead, the comparison may reveal that the legal concept diverges in important or interesting ways from the ordinary one,[23] or it may uncover striking similarities between the two,[24] or it may discover unknown features of the ordinary concept that could better explain the legal concept.[25]

II. Empirically Grounded Conceptual Analysis

The previous section argued that one of private law theory's central projects is the analysis of legal concepts; moreover, that project's methodology includes the comparison of ordinary and legal concepts. This section builds on these claims, arguing that the *empirical* study of (ordinary) concepts can offer new and important insights into private law theory. Moreover, such empirical study is essential to adequately understand some of the law's central concepts. In brief, the rest of the argument is this: Private law theorists may not know (from the armchair) all there is to know about ordinary concepts, and empirical studies can offer insight into the features of ordinary concepts; thus, private law theorists who employ traditional methods of legal conceptual analysis have good reason to consider empirical revelations about plausibly related ordinary concepts.

One set of relevant empirical studies goes by the name of 'experimental philosophy of law' or 'experimental jurisprudence'.[26] This work differs in its aims and ambitions from other types of empirically informed legal theory, which often seeks to best calibrate the incentives of legal rules in light of psychological and behavioural realities (for example, empirical studies of empathy gaps,

[23] eg Shiffrin (n 7) (describing the divergence of contract from promise).

[24] eg Keating (n 4) (arguing that legal reasonableness reflects our ordinary understanding).

[25] eg Yaffe (n 13) (suggesting that progress in the philosophy of mind and action on the ordinary concept of intent inform legal inquiries into the legal concept of intent).

[26] See generally Karolina Magdalena Prochownik, 'The Experimental Philosophy of Law: New Ways, Old Questions, and How not to Get Lost' (2021) 16 Philosophy Compass 12791; Kevin Tobia, 'Experimental Jurisprudence' (2022) 89 U Chicago L Rev 735. This term nods to 'experimental philosophy', a similar empirical approach to questions in philosophy (eg ethics and metaphysics). See Joshua Knobe and Shaun Nichols, 'An Experimental Philosophy Manifesto' in J Knobe and S Nichols (eds), *Experimental Philosophy* (2008) 3; see also Stephen Stich and Kevin P Tobia, 'Experimental Philosophy and the Philosophical Tradition' in J Sytsma and W Buckwalter (eds), *A Companion to Experimental Philosophy* (Wiley-Blackwell 2016) 5.

social influence effects).[27] Here again, think about updating legal theory for the 'bad man' into legal theory for the (behaviourally complex) 'good person'.

Experimental jurisprudence's principal motivation is not to fill in the empirical details relevant to law and economics. Rather, it seeks to make progress on a broader set of legal theory questions, including questions of conceptual analysis. For example, consider empirical research about *intent*.[28] Markus Kneer and Sacha Bourgeois-Gironde set out to study how laypeople (and French judges) ordinarily understand an act's consequence to be produced 'intentionally'. Specifically, they designed an experiment to test whether intentionality attributions depend on the apparent severity of the side effect.

Kneer and Bourgeois-Gironde randomly assigned experimental participants to evaluate one of two different scenarios: The first was a 'moderate' scenario, in which a mayor decides to build a new highway in order to improve the flow of traffic. However, the highway construction will foreseeably produce a moderate environmental impact, disturbing some animals in the construction zone. The mayor asserts that he does not 'care at all about the environment' and proceeds with the programme: Sure enough, some animals are disturbed as a side effect.

Kneer and Bourgeois-Gironde's second scenario was nearly identical to the first, except that the environmental effect was *severe*. In this 'severe version', it was foreseeable that the impacted animals would die. Again, the mayor asserts that he does not 'care at all about the environment' and the construction proceeds. Sure enough, some animals die as a side effect.

In both scenarios, participants evaluated the same question: Did the mayor 'intentionally' harm the environment? This experiment sought to vary *only* the severity of the side-effect (moderate disturbance or severe death) while holding the mayor's attitude constant to assess whether that factor (severity of outcome) influences judgments of intentionality.

This research uncovered that intuitions about intentionality are sensitive to outcome severity. The mayor arguably expresses the same attitude in both scenarios, but participants assess intentionality differently. In the severe case, compared to the moderate case, participants more strongly agreed that the harm was produced 'intentionally'.

[27] For an exceptionally helpful review of that work and its implications for legal theory, see Tess Wilkinson-Ryan (n 20). Many of the findings described are most compatible with instrumentalist approaches to legal theory. However, the end of that chapter discusses the study of norms as a promising area to '[move] past the thinner economic approach to individual preferences'.

[28] Markus Kneer and Sacha Bourgeois-Gironde, 'Mens Rea Ascription, Expertise and Outcome Effects: Professional Judges Surveyed' (2017) 169 Cognition 139; see also Joshua Knobe, 'Intentional Action and Side Effects in Ordinary Language' (2003) 63 Analysis 190.

This finding (outcome severity influences intentionality) has been replicated many times with lay samples. Unlike most experimental jurisprudence, Kneer and Bourgeois-Gironde's study recruited experts as participants: French judges.

Empirical work like this, which reveals features of ordinary concepts, is essential data for private law theorists. It helps make clear the underlying criteria of the ordinary concepts, which may (or may not) be the underlying criteria of the legal concepts. As Section I of this chapter outlined, private law theory regularly analyses legal concepts with reference to ordinary concepts.[29] Legal theorists, despite their rich expertise, may not know all there is to know about our ordinary concepts. For example, to helpfully analyse the law's concepts of duty, cause, intent, or reasonableness, the legal theorist cannot ignore the ordinary concepts of duty, cause, intent, or reasonableness.[30]

This 'experimental' approach is not radically different from more traditional approaches within legal philosophy. Legal philosophers often employ 'thought experimentation'. A theorist will propose a hypothetical scenario and offer their own intuitive response to the scenario, as bearing on legal theory claims.[31] Experimental jurisprudence proceeds similarly. It designs hypothetical scenarios and probes intuitive responses to those scenarios, taking those responses to bear on claims of legal theory.

It might seem that experimental jurisprudence and legal philosophy's thought experimentation diverge in their conceptual targets: The former studies ordinary (lay) concepts, and the latter legal (expert) concepts. This difference is overstated. For one, some experimental jurisprudence examines the judgments of legal officials (for example, judges)[32] or law students.[33] Often,

[29] eg HLA Hart and T Honoré, *Causation in the Law* (2nd edn, OUP 1985)(on causation).

[30] Again, this is a methodological claim, not a constitutive one. The legal theorist need not conclude that, eg, legal cause equates to ordinary cause.

[31] See, eg, Lucas Miotto, 'From Angels to Humans: Law, Coercion, and the Society of Angels Thought Experiment, (2021) 40 Law and Phil 277 ('[t]he "society of angels thought experiment" has received a fair amount of attention in contemporary analytical jurisprudence. Several legal philosophers—including prominent figures such as Hart, Raz, Finnis, and Gardner—have presented variations of this thought experiment while discussing the role of coercion in law. In this discussion, the thought experiment is supposed to both work as a counterexample to the claim that legal systems are necessarily coercive and to provide support for the view according to which non-coercive legal systems are possible.'); see also John Gardner, 'The Idea of a Pure Theory of Law' (2019) 10 Jurisprudence 118 ('H.L.A. Hart argued that the connection between the existence of law and the use of force is "contingent on human beings and the world they live in".. . Joseph Raz furnished a famous thought-experiment ... in support of Hart's claim. Many were persuaded, myself included.').

[32] eg Markus Kneer and Sacha Bourgeois-Gironde, 'Mens Rea Ascription, Expertise and Outcome Effects: Professional Judges Surveyed' (2017) 169 Cognition 139; Kevin Tobia, 'Testing Ordinary Meaning' (2020) 134 Harvard LR.

[33] eg Noel Struchiner, Guilherme Almeida, and Ivar Hannikainen, 'An Experimental Guide to Vehicles in the Park' (2020) 15 Judgment and Decision Making 312; Karolina Prochownik and others,

these projects recruit both experts and laypeople to examine the difference between ordinary and legal concepts.[34] Moreover, traditional legal philosophy regularly offers intuitions about *ordinary* (not technical) concepts. Thought experiments are regularly offered as tests of 'our moral intuitions'[35] or the 'intuitions of a community'[36]—a social or legal community. The legal theorist who offers intuition and analyses that intuition's legal import serves two roles: The legal theorist wears their 'ordinary person' hat in offering the shared intuition and their expert theorist hat in articulating the legal import of that common intuition.

However, there are *methodological* differences between experimental jurisprudence and traditional legal philosophy. The former most often recruits a large number of lay participants in an experimental study, while the latter generally reports the intuitions or judgments of one expert theorist. This sample size difference should be uncontroversially resolved in favour of the experimental approach. Traditional legal philosophy typically frames intuitions as 'shared' or 'common' and thus would do better to report that the offered intuitions are shared among multiple theorists. Relatedly, the *experimental* approach (randomly assigning evaluators to consider different versions of a hypothetical) is useful in identifying what factors impact intuitive appraisals.

A more interesting (and controversial) difference concerns the relevant population: laypeople or legal experts. Experimental jurisprudence usually favours the former, traditional legal philosophy the latter. One reaction to this difference is to strongly endorse the traditional methodology: Perhaps experimental jurisprudence has more intuiters, but traditional jurisprudence has better quality intuiters. Or perhaps only the views of the experts count.[37]

A common defence of this claim (only legal-expert views count) begins by positing that law is fundamentally created by expert legal officials—not laypeople—and we should restrict our theoretical inquiry to the views of those who contribute to legal content. However, un many legal systems, laypeople

'Not as bad as painted? Legal expertise, intentionality ascription, and outcome effects revisited' in S Denison and others (eds), *Proceedings of the 42nd annual meeting of the Cognitive Science Society* (Cognitive Science Society 2020) 1930–36; Kevin Tobia, Legal Concepts and Legal Expertise (Synthese) (forthcoming)).

[34] eg ibid; Prochownik and others (n 33).

[35] Kimberly Kessler Ferzan, 'Justifying Self-Defense' (2005) 24 Law and Philosophy 711, 749 (explaining the role of intuition in the proposed analysis of self-defence).

[36] Joshua Dressler, 'Does One Mens Rea Fit All?: Thoughts on Alexander's Unified Conception of Criminal Culpability' (2000) 88 Cal LR 955, 961.

[37] See, eg Felipe Jimenez, 'Some Doubts about Folk Jurisprudence: The Case of Proximate Cause' (2021) U Chicago L Rev Online.

contribute meaningfully to legal content. Consider the traditional role of the jury—both in the United States and other legal systems.[38] Even in the determination of 'factual' and 'mixed' questions, jurors influence law's development, articulating the scope of central private law concepts like causation and reasonableness. Private law theory in these areas should not neglect ordinary concepts and understandings. For example, the private law theory of tort negligence should (and often does) reflect on ordinary understandings.[39]

More broadly, it is not clear that legal theorists should restrict their focus to only the views of those who *create* legal content. Private law is fundamentally interpersonal, and we all need to know what to expect of people around us. Private law operates on our private lives; it is not implausible that private law theory should elucidate the understanding of all the subjects of that law.

All this said, even if legal theory restricted its focus to the views of legal officials or the legal elite (say, judges and law professors), empirical study is still useful. Legal experts often disagree about legal theory. Legal scholars recognize theoretical disagreement about public law theory,[40] and a survey of over 600 American law professors indicates disagreement about questions of both public and private law theory.[41] Given this disagreement about major theoretical questions, it is likely that there is some disagreement about some lower-level intuitions. Legal theory is littered with appeals to 'intuition', claims that *X* seems like 'the cause' or *Y* seems 'reasonable'. But even experts' intuitions can differ, and the source of these intuitions is often opaque.

These concerns have led to scepticism of intuition in traditional philosophy. The story in legal theory is different: 'In many areas of philosophy, doubts about... conceptual and linguistic analysis... have become common... but not so in legal philosophy.'[42] Empirical study can help assess whether an expert's intuitions are widespread or controversial. It can help assess the source of the intuition, which bears directly on the justificatory status that intuition should have.

[38] See generally Valerie Hans, 'Introduction: Lay Participation in Legal Decision Making', (2003) 83 Law & Policy.

[39] See, eg Mark Geistfeld, 'Folk Tort Law' in H Dagan and B Zipursky (eds), *Handbook of Private Law Theories* (Edward Elgar Press 2020); Christina Tilley, 'Tort Law Inside Out' (2017) 126 Yale LJ; Benjamin Zipursky, 'Reasonableness in and Out of Negligence Law' (2015) 163 U Penn L Rev.

[40] Courtney Cox, 'The Uncertain Judge', 90 U Chicago L Rev (2023); Emad Atiq and Jud Mathews, 'The Uncertain Foundations of Public Law Theory' (2023) Cornell J L & Pub Pol; Evan Bernick, 'Hedging Constitutional Bets' (unpublished).

[41] Eric Martínez and Kevin Tobia, 'What Do Law Professors Believe about Law and the Legal Academy', (Georgetown Law Journal) (2023)).

[42] Alex Langlinais and Brian Leiter, 'The Methodology of Legal Philosophy' in H Cappelen, T Gendler, and J Hawthorn (eds), *The Oxford Handbook of Philosophical Methodology* (OUP 2016) 671, 677.

Before turning to a case study, consider one final objection to this section: The argument supports that empirical study of ordinary concepts can reveal some interesting findings but has not supported the strong claim that empirical study is 'essential' to private law theory.

Laws are not expressed in a new, entirely distinct language or grammar. Instead, laws are traditionally written and expressed in the language (and grammar) of the people they govern. But this results in a potentially confusing state of affairs. For most legal concepts picked out by a term 'x' (for example, 'reasonableness' points to *legal reasonableness*), 'x' also names an ordinary concept (for example, *ordinary reasonableness*). And there are potentially overlapping and distinct features of those legal and ordinary concepts: (a) features shared by both the legal and ordinary concept, (b) features of only the ordinary concept, (c) features of only the legal concept, (d) features of neither. Insofar as 'conceptual analysis' is breaking down concepts into their constituent parts, and the features of the ordinary and legal concepts picked out by 'x' do not usually fall into only one bucket (a)–(d), it is essential (to fully break down the legal concept), to compare the legal and ordinary concepts.

Sometimes, that analytical work is easy, so the philosophical analysis is uninteresting. In other cases, the work is difficult, but it is possible to complete it through traditional methods of individual introspection and analysis. In other cases, there are subtle features of the concepts that cannot be fully or confidently gleaned through individual introspection and analysis—these cases call for empirical study. As empirical studies reveal subtle and surprising features of important concepts (for example, intent, cause, reasonableness), it increasingly becomes clear that the analysis of many important legal concepts falls into this third category. In sum, the empirical study of ordinary concepts is essential to private law theory because the study of ordinary concepts is essential to private law theory, and empirical methods (in some important cases) offer unique insights.

III. A Case Study: Cross-Cultural Empirical Study

Thus far, the chapter has argued that jurists engaged in legal conceptual analysis should consult empirical evidence about ordinary concepts. Section III makes this discussion more concrete by outlining some recent examples of that empirical work, all conducted across several countries. As such, this section concludes by reflecting on experimental jurisprudence of the cross-cultural variety.

As a first example, consider *reasonableness*. The term 'reasonable' appears frequently in US law, in many different contexts.[43] Reasonableness is perhaps most strongly associated with the negligence standard in tort law. As the Second Restatement of Torts (1965) explains:

> Unless the actor is a child, the standard of conduct to which he must conform to avoid being negligent is that of a reasonable man under like circumstances.[44]

Who, exactly, is this 'reasonable' person?[45] There are various legal theoretical answers to that question. One view associated with law and economics is that the reasonable person is a legal fiction that reflects cost-benefit reasoning. As the Third Restatement of Torts (2010) puts it:

> A person acts negligently if the person does not exercise reasonable care under all the circumstances. Primary factors to consider in ascertaining whether the person's conduct lacks reasonable care are the foreseeable likelihood that the person's conduct will result in harm, the foreseeable severity of any harm that may ensue, and the burden of precautions to eliminate or reduce the risk of harm.[46]

This formulation stops short of endorsing the Hand Formula (that is, one should evaluate whether the foreseeable likelihood that the person's conduct will result in harm times the foreseeable severity of any harm that may ensue outweighs the cheapest burden of precautions to eliminate or reduce the risk of harm). But the influence of law and economics is clear: on this definition, reasonableness is about the foreseeable likelihood of harm (P), the foreseeable severity of any harm (L), and the burden of precautions (B).

Consider two different ways to understand this account of reasonableness:

1. L&E Realism: "Reasonableness" in legal standards is simply a placeholder for external policy considerations. And cost-benefit weighing, rather than some other theory, reflects the best policy.

[43] Benjamin Zipursky, 'Reasonableness in and Out of Negligence Law' (2015) 163 U Penn L Rev.

[44] Restatement (Second) of Torts § 283 (1965).

[45] See generally Zipursky (n 43); Simon Stern, 'From Clapham to Saline: Locating the Reasonable Man' (2023) Law and Literature.

[46] Restatement (Third) of Torts: Physical and Emotional Harm § 3 (2010); see also Catherine M Sharkey, 'Modern Tort Law: Preventing Harms, Not Recognizing Wrongs', (2021) 134 Harvard LR 1423, 1424 ('The law and economics-inspired view of tort law is ascendant, not only in the legal academy but also in the decisions of influential state and federal courts, including the U.S. Supreme Court.').

2. L&E Conceptualism: Common law evaluation of reasonableness (for example, by jurors) reflects intuitive cost-benefit analysis.

L&E Realism falls outside of the scope of this chapter and stands in stark contrast to the non-instrumentalist position of the New Private Law. But L&E Conceptualism offers a theory that competes with the New Private Law on its own (conceptual-focused) turf. Perhaps the criterion of the legal concept of reasonableness, which reflects the law's internal logic, *is* cost-benefit analysis. This is a question informed by both analysis of doctrine and analysis of (the ordinary notion) of reasonableness.[47]

Empirical studies of lay cognition about what is reasonable can help inform this kind of legal theory dispute.[48] Consider, for example, an empirical study about reasonableness.[49] Drawing on cognitive science research on the ordinary concept of what is 'normal',[50] the reasonableness study randomly assigned participants into one of three conditions:

- 'Average': Participants reported their judgments of average quantities; for example, what is the average number of sugary drinks to consume in a week?
- 'Ideal': Participants reported their judgments of ideal quantities; for example, what is the ideal number of sugary drinks to consume in a week?
- 'Reasonable': Participants reported their judgments of reasonable quantities; for example, what is the reasonable number of sugary drinks to consume in a week?

[47] See, eg, Zipursky (n 43) 2165 ('Imagine a person who owns an all-wheel drive SUV, parked in his garage, and a brand new rear-wheel-drive sedan, parked on the street. He realizes it would probably be somewhat safer to drive the SUV, given the rainy weather conditions, but he is too lazy to switch cars and he feels like driving his new sedan anyway. Alas, a cyclist pulls out from behind a truck. The driver swerves, but hits the cyclist nonetheless ... Assuming a Hand formula ... would generate a plausible argument for breach ... But negligence law—at least as to ordinary people—is significantly less demanding than that. A reasonably prudent person would not think it necessary to take every last cost-efficient precaution and would not think it necessary to alter his automobile choice based on the risks to others. The argument that, if the SUV really would have reduced the risk of accident, his duty of care required him to switch cars has more than a touch of unreality. Reasonable people make such choices all the time, and a plaintiff's lawyer would be unlikely to suggest otherwise to a jury.').

[48] See eg Kevin P Tobia, 'How People Judge What is Reasonable' (2018) 70 Ala L Rev 293; Christopher Brett Jaeger, 'The Empirical Reasonable Person', (2021) 72 Ala L Rev 887 (2021); Mikaela Spruill and Neil A Lewis Jr, 'Legal Descriptions of Police Officers Affect How Citizens Judge Them' (2022) 101 J Ex Soc Psych'y; Kevin Tobia and others, 'What Is Reasonable? A Multi-Country Investigation' (unpublished); Christopher Brett Jaeger, 'Reasonableness from an XJur Perspective' in *The Cambridge Handbook of Experimental Jurisprudence* (forthcoming).

[49] See eg Tobia (n 48).

[50] Adam Bear and Joshua Knobe, 'Normality: Part Descriptive, Part Prescriptive' (2017) 167 Cognition 25–37.

Participants in each condition considered a large number of domains: the [average, ideal, or reasonable] number of sugary drinks to consume per week; books read per year; hours of landlord notice provided before entering an apartment; weeks to return a product ordered online; loud events held on a football field in a residential neighbourhood, per year; and so on.

A striking pattern emerged across these diverse domains at rates greater than chance. Averaging across all participants, the mean 'reasonable' estimate was *intermediate* between the mean average and ideal estimates in a given domain. For example, the mean *average* number of loud events held on a football field in a residential neighbourhood per year was thirty, the *ideal* number was eleven, and the *reasonable* number was sixteen (intermediate).

That paper interpreted this result to provide evidence about the ordinary concept of reasonableness. The data supports a 'hybrid' account of reasonableness as a concept that reflects both descriptive and prescriptive norms (that is, what seems typical and good). Importantly, this study does not prove that 'sixteen' is the legally reasonable number of loud events on a football field each year. The point is not to outsource to laypeople specific legal determinations (there was also great variation among participants' evaluations of what is average, reasonable, and ideal). Rather, the point is to gain insight into the ordinary concept of what is reasonable.

Other experimental research has provided further support that descriptive norms influence what appears reasonable—and that descriptive norms have a larger impact than economic cost-benefit considerations.[51] Many of these results offer points of intersection with non-empirical tort theory. For example, the 'hybrid account' has much in common with accounts of reasonableness (in negligence) as moderation.[52] And another empirical study has provided evidence that there is an ordinary distinction between the 'reasonable' and the 'rational',[53] one which is broadly consistent with the distinction posited by the legal theorist Greg Keating.[54]

As one final example, consider a large cross-cultural and cross-linguistic study. This study assessed whether the previously described 'hybrid' intermediacy finding characterizes reasonableness judgments in several countries and languages. The same study was conducted across Brazil, Colombia, Germany, India, Italy, Lithuania, the Netherlands, Poland, Spain, and the

[51] Jaeger (n 48).

[52] eg Zipursky (n 43) (emphasizing moderation and mutuality).

[53] Igor Grossman, Richard P Eibach, Jacklyn Koyama, and Qaisar B Sahi, *Folk Standards of Sound Judgment; Rationality Versus Reasonableness*, 6 Sci Advances (2020).

[54] Keating (n 4).

United States, translated into the relevant languages. The same intermediacy pattern emerged across many examples in many countries.[55]

Those results also suggest an interesting possibility concerning cross-cultural and cross-linguistic similarity. There is undoubtedly *variation* among the populations. For example, in the sample from the Netherlands, participants estimated fewer than ten loud events per year on a football field in a residential neighbourhood. The sample from Italy evaluated that there would be thirty loud events per year on a football field in a residential neighbourhood.

At the same time, there is a similarity above this variation: In the Italian sample, the conception of the *reasonable* number of events is also higher, and for both countries, the same intermediacy pattern emerges. Within each country, the reasonable estimates fall between the (respective) average and ideal estimates. In other words, although there are surely cultural differences (about drinking sugary drinks or hosting loud events), the results suggest an intriguing similarity in how people across these countries conceptualize averages, ideals, and 'reasonable' quantities.

This is only one study, but this pattern crystallizes new possibilities for comparative private law theory. Perhaps there are some general, shared features of ordinary concepts of legal relevance across many cultures. It may be difficult to detect those patterns from the armchair or from observing jury judgments in isolation. But, an *experimental* comparative method (that is, a study assessing average, ideal, and reasonable quantities) can reveal patterns of similarity in what otherwise might appear to be largely cultural relativity.

Altogether, this research supports that the ordinary concept of the reasonable reflects considerations about what is typical or customary and considerations about what appears 'good'. The evidence does not support that cost-benefit reasoning is the only criterion of ordinary reasonableness (contra L&E Conceptualism), nor does it support that cost-benefit reasoning is the most influential criterion. For private law theorists who seek to ground legal theory in claims about 'our' shared understandings, this data about the ordinary concept of reasonableness provides relevant evidence.

As a final note, this research may illuminate concepts more than terms. That is, its implications more likely concern the concept of reasonableness, not particular features of the term 'reasonable'. This is made clear by the cross-cultural research, whose translations use different terms. But it is also clarified by the similar results for US participants' evaluation of the 'normal'.[56] This is

[55] Tobia and others, 'What is Reasonable? A Multi-Country Study' (unpublished).

[56] Bear and Knobe (n 50).

significant for private law theory, insofar as some tort jury instructions use the term 'reasonable', while others do not.[57]

Beyond studies of what is 'reasonable', there are several other comparative experimental jurisprudence projects. For example, one paper replicates the severity-sensitivity effect described earlier. Across Brazil, Columbia, the United States, Japan, Germany, Italy, Lithuania, Netherlands, Poland, and Spain, the intent is severity-sensitive.[58] Others have found similarities in the ordinary concept of rule[59] and the concept of identity.[60]

IV. Conclusion

It is exciting to witness the growth of a New Private Law theory committed to the coherence and significance of legal concepts. Yet, that approach faces some scepticism about its methodology and the source of these legal concepts. Defenders of the New Private Law hold that '[p]rivate law is not a brooding omnipresence in the sky'.[61] This chapter agrees and offers empirical research about ordinary concepts as one tool to help make further progress in private law theory.

[57] As Zipursky finds, lay jury instructions across the country tend to reflect descriptions of ordinary care, reasonable prudence, and carefulness—but not the concepts contained within the Hand Formula. Benjamin Zipursky, 'Sleight of Hand' (2007) 48 Wm & Mary L Rev; see also Patrick J Kelley and Laurel A Wendt, 'What Judges Tell Juries About Negligence: A Review of Pattern Jury Instructions' (2002) 77 Chicago-Kent L Rev 587, 591.

[58] Markus Kneer and others, 'The Severity Effect on Intention and Knowledge. A cross-cultural study with laypeople and legal experts' (unpublished manuscript); see also Z Lin and others, 'Norm Status, Rather than Norm Type or Blameworthiness, Results in the Side-Effect Effect' (2019) 8 Psychology 513.

[59] Ivar Hannikainen and others, 'Coordination and Expertise Foster Legal Textualism' (2022) 119 Proc Nat'l Acad Sciences e2206531119. for work on one population, see also SM Garcia, P Chen, and MT Gordon, 'The letter versus the spirit of the law: Alay perspective on culpability' (2014) 9 Judgment & Decision Making; Noel Struchiner and others, 'An Experimental Guide to Vehicles in the Park' (2020) 15 Judgment & Decision Making.

[60] V Dranseika and E Lauraityte, 'Experimental Jurisprudence Cross-cultural Study Swap Consortium (unpublished data), Cross-cultural Replication of Tobia (2016)' (unpublished manuscript).

[61] Nathan B Oman, 'Private Law and Local Custom' in AS Gold and others (eds), *The Oxford Handbook of The New Private Law* (OUP 2020) 174. See also Holmes's critique of the general common law, as a 'brooding omnipresence in the sky'. *Southern Pac Co v Jensen*, 244 US 205, 222 (1916).

Index

For the benefit of digital users, indexed terms that span two pages (e.g., 52–53) may, on occasion, appear on only one of those pages.

Tables are indicated by *t* following the page number